A Forgotten Landscape

Ariana Mangum

Copyright 2002 by Ariana Mangum
No part of this work may be reproduced without written permission from author and the publisher.

The back cover illustration depicting St. Mary's Church is the work of Margaret Duke Lundvall and is used with her kind permission.

Righter Publishing Company, Inc.
1112 Rogers Road
Graham, NC 27253

www.righterbooks.com

Third Edition October 2016

Printed and bound in the United States of America

Library of Congress Control Number
2008939276

ISBN: 978-1-934936-16-0
A Forgotten Landscape
By Ariana Mangum

Acknowledgements

This book was written while I was living in Ireland for seven years. I wish to thank two friends, who guided me through some rough water and brought order out of chaos. Eva Cathair and Colbert Martin stuck by me when I felt very discouraged at finishing this manuscript. I also wish to thank two readers in Ireland, Ann Rovet and Paul Keatings. I had two typists in Ireland, Avril Alberti and Nan Blounie, who typed and retyped for me. Nan Blounie died shortly after I returned to America.

I also want to thank Noel who saved paper for me, and my sister, Holly Pulsifer, who had the manuscript copied on American-size paper.

I wish to thank the Bray Library for the use of their books on World War II, some which were out of print and hard to come by. I also must acknowledge my Father's manuscript about his G2 experiences with Omar Bradley and George Patton.

I also appreciate the help of Edith Bennett, a great friend who encouraged me and made suggestions and whose untimely death did not allow her to see the book completed. Her advice, her tape recorder and her help with Italian phrases all contributed to bring this manuscript to completion.

In America my stepmother, Eleanor Dickson and my brother Colin Dickson both offered advice and encouragement. My daughter, Alice Mangum edited the manuscript and my husband, William Mangum gave the book a final reading. Lastly, but not least my friend, Jean King, who corrected spelling and grammar, and enjoyed the story. Thank you all very much.

Ariana Mangum
Chapel Hill, NC

Table of Contents

Part I: Prelude to War - 1938-1939

Preface - Mrs. Houghton and the Birds — 9

1. The Coming of the Houghtons — 11
2. In the Beginning — 19
3. Traveller's Bees — 27
4. Mrs. Preston's Story — 35
5. Coming of War — 51
6. Troubled Waters — 57
7. Secret Feelings — 63
8. Special Nights in the Houghtons' Cottage — 69
9. At Henley's Store — 77
10. Fox Hunting — 87
11. The Last Peacetime Christmas — 97
12. My Trip to Philadelphia — 105

Part II: War Begins in Europe - 1940-1941

13. The Prelude Ends — 119
14. Thelma's Place — 127
15. War Troubles — 133
16. Changes — 143
17. The Duchess's Family — 153
18. Heavenly Peace — 163
19. Mr. Carter's Folklore — 169
20. Enter Rommel — 177
21. Lord Haw Haw — 183
22. Education — 187
23. Bundles for Britain — 191
24. Preparations — 197
25. Rommel Again (Maps) — 205
26. The Importance of Bills — 209

Table of Contents

27. The Pale Horseman	215
28. Afton Mountain	219
29. Mr. Houghton Fights a Fire	225
30. A Strange Meeting	229
31. An Interlude	235
32. Winter Offensive	239
33. Mrs. Haunch Appears Again	243
34. "To Hell with Babe Ruth"	249
35. Germany Calling	255

Part III: Trouble on the Home Front - 1942

36. "Nothing but Fear Itself"	259
37. Mr. Houghton's Wedding	263
38. The Night the Taliaferros' Barn Burned	277
39. Store Talk	285
40. Spring Cleaning	291
41. Jackie Disturbs the Peace	295
42. When Dr. Clery Went to War	303
43. Ilse	307
44. Angelo	313
45. Gossip	329
46. War News from the Pacific	335
47. The Battle of Midway	345
48. Mr. Taliaferro Dies	349
49. Afton Mountain Holiday	351
50. A Strange Christening	357
51. Mr. Houghton and Jackie	363
52. When the James River Flooded	371
53. Mr. Houghton and the Guimeas	383
54. War News	391
55. Cary Again	399
56. As the Year Ends	403

Table of Contents

Part IV: "We Shall Fight Them on the Beaches" - 1943

Letters	409
57. Mr. Houghton's War Effort	411
58. When Old Sally Died	421
59. Mrs. Houghton and I Worked at the Red Cross	425
60. Battle of El Guettar	437
61. El Guettar	441
62. A Letter from Tommy	445
63. Mr. Brown's Daimond Head	451
64. Angelo's Story	463
65. When James Broke His Arm	467
66. Sicily	475
67. Grandmother's Phone Call	479
68. The News	487
69. A Mystery at Afton Mountain	489
70. Growing Pains	501
71. Mrs. Haunch's Last Appearance	517
72. "Lilli Marlene"	523
73. A Day to Remember	537
74. Fool's Faces	543
75. Mrs. Carthage's Shopping Trip	547
76. Mr. Houghton's Birthday	551
77. Christmas	559

Part V: The End of the Beginning - 1944 — 561

78. "Thy Tents Shall Be Our Home"	563
79. "Is There Room Enough for Me"	571
80. Mother's Revelation	583
81. West Point	593
82. "The End of the Beginning"	607
Selected Bibliography	609

Part I
1938 – 1939

A Prelude to War

Harry and Clara Houghton*

* Pronounced Howton

Preface

Mrs. Houghton and the Birds

I had not thought of my dear friend from childhood recently, until I read an article in our local newspaper entitled, "Food for Birds". Then I remembered. Memories of my troubled adolescent years and the woman who befriended me came rushing back.

Mrs. Houghton possessed a special way with birds. Each spring when they returned from their southern winter, it was she who saw the first robin. In the early 1940's the *Richmond Times Dispatch* offered $25.00 to the reader who reported seeing this first harbinger of spring. Twice Mrs. Houghton sent a letter to the newspaper. But since we lived in the country, each year someone, who lived in the more sheltered city, had spotted a robin before she did. I was disappointed but kept encouraging Mrs. Houghton every spring to write again.

As spring came the cardinals returned. Once a special pair nested in my friend's garden for five summers. The male perched on the pine beside the kitchen window and squawked at her for a bread crust. When Mrs. Houghton threw one out, the cardinal, picking it up, would fly away - only to return a few minutes later to serenade her with a song of thanks. He did this every morning, and again at suppertime. Finally, one year when this pair of cardinals flew south in the autumn they failed to return. I remember my friend standing beside her window watching for them.

The next year a pair of titmice, black cap over white head, hopped through Mrs. Houghton's window and pecked at the crumbs she laid on the kitchen table. But when she tried to get these birds to feed out of her hand, they, being fearful of human beings, retreated.

It's February again. Many years have come and gone since my

friend passed away. But each spring when I see a robin, fat and sassy on my lawn, and hear it call to its mate, I remember those war years, the handsome prize the newspaper offered, and Mrs. Houghton in her garden feeding the birds.

I had not intended to write about those characters, real and fictional, who crowded my girlhood, but first the newspaper article, and then word of Mr. Houghton's death caused all those memories of my country life to come flooding back.

1

The Coming of the Houghtons

It was a Sunday, I remember - just an ordinary, plain Sunday in early April that an older couple appeared on our gravel road looking for property. Mother and Father had bought only seventy of the hundred acres offered for sale, and a small plot of thirty still remained.

The man wore a gray suit with a vest, and a gold watch chain looped through the middle buttonhole. On his head, at a rakish angle, perched a felt hat trimmed with a small red feather. Followed by his wife, his angular figure crossed our field with the longest strides I had ever seen. Right from the start I realized this man was different from any of Mother and Father's friends.

"I would like to inquire about the thirty acres for sale," the stranger came right to the point.

"It's that field over there," Father indicated the stubble field beyond our recently ploughed ones. "It lies between my property and a large farm next door owned by the Taliaferros."

"I see" he replied.

I watched as he surveyed the overgrown, pine-tree-scattered land. The expression on his tanned out-doors face indicated they were the most unpromising thirty acres he had ever seen. The land rose from Tuckahoe Creek so sharply it formed a bluff. From this promontory one had a glorious view of the valley below. Our farm lay partly on the promontory and partly on a level plateau adjacent to it. The rest of the ground dropped sharply down into the woods.

"It's very hilly and steep," Father commented.

"Not many spots to build a house," agreed our visitor. I noticed he spoke with an English accent, and I regarded him with renewed curiosity.

"Probably don't want much for this land, since there is no building site of any consequence."

"I've bought the remaining acreage, but quite frankly I could see nothing but work getting that other field cleared off. It's no use to me, and I am not sure it even has water," Father replied as a neatly attired lady approached us.

"I am Clara Houghton and this is my husband, Harry," she introduced herself.

Father gave a slight bow. "This is my daughter, Doc. I'm John Dickson. I am delighted to meet you."

The two men extended their hands in greeting. Shortly after this encounter in our corn field, we heard that the Houghtons had made a bid on the thirty acres. I was ten, and they were in their forties.

All the land around us, over two thousand acres, including our farm, had once belonged to the Randolph family. These early plantation owners had possessed many slaves to work the fields of tobacco and cotton. But as the Randolphs died out the land was sold, although their historic house, Tuckahoe, still stood amid its giant oak trees. A smaller Randolph place was located on our road. Considered even older than Tuckahoe, this house possessed two interesting ghosts. Ballyclare, standing at the end of a lonely, dark lane, was not only haunted, but was also believed to possess three unmarked graves of Revolutionary soldiers. Some of the county folks claimed there were Indian graves, but Gordon Carter, our local historian, said not.

"Indians rarely bury their dead," he insisted. "My Father once opened those graves and found buttons. Indians in 1776 never used buttons that I know of."

Although, they were probably not Indian graves, we did have an Indian ghost. A wicked brave often stood at an upstairs bedroom of Tuckahoe and stared out at us. Usually around four o'clock in the afternoon when long shadows fell upon the window in a certain way, they outlined a cruel face with a large crooked nose. Sometimes Father and I would ride his horse Cherry over to visit the present mistress of Tuckahoe, Mrs. Cummings, and she showed us this ghost.

Beyond Tuckahoe on the James River stood the ruins of Allen's Mill. Here a Yankee captain hanged a negro slave who, acting as a guide, mistook the location of the ford. Thinking this poor colored man had betrayed him, the captain hanged the hapless negro from a giant tree that still stands beside this ruined mill.

I remembered on summer evenings when riding in front of Father on Cherry, we often went down to the mill to watch the mist rise from the river. Hoping to find a cool breeze after the oppressive heat of a July day, we would let Cherry crop grass while we sat together on the bank. A chorus of tree toads and cicadas greeted us as they saturated the riverside with their evening song. Sometimes a fish, fat and lazy, would jump and create ever widening rings in the swiftly flowing brown water.

Some evenings I would dig around the old mill hoping, the way Mr. Carter often did, to find arrowheads. He told me that Cherokee Indians once hunted over our land and built a summer camp in what is now Taliaferros' railroad pasture, located high on a bluff overlooking the Lockawana canal, that runs beside the railroad tracks. In the woods nearby lived the mythical hoop snake Mr. Carter once discovered with its horn stuck fast in a tree.

For many years he kept that horn in a jar, and would tell us the story about this wonderful snake. Tradition says it rolls, tail held in its mouth, from place to place. But its horn, sharper than any brier, can become stuck, and unable to free itself, the snake finally dies. On special evenings, such as Midsummer, Father and I would ride out on Cherry to search for this fantastic creature.

A few weeks after our first meeting I was glad to learn that Mr. Houghton had bought the thirty acres. During the last days of April he started to clear a lot of the scrub pine and drew plans to erect an English cottage.

As the spring progressed I discovered that Mrs. Houghton and her husband had recently moved down from Canada where they owned a large cattle farm near Barrie, about a hundred miles north of Toronto.

"We no longer wish to raise cattle," she explained the first afternoon I offered to help her clear away some undergrowth, "but we would like to live in the country without the worry of animals. You might say we have retired from farming, now that we've moved to Virginia."

"We don't have any cattle either," I replied as we chopped at the brambles in her field. "But our neighbors, the Taliaferros do: White Faced Herefords. We own only a horse and a pony."

"So we shall be neighbors, Mrs. Houghton seemed pleased by this prospect. "It will be grand to have a young girl living next door. You see, Mr. Houghton and I have no children of our own."

After that first day I often helped her clear out the brambles and honeysuckle, and later we planted seedlings for vegetables. Sometimes when I got into trouble at home I would climb up my favorite apple tree in the very center of the orchard. From this vantage point I watched Mrs. Houghton work. When the tree became too hot and uncomfortable, I would climb down and seek her company.

"Well, Doc," she called as I approached from the orchard one scorching hot, July afternoon.

"Hello," I replied.

"What do you know about gardening?"

"Not much," I confessed squinting against the sun. "I can hardly tell vegetables from flowers."

"You'll have to learn more than that to become a good gardener."

"I suspect so," I conceded, not interested.

Mrs. Houghton stopped raking the parched earth and pointed to the string beans, carrots and sweet peas that prospered under her care.

"I have got a few vegetables growing in spite of the intense heat."

"Would you like some lemonade?" I produced a battered thermos and two squashed paper cups. "I made some to drink up in the apple tree, but was afraid I'd fall out."

She nodded in agreement, and laid down her rake. Carefully I poured out the cold liquid. Then we drank the sweetened lemon juice in great gulps as we sat, legs stretched out in front of us, on prickly pine needles in the shade of mimosa trees. Nearby, Peggy, Mrs. Houghton's brown and white fox terrier, lay panting under a bush. After regarding us with lazy interest she rose, poked an inquisitive nose at her mistress's cup, and started to lick the condensation from the thermos.

"She's thirsty," I said. "May she have some?"

"She'd love it. Poor little thing, it's unbearably hot today."

Again I filled my paper cup and offered it to Peggy who eagerly lapped up the lemonade.

After resting in the shade for several more minutes my friend picked up her rake, and under her gentle tutelage I began my apprenticeship as a gardener.

All that summer I watched with considerable interest the construc-

The Coming of the Houghtons

tion of the Houghtons' cottage. Although built on a concrete slab foundation and from a simple plan, seasoned lumber and suitable building materials proved difficult to come by. Locating just the right kind of shingles caused a long delay, as did finding the correct size pipes.

Lack of water on our hill, a major problem, caused Mr. Houghton to drill two wells. Now, in the field around the garden lay strewn various kinds of pipes from which water finally gushed, pumped from a well house cleverly concealed in the woods. From one of these pipes Mrs. Houghton watered her garden.

After unsuccessful attempts to buy the right building materials, Mr. Houghton's friend, Tom Harris, finally located a lumberyard in neighboring Fluvana County.

Here the owner promised to supply the shingles needed for an English cottage, and several lengths of the right size boards. The two friends, accompanied by black Grievous Sin Snead, a local carpenter, spent the greater part of a day riding up to Fluvana Court House in Mr. Harris's truck and returned loaded up with what seemed to me every kind of building material imaginable. After that Mr. Houghton worked steadily, helped solely by Grievous Snead. Only an occasional heavy rain storm, and a periodic wait for electricians and plumbers interrupted the cottage's slow progress. With much curiosity I watched as its clapboard walls, pitched roof and open back porch rose from a shaded knoll surrounded by two enormous oak trees.

One morning in late July, I gingerly put my head through the hole that was to become the front door. I could distinguish five rooms, excluding the porch. Upon entering the combination living-dining room, I discovered a large brick fireplace, its most distinctive feature. A front bedroom opened off this lounge, and a second bedroom, of about the same proportions, looked out the back onto the woods. Both of these rooms, I noticed, possessed three windows and good cross ventilation- an important feature in a hot climate. Off a small back hall I found the bathroom fitted out with a toilet. Curious, I gave the handle a tug, and to my surprise water-gushed forth and gurgled pleasantly in the tank. Beside the toilet stood a sink and a bathtub still packed in their crates.

"What a cozy place," I remarked, re-entering the living room.

"It's beginning to take shape. Watch out where you step," Mr Houghton warned from his perch on the top of a ladder.

"Do you think you'll be done by October?"

"We live in hopes," he replied.

In the front bedroom Grievous Snead crouched beside an open toolbox. I watched him select some nails, slip them into his overall pocket, and remount his ladder.

"Hello, Grievous" I said. "This room looks great."

"Yes, missie," the old man replied. I knew he didn't like my poking about.

He took up his hammer and started to nail some boards onto the ceiling. "We is powerful busy."

Feeling unwelcome I decided to leave. I stepped backwards to avoid the scaffolding and fell heavily into the toolbox.

"Ouch help! Ouch! Get me out of here!"

"Missie, you'll get yourself kilt. Yous best leave."

Grievous nearly fell from his ladder laughing. Furious, I scrambled around among hammers, saws and screw drivers trying to regain my balance. More angry than hurt, I stood up and marched from the house. I left Grievous strangling with laughter.

"Better stay away, Doc, or you'll hurt yourself. We are not ready to serve tea yet," Mr. Houghton chuckled.

Shaking with anger and humiliation I walked across the yard towards Mrs. Houghton, who was busy hoeing the baked earth around her vegetables, In the piece of corn field we had cleared now grew carrots, celery, lettuce and beautiful crimson tomatoes. Beans, peas and carrots had already brightened our dinner table, This morning I found her watering her thriving plants and breaking up the heavy parched soil so the moisture could soak in.

"Well, Doc," she called, "I see you got turned out on your ear."

"I fell over the toolbox and nearly ruined myself." I hoped to find some sympathy,

"Don't you start," she warned me. "All I hear about these days are ten penny nails, four by six boards, varieties of piping, shingles, broken hammers and lost screw drivers. You're much safer out here with me and, at least, we can talk of other subjects."

Since the spring when we first chatted across the stubble field, I had found out some interesting things about my new neighbors. Mrs. Houghton liked to talk of her early life in England. Even though it was

The Coming of the Houghtons

more than ten years since she had "come out" to live in Canada she still felt a great longing for home.

"I was born in Kent," she told me one day, "the garden of England, in the South east corner. And I attended school near Canterbury Cathedral."

"Where is that? " I demanded, uncertain about geography in England. "Is it near London?"

"Almost two hours' run in the train. About as far away as Washington is from here."

Several weeks after this discussion, she propped her hoe against the nearest tree and picked up an old photograph album. Leafing through it, she stopped finally at a picture, long faded, of a church with gigantic proportions, its massive front portal covered with statues, and its entrance gate decorated with various coats of arms.

"What a fantastic place!" I gasped with delight, staring at the yellowing black and white photograph.

"That's Canterbury Cathedral," she explained, "and that's the Bell Harry Tower."

"The tower's named Harry?" What a strange custom, I thought, to give a tower a man's name.

"No, that's what the bell's called. The tower was built to accommodate the bell.

In England we have bell ringers who ring in sets of peals, called change ringing."

"Do all the bells have names?" I wondered.

"Yes, that's right. And each has a different tone. Sometimes in a single tower you'll find ten or even twelve bells. So they're called Big Harry, Little Tom or Great Bob, according to their size to distinguish them."

"I've never heard of that before."

Thoughtfully she turned the pages of the leather bound album and paused at another photograph, faded brown, of an old man standing before some ruins set amid rolling fields.

"That's my Dad," she explained, "taken in front of Cooling Castle, near Rochester. Not far away is the parish church where, in *Great Expectations*, Pip discovered the convict in the graveyard. Here, too, are the numerous children's graves that Dickens said, 'lay like lozenges all in a row!' "

Taking the album from her, I studied the intense face of her father who smiled back at me from the brittle paper. Behind him stood the forlorn ruins of a crumbling castle. Both, it seemed to me, belonged to a world entirely foreign from my own.

"My parents," said Mrs. Houghton, "moved from Canterbury to a place near Cooling Castle shortly after I left home. I used to visit them on weekends and knew the surrounding countryside well. My dad died some years after I came out to Canada. I never saw him again once I left England. Nor have I ever been home since."

Tears suddenly brimmed over her clear blue eyes and dropped upon her blouse and light seersucker skirt. Embarrassed, I turned my back, pretending not to notice, while she, taking a linen handkerchief from her skirt pocket, blew her nose and regained her composure. Realizing for the first time how terrible homesickness must be, I felt extremely sorry for her.

She seemed different, somehow, from other people I knew; sadder, kinder, perhaps. Little things amused her, the dog's questioning eyes, a wren's song, a seedling tree she found trampled in the woods. Often she would tie it up with a stick and a piece of string, and visit it again. I discovered a desire to please her, and bought lemons with my pocket money so I could make cool lemonade on hot afternoons, to drink with her under a shade tree. Now, in the middle of July she had transformed one section of the stubble field into a prosperous garden, and together we drank gallons of lemonade. She did not seem to mind the sticky taste and always welcomed my company. The day she showed me her photograph album so filled with English memories, I knew we had become firm friends.

2

In the Beginning

With great optimism Father and Mother had bought our farm at the end of the depression. Long neglected, with a dilapidated old house, to make anything comfortable out of that farm I thought hopeless.

"This place will never look like home," I remarked when first I walked behind Father across the stubble-covered fields.

"Just watch," he replied, poking hopefully into the old barns; "We'll make it into a show place."

"Are you sure, "I asked in doubt. "There's nothing here to work with."

But together he and Mother remodeled the house and repaired the barns. Father hired Ben Walters, a Negro farmer, to plough the fields and to put in a crop of clover. We came out only on weekends; back then people who worked in town did not live in the country. The distances were too great and our automobiles too unreliable. Gradually the farmhouse began to change into an attractive home. Then, shortly after my tenth birthday, we sold the house in town and moved to the country.

A few weeks later Father bought me a pony.

"Doc," he greeted me one morning as I entered the dining room, "did you see what's wandered into our pasture? I think you and I need to investigate."

It was a cool day in early spring when Father and I walked across the yet bumpy lawn to the pasture. Here we found a bay Welsh pony with a white patch on his left side.

"Whose is it?" I demanded,, "Where did he come from?"

"I found him wandering about the countryside looking for a young girl to love him," Father winked at me. "I suggested he come and meet you."

"You mean he's mine?" I whispered.

"Only if he likes you and you like him. So you must ride him and find out if you can become friends. There's a little saddle and bridle just the right size in the barn."

Fifteen minutes later with the new pony caught and saddled I mounted him. First I made several turns at a walk around the stable yard. Then I trotted out into the pasture. Away the pony went across the rough grass, first at a trot and then at a canter, his ears pricked forward and his steady hooves rhythmic underneath me. Never had I experienced such joy. A pony all my own!

"He is great, Father, really great." I pulled the little fellow down to a trot and reentered the stable yard. "I shall name him Billy."

"I see you get along famously. When your legs become too long, and you are a more accomplished horsewoman, I'll buy you a horse." Father took Billy by his bridle.

Together we built our stable. I held the nails and passed them up to Father for him to hammer in. I also held the ends of the boards as they lay over two wooden horses while Father sawed the required lengths. He even showed me how to use a tape measure and a ruler. Soon I drew the pencil lines on the two-by-fours where Father wanted them cut. Together we watched the three-stall barn rise from the red clay beside an enormous pine tree that shaded our stable yard. The largest stall was for Cherry, Father's big hunter, a second for Billy, my bay pony, and the third stall we reserved for my promised horse when I grew big enough to own one.

Mother rarely played with me. I thought of her as the boss, all spit and polish. She reminded me of my gym teacher who shouted out orders and expected them to be obeyed on the instant. She liked to organize things and people, and became the president of various women's clubs.

My being a child bored her, and she did not know quite what to do with me. I wondered what her childhood was like, and if she had been happy.

"You can't wear that dress," she would remark. "It's much too short. And you can't wear a blue skirt with green socks. Go comb your hair and tie your shoes. When will you ever learn to be neat?" Even at breakfast Mother would regard me with disapproval.

"I am trying to grow up. But I can't seem to do anything right," I complained.

"You don't try hard enough. You must learn to organize. Really, Catherine, your behavior is impossible." She insisted upon using my real name.

Then my whole day would start off wrong. My bright, optimistic morning would be dashed to bits by her sharp words. Yet, as hard as I tried to please her, Mother always seemed to regard me as a hopeless misfit.

"Give me time to be a child," I would beg her. "Just a little while to have fun and no responsibility."

"You shall never amount to much with that lackadaisical attitude. Take some pride in yourself. Act as if you're important."

But I never could. She made me feel totally inadequate. She expected me to act sixteen before I was even ten. Father liked me the way I was, and preferred to call me by my nickname, 'Doc.' Although often he got mixed up and called me Son; I guess he was secretly disappointed I wasn't a boy.

We enjoyed each other's company. When I was eight Father bought me my first fishing pole. It was bamboo, I remember, with a bright red bobber and a sharp curved hook. Light and springy, this pole I found easy to handle and to land a fish. Holding the wriggling earth-worm between his fingers Father showed me how to bait the hook. Then I would throw my line into our pond and wait for a fish to come. Sometimes the red bobber would bounce up and down ever so gently. Often, on such occasions, when I pulled my line in the worm would be gone or just half covering the hook.

"Don't feed the fish, catch them," Father would laugh. "Maybe your worm crawled off."

So, hoping to avoid this eventuality, I very carefully would place the line into the water. 'Plop' went the sinker as it disappeared beneath the dark surface. Then I would sit on the bank and wait for the fish to spy my delightfully tasty earthworm.

"Walk your line slowly down the shore. Perhaps Mr. Perch and Mr. Sunfish like to see a moving object," Father would suggest after we waited, staring at the still bobber for several minutes. Then suddenly the line would grow taut; my red bobber would dive under the lilypads. Always my heart leapt in excitement as I reeled in my catch. I soon learned to take the fish off the hook without poking the sharp fins into my soft palms. Those companionable days, I thought, would never end. I felt marvelously happy in Father's company.

But sometimes Mother would object.

"You spend too much time with Catherine. You are indulging her. Really, John, you act as much of a child as she does."

"Allow Doc to be a girl, " Father would reply. "At nine you can hardly expect her to be an adult. Why do you want her to behave like an old lady? Don't you trust her? Let Doc enjoy her youth and experience a little fun."

"Fun? But life is a serious matter. She must realize that."

"She will," Father assured Mother with a sigh. "Don't mould her into an over-serious young woman. Let her enjoy herself."

Mother was never willing to leave things to chance. Not everything, of course, can be left, but when chance does play a part in matters the most delightful, unexpected happenings occur. However, Mother rarely allowed chance a hand in any of her affairs. She lived in a tight-fisted, self-controlled manner. Chance, however, allowed me to see her on rare occasions, as she might have been if she'd relaxed and embraced the unexpected.

One evening I remember when Mother, dressed to go out dancing with Father, appeared especially glamorous in a soft, blue chiffon gown.

"See how elegant our boss looks tonight," Father regarded her with admiration.

I nodded and smiled, watching the filmy chiffon swirl gently around Mother's slim figure as she descended the stairs. Her face suddenly softened and she twirled around the hall making the dress stand out like a silken balloon.

"How beautiful!" I whispered.

Mother, appearing younger and gentler, basked in our praise. Her voice, often too loud, dropped in pitch and sounded musical. For one breathtaking moment I experienced a fleeting glimpse of an entirely different person.

"You make me feel like a schoolgirl going out to her first evening party," Mother told us, her face radiant.

"You're as fresh as a debutante and especially alluring tonight," Father took her by the hand and kissed it.

"What a charming thing to do!" Mother cooed with happiness.

But such moments were rare. Only at times did my parents seem in tune with one another. These fleeting petal-like minutes when they expressed their love now happened less and less often. In recent months Father frequently retreated into his library in moody silence. He found Mother's desire to dominate us intolerable. At such times I would climb up into my special apple tree and remain out of the way.

"Come, Doc." As evening fell Father would seek me in the orchard. "We'll ride Cherry down to the river and watch the moon rise."

Silently I would climb down from my perch, and together we would slip away like two conspirators. Ever so quickly we saddled up the big chestnut gelding, and with my riding in front of him, Father would gallop down the silent road towards the Taliaferros' lowgrounds. The pace I found exhilarating, and with Father's strong arms holding me secure, I experienced a strange sense of freedom. A freedom born of flight and speed, but enhanced by my desire to grab and taste the richness of life.

Father, too, experienced this sense of freedom. "Some people don't hunger for adventure as we do, Doc."

I was nine.

By the time we sold the house in town and moved permanently to the country, I was ten. That fall Clara and Harry Houghton completed their English cottage and started to erect a beautiful six stall barn. In Goochland's rolling hills they created a tiny corner of Mr. Houghton's native Yorkshire.

A few months later Emma Craddock and her son, Cary, bought about ten acres across the road from us and converted an old cabin into an attractive home. Just before I reached my eleventh birthday, in the spring of 1939, our country neighborhood was complete.

The arrival of Cary I considered a major event. Since many of my neighbors had moved out to the country after they retired, few children lived near me. Although Cary was five years my senior, I found him terribly interesting. He was handsome with great blue eyes and dark curly hair. He adored football and played on the school team. After classes he remained late at St. Lawrence's School to practice and came home exhausted and unbelievably dirty - even for a boy.

"What's so great about football when you nearly kill yourself running after a stupid ball?" I demanded one afternoon as we fed our horses.

"It's great fun, with lots of action. But I suppose it's not something a girl would play," Cary replied laughing as he measured out the oats for Killybegs, his Connemara pony, and for his mother's hunter, Mistress.

"It's dumb to hurt yourself," I insisted, "and to come home every day tired out and cut up with someone else's cleats."

"I also like to ride horses. Both Mistress and Killybegs are fun to hunt.

Cary picked up a water bucket, washed it out and rehung it in his pony's stall.

"I've hunted too, but not on Billy. He's too small. Father's friend, Doug Fraser, loaned me a larger pony."

I turned on the hose; we watered the horses and finished the chores. Then we slapped each other on the shoulder and walked home.

Why Cary even spoke to me I never knew. But he did. Like most eleven-year-old girls, I was still a kid and considered myself pretty boring company for a sixteen-year-old boy. Cary was always kind and seemed to accept me in the same casual manner he treated the rest of our neighbors. And I idolized him. He had everything a grown up boy should - charm, good looks and a quirky sense of humor.

I was delighted when some weeks later he began to drive into school with me while his mother, who worked for Miller and Rhoads, was away in New York on a buying trip. I thought she owned this department store since it took up so much of her time, and was very disappointed when I found out she only worked there. With Cary accompanying us to school, the thirteen miles seemed much less long and boring. Then Mrs. Houghton began to come along too when she decided to consult a doctor in town. And with both she and Cary in the car the long drive was actually fun.

"Goodbye, for now," Cary remarked as he got out.

"Don't get killed on the football field," I teased.

Mrs. Houghton always wished him a pleasant day and waved until we turned the corner. Usually Father drove us, and he kept the conversation lively.

"What position do you play?" he asked Cary. "I was a linesman."

"Sir, I play full back, and sometimes running back. I'm not big enough for the line."

"You'll have to eat more spinach, that's all, Cary, and potatoes, they'll put fat on you."

In the Beginning

But sometimes Mother drove us. Then the car remained silent except for a few whispered remarks between Cary and me. If Mrs. Houghton went along Mother addressed the conversation to her and left us out. Sitting together on the back seat we wrote notes to each other and played tic tac toe on our school books. Even Mrs. Houghton sounded strained and spoke politely on boring topics.

Mother drove with the radio on. First we listened to Douglas Freeman give the morning news, then to Polly Dafferin who told us about the latest fashions. She spoke in a high squeaky voice and gushed over cotton, silk and wool as if they were gold. I disliked both these programs. Cary made wry faces, and I giggled uncontrollably behind Mother's back.

"Stop that nonsense, Catherine. You're acting silly. Behave." She turned around and glared at me.

Cary made faces mimicking her. I nearly strangled from laughter. Mrs. Houghton, who was in on the fun, turned and winked. I liked it when Miss Emma, Cary's mother, drove us. She made things lively, but Mr. Houghton was the best.. He complained about everyone else's driving and shouted at the red lights. Every time he stopped for a cat or a dog, he nearly threw us through the windshield. This made Cary and me double up with laughter.

That fall I entered the seventh grade and changed classrooms throughout the day. This at first seemed very confusing because the Upper School's room numbering was not consistent. That previous spring Mrs. Genevieve Owens came into my life and taught me what it meant to be a Virginian. I realized she disapproved of me because I was not born in Richmond - a terrible oversight on my parents' part. This school year she was my homeroom teacher. I was doomed to become a Virginian; there was no escape.

Although my forefathers were Virginians, it didn't count because my great grandfather had moved to Indiana before The War Between the States, called The War by correct Southerners. My family had deserted its heritage, and therefore I was suspect in Mrs. Owen's eyes. She was probably right because I flaunted Richmond conventions because I didn't understand them. We had no picture of Robert E. Lee in our house, and I hated wearing hat and gloves down town to Miller and Rhoads tea room. We celebrated May thirtieth Memorial Day and not May tenth. I didn't know Lee's middle name and constantly forgot it on tests. I wasn't even sure where William Byrd's Westover Plantation was located although it was less than twenty miles from Richmond. I had no idea who the beautiful Evelyn Byrd was and where her ghost walked, To make matters worse I mixed up John Smith with John Rolf, although I knew they both had something to do with Pocohontas. I even pronounced Powhatan wrong. I was Indiana Come to Town even though I'd never lived there. Mrs. Owens found my manners appalling and my speech unacceptable. She started right off trying to put things right.

"You must say aunt to rhyme with haunt not ant. It is not correct to say, 'tomatoes.' It's tomatoes to rhyme with mulattoes. Now don't forget that. Where is your father from? He has a southern accent."

"He was born in Georgia. His mother was from Atlanta," I replied. She left me alone for awhile after that.

3

Traveller's Bees

My school was situated on Monument Avenue, that historic thoroughfare interspersed by numerous statues of Confederate heroes. Monument School for Girls occupied two three-story Edwardian buildings separated by a playground. Architecturally these buildings blended well with the turn-of-the-century residences that lined this stately avenue. Two rows of large maple trees promenaded like lovers on a warm day up the grass plot in the center of the street. Two more rows of maples grew on the wide sidewalks in front of the gracious houses and formed a leafy canopy in summer.

For several years I studied my lessons between the statues of two of the South's most illustrious generals, three churches, and a hospital. It was an historic spot in a city filled with history. At one end of the block stood the enormous statue of Robert E. Lee on Traveller, and at the other end pranced J.E.B. Stuart on his noble charger, Firefly.

When I first came to Richmond and entered school there, I found some of the patriotic holidays celebrated at different times. In Virginia Memorial Day was May tenth. When I was in third grade I walked down with my class to J.E.B. Stuart's statue to place Confederate flags on the cast iron fence that surrounded it.

The Indiana Memorial Day was the thirtieth of May - the day of the big race, The Indianapolis 500. We looked forward to this event every year. There were parades with brass bands and festivities which lasted for a whole week.

Now at eleven I considered myself a native of Richmond. But I still found some of the traditions held by older Virginians archaic. Their recitation of each other's family genealogy bored me, and they avoided talking of bad things such as illness or divorce. These they hid under euphemistic phrases. People felt a divorced woman was somehow to blame for the breakup of her marriage, and she tended to marry again as soon as possible. If someone suffered a mental breakdown it was whispered, " nerves were bad." Or it might be said he had gone away for a long rest. How Virginians swept everything unpleasant under the carpet intrigued me.

To become a lady was stressed above all else. That meant your behavior must be impeccable, your dress neat and in good taste, and you must always be clean. Above all it meant that money, no matter how rich you were, must never be flaunted. Driving big cars or wearing too many jewels was considered in poor taste. A lady was something every girl aspired to become. We prayed at night that one day we would achieve ladyhood. I held little hope of ever reaching this magic pinnacle.

The worst thing anyone could be was a Yankee. North Carolinians came next. They were considered tacky people with little breeding. They drove large ostentatious cars when the women came up to Richmond to shop or to attend a funeral. Many North Carolinians, it was said, were professional funeral-goers, especially the tobacco people, who would brag how many times they had driven up to Richmond in a year to bury their departed colleagues. Little wonder Virginians found this practice offensive. A South Carolinian was regarded as a little more acceptable. He might pass the rigid test of propriety if he came from Charleston or Georgetown and, like the Chinese, he ate rice and worshipped his ancestors. The people from South Carolina felt very superior to their northerly neighbors. It was all very snobbish, and I could not keep it straight who I was supposed to like or dislike. The people from the rest of the state we considered hillbillies. I soon got the idea that being a Virginian was like being in the antechamber of heaven. It was something you earned by hard work, unless you happened to be born there.

The greatest challenge of 7th grade was the history teacher, Mrs. Genevieve Owens. She was neither young nor old, but appeared to be somewhere in between. I felt sure she dyed her hair. Some days it looked considerably redder than on others. She often experimented with new styles. Most I thought very unattractive.

Mrs. Owens felt great pride in being a Virginian. She never let us forget she was a direct descendant of Martha Custis Washington, the wife of our first President and explained this connection on several occasions in great detail. I remained very confused just how it worked although I was convinced it was important. In the fall the weather remained unusually warm so some afternoons Mrs. Owens took us out under the trees on the grass plot that ran down the middle of Monument Avenue. There in the coolness of the shady maples we studied our history. The warm atmosphere seemed filled with the buzzing sound of bees. They flew around our heads with such persistence that my classmates squealed in fright. Finally Mrs. Owens led us up the grass plot closer to the statue of Lee on Traveller. Here the bees seemed thicker, and we ran around trying to rid ourselves of these buzzing pests.

"Look, Mrs. Owens, the bees are flying in and out of Traveller's mouth," cried Mary Ann.

"Bees in Traveller's mouth? Surely not!" She gazed up at the bronze statue.

"Yes," insisted Frances James, "there are,"

I stared at Traveller with new interest and wondered if the bees really had found a home. His lips seemed dark with strange spots, and as I watched these spots moved.

"There is something dripping from the statue's mouth," I said, crossing the street to the wrought iron fence that surrounded the monument.

"Catherine, come back onto the grass plot. We shall sit here for our history lesson," Mrs. Owens called me.

"But there is honey, coming from Traveller's mouth," I insisted.

The others followed me, and eagerly we all pressed against the iron railings that surrounded the statue of the South's most famous general and strained our heads back, looking upwards sheltering our eyes from the sun.

"See that?" Mary Ann pointed. "Something wet and thick seems to be falling from the horse's lips."

Mrs. Owens regarded Traveller in horror.

"If bees are nesting in Lee's statue, how very unpatriotic of them. Don't they realize they're defacing a monument of one of the South's greatest heroes?"

"Probably not," I replied giggling. "It's just a good place to build a nest high above the street away from people."

The seventh grade history class, now completely out of control, studied the statue's mouth. After a long look at Traveller's spots the fourteen of us girls returned to the grass plot where we sat down under the trees and opened our books.

"I plan to assign you each a project upon which you shall write a paper. Now since Richmond is the capital of the Confederacy we shall study places of historic note in this city."

Mrs. Owens regarded me with a pained look.

"My dear," she said curtly, "you are not from Richmond."

"No," I replied, "I was born in Indianapolis."

She arched one eyebrow as if I had done something terribly wrong.

"That explains many things," my teacher replied looking considerably relieved. "You are not a Virginian."

"I moved here when I was only six years old, and I have Virginia relatives." I hoped that would please her.

"Yes, but my dear, (she always prefixed important pronouncements in this manner) you must be born here to be a Virginian. We learn a lot of things from the cradle."

"Although the bees were born here they don't seem to realize that Traveller's mouth is sacred," I retorted.

I was saved by gales of laughter from my classmates. But Mrs. Owens frowned and regarded me with her piercing dark eyes. I felt she did not quite trust me, since I was born in Indiana. That made me a Hoosier which she seemed to feel was almost as fatal as being a Yankee. And Mrs. Owens hated Yankees.

"There are some things, Catherine," she said finally as I returned her gaze, "that someone born outside the Old Dominion cannot understand. But at least you are not from North Carolina."

"Yes, Ma'am," I replied, "I've heard that it's a vale of humility between two mountains of conceit." Taken aback, Mrs. Owens raised her eyebrows in an alarming fashion and continued.

"So in order to help you overcome this deficiency you and Mary Ann together will study the little museum at the Home for Confederate Wives and Daughters. See if you can interview one of the ladies as well as visiting the exhibits at Battle Abbey. That includes the Stonewall Jackson memorabilia. His horse, Old Sorrel, now stuffed, is displayed at the museum with Jackson's saddle and field equipment. Flurry Cartwright, you and Christina Morris will do the President of the Confederacy, Jefferson Davis," Mrs. Owens went on with her assignments.

Later that week, the *Richmond Times Dispatch* featured an account of the bees in Traveller's mouth. I read this article with considerable interest. Apparently beekeepers had been consulted. The Fire Company had offered one of its tall ladders with a basket so the enormous statue could be reached and the bees removed. There was actually an argument as to who should take the bees down, and if the mouth of Traveller should be plugged up so that another swarm could not enter it. Letters to the Editor arrived from people all over Richmond offering their suggestions of how to rid Traveller of his honey.

"Our monuments are precious and the sooner those bees are out the better," Mrs. Owens told her history class the next Friday afternoon as we sat in the stifling classroom.

"But," I objected, "the bees have a right to make their honey. Why can't they stay there until the honey-making season is over?"

"Then we could gather Traveller's famous honey and sell it for a dollar a pint," suggested Sarah Ross, who was always enterprising.

"Yes, Mrs. Owens, and let our history class set up a booth down on the grass plot to sell the honey. Just think of the money we could make," Mary Ann laughed.

"And the traffic jam we would cause," giggled Frances Jones.

"We could call it Lee's Honey Pot and dress in old fashioned clothes as they do in Williamsburg," Flurry Cartwright suggested.

"Girls, girls, come to order," Mrs. Owens pulled her history class to attention. "Flurry, it is very hot in this room, would you please open the French doors?"

Flurry not only opened the doors, but burst right out onto the balcony, something that was strictly forbidden.

"Mrs. Owens, look! Some men are riding in a basket at Lee's statue," she cried.

In an instant the whole class ran to the windows. We pushed and shoved each other in order to see what was happening at the end of the block. Mrs. Owens apparently feared for our lives.

"Come girls, we shall go outside."

Then with her aristocratic head held high she led us from the classroom, down the stairs, and out onto the grass plot.

At the statue we found the fire department and several beekeepers. Two men covered in hats with nets and wearing gloves rode in the basket at the end of a long ladder being winched from an enormous fire engine. Below, inside the iron fence, stood various people of importance. Newspaper reporters and photographers were easily recognizable, but several other men were not. Everyone stood with his head back looking skyward, sheltering his eyes from the sun.

Mrs. Owens led us across Monument Avenue into the acre of ground that surrounded the statue. She marched us right up to the most important-looking person she could find and inquired.

What's going on? Are Traveller's bees coming down?"

The man regarded her with some amusement, and then looked at the fourteen girls who followed.

'I am Mrs. Owens from the Monument School, and this is my seventh grade history class," she introduced us. "We are extremely interested in Traveller's honey bees."

"I see," replied the fire chief, for so he turned out to be.

"We are trying to decide what can be done. Since we are unable to burn them out, because it would damage the statue, we shall have to wait for the bees to become sleepy, and take them down - hive, honey and all."

"Who are those men?" I asked pointing.

"They're bee keepers from The University, here to investigate the problem."

Fascinated, I watched the two men high up in the basket working at the great horse's mouth. At last their basket was lowered, and they climbed out.

"Well?" asked the fire chief, as the two bee experts approached and removed their protective clothing.

"We shall have to wait until it's a little colder. There is a great swarm up there with lots of honey. If we wait a week or two, the bees will become sleepy, and we can remove them quite easily," the younger expert suggested.

"I quite agree. Then we can plug up the mouth to prevent any more bees invading Traveller." The second man regarded us with amusement. "This is quite a delegation you have here."

"I am Mrs. Owens from the Monument School and this is my class.

We are very interested in the bees."

"So are we all," laughed the beekeeper. "Traveller's got a real sweet tooth and quite a honey pot."

"The girls thought they might set up a stand and sell it," continued Mrs. Owens, as Frances and Christina blushed scarlet.

"When do you think you'll be able to take the bees down?"

"Perhaps next week, or the week after. We'll let you know," the fire chief promised.

Little did I dream then what trouble this two-week's delay would cause. Mary Ann and I had arranged for me to spend the night at her house, so we could visit Battle Abbey and the Confederate museum on Saturday morning to complete our assignment.

I found this museum awe-inspiring. It contained not only Stonewall Jackson's camp gear, as well as Old Sorrel's remains and his saddle and bridle, but also maps of the famous Valley Campaign. That classic campaign in which Jackson hit the enemy quickly and hard before he disappeared to suddenly strike again.

Behind the museum, on the Boulevard, was the Home for Confederate Wives and Daughters. In this handsome building lived Mrs. Preston, Mary Ann's aunt's friend. We were invited to visit her on Saturday afternoon.

Mary Anne's Aunt Jojo, a Latin teacher in the public schools, arranged for us to visit Mrs. Preston, whose father had fought and died for the Confederacy. He had been wounded several times and was finally laid in a hero's grave after the Battle of Gettysburg, that terrible battle in a tiny Pennsylvania town where General Lee's army was cut to pieces. It was the high-water mark of the Confederacy. But for two more years the brave Southern Armies had continued to fight and die for The Cause.

Mrs. Preston was now an old lady in her eighties. And Aunt Jojo told us her friend was not only as bright as a new penny, but also a fascinating person. I was looking forward to meeting her. At three-thirty Mary Ann and I, dressed in clean skirts and blouses, took the bus up to the Boulevard, walked through the grounds of the museums and arrived at the Home for Confederate Wives and Daughters at just four o'clock.

A Forgotten Landscape

4

Mrs. Preston's Story

A Negro porter with closely cropped gray hair opened the door for us. As soon as I crossed the threshold of that elegant building, I felt as if I had stepped back into the past.

"We have come to see Mrs. Agnes Preston," Mary Ann said.

"Yes, miss, she is expecting you," replied the courtly old servant. He led us down the corridor into a bright cheerful sitting room furnished with several groups of chairs and love seats decorated in flowered chintz of pretty blues and yellows. Plain blue curtains with yellow fringe hung at the tall windows. Seated at one of the love seats was a very old lady dressed in a high collared white blouse and a plain brown skirt. Her ivory colored hair she wore piled high on her head. And in her hand I noticed she carried a fan to create a little breeze for herself on that hot, humid September afternoon.

"Mrs. Preston, here are the girls you were expecting," the porter introduced us.

The old lady smiled and seemed very pleased to welcome us.

"Do be seated. Mary Ann and Catherine, how nice of you to wish to interview an old lady on such a hot afternoon."

Mary Ann sat in the chair across from Mrs. Preston while I stood fascinated and stared at her. She was the oldest old lady I had ever met. She could have passed for a much younger woman, as her appearance belied her eighty-two years. She had deep brown eyes and beautiful skin, which was gently wrinkled.

Her quick glance regarded me as she sat like a queen before us on the love seat.

"Would you like to sit down, Catherine?" She offered again.

"Mary Ann, I understand from your Aunt Jojo you are doing a history project on Richmond's part in the War Between the States."

That was how the older Southerners always referred to the war that so changed their lives. Only Yankees and the uninitiated dared call it the Civil War.

"Yes, ma'am," Mary Ann replied. "We wondered how it affected your life."

"Well, I was a very small child, about three years old, when Papa was wounded at Gettysburg and died shortly after that great battle." I noticed she said Papa with the accent upon the second syllable and used the old-fashioned pronunciation, referred to by Virginians as the broad A.

"Mama and Grandmama lived in Richmond during the war, just outside of the city on a farm. My grandmama was a widow with two daughters, Mama, and her younger and extremely pretty sister, Aunt Belle. She was nineteen in 1863 and a flirtatious girl with her eye on a handsome Confederate major from Fredericksburg. Grandmama was determined Aunt Belle would train to become a teacher and would delay marriage until after the war. Mama's early widowhood, the deaths and terrible wounds suffered by other young relatives and friends with wives and small children had been devastating. Grandmama decided to spare her younger daughter this kind of loss.

"But Aunt Belle, in spite of her mother's dictates, considered herself engaged to John Taylor and, as soon as the war was over, she was determined to marry him. Quite as strong-willed as her mother, Belle usually got her way.

"Confederate paper money by 1863 was hardly worth the paper it was printed on. Many Richmond families began to hoard gold coins. But as money became scarce and the pawn shops on the wrong side of Broad Street, (you know, the north side where the saloons used to be) became filled with family silver and every conceivable thing of value, the pawn brokers stopped buying. Mama buried her silver in the garden near the old apple tree, and swore she would never pawn it. Times were very difficult for my family, and Grandmama decided to send Aunt Belle to Washington, D.C. to meet our Uncle Franklin Preston. He lived in Troy, New York, and was a professor of economics. He also had a small investment business. It was a daring plan, because Aunt Belle would be

Mrs. Preston's Story

passed through the lines under army escort. And she was to carry all the gold coins that my mother and her friends could hoard. After much discussion Grandmama finally persuaded her brother-in-law, Judge Joseph Smith, to arrange the trip.

"The plan was for Great Uncle Franklin to invest the money in Northern securities. Mama had to be very careful, because Richmond was a nest of spies and of rumors. Only very close friends were let in on the secret. For weeks during the summer of 1863 these families collected their gold coins and brought them to our house in great stealth after dark.

Grandmama had buried some gold coins in the box with Mama's silver, and so one moonless night the two women went into the garden and dug up the earth around the apple tree. They took the gold coins from the box and reburied the silver. I can still remember behind an old portrait of Grandpapa, there was a small map folded up into a tiny square and hidden under the wooden stretchers covered by the enormous gilt frame. This map told the location of the silver.

"Aunt Belle was allowed to carry only one small trunk. In it she packed the barest necessities. Since all her dresses were three years behind the current fashion she very much wanted new ones. The crinolines that ladies wore before the war had given way to a new style. Because of the war, few ladies' magazines and fashion supplies reached Richmond and Aunt Bell could not wait to have a new outfit. Always resourceful, Grandmama made a lovely traveling suit from an old dress of hers. In it, she hid the gold coins, skillfully using them as weights in the skirt and in the jacket hems. She even put some coins in the cuffs of the coat with the utmost assurance of an expert seamstress. The navy suit was considered very fashionable by Richmond's standards, and what Yankee would dream that such a charming young woman could be carrying five hundred dollars in gold?

Mr. Gambini, the local shoe man, made over a good pair of leather boots for the journey. Mama offered a perky bonnet to finish off the costume and in its quilted lining more gold coins were carefully sewn. The morning of her departure, Aunt Belle looked the height of fashion, even without a crinoline.

Great Uncle Joseph made careful arrangements for two Confederate soldiers to escort Aunt Belle to Fredericksburg on the train. There she would be passed over to two Yankee soldiers who would take her by packet boat on to Washington. Aunt Belle, who expected an exciting adventure, looked forward to going. But she was terrified by the thought of being passed over to Yankee soldiers for the remaining part of her trip.

"Finally everything was ready. On the morning of Aunt Belle's departure Great Uncle Joseph arrived at our house early with his ancient horse and trap. After a great many good-byes and promises to write, uncle and niece finally drove down Cary Street Road towards Richmond and the railroad station.

"At Main Street Station Great Uncle Joseph, after some difficulty, found the two officers who would escort Aunt Belle to Fredericksburg. Not only did she find them charming, but they in turn seemed delighted to take such a fashionable young lady into their charge. She was a terrible flirt, you know.

"The cars were overcrowded with soldiers and their equipment. On the platform several Richmond women helped the wounded, the remnants of General Lee's army, from the train and led them towards the waiting ambulances. Uncle Joseph finally located three places in a forward carriage and secured Aunt Belle's little trunk under the seat. He hugged his niece affectionately and then waved goodbye from the platform as the train pulled out of the station.

"The first fifty miles to Fredericksburg Aunt Belle found the most uncomfortable part of the whole journey. The train stopped at every country crossroads and only crawled at a snail's pace after long delays. Although the windows were opened the carriage soon became hot and dusty. Fear nearly choked her when Aunt Belle found herself surrounded by hordes of men of all conditions. Some of them looked no more than boys who regarded the fashionably dressed young woman with dull weary eyes. Laying their caps and guns beside them, and with their torn, dirty tunics folded under their heads as pillows, these exhausted youngsters slept. Aunt Belle felt shocked to see the proud Richmond Blues reduced to such tired, battle-scarred men.

"Along the railroad line she saw twisted parts of abandoned cannon and wagons. A dead horse lay in a farmyard, its barn and house reduced to ashes, burned to the ground by the retreating army. Never had Aunt Belle seen such devastation. Suddenly she found herself shaking with sobs as the distance between her and her dear ones in Richmond multiplied by miles. The desolate countryside frightened her, and she wondered if she would ever be able to return home again. Quickly she brushed away her tears, determined to stay as brave as she could manage until she reached Washington, as she had promised John Taylor. Even though she had no idea whether he was still alive, she prayed he would come back safely to Richmond.

" At Fredericksburg, Aunt Belle felt relieved as she climbed down from the crowded dusty train with her escort, and walked up the station platform overflowing with men, guns and ambulance wagons.

" 'Who's that Southern belle?' asked a bearded half-drunken soldier leaning against the waiting room door. "Good morning, dear."

"The two gray-.clad lieutenants closed ranks on a terrified Aunt Belle and hastened down Fredericksburg's main street towards the Rappahannock River. From here the packet boat under Captain Patrick O'Neal would take her to Washington. He was instructed to take Aunt Belle in charge, although she would also be escorted by two Yankee officers who would hand her over only to Uncle Franklin in Washington.

"At the quay under the high cliffs of the river waited a small flat-bottomed skipjack, the kind of boat used by the fishermen on the Chesapeake Bay. At the water's edge stood two smartly dressed Yankee soldiers in blue uniforms talking to a wiry man with bushy eyebrows and a brilliant red mustache. As Aunt Belle regarded them her heart fell into her boots. The Captain appeared to be an Irish fisherman, as he wore no uniform. Apprehensively she wondered if the two Yankee soldiers would harm her. For one fleeting moment she wanted to run back up the street and return to Richmond.

" 'Miss Belle Smith?' inquired the Captain, his blue eyes not unkind. 'We are expecting you. Please show me your travel documents.' With her fingers trembling she opened her pocket book and withdrew her pass and her identification papers. The Captain and the two officers read them over carefully.

" 'Everything is in order here. I understand, Miss Smith, you will be met in Washington by your uncle, Mr. Franklin Preston,' the first officer remarked, regarding her quizzically.

" 'Yes, that's right,' replied Aunt Belle.

" 'How do we know you are not a Confederate spy?' teased the second officer as he picked up her trunk. "In the North we shoot spies."

" 'Yes, I've heard.' Her Southern pride took over. 'We in the South are more gracious. But I am no spy, just a Southern girl traveling to meet my uncle from Troy, New York.'

"Apparently satisfied with her papers, the escort returned them. Then the two Yankees saluted smartly the two lieutenants in gray and without another word took Aunt Belle by the arm and led her up the gangplank.

" 'Goodbye and thank you,' she called to the retreating backs of her Southern guards, and stood in line behind several other passengers.

"A few minutes later the ropes holding the packet to the pier were cast off, and Captain O'Neal expertly backed his little craft out into the channel of the river. Swift and deep, the Rappahannock ran like a dark snake towards the Chesapeake Bay. Aunt Belle stood on the deck and watched the numerous boats filled with troops, guns, horses and mules pass her on their journey South. She realized that the Yankees must be planning a new offensive. The amount of guns and troops alarmed the Southern girl. They presented a marked contrast to the exhausted soldiers she had seen on the train between Richmond and Fredericksburg. Fighting back her tears, because John Taylor would wish her to be brave and dignified, Aunt Belle understood for the first time that with all these munitions and men the Yankees could quite possibly win this terrible war. Whatever would become of her family in Richmond if these troops captured the city? Presently she noticed that the two officers escorting her to Washington were regarding her closely. This caused her considerable alarm. In all her 19 years she had never traveled without a companion of her own sex, no matter how short the journey. Being in the charge of men she did not know made her feel apprehensive - especially Yankee men. As the little boat slipped through the water a gun placement on the southern bank opened fire.

"The Captain turned the skipjack first to the left and then immediately back to the right. In the next instant Aunt Belle found herself lying flat upon the deck as shells whizzed over her head and landed in the water in front of them. The young officer had pushed her down with his strong hands and held her pinned against the boat's planking.

" 'What are you doing?' the frightened girl demanded as she struggled to free herself. 'Let me go, sir.'

"Not knowing what she might expect from a Yankee soldier, Aunt

Mrs. Preston's Story

Belle wondered anxiously what he was up to.

" 'Your rebel guns along the river have opened fire upon us. Do you want to be killed?' The young man held her fast.

"Terrified that he should discover her dress was filled with gold coins Aunt Belle continued to struggle.

" 'Unhand me, sir,' she demanded, feeling her sense of propriety outraged. 'I shall report you to the Captain. How dare you touch me!'

" 'Sorry, miss, but you are a perfect target in your blue dress. You look just like a Yankee.'

"Blinded by fury that she could possibly be mistaken for anything other than a true Confederate, Aunt Belle sank her teeth into the strong hand which restrained her.

" 'I'll take my chances,' she retorted. 'You are no gentleman!'

" 'Ouch,' came a cry of pain. 'In Pennsylvania, ladies do not bite.' "The surprised officer regarded his pretty attacker in disbelief.

"After another deafening salvo the firing stopped as the little skipjack scooted out of range. The boat, piloted by its able Irish captain, whacked the waves and moved steadily seaward. Tricky winds and sudden storms make the Chesapeake Bay one of the most dangerous bodies of water on the East Coast. Only the flat-bottomed skipjack is seaworthy in such currents. These tough little fishing boats are designed to sail on the bay and in its tributary rivers. Captain O'Neal knew these waters well and was considered an expert sailor. Few civilian boats continued to make this run through Confederate held country, but he still ferried important people deep into enemy territory. As a special favor, he had consented to take the Southern young lady to Washington to meet her uncle. He had carried several other young ladies, from both the North and the South, during the three years of conflict, and he had been well compensated for his trouble. With General Mosby's irregulars sabotaging the railroads throughout Northern Virginia, and with the Union forces in control of the coast, a boat was considered the safest means of travel.

"After the firing stopped, still furious, Aunt Belle stood up, and smoothed down her dress. Her cheeks flushed scarlet and her eyes sparkled with anger. Although she felt humiliated, she quickly regained her dignity and walked around the deck to the lounge door. Inside she found a chair away from the other passengers and sat down. Her escort maintained a respectful distance. Neither spoke, but she regarded the two men sent to watch over her with open hostility.

"She noticed the passengers numbered just ten. Two men in civilian clothes spoke together in hushed tones, apparently deep in conversation. Aunt Belle wondered if they might be Yankee spies. She watched with interest as three Union officers entered the lounge. One of them walked on crutches. He looked tired and sick, but his uniform appeared new and well pressed. Considerably alarmed for her safety Aunt Belle was horrified when she realized she was the only woman on board. Fear caused her to raise her head higher, making her appear quite haughty.

" 'I earnestly hoped nobody dared speak to me because my reply would be rude or, worse yet, I might burst into tears.' She told me this years later.

"Aunt Belle did not know it, but their route was an extremely dangerous one. It was fifty miles to Washington on land, but Aunt Belle had no idea how far by water. The Rappahannock flowed south through Virginia's northern neck. The few Confederate guns that lined the bank several times sent salvos across the skipjack's bow. Boats equipped with cannon answered. And for several minutes the little packet boat scudded to and fro trying to avoid being hit. But as dusk gradually fell, the gun emplacements became silent. Traveling without lights, Captain O'Neal ran his sails up and slipped past the landings at Urbanna and Irvington. Now the Rappahannock widened, and under cover of darkness the skipjack sailed by Deltaville at the mouth of the river and finally out into the bay.

"Allowing plenty of space between his boat and the hostile batteries on the shore, Captain O'Neal rounded the eastern most point of the northern neck. He kept a sharp lookout for the channel buoys that marked the mouth of the Potomac River. Swiftly the sturdy craft glided northwestward through the dark night headed towards Point Lookout near the Yankee Prison Camp on the Maryland shore.

"As the evening progressed Aunt Belle found the Union Army's presence on the Rappahannock River overwhelming. Feelings of concern for her family's safety finally drove- her into the solitude of her cabin. In the sheltering darkness she fought back her tears. The immediate danger of the packet boat and its passengers seemed trifling compared to what the future might hold for her family. She thought of John Taylor and prayed he was not dead, but safe somewhere, perhaps in a northern prison camp or even back with his own regiment. Lying in the dark, gently rolling to the ship's motion, Aunt Belle suddenly realized how naive she was just twenty-four hours earlier. Until today she had never doubted that the South would win its glorious Cause.

" 'How terribly brave I've been.' she remarked aloud. 'And I'm only a girl.'

"Now nothing seemed to make sense to her anymore. Even the boat sailed south down the Rappahannock to take her north. No one had told her Captain O'Neal would come under enemy fire. Suppose she, a Southern girl, should be killed by Confederate cannon shot? This very afternoon a Yankee soldier had knocked her onto the ship's deck in order to save her life. She felt everything had suddenly become upside down and deathly ironic. Then finally she slept.

"During the night the skipjack, still running without lights, rounded Far Port on the Virginia Coast. Just before they reached Port Lookout on the Maryland side of the Potomac River, Captain O'Neal turned west towards Washington. At dawn Aunt Belle awoke to the sound of gunfire. A second battery answered. The sturdy craft bounced like a toy as the shells exploded around it. Almost tossed out of bed onto the floor, Aunt Belle tried to remember where she was. Suddenly she lay in the dark blushing as she recalled how she had bitten the Yankee officer's hand. No Southern lady, unless seriously provoked, would do such a thing.

" 'How could I've acted like such a vixen?' Then she remembered the gold.

Eventually the firing ceased and the little boat continued on its journey up the Potomac River towards Washington and Uncle Franklin.

"At eight o'clock Aunt Belle dressed and went upstairs to the main deck. With her she took a hamper of food. When she entered the lounge in search of coffee, her escort was already there waiting for her.

" 'Good morning, Miss,' greeted the man whose hand she had bitten.

" 'Good morning,' Aunt Belle replied blushing. She carried her head a trifle higher to cover up her true feelings. She felt, being a Virginian, she must maintain her dignity and her loyalty to The Cause.

" 'There is some hot coffee. Let me get you a cup,' the other young officer-suggested.

" 'Yes, thank you,' she replied.

"As they ate their breakfast the sun climbed higher, promising a warm September day.

"The Potomac River twisted and turned as the Captain expertly guided his boat up stream through a great number of barges that carried supplies towards the Chesapeake Bay. Along the banks Aunt Belle noticed the many guns and troops assigned to protect the nation's capitol from the rebels.

"Late that afternoon when the skipjack tied up at the docks of Washington, Aunt Belle felt she had entered another world. Despite the war Washington had its lights on, and campfires glowed along the waterfront. Soldiers and stevedores crowded the docks, and guns, wagons and cannon lined the quays. How would Uncle Franklin find her in all of this multitude, Aunt Belle wondered. The docks looked dangerous with rough seamen, armed soldiers and the common rabble usually found at river piers. Rough, uncouth men who held Southern womanhood in little regard watched her from the pier. Aunt Belle felt suddenly thankful for her escort.

"Although she strained to catch a glimpse of a familiar face amid the crowds upon the banks, Aunt Belle saw nobody she recognized. Tears welled up in. her eyes, and fear made her catch her breath. Defiantly she brushed the tears away. No Yankee would ever see her cry. But what would become of her now? she wondered. Suppose Uncle Franklin did not arrive to claim her? Would the Yankees find the gold coins she had hidden in her dress? And how would she ever get back home again?

"Suddenly a familiar voice called her name. Aunt Belle had never experienced such joy in her entire life. Before her stood Uncle Franklin, solid and serene. She threw her arms around his neck and burst into tears.

" 'There, there, my girl,' he comforted her. 'I just could not get through the crowds, that's all. Let me see your papers.'

"From her handbag she took out the travel permit documents. They were stamped by the Confederates with red seals and by the Yankees with blue ones. The port official took them from her uncle.

" 'Everything is in order here, Miss.' smiled the Captain.

" 'Goodbye now.' The official read the documents and stood aside to let her pass.

" 'Goodbye, Sir,' replied Aunt Belle, drying her tears.

" 'Thank you for a very comfortable journey.'

"Still under escort she and Uncle Franklin left the ship. They walked down the dock to an awaiting carriage, and the young officer, with his hand still red from the bite, hoisted up the trunk to the driver. Once inside Uncle Franklin gave the two soldiers the necessary papers and instantly the horses stepped forward at a brisk trot.

" 'Oh, Uncle Franklin,'" sobbed Aunt Belle, quite overcome with relief. 'I am so happy to see you!'

" 'My dear girl,' he put his arm around her, 'What a brave thing you have done.'

"Belle dried her tears. 'Yes,' she replied, amazed at the thought, 'I suppose it is.'

"Her uncle laughed. Then regarding the frightened girl in her unfashionable dress he drew her close to him and hugged her.

"They remained in Washington for three days. Uncle Franklin needed time to make arrangements for their transportation to upper New York State, and Aunt Belle was dying to buy some new clothes. Together they visited several shops and found two very pretty dresses, copies of the latest styles from Paris. Then Aunt Belle was fitted for a fine pair of leather boots, and a fashionable bonnet. She felt quite a new woman when she and her uncle boarded the train for Troy, New York. Uncle Franklin appeared equally delighted to have such a pretty, flirtatious niece.

"With great care he invested the money Aunt Belle had brought sewn in her dress. These investments kept us and our neighbors from starving during the devastating reconstruction years.

"But Grandmama was very displeased, because her brother had invested in companies engaged in manufacturing war goods. For many years she felt Uncle Franklin had turned against his family, and may have caused the deaths of some of his own people. Although he continued to visit us after he brought his niece home, in her heart Grandmama never forgave him.

"She almost did not come to my wedding, because you see, I married my third cousin, Thomas Preston. And Grandmama thought anyone with that name was a traitor to The Cause. Although, I will admit, she enjoyed the fruits of Aunt Belle's golden suit, as we called it.

"That flirtatious young lady remained in the north for three years. She trained to become a teacher and was happy during her long visit in

Troy. When she did return to Richmond, Aunt Belle worked very hard teaching school, even after she married. Her young man survived almost two years in a Yankee prison camp and came home with his health broken. Unable to work and with little money, he spent the first 18 months after the peace trying to regain his former vigor. Three years after the war, when things at home became easier Aunt Belle finally married her proud Major John Taylor from Fredericksburg. And even Grandmama approved."

I sat fascinated as Mrs. Preston finished her story. She was an excellent storyteller. She lowered her voice in the exciting places and her eyes took on a very serious look. I could hardly believe when the porter interrupted us with a tray of tea cups and a silver tea service, that we had been there for over an hour. Sedately the aged servant poured us each a cup of hot tea and offered milk and lemon. Then he passed a plateful of elegant~looking cookies, first to Mrs. Preston, then to Mary Ann and me. I hesitated and held my hand over the plate, undecided which one to take.

"Have two," Mrs. Preston offered. "They are extremely good, and one hardly seems enough - especially on a hot afternoon."

I smiled at her gratefully and did as I was bidden, and found these some of the most delicious cookies I had ever eaten.

It was about five-thirty when Mrs. Preston stood up and walked with us down the corridor towards the front door. She chatted happily to Mary Ann about her Mother and Aunt Jojo. Then standing in the open doorway she waved us goodbye in her friendly, yet stately manner.

"I hope the history project goes well," she smiled, "do come again if you need any more help. I have so much enjoyed meeting both of you this afternoon."

Then Mary Ann and I stepped out again into the modern world.

Part II

All the next week we worked on writing the paper. I took one part, my friend another - until we finally put together a project that we both felt was good. Each afternoon I did my homework on the grass plot in order to keep an eye upon Traveller's bees. I was afraid that the fire chief

Mrs. Preston's Story

and the beekeepers might forget to tell Mrs. Owens when they planned to take down the nest. And I was determined not to miss a second of that exciting occurrence.

On Friday, before the paper was due I planned to spend the afternoon with Mary Ann so we could put the finishing touches to our project. The paper was due on Monday, and we had to copy it over in ink in our best handwriting. Since it was a very hot afternoon I decided to go down to the grass plot near the Lee monument and write the final copy out under the trees.

"They won't take those bees down on a Friday," Mary Ann insisted. "It looks like rain, so I'm going to walk on home."

"I'll be there in an hour or so," I promised. "I must keep a watch on those bees. I would hate to miss all that excitement since I am staying in town."

So we parted. I took my ink bottle, two fountain pens, a packet of fresh paper and my notebook down to the grass plot and found a pleasant place where I could write. Carefully I copied over the notes, made a very bad blot and started to copy the story again. A strange noise attracted my attention. Suddenly behind me at Lee's monument stood a fire truck with its long ladder. Two men in protective masks and gloves appeared and climbed into the basket. The gates into the grassy knoll upon which the statue stood were flung open and several men entered carrying cameras.

Excited by the prospect of seeing the bees and the honey being taken out of Traveller's mouth, I folded my papers into the notebook, put the ink bottle on top of it so they would not blow away, and ran towards the fire truck. As the cameras clicked, the two beekeepers gently removed the honeycombs, and placed them into a large covered box. The bees swarmed and then settled in the box with their queen. Afterwards the beekeepers in their basket were lowered back down to the ground.

Next two firemen entered the basket and were winched up to Traveller's mouth. They cleaned the statue of wax and honey before they put a plug in to keep another swarm from nesting there. I strained my eyes, shading them from the sun, to see what was going on.

"Are you from Mrs. Owens's class?" the fire chief inquired.

"Yes," I replied. "I would not have missed this for the world. I'm sorry the rest of the girls couldn't see it."

"It is too bad, but we couldn't get those fellows from The University except this afternoon." The fire chief regarded me. "I think it's starting to rain."

Sure enough, great wet drops fell on my head and splashed down upon my dress. A cooling breeze began to blow, and leaves, limp and dusty, moved lazily on the trees.

"Oh," I cried, "my paper. I must go. Thank you very much for allowing me to see this."

"Don't go," called the fireman, "let me show you the honey we got. Maybe your friends could sell it," he laughed.

"I've left my papers under the trees on the grass plot," I ran towards the blue square that was my notebook.

But the rain was faster than I was. It splashed down in sheets as I gathered up my belongings and tried to find some protection under the trees. Finally, dripping wet I sat down on the notebook to keep my precious report dry. I prayed the washable blue ink we were instructed to use would not run and spoil my notes.

Half an hour later I arrived at Mary Ann's house soaking wet and clutching my notebook folded in a sweater.

"Doc, where have you been?" laughed Mrs. Thornton. "You look like a drowned rat."

She brought me inside and took the notebook from my arms. Then she made me take off my shoes.

"Go upstairs immediately and get into a hot tub," she commanded.

"Mrs. Thornton," I pleaded, my heart thumping in my chest, "just open the notebook and see if the ink on my report has run."

When she removed the sodden cover, I gasped. Inside we found some of my carefully written pages wet beyond repair. But others were still in fairly good shape. I burst into tears.

"Oh, no," I wailed, "our report is due on Monday. I'll have to rewrite it."

Mary Ann ran into the room, and regarded the dripping pages. Then she stared at me in disbelief.

"How could you?" she demanded. "Really, Doc, you are impossible."

"You girls go upstairs while I put these papers on the kitchen table. I'll open the oven door and the heat should dry them out." Mrs. Thornton took charge. "Mary Ann, find Doc something to put on while I dry her clothes. Go on girls, move."

We scurried up the stairs, and I was soon soaking in a hot tub while Mary Ann found a skirt and blouse of hers for me to wear. I had just brought a change of under clothes and a nightgown with me since I was going home on Saturday afternoon.

Mrs. Thornton, meanwhile, laid out the soggy papers and turned on her oven. Slowly the report dried and the ink did not smear any more.

"It will be all right. But you'll have to copy it over," she told us after I reappeared dressed and warm.

And so we started to copy the report. Mary Ann and I sat up at the dining room table with our notes, my wet papers and her neatly written copy — and wrote. We read aloud the pages that were smeared and tried to make out what I had said. Then we compared my notes with hers and copied out the pages carefully in a neat hand. After consuming numerous glasses of iced tea Mrs. Thornton made for us, and making many mistakes with inkblots, we finally finished the paper at four o'clock the next afternoon. Our whole Saturday was spent at the table writing. September can be very hot and humid in Virginia, and we drank tea and ate ice until Mrs. Thornton feared for our kidneys. Finally we finished. We read the report over. Mrs. Thornton read it too and after a few corrections in punctuation, we finally placed it in a cover and collapsed into living room chairs. It was only then I noticed the clock.

"Oh, glory, Miss Emma will be waiting for me at school. I've got to go."

Grabbing my things I darted out the door and ran all the way to the Monument School. Just as I rounded the corner a block away I saw Miss Emma's car. She pulled out from the curb and headed east toward J. E. B. Stuart's monument, then turned around it to come up on the other side of the grass plot, I crossed the street and ran down the grass plot, but she didn't see me waving at her frantically to stop. I was left behind. Angry tears streaked down my face as I walked back to the Thorntons.

"I'll be in almighty trouble now," I told Mrs. Thornton as she opened the front door, "I've missed my ride home."

"Never mind, dear, I'll call your mother, and Miss Emma too, and explain. You will just have to spend the night. Mary Ann, we have guests." I stayed for the weekend, and worried a good part of the time how to make it up to Cary's mother.

On Monday morning dressed in Mary Ann's clothes, I walked to school with her. She carried the paper because she didn't trust me with it.

"You never know, it might rain again or you'll forget it and leave it behind," she teased me. "You look rather nice in my skirt and blouse."

Mrs. Owens was in high spirits that afternoon. She accepted our papers one by one, listening to our explanations about them.

"Oh, by the way, girls," she opened her history book, "the newspaper had quite an interesting account of the removal of the bees from Traveller's mouth. It seems that it was done late Friday afternoon. It's a pity we could not have been there," she regarded me "because it's a nice postscript to our studies."

I withdrew my eyes from her gaze, and glanced at Mary Ann. Her face looked grim.

"Yes ma'am," I replied, "I might have learned a little more about Virginia's history." I didn't dare tell her I was there because Mary Ann would kill me.

"These are things you'll remember, Catherine," Mrs. Owens gave me a knowing smile.

I agreed.

5

Coming of War

Just before school opened in September we heard on the radio that the Nazis had marched into Poland. Britain objected because she had a treaty with Poland and promised to come to her aid. Neville Chamberlain waited over a nerve-racked forty-eight hours. When Hitler made no response and the invasion of his small neighbor continued, the Prime Minister told the British people over the radio, "We are now in a state of war." A few hours later the French Prime Minister, Edouard Daladier, also declared war on Germany.

Father turned his short wave off. He leaned back in his chair in our library and closed his eyes. His face looked drawn; his lips were tight. He opened his eyes and saw me standing in front of him. Then taking down the Atlas from the shelf, Father opened it and showed me a map of Europe and pointed out the countries involved. He told me about Hitler and his enormous military buildup since the Great War which had ended in 1918.

"I was in Russia with the American Expeditionary Force stationed in Archangle and Mermansk. We lived in boxcars. I don't fancy doing that again in winter. We can't afford to go to war every twenty years," he said.

Father tried to explain to me there would be a war in Europe, and America would also get involved. "Since I'm in the military reserves, I'll have to go and most likely be sent overseas to fight with Britain."

I tried to understand all he said and listened very carefully even though I felt terrified. It was September 3rd, 1939, I remember, the day I lost my childhood ona bright Sunday at the end of the summer.

Finally, he decided to saddle Cherry, and we rode down to the James River together. We tied Cherry to a sappling and sat down on a grassy spot to watch the brown water flow towards Richmond. Neither of us spoke. About an hour later as dusk came over the land Mr. Talliaferro's foreman, Clyde Brewer, stopped by in his truck to tell us he must lock the gates to the low grounds, and we had to leave. Then Mr. Brewer lifted me onto the saddle in front of my dad, and we started back up the dirt road at a brisk trot.

"It's a good thing he was there to help us," Father told me as we rode along. "He's white so he's allowed to touch a white child. A Negro man must never touch a white child or a woman, and they must never touch him. Remember that, you young rebel, it's just not done."

I was thinking of other things. Mrs. Houghton cried that morning when we returned home after church, because she feared the war would never allow her to return to England and see her mother again. Mr. Houghton got cross with his little terrier, Peggy, for no reason, because he worried about his family in Yorkshire. Only Mother seemed unaffected as she went off to some function with her friends.

During the next week grainy pictures made of dots appeared in the newspapres showing the Polish defenses. I couldn't believe what I saw in the those photographs.

"They're sent by radio or wire," Father explained, "that's why they have that grainy quality. The poor devils are using horses against German tanks."

I wondered how the war would affect me, but although these events seemed far away, I realized that my world was about to change.

At church the following Sunday Mrs. Harrison, our elderly neighbor, knew her world was ripped apart and she cried openly.

"The War Between the States destroyed my father's family. They lost everything; their farm, their livilihood and six of their young men. My own brother was killed in the Spanish-American War, and my sister's son died in France in 1917. We were just getting back on our feet when the Depression came. Virginia must keep her old traditions in order to avoid choas. I remember the time when Yankee soldiers policed Richmond. Men no longer could vote or hold office, and they hardly had enough to keep their families together. We were poor, dirt poor. All we had were our traditions and our good name. I lived through those times, and now in my nineties I am forced to live through it again. Our way of life will be destroyed. Everything that has endured and been rebuilt will be swept away. This time forever. I can't face it at my time of life. Oh, God it's too much."

I listened to her amazed, understanding only part of what she said. Yet the meaning of her distress was clear, and the horror she felt scared me. Mrs. Taliaferro gently put her arm around Mrs. Harrison and offered to drive her home. I recognized her church handkerchief with the lace on it lying crumpled and wet in her hand as she mopped her streaming eyes.

Father took my arm and held it tight. He hurt me, yet I couldn't speak. My shock at seeing Mrs. Harrison in such a state quite unnerved me. The sun went under a cloud and the shadows in the churchyard felt cold. Father released me; he bent over and kissed me on the cheek. Then we walked to the car in silence.

That afternoon Mrs. Taliaferro came to call on us carrying a large basket. I opened the door for her.

"Is your Mother home?" She inquired.

"No, but Father is. Please come in, and I'll get him."

I escorted her into the living room and opened the shade to allow in some light. In summer the room was closed to keep the sun from fading the curtains and the furniture. Then I excused myself and found Dad upstairs reading. When I told him Mrs. Talioferro was waiting, he came immediately.

"I've come on account of Daisy Harrison. She's in an awful state since war was declared. She's lived through three wars and a depression and is sure Hitler will march up River Road next week. I've brought a basket, would you like to fill it with what-ever you can give to the poor old soul to provide her with a little security that we are not being invaded."

"Of course," Father said, "we'll send whatever you suggest. What would she like: fruit from the orchard or vegetables from the garden?"

"She's not got two coppers to rub together. All's that left of her family's past life is it's good name. Do you have any material left over, Doc, after making your school clothes? She'd love a new dress, and Mrs. Jones on River Road said she'd make it for her," Mrs. Taliaferro replied. "These old aristocratic families are pitiful because all they have left is their pride."

"Yes," Father agreed, "I've known a few. They follow Richmond's social conventions to the letter in order to maintain that pride. It's all they have left of a vanquished way of life. Mrs. Harrison remembers the Yankees' coming and how they burnt down her home. She knew a world that was totally destroyed seventy-five years ago. Although, she was a small child at the time, she's never forgotten."

I realized suddenly what I'd puzzled about for several weeks. Mrs. Houghton couldn't help me because she was English: Virginians' way of dressing: the ladies' print dresses, their hats and white gloves, and the men's seersucker suits. The strict adherance to outmoded codes of behavior gave these dispossessed families a form of status. The division of the races, the people one could touch or not touch, had all seemed baffling. The things ladies could and could not do, such as wear shorts to the movies at eleven years old which was forbidden. These all now made sense. The structure gave the chaotic world a feeling of order, of predictability. Yet I hated the restraints of all those silly rules.

No wonder Mrs. Owens disliked me. My family left Virginia in 1870 in her hour of need and only returned two generations later when the south was no longer defeated by war and reconstruction.

"Maybe my Atlanta grandmother will make a difference," I said aloud. "After all, Atlanta's famous because of *Gone With the Wind*."

Mrs. Taliaferro looked at me rather strangely not comprehending my newly acquired understanding of Virginians. I smiled and taking the basket left the room and filled it. A few minutes later I returned with some fruit and vegetables from our garden and two jars of Berta's watermellon pickles. She was known for her pickles which she made at our house every summer on our electric stove and put down in the basement in glass jars. I also found some leftover material from a school dress and a second piece left over from a Sunday one. These I added to the basket wrapped in tissue paper. I wondered if Mrs. Harrison would mind if we wore matching dresses to church one day. Then, feeling very virtuous, I returned to our guest.

"Well, Doc's got you amply supplied," Father greeted me. "I hope this will help."

"Thank you, my dear," said Mrs. Taliaferro as she took her basket. She seemed delighted with my offering. "You've been most generous."

"Do you think the war will last long?" I ventured as we escorted her to the door. "It's scary to see all those German tanks and soldiers in the pictures in the newspaper. Hitler's army looks mighty powerful."

"They are powerful. They are the most formidable military force in the world," Father replied.

"And the most deadly." Mrs. Taliaferro added. "it's a very frightening time, I agree. We must all pray to God that we can defeat them."

She smiled and was gone carrying her basket down our drive and walking very fast. I watched her thanking her silently for teaching me more about Virginians.

A Forgotten Landscape

6

Troubled Waters

Shortly after our arrival in Richmond Father met Rudy Melton at a party, and they became friends. I never understood why. Father enjoyed an adventurous life. After graduating from West Point he had served with the American Expeditionary Force in Russia during World War I. He spoke both French and German fluently and even remembered a smattering of Russian. During his trip to Austria and Czechoslovakia right after I was born, he had flown from Paris to Hamburg long before commercial flights were introduced.

Rudy Melton hated to fly and thought speaking German beneath him.

Although he had studied engineering at MIT, Father did not like business and secretly wished to become a war correspondent. Instead he'd taken a job with an engineering firm.

"Doc," he often told me, "for God's sake do what you want. I'll stand behind you all the way. My father insisted I become an engineer. It's all right, but not exciting."

Rudy, on the other hand, liked engineering. He built bridges, and roads, and tall buildings. His conversation included such expressions as tension, torque, stress and other construction terms. But when he rode Cherry one day and nearly fell off, and he got his fishing pole caught up in a tree causing Father to cut the line to free it, I thought Rudy hopeless in the country. His shoes were much too expensive for walking through mud, and his hats looked ridiculous. He loved to wear grousers hats and deerstalkers that made him appear like a fat Sherlock Holmes. He even carried a folded umbrella and fancied himself English.

"Who's that peacock?" asked Mr. Houghton one Sunday afternoon as he peered through his front window. "He looks like an actor."

"It's just Rudy Melton out walking with my parents."

"He's a bit of a clown, if you ask me," Mr. Houghton continued to stare.

"For goodness sake, Harry, close that curtain before some one sees you. Have you no manners?" asked his wife.

"Well, I've never seen anything quite like it," he sounded offended, "have you?"

"No, but that's no reason to be rude," Mrs. Houghton jerked the lace curtain from his hand and let it fall across the window. "Don't be a Peeping Tom."

"Where did he come from, I wonder? He's a new sight around here. Look at the get-up, will you?" Mr. Houghton went to the front door and peeked out.

"It's awful," I agreed. "He's an incredible bore. I don't know why Father likes him. Did you ever know Father to suffer bores gladly? He usually ignores them. And there's something fishy about Rudy Melton. Did you know his name used to be Rudolph Mueller? He came here from Milwaukee and works as an engineer with a construction company, " Father said he changed his name to hide his German origin."

I disliked Rudy Melton from the first day I met him, because he tried to pass himself off as something he wasn't.

"You know," I continued, "last summer Rudy tried to call himself Randolph, an old Virginian name. But Father stopped him. 'A bit pretentious!' he said, 'don't you think?' "

"The next time he came out he'd dropped the Randolph and was just plain old Rudy again. Now I want to know what you think of that?"

"He's up to no good, that one. I peg him as a social climber, if not worse. He's German, you say? Well, that may account for it then. Germans can be pushy, and they're very clever." Mr. Houghton watched as the walkers turned into the woods.

"Come away, Harry. You've heard nothing about that man. He might be an upright character, for all we know," Mrs. Houghton handed him part of the Sunday paper.

"He's sly, and up to no good, Mrs. Houghton," I told her. "He's out for what he can get. There's something sneaky about him, I feel sure."

"Well, of all the back-biting from the two of you. Really, you're as bad as Harry. Where do you get such ideas?"

She regarded me from over glasses allowing the *Richmond Times Dispatch* to fall across her knees. "Sit down, Harry, and read the paper. Doc, here're the funnies. Now no more talking about Rudy Melton' it's unkind."

"All right," I said under my breath, "but it's true."

Gradually Rudy began to accompany my parents to some of the more fancy parties at the Country Club. I thought this strange, but he was an excellent dancer, which Father was not, and Mother adored dancing. Soon Rudy made no secret of his admiration for Mother and openly praised her wit and beauty. Flattered by this attention to his pretty wife, Father joked about it. He apparently saw nothing unusual in their threesome. But I did and silently disapproved.

The weather remained fine and warm, so I spent a great deal of time with Billy, riding him and grooming him until he shone. I also took horseback riding and piano lessons twice a week. School kept me busy in between. Mary Ann had invited me in twice to spend the night, and she had come out one weekend to stay with me.

During this time I didn't see Father much, but he seemed silent and worried.

"Come, Son", he said one evening, "let's ride down to the lowgrounds, I need to talk to you." He called me "son" when there was something important he wished to tell me.

So we saddled up Cherry, and rode off together. I sat in front, held safely by his strong arms as we cantered over the road. He didn't say much, just spoke gently to the big hunter, encouraging and restraining. Finally we pulled up under the trees beside the river, and I slid off.

"I don't know how many more evenings we'll have like this," Father commented as he dismounted and tied Cherry's reins to a sapling. "So we'll enjoy ourselves."

"October's often warm" I replied, "so we might have more."

"What do you think of Rudy?" he asked.

Taken unawares, I didn't answer right away.

"Well?" Father asked again.

"I don't like him. He's sneaky."

Father laughed a great roar of a laugh. Cherry jumped in alarm. I caught his reins and held him.

"Whoa," I cooed, "whoa, it's okay, Cherry."

Father took the reins and secured them more tightly.

"Yes, you're right," he said. "You're a good judge of character for one so young."

"Mrs. Owens, my history teacher, thinks I'm strange because I'm not a Virginian."

We sat on the bank in a patch of grass and watched the brown river flow down towards Richmond.

"Then Mrs. Owens hasn't much sense. There's nothing strange about you, my dear."

Father crossed his long legs and laid his riding crop on his boots. "I think you are right about Rudy. A social climber and possibly a wife stealer, and a Yankee. Does Mrs. Ovens like Yankees?"

"Hates them. And North Carolinians next. She calls them ricky, ticky, tacky Tar Heels."

"Rudy's a Yankee, but he's ricky, ticky tacky all the same," Father replied.

"Mother likes him. At least she enjoys going to dances with him and you."

"Yes, that's the trouble. She can't see through him, what he's after."

"What is he after?" I asked, throwing a rock into the river.

"Money and social position. He's very interested in both. He's causing trouble"

"What kind of trouble?" I stood up in order to skim a flat stone across the water.

"Trouble between your mother and me."

I turned and watched him still stretched out on the riverbank supporting himself with his arms behind him, legs crossed. How tall he seemed, how handsome he looked in riding clothes. They were not new and flashy like Rudy's shoes, but were well worn and fit him comfortably. He looked a part of the country, easy in his manner, and relaxed. Rudy, by contrast, was always trying too hard to fit in. He had a shallow quality. He seemed a big city man trying to act like a country gentleman. I distrusted him and so did Mr. Houghton.

I ran down the bank pretending to find a flat stone, but really running away from the disturbing news Father told me. Deep inside me I knew things were wrong. The long silences at dinner, the sharp words when they thought I was out of ear shot. Finally in the last weeks, arguments, with both of them shouting. I was neither blind nor deaf. I had figured it out, and knew things had reached a breaking point. But I didn't wish to admit it, nor hear it this evening from Father.

"Come," he said at last, "we must be getting home. Cherry's restless and wants his hay."

He boosted me onto the chestnut horse's saddle and easily swung up behind me, riding double. Then we flew down the lowlands road at a gallop. Finally at the creek Father pulled the horse up. We crossed the bridge and I opened the gate into the pasture, held it as we went through and closed it. Again we galloped up the road towards the railroad tracks, and again we stopped to open a gate. After walking Cherry across the tracks we flew up the hill at a gallop and finally walked the last half-mile home.

"Never bring a horse in hot, it's very bad form," Father reminded me. "Cherry's coat is getting heavy and he needs to blow and cool out."

"Yes, sir," I replied, feeling the great muscles under my legs. "I know." I loved riding in front of Father and feeling the powerful animal under me.

"I hope you'll remember this evening - the river, the stones, and Cherry's exciting gallop up the hill. And me."

"You?" I asked, "I'll always remember you. We've something special between us, you and I. Something precious."

"Yes," he replied, his voice deep with emotion, "something very precious."

Slowly and carefully we unsaddled the big horse and gave him hay and oats. Father put on his sheet, patted him affectionately on the neck and closed the stall door. I carried the heavy saddle and bridle to the tack room. In the darkness I found the rack and hung them up. Then hand in hand Father and I walked across the bumpy grass towards the house. After that night nothing would remain the same.

A Forgotten Landscape

7

Secret Feelings

The autumn weather continued fine. Mary Ann and I took riding lessons at the Hunt Club on Broad Street once a week. Every second week we rode out on the trails and jumped over logs and ditches. Since I could jump now with adequate form and less fear, these were the lessons Mary Ann and I looked forward to. Our teacher, Major Kepler, was a German cavalry officer, who fought in the Great War 1914 -1918.

"Catherine, don't post so high. Dat's right. Mary Anne look up, look up, pretend you are a snob. Frances sit straight."

Around the ring we went, the Major insisting upon perfection. His methods were good, but he was terribly strict.

Occasionally we went on the weekly drag hunt.

Since the city was growing up, the Hunt Club's grounds were squeezed, surrounded by roads, the trails and streams were now threatened by encroaching buildings. There was talk of moving the Club out to Goochland, and Colonel Hollis and his committee had looked at land and made a proposal. Now with war threatening, this had been put aside until things worldwide were more settled.

"Sit down in your saddle more," Major Kepler instructed; "Catherine, make your stirrups a hole longer."

We used to make fun of his accent. He had a lisp as well as the Teutonic trouble with th and W. We thought his pronunciation terribly funny. But suddenly we realized in Hitler's Germany, Major Kepler's daughter, a student in Berlin, was having difficulties getting out.

"I hear the Nazis arrested her," Frances confided one afternoon as we tacked up our horses.

"What for?" I asked.

"For wanting to come home, I suppose," Frances replied. "Anyway, the Major's been in Washington at the German Embassy to see about her."

"How do you know that?" Mary Ann inquired.

"I heard it from Ezzy," (the colored groom). Frances led her horse out of its stall. Mary Ann and I followed.

"We'd better be good today and not tease him. It's awful sad because she's his only daughter, Mary Ann said.

We entered the ring full of good intentions.

"Are they Jews?" Frances asked as we mounted. "I hear they are being persecuted. Did you see the pictures in *Life Magazine*?

"I don't think so, at least the Major wears some kind of medal. You know, like a Catholic," I replied. Mrs. Houghton had shown me a beautiful medal a Catholic friend had brought her from Rome. It had a picture of Mary on it and was of sterling silver. Occasionally on Sundays she wore it, and I though it looked pretty.

We worried about the Major's daughter for several weeks until Ezzy told us, "Dey got her out. Dey surh did.. She's comin' home."

"How did they get her out?" We crowded around the elderly groom.

"I don't know for shuah, but she's in Sweden now. Dey making 'rrangements for her passage home to America. And the Major's bloomin' like a peach."

Now that everything seemed normal once more we started teasing him again.

German Jews began arriving in Richmond, sponsored by rich merchants and the local synagogues. A deli opened on Cary Street with meats hanging from their strings in the window. We thought this very old-world-looking. Richmond noticed these newcomers because it had never been a very Jewish or German city. Curious, Mary Anne and I sampled this new deli and discovered marvelous new foods.

One Saturday in the middle of October, Father and I went up the country to a picnic at the Fraisers. They lived beyond Manakin (where Clarke's store was) on a big farm and had six children and lots of horses. Doug Fraiser had been Father's friend since their bachelor days and was great fun. His wife was sweet, and I enjoyed their children. I loved going to the Fraisers because we always had a good time.

That same evening Mother was invited to a dance at the Country

Club, where she and Rudy had danced in several contests and won.. Tonight was the final competition, when the winner would receive the grand prize. Mother and Rudy had the most points so far and could win. It seemed to mean an awful lot to her to go.

"Do come with us, John," Mother begged Father. "We need your moral support.."

"I've told Doug we'd join his picnic, and Doc's expecting to go."

Father sounded cross, and Mother, resigned to go without him, put on her coat.

"Well," she commented, "if that's more important than my winning this contest, go ahead then, enjoy yourself."

Without another word she and Rudy crossed the front hall and went out the door.

I watched from the landing and hoped they didn't see me. Then ever so quietly I slipped upstairs to my room.

"Come, Doc," Father's cheerful voice sounded from downstairs. "Let's go. Are you ready?"

Tugging on my sweater I stood in the upstairs hall and looked down at his upturned face in the foyer.

"I'm quite ready, Sir," I said, "I'm just changing my clothes. I'll meet you in the car." He disappeared into the dining room, and I finished dressing, and slid down the banister to the landing. Then remembering what Mrs. Owens said about being a lady, I walked the rest of the way. In the kitchen Father gathered our share of the picnic together, and carried it to the car.

Doug Fraiser built a fire outside, and we roasted hotdogs and hamburgers. All six of the Fraiser children and I positively stuffed ourselves with potato chips, homemade pickles and ice cream. After supper we played kick-the-can. About ten o'clock Father drove me home.

"It's terribly hot tonight," I complained. "I can't sleep in this stuffy room."

"I'll get you a fan, it'll stir the air," he said.

He brought a small oscillating fan from the library and plugged it in. The humid air lifted enough for me to drift off to sleep. It was dark when I awoke again, and heard the front door slam, and muffled voices in the hall. I listened, recognizing Mother's firm tones as she told Rudy goodnight. His voice sounded too loud in the stillness, and I thought he was drunk.

"Oh, Nancy," he said, "you're a remarkable woman."

"How you love to flatter. Rudy, I don't believe a word you say. But we did win the grand prize, didn't we?"

"I wish to God you weren't married with a child. You're the only woman I've ever loved."

"Don't say such things," Mother giggled. "John might hear you. And you and I both drank more than we should."

Her high-pitched laughter disturbed me. Presently I heard their footsteps in the living room. I slipped from my bed and crept out into the dark hall. Curious, I crouched down and could just make out two people through the half-opened door.

"I wish John were more interested in social gatherings. He'd meet people who might further his career. But he'd rather go on a picnic with Catherine than with us to the Country Club," Mother said is a low tone.

"Oh, Nancy, why didn't we meet sooner?"

"Yes, it would've been nice," Mother replied.

"How grand to just be here with you alone," Rudy's voice sounded slurred.

I heard Mother giggle; their voices became muffled. Silently I crept closer to the banister so I could hear.

"You're a good dancer, Rudy. It's lovely to have a partner like you."

"You're such fun to dance with, Nancy, Let's be partners forever. We would dance together with perfection."

For a few minutes I heard nothing, no matter how hard I listened.

"Such a waste of a good mind," Rudy said. Mother giggled. "You'll be the power behind the throne."

Again their voices muffled and only the sound of their suppressed laughter reached me. I couldn't make head nor tail out of this conversation. It faded in and out like a bad radio.

"Don't Rudy, you shouldn't do that, you know. I ought to slap your face," Mother's harsh words dissolved into giggles.

"Oh, Nancy, I'm crazy about you," Rudy replied. "How I long to kiss you."

The library door burst open. Father appeared still dressed. He strode across the front hall and invaded the living room.

"What the hell are you doing here at two o'clock in the morning?"

His voice resounded like a thunderclap as he slammed the French doors behind him.

Their angry voices rose to a crescendo, I couldn't understand what they said. Feeling sure Father would take care of things, I crept softly back to my own room and into bed. Car tires screeched down the drive and footsteps sounded upon the stairs. The house became deathly quiet. For a long time I lay still and listened. Finally I dropped off to sleep.

In the morning I awoke later then usual with the hot sun streaming into my room. It was Saturday so there was no school. I got up and listened for voices; it was so quiet, I thought everyone must have gone out somewhere. I slipped on my robe and went downstairs. In the dining room I found Mother arranging flowers.

"Where's Father?" I enquired. "He promised to take me out riding this morning."

"He's gone," Mother replied without looking at me.

"Gone where?" I asked. I noticed her face was streaked with tears. "Where has he gone?"

"I am not sure. He said something about Philadelphia." Mother's voice sounded dull and lifeless.

"Philadelphia? But he doesn't know anyone in Philadelphia." I couldn't believe Father would leave without telling me goodbye.

"He's got a cousin there, and your father has gone to stay with him." She picked up the flowers and left the dining room.

"He'd never go away without saying goodbye," I protested following her. "Surely he hasn't left me without his love."

"Yes," Mother replied, her voice shrill. "He's left you his love."

"Did you win the dance competition?" I asked, changing the subject hoping what she said wasn't true.

"Yes, we won," she said. "But I don't wish to discuss it with you. And what happened between me and your father is my business. You are never to mention it. Do you understand?"

"But," I protested, "this is awful. How do I get in touch with him? Surely he wouldn't go and leave me."

"Where do you think it leaves me? You're not to mention John Dickson's name again in my presence. I forbid it." Then quite suddenly she burst into tears and raced from the room.

Dumbfounded I stood in the front hall and heard her bedroom door slam. Then feeling hungry I headed towards the kitchen with tears streaming down my cheeks and sobs strangling my throat.

"Not speak about Father?" I asked aloud. "Never mention his name? Surely she didn't mean it."

But she did. Bereft and miserable I poured out milk and cereal, then pushing the bowl aside gave way to my anger and grief.

8

Special Nights in the Houghton's Cottage

"Hello, Mrs. Houghton," Cary bounced in through her front door later one afternoon. I noticed he was carrying a zipper bag and a jar of pickles. "Mom sent these for you." He handed her the pickles. "They're watermelon."

"Hi, Cary," I greeted him. "What are you up to?"

"Playing football mostly. I've made the team again this year. Well, the second team. But it's fun just the same."

He dropped his overnight bag in the front bedroom, and came back to us in the kitchen.

"What are you doing here, Doc? I thought you were off to Florida for a house party."

I realized my face must look ruined and puffy from tears. Mother and I had been invited to Florida, but she decided to take Rudy, not me.

"How's Killybegs? When do you start to hunt?"

"I have been out once or twice this fall, but now that football is over I shall have more time for Killybegs. I enjoy hunting; it's a great sport, too."

"Supper will be ready in a half hour, Doc, you and Cary set the table." Mrs. Houghton's voice, disembodied, came from the back porch. "And, Cary, I would appreciate it if you could bring in that coal scuttle. I need to stoke up the fire in the kitchen stove to heat the water. We shall have lots of baths tonight."

I did as she bade me and placed mats, silver and chairs around the table, pulling it out from under the window.

"Things look serious in Europe with Germany and Russia dividing up Czechslovacia and now Poland's invaded by Hitler and occupied," remarked Cary. "It seems there is to be an all-out war."

"Yes," agreed Mr. Houghton. "I'm very much afraid there'll be fighting in France by Spring. If Hitler keeps stirring up trouble we'll have to defeat Germany all over again."

A shadow fell over our pleasant meal. Both England and France had declared war on Germany after she marched into Poland, but I prayed they wouldn't fight. Recent photographs in *Life Magazine* showed Jews in Germany, beaten up, and their storefronts smashed. These pictures made the troubles in Europe seem real. I shivered, as fear for the world's future oppressed me.

Mrs. Houghton changed the subject. "Let's enjoy our meal. I've made a special dessert."

"What is it?" I asked. "Is it cake?"

"No, not a cake."

"I like pie," said Cary. "Did you make a cherry pie?"

"Then special pudding? Your very special apple pudding with custard!" I asked.

"How did you guess?" Mrs. Houghton laughed.

"I smelt it. All of those wonderful apple smells."

"You're all wrong," declared Mr. Houghton. "We're having bread-and-pull-it."

"Bread-and-pull-it, what's that?" laughed Cary. "Some English specialty?"

"That's right," Mr. Houghton said, "they eat bread-and-pull-it in London at all the posh places like Claridges."

"Pudding," I corrected. "It's got to be pudding."

Mrs. Houghton rose stiffly to clear the table. Cary helped her and brought in the dessert dishes. Then the pudding, full of apples and raisins, piping hot, was borne in by Mrs. Houghton. Warm custard in a large pitcher accompanied it. A marvelous treat! Both Cary and I ate two helpings.

When supper was over, we all helped with the dishes. Later, accompanied by our host, Cary and I walked through the dark November evening to check our horses and Mr. Houghton's chickens. He only had six hens, but they were special and he gave them a great deal of care.

Special Nights in the Houghton's Cottage

Also, he had bought a team of black mares recently at a sale in Richmond and named them Lindy Lou and Susie Q. They were the closest things he would ever own to cattle. Not only was his place too small, but Mrs. Houghton strenuously objected.

"We are retired from cattle raising," she maintained. "Horses and a few chickens are all I can handle."

After watering Mr. Houghton's horses and checking on Mistress and Killybegs in Cary's stables, we threw down some fresh hay for Billy and our young donkey, Jackie, recently sent to us by an uncle.

"Look at the stars," Cary pointed skyward. "There are masses of them."

"That's the Big Dipper, and over there is the little one. Above is Orion's Belt - he's the hunter, you know." Mr. Houghton pointed out the constellations. "And that's Polaris, the North Star."

"It's the star that sailors navigate by," added Cary.

"That's right. Although it is several degrees off dead north," Mr. Houghton explained.

I felt magic in the air that evening as I sang an old song about the moon drinking from the Dipper. Cary must have felt the same magic, because he linked arms through mine and Mr. Houghton's. We walked briskly down the dark, unlit road towards the English cottage. Cozy and warm before the open log fire, Cary and I spread out our books while Mr. and Mrs. Houghton turned on the radio and opened their *Richmond Times Dispatch*, which they divided between them.

I hoped he would tell us a story.

Winter evenings were the best time for storytelling, usually just before starting to bed, when the hearth fire burnt low, making weird shadows upon the cottage walls. When the mantle clock struck ten Mr. Houghton laid his newspaper aside, pushed his little dog, Peggy, from his lap and began:

"Did I ever tell you about the time ...?" He always started in the same way, "When I was a lad of sixteen, before the First World War, and came out to Canada from Yorkshire to work in the nickel mines? There was no work in England, and I wanted to seek my fortune. Three of us lads came out together. It was a hard life, but we had money in our pockets."

A Forgotten Landscape

Mrs. Houghton sighed, because she realized we would be late getting to bed. Cary and I sat on the floor with our backs to the hearth, not wanting to miss one word. The fire crackled pleasantly throwing sparks, and this cozy home filled with magic as we soared on wings of gold and silver to Canada, to England, even to Alaska. We met trappers, lumberjacks, pickpockets, and beautiful women. (They all seemed to resemble Ann Sheridan for whom Mr. Houghton expressed a special fondness.) In the course of the evening we encountered magically swift horses, even grizzly bears and timber wolves before the last ember died, and we all rose stiffly to go to bed. Neither Cary nor I spoke, but slipped quietly under the covers to dream of high mountains and snow-covered valleys thousands of miles away in western Canada. What a night of enchantment we'd enjoyed. Another evening Mr. Houghton told us about his boyhood experiences on a Yorkshire farm where he helped to birth several crops of new lambs on cold February mornings, often in open fields. On his father's farm Mr. Houghton fell in love with the massive Shire horses, those gentle giants who did the heavy work. It was a love affair that would last throughout his life. Often he gambled recklessly, hoping to raise a stake to buy such a team. But it was not until after his emigration to Canada to work in the nickel mines that Mr. Houghton managed to win a stake large enough to buy a team of those grand horses. In the early twenties, he moved to Alberta to homestead, and wrangled his team into a boxcar on the same train he rode out to the Canadian west. Eventually, after enduring five extremely rough winters and several poor harvests, he sold out his homestead and moved with his horses back to Ontario.

"There, following an extended search," he said, "I bought a farm, run-down and neglected, near Barrie, a hundred miles north of Toronto. Angus, at that time, was a tiny crossroads, but here I lived for several years and raised Hereford cattle."

Here, too, he brought his bride in November 1928 taking her across the prairie in an open cutter (a sleigh with two horses) in the dead of winter.

"I've had an adventuresome life," Mr. Houghton said from the depths of his armchair. "I'd take nothing for it. It was wonderful. I like to get the goodness out of things."

How Cary and I envied him. How marvelous we found his tales of the great world beyond Virginia. We dreamed, each in our own secret way, of becoming rich and famous, with money enough to give the Houghtons the luxuries their life denied them. We also hoped all the adventure in the world hadn't been used up, and that we'd get our share.

"Where can we have experiences like that?" we asked each other. "Life in Virginia seems so tame."

During our stay we met Mr. Houghton's friend, Tom Harris, who reminded me of Clark Gable. Tall, thin, with an elegantly trimmed moustache, Mr. Harris's deeply tanned face was framed by a thick shock of wavy hair. His eyes were an unusual violet color; his sensitive fingers those of a good horseman. Although much admired by us, he was not a close neighbor since he lived on the other side of Manakin where he owned a dairy farm. Quite unexpectedly, he dropped by to see Mr. Houghton.

"Hello, there," Mr. Harris greeted me. "You're John Dickson's kid, aren't you?"

Although I didn't like the name 'kid', I replied "Yes," and exchanged a few words with this neighbor. Cary shook hands and returned to his homework. Seated upon the hassock in front of the fire I regarded Mr. Harris with interest. His good looks contrasted with Mr. Houghton's craggy features. Mr. Houghton was not handsome, yet his face reflected a certain character, and his blue eyes usually danced with mischief.

Mr. Harris had come to ask his friend's help, and when these farm matters were completed, he got up to leave.

"It looks as if Adolf Hitler is grabbing every country in Europe," he commented. "You can't appease that man."

Then not waiting for us to reply, Mr. Harris left the house and drove off in his battered old car.

"It's a bad situation," Mr. Houghton agreed as he pulled himself out of his chair.

I watched him bank the fires. The heater in the sitting room burned coal and wood. Cary closed his books and brought in the scuttle from the kitchen. Fascinated, I watched Mr. Houghton shovel the coal to the back of the stove. With luck and skill the fire would smolder all night and some coal would still be lit the next morning. Since the coal stove in the kitchen only heated the water, it was allowed to burn out.

"Come along, Cary," Mrs. Houghton rose from her love seat. "You take your bath tonight. There is plenty of hot water. Boys use so much of it, somehow. Doc, you take your bath in the morning."

"Here, Peggy," Mr. Houghton whistled from the back door. "My, it's cold tonight. Feels like frost, maybe snow. Clara, these kids may need some extra blankets."

Quickly we each set about the business of going to bed. The hearth fire burnt low, protected by a screen. Well banked, the heater glowed in a comfortable manner as Cary, pajamas in hand, entered the bathroom. I slipped into Mrs. Houghton's bedroom, put on my flannel pajamas before I scampered across the living room and into the warm kitchen. Here I gave my hands and face a vigorous washing and brushed my teeth. I realized Cary would remain in the bathroom for hours, in front of the mirror combing his hair. I didn't consider his hair anything special. It looked to me like ordinary, curly brown hair that framed his handsome face and fell into his blue eyes. But Cary thought differently.

I ran tip-toe back across the living room, into the chilly bedroom and slipped under the covers. Sometime later Cary entered the darkened room, illuminated only by the dying embers of the hearth.

"Goodnight, Doc," he said. "Sleep well."

"Goodnight," I mumbled from under the blankets.

"Perhaps we shouldn't share the same room," Cary replied. "You being a girl and all."

"It's okay. Mrs. Houghton wouldn't let us if she thought it was wrong. I won't bite you."

I heard a suppressed giggle as Cary settled himself for the night. I lay on my back and watched the firelight play on the ceiling, creating weird dances. The threat of war worried me. I couldn't make sense out of Germany's aggression, and its soldiers' goose-stepping. I thought of Cary, now sixteen. Would he have to fight if Americans were sent overseas? What about Father? A graduate of West Point who fought in the last World War, surely he would be among the first called. I decided to write Grandmother and ask her to take me to Philadelphia. A log shifted on the hearth and a shower of sparks illuminated the bedroom. Peggy stirred in her basket; a few minutes later, I slept.

Special Nights in the Houghton's Cottage

It was still dark when I awoke at six o'clock. Mr. Houghton rose and appeared clad in a sweater and a heavy dressing gown. I watched him add a rolled up newspaper and wood to the still glowing coals in the heater. Later, he would shake down the ashes and do a proper job. Now he padded across the living room rug noiselessly in his broken leather slippers to fire the coal stove and heat my bath water. The cottage was freezing, and I snuggled back under the blankets. The hinges on the back door squeaked as it opened for Peggy to go out. I heard water from the tap strike the metal tea kettle, the pipes shivered, and a match box rattled. Presently, Mr. Houghton reappeared. He padded back across the living room rug and entered the darkened bathroom.

Cary groaned and turned over. In an hour and a half's time we must start for school. When Mr. Houghton came out of the bathroom, Cary tip-toed in. Lights illuminated the kitchen. The teakettle sang, and Peggy barked sharply at the back door. Mr Houghton opened it. Then I heard the rattle of pans and dishes as he started breakfast. Cary took a long time brushing his teeth, but I knew when he reappeared, I must get up in that frigid room and take a bath. I prayed the water was sufficiently hot. A few minutes later, when Cary returned, I heard his teeth chatter.

"Good morning, Doc," he whispered. "The bathroom's all yours."

Silently I gathered together my skirt and sweater, and bundling up my underclothes I left the room. Hot water trickled from the frozen tap and, shivering, I climbed into the tub. I washed quickly, toweled and dressed. My teeth chattered so hard, I could hardly brush them. I returned to the living room, stood beside the heater and pulled on my socks and shoes.

"Hurry up, Doc," Cary called softly. "Make your bed. Breakfast is ready."

Tray in hand, Mr Houghton appeared, carrying his wife's morning tea. Now, fully dressed, with beds made, Cary and I entered the cozy kitchen.

Mr. Houghton, clad in his heavy jacket, trousers and boots, let himself out in the cold morning to do the chores.

"Be back in a minute," he promised, and departed.

I noticed the clock on the wall said quarter after seven. Outside the black morning became tipped with grey as the sun peeked over the horizon. Inside on the kitchen table lay three plates heaped up with bacon, eggs and brown buttered toast. A battered teapot, covered with an old green cozy sat on one end of the stove. Cary raised this cover and poured us each a cup of tea. Mr. Houghton opened the door; his boots muddy, in silence he sat down to breakfast. At seven-thirty, bundled in coats, and snuggled under a heavy lap robe, Cary and I started for school. Gently coaxing the 1932 Chevrolet to life, Mr. Houghton with Peggy seated on his lap drove us through the darkness towards Richmond.

9

At Henley's Store

One Saturday morning, I trotted up to Henley's store on Billy, and recognized several of the farmers who sat out under the trees. Even though it was November the day was warm and some leaves still clung to the maples. I had come on my pony for an ice cream cone, and broke Mother's rules by crossing River Road. I trotted up to the store knowing full well it was out of bounds.

"Hello, Doc," welcomed Grievous Sin Snead from the yard. "I'll hold your pony for you."

"I won't be long. Billy can just graze and enjoy the grass."

I jumped down and handed Grievous the reins.

"Take your time, I ain't got nothin' better to do. I's waitin' on Mr. Harris to carry me up to his place for a day's work." The colored man patted the pony's head, then squatting down on his haunches to puff his corn-cob pipe.

Mr. Pillar drove up, switched off the motor of his pickup, and let fly a dark stream of tobacco juice. It landed at Grievous's feet; he glanced at the spitter warily.

"Over there, boy, away from them trees. We don't want no horse shit smellin' up the place," Mr. Pillar thumped Billy on the rear making him jump.

"I's grazin' Miss Doc's pony."

"Leave him, Jed, they aren't in the way," Mr. Henley intervened.

I watched as with great dignity Grievous picked up his hat and placed it firmly on his head, before he led the pony away.

"You got to learn a colored man, Arthur, specially one like Grievous. Him being so dignified and all - so he don't get ahead of hisself, and think he's better than a white man."

"Before you knows it they'll be shoppin' at Miller and Rhoads," added Mr. Allen, "where they ain't allowed to try on."

I started back considering I'd better forget the ice cream, until Mr. Henley stopped me.

"Get your cone, kid, the pony's all right. Ask Mrs. Henley to come out and pump Jed some gas."

"Yes, sir."

I never liked Mr. Pillar. He made me afraid. I hated his mean pig-eyes, and his rough way of talking. Fat, and foul with tobacco spit, he smelled bad most of the time. His only redeeming feature was his family. He had a pretty wife and a lively young daughter, three years younger than I. But Mr. Pillar acted high and mighty because he was white. We all knew he hated colored people, and most of them were wary of his rough ways because he liked to fight and carried a gun in the back of his pickup. Mr. Houghton believed he belonged to the Ku Klux Klan.

"Good morning, Mrs. Henley," I flung open the door of her general store. "Can I have an ice cream cone, please? Mr. Henley needs you outside."

Four faces twisted towards me: Mrs. Henley, Anita Sparrow, Catherine Hollis and Mrs. Crosbie's. I slammed the screen door shut, making the stick Mrs. Henley used to pick down packages of cereals from their high shelves leap up off its rack.

It lay cradled between two hooks under the photograph of President Roosevelt.

"Really, Doc, where're your manners?" Anita Sparrow asked sharply. "You must wait your turn."

"Excuse me," I blushed, "but I scoop the ice cream myself. After I've asked, of course."

"Go ahead," said Mrs. Henley kindly. She caught the rolling stick and straightened Mr. Roosevelt's picture "Help yourself."

I laid my dime down on the wooden counter and escaped to the ice cream freezer at the back of the store. After scooping out a generous double portion I sat down upon the bottom shelf amid the work boots and licked the cone's streaming sides. I heard both the front and back doors slam shut, and peeked through the crack between the freezer and cold case to see Mrs. Henley in the yard pumping gas into Mr. Pillar's truck.

"Well, I never," Mrs. Sparrow's voice floated over the freezer. "That Doc has the manners of a goose. Really an oaf of a girl, all arms and legs."

"Have you ever seen such clumsy feet? She must wear a size ten!" Mrs. Crosbie chimed in.

"She's a sweet person all the same," Catherine Hollis said, "and very thoughtful for all her awkwardness."

"Well, if you ask me," Mrs. Sparrow continued, "if she's anything like her dad, for all his charm, she'll end up an irresponsible clown."

"I've heard he's left his family and disappeared. Just ups and went one night without so much as a fare-thee-well."

Stunned, I leaned forward to listen.

"Why, Sarah, do you say such things?" Catherine Hollis sounded shocked.

"He's taken an engineering job in Philadelphia."

"It's true, John Dickson's deserted his wife and child. Nancy's such a lovely young thing; it's a pity. She'll have to raise Doc on her own, and that's not easy." Mrs. Crosbie's voice dropped to a conspiratorial tone. "I hear there's another man involved. A Yankee from Wisconsin or Michigan, or some such place. Very unsavory scandal if that ever got out."

"Very unsavory, if what I hear is true," Anita Sparrow added. "This Yankee escorted Nancy to dances at the Country Club, of all places, without her husband. Now I ask you, what is this world coming to? Yankees have such little breeding."

"Anita, don't generalize on Yankees. My daughter married one, and I must admit he's quite charming," Mrs. Hollis protested.

"But his mother came from Atlanta. That makes all the difference," Sarah Crosbie pointed out.

"Yes, I expect so, but I like Edward's father too. He's from Upper New York State and works at Corning Glass in the Stuben division." Catherine Hollis defended her Northern family. "In fact we just returned from New York last week. We went up to do some shopping in the City. I just had to see that famous statue of General Sherman being led by Victory. You know, the one they joke about? A Southern wag remarked, upon seeing it, 'Just like a Yankee, to ride while a lady walks'." Polite laughter filled the store.

I sat very still among the boots and listened. The neglected ice cream ran down my fingers and felt sticky. I licked my hand of the white streams, and finished the cone. How dare they speak of my family in such a way? Mortified, I blushed. How could I ever face these ladies again?

"It's a nice bit of scandal to enliven the county. I like Nancy in spite of her airs and graces. I like John too, he's a great charmer and ever so handsome. But another man lurking in the background sounds in very poor taste," Mrs. Sparrow continued.

"You know what they say, variety is the spice of life," Mrs. Hollis's voice dropped to a whisper.

"Catherine, what a thing to say! How naughty! But it's true, I suppose. All our men drink too much and chase women, and we're not supposed to know."

Mrs. Crosbie started towards the door. "I'll see you folks later. We'd better keep this information to ourselves. If Alvira Carthage finds out, the whole county would know in an hour."

Peering through the crack I watched her depart. I wished the others would go too, as I must remain imprisoned in my corner until they did. Mrs. Henley sure was taking a long time. And where was Ethel? Answering footsteps sounded overhead in her apartment. I waited impatiently for her to come down.

"Poor Doc", Mrs. Hollis said, "it'll be hard on her if there's any hint of scandal. A second marriage could spell disaster, especially if there're other children. I don't think Nancy, with all her goings and comings, has much time for Doc. She reminds me of a little gypsy, that girl, full of tricks and as wild. But she's a kind person all the same. Clara Houghton is very fond of her. And Harry positively dotes on her. Doc's fond of them too, so perhaps she'll find someone who cares."

"Let's hope so. Goodbye, Catherine, I'll see you on Tuesday at the Garden Club." Anita Sparrow let herself out, banging the door.

I watched Catherine Hollis select a loaf of bread and a dozen eggs, and place the money on the counter before she followed her neighbors into the yard. At the same time Ethel entered the store through the back door and saw me sitting beside the freezer.

"Are you still here?" she asked, startled.

"Yes, may I please wash my hands. I've got ice cream all over them."

Unaware I was hiding, Ethel led me back into the feed room, and handed me soap and an old piece of towel.

"Here you are, Doc. Just close the door when you finish." Ethel, who was often slow and rather hesitant with adults, felt at ease with me.

I scrubbed my dirty hands and washed the ice cream from my nose and mouth. Then I laid the towel and soap on a table in the hall and pulled the door shut. I re-entered the store and found only Mrs. Henley and Ethel. Relieved to avoid the ladies, I thanked the sisters and departed.

Outside Grievous Sin still held Billy. The pony raised his head as I approached. Mr. Pillar's truck stood idling close by with Mr. Pillar's head stuck out of it talking to the men.

"'Bout time you got here, kid. That boy's got better things to do than hold your pony," he snapped.

"It's all right, little miss, he's enjoyin' the grass," Grievous smiled. His broken teeth I saw were stained with tobacco." I's enjoyin' my pipe waiting for Mr. Harris to come." I felt angry at Mr. Pillar for calling a grown man a boy as I took the reins and mounted Billy.

"I 'spect I'll walk with you to Mrs. Haunch's road," Grievous said. "There's a smart amount of cars comin', and I 'spects you ain't supposed to come this far."

"Don't tell, Grievous. Please don't tell. The end of Mrs. Haunch's road is my limit. But I just couldn't resist the ice cream, and Henley's store is only a little way out of bounds."

"Good long way, if you axes me," the elderly Negro replied.

Grievous turned the pony, and we started down the road together. Then he stopped and asked Mr. Henley to keep a look out for Tom Harris.

"Sure thing, I'll hold him here 'til you return," the storekeeper promised.

"Dis heah pony ain't all that quiet, Miss Doc. He don't take to cars easily. Ain't you perhaps foolish comin' out this far. And Jed Pillar would love to find somethin' out dat he could punish you with."

Billy walked along the grass shoulder shying at the water in the ditch and looking suspiciously at the mailboxes. The colored man held the bridle, his face gentle; the pony responded and dropped his head.

"I know it's foolish to get into trouble. But it's fun defying Mother's orders. She has too many, and I don't break them often."

"Be careful, Miss Doc," Grievous warned. "It ain't good for a young girl to be out alone. Somethin' might happen, that's what's worryin'." I knew he felt concerned.

A car horn blasted. Billy jumped. I grabbed his mane as I almost tumbled off his rear. Mr. Pillar flew past us, his head stuck out of the window, laughing unpleasantly as his truck tires squealed around the curve.

"Some white men think they's big 'cus they's white. They ain't no better than a colored man. That's a fact. They ain't better than a field hand who eats with his fingers and ain't never washed." Grievous spat contemptuously. "Take no notice of him, little miss. Old man Pillar's got a lot to learn 'bout life."

"But I'm afraid of him, Grievous. He can be mean."

The Negro laid his hand upon Billy's neck as he walked along beside me.

"Don't be afeared, 'cause Old Man Pillar is afraid too. He don't talk big around Tom Harris, Colonel Hollis, or even Mr. Houghton. He just talk big when he can get aways with it. He ain't worth bein' afeared of, Miss Doc', he sho ain't."

Grievous brought the pony to a halt before we crossed River Road and entered Mrs. Haunch's lane.

"Go through them old saw mill trails, scurry on home now, 'fore you's discovered."

"Goodbye, Grievous," I called.

He tipped his hat and started back up the road towards the store. I galloped down the trail for home, thinking of what the ladies had said.

Apparently Mother'd caused a scandal by going to the Country Club with a Yankee without Father. Now she planned to marry Rudy Melton as soon as her divorce came through.

"How awful!" I thought. "What would the neighbors think about her trip to Florida? And Rudy's going too? Maybe now that the whole county's talking about her she won't marry him after all. Surely she can't love him, with his being a Yankee and all. And Richmond people don't have second husbands. It just isn't done."

Three days elapsed before I mentioned anything to Mother. Since I wasn't sure which way to approach the subject, I spent hours working out ways to open the conversation. It was finally decided for me.

"Well, it's all set," Mother told me the next evening at dinner. "I shall marry Rudy in the spring at a home wedding."

"It's much too soon," I replied, furious at her.

"Too soon?"

"People are bound to talk because no one gets married twice in Richmond. Only one of my friends has a stepfather. Although Mary Armstead's father is dead, her mother's not remarried again." I studied the creases in my napkin, hoping not to make her angry.

"Mrs. Armstrong has nothing to do with me," Mother shouted.

"Armstead," I corrected. "You know Mary Armstead."

"I don't care in the least what other people do. And it's none of their business what I choose to do." Mother glared at me over her soup. I noticed her hands were shaking.

"But people talk."

"What people?" She demanded.

"Just people. You know at the general store, at church, in town," I said airly. "We'll be the laughing stock of the county."

"Well, my friends would never talk, as you call it. They wouldn't be so rude as to gossip. Where do you hear such things?"

"I don't really want a stepfather," I tried another tack, "I've a perfectly good father of my own, and don't see the need for another one. You don't really love Rudy, do you?"

She dropped her spoon, eyes blazing, her face crimson. "What business is that of yours?" She demanded. "I need someone to take care of me. I need someone to love me. I am now a woman alone with a child. That causes talk, lots of talk and my friends feel awkward because they think I might be after their husbands."

"Are you?" I inquired boldly.

"How dare you? How dare you address me so? What can you possibly know about love?" She threw back her chair and tried to hit me. Instead she tripped and fell back into her seat.

"Now see what you've done," she shouted. "Finish your supper and keep quiet. You're the cause of my remarrying. I can't remain single with a child. It's bad form." She attacked her soup.

"It's bad form to marry someone you don't love. People will talk about us, and you can't stop them by marrying Rudy. Besides he's far too short, and he wears outlandish clothes."

"You don't understand anything. You're a willful, stupid, ungainly girl. I shall marry Rudy, if I like. Your father's not coming back."

"I realize that. But why complicate things with a second husband? My name will be different from yours. It'll cause problems."

"Then we'll change it to Melton. It's a perfectly respectable name and goes well with Catherine. We'll just do that." Mother glared at me.

"No!" It was my turn to be angry. "I won't give up Fathers s name. It's mine by birth. You and nobody else will take it from me." I slammed down my soup spoon, jumped up and raised my hand as if to hit her.

"Why do you treat me so?" she wailed. "I've tried to make a home for you. But you oppose me at every turn."

"It's not a home without Father," I shouted. "You sent him away because of Rudy Melton. And you won't let him come back. It's you who broke up my home. I hate you for that. I really hate you." I ran from the table, dashed out the front door and into the woods.

"Catherine," Mother called after me, "Catherine, come back and finish your dinner."

I found a mossy spot under an oak tree and sat down. I hadn't meant to say all those hurtful things. I hadn't meant to fight. I felt ashamed. I just wanted her to know people were spreading gossip. I wanted her to know I cared. Yet deep down inside me I wanted to hurt her because she'd sent Father away. Her bitterness now infected everything she did and said.

"She mustn't love Father anymore. But how could she love Rudy Melton, a Yankee from Wisconsin?" I asked myself aloud. "Perhaps she no longer loves me either. Can you turn love on and off like a spigot?" I wondered.

December in the woods is cold, and the night felt frosty. I shivered. Then feeling hungry I got up and returned to the house. I found the table cleared and Mother gone. In the kitchen everything was put away, not a scrap of dinner remained. I took down a jar of peanut butter and scraped it thickly upon two slices of bread, folding them in half. Slowly I ate these with a glass of milk. In the pantry I discovered some stale cookies and helped myself to several and an over ripe banana. Then I tiptoed silently out of the back door and headed for the Houghtons.

"Well, Doc," Mr. Houghton greeted me, "your face's as long as a buzzard's. What's the matter?"

"Mother's marrying Rudy Melton, and the whole county's talking about us. What a pickle I'm in! I'm sure she hates me." I stared up at him with tearful eyes. "Whatever am I to do?"

"Big trouble, eh? And Rudy's no Clark Gable, even though he dresses like one. He's kind of fat and dumpy, if you ask me. And terribly short." Mr. Houghton took me by the hand and led me inside.

"That's about it." I sat down on his bony lap and buried my face in his chest. "It's awful, really awful. Father's never coming back. I miss him terribly and no one seems to care."

"I care, Doc, I really do. I realize his departure has left a big hole in your life."

"An enormously big hole. Why can't they live together as before?"

"I don't know," Mr. Houghton put his comforting arms about me. "But sometimes it's like that."

"It hurts," I protested, "it hurts me deep down inside. In the in-most part of me. Is that your soul?"

"I expect it is, Doc. You've suffered a terrible hurt if it's that deep. But you can do nothing to change things."

"I've tried, but Mother won't listen to me. She just gets angry. She never listens to me. She even called me stupid. I'm not stupid, am I, Mr. Houghton?"

"No," he agreed, "you're not. Maybe you're other things, but stupid is not one of them. You're pig headed, and dirty most of the time, and a sneak and a liar, but never stupid."

"I am? You think I'm all those awful things?" I asked sitting up right on his lap.

"Yes," he teased, "and a whole lot more. Let's see. You're growing up much too fast. We need to put a brick on your head to slow you down. You leave me quite breathless."

"Oh, if that's all I am, then I needn't worry. I'll grow out of those things. I shall become so clean you'll think I'm sick and so truthful you'll hate me. Because I'll tell things I shouldn't. I'll be so easy going that you'll think I'm a great big turp. How would you like that?" I tickled him.

"If you start that, you'll have to get down." Mr. Houghton twisted from side to side. "I mean it now."

"Okay, I'll be good,"

"Now, young lady, dry your eyes, and go wash your face and hands. The Missus has made some scrumptious cake and you shall have some. Hurry, now, while I call her." I jumped down as he stood up.

A few minutes later, washed, with my hair combed, I sat at the table in front of a huge piece of sponge cake and a cup of tea.

"There you are, Doc. You'll not go hungry tonight. It's the finest cake I've made since June, so eat up." Mrs. Houghton encouraged me. "Then off you go home and make up with your mother."

10

Fox Hunting

Mother didn't say much when I arrived home that night. And since she never asked me where I'd been, I didn't mention it. Rudy seemed to pop in and out of the house like a jack in a box, but their wedding had been postponed until late spring. The divorce seemed complicated, because Father wanted custody of me, and Mother opposed it.

As for the wedding dress I'd burnt up after I'd returned from the Houghton's, Mother apparently forgot she'd bought it, and of course, I didn't remind her. But I began to feel guilty about tearing it up. It was wasteful, and Mrs. Houghton had impressed upon me that it was a sin.

One Saturday afternoon about two weeks later I told her what I had done. We were sitting in her living room while she helped me with my knitting.

"You know, Mrs. Houghton, I'm a great sinner."

"You are, my dear? I wouldn't have thought so," she replied without looking up. "I'm trying to count these stitches."

"I've done something terribly wasteful, and I did it deliberately."

"What have you done?" She put down my socks and studied me.

"I Cut up a brand new dress and burnt it in the furnace."

"Whatever possessed you to do that?"

"Mother bought me a dreadfully ugly, blue thing to wear at her wedding. It was a lady's dress with bosoms. And look at me! I'm as skinny as a rail, and it looked just awful."

"And you burnt it?"

"Yes, but first I cut it into strips. I destroyed it on purpose." I felt this the greater sin. "You said never to waste anything because someone else might use it."

"Now the wedding's delayed." She picked up her knitting, "You won't wear that dress, you've seen to it. But you shouldn't have cut it up."

"I know. That's why I'm a great sinner." I sat on her old hassock and rocked back and forth. "I feel terribly guilty. Someone could have used that dress, in spite of its being ugly. But cutting it up felt awful good. I just loved doing it."

"I expect you were very angry," Mrs. Houghton continued, "to have done such a wasteful thing."

"Ever so angry, and furious too at Mother for not listening to me."

"I see," she said, "and you got back at your mother by burning the dress in the furnace. Doc, I understand your feelings. You took them out on the dress; that's better, I suppose, than cutting up Mother and throwing her away. But she'll marry Rudy in the finish, and you'll have to face it. She'll find out what you've done eventually, but let's keep this to ourselves for now. When she does get married, maybe you can have the dress you want. Perhaps your grandmother can help you choose one."

"That's a splendid idea. I'm sure she'd buy me one I'd like. You are a wonder, Mrs. Houghton. You're the smartest person in the whole wide world." I jumped up from the rolling hassock and hugged her.

"My dear! Don't choke me. Now we must get these socks finished for the Red Cross. I've turned the heels for you. Stop worrying about the dress. You're not such a great sinner. I've known greater. Now Mr. H. will be trotting in here soon wanting his tea. Come in the kitchen, and we'll prepare it."

Just before Christmas, Colonel Hollis came to call - not on Mother, but on me.

"I'm looking for a young lady named Doc. Or perhaps, Catherine Dickson." He announced in his breathless tones.

"Sir, I'm Doc," I showed my visitor into the library. "I'll go call Mother."

"No, it's you I wish to speak with. How would you like to come hunting with the Silver Creek Club during the Christmas holidays? We need some more young people. And I hear you're an excellent rider."

"I am taking lessons with Major Kepler. He thinks I'm terrible. But I am sure I'm good enough to hunt."

"Yes, he told me you were coming on nicely, and he has a quiet horse he'd lend you. Would you like to come out with us?" The Colonel took a seat in one of the deep library chairs. "We have a Second Flight, you know, that I lead with all the ponies, old ladies, and young children. I lower the jumps if need be, and we have a great time."

"Yes, I'd love to. I do ride rather well for my age, and I'd get along fine with a borrowed horse," I announced. "It's much nicer than riding a pony." Fox hunting sounded like the most exciting adventure I'd ever experience.

Colonel Hollis laughed. His ruddy face twisted in mirth, his breathless voice exploding in gasps. How astonishing, I thought, watching him somewhat alarmed. But then he was an astonishing man.

He had lived all over the world, and for a while outside London after his Army service in Burma and India. Then he'd married an American girl and joined the Imperial Tobacco Company, whose headquarters was in Richmond, and moved to Virginia. Immediately he put new life into the veins of the staggering old Hunt Club, and combined it with a fledgling one that had just purchased land in Goochland.

He now stood before me in an old tweed jacket, an almost shapeless garment, worn over a pair of baggy trousers, their knees grass stained, their cuffs muddy. A pipe, held firmly between his teeth, remained unlit. I noticed he spent a great deal of time preparing this pipe, but rarely smoked it. In the pockets of his jacket he crammed the most amazing stuff: a dog lead, a broken noseband for his horse, an enormous creature named Brutus, that the Colonel always rode. I watched him pull out several articles looking for his matches: a packet of shotgun cartridges, various sized horse shoe nails, and a watch with a broken strap. Seeming surprised to find these things he put them back and rummaged through his trouser pockets. Here he discovered a half-used book of matches. These he opened and lit his pipe. The sweet aroma of burning tobacco filled the room as he puffed hard to keep it lit.

"I'll speak to your mother about this later. But these arrangements stand, and Major Kepler will give you the details. I think your friend, Mary Ann, is also going to join us. So you won't be alone."

The Colonel stood up, and I did likewise. He was a big man with long, slim legs that looked well on a horse. His pink coat was custom tailored; in it he looked trim and immaculate. Such a contrast to the baggy, shapeless clothes he wore now. A retired army officer, he rode fearlessly and well. His motley crew of children, old ladies and timid riders he commanded with a firm hand. Consequently, he rarely had an accident. An invitation to ride with the Second Flight, I considered the highest compliment. Later Cary informed me that the Colonel's commands must be obeyed on the instant, or you would never be asked to hunt with him again.

Now I walked with him to the door, and shaking his hand politely, showed him out. I watched his tall figure go down our steps and enter his car.

"Goodbye," he called, "see you on the hunt field."

Then he drove away.

Saturday morning early, Cary, his mother and I, joined by Mary Ann, started out for the Hunt Club with Killybegs and Mistress in the trailer. We found the Club's drive crowded with horses and riders, all trying to get ready. Colonel Hollis met us by the stables and instructed Cary where to meet the Second Flight.

"Hurry up now, and get mounted," he commanded. "We'll be ready to leave in fifteen minutes." How elegant he appeared attired in his riding clothes, which he wore like a uniform, correct down to the minutest detail.

"Oh, Cary," confessed Mary Ann, "I'm scared."

"Don't worry, it'll be fun," he encouraged her.

Emma Craddock skirted the other trailers and parked near the riding ring. She and Cary backed their horses out, already saddled, and put on their bridles.

Mary Ann and I crossed the field and walked down the stables' row.

"Doc, look at everyone. How well dressed they are," she observed.

"And we're almost as well turned out as the Colonel."

"In these borrowed clothes? This coat is much too big, and besides it's a boy's."

"Come on, Mary Ann, you look first rate, and it's a great compliment to ride with the Hunt."

Attired in borrowed stocks, tweed coats, and riding shirts belonging to Cary, I considered we looked quite smart. Our breeches and boots were new. (Only our hunt caps looked worn, their black velvet faded brown.) Dressed correctly after a great deal of trouble, I couldn't understand Mary Ann's objections to wearing boy's clothes.

"There you are," greeted Colonel Kepler. "Doc, you take Little Man, and you, Mary Ann, ride Lady Jane. Let's have a look at you. Yes, yes, very good. Now get mounted, and I'll wipe the mud off your boots." (Muddy boots made our stirrups slippery.)

"It's a wonder he approved of our outfits," Mary Ann said as we brought our ponies from their stalls and mounted.

Both Little Man and Lady Jane sported hunting array, their manes braided, their tails tied up to keep them out of the red mud.

"Look at them!" I gasped at the ponies' transformation.

"They look like show ponies. I can't believe they're the same brown nags we ride in lessons," Mary Ann replied.

(They were ponies, since both Little Man and Lady Jane were 14:2, just under horse size.)

Once mounted Major Kepler wiped off our muddy boots, and we looked around for Colonel Hollis. Correctly dressed in a black melton coat and mounted on his gray pony, Cary waited for us at the end of the shed row.

"Follow Killybegs," suggested the Major as he got on his large black gelding. "I think we meet at the riding ring." Horses and riders milled around anxious to be off.

"Goodbye, girls," waved Emma Craddock. "I'll see you after the hunt. Have fun."

She trotted Mistress towards the front. A bold and daring horsewoman, Miss Emma always out-rode most of the men. Mistress was a strong fencer. Although not large she could out stay most of the heavy geldings ridden by the Whippers - In and the MFH. Most of the regular members who hunted every Saturday morning during the season, admired Miss Emma on her brown mare. Cary felt proud of his mother and enjoyed accompanying her.

At the ring we found assembled ten children on various size ponies and two older women riding veteran hunters. Colonel Hollis trotted up on Brutus.

"Good morning, Members of my Second Flight. Allow me to welcome you." He rose in his stirrups and saluted us with his hunt whip.

Ten anxious ponies stood stock-still; the boys doffed their hunt caps. The older ladies stopped talking and paid attention. Beside me Mary Ann sat anxiously erect, her face flushed with excitement, her restive horse's ears pricked forward. Little Man tossed his head, eager to be off, and my stomach turned flip-flops in an electric thrill of anticipation. The colorful riders mounted on their gleaming horses; the bright winter sunshine, and the earthy smells of animals and woods made me shiver with joy.

"Good morning," we all replied.

We rode behind him down the drive towards the open fields. The Master and his Whippers—In led with the hounds; behind them came the Huntsman and Mistress prancing at his horse's heels. Twenty eager horses and riders followed. Some of them wore pink coats, some clad in black and in tweeds, but Mrs. Henderson, riding her brilliant chestnut, sidesaddle, outshone them all.

"Look," I said to Mary Ann, "isn't she wonderful? That's what I want. How grand she is all in black, how gorgeous in that veil and top hat!"

We watched Mrs. Henderson trot down the road before us. Few ladies now rode sidesaddle, and few were as accomplished as this erect figure or more elegant.

"We are off," yelled Mary Ann.

"Great," I yelled back, "Little Man knows the ropes."

The old pony neither pulled nor shied, but galloped along as if enjoying himself. Ahead I could see the Colonel, an elegant figure on Brutus, taking the jumps easily. Behind us rode Major Kepler, keeping an eye on us. Suddenly we pulled up, and Colonel Hollis spun around.

"Anyone want the jump lowered?" He shouted.

"No!" we all chorused.

"Come along then." Brutus flew over the chicken coop. We jumped in single file, (first the smaller children, the older women, and finally Cary, Mary Ann and me), landing in a muddy pasture. Mary Ann took the jump well with Lady Jane's clever hocks tightly folded. Around the edge of the field we galloped, plunged into the woods, crossed a stream, water splashing cold over my riding breeches. Little Man scrambled up the bank, and we headed towards the next fence. Lightly I held him, gave the signal, we rose in the air just skimming over the felled tree, and raced after the Colonel's retreating scarlet back.

We entered, at a gallop, a woodsy trail cut up by heavy saw mill trucks.

"It's slick through here," yelled Cary at me from behind. "Pull your horse up. Slowly, so he doesn't trip."

Too late I obeyed. Little Man fell to his knees and slid across the slimy ground. Clinging to the saddle, I tried to steady him, being careful not to shift my weight or to jerk his head. With a tremendous effort the little horse struggled to his feet. Red mud covered his belly and streamed over my new boots. Tingles of fear shot down my neck, dangling stirrups bruised my ankles, but I hung on. As the clever pony stopped, Major Kepler grabbed my reins. Killybegs slid to a halt behind us, plunged into the woods, and galloped on.

"Well done. You ride like a trooper," said the Major pushing me back into the saddle. "Get your stirrups. We can't stop."

Gasping for breath, I caught up my stirrups, and raced down the trail after Killybegs. The gray Connemara looked like a dappled carousel pony with red clay clinging to his coat. Ahead Cary sailed over the post and rail and landed safely on the other side. Wanting to catch up, I urged Little Man forward; I could hear the Major's big horse galloping behind as over the jump I flew. Now I felt more secure. Fear left me, replaced by the excitement of adventure.

"Like riding Cherry on summer evenings with Father," I thought.

When we pulled up at the check, Major Kepler complimented me.

"Not bad horsemanship, for one so young," he smiled a rare smile. "And Cary too, avoided hitting us."

I basked in his unaccustomed praise.

"I'll ride in front of you next time, Doc. Killybegs ran me over several trees. Is my face bleeding?"

"Just scratched," I laughed. "You look ten times worse after a football match."

Cary raised his crop as if to hit me, Colonel Hollis glared at us with fierce disapproval, making Cary drop his arm.

"I'll get you later," he whispered. "Just you wait until we're home."

"Really, Cary," said Mary Ann, "you know Doc's scared to death."

We followed Colonel Hollis across the highway, and entered the pine woods on the far side. Mud caked Little Man's brown coat, his neck felt sticky with sweat, he resembled a plough horse more than a well-groomed hunter. The tired horse waded through the stream, at a trot, spraying water over us, and cantered down the hill to the cornfield.

In sight of the Hunt Club, Little Man seemed anxious to get home. Sweaty and tired, the Whippers-In gathered up the hounds; the Huntsman brought his field together as we reined for a gate. Their tired horses jumped the final chicken coop and headed towards home. Colonel Hollis collected his Second Flight as we pulled up at the stables.

"We had a good day's sport, congratulations." He raised his whip and saluted us.

As Christmas approached I missed Father more and more. Since war was declared between England and Germany on the third of September everyone realized this would be the last peacetime Christmas, perhaps for several years. Americans, afraid they'd be dragged into Europe's conflict, began to prepare.

I wrote Father a long letter about fox hunting with the Colonel, and how I'd almost caused Cary and Killybegs to run over me. In return I received a cheerful letter full of news.

Grandmother came briefly for a visit. She'd planned to stay longer, but she and Mother got into an argument. She disapproved of Mother's marriage to Rudy on several accounts.

"He has no room for Doc in his plans. You can't marry someone who dislikes your only child," I heard Grandmother say as I stood in the upstairs hall and listened.

"He's ambitious to get ahead in the world. That's more than John was. He only cared about the country and his daughter. He even neglected my interests for hers." Mother's voice sounded angry.

"Then let me take Doc back to Indianapolis. There is no life for her here. You and Rudy won't make her happy," Grandmother's voice pleaded. "You don't seem very interested in her welfare."

"I'm not," Mother's voice was ice cold. "I don't want John to have her. I won't give her to you or anyone as long as John's alive. He left me, just walked out and left me humiliated before all the world."

"Nancy, you are making an awful mistake. You will regret this decision later. You will lose Doc's love as you lost John's by being unreasonable. Consider what you are doing - to yourself and to your child." Grandmother's voice was filled with tears. The next day she packed her bags and quietly left for Indianapolis.

I didn't see her for several months, although she wrote me frequently and I corresponded with her. She rarely called us on the phone now, and when she did her conversation was brief. She never mentioned that she wanted me to go and live in Indianapolis with her, and I never told her what I'd overheard. Only Mrs. Houghton knew, but we never discussed it. I just told her one day, - that was all.

A Forgotten Landscape

11

The Last Peacetime Christmas

Christmas that year of 1939 felt strange. First of all, Mother's sister and her family planned to come, an event in itself.. They rarely visited us, and we usually saw them when we went to Grandmother's in Indiana. But this year everyone wanted to be with everyone else, and families traveled great distances to spend the last peacetime Christmas together. Grandmother also came, and after Christmas she'd arranged to take me to Philadelphia to see Father.

Although Hitler made no effort to attack France or Belgium on the continent or England's island off shore, we lived in dread. Everyone knew this phony war could not last for long. We were certain the Germans would attack, but when or where was only guessed at, and the uncertainty made us all nervous. Father said it would be in the spring. Meanwhile, England tightened her defenses and France prepared for war. The time of appeasement was over, and the world braced itself for another conflict of arms. The uncertainty was nerve-racking ever since the third of September when war was declared.

Grandmother wrote me that she was coming to take me to see Father. She also wrote that he had a new girlfriend named Frances. "I've known her parents," she told me; "they lived in Indianapolis and were extremely nice."

Confused by all these new people in my life, I wrote back and asked, "What do I call her?"

Then Grandmother explained about stepmothers and their roles in fairy tales. "Some stepmothers are wicked in stories, but some are very good people in real life. Why don't you call her Frances?"

"Yes," I wrote back, "I like that name. It sounds friendly, and the only other Frances I know is very pleasant. She's two grades ahead of me at school and is fun."

I hadn't thought of Father having a girlfriend or getting married again. But men do, I supposed, usually like a lady to escort to dances and parties.

Grandmother wrote, "He might marry her soon, my dear, with the war starting. He'd like to marry. It's lonely being a bachelor. Be happy for him, Doc, and learn to like Frances."

This had never occurred to me. I felt unhinged like a broken door, unsupported by the doorframe. In fact, I went to the stables and swung a door with only one hinge to see how it worked. Not very well, I discovered. This upset me. I didn't wish to become an unhinged door. Mr. Houghton found me there, and when he asked me what I was doing, I couldn't explain.

"How long do one-hinged doors remain workable?" I asked him, feeling I must explain myself.

"That depends upon several factors: how strong the remaining hinge is, and if the screws are in tight," he told me.

"I'm afraid they're rather loose," I replied; then I burst into tears.

Flabbergasted at causing such strong emotion, he retreated. I took his hand.

"The world's terribly mixed up with Christmas visitors and Father's new girlfriend, and Hitler and war. I can't stand it," I cried.

He took me in his boney arms and hugged me, then handed me a bit of rag to dry my face.

"It's clean," he assured me; "it's a piece of the Missus's torn tea towel. Dry your eyes. Old man Hitler isn't coming to Virginia. So stop worrying and enjoy your holidays."

"I know," I said wiping my eyes. "It's Father, you know, he's getting married."

"Oh, I see what's caused those tears. He's in the Reserves too, isn't he?" Mr. Houghton took the rag and put it in his pocket. "It's pretty serious stuff for a young girl to cope with."

I nodded. "Yes, it's serious. Frances is her name, and Grandmother says she's nice. She knew her parents. You know, in Indianapolis when Frances was young. I must call her Frances because it sounds more friendly than Aunt Frances, Grandmother says."

"I see," Mr. Houghton said, "it's a big change and difficult to accept. This war that's not a war has everyone nervous. Hitler's got to be stopped, and Europe will suffer. No, Doc, these are difficult times for adults much less a young girl. Your father loves you and when things are hard, remember that. Love's a big thing, you know. It keeps people safe."

He looked embarrassed as he squeezed my shoulder and walked away. He'd found it hard, I realized, to express these sentiments, and I felt grateful. It was hard for me to tell people my feelings; so I understood. I could express anger, but not other emotions which seemed to choke me. I loved Mr. Houghton for what he'd said.

Later that day I wasn't so sure. I had a friend, Doris Symonds, who was passed around like a football between her parents. One lived in Florida and the other in Richmond. I felt extremely sorry for her, because, at Christmas, she had to decide which place she wanted to go. It was all very confusing, and it seemed she hurt one or the other of her parents no matter which way she decided. I didn't want to be like her. I decided not to think about it; so I put the saddle and bridle on Billy and went off into the woods to ride in peace and to think.

About four o'clock when I entered the Houghtons' kitchen I found them arguing about the war. In haste I retreated, but Mr. Houghton caught me by my jacket and held fast.

"Just a minute, young lady. Come in. We are discussing the war."

"So is everyone else. I'm tired of it. Can't you think of something besides the troubles in Europe?"

"It's only a phony war," Mr. Houghton explained. "A non-shooting war. Britain is too poor to make battle against a flea."

"Why does Hitler have to go and spoil everything? Things are fine as they are. Really, he's going to tear everyone's life to pieces." I felt if the war were delayed, perhaps Father wouldn't marry right away.

"Hitler wants to get back the land that the Allies took from Germany in the Treaty after the Great War," Mr. Houghton explained.

"That man's a menace if ever there was one," Mrs. Houghton replied.

"I agree, and that's why I should buy some cattle," Mr. Houghton let go of my jacket.

"Now, Harry, we decided if we lived in the country, we would not raise cattle. We left Canada to get away from the severe weather and the responsibility of a large farm. My health isn't robust enough to take on cattle." His wife's tones sounded sharp. "Horses are fine, but no other animals. I don't want to be tied down again to a large operation. It's too confining."

"All right, dear," her husband acquiesced. "Suppose I buy some chickens?"

Mrs. Houghton sighed deeply then asked, "How many chickens?"

"Oh, just a few so we can sell eggs and have some for ourselves. It will help the war effort when the shooting starts Chickens will produce food. Remember the last time everyone had to grow something. We'll get into this conflict soon enough, you'll see"

"Okay then, chickens it is, but not too many. I'm not staying up at night bottle-feeding them as I did with the calves A few chickens would come in handy, I suppose."

Mr. Houghton washed his tanned arms and hands under the tap in the kitchen. "I'll order some baby chicks from Southern States and we'll go into business with a hundred biddies. That will be a good start.."

"Do you think we'll get into this war?" I asked Mrs.. Houghton, hoping to find a way to keep Father from marrying Frances and from going overseas with the Army Reserves.

"I don't know. It looks pretty serious. But maybe things will get sorted out in spite of Mr. Hitler," she said kindly.

Somehow I doubted it.

Soon after this conversation a hundred baby chicks arrived in a large cardboard box. Mr. Houghton fixed up an electric light for heat in an empty stall. Then he bought feed troughs, growing mash and water cylinders.

"This is sort of jerry-rigged," he confessed to me one evening after school, "but I've decided to build a chicken house. You can get a shell sort of thing from Sears Roebuck."

"What do you mean, a shell sort of thing?" I asked him.

"You put it together with directions. But it mightn't be any good. I'll have to look into it more and find out what is the best breeding house. I want to get the goodness out of whatever I buy. It's got to last the duration of the war as things might get scarce."

"What do you mean - you put it together with directions? What kind of house would that be?" I replied, confused.

Within a week's time he built a proper chicken house that rose from the red earth with the help of Sears Roebuck's catalogue and Grievous Sin Snead.

"That's more like it," Mr. Houghton stood admiring his new building one late December afternoon. "It's my birthday present from the Misses. You know my birthday is the twenty-first of December, the shortest day and the longest night I only get a half a birthday because it's dark most of the day."

"How old are you now?" I asked him boldly, knowing it was a personal question and forbidden by good manners

"As old as my tongue and a little older than my teeth," he replied. "I've got a place now for a hundred chickens with a feed room, water tap and everything included. All I had to do was read those directions." He indicated a dirty roll of papers stuck behind a two by four.

"It's all okay," I said, amazed. "Do you plan to paint it white?" Not impressed by his litany of facilities, I walked away. "It looks too new standing up there without shrubs or paint."

Mr. Houghton circled his chicken house with a more critical eye.

"Yes," he repeated, "It's a fine-looking building. Who would have thought it came out of a Sears and Roebuck catalogue? The Misses was right. It will do nicely. Tomorrow I'll get Grievous Sin to paint it white with forest green trim."

"Tomorrow's Christmas Eve," I reminded him. "I doubt if Grievous will come."

"Yes, green paint around the windows, and white sides will look handsome, for sure. Don't you agree?" He ignored my remark about Christmas Eve.

Mr. Houghton's new chicken house caused quite a stir in the neighborhood Miss Emma and Cary were given the 'Cook's Tour,' and even Mr. Harris drove down from Manakin to look over the new building.

"It's a credit to the war effort, if war comes," Mr. Harris pointed out after being conducted through the feed room, the nesting boxes and the little pump house.

"Yes, sir," agreed Mr. Houghton with pride, "I am raising a new variety of chicken called Indian River Cross. They're just being tried out before they are sold for general production."

"I've heard of them. You should get plenty of eggs and meat with that breed. A very superior chicken, I hear," Mr. Harris said with authority.

Often during that first winter I 'd find a boxful of baby chickens beneath my neighbor's stove. Huddled together under an old towel for warmth, this corner of the kitchen became their incubator. Over the years Mr. Houghton would raise not only chickens, but also guineas and even a pheasant under that stove - usually ignoring his wife's objections. As the Christmas Season came and went, Mr. Houghton seemed contented with his hens and his horses. Although the black mares did little work except to plough our gardens and to pull a wagon to bring in the Christmas tree, they lived contented lives.

As the nation's families assembled for this most special holiday, the clouds of war gathered in Europe. My cousins, Sarah and James, kept saying, "Let's do that one more time, because nobody knows where we shall be next year."

"Here," I told them firmly. "I shall be here."

"You don't know that," said James. "Not for certain. So I'll eat some more chocolates just in case."

"You'll make yourself sick. And, anyway, I'm not going to let old man Hitler spoil my holidays," I replied with determination.

We all ate too much candy, turkey and plum pudding. I felt as if I'd celebrated ten Christmases all rolled into one. I just couldn't believe that this would be the last time I would open my stocking or trim the tree or eat turkey and dressing. I soon grew tired of food and took my cousins to the barn to hook up Jackie, our donkey, to the pony cart and drove them up to the Taliaferros' house for a visit. The adults acted just as crazy as the children. They drank and ate too much, and sang too loudly the old familiar carols at church. Everybody kissed everybody else and slapped each other on the back. After a while it all became rather silly.

"Goodbye until the war is over," the men greeted each other. "Let me have a little kiss now, before I go to war," they coaxed the ladies.

Behind all this forced merriment lay a fear, unspoken but real, that next Christmas some of these partygoers would lay dead upon an unknown battlefield in France. I realized that this might be true since a lot of British people who worked for Imperial Tobacco Company planned to return home in the New Year. Colonel Hollis announced he was joining the Canadian Air Force shortly after the holidays. Christmas night I lay in bed and pondered over the events of the day. The dancing, drinking adults who wished each other Merry Christmas and laughed too loudly to cover up what lay in their hearts disturbed me. They acted as if all their frantic merriment would delay the war. Underneath all this false good will, I realized that they were afraid. I was afraid too that my comfortable world would be blown to bits. Father warned in his letters that an all-out war involving many countries was coming. I tried not to think about it. Yet it was there, the fear and the resentment that one crazy German could bring destruction to the whole world and to my life which had hardly begun. I knew one eleven-year-old girl, in America, counted for very little in the big scheme of things. Still I must believe in the ability of good people in the world to counter the evil that crept up behind us. The devil always worked by stealth and in the dark, somebody once told me, and he usually came from behind us unnoticed. I decided to think of other things. Next week I would visit Father, and then I hoped all this mess about war and Hitler would be placed in a different perspective. Father wouldn't act silly and afraid. He'd show me how I could "deport" myself. Mother always told me my deportment needed to be improved.

But I think it's what I feel inside, and the way I show my love and affection that's really important. I just can't express the same feelings of love for Mother as I can for Father. I've tried, but she rejects me. Perhaps she doesn't love me. Maybe I'm not very loveable in her eyes. Mr. Houghton and Mrs. Houghton love me even when I climb trees and get terribly dirty. Father loves me and calls me Son, because he felt disappointed that I wasn't a boy. He loves me though, very much. I wonder if he marries Frances if he'll still love me. I'm sure he will, because we ride down to the river together and share secrets. That's why I love Father and the Houghtons - we share lots of interesting secrets. Safe in the assurance that I would always be his girl, I dropped off to sleep.

The next day Grandmother drew me aside and told me I must not mention Father's getting married to anyone.

"Your mother will lose face if people know," she said. "There's enough talk about her relationship with Rudy."

"I don't like him," I replied crossly.

"Yes, I can see why," was her curious reply. "But you must never discuss it. That's something better swept under the carpet."

"How very Virginian," I thought, "all these rules that make no sense one must know. I hate rules and things one can't speak about. Mrs. Houghton will understand when I tell her."

Grandmother and I sat in the guest room opposite mine off the upstairs hall. I could see she felt uncomfortable with the situation. She picked up her knitting, but after dropping several stitches she put it down again. I sat on the floor beside her chair rocking back and forth. A favorite position when I wished to think.

"You promise you won't say anything," she placed her hand on my shoulder. "Some things are better left unsaid. Gossip can be a hurtful thing, and we don't need any gossip. Promise me."

I promised, knowing full well I would discuss it all with Mrs. Houghton who would explain things to me. Once I understood the situation, I would refrain from asking questions. Grandmother seemed happy enough with my promise.

"Tomorrow we shall go see your Father and Frances in Philadelphia!" She hugged me.

12

My Trip to Philadelphia

As the train pulled into Broad Street Station I saw Father sprint along the platform to meet us. Grandmother stood aside to let me get off first, and with one jump I landed in Father's arms and was smothered in a bear hug.

"What a young lady you've grown into," he exclaimed. "You're no longer a little girl. Don't change too much, Doc. Remain your own sweet self. I like you the way you are."

"All little girls must grow up," Grandmother reminded him as she stepped onto the platform. "You don't want a case of arrested development now, John."

"I know you must become a lady," he winked at me. "But not too quickly. I am missing out on your girlhood, Doc. And I don't want to miss a single minute." We strode up the platform together, Father carrying our suitcases.

"Did you have a good Christmas?" he asked, looking down at me with his hazel eyes. "What did Santa Claus bring you?"

"He brought Mr. Houghton a new chicken house from the Sears Roebuck catalogue," I said. "It was the talk of the neighborhood. Even Mr. Harris drove down from Manakin to admire it."

"But what did he bring you?" Father asked again.

"A book, some stationery, a pen and pencil set. It's really beautiful. I like it. And a bracelet and a lovely blue sweater from you. I've brought it with me."

Grandmother packed it, knowing Father would be pleased.

"It fits all right?" he asked.

"Perfectly," I said. "it's going to be shown off tomorrow. So you can admire me."

At the end of the platform we climbed down several steps to a cab stand.

"Bellevue-Stratford," Father told the driver, settling us in the back seat. "We'll have some lunch there before you go out to Haverford."

The city of Philadelphia looked enormous. I saw William Penn's statue atop the City Hall as we sped by and entered a wide street filled with movie houses. After dodging through lunchtime traffic, we jerked to a halt in front of the elegant Bellview Strafford. How formidable it appeared with large rooms and uniformed waiters.

"What a treat," I said as we followed the maitre d'hotel to a stiffly starched linen-cloth covered table. "I've never eaten at a hotel."

The surroundings were splendid. Heavy curtains framed the windows and a deep pile rug muffled the sounds of feet as various groups of businessmen and ladies entered the dining room. The waiter handed me a huge menu. I opened it and was confronted by myriad choices of French food.

"We'll have the roast beef," Father took charge, "with soup and coffee. We'll order dessert later."

"That sounds good to me," said Grandmother, unfolding her linen napkin.

"Yes," I agreed, relieved I didn't have to choose. "It's great."

"Well, my child, what've you been doing?" Father turned to me.

"I am taking riding lessons, and piano lessons, but I'm not very good. My teacher thinks I have a tin ear."

"No doubt inherited from me," he laughed. "I love music, especially opera. And I can hum some of the arias, but hopelessly off key."

"I don't expect there's much chance for me." I unfolded the large napkin and placed it in the band of my skirt.

"I remember when I visited Prague and Vienna shortly after you were born we went to the opera house in Vienna and heard 'La Traviata.' What melodious music! For days afterwards I hummed the melody of the opera's drinking song and of the love theme."

"Why did you go to Prague and Vienna after I was born," I asked.

"It was planned months before, but your arrival delayed things. After I'd peeked at you and put down my stamp of approval, I went off to Europe with James Dennis for three weeks."

"Were you disappointed I wasn't a boy?" I watched him to see.

"Of course. Everyone wants a boy. But then girls are nice too. I have to admit."

"Did you go to Vienna and Prague because you were displeased I was a girl?" I asked him.

"Not a bit. And after all you've turned out all right, I must say." The waiter served our soup. "Yes, you'll do, I suppose."

I laughed and accepted his teasing. We ate for a while in silence. Father got soup on his moustache and wiped it with his napkin. Grandmother ate with her little finger stuck out in the air, and I tried ever so hard not to spill on the pristine tablecloth. The dining room had filled up, and the waiters scurried to and fro with great trays held high above their shoulders. Christmas decorations glistened and reflected the lights turned on now to dispel the gray afternoon. It was all very festive, I thought, so different from Richmond.

"I want you to meet Frances Rolash, Doc. I think you'll like her." Father broke the silence. "She's a great gal, charming and delightful."

"Grandmother told me you might get married again."

He regarded me sharply, but said nothing and returned to his soup. I watched his face, but saw no flicker of displeasure.

"It's all right, sir, if you wish to get married. As long as I'm still your girl."

He laughed. It was a great laugh that caused me to jump.

"So I've got your permission, have I?" He chuckled.

"I thought you might like it, that's all." I placed my spoon in my soup bowl and wiped my mouth. "We shouldn't have any misunderstanding."

"No," he replied, seriously, "we shouldn't."

The waiter came and took our empty bowls, then brought a great tray filled with covered dishes. These he removed and placed steaming plates of roast beef and vegetables before us. Then, after filling our water glasses, he departed. At last Father spoke.

"I'll probably get married around the first part of the New Year. Nothing definite has been arranged as yet. But that's when we think we can manage the free time. She works in New York and must make some arrangements there," he explained.

"Oh," I gasped. "So it's all planned."

"Not exactly, just talked about. Nothing definite, yet."

"That's grand, John," Grandmother added, "I'm very pleased. It's time you were settled again."

I glanced at her quickly then down at my plate. I wondered where this left me, being a part of two families. I realized how Doris Symonds must feel when confronted with her plans for Christmas. I felt Father's eyes upon me, so I looked up at him and smiled.

"It'll take some getting used to, yeah, Doc. All these different families with cousins by the dozen, and aunts and uncles coming out of your ears." He winked.

"Yes, sir. That's exactly what I've been thinking. It will seem strange," I admitted.

"Never mind," Father changed the subject. "I am more concerned about this phony war right now. Being in the Army Reserves I've been taking some courses in tactics at the War College. I trip down to Washington once a week. These classes are extremely interesting. I'll show you my map with the red and blue armies I am working on."

"Do you think there'll be a war?" I asked him.

"By the time you are thirteen we shall be involved in another World conflict."

"I shall be twelve in the spring. That's not very long."

"Mark my words, Doc, by spring the British will be in France fighting the Germans again." He picked up his knife and thoughtfully cut his meat.

"Are you sure?" I insisted. "Are you sure?"

"Yes, my dear girl, I am sure. And make no mistake about it, I'll be among the first called. I saw action in Russia during the last war and was trained at West Point Military Academy, so I'll be in this new conflict."

"But what about me?" I said just above a whisper.

"I've a duty to defend my country if it's threatened. That's a higher calling. And you as a Captain's daughter must never forget it." Father sounded firm.

"Yes, sir," I replied. "But what of us?"

"Us? Us?" he questioned. "By us you mean Americans?"

"No, sir, I mean you and me." I hated his patriotism.

"But, Son, bigger issues are at stake now. Issues that you and I

My Trip to Philadelphia

must realize we can't control," Father replied.

I sat quietly. Whenever Father called me "Son" in that tone, it meant not to pursue the subject further. I knew he loved me, but I wanted him to say it.

The waiter removed our plates, crumbed the table with a silver crumber and offered us the menu once more. Out of the corner of my eye I noticed a trolley filled with cakes and lovely tiny iced confections.

"Oh, Father," I gasped in delight. "What are those?"

"French pastries," he replied. "Would you like one?"

"Oh, yes, please."

"Then your wish is my command. Waiter, one of those pastries, please."

The dark haired waiter rolled the trolley over to my place. Never had I seen anything so wonderful.

"Which one would you like, miss?" he asked.

"I can't decide," I said, confused by the choice. "That one there, please." I pointed to something that looked like a fairy castle.

Father looked amused, and watched me take the first bite. I rolled my eyes skyward with pleasure, and rubbed my tummy.

"Don't they—have French pastry in Virginia?" he asked me.

"I am sure they don't. I've never seen any there," I told him. "I've never tasted anything so wonderful."

In tiny bites I devoured the pastry and looked hungrily at the trolley. In a small voice, knowing full well my request would be denied, I asked for a second piece.

"Well, who ever heard of eating two French pastries at one time?" Father roared with laughter. "Waiter, please bring her another."

The waiter appeared terribly amused as he brought me the trolley once more. From its gleaming tray I selected a second confection. With a flourish he placed the second dessert in front of me. It was even better than the first. Nuts, cream and brown sugar simply melted in my mouth. The waiter gave me a little bow when he brought Father the bill. Absolutely thrilled with the meal at the Bellevue-Stratford, I bowed in return.

"I call that a very satisfactory lunch," said Father as we prepared to leave. " 'Twas a great success. Don't you agree, Son?"

"Oh, yes, sir!" I followed Father and Grandmother out of the dining room.

"I'll return to the office now. But I've asked Virginia, my housekeeper, to take care of you. So if you want to do some shopping or go straight out to Haverford give her a sound on the horn. Frances is coming down from New York to meet you. Since it's Friday she may even come after work this evening. I'll see you at the apartment about six o'clock."

"Fine," Grandmother told him. "I'll take Doc to Wannamakers to see the decorations. She needs some good Oxford shoes and we might find her a pair. We'll see you again this evening."

I watched Father walk briskly up the street and disappear around the next corner.

Grandmother, with me in tow, walked back around the City Hall to Wanamaker's Department Store. It was enormous. An organ played above me in a mezzanine and a large eagle stood in the middle of the main floor. Later I learned it was a famous meeting place. I clutched Grandmother's hand afraid I might get lost. The Christmas decorations were positively beautiful, and I walked around with my head in the clouds.

At the shoe department on the second or third floor - I can't remember which - Grandmother bought me a pair of Oxfords with silver buckles. These were by far the finest shoes I'd ever owned. I kept them safely in their box and hugged them against my chest like a prize.

"This place is wonderful," I gasped. "I've never seen such things: books, toys, dolls, made in Germany, you wouldn't believe existed, with gorgeous clothes. What a Fairyland!"

After looking around for an hour, Grandmother and I returned to the Bellevue-Stratford. We picked up our luggage, and we took a cab to Suburban Station to catch a train for Haverford.

"We'll get the Paoli Local. Come on, Doc. Let's hurry. It's on track Number 10, I believe."

Carrying my suitcase and the precious shoes I followed Grandmother. She bought us each a ticket, and headed down a long flight of stairs to the train. The whistle blew, we pulled out of the station, and headed towards Philadelphia's Main Line.

At Haverford we got down, and took a cab to Father's apartment where a beaming Virginia opened the door.

"Oh, Mrs. Ferrell, how nice to see you."

"It's nice to be here," Grandmother replied, laying down her heavy suitcase. "I am exhausted. Could you fix us a cup of tea?"

"Hello, Doc."

"Hello, Virginia," I greeted her.

Virginia, who looked after my grandfather, was now Father's housekeeper.

Ten minutes later, our hands washed and slippers warming our aching feet, Grandmother and I sat down to a beautifully appointed tea tray. I felt I was home in Virginia with Mrs. Houghton as we poured the hot tea. Still full of French pastry, I declined a cookie and the piece of cake offered me.

"No, thank you, Virginia, I just can't. Because I ate two pieces of wonderful pastry for lunch."

"Oh, I see," Virginia, sounded hurt. "Mine's not fancy enough."

"Don't worry, she'll have them tomorrow," Grandmother reassured her. "Your cakes are always perfect."

As we sat in the deep leather chairs of Father's living room enjoying ourselves I forgot about the war and his forthcoming marriage.

Later that evening, shortly after Father's return, Frances arrived from New York. She breezed in and in front of us kissed Father with great affection; I felt awkward and silently tiptoed out to Virginia in the kitchen. But Father followed, he wished to introduce me to Frances.

I re-entered the sitting room with him to shake hands, and suddenly felt our special relationship would never be quite the same again.

"Hello, Doc, I've heard so much about you and your farm in Virginia."

"Oh, yes?" I stammered.

"How nice to meet you at last," Frances continued. "You're quite a young lady."

"Not really," I blushed.

"Let me fix us a drink," Father offered and disappeared into the kitchen to tell Virginia, who arrived with a tray already set up with glasses and ice.

I sat politely and listened to their conversation sipping thoughtfully my glass of orange juice decorated with fruit slices. Frances, I noticed, appeared extremely well dressed in a black silk crepe. She possessed long, very shapely legs which she crossed around twice. Yet, for all her New York clothes and manner, she seemed kind. The conversation sparkled. Father loved to use words, and Frances also had this flair. Laughing and talking easily together, they spoke of a life I had known only in books. Little by little I found myself fascinated and eventually charmed by this strange, rather worldly woman. "Now, my dear, we must eat supper," Frances finally exclaimed. "Doc, you must be famished."

"Not exactly," I confessed, still full of tea and pastry. "But it is rather late."

"Come, Mrs. Ferrell, let's go into the dining room," Frances invited. "Really, John, we must not talk all night."

After placing my empty glass on the tray I followed the adults. Frances seated us on either side of the table while she and Father sat at the ends. Virginia served, and I recognized the best china for this occasion. Again I listened to the adults' conversation, feeling tired and unsure. Father laughed his big laugh Frances and Grandmother giggled while I watched these proceedings with considerable interest.

Frances, I decided, would make Father a good wife. She was fun and entertaining and extremely elegant. In her company, Father again seemed his old self. His brooding nature had changed, and his eyes sparkled with happiness.

"What did you do today, Doc?" Frances addressed me suddenly. "How do you like Philadelphia?"

"Oh, fine," I replied. "It's terribly big, much bigger than Richmond and dirtier, too."

"Did you see the little push carts with pretzels and chestnuts? They're usually out along Market Street near the City Hall."

"I'm not sure," I confessed. "But we did go to Wanamaker's to buy some shoes."

"And were the decorations as gorgeous as ever?" she asked.

"They were fantastic. And the organ played carols, and we saw marvelous dolls from Germany dressed in velvet and lace."

"Wanamaker's a fairyland at Christmas with toys and music and excited shoppers," Grandmother interjected.

"Yes," I agreed. "It certainly is."

Dinner over, we thanked Virginia and returned to the living room. Father lit the fire; we sat around it while the adults drank coffee, and I had a cup of hot cocoa. Their talk swirled around my head, laughter and chatter blended together. Sitting relaxed in the big wing chair I fell asleep.

My Trip to Philadelphia

The next morning at breakfast Frances appeared looking elegant and fresh.

"I've arranged for us to go to a matinee this afternoon," she told me before she had finished her first cup of tea. "We shall leave here about one o'clock for a two-thirty curtain."

Father put down his newspaper. "Yes, and Mother Ferrell and I'll visit the Rochesters in Gladwyne. These squirrels of politicians in Washington are a bunch of jackasses. They will squirrel around and do nothing. No wonder the world's in a mess."

"That'll be splendid," Grandmother replied.

"You mean I shall go to the theatre in Philadelphia?" I asked Frances. "To see a real, live play on the stage?"

We ignored Father's outburst against the government.

"That's the idea, Son." Father went back inside his *New York Times*, still muttering about the incompetence of politicians.

"Yes, and I've arranged for you to go back stage. An old friend of mine is appearing in a new play, and I want you to meet him."

"You know real actors?" I asked, amazed by this newest revelation.

"I was in the theatre once upon a time, back in the twenties before I discovered I must eat three times a day and pay the rent." Frances said kindly. "You've never been to the theatre before?"

"Oh, yes," I lied, "in Richmond we have road companies at the Lyric Theatre downtown."

"I see," said Frances doubtfully, attacking her boiled egg.

At one o'clock, dressed in Father's Christmas sweater and my new shoes, and accompanied by an elegant Frances, we boarded the Paoli Local for town. She not only dressed in style, but she also smelled good. Perfume wafted from her and settled around me. She looked absolutely marvelous in a trim suit with a fur collar.

"Well, this is just great," she assured me when we found our seats in the train. "I love the theatre. I really adore it. What fun to go with you."

"You think so?" I asked her incredulously. "I thought you'd want to stay home and talk to Father."

"I'll see him this evening. Anyway, he and your grandmother are busy with their own plans."

We rattled along the Main Line tracks and thirty minutes later pulled into Suburban Station. Here Frances hailed a taxi and told the driver where she wished to go. When we got out in front of the theatre, greatly excited I pushed through the matinee crowds, as we entered the foyer and were directed upstairs to our seats in a box. How special I felt!

Frances handed me a program and settled herself in a very uncomfortable chair. After crossing her legs twice, she opened her playbill. Fascinated by the theater's lights and its fancy curtain, I remained standing, precariously leaning over the box to see what was underneath. Below, people dressed in their finest clothes moved along the aisles to their seats. The sounds of voices created a pleasant hum of anticipation. Above me a great chandelier illuminated the auditorium casting fantastic patterns from its prisms. Remembering I must act like a lady, I removed my coat and took my seat. The house lights dimmed, the audience hushed and the curtain rose.

The stage was transformed into a wonderland. Actors appeared, spoke their lines and the play started. For an hour I sat transported beyond the confines of the theatre into the magical world of imagination. Quite suddenly the curtain descended, and I was returned to the theatre. Frances stood up. I followed her into the lobby where she lit a cigarette.

"Are you enjoying it?" she asked me in her usual voice.

Not wishing to break the magic spell, I nodded in assent. She hardly had time to finish her cigarette before the usher signaled us back to our seats. The curtain rose, and once more I was transported into the marvelous world of fantasy. When the lights came on for the last time, and the curtain rang down amid shouts of "Bravo" and thunderous applause, I remained glued to my chair.

"Come, dear, I want you to meet Alexander Roman, an old friend of mine."

Still in a trance I followed Frances out of the box and down some stairs. Then quite suddenly we found ourselves back stage amid scenery, prop men and actors. Frances knocked on a dressing room door, which opened with a flourish and before us stood the most handsome man I had ever seen. His face still covered with makeup, he greeted us warmly and invited us in.

"My dear Rolash, this is a surprise. How nice of you to come. And who, pray tell, is this young lady?" Mr. Roman turned to me.

"This is Catherine Dickson, John's daughter from Virginia. She has not been to the theatre before so I brought her this afternoon when I found out you were here."

"How do you do?" I stammered, extending my hand.

"Delighted to meet you. A real Southern belle, I suppose."

I blushed scarlet from my neck to the roots of my hair. Frances continued to talk and asked her friend about the play's run and when it would open in New York.

"Probably next month," Mr. Roman replied. "It's doing quite well, you know."

As they chatted together, I looked around and discovered to my surprise various costumes and wigs sitting on a shelf above my head. Before the long dressing table Mr. Roman sat down, and I watched spellbound as he removed his makeup. To my great surprise, underneath he appeared to be a man just like anyone else. Frances moved towards the door.

"We must go," she said. "Perhaps I'll see you in New York when you open there."

"Yes, we must get together. How nice of you to come, and what a pleasure to meet this young lady." Clicking his heels, Alexander Roman bowed to me.

"Thank you, sir," I replied, out of my depth.

In a twinkling we left the dressing room, crossed beside the now-darkened stage, and entered the auditorium once more. Then, with me following, we walked out of the magical world of the theatre and back onto Philadelphia's darkening streets.

"What a wonderful afternoon," I took Frances's hand. "Thank you."

"It was nice, wasn't it? I enjoyed it too." She consulted her watch. "We can make the next train if we hurry. I'll hail a cab."

Retracing our steps we headed back through the station and caught the Paoli Local once more. But I, although walking on the ground in my new shoes, which now hurt, felt somehow no longer part of it. I still remained in that wonderful world of make believe I had discovered that afternoon in the theatre. This had been the most exciting day of my life.

A Forgotten Landscape

Part II
January 1940 – December 1941

War Begins in Europe

A Forgotten Landscape

13

The Prelude Ends

The phony war continued. Winter finally gave way to spring. And with the spring's arrival my neighbors began to prepare the fields for planting. In the woods the leaf buds burst into flower, and suckling calves wobbled behind their mothers in the greening fields. Even though the sun warmed my back, somehow it didn't seem as friendly as in previous years.

A feeling of tension affected us as we waited expectantly for Hitler's offensive. "It'll come in the spring," Mr. Houghton said.

In April of 1940 German troops invaded Norway and Denmark. Father wrote from Philadelphia that he with other members of the Army Reserves continued their classes on military tactics. A new kind of dread invaded my heart and refused to retreat. This prelude to Europe's war scared me.

Then, quite unexpectedly, Jean Taliaferro telephoned, and asked me to come horseback riding with her. Jean and her sister, Sally Anne, were ten and twelve years my senior and out of school. They had lived in the country for a long time; their father bought his farm shortly after the last war, when Mr. Taliaferro retired from his job in Richmond he moved his family out to the farm where he raised beef cattle: White-faced Herefords.

He insisted that his daughters learn to keep the farm's accounts, and to accompany him to cattle sales. I admired Jean, who knew more about beef cows than most men. I rarely saw these girls, and their invitation to go riding surprised me. Since Billy couldn't keep up, I sat in front of Jean on her big, powerfully built half-breed. Exceedingly strong and over sixteen hands, Huck traveled on magical hooves, and appeared to float over the ground with long, steady strides. Plain and down-to-earth, Jean loved the country and liked helping her father on the farm. But her younger, prettier sister, Sally Ann, preferred going to dances in Richmond. Often on weekends she entertained several of her friends, and enjoyed an active social life.

"It seems a different spring this year," I confided to Jean as we rode through the woods. "It has an unsettled feeling."

"Yes," she agreed, but I wasn't sure she understood. "Spring can often seem that way."

Sally Anne followed on Tom; although bigger than Huck, he was quieter and easier to ride.

"The woods are beautiful today," she called to us. "I see numerous wild flowers, and the dogwood trees are starting to bloom."

"Come on, Sally, stop admiring the scenery. Let's have a gallop." Jean urged Huck forward into a canter, and we left Sally Anne behind. Under me I felt the great muscles tense and uncoil, and heard the rhythmic hoof beats upon the forest floor. Behind us Tom's eager feet pounded over the soft earth, and suddenly I forgot about the war and experienced an exhilarating sense of freedom. Jean pulled Huck up in front of Mrs. Haunch's gates. She, also, lived on our road. But this neighbor remained for me an intriguing mystery.

"Have you ever seen her?" I asked. "I've lived up here for two years now and never laid eyes on her."

"Mrs. Haunch?" Jean replied as she settled Huck into a walk. "She's a small, birdlike woman who wears dirty riding breeches most of the time."

"Is she a witch?"

"No, I don't think so. But she is terribly eccentric. And shortly after her husband died she became a hermit," Jean explained.

"She scares me. I'm sure she's a witch. Next to the German Army invading America, I consider Mrs. Haunch the most terrifying person in the world."

Jean laughed and urged Huck over a small stream, and across the dirt road.

"She's not that frightening, just an old lady who lives with her dogs, and dislikes people."

But I knew different. Nothing would ever convince me that Mrs.

The Prelude Ends

Haunch's place wasn't haunted.

"What an imagination you've got," Sally Anne remarked as we turned towards home. "She is a scary old lady, I agree."

I confided my fears to Mrs. Houghton.

"She's not a witch, but Mrs. Haunch could cause you a great deal of trouble. Do you hear me, Doc? Don't go near her place." But it was my secret wish to pluck up enough courage and walk up that dark driveway, right to Mrs. Haunch's front door and ring her bell.

"I wish I had raven locks like the Taliaferro girls." I sat at the kitchen table in Mrs. Houghton's cottage helping her with supper. "My hair is much too short, and I don't like its color."

"No wonder those girls are good looking. In her youth, their mother, Laura Taliaferro, was considered a great beauty, and the belle of Richmond."

"I think she is beautiful now and ever so stately with her tall, slim figure."

Mrs. Taliaferro's brown eyes always seemed kind, her grey hair she wore swept up from an elegant neck. Often she selected hand-embroidered blouses, sometimes set off with an old fashioned pin of pearls and diamonds, to wear with her tweed skirts. I considered her perfectly beautiful, even in gardening clothes.

"Apparently," Mrs. Houghton continued, "during their courtship, she dazzled John Martin Taliaferro who chased her to Italy. There, after some months, he married her."

"How wonderfully romantic. Fancy being married in Italy, miles away from Virginia." I dreamed wistfully one day this would happen to me.

Shortly after this conversation, early in the morning of the tenth of May, 1940, the Germans parachuted into Holland and Belgium. Now, Hitler's great armies, reinforced with tanks, attacked through the Ardennes Forest and headed towards Paris. The phony war had ended and the mighty German offensive rolled across Europe. Soon the Low Countries and then France fell into Nazi hands. In great confusion, the British and French Armies now raced towards the sea, with the Belgian Army covering their retreat.

One evening after hearing this news on his radio Mr. Houghton and I drove down to Henley's store for a loaf of bread. Since it was unusually warm, Mr. Henley placed chairs in his yard under the trees. Here, several farmers gathered to talk over these alarming events. For the past week everyone spoke of little else except the war. As Mr. Houghton and I pulled into the forecourt, a robin sang his evening song. He made the twilight seem idyllic and peaceful.

Inside, we found Mrs. Henley and her sister, Ethel, who scooped out mounds of ice cream into cones for three dirty-faced children. These children and two of my neighbors seemed to fill the little store. Mrs. Carter placed her groceries on the brown wooden counter, which was stacked with pyramids of fresh bread, country eggs and Chesterfield cigarettes. Behind this counter long, high shelves reached to the ceiling. Neatly stacked canned goods, including Campbell's soups, potted meats and various kinds of vegetables lined the middle shelves. Beside these stood rows of aspirin, Ipana toothpaste, deodorants and shampoos. Nearby lay a brown box filled with buttons, spools of various colored threads, needles and rolls of red and white hair ribbons. On the bottom shelf lay sticks of paraffin (a wax used for covering jellies and preserves). Next to these, I saw several bolts of cotton prints for dressmaking. Above them, large boxes of Kellogg's cereals lined the top shelves, and created a crazy-quilt pattern.

A black pot-bellied stove stood in the middle of the room, resting firmly in a protective box of sand. In winter, around this stove the farmers sat and chatted with their neighbors. This evening the stove remained unfired. Nearby several nail kegs made handy stools. I perched on one of these and watched Mr. Houghton test a hammer for weight and balance. Apparently the first one did not satisfy him, because he replaced it and tried another.

"The war news sounds more terrible each day: all those poor Allied soldiers getting killed," commented Anita Sparrow as Mrs. Henley added up the price of the groceries on the corner of a brown paper bag. "I feel sure America will remain neutral. I see no reason why we should fight Europe's battles."

"Neither do I," agreed Mrs. Henley taking the ten-dollar bill Mrs. Sparrow offered her and making change. "Let them fight over there if they wish to. We've got no argument with Germany."

"I heard on the radio that British troops are running for their lives. They're right against the English Channel on the beaches of France,"

The Prelude Ends

Mrs. Carter joined in. "We Americans won't stand by and allow the Germans to overrun England. We shall get into this war yet; just you wait and see."

"Not on your life, Mary," Mrs. Sparrow countered. "There isn't a particle of need for us to fight in Europe. We have enough to worry about right here with the Depression and everyone out of work."

"Mrs. Henley, I need some washing powder. I think Ivory Flakes will be okay." Mary Carter read from the list in her hand. "And a package of La France blueing. That's about all."

"Have you heard about Alexander Forest's son?" Anita Sparrow continued.

"No," Mrs. Carter replied, "What's he done?"

"Lied about his age and upped and joined the Navy. Flunked out of the University, of all the stupid things."

"Well, I never. He's a strong-minded boy, that's for sure," Mrs. Carter picked up her groceries.

"And what's more, that awful Wallis Simpson's caused a creation in New York."

"That woman! Wallis Simpson wanted to become queen. And when she didn't, she acts like one anyway. Who ever heard of traipsing around the world with a dozen trunks?" Mrs. Carter spat out the words in disgust.

"She's positively awful. What an ambitious adventuress! And he's not much better giving up his throne," Mrs. Henley agreed. "What ever got into him, thinking he could make Mrs. Simpson his queen?"

"I hear she's awful high and mighty," Mrs. Carter said.

"They're a sad couple. Nobody wants them." Anita Sparrow selected a loaf of bread and a dozen eggs.

As Mr. Houghton listened to the ladies' conversation, he became exceedingly annoyed. Silently he tested the hammer allowing it to fall on his palm, and then laying it across his finger at the end of the wooden handle for balance. From my perch on the nail keg I saw all the danger signals, the pursed lips, the nervous grinding of teeth until he could contain his temper no longer.

"Don't you realize what will happen if Hitler conquers all of Europe including Britain?" he thundered as he spun around, hammer raised.

In peril for their lives the women squealed and fled towards the door. Surprised at the fright he'd caused, Mr. Houghton lowered the hammer and standing in the middle of the store, his face flushed, continued:

"America would be isolated from those countries. She trades with Europe, you know. And Hitler, with all of Europe under his command, could defeat us economically. There's no such thing as remaining neutral if England's gone."

Anita Sparrow, ever bold, held her ground, with eyes ablaze, and cheeks crimson.

"You British just can't fight your own wars; that's your trouble. Why should our boys be sent to France again to get killed? We've no quarrel with Hitler. Who cares about such places as Austria, Poland and Czechoslovakia? I surely don't."

"Nor I," concurred Mrs. Henley. "They don't even speak English there. Who knows what they're dreaming up?"

Mr. Houghton placed the hammer on the counter and took out his money.

"Mark my words," he said, his voice still edged with anger, "there will be war. Another world conflict more terrible than the last. And America will be forced to get in. She'll not allow England to fight alone."

Mrs. Carter placed her hand on Mr. Houghton's arm, gently turning him towards her. "You're right, I know. I hate to admit it, but you're absolutely right. It's coming no matter what you say, Anita Sparrow."

Mrs. Sparrow stood, groceries in hand, blocking the door. I watched her as she stepped forward, face contorted, furious she'd lost Mary Carter's complete obeisance. Mary of all people, timid and shy, who believed everything Anita said was gospel. I realized that Mrs. Sparrow refused to leave before she had the final word.

"Maybe not, Mary," she said wickedly. "You'll see, Mr. Roosevelt will keep us out of foreign wars and our boys safe at home."

Then she turned on her heel and left the store, slamming the door causing our President's photograph that Mrs. Henley prized so much to swing dangerously on its thin nail.

"What's got into her?" Mrs. Henley asked as she caught her flying picture. "She didn't need to get so het-up."

The remaining customers shook their heads in disbelief and finished their shopping.

"I'll have some of those ripe tomatoes, please," Mary Carter, visibly

The Prelude Ends

shaken said. I knew she considered Mrs. Sparrow extremely important, much more important than the Houghtons and me. So much so, in fact, that Mrs. Carter often didn't speak to us when she was around. But this afternoon was different, this afternoon Mary Carter, timid, plump and out of fashion, had taken on a new dimension. It was then that I began to like her and to look at her from a different point of view.

"These are greenhouse grown," Mrs. Henley replied, turning towards me. "Doc, I've saved some ice cream tops for you with movie stars on them. Here is a rare Clark Gable and two Bing Crosbys, to trade or add to your collection."

"Thank you," I said, jumping down from the nail keg. "I've a friend at school who needs a Bing Crosby. And I've never seen a Clark Gable before."

Mr. Houghton selected a loaf of Wonder bread from the pyramid and some jam.

"I'll have these," he said, putting down his money. Then, bidding the ladies goodbye he left the store. I followed.

"You know," I remarked, "this evening seems perfectly natural and usual. Yet, I know in Europe people are dying and fighting like hell. It doesn't seem real, somehow."

"It's real, all right – just far away. It'll be real enough once we get mobilized. This war is downright frightening. We've got so much to lose, and people like Anita Sparrow aren't helping." Mr. Houghton climbed into his car.

"I've written Father. Time seems so short now with the war. He and Frances are getting married, you know."

"I know," said Mr. Houghton turning the car onto River Road.

"I don't think this world's very fair, separating us, with people getting killed - even children and old people who never did the Germans any harm. If God loves us why does He make bad things happen?"

"I don't know why, but this world's going to be shot to hell!"

The car jumped forward as he angrily pressed the accelerator. I felt grown up using the forbidden word, "hell." I'd done it purposely because I realized Mr. Houghton was too angry to notice.

A Forgotten Landscape

14

Thelma's Place

The news from Europe broke over us like a giant tidal wave. At a place on the French coast called Dunkirk over two hundred thousand French and British troops crowded onto the beaches. Then, a flotilla of small boats, called forth from all over Britain, streamed across the Channel and plucked thousands of young men off the sands right in front of Hitler's nose. For three days and nights, in spite of great confusion, poor weather, and German air attacks, the British Army's rescue continued. Over the radio Winston Churchill's now familiar, deep, gravelly voice inspired his countrymen with ringing phrases:

"We shall not flag or fail - we shall fight them on the beaches; we shall fight them on the landing grounds; we shall fight them in the fields and in the streets; we shall fight them in the hills; we shall never surrender."

For several days during these great events we sat with our ears glued against the radio. We rejoiced that the British Expeditionary Force was saved. But within three weeks France fell. Finally, on the twenty-second of June when the Franco-German Armistice was signed, a feeling of great uncertainty as to our own future settled over America.

Again, we waited in fear as Hitler's air force pounded England's major cities. In the late summer, when a fierce air battle started, we hoped the Germans would not invade Churchill's "island kingdom." It was around this time, I remember, that Mr. Houghton ordered his second batch of a hundred baby chickens.

"What was it Mr. Churchill said? 'Let us therefore brace ourselves to our duty and so bear ourselves that if the British Commonwealth and Empire last for a thousand years, men will say, 'This is their finest hour.'"

Mr. Houghton read aloud the words he had copied out of the newspaper.

"But surely," I protested, "the Prime Minister didn't mean chickens."

"Of course he didn't mean chickens. But what else can I do? They're my countrymen who are being murdered by those devils, and I've got to help. Some of the men taken off at Dunkirk are my own blood and kin."

Only then did I realize how very serious Mr. Houghton felt about the war. In two days he converted a second empty stall into a grand place to raise this new crop of baby chicks. Since the first batch had already started to lay, he began to consider ways to market his eggs.

"Those Indian River Cross hens are great layers, and I usually get several double yoked eggs each week," he confided. "I am sure the general stores here and in Manakin could sell such a superior product."

First, Mr. Houghton consulted Arthur Henley who agreed to take three dozen eggs a week for his store. Then we drove up to Manakin and made arrangements with Mrs. Clark and her daughter, Mary, who ran a combination general store and post office. They decided on four dozen eggs a week, and Elizabeth Harris wanted another dozen. Slowly but steadily Mr. Houghton found outlets for his eggs. And to his great surprise, by the spring, we would be selling eggs to several customers in Richmond.

As the chicken business progressed successfully, Mr. Houghton found he needed additional help. He first approached Cary. But when Cary declined, the job was offered to me.

"How about delivering eggs with me on Saturdays? I'll pay you a quarter a week."

"That sounds great. I've never earned money before."

"First, I'll check with your Mother."

"Please don't tell her anything about money. She won't like that," I warned.

Mr. Houghton agreed, and wrote the letter.

The next Saturday morning I entered into the chicken business, as a salaried employee. An extra dollar each month would boost my flagging finances, and I rejoiced at this good fortune.

I found delivering eggs proved a lot more of a job than I had at first expected. At least the way Mr. Houghton delivered them. I earned my dollar every month from hard work and patience. Usually we left the house about nine o'clock with the car bulging with egg cartons nestled in wooden crates. Most weeks we carried about twelve dozen eggs, and

Thelma's Place

the wooden crates prevented the cartons from jolting and breaking our cargo. The first call was at Henley's store on River Road. Here we bought gas, a soft drink, and enjoyed a little chat with the proprietors. Then we continued on towards Manakin and Mrs. Clark's. Although pleasant, she never possessed the right change until Mary opened the post office strong box; Mrs. Clark could never find anything less than a five-dollar bill. Since her regular order of four dozen eggs came to about two dollars, we always returned on the way home to collect what was due us.

"That woman is a pain in the neck," Mr. Houghton complained. "Did it ever occur to her to change her money on Friday evenings before Mary locks up the strong box?"

"It doesn't," I replied as we drove down the narrow road towards Tom Harris's dairy farm.

This was our last stop. Elizabeth Harris usually insisted we come in for a cup of tea, and her husband would arrive from his barn to enjoy our visit. Sometimes we would remain talking for more than a half hour, and on occasion Mr. Harris would give us additional orders.

"My neighbor up the road, Mrs. Sealey, needs two dozen; she plans to bake this week for company. And my colored tenant farmer, Ralph, wants a dozen. I'll pay you for them now and collect the money myself. That'll save time, Miss Doc, won't it?"

I nodded in assent, knowing we wouldn't get home before noon.

"You know Thelma, who owns the beer joint and little eating place on Route 6?" Mr. Harris asked one pleasant morning.

"You mean the colored woman who owns Thelma's place? Yeah, I know her," Mr. Houghton replied.

"That's the one. I heard this morning she needed some eggs," Tom Harris told us as we walked towards the car. "Call on her, Harry; she serves a noonday meal and could become a good customer."

"I'm not sure I am allowed to go into such places," I said as we drove away. "Doesn't she serve beer?"

"Yes," concurred Mr. Houghton, "she does."

But Thelma's small eating establishment was often frequented by white people. Occasionally, when Mr. Houghton went to Manakin alone, he'd stop at Thelma's Place for a cold beer.

"It's all right," he reassured me; "it's not rough. And she might become a steady customer."

After stopping at Mrs. Clark's to collect her money in two dirty dollar bills, Mr. Houghton turned parallel to Route 6 and continued down a bumpy dirt lane. Here, we found a neat looking building, painted white and bearing a large sign. Mr. Houghton pulled his 1932 Chevrolet to the side of the road. Then, with three dozen eggs cradled in his arms, we entered the little cafe. Bright cherry red and white curtains hung at the windows and on the tables lay matching cotton cloths. Feeling unsure, I stopped in the doorway, until Mr. Houghton pushed me gently forward.

"Well, there is a great, grown white girl for you," Thelma greeted me with considerable surprise.

I blushed scarlet as Thelma offered us stools at the counter and asked what we would like to drink. Placing the egg cartons across his knees, Mr. Houghton motioned me to sit down, and ordered a beer.

"What do you want, Doc, a Seven Up?"

I nodded, and accepted the soft drink Thelma brought, still in its bottle.

"Do you want a cup?" she asked. I wasn't sure it would be clean so didn't reply. She placed a glass down on the counter next to the drink.

"It's clean as white folk's glasses, honey," Thelma insisted.

"I hear you might need some fresh country eggs," Mr. Houghton came right to the point. "And I have some nice ones."

He laid his cartons on the counter, and I watched as the light skinned negress opened them and inspected their contents.

"Yes," she replied. "How much are you asking for them?"

"Fifty cents a dozen this time of year: more in winter when the chickens aren't laying as well. We deliver each week on Saturday mornings," Mr. Houghton explained.

I found something offensive in Thelma's manner. She acted differently from the elderly Bertha who washed our clothes - more sure of herself, more abrupt. She wore a brilliant red blouse with her tight fitting navy skirt. Lipstick, thick and red, outlined her mouth. Her dark, straightened hair glistened with pomade and was arranged with a certain style.

"I'll take three dozen a week to start with. Later, I might need more. Here's your dollar-fifty." Thelma handed him the money. "I expect several men in for dinner; you'll have to excuse me."

Farmers and telephone workmen from Richmond, who found her place clean and convenient, and several men of her own color appeared regularly for their midday meal. I never saw any white people eating there; the telephone linesmen would order their dinner and eat it in their trucks.

Mr. Houghton got down from his stool, finished the last drop of beer, and turned to me. "Come along, Doc, we must get on home."

I have no doubt this little eating place, tucked away in the country, was unique for its day. Thelma certainly was. After this first encounter I enjoyed going, especially because I knew Mother would forbid it. And like the extra dollar pocket money, I considered these visits to Thelma's Place all a part of my job.

June 1940.
Philadelphia, Penn.

Dear Doc,

Frances and I are married. We went up to Goshen, New York to see her ancient Aunt Maltilda who has been ill. Afraid she would die before we got married, this intrepid lady arranged for everything in her church last Saturday morning.

We invited a few relatives and friends and got the job done. After three days in a country inn we returned to Philadelphia on Tuesday. It all happened too suddenly to make arrangements with Mother Ferrell to bring you up. But both Frances and I want you to visit us as soon as possible. You are still my best daughter, Doc; never doubt that I love you.

Dad.

I closed the letter and put it in my pocket. How could he get married without me? I hated Frances's aunt for being so sneaky. For three days I carried his letter around, reading and rereading it. Finally, unable to resolve my feelings, I sought Mrs. Houghton.

"I want your opinion," I said, handing it to her.

She looked up from reading my letter and smiled.

"He's no longer lonely, Doc. How nice. But I realize you must feel terribly hurt."

"Yes," I replied, sitting on the hassock, "that's exactly how I feel."

I was amazed at her perception.

"You've a right to be hurt. His marriage changes things, and you should have been forewarned. But with the war's coming, there's little time left, and people behave differently in wartime. He still loves you, Doc, don't ever forget it."

"It's not natural, somehow. First, Rudy and now Frances. That isn't how a family should be with two extra people. Where do I fit in?"

Mrs. Houghton, sitting on the loveseat, put down her knitting; she took my hand and drew me to her. The hassock spun as I dropped on my knees and allowed her to hug me.

"There's room for you here, my dear. Mr. H. and I never change and our affection for you remains the same and always will."

I knew she meant it, and deep down I realized Mrs. Houghton herself felt lonely. Her deafness isolated her. Her leaving England to marry in Canada cut her off from her family. She had never felt comfortable in North America and prayed she would one day have money enough to return home. She understood my loneliness and how my acquisition of so much family left everyone with too little time for me.

"I love you, Mrs. Houghton," was all I could say.

"Now," she replied, always practical, "write and congratulate your Dad on his marriage. Don't let him know you're hurt; it'll only upset him. Make him feel good about Frances. After all, you like her, don't you?"

"Yes," I sat back on the hassock. "I'm not sure I want to write."

"Do as I say, and it'll come all right in the end.

Forget about the 'poor Me's;' they never help."

So I brought out pencil and paper and sat down to write.

Mrs. Houghton corrected my spelling before I copied the letter over neatly in ink. Thoughtfully, I addressed the envelope wondering if anger wouldn't have been more productive.

"Now," she said when I'd finished, "you'll feel better. Never forget, Doc, he loves you."

15

War Troubles

Once again the events in Europe appalled us. Although Britain got most of her troops and a great many of France's off the beaches at Dunkirk, she needed America's help to continue fighting. In June 1940, Mussolini declared war on Britain and France. Four days later the Germans occupied Paris. On the twentieth the French government, under Marshall Henri Petain, signed the Armistice.

Father wrote me with considerable alarm.

"Son,
Gird up your loins. We are marching to war. We shall be involved soon.
Love, Dad."

"The isolationists won't hear of it. They'd kick up a hell of a fuss. Why they hardly let Britain buy arms," Mr. Houghton reassured me.

Only after Dunkirk did Roosevelt allow British ships to call at American ports for repairs. Finally in September we gave fifty average-size destroyers to Churchill in exchange for air bases in the Atlantic. Later that month when Congress passed the first peacetime draft bill Mrs. Sparrow got into an argument at Henley's store.

"Mr. Roosevelt has overstepped himself. Mrs. Henley take that picture down at once. It's offensive!" Anita Sparrow, flaming angry, insisted. "Who ever heard of calling for a draft law in peace time? It's never been done before. I'm sure it's unconstitutional."

"Mr. Roosevelt's picture stays. He's our president, and he kept us out of war." Mrs. Henley stood in front of her photograph, and took down her long stick.

"You don't understand. We are neutral, and we're drafting young men into a peace-time army? Nobody needs a draft unless there's an armed conflict. And that's where we're headed. That old Yankee president's leading us to war," Mrs. Sparrow cried. She voted Republican, a rare thing in the solid South of the time.

Mary Carter took her arm.

"Come on, Anita. It's not Mrs. Henley's fault. She's just being patriotic, that's all, hanging up her picture."

"Yes," Mrs. Henley agreed, "I am."

"You take that picture down or I'll never set foot in this store again," challenged Mrs. Sparrow.

Suddenly Mr. Henley banged open the screen door and stood at the counter.

"What's going on here?" he demanded.

"The draft bill's upset Anita," explained Mary Carter. "She objects to Mr. Roosevelt's picture."

"The draft bill's upset everyone. We all know the war's coming. It's got to come. But Mr. Roosevelt stays. I'll put your groceries in the car for you." Without another word he picked up the brown paper sack and escorted Mrs. Sparrow out.

For about a week she stayed away. But a country store is a meeting place, a gossip-swapping place, and soon she was back again as usual. She never mentioned Mr. Roosevelt's picture, nor did Mrs. Henley take it down.

At the end of June Mother married Rudy, and although I didn't consider this such a major event, it brought changes. Grandmother came and gave me a dress, which I felt was all to the good because I never bothered mentioning the one I'd cut up.

But Rudy's family was a different story. Real Germans, they acted like battle axes: his much younger sister and his boss of a mother. When Rudy's father had died, several years ago, Mrs. Meuller took over the family business. Typical Midwesterners, they held the isolationist attitudes of middle America. Both appeared over dressed, preferring ruffles and bows, and both wore outlandish hats. These women seemed even more out of place than Rudy with his expensive shoes and his hard-edged accent. I instantly disliked them.

War Troubles

One afternoon when I entered the living room, I found Rudy's sister Louise reading a magazine. Never talkative, she often retreated there and let us know she preferred to be alone.

"Hello," I said, stopping abruptly. "I didn't realize you were here."

"Reading about the war. It keeps getting worse."

"Yes," I agreed, "it's very bad. Before long we'll be involved."

"It's silly to fight Hitler. He's not all bad, after all he made the trains run on time, and brought work and prosperity to Germany."

"Mussolini fixed up the trains," I corrected, "in Italy not in Germany."

Louise's hard pig eyes reminded me of Mr. Pillar's, a local farmer I disliked; her ample figure overflowed the chair.

"How do you know it wasn't Hitler'?' she asked, her voice combative, her eyes gray glints full of distrust.

"Mr. Houghton told me. He keeps up with such things."

"Oh, that English person I met, your neighbor. We need to stay out of this war. It's none of our affair. We should all be grateful to Roosevelt for keeping us out of war. Let's attend to our own garden and leave other people's alone."

"I'm not sure we can," I replied. "Besides, Mr. Houghton says Britain can't go on alone, so we'll have to get in."

"That's an Englishman's opinion. In Wisconsin we're opposed to getting involved. Let Europe fight her own battles." She pushed her ponderous figure from the chair. "We should keep America for Americans. We got involved once before and helped them beat the Germans. We shouldn't do it again."

"My father would have to go. He's in the Reserves, you know, and an officer. He'd be called up first. You can't just pretend it's not coming, because it is." I felt my temper rising. How could she be so stupid?

"That's the trouble with the East," she continued, "it's always looking towards Europe. In the Midwest we look towards the East, that's true, but we don't need to get involved with the rest of the world."

"There's no way we can't get involved," I persisted, "we can't allow England to go under."

Louise didn't reply; she seemed interested in her magazine. Realizing the conversation had ended, I left the room.

In the kitchen Bertha fussed at me for being rude to my guest.

"That ain't no way to behave, Miss Doc. She's company," the old negress upbraided me.

"She's stupid," I replied. "Everyone knows the war is coming."

Disgusted I went outside and banged the door.

Part II

After the wedding Grandmother took me to visit Father in Philadelphia. Still hurt to be excluded from his wedding I was prepared to hate Frances. But when I saw them together, so happy and cheerful, I gradually forgave her. Yet I felt awkward. I wasn't sure where I fit into this twosome. Their complete absorption with their new life and with each other made me feel like an intruder, an outsider looking in, but not a part of their lives. Grandmother wasn't any help; she obviously felt comfortable with the situation. I thought Frances tried too hard to make us welcomed, and Father seemed careless about my feelings. He hugged me with affection, and then ignored me when the conversation drew his attention.

When I spoke he talked over me and wouldn't listen. Feelings of anger and hurt enveloped me. I sat in the chair and sulked, unhappy in my rejection.

"How do you like our new house, Son?" Father's voice broke over the waves of conversation. "You're mighty quiet this evening."

The mill, set back from the road and surrounded by old trees was constructed of Pennsylvania field stone, long mellowed. Although the rooms were small, each had a fireplace and deep set windows. It looked very different from Virginia houses and was furnished with a charm and warmth that reflected Frances's good taste.

"It's great," I replied, "And I love the stream with the ducks. They're the best. It's like living in the country."

Father kissed me on the forehead as he used to before his marriage when we shared our good times. But now he had Frances to share things with, and might not need me. I sipped my orange juice huddled up in my chair, and considered things. She's very pretty, really very attentive. How could he like her better than me? Maybe she's more fun. Maybe it wasn't Aunt Matilda, but they just couldn't wait to get married. Maybe it wasn't the war at all, maybe, maybe. Mrs. Houghton said not to question things, but to accept them. She's right about Father's loving me. I know she is, and I must believe it. How happy they look! Everything about them is perfect and beautiful. Maybe that's what love is. It changes you and makes you a whole person. I'd like that. I guess I'm happy for Father, and for Frances too, of course.

"Yes, Frances, it's charming," Grandmother's voice broke into my thoughts. "The two of you look radiant. Have you already forgotten New York?"

"No, I still miss the city, but I'm enjoying Philadelphia. It's nice to have grass and trees after the noisy streets. I've found a job here, and have started working. That's the way to meet people; don't you agree?"

"How practical you are!" Grandmother said admiringly. "You'll do well here; I've no doubt."

The next morning Frances appeared early in the kitchen, fully dressed. Rarely able to sleep beyond seven o'clock, I had slipped quietly down the stairs and helped myself to cereal.

"Good morning, Doc," she greeted me. "How would you like to visit Independence Hall where our Founding Fathers drafted the Constitution and the Declaration of Independence? Perhaps we can see Betsy Ross's house as well."

"Who's Betsy Ross," I asked, not interested.

"She folded some blue material just the right way and with one snip of her scissors created our first flag. If you cut it right, you can make a perfect six-point star."

"With one cut of the scissors. She must have been very clever." I helped myself to more milk, pouring it over the corn flakes and adding another banana. "Will Grandmother come too?"

"If she likes," Frances replied. "Please set the table for breakfast."

Amazed by this unexpected request I sat still.

"Where is Virginia?"

"Gone back to Germany. She's in love with some man in the German Army and went home to marry him. She's a real Nazi." Frances laid out the mats and silver for me.

"How do you know?" Disbelieving, I questioned her. Then taking up the things she laid out, went to set the table.

"Don't you remember how she was always saving tin foil from gum and candy wrappers? These she sent off to Germany for its war effort.

Her connections there were decidedly dubious, and she was working here for an American army officer. I doubt if she'll be allowed to return."

"I can't believe it, she made such wonderful cookies," I protested.

"Even bad people can do good things." Frances laid out the cups and plates. "Here, put these around."

"You mean she actually was a Nazi like those people you read about in magazines?"

"That's exactly what I mean. She was here feathering her nest by being an excellent cook and housekeeper for your father."

Frances and I finished setting the table. She went back to the cold pantry for eggs and ham before she sent me out to get the newspaper, at the bottom of the garden. Walking slowly, and watching the tips of my shoes I thought about Virginia.

How could she work for Father and still believe in the Nazi cause? Father who was always so upright and patriotic must have never suspected her treachery. Suddenly I hated her with all the strength I possessed. Even Rudy seemed pale by comparison. Angrily I remembered helping her save the gum wrappers which she pressed into a large silver ball. I was guilty too. How could she've implicated me in Hitler's war? I felt betrayed. I reached the bottom of the garden and stood shivering in the warm morning air. Finally I picked up the paper. How many other Germans, I wondered, had returned to fight for the Fatherland? How many other Virginias were there? Anger and fear overwhelmed me. I knew as I carried the paper towards the house that Mr. Houghton was right. We would go to war. Nobody was safe, not even in America.

When I entered the dining room, Father was talking with Grandmother and Frances about visiting Valley Forge. It sounded like it was all planned to take a picnic.

"What's Valley Forge?" I interrupted, not interested in going.

"A Military Park where Washington and his men lived during a terribly cold winter when the British Troops occupied Philadelphia. There're breastworks, some huts and a chapel. It's a great place for a picnic." Father took his paper and gave me a kiss. "How are you this morning, Son?"

"All right, I suppose. But I'm not much interested in picnics. Isn't there something else we can do?"

I took my place at the table. Father opened his paper, read the headlines and folded it again. Grandmother was busy passing things, first the sugar, then the cream. She didn't look at me, but I could tell she was displeased. The plans were arranged, and I mustn't object. It was Frances who broke the silence. "Those poor soldiers must have frozen, living in huts all winter."

"They wrapped their feet in rags and depended upon the country folk to feed them," Father explained. "What do you know about the Revolutionary War, Doc?"

"Not much," I replied, "I prefer the Civil War with all those dashing generals. It's sissy for men to wear pigtails done up in ribbons like that Marquis de Lafayette. He looks positively ridiculous."

Father laughed. "So much for the history lesson."

After breakfast we started out squeezed into his little roadster. Grandmother rode in front in consideration of her age, so Frances and I sat cramped into the back seat. But Valley Forge proved a lot more entertaining than I'd anticipated. June can be golden with clear blue skies and warm days. Insects and song birds created unfamiliar noises. Rolling green fields bisected by Valley Creek made a perfect place to run. I raced ahead humming, trying to shake off the eerie feeling of Virginia. I wanted to talk to Father about her, but not in front of Frances and Grandmother. Finally, out of breath, I stopped running and sat down on the cool grass.

"What are you sitting here for?" Father asked catching up with me. "Are you thinking about our soldiers who lived in the toughest conditions while Cornwallis and his boys lay billeted in Philadelphia?"

"Not exactly," I confessed. "I'm thinking about Virginia."

A frown clouded his handsome face as he helped me up. "Oh," he said simply and we continued to walk in silence.

"Did you know she was a Nazi?"

"I'm not sure she was, but definitely pro-Hitler. I knew she was saving string and tinfoil in great silver balls, and read all the German language newspapers she could put her hands on. I read them too. Hitler's a funny-talking guy, and he gave me a good laugh. But she took him seriously."

"Frances said she was in love with someone in the German Army," I said, trying to sound casual. I wanted him to go ahead and explain.

"That's right, she was. Hans something or other. I forget his last name. He was a professional soldier, so was her brother. I got some dope on him and realized Virginia must go home." Father looked away out over the fields. "She didn't have the money, so I loaned it to her."

"Loaned it to her, a Nazi?" I gasped, unbelieving.

"No, as a friend who has taken care of me since I left your mother. Virginia wasn't all bad, just misguided. I felt she needed to return to her own country where her loyalties stood. They surely weren't here. Don't forget there're lot of Germans in America like your riding master, Captain what's his name, who are loyal citizens and should be treated as such. Others who hold the sentiments of their own country should go home. Don't confuse the two. There's a vast difference." Father's voice sounded stern, his manner abrupt. "I miss Virginia, but she was unfaithful to this country's ideals."

I didn't speak for awhile trying to allow the tension to clear. Finally I asked, "You mean Washington didn't live with his troops in a cabin? He didn't wrap his feet in rags, did he?"

"No, he and his staff had better accommodations. He was a Virginia gentleman, you know, and a snob."

"Then he must have brought his servants, and his mammy," I laughed.

Father stopped and waved at Frances and Grandmother who sat on the grass in the sun, and returned his wave.

"They'll catch up eventually. Let's walk on. Did you know Washington had false teeth made of wood?"

"How uncomfortable! Wooden ones, how did he eat?"

"Without them, I suppose. He just used them for show, don't you think?"

"Lafayette, what did he have?" I enjoyed this game. "And what language did he speak to Washington in? French or English?"

"I'm not sure. I expect Washington spoke French as most educated people did. Perhaps Lafayette spoke some English," Father looked amused. "I've never thought of it before."

"I'm not that all fired up about Washington, but he did cross the Delaware on Christmas Eve and caught the British with their pants down celebrating. Do you really think he went into battle with that silly wig?"

"Probably just used it for the painting. It'd get in his way, you know, while he was fighting. He might lose it and confuse his troops."

Father laughed.

"Is that what war is like? It's pretty terrible, I guess, living in trenches and eating bad food."

Father stopped and looked down. I'd startled him because he regarded me with infinite sadness, an expression I'd never seen before. For a long several minutes we stood there then he took my hand and squeezed it. Finally he spoke in a voice that was filled with a strange emotion.

"Virginia's being pro-Nazi has got to you, hasn't it? My paying her fare doesn't set well. Son, nothing is ever black and white; it would be a lot easier if it was. Not all Germans are Nazis; just like not all Americans are Democrats. But it's a very dangerous time we're living in, and you must grow up in. Do you know why Mother Ferrell always brings you? Your mother won't allow me to have you unless she comes. She doesn't trust me, I suppose, to send you back. And she's not a Nazi. A year from now, or even six months we could be at war. I will go overseas for two, maybe three years, who knows how long? I could be wounded or killed; whatever the Fates decree, it could happen." He let go my hand and seemed lost in his own thoughts, his long steps causing me to run to keep up. "Nothing will ever be the same again," he said savagely.

I felt afraid of him. He'd changed suddenly into someone I didn't know. His eyes, hazel and deep set, appeared hard and cold, his head tilted back as if looking at something a long ways off.

"You see that hawk," he asked more gently. "He lives by killing and he's vicious. War changes men; they're no longer boys when they come back."

"Father," I said softly. "I'll remember this day forever as the one when I grew up."

Returning from some far off place he looked down at me, once more his familiar self. Again he took my hand, and we continued to walk over the June-bright fields. Behind us I heard Frances and Grandmother laughing, enjoying themselves. They seemed unaware that I had just experienced a new reality, and would never be a child again.

A Forgotten Landscape

16

Changes

One afternoon when I returned home Mother and Rudy called me in for a little chat. I never liked these 'little chats', as she called them, because they usually ended in an argument. With great reluctance I entered the library.

"Hello," Rudy greeted me roughly, "take a seat."

"Yes, sir," I complied, sitting in an uncomfortable chair.

"How's school?" Mother asked.

"Fine," I knew school wasn't the reason for this conference but decided to play along. "Mary Ann and her mother went to South Carolina last weekend to visit a friend in Charleston. It's a beautiful city on two rivers."

"And extremely hot in summer, the humidity's even worse than Richmond's," Mother replied pleasantly.

"Nothing's hotter than Richmond, even the tropics. And I despise hot weather."

"I expect Mother's informed you we're moving to Washington," Rudy interrupted. "I've taken a government job there of some importance for the duration. We'll be expected to attend certain social functions. It's no place for a young girl; you're better off here. Besides you'd have to change schools."

"Aren't there schools in Washington?" I inquired.

"Of course there're schools. Don't be impertinent!"

"I'm just asking, that's all."

"You'll finish in another six years, and we think it best you should remain at The Monument School until you graduate."

Mother's voice sounded nervous; I noticed she fidgeted with her handkerchief. "You must get a good education."

Rudy crossed the room, glanced out of the window and paced back towards the bar. Here he stopped and fixed himself a drink, without offering Mother one.

"You don't understand, Doc, you don't fit into city life. Your mother and I want to dance in contests again, and cut a fine figure in society. This job might lead to other things, big things, after the war. I want to further my career, make a name for myself." He paused to sip his drink. "You're not included in my plans."

"Not included?" I repeated in disbelief. "Have you asked Father about this? What's to become of me?"

"Your Father's not here. It's none of his business," Rudy replied shortly. "This is my house now, I'm running things. I've leased our two cornfields to Harrison Moore, and Mr. Houghton will look after this house and the livestock. He's well compensated for his trouble, and for looking after you. Apparently, he doesn't object, and you seem to like him."

"Yes," I agreed, "and he likes me too. We're friends." I couldn't believe they'd just leave without discussing the plans with me first.

"Excellent. You fit more into his way of life, than into your mother's and mine. I've never understood you, Doc."

"No," I concurred, "but then you've never tried."

"How dare you speak to me like that? Have you no manners?"

"Really, dear, you're extremely rude," Mother added supporting Rudy.

"You've come into my home and taken over. How else should I feel about you? What did you expect?" My anger flared as I voiced my pent-up feelings.

"Don't be insolent," Rudy sounded threatening, glaring at me with his round, dark eyes. "I should slap your face for that remark, but I'll overlook it since your mother's present."

My anger knew no limits. Only with great difficulty I held my temper, knowing all would be lost if I didn't.

"Father'll have something to say about this," I cried with abandon. "I don't give a tinker's damn if you go to Washington. I hate you, Rudy: I hate you more than anyone in the whole world."

Before he could stop me I fled from the room, I slipped under his arm, dashed from the room, and ran upstairs. I locked my door, sat down on the bed, tears streaming from my eyes, great sobs strangling me. How could they treat me like a colt turned out to pasture and forgotten?

Neither Rudy nor Mother discussed this matter again. But the house was turned upside down and packing boxes appeared for the move to Washington. I made myself scarce. Mary Ann came out for the weekend, and we took Jackie and Billy prospecting for gold in Tuckahoe Creek. Of course we didn't find any, but then we didn't expect to either.

"I wish old Rudy would drop dead," I confided. "He's behind all this."

"That do make it nice!" Mary Ann loved army expressions. "Honestly, Doc, he doesn't like you."

"Hates me is more like it. And I commenced hating him the very first day I laid eyes on that Yankee numbskull."

We knelt beside the creek panning with an old sieve, and catching pieces of twigs and roots.

"The water's supposed to flow over rocks," Mary Ann pointed out. "This isn't the right kind of water for gold."

"Who says so? They've got gold and garnets in North Carolina, and rivers there aren't much different from ours." I shook dirty water from the sieve. "Look, there's some glittering stuff."

"It's not gold," Mary Ann laughed.

"Let's pretend this is the Comstock Lode, and we're panning for silver." I scooped up another sieve full of mud. "I'm sure this is silver, or at least something like it."

We sat on the bank and separated the mud. All we found were several pretty stones, and these we piled to one side.

"Let me fetch another sieve full." Mary Ann started through the high grass for the creek. A copperhead, as long as a rope, lay on a rock sunning himself. It's diamond-back markings were easily recognizable; it's white mouth looked like cotton.

"Run, run," I screamed. "There's a copperhead."

Back and forth flicked its long blade tongue, its head raised to strike, its poison fangs full. Mary Ann stood paralyzed with fright. The copperhead wriggled across the rock through the grass towards us.

"Run, you jackass," I yelled at her; "for God's sake, run."

Mary Ann fled up the patch screaming blue murder, as if seven devils chased her. Picking up the sieve she had dropped, I tossed it at the snake and watched it slither away into the tall weeds. "Come back, silly, you've scared that snake all the way to Richmond."

"Get the ponies and the stones. I'm not stepping an inch closer. You're sure there're no more snakes around here?" She started to climb a low tree.

"Come on, don't be a scaredy-cat," I coaxed her.

"Not on your life. Besides," she insisted trying to balance herself on a thin branch, "there's no gold in that old creek."

"Get down before you fall. See," I picked up a stick and beat the undergrowth to prove the snake had gone, "he's miles from here. Your screaming gave him a heart attack."

"Get the ponies, and bring Jackie here so I can get on him. Don't forget my stones."

I brought Jackie and placed him so Mary Ann could slide onto his back.

"Get the stones yourself," I insisted, riding Billy up the trail.

Gingerly she got down from the tree onto Jackie; then she went back for her treasure. This she stuffed into the pockets of her slacks and rode like crazy towards higher ground.

"You ain't much of a woodsman," I teased. "What did you learn in Scouts? I didn't think you're afraid of a little old snake."

"It's poisonous, you fool. Don't you realize we could get bitten and die?"

"Not likely," I said. "I'm hungry, let's eat. Tie Jackie to a tree. That old stump will make a grand table."

I sat down and took out two peanut butter and jelly sandwiches from my knapsack. "They're good," I assured her offering one, "but they're sort of squashed."

"Look at all those ants. We can't sit here," Mary Ann objected.

"Brush them off, and sit down. Ants won't hurt you."

She scraped the ants away with her foot and sat beside me. She took two Dr. Peppers from her knapsack and opened them with her scout knife.

"They're warm," she apologized, "but they're wet. I also brought some cookies."

We sat for a while in silence eating.

"I'd miss you if you moved to Washington, Doc. It wouldn't be the same around here, you know," Mary Ann said suddenly. "I'd lose my best friend."

She sat on the stump, her mouth full of sandwich, looking out across the woods. Then she turned and hugged me.

"I appreciate your caring," I told her, feeling I might cry. "You've got lots of friends. What about Flurry Cartwright?"

"Flurry's all right, but she's not half as much fun. Who else would think of panning for gold in Tuckahoe Creek?"

"Well, we didn't find any, and I'm all over mud." I poured some Dr. Pepper on my hands trying to clean them.

"And Mrs. Ovens wouldn't have a Yankee to tease," Mary Ann continued, licking jelly from her shirt.

"I'm a Hoosier," I insisted, handing her a napkin. "I'm a Hoosier hot-shot because I was born in Indiana. That's not a Yankee; that's Midwest."

"Well, Mrs. Owens would be lost without you, and so would I." She lay back on the grass. "Invite me out when your parents go away. Why can't all days be as nice as this?"

"The Houghtons don't have room, but I suppose we could stay in the house. Do you really think it's okay, my being left and all?"

"It's great," Mary Ann's dark eyes grew wide. "You're rid of Rudy and your mother both. What more do you want?"

"I want to be loved, not just passed around like a football."

"You'd hate the city, Doc. You'd be in high cotton."

"High cotton, what's that?"

"Lots of senators and bureaucrats, and other rich and important people." Mary Ann explained.

Thoughtfully I put my empty pop bottle in her knapsack.

"Besides," she went on, "the Houghtons like you, and I am sure they want you."

"Yes, we're friends," I agreed. "But I might like high cotton."

"That would bore you to death, all that cityfied life. Doc, as much as you like freedom, you'd die all cooped up."

I sat on the stump hugging my knees, thinking about what city life might be like. Perhaps I'd find it exciting for a few months. Yet I knew I would miss the country. Mary Ann sounded convincing but still I deeply resented being left.

Billy and Jackie grew restless. I stood up, untied their reins and handed Jackie's to Mary Ann.

"Let's ride to the store for some ice cream," I suggested mounting Billy.

"Got any money?" Mary Ann asked.

"A quarter and three pennies. It's enough, come on." We trotted up the path, dropped down below the stables and headed towards the pond.

"Shouldn't you tell your mother?" asked Mary Ann.

"I'll leave a note for Mr. Houghton. It's easier." Leading the way I made a wide circle and came out behind his chicken run, unseen. Quickly I penned a cryptic note scribbled with Mr. Houghton's stubby pencil that hung on the feed room door.

"Store, ice cream. No gold in creek, Doc." I tacked it over his chicken calendar on which he marked each day's number of eggs.

"He'll understand," I assured her, remounting Billy and urging him forward.

We entered the woods and cantered down the trail.

"No wonder you're always in trouble, Doc," Mary Ann reined in Jackie.

"Mother makes up new rules every day, so I don't pay any attention. I guess that's being sneaky."

"You're the biggest sneak in the whole world. Really, you are the sneakiest person I've ever known. But you have such fun doing it," she laughed.

We rode along single file, jumped two felled logs and came out on Mrs. Haunch's road just below Ballyclare. We crossed over and re-entered the woods, riding on old saw mill trails that led straight out to River Road.

At the store we found Alvira Carthage chatting outside with Anita Sparrow.

"Hello, Doc, who's your friend?" Mrs. Carthage greeted us.

"Mary Ann, she's from town," I introduced them.

"What's this I hear about you?"

"I don't know. I hope it's nothing bad," I let Mary Ann in the screen door.

"I hear you're off to Washington for the duration." Mrs. Carthage followed us.

"Yes, at the end of the month," I replied.

"You'll love Washington; it's such an exciting city. I worked there once, ages ago, before I married."

"I hear the cherry blossoms are gorgeous in the spring." I didn't want her to know I wasn't going. Where on earth did she pick up this gossip? Her ears must be as large as an elephant's.

"They've good schools there," she continued, "some filled with millionaires' children. Washington's bursting with money. Don't you come home now stuck up."

Mary Ann piled ice cream on two cones, and I laid twenty cents down on the counter.

"Miss Doc," said Ethel, "are you really moving to Washington?"

"Yes, Rudy has taken a job there with the government. We leave early next month. Nothing's settled yet, about schools and all." I didn't wish to tell Ethel a lie because she was simple. Besides she'd never forgive me, and I needed her friendship.

"You won't like it as much as Richmond," she said opening the cash register.

"That's what I've told her," Mary Ann agreed as we left the store.

"Wait, I want to hear more about it," Mrs. Carthage called us.

"That's all I know. We must get on home before Mother commences worrying."

"Goodbye," Mary Ann said politely. We mounted Billy and Jackie and urged them up River Road as fast as they would trot.

"Of all people, Mrs. Carthage!" I said furiously. "She knows everything, most times before you know it yourself."

In three days the whole county knew of my parents' plans. But I managed to keep my staying home a secret. Every room was piled high with mess, boxes and suitcases. Rugs stood rolled up in corners of rooms, chairs, tables and draperies were stacked in the library. Only my room remained its own comfortable self.

Bertha would still come as usual on Thursdays. Laundry would be sent home in a special box and mailed back. Mrs. Houghton would check on things in the house, and Mr. Houghton would look after the furnace, water pipes and such things. Finally on a Saturday less than a month later Mother and Rudy left, the car piled high with suitcases, kitchen stuff and the best china. A moving van took the rest.

"I'll see you at the end of the month," Mother kissed me lightly on the cheek. "Behave yourself, and do your homework. I can't worry about you in Washington, as you must learn to act responsibly. Goodbye, Doc."

Suddenly I felt sorry for her. She appeared distressed at leaving me, and came back a second time to hug me. Embarrassed by this unusual show of affection, I kissed her. Then she climbed in the car and Rudy started the motor.

"We'll be fine," Mr. Houghton assured her, taking my hand and squeezing it. "You'll have a young lady when you return."

"I really think she's sad to leave me," I commented as the car drove away.

"You? Who's worried about a big girl like you?"

"I'd like someone to be for a change." Loneliness enveloped me.

"Come on, Doc, isn't this your sacrifice for the war effort? Just think of the great times we'll have. It'll be fun to have a daughter."

Reassured, I followed him across the orchard.

Several days later I wrote to Father and explained I was staying with the Houghtons. Not wishing to worry him I mentioned the need for me to remain at the Monument School and graduate. His return letter was filled with his own move to Washington.

Mrs. Houghton made the change from home fun. She brought an extra pair of curtains over and my bedspread. Then gathering up my clothes she piled them in a wheelbarrow, which we pushed across the lawn. Selecting two floral pillows we found in the attic she fixed up her room with new curtains and made it into mine. I was delighted and helped her move her things into a chest of drawers in Mr. Houghton's room. We shared the closet and hung our heavy coats from pegs in the hall beside the bathroom behind the heater. It made them all cozy and warm when we put them on. Although not large, the cottage had ample closet space, and we didn't feel cramped.

"It's gorgeous," I exclaimed in delight admiring my new room. "It's just as beautiful and feminine as Mary Ann's."

We all felt this arrangement would be temporary. The war would soon be over and life would return to normal. Yet behind our optimism an unspoken fear prevailed.

"This state of things can only get worse," Mr. Houghton predicted. "We shall all be older and wiser when it's over."

A Forgotten Landscape

17

The Duchess's Family

Late that summer the Germans pounded the English coast, the Lufwaffe continually bombed London; the East End lay in ruins. Any day we expected the enemy to invade England. Fierce air battles began all over Britain and in mid September the R.A.F. scored a thrilling victory. A victory later known as the Battle For Britain.

The Atlantic bristled with German U-boats, and we in America held our breath, worried we would be drawn into Europe's war. Early in October Father wrote that he expected soon to be put on active service, and Mrs. Houghton received word that Allen's (her favorite nephew) ship was hit.

"He's such a fine young lad," she told me. "He's always promised to come out and visit Auntie in America. How I wish he had."

"After all, the ship wasn't sunk," Mr. Houghton consoled her. "And you'll hear in a few days that he's all right. Don't worry, dear, until you're certain."

"That sounds like a good idea to me," I added, trying to be helpful. "I'm sure he's just fine."

"Perhaps you're right, Doc. We shall hope so." She put on a brave face and continued to wash the dishes.

We waited anxiously until her "handsome brother," Tommy Phillpot, wrote to say that Allen's ship had returned to England badly crippled, but under its own power.

"My dear Duchess," Tommy always addressed his sister in this way, "put away your worries."

"You're not really a duchess, are you?" I asked.

"Not really, but Tommy thinks I am. He's called me that ever since we first entered service. He works for the Rothschilds, you know."

Tom Phillpot became a remote, romantic figure in his butler's morning coat and his elegant trousers. And although he lived a long way across the Atlantic, I felt I knew him.

His photograph hung in his sister's bedroom, and I had, on several occasions, studied it minutely. Of medium height, he possessed a thick mane of dark wavy hair, a long straight nose, and azure blue eyes. Even though the picture was done in sepia tones, the features were painted in. Tommy's face like his letter sparkled with laughter and good humor. I found him fascinating and longed to meet him.

"We both entered service about the same time," Mrs. Houghton explained. "I'm two years older than Tom, the second of ten children."

"Ten children!" I echoed. "How did you find enough beds for ten children?"

"We weren't all home at one time." She laughed, hastening to explain. "But there was a crowd of us, I must agree."

Both Mrs. Houghton and her husband were the second of ten children, and both were born in the last glimmer of Queen Victoria's reign. I thought it rather wonderful, having been born in a different century.

Clara Houghton, who was three years older than her husband, grew up in Kent and went to school in the shadow of Canterbury Cathedral.

"We've known difficult times," she remembered, "But we all managed to attend school and to earn our living. I was barely thirteen when I first entered service."

"When did you finish school?" I asked, surprised that she could leave so young.

"Twelve, almost thirteen. During the first few months of the Great War I worked in a munitions factory filling bullets with gun powder. When the foreman discovered I was hard of hearing, he dismissed me. That's when I entered service as a maid in the London home of Lady Crystal."

"Well, go on, finish the story," I coaxed, hating it when she stopped in the middle of something interesting.

"At night, three flights up above the family, I'd build a small fire in the grate and read. I wasn't allowed much coal, so I'd put on my gloves. How I loved the Scarlet Pimpernel stories! He always made such fantastic hair's breadth escapes. Often it was in the wee small hours before I'd put the book down."

"And?" I prompted.

"And begin work at six o'clock the next morning exhausted!" She continued. "Lady Crystal was a Jewess, and extremely demanding."

I stayed with her for most of the war, but the staff quickly dwindled from six to just two of us; the old beadle-nosed cook and me."

"Why did she have a beadle nose?"

"Into everyone's business, she was too old for war work and a petty tyrant. Even Lady Crystal feared her."

"Do you remember her name?"

"Longacre, Hortense Longacre." Mrs. Houghton laughed. "She used to run me a merry chase! Hortense wasn't her real name, I believe, but she fancied it went well with Longacre and sounded French, although her cooking was decidedly plain English."

"How long did you stay in London?"

"Until just after the Armistice, and then I moved to a place in the country."

"Come on, Mrs. Houghton, don't just tell driblets. I'm interested because it's fantastic and so different from my own life. Do go on and explain." I begged.

"Lady Crystal moved in with her son, and soon afterwards her London home was sold. Mrs. Longacre got another position as cook, but I went home to Kent to a family with three young girls."

How I loved to listen to these stories of her life in England.

But one afternoon she mentioned something that disturbed me. When her dad died unexpectedly several years after she "came out" to Canada, she felt devastated.

"I'd always hoped to return to England for a visit and see him. I never considered our separation final. When he died, I cried for three days. Tommy understood and placed my photograph in Dad's coffin. This touched me deeply and made his death bearable. Although I'll never see him again, I feel I didn't desert him."

"How terrible for you to be so far from home," I realized suddenly how I might feel if my own father died.

"It was terrible. I felt trapped in Canada and cried for months. But we simply didn't have money for me to go home." She busied herself preparing her husband's dinner, while I sat at the table shelling butter beans and feeling very sorry for her.

On November fifteenth the war came closer. That morning before dawn Coventry Cathedral went up in flames. German planes devastated that city by dropping thousands of incendiary bombs. Fires could be seen for miles and for hours the Cathedral burned.

"The casualties are feared to number nearly a thousand with considerable property damage as well." At breakfast we sat beside the radio horrified by this latest German outrage.

"Numbers of civilians have died; in this Cathedral city, fires are still burning, and in the Cathedral, human bones, buried for centuries, lay exposed. The ancient church lies in ruins as do numerous shops, businesses and homes," reported the funereal voice of Douglas Freeman.

"My sister, Jessie, lives near Coventry. She and her husband have a home there. Dear God in heaven, let them be all right!" Mrs. Houghton prayed.

We waited for three weeks for a letter from England; dreading its coming, yet anxiously anticipating its arrival.

"Maybe they're dead," she sighed deeply one afternoon her voice shaking.

I stood in her kitchen not knowing how to comfort her, afraid I might say the wrong thing. Yet unable to remain silent, I ran to her, put my arms around her waist and hugged her. Great sobs shook her body as she drew me closer.

"Oh, Doc," she said between her sobs, "whatever would I do without you?"

"Please, don't cry, Mrs. Houghton. You'll hear soon, I'm sure. A letter will come. I know they're not dead. They can't be."

She released me, put her head in her apron and sank into a kitchen chair. Finally when the tears subsided she stood up, splashed water on her face from the tap and regarded me with a tenderness I'd never seen before.

"How kind and understanding you are for one so young," she remarked.

When her letter finally came she placed it unopened on the kitchen table, and studied the stamp and the handwriting.

"It's from Tommy," she said. "He's good about writing. Scarcely a fortnight goes by without a letter."

"Open it, Mrs. Houghton," I told her, impatiently. "It's good news; open it and see."

She slit the envelope with a paring knife and unfolded the single sheet of paper.

I was conscious of my heart pounding.

"They're all right. They've lost their home, but they're all right and staying in Chester with their daughter." Her eyes were filled with tears, but she smiled. "Thank God I can stop worrying."

All that autumn fleets of German bombers kept coming across the Channel. Spitfires and Hurricanes scrambled to intercept them; anti-aircraft guns sought their target. Britain now stood alone against this German onslaught. The blitz racked London night after night, but British morale remained high as the R.A.F. and the ack-ack guns took their toll of Nazi planes. Still, night after night the planes kept coming.

Tommy Phillpot wrote me at Christmas, his cheerful letter scarcely mentioned the war. Rather he preferred to describe the London he knew before it.

"We have wonderful street names," he told me, "Pudding Lane, Threadneedle Street, Piccadilly Circus and Petticoat Lane."

"A circus in the middle of London? How strange," I thought.

He also described the Kentish countryside with its distinctive oast houses.

"As a boy I picked hops from which beer is made for pocket money during the long summer holidays. It was hard work, but good fun with other young lads for companionship. The money came in handy, although it was really very little." He continued, "of course we see your War of Independence from a different perspective. Let's not go into that. Doc, we view life from the opposite sides of a very large ocean. I, as an Englishman, and you, as a young, American girl. But it's such differences that make life interesting."

I wrote him back and asked about fox hunting in England, and the various kinds of ponies raised there. I wanted to tease him about our Revolutionary War, but afraid I might offend him I just commented on the strange-sounding street names and asked him how many circuses London possessed.

"Surely, they aren't like American ones with elephants and clowns.

Your English type must be very different if they have them in London in war-time."

Imagine my surprise when by return post I discovered Oxford and Piccadilly Circus were not circuses at all, but old Roman sites.

"You know," I confided to Mrs. Houghton, "I've learned some very curious things about London. Tommy's told me heaps of places like Kensington, Chelsea and Kew Gardens with its glass houses. One day I'm determined to see them."

Mother and Rudy arrived from Washington and reluctantly I moved back into the house. Although she lectured me the first day on responsibility, Mother and Rudy filled their week's holiday with social obligations and generally ignored me.

"You're doing poorly in Math," Rudy commented one afternoon when Mother was out. "Don't you study?"

"Yes, Sir, I study very hard," I replied.

"And a "C" in French is not good enough to get into College. You must consider your future. I expect your Dad'll put on a uniform soon."

"I haven't heard anything."

He poured a healthy Scotch whiskey and drank it neat.

"You must stop making pencil marks in the dictionary. Just look at the mess you've made."

"It's easier," I replied; "we study here."

"We?" Rudy raised his eyebrow quizzically. "Do you have a boyfriend?"

"No, just Mary Ann and me."

What a stupid question, I thought; at twelve, girls didn't have boyfriends. I felt hot and uncomfortable as I watched him drink his whiskey.

"You're too young, I suppose," he continued, flustered. "You need to take more responsibility and help Mrs. Houghton."

"I do," I answered, "I work at the Red Cross and deliver eggs and help with the house work. What else should I do?"

He grunted, and not knowing what to say dismissed me. This was our only conversation during the holidays. He simply ignored me. And Mother's attention to my needs was only a little more helpful. Feeling left out, I sought Cary and the Houghtons.

That Christmas I received a young mare, Lady. Finally even Mother agreed to what was long apparent; Billy was too small. I needed a horse in the country where horses were considered transportation. A few days before Christmas I thought things seemed awful fishy when Cary wouldn't let me in his barn. "What's up?" I demanded. "Is Killybegs sick?"

"Not exactly," he admitted.

"Well, come on, Cary, don't act stupid. Why can't I go in?" I tried to push my way through.

"Not on your life, Doc, do you get in this barn." He shoved me away and padlocked the door.

Realizing something was up, I didn't press it. Anyway, I loved surprises - and they made Christmas a lot more exciting.

Early that morning Cary tied a red ribbon around Lady's chestnut neck and led her down my driveway. Hearing the rhythmic sound of a horse's hooves upon the gravel, I raced to the window, and there below me stood the most wonderful hunter I'd ever seen.

"It's a Thoroughbred!" I squealed, "A Thoroughbred hunter! I can't believe it."

Grabbing a coat and shoes, I raced downstairs and outside.

"How beautiful," I gasped, "Is she really mine?"

"Don't wake the whole county," cautioned Cary. "There's a bridle and saddle, too. Isn't she a beauty? She's a dream to ride, comfortable and well mannered. The name, Lady, suits her exactly."

"Oh, Cary, I can't believe it. Now I can hunt with you and Killybegs." I ran my appreciative fingers over the elegant neck and down her nose. "Will you take me?"

"Sure. But this afternoon we'll try her out. After all the turkey and dressing are over."

As Cary led my beautiful new mare down the drive towards the barn, I skipped joyously along beside him.

Later, stuffed with Christmas dinner, we rode Lady and Killybegs through frosty trails in the woods. Lady I found perfect in every way, and couldn't believe my good fortune. Even Mother smiled on that day.

Later I wrote Tom Phillpot, "You can't possibly guess what's happened. I got a Chestnut Mare for Christmas, about 15.3 hands, and Cary took me hunting at the Silver Creek Club. Lady's heels grew wings, and I felt like a fairy princess riding through the woods on a magical steed."

Suddenly I remembered that his Christmas must have appeared grim compared to mine.

"It was a wonderful gift. But I hope your holidays were happy too. I sent in "the Duchess's" parcel some candies for you. I hope you enjoyed them, and Cary sent you some gloves. He received them before Christmas from his great Aunt Margaret who got the size wrong – miles too big. He thought they might be cozy in your damp English climate and perhaps fit you better. He asked me to mention it. I wasn't to tell you about his great Aunt Margaret. But I was afraid you'd think Cary'd spent all his pocket money and be embarrassed and not enjoy his gift. They're really handsome gloves, fur lined and beautiful soft leather. So I hope you like Aunt Margaret's gift."

Tom Phillpot didn't disappoint me. He understood and replied, "What lovely candies you have in America! And how we enjoyed them. What an exciting Christmas parcel. Cary's gloves are the finest I've ever owned and are perfect fit. Aunt Margaret must have known my size. How lucky we all felt to have such friends as you and Cary in America.

"When I write to Cary I shall not mention your explanation. That's our secret. I am extremely happy Aunt Margaret can't judge sizes because you should hear the compliments I've received. Your parcel gave us all a joyous Christmas."

I confessed this little secret to "the duchess," and although she had not questioned Cary's generosity, she was curious.

"What a naughty pair you are." She laughed, her eyes sparkling. "Giving away leather gloves and candy to some unknown chap in England! What kind, thoughtful neighbors I have."

Of course, I've told Cary all about Tom and read his letters. "Cary's terribly interested in England, you know," I assured her. "He claims they make the best saddle leather."

"And woollens, china and literature," Mrs. Houghton added, sitting down on the love seat.

I perched beside her on the hassock.

"I'm glad Tommy's pleased; now I don't feel guilty about getting a new horse. I'm happy we sent the gloves and candy."

"Maybe next time we can bake cookies and send them," Mrs. Houghton suggested picking up her knitting.

Soon afterwards Tom Phillpot wrote me.

The Duchess's Family

"You have inquired about horses here. We have Thoroughbreds and various ponies, but no burros like your Jackie, although we have donkeys at the seaside. At one time," he continued, "the Rothschilds kept a pack of hounds - the Waadom Chase, and my, did they make work! I hope you enjoy a gallop today, and perhaps tea with "the Duchess." She used to make such lovely teas, Doc. Does she still?" he asked me wistfully.

"Such a special man," said Mrs. Houghton when I showed her this letter, "to take time to write a young girl he's never met. I've always called him my 'handsome brother,' and so he is."

We shared Tommy's letters from Bedfordshire, awaiting eagerly for their arrival. Soon I recognized the foreign stamp, the straight up and down writing and the poor quality envelopes.

"These are happy days," I confided as 1940 blended into the New Year.

A Forgotten Landscape

18

Heavenly Peace

Just off River Road in the woods behind Red Jones's house lay three little graves. Few of us knew these children's graves existed. But one day when out riding with Jean Taliaferro, we discovered their broken headstones hidden by brambles. Jean put a chop on a tree nearby with her hatchet to mark the spot. At one time, years ago, people had private cemeteries on their own farms. But as churchyards became more popular these old cemeteries were no longer used. Today, in our section of Goochland, although private cemeteries still remain, only those people who died in mysterious circumstances lie buried in unmarked graves on their own land. Local tradition says that these poor children died of measles. Within four days of each other their parents lost three little girls. And because they died of an infectious disease these children were buried on their family farm.

Now several months later, I had forgotten about the graves, a county official arrived at the Taliaferros' door trying to locate them.

"The land's been sold," he told us, "and the new owner wants to move that graveyard. Can you find it for me?"

Jean and I weren't sure. No one else, it seemed, knew the exact location. Our colored laundress, Bertha, upon hearing about the matter, remained adamant.

"Don't let them move those children's graves, Miss Jean; we shall all be haunted the rest of our lives."

In the minds of the colored people, and also some white folks, to disturb any grave was considered bad luck. But to move someone who had died of an infectious disease always caused serious consequences. This, in popular tradition, was referred to as a "fever grave".

"I am afraid there isn't much I can do," Jean replied, "except locate the chop I made on a tree."

Although we tramped through the woods with the county man most of that afternoon we could find neither graves nor chop mark. The next morning when a team of horses appeared upon River Road pulling a large harrow, Jean and I rode Huck and Lady down to find out what was happening.

"We plan to cut out that undergrowth and find those graves," the man from the county told us as we trotted up. "Please go in there and see if you can remember their location."

As the big team of horses swung into the woods with its harrow, Jean tried to direct the driver towards an old stream bed. Dismounting near a clump of trees we found the ground muddy. I'd walked only a few steps when I heard a sucking noise beneath my feet and saw water flowing over my boots.

"Here's the stream," I called.

"Can't they just build a fence around the burial ground and leave the graves?" Jean asked, as we remounted our horses.

"Aren't there laws about digging up old graveyards? Bertha says we'll be haunted if we move those children," I added.

"Come along, Doc," Jean said, "we can help no more here."

Turning our horses we trotted down the path, crossed River Road and headed into our own woods.

"Don't go, Miss Jean, we need your advice," the county official called after us.

"I can't say any more. I suggest you leave those children where they are and build a fence," Jean replied reining in Huck.

The big team entered a dense thicket, with honeysuckle entangled in the harrow, and standing in mud and goo up to their bellies, the horses stopped. A loud scraping sound told us they had hit a rock.

"We found the markers," the workman's voice rang through the woods. "Better come here and have a look," the county man called to us.

We turned our horses, dismounted, and once more entered the woods on foot. Sinking into mud with each step, we made our way through the tangled briars as Jean chopped at the thick underbrush with her hatchet. After some difficulty we reached the team. There, sticking out of the honeysuckle half exposed in front of us lay a headstone. About ten yards away we found a second, cracked and broken. Scraping off layers of mud with a stick, I read, "Hazel and Annie". On the second one I deciphered the name, "Mildred."

"Pull the team up, Grievous, I'll cut down the brush," said Jean.

The great horses, their traces encased in mud, pulled forward again, dragging the entangled harrow. Briars, jerked up, and hung around its giant spikes. With the county official's help we dug, using his shovels, beside the stream bed and found the graves. The head and feet were marked by little round stones.

The county official identified the place with a red stake, Grievous and the team, their work completed, struggled back onto the road. A few days later the three little girls were dug up and moved into St. Mary's churchyard. The remains of Annie and Hazel and their older sister, Mildred, were placed in a pine coffin and made ready for reburial.

That same week, in late January, it snowed. I watched it start in the early morning on my way to school, and slowly cover the landscape with a fine white powder. By evening I knew the roads would become slippery and our country ones especially dangerous. When Mr. Houghton came for me that afternoon we chugged ever so slowly down River Road in his old 1932 Chevrolet, taking no chances. As we passed St. Mary's church he suddenly asked, "Who died? I can't believe there's an open grave in this storm."

"Nobody died, that I know of. Why?" I replied, curious.

"Let's stop a minute and see. Something strange is going on here."

We pulled over and got out of the car. Through the snow I ran towards the cemetery and met Ben, our colored sexton, coming up the path, his face almost white from fear.

"Mr. Houghton, I sure is glad to see you. Come here and look at this. I ain't never seen nothin' like it. Those children we buried yesterday is gone."

"Gone? Where could they go?" Mr. Houghton looked puzzled.

"They is gone, Miss Doc, as sure as I am standing here," Ben's eyes seemed suddenly enormous in his dark face. "We put those three fever children in this here grave, and I put the earth back over them myself. Miss Doc, I swear I ain't had no whiskey."

Before us in the red earth, now powdered with snow, lay the open grave - empty. Nor could we find the coffin anywhere. Nothing in the churchyard gave us a clue: No tire tracks, no foot prints, not even a scrape mark.

"I can't believe it, Ben. Where could that coffin go?" I shuddered with fear. "This is downright spooky."

"It's jumped. Those children have settled back into their own woods," he whispered mysteriously.

"How can a casket jump from one place to another? Unless, that is, some one jumped it," Mr. Houghton asked, looking into the empty hole.

"You can't disturb a fever grave. Those little ones weren't buried in holy ground." Ben stood in the snow before us, cap in hand. "Go look in the woods across the road, Miss Doc, and see if they ain't jumped there."

I realized old Ben addressed his remarks to me because I was a child and might still believe in ghosts and fairies. About Mr. Houghton's attitude towards these strange happenings the sexton felt unsure.

We slid across the icy road and entered the woods about a hundred yards below Red Jones's house. There lying upon the soft earth, its lid covered with fresh snow, we found the small coffin. Not a soul was anywhere in sight. Only old Ben, Mr. Houghton and I stood there beside the lonely country road.

"I thought so," whispered Ben. "It's jumped!"

"Who moved it?" I asked looking at the pale cream-colored box in the blowing snow.

"No one, little Miss. It's jumped back out of holy ground."

The next morning when Mr. Houghton drove us down to St. Mary's everything was exactly as we left it. The grave lay open, now half filled with snow. And on the other side of the road, the small coffin still rested on the boggy ground. Baffled, we drove into Westhampton, the nearest suburb, and found an Episcopal church.

"You'll have to explain what's happened, Doc. They'll think I am crazy, and lock me up," Mr. Houghton said as we got out of the car.

The Reverend Francis Scott welcomed us into his office at St. Luke's, and listened patiently while I explained about the jumping coffin.

"You see," I concluded, "these were fever graves of three small children. Ben and old Bertha told us you can't move such graves, out of "non-holy" ground into ground that's blessed. And they both consider it's very bad luck to disturb them."

"Yes, I've heard of that," replied the priest. "But how do you know it's unblessed ground those children lie in? Some old family cemeteries have sacred ground. Can you be sure?"

"No, sir," I thought this over. "But why else would a coffin jump? I mean they move old cemeteries sometimes and re-bury the people in other places. I have never heard of coffins jumping back. And anyway, nobody seems to care about these old graves. Few of our neighbors even know where they are, so we might never find out if the ground's been blessed."

Later that afternoon, the Reverend Scott, accompanied by his superior, drove up to the Houghton's cottage. In the car with them sat Jean Taliaferro.

"Doc, we need you to come to the cemetery with us. Can you remember the names on the two grave stones?"

"Yes, there were Hazel and Annie on one stone, and Mildred on the other. I don't know their last name. But they died within a week of each other," I replied climbing into the car beside Jean.

At the cemetery old Ben carried the coffin over the road once more and laid it gently in the churchyard.

"It ain't going to stay here, Miss Doe, unless it goes inside the church," Ben commented, shaking his head. "No sir, it'll jump again."

"How can you be so sure?" I asked.

"Cause that's the way with them jumpin' coffins."

Ben and the two priests held a brief consultation.

"Do you think there're any markers still in that muddy bog?" The superior wondered.

"We've got to find them. And we needs a grave exactly like it was on the other side," Ben insisted.

Jean and I went in search of the headstones while Ben and the two priests entered the church. After some digging we found three small rounded stones and a cracked marker.

"That one's Mildred's," I explained. "Annie and Hazel's leaning against the tall pine tree over there. They died on the 6th and 10th of May, 1929. How very sad."

Together Jean and I carried the markers and the round stones back across River Road and laid them against a tree in the parking lot. Then we all entered the church.

"How old are you?" Reverend Scott asked me.

"Twelve, sir," I replied.

"Then you're old enough to hold the candle and the Prayer Book. Do as I tell you."

"You mean you plan to conduct a service. This church is freezing cold," I protested.

"Precisely. Ask your friend here," he pointed to Ben, "what is needed to make those children stay put."

We started the Office of Burial, with my holding the candle to provide light, and Jean, helping at the altar, turned the pages of the Prayer Book. Softly Ben sang an old hymn. Then we intoned the prayers, offering our petitions to the Lord for the souls of three small children none of us knew.

Afterwards Ben lowered the little casket into the grave and covered it up. I helped throw in some red earth with my hands. Then we placed the rounded stones at the foot of the little mound and laid the two markers at its head. This strange funeral completed, we all drove home.

On the way into school the next morning I asked Mr. Houghton to let me inspect the grave. We found it quite easily although covered with snow. Relieved the coffin had not jumped, I regarded the stones. Somehow they seemed different, more settled, perhaps.

"They'll stay now," Ben assured us. "We said the right prayers, and laid those children to rest like Christians, in sacred ground. Now they'll sleep in heavenly peace."

19

Mr. Carter's Folklore

Shortly after we buried the three fever children, Jean Taliaferro invited me up to her house for an evening of story telling. She rigged up a recorder and hid it under the loveseat where our local historian sat with his wife and son, Dabney.

"Don't talk, Doc, just listen to Mr. Carter's stories and ask questions about them," Jean instructed upon my arrival.

Everyone thought Mr. Carter's stories fascinating, and I was perfectly willing to listen. On the heated porch, I found Sally Ann and Mrs. Taliaferro, who offered me a seat next to her on the sofa. Then the evening's entertainment began.

"When I was a boy of perhaps ten," Mr. Carter slowly returned to the Tuckahoe of his past, "everyone was afraid to visit Ballyclare, Mrs. Haunch's present house. Old Thomas Randolph's eldest son, Peter, added to the first part of that house and brought his bride there. And a more wicked man never set foot in Virginia. He courted and finally married Nellie Fitzhugh, from James City County, and brought her out here as a bride. The house, at that time, was hardly more than a cabin placed in a swamp, and possessed three out buildings; a stable, an office and a brick kitchen.

"It was not long before Miss Nellie lived in mortal fear not only of the swamp, which was infested with snakes, but also of her husband. He drank heavily and gambled away his land, which the elder Randolph bought back. Finally his father became disgusted, and took away Peter's inheritance to bestow it upon a younger, more favored son.

"One day shortly after he'd married, Peter went out on his farm to inspect the corn and tobacco. He rode a handsome young horse, and carried a brace of dueling pistols. He was a crack shot as well as a good horseman. After riding across his property Peter often ducked into the woods to practice his marksmanship.

"That same afternoon old Thomas Randolph arrived at the cabin inquiring for his eldest son. And when Miss Nellie told him that Peter was out on the farm old Mr. Randolph decided to wait. Father and son both fancied the same young slave girl in the quarters, and Thomas Randolph meant to speak to his son about this. Also, young Patrick Randolph was expected that afternoon, and the older Randolphs planned a dinner party in their younger son's honor.

"When Peter rode up on his handsome colt, the father went out to greet him. The two men remained talking in the front yard for several minutes; when, suddenly, their voices rose in anger.

" 'First you take my land, and now my slave girl,' Peter shouted. 'And you wish me to rejoice at Patrick's return?'

" 'Your mother is expecting you at seven sharp for dinner', the older Randolph mounted his horse. 'I want you to sign some deeds this evening, so be there.'

"All afternoon Peter remained in a black fury. About dusk Miss Nellie and her maid heard him leave, headed down the road towards his father's house. They were surprised when a half hour later Peter returned with a handsome negress riding double behind him. From a window Nellie watched as the slave girl dismounted and entered the outside kitchen. Peter followed after tying the colt. In his hand he carried a pistol.

" 'You're mine,' Peter told the frightened colored girl. 'I shall dress you up in fine clothes, and give you jewels. Then we shall drink wine together'.

" 'Master, please let me go home,' pleaded the young slave. 'Suppose old master finds me here. Please, sir, let me go home.'

" 'You'll do as I tell you,' Peter's voice rose in anger as he flung himself out of the kitchen and banged the door.

"Nellie cringed when her husband entered their cabin, jerked open her cupboard door and snatched down her best dress. When she tried to protest Peter pushed her aside with one wave of his pistol and left the house.

" 'Put this on, my pretty; then we'll drink some wine,' he commanded the frightened negress.

"Soon the kitchen was filled with song, and then shouts. A scuffle broke out as the girl tried to free herself from Peter's drunken embraces.

" 'Come here, give me a little kiss,' he coaxed.

" 'Oh, no sir, please master,' cried the terrified girl. 'I'd better get dressed in my own clothes and go back home.'

" 'You shall never go back. You are mine to do with as I like. Come here,' I said.

"Sounds of struggle - a scream - followed by a shot. A long protracted wail filled the still evening and then - silence. Miss Nellie didn't wait to find out what happened. She fled from the house, running through the woods, catching her long dress upon briars as she struggled across the swampy land towards the big house. Emboldened by fear, her flight took her deep into the swamp. The weight of her dress, now wet from the marsh, pulled her down. Finally, entangled in the undergrowth, in her panic to free herself she slipped into the swamp. After a brief struggle the waters closed over her.

"In the morning they found Miss Nellie where the bridge is now. Her father, Raymond Fitzhugh, accompanied the body back to James City County to bury it amongst her own people. In the summer kitchen old Thomas Randolph found the dead negress, still clad in Nellie's gown, shot through the heart. Beside her lay Peter's dueling pistol. But he had fled. The only witness to the murder was Nellie's slave who had gone with her mistress's remains back home to Tidewater, Virginia. The distraught girl refused to talk about that terrible evening. So when Peter returned home a few days later, although everyone knew what had happened, he was never brought to trial. From that day on he became a disgraced man and one to avoid.

"Although he lived for another thirty years, Peter rarely left the solitude of his plantation. His younger brother, Patrick, inherited Tuckahoe and carried on the Randolph name. When Peter died his branch died with him, a twisted and crooked limb of a great old family. He lies buried in an unmarked grave at Tuckahoe, a man who destroyed his wife, as well as himself by his terrible crime. For years Peter was shunned by the neighborhood that claimed he was mad - a product, it was whispered, of cousin marrying cousin.

"Today when you cross the bridge on Mrs. Haunch's road, the air is always cool in summer and warm in winter. This is Nellie Randolph's troubled spirit who walks beside the bridge.

"At the house a more sinister ghost haunts the kitchen now boarded up and no longer used."

No one spoke for a moment as Mr. Carter concluded his story. Jean offered us a cup of coffee and a cookie before she secretly checked the recorder and sat down once again.

"What about the Indian graves you opened with your father years ago?" invited Sally Anne.

"They were not Indian graves, but those of Revolutionary soldiers. No Indians wore buttons in 1776. Unless, that is, they were half-breeds or Scouts. These graves lie in the woods near Ballyclare. My father opened them, but all we found were a few bones and several buttons. However, shortly after these graves were opened the headless horseman began to ride at Black Bottom."

"Where is Black Bottom?" I asked, curious, for I'd never heard of it before.

"Where the bridge on River Road crosses Tuckahoe Creek. It's still a dark and forbidding spot, even on a day when the sun shines. But when I was a boy the woods there were very thick, and it was a fearsome place," Mr. Carter replied.

"I remember one winter morning, when I rode my little mare the five miles to Pelham's Crossroads to fetch the newspaper, a crescent moon was just visible and partly covered by fast-racing clouds. All at once the woods became still as I rode along, ominously still. No songbirds chirped in the trees; no squirrels played in the undergrowth. The atmosphere seemed to be listening, as if it expected something strange to occur. The mare felt it also and shied at a dark shadow in the road. Then she leaped forward and galloped for all she was worth towards the bridge.

"Icy fingers seemed to clutch at me and to pull me from the saddle. I clung on with all of my might as the little mare started down the hill towards Black Bottom. On either side of the road the pine woods looked dark and swampy. Brambles appeared unusually thick, and pine needles on the forest floor were so soft and deep I could ride hardly making a sound. Suddenly in the woods behind me I heard hoof beats, soft and rhythmic, coming at a gallop. I glanced back and saw a headless rider. In spite of his great speed the ghost horse made little noise. My mare leaped forward as if the devil was after her. Furiously we raced for the keystone of the bridge at Black Bottom. Ghosts cannot cross over water, you see, because it's a life force and purifies them. The great black horse galloped up behind us, his hooves flying like leaves before a storm. When we reached the bridge I raced over it, galloping towards Richmond. The headless horseman disappeared, wallowed up in the darkness of Black Bottom.

"I didn't look back or draw in on the reins until we reached Pelham's Crossroads. When I jumped down to collect the newspaper, I found the mare trembling and covered in sweat from head to tail. She appeared as nervous as a cat and jumped at her own shadow.

"Believe me, I hated to start down that road again. Black Bottom and the headless horseman lay between me and home. Slowly I walked the frightened mare, and just before I reached the bridge I pulled her up. The road ahead wound through the woods and disappeared at the crest of a hill. Nothing seemed out of the ordinary. The slip of a moon disappeared as morning broke, and the dawn stars burnt out in the gray sky. Crows called to one another in the woods, as the world returned to life.

"Everything appeared quite normal as the mare walked over the wooden planking of the bridge. We galloped up the road fairly flying until we reached St. Mary's where I pulled my horse down. I was scared to death of Black Bottom after that morning. But I continued to ride over it for more than six years to fetch the newspaper for my father. Only one other time did I encounter that ghost again, and that was on Black Friday in 1929.

"Early on that October morning as I rode after the paper, again at the bridge I heard a rustling noise like the wind. But the trees did not move. Then I heard the sound of galloping hooves coming up behind me. The ghost passed us effortlessly as if my mare and I were standing still in her tracks. The great black horse lifted himself into the air, and both horse and rider vanished into the woods.

"Believe me, I was scared. I spent some minutes calming my usually docile horse who leaped forward at the sight of her own shadow. The sound of an old owl hooting near the bridge quite startled her. And I was forced to dismount and lead the mare. When we reached the crest of the hill I remounted and rode on.

"After collecting the newspaper, on the way home, again I

dismounted just before reaching the bridge. I was curious about Black Bottom. Along the roadside the leaves lay in thick masses; then suddenly I came upon a place with no leaves: only the soft earth along the road's muddy shoulder. Here I discovered a print made by a massive hoof, and beside this print lay a clump of horse hair. I kicked it aside. Underneath something bright shone in the rising sun. With great excitement I picked up a five dollar gold piece. I couldn't remember ever having seen one before. I placed this coin in my pocket and quickly mounted the mare. Looking around me to make sure the headless horseman was no longer about, I flew up the road — towards home. Later that afternoon the stock market collapsed. Here's the coin I found along the roadside that morning," Mr. Carter said as he laid the gold piece on the coffee table in front of us.

"I've never seen one of these before," I exclaimed, picking it up.

"It's no longer legal tender. But you find one from time to time," Mrs. Taliaferro explained. "Have you seen the ghost since, Mr. Carter? Go on with your story."

"The last time I saw that ghost at Black Bottom was in September 1939. I had been in Richmond for the day and was on my way home. It must have been around six o'clock in the evening when I crossed the bridge. This time I drove my old Ford car. Just as I reached the middle of Tuckahoe Creek, I heard a wind-rushing sound and saw the headless horseman on his big ebony steed fly over my head. From his hand dropped three objects: one golden, one silver and one brass. Instantly I put on my brakes and got out of the car. In front of me on the bridge lay three coins. I have them here," Mr. Carter laid three curious foreign coins down in front of us.

I shall never forget them. One was an English sovereign, gold in color and badly worn. The second one was a French coin made of silver, and the third was a German one of brass. All the coins were old and out of circulation.

"The next day these countries declared war," Mr. Carter concluded. "I have not seen the headless horseman since."

But I knew of another sighting. One morning recently when Mr. Houghton drove to Hall's store he found an enormous hoof mark near the bridge and a silver dollar half buried in the soft earth. I didn't mention this, because Mr. Carter began to speak again. And once more we all listened spellbound.

"You see," he explained, "the headless horseman only comes in times of great peril. I counted back over the years when my dad disturbed those Indian graves. It was around 1914 or 1915 just before we entered the First World War. I remember I must have been about ten. That's when the ghost first started to ride. Even so, it's safer to stay away from Black Bottom after dusk."

Leslie, the Taliaferro's colored maid moved uneasily in her chair beside the fireplace.

"I knows about that ghost, Miss Doc," she whispered. "Colored folks don't never go down to that bridge walking after dark. It ain't safe. I've never seen that headless horseman, but I don't want to see him neither."

Mr. Carter then told us about the hoop snake, and of the Indian arrow heads he used to find when the ground was turned by the plough on what was now the Taliaferros' low grounds. Finally the evening's story telling was concluded, and we all drove home together. Just in case there might be a ghost, Dabney Carter even walked me up the front steps and saw me in the Houghtons' door.

After that evening I was fascinated with the story of the headless horseman and against my better judgment I rode Lady down the road to the bridge at Black Bottom. I waited until Sunday when there was little traffic, and taking no chances went about mid—afternoon. As the mare and I crossed River Road after a fine gallop through our woods we trotted along the shoulder. We passed a ramshackle Negro cabin, and started down the hill towards the bridge. Before us ran Tuckahoe Creek, dark and ominous. I knew it was inhabited by poisonous snakes like water moccasins and copperheads. Shivering, I continued on until I reached the wooden bridge. Here I pulled the mare down.

"There is nothing here, Lady," I shouted over the black water. "Only broken trees and snakes."

I decided not to cross the bridge because its wooden planks sounded hollow under the hooves of the fractious mare and might frighten her. Instead I turned around. When we trotted back up the hill a sudden wind seemed to strike me from behind. Cold fingers nearly pulled me from my horse. Frightened, the mare broke into a wild gallop and dashed into the woods. Unable to pull her up I clung to the chestnut mane and prayed.

The bit between her teeth, Lady ran, out of control, to St. Mary's church. Here, only a fence covered with honeysuckle stopped her flight, and she skidded to a halt. Trembling, with her chestnut coat lathered in sweat she reared, pawing the air.

"Walk, girl," I cooed, trying to calm her. "Walk now."

Jig-trotting through the woods, Lady didn't walk until we reached our long hill. I felt her great muscles coiled as if ready to spring. Sweat frothed up over the reins and covered her like a blanket. Before reaching the top of the hill I turned into our woods and dismounted. Here I found some clean pine needles upon the forest floor and wiped down the dripping mare and dried her steaming coat. Lady trembled all over and kept looking behind her. It took me an hour to get her quiet. Only after I had her safely bedded down in her stall did I realize how shaken I felt. I never told anyone about my experience at Black Bottom, not even Mrs. Houghton. For days afterwards I was afraid even to ride over Tuckahoe Creek in a car. And although I have never seen the ghost since, I firmly believe in the headless horseman.

20

Enter Rommel

In December the Italians were routed in North Africa. The year began with the British taking Cyranaica after its coastal defenses fell. Generals O'Connor and Wavell captured Sidi Barrani in Libya in less than an hour and took 4000 German prisoners.

"At Camp Maktila, also in Libya, on the northern coast the 1st Durham Infantry found 500 Italians in parade formation standing at attention. A general stood in front waving a white flag. He wished to surrender to the first British officer who appeared. Shortly afterwards the Italian Army was destroyed. The Allies took 5 acres of officers and 200 acres of other ranks," Mr. Houghton quoted one English officer's remark.

Although Mussolini had over 500,000 men in Africa, they were no match for the mechanized British with their tanks, airplanes and big guns. The Italians had very few tanks and these were of World War I vintage. They also had inadequate artillery pieces and anti-aircraft guns.

"Their tanks are called 'self propelled coffins'," Mr. Houghton told me.

On January 4, 1941, when the British and Australians captured Bardia after only a two-day assault the Italians were devastated. When Bardia fell they believed it was the most heavily fortified town in Libya. Beda Fomm fell on February 5 and Benghazi on February 7.

Then the British turned on the seaport of Tobruk. They captured its fortress with its two rings of fortifications in 48 hours and took 25,000 prisoners. Tobruk, although a small town of 4000 people, had a large port and sat at the crossroads, which gave access to the south, the west and the east. A few days later Dema and Sollum fell; then Benghazi, the capital of Cyranaica, was taken. At Beda Fomm only 3000 British and Australian troops destroyed the Pavia, the last of the Italian Armored Regiments.

We rejoiced. The British Generals O'Connor and Wavell became heroes. When Benghazi fell on February 9, even the funereal sounding Douglas Freeman, who read the morning news, sounded jubilant. By the middle of February the desert roads became a sea of mud, so reinforcements were brought into Tobruk by sea. Only the coast road was paved, but it was stony and at times unable to carry traffic and the materials needed in war. The desert was also subject to dust storms, which blew sand and covered this road. These storms and the terrific heat gave the troops on both sides plenty of trouble. Along with the heat were insect pests of all kinds. North Africa had plenty of these.

The Germans, meanwhile, left Belgrade in ruins, and the swastika fluttered above the Greek Acropolis. In North Africa General Wavell's troops gave us renewed hope that the Allies could win battles. Then suddenly Churchill ordered Wavell's victorious troops to Greece leaving only a skeleton crew in Africa.

Then entered General Erwin Rommel upon the world's stage. He flew into Tripoli in early February and took command of the German Afrika Korps. On the 31st of March to our amazement using air cover, including Junker dive bombers, Stukas, Heinkels and Messerschmitts, Rommel turned his full German force towards the British defenses. Within days he recaptured Benghazi and destroyed the British 2nd Armored Division in an unrelenting pursuit. He captured Generals Richard O'Conner and Philip Meane.

The 9th Australian Infantry under General Moreshead retreated as fast as it could to Tmimi fifty miles west of Tobruk before Rommel cut them off. The 7th Australian Division which was on its way to the campaign in Greece was diverted to Tobruk. Churchill wanted it held at all costs. It was the only seaport worth defending in Libya.

Rommel divided his forces. A small armored force under General Van Schwerin went south to Agedabia. He picked up part of the panzer Korps setting off towards Derna and Tmime. With the 5th Light Division he reached Mechili. The 5th Panzer advanced from Msus against Mechile

Enter Rommel

and a third division marched east from Benghazi and repulsed the Australians at El Regima and joined the other British columns at Mechili.

Colonel Von Pineth's spearhead launched an attack against Derna and blocked the British retreat. They could not reach the main road, Via Bebia, which led out of Derna. It was by this route that the British troops escaped. The 9th Australian Division crossed the desert by way of Martuba and reached Tobruk which they defended.

Mr. Houghton couldn't believe the swiftness of Rommel's attack and his victories. He bought a new map and showed me where things were. Sirte on the Gulf of that name was 300 hundred miles from Tripoli. From Agheila on the north, to the southern-most part of the Gulf of Sirte was 200 miles. It was another 200 miles to Benghazi, the capital of Cyrenaica. From Tripoli on the coast to Egypt was 1000 miles. One hundred miles form the frontier stood the fortress of Tobruk. Built by the Italians it had two lines of defense made up of trenches, cement poles and barbed wire. The Italian defenses stretched from the Gulf of Sirte to the Egyptian border. Libya was part of Italy's colonial empire and well fortified. Tobruk guarded an important seaport and the crossroads of three main tracks through the desert. One came from Bardia in the east, a second came from Derna in the west, and the third came from El-Adem from the south. Sandy and stony these roads were often unfit for travel part of the way, but they allowed whomever held them access to the interior and to the sea. Rommel wanted Tobruk so he could control the three roads and turned his full force against it. But Tobruk, defended by the Australians and a small British force, held. Mr. Houghton explained this to me using his map.

For this we rejoiced. But Rommel's victory left us speechless and disbelieving. The radio must have got it wrong. When *The Richmond Times Dispatch* printed a map, it made our disbelief even greater.

"How can this have happened?" I asked as we sat in the living room in early April.

"This Rommel chap means trouble," commented Mr. Houghton. "He's a World War I soldier and knows his stuff."

"All those young British boys lost. It's a terrible defeat. We thought we had the Italians out of this war. Now it's worse than ever." Mrs. Houghton said opening the newspaper.

A Forgotten Landscape

We sat in our usual places. She was on her loveseat by the window. Mr. Houghton sat in his deep chair, and I perched upon my favorite hassock. It was a battered, old footstool made of crumbling leather, and was all right for my weight, but not for an adult's. It also was handy to set a book on or a cup of tea. Mrs. Houghton used it for this purpose. I loved sitting on it because I could roll it around. I also did my homework on it and considered the battered stool mine. I'd never had my very own place before, so I thought it special.

Mr. Houghton handed me a new map he had bought that afternoon. It showed Egypt, Libya, Tunisia, Algeria and Morocco. I laid it on the floor and studied it. I found Tobruk, Alexandria and Benghazi. Alexandria in Egypt was a large important port city. Since the British controlled Egypt, they relied on this port to bring in troops and war material. Mr. Houghton had explained that before. I also found Tripoli and the Gulf of Sirte. I could see how cleverly Rommel executed his attack by splitting his forces.

"I heard that when Rommel visited the Civil War Battlefields during the 1930's, the American General George Patton showed him around," Mrs. Houghton said. "He's studied Jackson's Valley Campaign tactics you can tell."

She'd read everything she could about the War Between the States. Our branch library had sent for inter-library loans for her. I realized she spoke as an expert. Still it was a new thought: Rommel in the desert using the same tactics as Jackson had done in the Shenandoah Valley. I could hardly believe the Desert Fox was that clever.

"It's a mess," I agreed. "After all our winning. At least the fortress at Tobruk held out. That's something Rommel didn't get."

"Give him time, Doc. That German is a professional soldier. He will give our boys hell." Mr. Houghton picked up the map. "Why can't those Arab towns be more pronounceable? Have you ever heard of such names? Halfaya Pass, El Alemain, Benghazi, I can hardly get my tongue around those names. They make my mouth hurt."

"The paper says, 'Rommel attacked Tobruk twice and was twice repulsed. The British tried to relieve the besieged garrison, but they were thrown back suffering heavy loses.' Now Rommel has out-run his supplies," Mrs. Houghton said.

Enter Rommel

"Why all this fuss about Africa?" I wanted to know. "It's just a lot of sand and windstorms."

"The windstorms are called 'ghibli.' I'm not sure how to pronounce it." Mrs. Houghton replied.

"Oil," Mr. Houghton shouted making us jump. "It's oil. The Suez must be kept open to bring oil to supply the British War Machines. Our shipping must remain free to travel to the Middle East, and to India on beyond. Our navy must control the Mediterranean Sea."

"And the Germans want the oil supply?" I continued.

"Exactly. Now you've got it. This fellow Rommel is after oil. That's why this see-saw affair has continued all winter. It's oil that runs a tank; it's oil that runs the planes; it's oil that runs the whole show."

I didn't ask any more questions. I understood. I decided to keep my eye on this fellow, Erwin Rommel. He was dangerous and - interesting.

That spring I celebrated my thirteenth birthday. I felt glad America remained neutral because I remembered Father once told me, "Before your thirteenth birthday we shall be at war." I dreaded becoming thirteen all year because I knew with Rommel's raging about North Africa, we had little hope of peace.

A Forgotten Landscape

21

Lord Haw Haw

Mr. Houghton's short wave radio played at all hours. London was six hours ahead of us because they were on summer time, all year round, so we had to listen to the BBC at six o'clock to get the midday news. That spring we came to know the German propagandist, Lord Haw Haw. He had an oily, upper-class voice, and we hated him.

"Jairmany calling. Jairmany calling. Here are the Richssender Hamburg, Station Breman."

"Listen to him he can't even pronounce Germany correctly," Mrs. Houghton interrupted.

"Once more, I say to you, People of Great Britain, just think for a minute, and you will realize how much you are losing, individually and as a nation as a whole. The sooner we stop this senseless slaughter and come to our right senses and forever kick the Jooees out of our country, the sooner we shall be able to secure peace for ourselves –"

"What are Jooees?" I asked.

"Jews," Mrs. Houghton explained. "It's his fake posh accent; it's hard to understand. We used to call that a West Brit accent from Ireland. I lived in London for several years, and I know a posh accent when I hear one."

I said nothing. We had Jewish girls at school. After (Krystallnacht) in November 1938, when 800 Jews were killed and their shops broken in to, our Headmistress had told us that we must respect all people no matter what their religion or color. When Flurry Cartwright said something rude to the School's colored maid Pearl, Flurry found herself in the principal's office before she could turn around good. Prejudice of any kind was not tolerated.

Lord Haw Haw continued:

"Our children will only be able to turn 'round and say that we delivered the Empire to the Jooees. United we fall."

"Turn that oily voice off," Mrs. Houghton demanded. "Doc doesn't' need to hear that kind of stuff. That man has enough oil in his voice to grease the whole German army."

"Wait, let's hear him," Mr. Houghton replied.

The evil sounding voice went on.

"When it's just good night,
There's not a flight of birds
Who'll take to the sky,
But when the moon is bright
On a good, good night
There's many a man will try,
A good night all is just the call
For brave men good and true,
But a good night to every one
Is the best good night of all."

Mr. Houghton turned his radio off, and we sat in silence as Lord Haw Haw's spell hung over us.

I hated his voice and his evil words. He sounded more scary than Erwin Rommel whom Mr. Houghton and I secretly admired. We never mentioned this to Mrs. Houghton because she would disapprove. We discussed it between ourselves out in the barns and chicken house.

"Sssh," he warned me, "never breathe a word of this to the missus. She'd skin us. The newspapers call Rommel, 'The Desert Fox,' a name that surely fits him. He's really fantastic, that sly bird."

As the siege of Tobruk went into a third month, it was Lord Haw Haw who dubbed the brave defenders, "The Rats of Tobruk."

"Why are they called 'The Rats of Tobruk?'" I wanted to know as I followed Mr. Houghton into his chicken house to gather eggs.

"'Cause they're living like rats and probably eating them too," he replied.

"Eating rats? How disgusting: What do they taste like?" I demanded as we collected the eggs.

"Like chicken, but all dark meat," Mr. Houghton said. He pushed a clucky hen off her nest. "Rats make a grand stew."

I made a face and did not believe him. We placed 60 eggs into straw-filled baskets, and I watched as he took his stubby pencil and marked 60 on his egg calendar.

"We need to take three extra dozen to Richmond to Bill Hughes this week. He has three professor friends who want eggs." Mr. Houghton told me.

"The soldiers at Tobruk are not really eating rats, are they?"

I followed him out of the chicken house and into his barn. He fed Suzie Q, and Lindy Lou, while I tagged along getting in his way.

"Take that pitch fork and throw some hay down for these horses," he commanded.

We worked in silence for a minute or two.

"You don't really think those boys at Tobruk are eating rats?" I was deeply troubled by this revelation.

"Rats, mice, snakes, too, no doubt. Rattlesnake meat makes a good meal. It's a delicacy like snails.

"Do they have snails in the desert?"

"I should think not."

"Snails, who eats snails?"

"The French love them. We ate them during the last war. I didn't like them much. Too slimy."

That night I made a special flag for the fortress at Tobruk with a big red rat on it. I left off the snakes and the snails although Mr. Houghton thought I should have drawn all three.

"I'm not that good an artist. The rat is enough. He looks like a rat, and I am not sure how a snake and a snail would like his company."

"The rat is sufficient," Mrs. Houghton said. "It's symbolic. Goodness, Harry, you do carry on so. Stop teasing the poor girl."

A Forgotten Landscape

22

Education

Rommel once again messed up our flags with his spring offensive and pushed the Allies, in a whirlwind battle, to El Alamein near Alexandria on the Egyptian border. Rommel's thrust pushed the allies back 300 miles in a week. Mr. Houghton spent most of that time moving our flags on his map of North Africa.

"I wish the British would win a few battles," he commented as we sat in the living room. "Now they are spread out all over the desert. Why can't they concentrate their forces and fight as a unit like the Germans?"

Mrs. Houghton looked up from her knitting.

"I had a letter from home today," she said, "and rationing is very severe. Few eggs, a little milk and a tiny bit of tea. We must pack another box. Mother looks forward to them so much."

"What do you know about French?" I asked. "This stuff is hard. All those irregular verbs, I can't get them." I sat at the table with my homework.

"Oh, Doc, I don't know any French except, Voulez vous m'embracer, ma cherie."

"What does that mean?"

"Will you embrace me. That's my sole knowledge of French," she said laughing. "I'm supposed to have a good accent."

"That won't help," I replied. "I have to translate these sentences."

"Get the goodness out of the dictionary we bought you. It cost enough to have everything in it." Mr. Houghton looked up from pinning our flags to his map.

"Madame likes it perfect," I replied, "letters, accents and all. I'll ask Mrs. Taliaferro."

I rang her on the telephone, and we did my French homework together. She spoke it fluently and explained the verbs. I felt delighted.

Mrs. Taliaferro invited me up to Alder's Point the following afternoon and showed me some beautiful books on Paris written in French which she read aloud to me. I translated it as best I could into English. Paris looked beautiful all wide streets and circles. It possessed fascinating buildings and gardens. I was enchanted. I hated the Germans even more for occupying it, but felt sure one day I would visit it when Paris was once again free.

"This is the Abbey of San Michelle," Mrs. Talliaferro showed me a most wonderful photograph of an Abbey surrounded by water. "It was here William the Conqueror stayed the night before he invaded England in 1066. It's on the coast of Normandy across the Channel from the Island of Jersey."

I was haunted by that picture with its medieval Abbey, part fortress and part monastery, built on a rock in the sea. I dreamt of knights in armor and monks in cowls all mixed up together. I also learned my French.

Another evening Mrs. Taliaferro read part of William James' Mont San Michele and Chartres, and I was enchanted I couldn't wait to see France.

"Now that's a good reason to learn French," Mrs. Taliaferro told me. "Some day you'll travel and see these places. Some day when this war is over."

"Oh yes, I shall go on the first boat when tourists are able to go again," I struggled on with my French with a new determination.

Mrs. Houghton helped with math and history. She was an expert on the War Between the States. Mr. Houghton and I did sums with chicken and egg money. We added and subtracted the cost of feed to see how much profit we made. Somehow this all made perfect sense. I could never get gallons of water flowing in and out a hole in a tub at such a rate per minute the math book told about. No one would put water in a leaking tub. So everything was translated into chickens and my grades improved.

Education

"Now Jackie and Lady are all expenses. Billy is expenses and work. Jackie is all trouble letting the horses out, cutting up the grass and eating up the flowers. He's hopeless. Forget about the horses and concentrate on chickens. They make a profit."

If a hundred baby chicks cost $75.00 and growing mash is $3.00 a hundred weight, and corn scratch is $5.00 then we can figure how much it will cost a month to grain a hundred chickens. It takes about six months to make a layer and bout three to make a broiler. We turn profits on broilers more quickly than on layers.

Apples and oranges were turned into chickens and their expenses and slowly I got the hang of algebra. I don't think Mr. Houghton knew a lot about it, but he knew how to figure profit and loss down to the last penny. The chickens didn't get away with much margin, and I learned a lot about the business. My education advanced slowly and successfully under this method. I was not a brilliant scholar, but if I found something interesting I pursued it. Mrs. Taliaferro opened my eyes to a different world with her stories of Virginia and her picture books of France.

Emma Craddock allowed me to browse in her library. She had books of all sorts. I especially liked the ones on horses and places in Virginia. I also borrowed some books for Mrs. Houghton on the War Between the States. Cary gave me books on fox hunting with wonderful old prints. These I studied in detail.

"These pictures are great," I exclaimed excited by such treasure as we browsed in the library one day after school.

"These are also some horse stores and some novels," Cary handed me an old leather bound volume. "There are some dirty ones by D. H. Lawrence which Mom reads."

"I don't think Miss Emma reads dirty books. Really Cary stop teasing."

"She does, you know, late at night when nobody can see her," he replied.

He pushed the stool to a certain shelf high up which he swore contained terribly dirty books. "They are strictly forbidden," he said.

He pulled down a volume by Robert Louis Stevenson entitled, *The Black Arrow*, and we sat together on the library floor and read it aloud to each other. He read one chapter and I read the next. Miss Emma found us there when she called Cary to supper. Together we read *Robin Hood*, *Kidnapped*, and *Treasure Island*.

"You do spend a lot of time at Cary's house," Mr. Houghton told me one snowy evening as I walked home. "What are you doing that's so interesting?"

"Reading books. It's too cold and wet to ride Lady and Killybegs, so we read books together." I'm not sure he believed me.

One afternoon when we finished *Robin Hood* Cary said in a soft voice, "I shall join the Army Air Corps when I graduate in another year. We shall get into this war, and I plan to be a part of it. I've not told Mom yet so keep it quiet."

"Aren't you afraid?" I asked him. "You might get killed."

"I don't think so."

"I'd be afraid to go fight. It would be awful."

"That's because you're a girl," he teased me. "This is a man's war."

"There are women in it too," I reminded him. Don't forget women are also brave."

"Yes, I know," he said, "But I love flying. You have to love what you're doing to be safe."

It's awful risk, Cary."

"Flying is safer than being a foot soldier."

"Oh, Cary, you frighten me. I never thought the war would touch us here in the country. I never thought it would come right up to my doorstep. I feel so helpless." I felt the tears come and prick my eyes.

"It's all right, Doc, let's finish our book. We have another whole year before I join up."

23

Bundles For Britain

My first job at war work was packing bundles for Britain. Some of my younger friends got them mixed up with bundles from heaven, but I knew the difference. During those dark, grim days when England lay almost exhausted under constant pounding from the German Luftwaffe, we began packing Bundles for Britain at the Red Cross in Manakin. Food and fuel were scarce, clothes hard to buy as every night great fleets of enemy planes bombed London and left the East End in cinders. Still the planes came, and still the British held their heads high.

Our parcels contained gloves, socks and sweaters knitted by our little Chapter on winter evenings according to special patterns. Canned goods, cigarettes and toilet articles were added and fitted like a puzzle into a tiny box. But Americans poured out their friendship and their material goods in these boxes. However, individuals were allowed only one package a month; it must be packed in a regulation box and not weigh over five pounds. No parcel could contain whiskey or more than two packs of cigarettes. Mrs. Houghton used her kitchen scales to make sure her boxes weren't an ounce too heavy.

Her mother, now an old lady in her seventies, lived in Kent near Cooling Castle. This part of England was hard hit by Hitler's air force because here the Germans dropped their leftover bombs before the planes flew back across the Channel. We followed these raids with interest, marking them on our map of Britain with a black pen. Anxiously Mrs. Houghton waited for letters from her family and we listened to Mr. Churchill on the radio. After his recent speech she had cut out an especially good picture of him from *Life Magazine* and hung it up in the kitchen above her calendar.

In early April, Tommy wrote his mother wasn't well and his youngest sister, Beatrice, had gone to live with her. But as she worked in Rochester and left early each morning and didn't return until late evening, this arrangement was not wholly satisfactory. Mrs. Philpot insisted on making the evening tea although her failing eye-sight prevented her from using the oven and their meal was often skimpy. When Beatrice complained, her mother felt offended and sulked. After several weeks of an uneasy truce things had settled down. Tommy wrote fortnightly and kept us informed how they were getting on. Concerned about her mother's failing health, Mrs. Houghton now sent her a parcel every month. I considered this great fun and usually helped to pack it.

One afternoon when I returned from school I found Mrs. Houghton seated at the kitchen table, tears streaming down her face. A letter lay open in front of her, and I recognized its English stamp.

"Mother's gravely ill in hospital," Mrs. Houghton sobbed. "I received a letter from Beatrice. Why must I be so far away? How can I possibly help?"

"We could pack a parcel," I suggested handing her the Kleenex to hide my embarrassment. "I'll be glad to stop after school tomorrow and pick up the regulation box. I could even buy some candies."

These boxes with tape and labels were sold at Woolworth's. Mrs. Houghton dabbed her eyes and blew her nose.

"What use is a six inch box?" She wondered. "I can't put my arms around it and tell it I love it." Again the tears streamed down her face.

"You can send useful things like toothpaste and handkerchiefs. And we could send fun things like chocolates," I continued, hoping the tears would stop. "We could make a list. You told me chocolate was very scarce now in England."

Mrs. Houghton wiped her eyes, and pressed her handkerchief, always made of white linen, against her mouth. Presently she rose and entered her bedroom. I followed and watched her mask her face with powder. Then she added lipstick and combed her hair. How gentle her face seemed and how kind. Her nose was, perhaps, too long, but I considered her beautiful. At fifty and no longer young, she wore what she called "dressmaker suits" with open neck blouses set off by a single strand of cultured pearls. On special occasions she wore pearl earrings to match.

"You're right, Doc," she said at last, "we can pack a parcel. Tomorrow I'll go to Richmond and shop. Can you go by White's and get a small box of chocolates?"

She handed me three dollars from her change purse. "I know they don't travel well, but Mother loves them."

"Oh, that reminds me," I remembered. "Mother's home for the week, and I'm supposed to move back to the house. Please ask her to let me stay here."

Mrs. Houghton returned to the kitchen, I followed like an expectant puppy, and noticed my case was packed and sat ready at the back door. Anxiously I waited for her to reply.

"Mr. H. and I are playing cards with the Harrises tonight," she said finally. "It's our bridge club, and you know how much Harry loves bridge. Stay with your mother, Doc; she's here only a short time and wants to see you."

I felt hurt. Usually when the Houghtons went out several times a month I stayed with Cary. I had learned to respect their social life and never asked to go with them. However, this evening was different, I didn't want to stay with Mother.

"Why can't I have a family like other people's?" I picked up my books and case knowing it was useless to argue.

Mrs. Houghton kissed me lightly on the cheek and then hugged me.

"That's a good girl," she said folding her letter and putting it back in its envelope. "Sometimes we each need to just be by ourselves. But tomorrow we'll pack our box."

Disappointed she wouldn't intervene for me with Mother I let the kitchen door slam shut. The grass felt wet and slippery as I climbed over the fence and walked slowly through the orchard towards the house. I resented Mother's intrusion each month. She always came when something exciting was about to happen and spoiled it by insisting I return home. Sometimes she stayed only for a weekend, and that was better. It wasn't as disruptive. But I wished she wouldn't come at all. Occasionally Rudy joined her, but he never remained for more than three or four days at most. His job at Lend Lease was time consuming, and ever anxious to become a success, he worked hard.

In the living room I found Mother busy talking with Mrs. Taliaferro, so I went upstairs to my own room and closed the door. I spread my books out on the bed and did my homework. Later that evening we had an uneventful supper together and afterwards Mother spent a great deal of time on the telephone. Feeling ignored I returned to my room and switched on the radio. Nothing much was on, so I finished my French translation and went to bed.

After school the next afternoon I skipped along to White's, an exotic candy shop, and bought the chocolates. Then I stopped in Woolworth's for the parcel-boxes. On the way back to school I went to the drug store and flipped through the movie magazines to pass the time until Miss Emma picked me up at four-thirty.

"Hello, Doc," she greeted me, "How's Mrs. Houghton's mother?"

"She's ill, and that's why I've got this box," I explained as we drove out of town. "I wish Cary would come over more often; we hardly ever see him."

"I'll tell him," she promised. "He's pretty busy these days. Now he's talking about joining the Air Corps."

"Cary wants to fly?" I protested. "He's not old enough."

"It doesn't seem possible, but he's eighteen in the summer, and graduates next June. He plans to join up then," she replied, her voice sounded worried. "What will I ever do without him?"

For several minutes I sat considering this. My thoughts went back to Virginia in Germany. Never would I forgive her for allowing me to help her collect lead foil from my gum and candy wrappers. How could she have involved me in her Nazi cause? Me, a true American, born and bred.

When Miss Emma stopped at Cary's school, he bounded into the back seat throwing his books and lunch box on the floor.

"Hello, Mom, I got an A on my math test!" He squeezed in next to me. "Move over, Doc, and let me in."

"That's great news," said his mother, obviously delighted. "How was the French composition I helped you with?"

"Okay, I got a B. She didn't think I covered the subject well enough." He glanced down at me. "What's wrong with you, Doc, cat's got your tongue?"

"Just thinking," I replied, as we turned into River Road. "Cary, do you know anyone who's a Nazi?"

"A Nazi? No, I don't think so," he said laughing. "Do you?"

"Virginia, Father's housekeeper. She's gone and returned to Germany to get married. Did you know she saved lead foil from candy wrappers for Hitler's re-armament? That's what bothers me."

Cary suddenly realized I was serious and looked at me quizzically. I guess he knew I wasn't telling everything about Virginia.

"What's worrying you?" he asked kindly.

I dropped my voice so that Miss Emma couldn't hear. "She got me to save it too."

"You didn't know it was for old man Hitler?"

"I did; that's what's so awful. We rolled it on a large silver ball with a lot of other wrappers. When the ball got to a certain weight, she packed it up and sent it to her brother in Germany. She told me it would be made into airplanes, but I didn't believe her."

"You've done nothing wrong. A ball of candy wrappers isn't going to help Hitler much," he reassured me.

"I don't know; I wish I could be sure. Besides, Father says there're good Germans and bad ones, and I mustn't confuse them. Colonel Kepler is a good German and so are those Jewish refugees who opened the new deli. And even though I don't like them, I guess Rudy's family can be considered good, since they're against the war. But Virginia's a bad German, yet she baked wonderful cookies. It's hard to distinguish the differences."

"And now we're having trouble with the Japanese. They're taking their ships into the Gulf of Siam and causing trouble in the Far East. I hope we don't go to war with them," Cary observed.

"I like things black and white, not all this fuzzy stuff in between. You don't know what to think."

I pulled Cary's head towards me and whispered into his ear.

"Father helped her too. He gave her money for her passage home. Can you believe it? Considering his position and all. But he felt she should go home where her loyalties lay."

"He's right too," Cary looked at me, a fierce expression on his face.

"We don't need any Fifth Column Germans hanging around causing trouble. Stop worrying, Doc, let's play tic, tack, toe." Then considering the discussion closed, he took a page from his notebook and drew the box.

Once home I scampered across the field and arrived breathless at Mrs. Houghton's kitchen door.

"I've got the dark ones you like," I gasped, holding out the box of chocolates for Mrs. Houghton's approval.

I opened my parcel and showed her the candy, the regulation boxes, tape and labels and a small book of poetry I thought her brother, Tommy would like.

"It cost a whole dollar," I told her pleased with my purchases. "I saved the money for weeks to get it. I hope Tommy likes poetry."

24

Preparations

Winter finally gave way to Spring. The farmers no longer burnt their crops, but sent them off to Britain on the Lend-Lease Plan: Buy now; pay after the war. Tommy Philpot wrote he had used the concentrated orange juice, the powdered eggs and milk.

"He claims they're not too bad," Mrs. Houghton assured me. "But I don't fancy them."

President Roosevelt took office again after defeating Wendell Willkie, and the defense of the nation became his primary concern. In Newport News, the ship yards wanted more men after being awarded new government contracts and several local people went down to apply for jobs. But this up-swing in the economy didn't hide the average American's increasing alarm as we edged ever closer to war.

"Things look terrible," remarked Mr. Houghton one evening. "Japan's at war with China, and threatening to close the Burma Road. Congress has appropriated funds for 200 warships and a whole fleet of planes. I'm too old to work in the ship yards; all I know is farming."

He fussed at Peggy for getting on his lap, then fussed about his slippers which had got lost under his bed. Anxiously he paced through the house looking for them, ending his search in the kitchen where he banged open all the closets.

"For heavens sake, Harry, get settled. What's wrong with you?" his wife complained.

I'll tell you, Clara, I'll tell you what's eating me. I'm too old to fight those devils. I'd go back to Canada and join up if I weren't too old. Between the Japs and the Germans this world's getting blasted to kingdom come."

"Harry, you did your bit in the last war; isn't that enough?" Mrs. Houghton picked up his fallen newspaper and sat down again.

"And besides you've got me to take care of and all those chickens," I added, watching his restless progress through the house with interest while pretending to study at the table.

"I don't care a tinker's damn about chickens. I want to raise cattle; that's what I know. I'm just an old crock, and who wants old crocks anyway?" His voice sounded close to desperation.

"We need people on the home front. I hear there's gong to be airplane spotting. Why don't you call Jean Taliaferro about it? She's signing people up," I suggested.

Finding his slippers at last, he complained, "I need a new pair; these are worn out." He sat down and picked up his paper. "What's this about airplane spotting? What do you do?"

"Just sit in a spotter's box with a stove and a telephone and report the airplanes to Richmond."

"Who do I get onto?"

"Civil Defense, Jean said. She's got the information because she spoke to Mr. Henley about it the other day at the store. But since he knows nothing about enemy planes he wasn't especially interested," I told him.

"That's a good idea; now I'll get onto Jean in the morning and find out. That's something you can do," his wife sounded pleased.

Mr. Houghton thought it over a minute. I could tell he wasn't sure about it, and perhaps was studying in his mind the differences between German Stukkas and Meserschmidts, and British Spitfires and Hurricanes. I didn't believe he'd find many of those. Still he sat quietly for several minutes, and Peggy cautiously crept back onto his lap.

"I'll ring her in the morning," he said finally and putting on his glasses took up his paper.

A few days later Mr. Houghton became a registered Airplane Spotter and went out two days a week for the afternoon to take up his position in the little box near Henley's store. He was soon disappointed not to see anything more exciting than a few American planes he didn't know the names of. So he bought a pamphlet and studied our aircraft. I considered the best thing about the job was his armband which said CIVIL DEFENSE in large white letters.

Mr. Houghton's happiness was short lived when his car began to give him trouble. After trying to get it repaired without much success, he decided he needed a newer model.

"I'll just have to buy a secondhand one, that's all," he told us one night. "My Chevy is ten years old and parts are hard to find. I hate to put out the money, and this car is such an improvement over our old 1928 Essex I don't want to sell it. Look at the goodness that's in her."

He was fairly dancing around the kitchen trying to avoid Mrs. Houghton's sudden movements from the stove to the table.

"For heaven's sake, get out of my way. How much does a new one cost?" she said trying to serve our dinner.

"I don't know. Different prices, but if we buy a car there goes our savings."

"Maybe this car will last, why wouldn't it?" she barked.

Mr. Houghton banged his fist on the table, making me jump.

"Don't ask stupid questions. How am I supposed to know? Really, Clara, you'd think I was made of money."

"Doc, get your books off the table and come help." Mrs. Houghton side-stepped her husband and brought in our plates. "Find the mats and silver, I'm ready to serve."

Mr. Houghton slipped his feet into his broken slippers and entered the dining room. Peggy followed and eyed us hopefully as we took our places. After he carved the small roast and filled three plates, we helped ourselves to vegetables, then bread and butter.

"But maybe my old car won't make it. But, again, maybe she will. What do you think?"

"Well, go have a look. Perhaps you can find something you like better, if it's not too dear." Mrs. Houghton said no more about it.

"I wish I could go to Washington to visit Father. He's living there now, you know," I commented.

"You can't go up without your grandmother," Mrs. Houghton replied.

"But it's only a hundred miles, and I'd be fine by myself." Then I had an idea, "Why doesn't' he come and see me?"

Mrs. Houghton looked doubtful, but Mr. Houghton appeared delighted.

"That's a great idea," he said, "We'll arrange it."

"And what will her mother say if she finds out?" Mrs. Houghton wanted to know.

"She doesn't have to find out. You wouldn't tell her. I'll write Frances and ask them to come for a weekend. That would be really great. I'd love it." In my excitement I stood up and beat the table.

Mr. Houghton laughed. And Mrs. Houghton joined in.

"Sit now, and finish your dinner. Perhaps we can arrange it. Of course they'd have to stay in town. And come out here to see you. We could work it out, couldn't we, Clara? It might be nearly the last time you'll get to see him, and it is such a short distance to Washington."

I sat there amazed they would agree to such a deception.

Like conspirators we worked out our plans. Only Mr. Harris was taken into our confidence so he could arrange the hotel in town. But Mary Ann became suspicious when I declined her overnight invitation. Luckily Cary and Emma Craddock planned to go away that weekend.

On a Friday evening in early April, just after my birthday, Father and Frances arrived by train from Washington. Mr. Houghton met them. Apologizing for his old Chevy, he drove them first to the hotel and then out to the country. Unable to contain my excitement, I ran down the road to meet them waving my arms and crying at the top my lungs.

"Welcome home, welcome home."

Father leapt from the car and took me in his arms. He was crying. Gently he put me down and surveyed the farm that had once been his home. He didn't say anything, but together we walked up the drive just the two of us like old times. Finally he spoke.

"The Houghtons could get into real trouble for allowing me to come here."

"I know, but they won't. We've planned it ever so well. Only Mr. Harris knows and in town it won't matter who sees you. You could be here on business," I replied, feeling for the first time since he left, I belonged.

"How I've missed you, and this place. I sold Cherry, you know. Doug Fraiser bought him. On occasion Doug comes to Washington, and

Preparations

we have lunch together. I've met Colonel Hollis recently. He came up to see about joining the Canadian air force. But there're other friends I don't hear from at all."

We strolled hand in hand across the lawn towards the barn. I showed him the new Christmas horse, Lady, Jackie, the donkey and Billy whom I still rode occasionally.

"It's very much the same," I reassured him. "Like it was when you lived here."

"Rudy's made few changes, then?"

"He's not here enough. He comes on holidays, but rarely when Mother comes once a month. He's not really interested in the farm or in me. Oh, it's so wonderful to have you here."

Mrs. Houghton made a special dinner, and we all stuffed ourselves. Frances, ever gracious, helped with the dishes, and all too soon Mr. Houghton drove them back into town. Saturday I was to go with them to the Fraisers. We planned to spend the day, and give the Houghtons plenty of time to look at a new car.

"He's not sure he wants one, now," Mrs. Houghton confided as we got ready for bed. "He thinks they're too expensive."

For a week this conversation had gone around and round. They had consulted friends, neighbors and finally the car dealers. But nothing satisfied them. At last, Mr. and Mrs. Harris had arranged to drive them down near Petersburg to see a friend of theirs who had a car for sale. Father and Frances planned to take us all out for dinner at Bert's Place, some restaurant where Mr. Houghton knew the owner who arranged for a private room. That way we wouldn't be discovered, and Mr. Harris could bring us home.

It worked like a charm. The day at the Fraiser's was great. I hadn't seen them for almost three years, but they welcomed me and made me feel at home. Frances and Father enjoyed themselves. It was her first time in Virginia and Father was anxious for his friends to know her. Jenny Fraiser and I played in the hayloft, rode her ponies, and finally we ended up in the shower being scrubbed within an inch of our lives. At six o'clock we drove to town with Doug Fraiser to meet the Houghtons. Mr. Harris was a few minutes late, but we found our private room and had a drink while we waited. Then Doug Fraiser excused himself and went home. Mrs. Harris had made me a pink birthday cake, and brought candles, party hats and crackers to help me celebrate. Mr. Houghton stood up to make a toast.

"We've decided to keep our old car," he announced amid cheers. "All I can do now is hope she'll get us through this war."

"We found nothing better," confided Mr. Harris. "Harry's taken such good care of her that she's hard to beat."

Father laughed, his great roar of a laugh. Mrs. Houghton ordered a champagne cocktail and offered me a sip.

"It's not very good," I objected, tasting it.

"It's lovely, Doc, and such a treat," she exclaimed. "Happy Birthday."

"Thank you for bringing Father home. It's not the same seeing him in Philadelphia. He belongs here."

Then I remembered Frances. I felt sorry for her because she wasn't a part of Father's life in Virginia. She belonged in Father's new life up North. Getting up from my chair I went over to her and put my arms around her.

"It's all right," I said gently; "we love you too."

She must have felt touched by my impulsive gestured because she showed me real affection.

Sunday passed off pleasantly without church but with a big Sunday lunch at the Houghtons'. Finally at three o'clock Mr. Houghton drove Father and Frances to the train.

At the station Father bent down to kiss me. "Goodbye, Son," he said softly. Then, seeming overwhelmed by emotion, he mounted the train.

Frances waved, and then they were gone. My special birthday was over. Nobody ever knew of their visit, or if they did, they never told.

25

Rommel Again

On Good Friday, April 11, Rommel attacked with probing thrusts. The garrison at Tobruk was manned by the 9th Australian division under General Morshead. It had returned safely from the Benghazi area. The 18th Infantry Brigade (7th Australian Division) arrived by sea and was followed by a detachment of a British Tank Regiment. This and a Polish Regiment made up the defenders of Tobruk.

Mr. Houghton's nephew, Andrew, was in the 9th Australian. So the Battle of Tobruk became for us a major concern. After Mr. Houghton bought the new map, I made a whole candy box full of flags: black ones for the Germans, blue ones for the British, red ones for the Australians and yellow ones for the Poles. Even Mrs. Houghton admired our maps.

On Easter Monday, April 14th, a holiday, the main German attack came. It broke through the British and Australian lines and drove two miles to the north where it was stopped by Allied artillery. The Italians attacked on the 16th, but this fizzled out when the Australians counter attacked. Nearly a thousand Italian prisoners were taken.

"I knew those Italians couldn't fight worth a tinker's darn," Mr. Houghton commented. "But that Rommel is dangerous. He'll give you nightmares."

On April 30th, a new assault was mounted on Tobruk by the German 15th Panzer Division which reinforced the 5th Light Infantry Division. By daylight of May 1st the German infantry made a breach a mile wide in the British Defenses and Rommel's tanks threatened Tobruk. A minefield suddenly stopped the Germans after some tanks blew up. Then British tanks counter attacked. At Tobruk the Australians put up a stiff resistance and knocked out some more of Rommel's tanks. The Germans took some ground but they couldn't capture Tobruk. The garrison held. The British General Wavell tried to relieve the port and the fortress, but could not reach it. We cheered for the brave Australians and Mr. Houghton took us out to dinner to celebrate his nephew's victorious division.

Our rejoicing was short lived. On May 26th the 15th Panzer Division of General Cruewell was on the move. These troops were veterans of the French Foreign Legion, and although ill-disciplined, they proved great warriors. Rommel turned south and by marching through the night surfaced on the British rear. At 6:30 the 3rd Indian Motor Brigade was attacked by the Ariete, the best of the Italian divisions, plus part of the 21st Panzer Division. The Indian regiment was overwhelmed. Next the 7th Motor Brigade was taken by surprise and the Germans broke through. The British Brigadier Rentor saved some of his troops and went to Bir el Gubi to find part of the garrison on leave in Tobruk. He had not enough men to fire his guns. Suddenly the German 4th Armored Division attacked. It defeated the 8th British Hussars, and almost completely destroyed them.

Rommel was knocking on the door of British –controlled Egypt. Beyond that was Palestine, also in British hands. Beyond these was Middle Eastern oil. Its control was vital to the war. The Germans must be stopped.

Secretly Mr. Houghton and I admired Rommel. He was so unpredictable and his tactics and strategy reminded us of Stonewall Jackson who was a hero of ours. We felt like conspirators, or worse yet spies. We knew it was wrong, but we found Rommel fascinating.

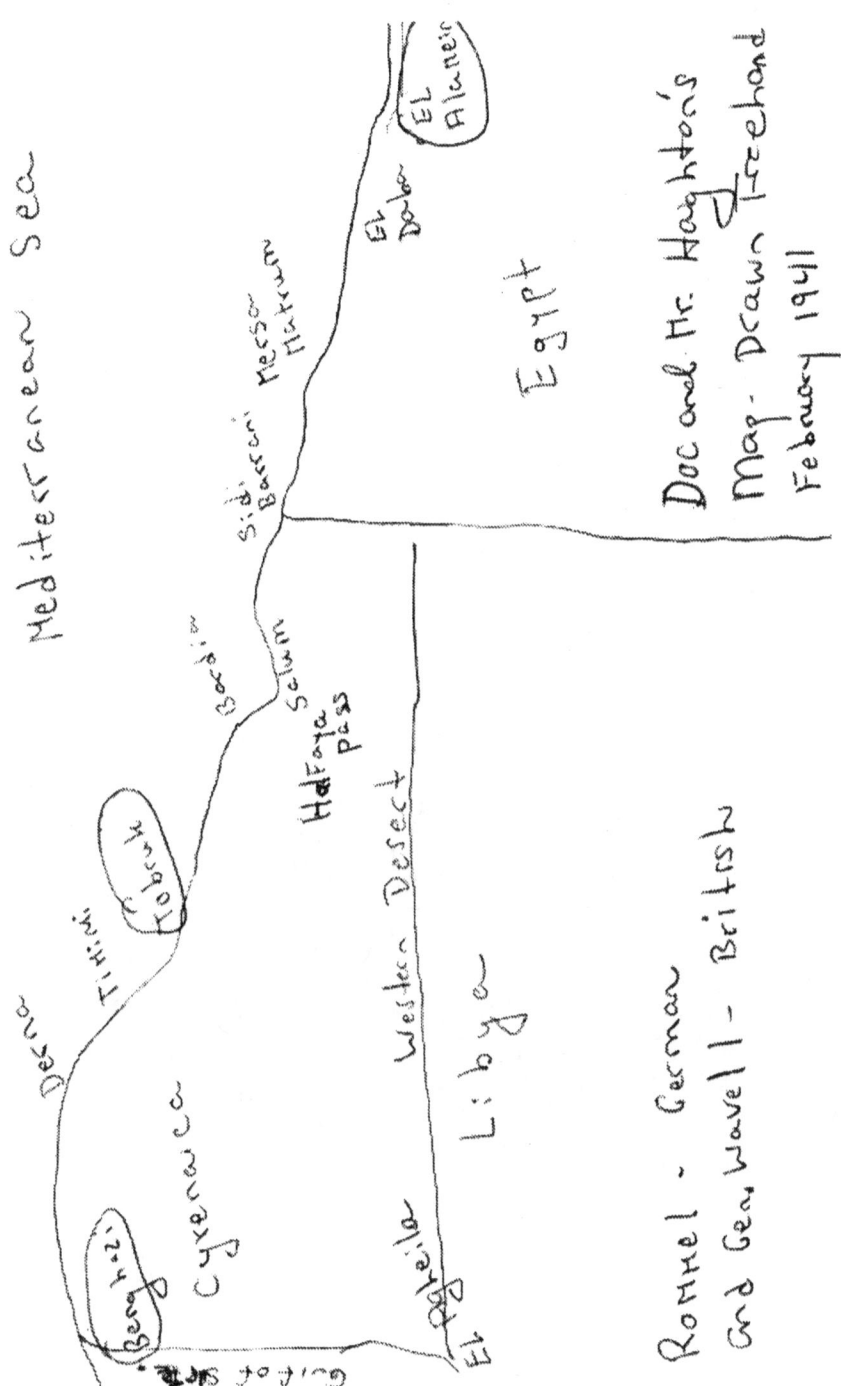

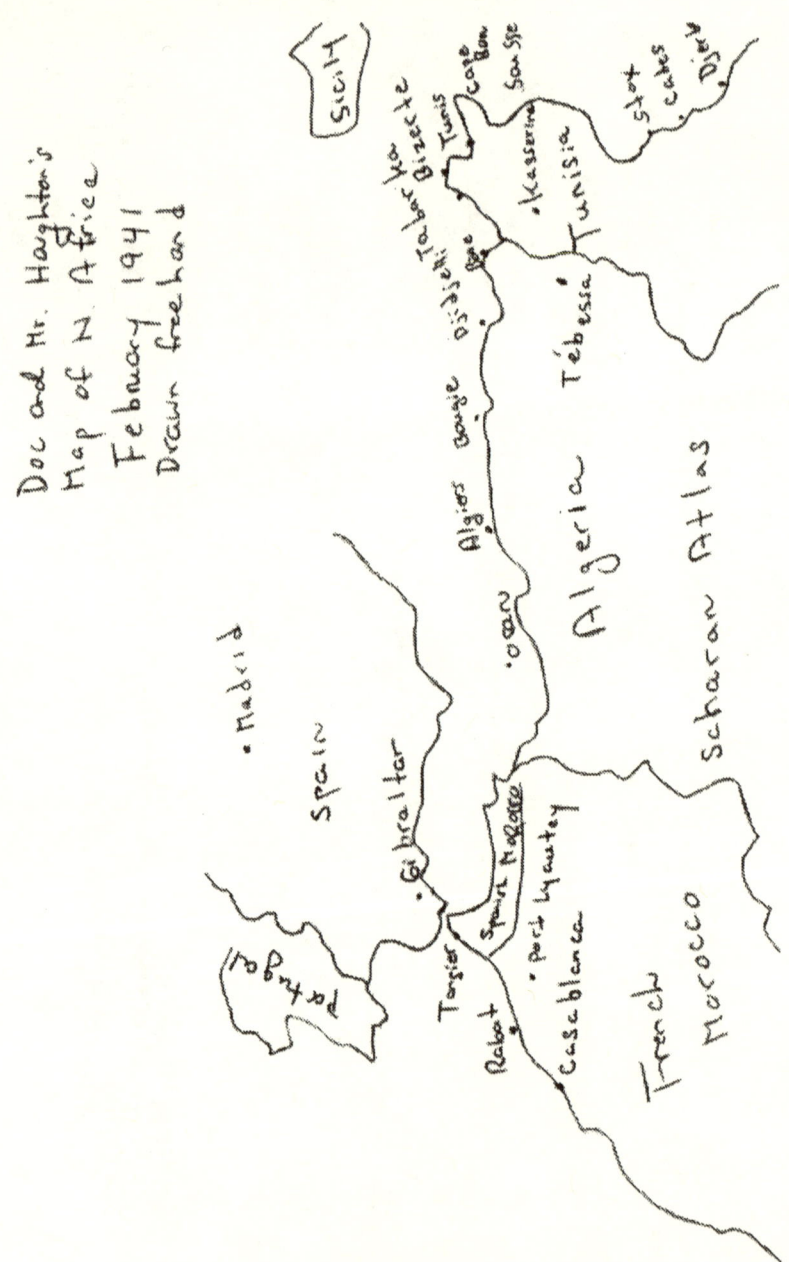

Rommel Again

Letters

April 20, 1941
Washington, D.C.

Dear Doc,

What a grand visit we had! And at thirteen you are quite a young lady. Never Mind Mrs. Owen's predictions; you'll make it.

A new man has appeared on the world scene. This Erwin Rommel is beating the pants off the British in Africa. He attacks and hangs on with his Afrika Korp of Germans and Italians like grim death. He has taken Cyrenaica with the exception of Tobruk on the coast. Bengahazi has been evacuated. What an impressive sort of guy. I must admit of course the importance of Africa depends upon the Suez Canal, and its access to the Persian Gulf. And beyond it the oil fields of Iraq and the Arab States. With the large shipping losses the Canal is closed, but it must remain in Allied hands. Keep your eye on that bird Rommel; he's going to make things hot for a while.

It was wonderful seeing you and being at home again. What kind friends the Houghtons are!

Love, Dad.

He also sent Mrs. Houghton a note and sent her a large box of dark chocolates, the kind she likes best. But I ate some too and so did Mr. Houghton. Shortly after their arrival I sat down and wrote him.

May 7, 1941
Richmond, Va.

Dear Dad,

Thank you for the lovely chocolates. We all enjoyed them.

Mr. Houghton agrees with you about Rommel. He's playing havoc. We've got our eyes on Tobruk. The Australians defending it are like Americans, full of grit. Look at the way they repulsed Rommel's recent attack. Mr. Houghton's nephew is with the 9th Australian and is in Tobruk. He went out to New South Wales about ten years ago and joined up out there. Mr. Houghton's made a large map with flags on it and we hung it up in the kitchen. Every evening we move the flags around and that's how we follow the war. Yesterday I cut out twenty new flags and Mrs. Houghton put pins in them. How colorful our map looks when we mark the battles.

Have you ever heard of such funny names? How do you pronounce Rezegh or Gobrsaleh? I can't pronounce them, and neither can Mr. Houghton. So we make up our own names and call them Rezi and Gooloosh. What a strange kind of war with first the British capturing a town and the Germans getting it back the next day. But this Rommel's a hard-hitting guy. I want the war to end and allow things to get back to normal. And I wish you could come see me again.

Love, Doc

P.S. Mrs. Owens wouldn't approve of the word "guy." She says it's vulgar and ladies don't use it. She doesn't approve of slang either. So you see why I'm always in trouble.

26

The Importance of Bills

That spring one of the teachers at Monument School announced her engagement to Bill Lennox. She came into class one day and showed off her ring. It was a great diamond set with smaller diamonds clustered around it.

"It's simply gorgeous," gasped Mary Ann who always loved beautiful things. "When's the big day?"

"That remains to be seen," Miss Allen told us beaming.

"How exciting," we all agreed. "Will you invite us?"

"Why, of course," said Miss Allen, pleased as a peacock that we admired her ring.

One of the senior girls also had a boy friend named Bill. She talked about him all the time in the lunchroom. Bill this and Bill that, until I got tired of listening. Then in Biology class we heard more about Miss Allen's Bill.

"He's so very handsome," she told us, "really lovely to look at. We went to a party last week and he wore tails. It was really super to see him in such elegant clothes."

At first I enjoyed hearing about Miss Allen's beau. She was so in love that she seemed to sparkle with happiness. She made her classes fun, and kept us busy dissecting earth worms and frogs. When we were engrossed in our work, she described her wedding dress.

"How simply beautiful!" cooed Sara Timmons. "It's exciting to think of wearing such a dress. And the veil, tell us about the veil."

"It's French lace. It's very old because it once belonged to my great grandmother. It falls from a lace cap and comes down to my toes."

"Tell us more about your dress. Is it satin or tulle?" Mary Ann wanted to know.

"Satin, of course, antique white. It belonged to both my grandmother and mother. I thought I would never get into it, but I've lost some weight so I can."

Finally I grew tired of these wedding plans. The senior girl, Florence Crouse, simply never let up about her Bill. I felt there must be other things to talk about.

"Really," I confided to Mary Ann, "I am sick to death of hearing about Bills."

"Yes," she quipped, "Miss Allen and Florence are the only people who like to see Bills come at any time during the month."

"It was all very exciting at first, but now I am thinking about the summer holidays and what we'll do."

"What will you do?" my friend asked as we walked to her house from school one afternoon. "I guess I'll go down to the beach for a couple of weeks."

"We usually go away," I told her. "But until then I'll probably help Mr. Houghton with his chicken business. It gives me extra pocket money."

"Oh, that's good." I could tell city-bred Mary Ann was not in the least interested in the chicken business. "I'm sure it helps the war effort."

"You know, I've decided," I confessed as we stopped for the red light on Park Avenue, "I've decided if ever I have a boy friend, he should be called Maxim, like Maximillian in the movie, Rebecca. And he shall look just like Laurence Olivier. None of this plain Bill stuff for me."

I agree; we can do better than that," Mary Anne crossed the street. "My husband's going to have a more patrician-sounding name than Bill."

"Patrician?" I questioned her.

"You know, opposite from plebeian in Roman History. The patricians were the rich nobles and important people. The plebeians were the poor folks." She explained.

"Why must you use such big words? Really, you do like to show off."

"I believe in building my vocabulary. As the headmistress says, 'a word to the wise is sufficient.'"

The Importance of Bills

"That's not what she means, silly. She's talking about getting our home work done and handing it in on time. You talk like a professor."

"That's better than being a hick from the country."

"Touche," I replied. In English class we had just finished reading *Cyrano de Bergerac*.

In June after school let out, we all went to Miss Allen's wedding. It was held at St. Andrew's Episcopal Church in Westhampton. We all agreed she looked simply gorgeous in her grandmother's gown. It was a really elegant occasion. We attended the reception at the Country Club, and stuffed ourselves with goodies.

"Don't tell mother we broke into the receiving line," I warned Mary Ann. "She'll skin me. She's always on me about my bad deportment, and my dirty finger nails."

"Let's sample some of the champagne," Mary Ann suggested.

"That's terribly daring. Will they give us some?"

I followed Mary Ann who deftly, with great sophistication, picked up two glasses filled with white bubbling wine.

"Here," she said, "try this."

"Should we?" I giggled. "The fizz tickles my nose."

Mary Ann found a table, sat down, crossed her legs and tried to look twenty-one. Sarah Timmons, Frances Jones and Flurry Cartwright joined us.

"What are you drinking?" Sarah asked, regarding our wine with interest.

"Champagne, of course," Mary Ann replied. "Everyone drinks champagne at a wedding."

"Really? Do you think we should?" Frances looked uncertain.

"Why not? Go get yourselves some."

Frances found a waiter, selected three glasses and offered them to Sarah and Flurry. Then the girls sat down, crossed their legs in what they considered a sophisticated pose and tentatively sipped their wine.

"It tastes good," said Frances. "I like it."

"I don't," coughed Sarah, putting her glass down. "But I'll drink a little just to say I had champagne."

"Oh, what fun," giggled Flurry, sampling her glass. "After all, we are thirteen. We're really adults and will enter eighth grade in the fall.

It's grown up to try new things, don't you think?"

"Yes," we agreed, then slowly, steadily finished our glasses.

The dancing began as the groom with his new bride stepped out onto the floor. The band struck up a Tommy Dorsey tune. Couples, one by one at first and then several joined in.

"Come on, Flurry," said Mary Ann. "You're a good dancer. Let's try it." And away they whirled around the floor.

The champagne gave Sarah the hiccups. She coughed and hiccupped and coughed again.

"Go get another glass of champagne," Frances suggested. "It might help."

"Do you think she should?" I asked. "I hear champagne is very potent."

"That stuff! Don't be silly, Doc," Frances chastised me. "It will do her good."

I was not so sure. But Frances insisted and brought Sarah a second glass. Meanwhile, Mary Ann and Flurry came waltzing back towards us.

"Change partners; come on Doc," Mary Ann grabbed me as Flurry took Frances.

We went swirling around the dance floor - first doing the waltz, then the polka. I loved to polka. Heel and toe and away we go. We galloped up and down the floor, bumping into each other and giggling.

"Now it's Sarah's turn. Come on; put that glass down. Let's dance."

Mary Ann went off dragging a reluctant Sarah and together they started to jitterbug. The music changed to a Glenn Miller tune and I watched the girls go around the floor at a fox trot.

"Oh, no," gasped Flurry. "Oh, no," she repeated.

Frances gave a startled squeal and dashed towards Sarah. They were best friends. Clinging to Mary Ann in a desperate effort to stand upright, Sara looked decidedly drunk. We gathered around her and supporting her between us, we slipped quickly into the ladies room.

"We need some coffee," Mary Ann ordered, making sure I understood. "You heard me. Now go."

I fled. Nor did I look around until I found a waiter and asked him as politely as I could in the circumstances for a pot of black coffee and

The Importance of Bills

some cups.

"Cups?" he asked.

"Yes, please. Five." I repeated, "and plenty of coffee. I'll wait for it here."

A few minutes later he brought the coffee, and the check. I had not thought about paying for it – just getting it. In haste I signed Mary Ann's mother's name and prayed I would not get into trouble. Then carrying the tray before me, I skidded over the waxed floors towards the ladies' room.

"She's sick," Mary Ann announced when I reappeared. "Pour out the coffee for the rest of us."

"I signed your mother's name," I told her.

"Why not your own mother's?" she demanded.

"Because she knows I don't drink coffee. And a pot for five would be very difficult to explain."

We drank several cups of black coffee, and forced a cup, laced with plenty of cream, down Sarah. She looked ghastly, her face white, her dress spotted. But she seemed more like herself, and I felt less worried.

After an hour, still supporting her, we rejoined the party.

"Oh goodness," said Mary Ann, "I forgot. Mints."

"Mints?" I asked. "Whatever for?"

"To get rid of the smell," she explained.

"But do they really help?" Frances asked.

"Yes," Mary Ann sounded very sure. "We all must eat some. Or else parsley."

"There's not much hope in finding parsley here," Flurry looked doubtfully about the ballroom. "Let's try the mints."

So we stuffed ourselves with peppermints, even Sarah.

With after dinner mints, and some more hors-d'oeuvres, we hoped our secret would not be discovered. When our mothers arrived Sarah at least seemed her old self. Mary Ann, sober and in command whispered, "Upon the pain of death never breathe one word."

"No," said Flurry and Frances crossing their hearts, "We'll never tell a living soul."

I wasn't so sure about Sarah's telling, but Mary Ann knew wild horses couldn't drag this out of me.

A Forgotten Landscape

27

The Pale Horseman

Hitler attacked Russia on the 21st of June and drove toward Stalengrad. England's threat of invasion was over. Mrs. Houghton wept from relief.

"It's a suicidal step," Father wrote me from Washington. "Hitler's made a grave mistake. The Russian winter will defeat him just as it defeated Napoleon."

"Only a damn fool would invade Russia," Mr. Houghton agreed. "At least England gets a breather. The Missus is greatly relieved."

"If Hitler thinks he's broken the English spirit, he's wrong. Our people are stubborn and don't know when they are defeated," Mrs. Houghton told me. "Let the Germans invade Russia. They will never defeat her."

We sat in the living room with two fans running and listened to the radio. H. V. Kaltenborne's news program was Mrs. Houghton's favourite while Mr. Houghton preferred the B.B.C. or Bob Trout. Then we listened to "Fibber McGee and Molly" and "Mr. Keen, The Tracer of Lost Persons." Mr. Houghton also liked the soap opera, "The Romance of Helen Trent," who could find love after thirty-five.

"Thirty-five!" I said, "How is someone that old going to find a man?"

"It's not that ancient," Mr. Houghton told me, "at thirty-five you're just starting to live."

That summer I collected cotton feed-bags to make tea towels, and Mrs. Houghton set me to work knitting socks for the Red Cross. She also taught me how to hem the towels which we put in our Bundles for Britain boxes.

"I hate all this sewing and knitting," I complained to Mary Ann when she came out for the weekend. "I have to knit a pair of socks a month."

She and I ran through the garden hose to cool off. I'd attached it to the largest sprinkler I could find so the garden would get watered too.

"You work all the time," Mary Ann said, her bathing suit wet and her brown hair soaked. "You're always busy."

"Yes," I agreed, "but that's life in the country."

She invited me to stay with her in town. We always ended up shopping and meeting boys at the drug store of which Mrs. Houghton disapproved. She didn't like my hanging around the drug store on Park Avenue or spending money down town. So Mary Ann came out to us more often.

"We buy groceries once a week, and that's enough. You don't need to shop for entertainment," Mrs. Houghton told me.

Mary Ann and I had to find other ways to amuse ourselves. We visited the Virginia Museum and rediscovered Battle Abbey and the Confederate Museum. We soon learned our way around Richmond and felt very independent.

All this freedom suddenly came to an end when Ida Jubert, who lived in Goochland, came down with polio. She'd been swimming in the local pool which was immediately closed and drained. Now we swam under the sprinkler.

"Town's boring," Mary Ann said as we dried off. "We can't play tennis or swim anymore."

"We still go to the movies once a week, but we only eat out in certain places where Mr. Houghton knows the owner. He thinks polio comes from food that's been left out for flies to get at. The Houghtons still play bridge, and I go to Cary's house and to Henley's store. We hope to go up to Afton Mountain soon."

"Mother's canceled our trip to the beach. She wants to visit her friend in Washington, but she's afraid to take me into a city," Mary Ann told me as we took off our wet suits. We dressed in the shed and hung our suits on the clothes line.

Mr. Houghton's car pulled up in front of the house. He got out and went inside directly without stopping to speak to us. We followed.

"Something's up," I told Mary Ann, "he's going to tell the Missus."

"Clara, Clara," Mr. Houghton called, "Where are you?"

Mrs. Houghton appeared from her bedroom.

"I just heard at the store that Ida Jubert died yesterday, and two more polio cases have been reported in Richmond."

"Who told you this?" his wife replied.

"Alvira Carthage, of course. She knows everything, that woman. But it's true. Mrs. Henley heard it on the radio."

"We'll have to go to Afton as soon as possible and get out of this heat." Mrs. Houghton looked at Mary Ann and me. "Stay inside and we'll have some cooking lessons. You might as well learn something worth while. It's too hot to be out. You can plan dinner tonight and set the table correctly; we'll make it look like Lady Crystal's for whom I worked in London."

She chased us into the bathroom to gargle with salt water and to wash our hands.

"I hate polio season," Mary Ann complained; "my hands always end up raw."

We planned our evening meal. When the sun dropped low in the sky Mrs. Houghton allowed us to enter the kitchen. She turned on a rotary fan and set us to work making an apple pie. We peeled the apples and measured out sugar, butter and cinnamon while she made the crust. Finally as the sun sank below the trees, we turned on the oven.

I usually make pies in the early morning when it's cooler. We'll just have to manage." She told us.

We sliced garden tomatoes and onions and celery to make a salad. Then we sliced cold meat and heated a few peas left over from yesterday. She made hot tea for herself and Mr. Houghton and iced tea for Mary Ann and me. Finally everything was ready.

"You'll have to come more often, Mary Ann, so that I can feast like this every day," Mr. Houghton teased.

"Mother will probably insist I get out of the city if there's going to be polio. It's scary when we have an epidemic." She helped Mr. Houghton to seconds. "No one knows how it's spread or what causes it."

"You come here anytime. With all the gargling that goes on here, polio wouldn't dare show its face," Mr. Houghton assured her.

We continued with our usual weekly shopping trips and going to the movies. We now ate at a friend's house and avoided restaurants. Several private pools were closed and drained. Mrs. Houghton didn't want me to go to the store because she was afraid other children might pass polio on to me there, but Mr. Houghton took me anyway.

"You can't lock her up in jail. The girl's got to have a social life. She's only Cary around here, and he and Miss Emma are away. It's terribly lonely." He protested.

"Get in touch with Mr. Harris then and find out if he can get his nephew to stay so we can go to Afton for our holiday," Mrs. Houghton commanded. "This polio scare has unnerved me. It's all Alvira Carthage can talk of these days. She told me another child died this week in Chesterfield County."

"It's the heat. We're desperate for rain," replied Mr. Houghton. "I'll get onto Tom and see what we can work out."

Mary Ann and I said nothing. We knew that there was no arguing about polio. It was the summer scourge and had to be dealt with every year. This epidemic was going to be bad and our fun would be restricted.

28

Afton Mountain

July 1941

On the first of July Mr. Houghton arranged for Mr. Harris's nephew to come and look after our animals so we could get away. Mr. Houghton preferred the mountains, and Afton had a pleasant inn that was not expensive. It also had the advantage of being less than a hundred miles from home. It took a week's preparation to get ready to leave.

First, Mr. Houghton's car had to be serviced. Then we filled four or five jugs with water for the radiator. Often it boiled over pulling the hills, and the road to Afton was straight up. Then we packed our clothes, extra boots for hiking and a long-handle-shovel as a protection against snakes.

Finally we made a picnic and filled the thermos with hot tea. Mrs. Houghton, being English, felt ice tea was sinful.

"Who ever heard of freezing a good cup of tea?" She'd ask me. "Make ice tea if you like and get another thermos from the house." Which I did.

We locked up Mother's house, or rather double locked it. Then we wrote out instructions for our "chicken sitter" about eggs and deliveries. Although Mr. Houghton had invited the young man down and gone through everything with him, nothing would do until I'd typed it all out on a long sheet of paper so he could read it clearly.

"You can never tell about handwriting," Mr. Houghton insisted. "You can very easily misread it. So I want it all typed out. Maybe then there will be no mistakes."

A second list of instructions explained how to feed the horses and let them out in the pasture at night. There were also memos about padlocks on the feed room doors for the horse barns and for the chicken house.

Finally when we felt nearly exhausted with preparations, we climbed into Mr. Houghton's old car about six o'clock on a Friday morning ready to go. Mrs. Houghton sat in the back seat as usual, and Mr. Houghton, Peggy and I sat in front. It took hours to drive to Afton. Mr. Houghton's car could not go faster than fifty miles an hour and even that he felt was dangerous. We stopped often. Peggy needed to go out or we had to cool down the radiator. We ate our picnic near Charlottesville which took us at least a half an hour. That allowed time for the radiator to cool before we climbed slowly up Route 250. Halfway up we stopped again to cool the overheated radiator and to add water. Finally after four hours of stopping and starting the car brought us to the Blue Ridge Inn. We all nearly keeled over from exhaustion.

We were surprised to find an English family staying there. Gill, Jenny and their younger brother, Hugh, were refugees. They'd come the previous year with their Nanny Grace to stay with an aunt, Miss Hilda Morrison, who lived near Washington. She had insisted they get out of England and took the family under her wing. Although unmarried with no children of her own, she knew all about raising them.

"It would be nice," she told Mrs. Houghton our first evening, "if you'd allow Doc to join us on a hike tomorrow. We shall go into the National Forest and learn something about the flora and fauna."

Bright and early the following morning we started out. Miss Hilda, as she wished to be called, was in command. We must identify three different kinds of trees and three different mosses. We were marched off with drawing materials, books of native plants, cold water and a sandwich in our knapsacks.

Miss Hilda showed us various trees, then told us to pick a leaf and draw it, label it and tell if it was a hardwood or a soft wood. We sat on the ground and did as we were told. Meanwhile Miss Hilda sat nearby sketching.

Although shy, Gill was pretty with golden hair and blue eyes. She was twelve and Jenny had just celebrated her eleventh birthday. She was anything but shy and liked to run ahead of us when we marched single file along the mountain trail. Hugh, their brother was three, and he came with Nanny Rosa only a short way before they turned back.

"Where did you live in England?" I asked.

"In Lavenham, one of the wool villages in Suffolk. It's not safe there because it's near the coast. We got a few bombs when the Germans hit Ipswich. So Auntie decided we should come to America," Gill explained.

"Do you like it here?" I didn't like asking personal questions, but felt curious about her English life.

"It's all right. I miss my parents. We have a farm and since people who grow food have priority, our father is not in the fighting. Mummy is even driving the tractor." Jenny told me. Her dark hair gleamed in the sun, her eyes were full of mischief.

"I miss my friends," Gill said, her face sad. "Our school here is very different from England. We wear uniforms, you don't. You have grades, we have forms. You play basketball, we play hockey."

"Even the spelling is different," added Jenny laughing. "You don't use o-u in favourite, colour and neighbour. We call arithmetic, maths; you call it math. We go to school in July, and you break up in June."

"Come along, girls," Miss Hilda broke in, "there's a pleasant stream here with some picnic tables. Let's have our lunch."

She selected a table and opened her knapsack. "Doc, I bought ice tea and some cookies. Would you like some?" Miss Hilda invited.

"She means biscuits," Jenny explained. "We don't use the word 'Cookie'."

"I forget," her aunt admitted as she spread a cloth on the wooden picnic table and poured out ice tea in paper cups from her large thermos. Then she set out paper plats, spoons and napkins. She offered us each a piece of chicken and sat down to enjoy her own lunch. We sat in a woodsy glade cooled by overhanging branches.

I decided after studying her that Miss Hilda must be about forty-five as her short brown hair was flecked with grey. She wore blue slacks, a white cotton blouse and hiking boots. She seemed a little overweight; yet I found her attractive. She taught science at the girls' school her nieces attended. She was definitely all spit and polish. She insisted we didn't waste time merely tramping through the forest, but that we must learn something. So she taught us about the trees, the wild flowers and the small animals we encountered. At night she organized games while the adults played bridge. In the morning, the next day she insisted I accompany them to Luray to visit the caverns. The following day she drove us to Front Royal.

"See those markers?" She pointed to several state historical signs. "They tell of Jackson's Valley Campaign."

"Like Rommel in Africa," I said without thinking. "He uses Jackson's tactics."

That's all it took. Miss Hilda drove us to Winchester, then down to Harrisonburg and over to Staunton. She showed us Lookout Mountain from where the Confederate scouts watched the Yankee troop movements. We drove over the newly constructed Skyline Drive so we could see the Shenandoah Valley below. We spent two weeks in the mountains learning history.

Mr. and Mrs. Houghton also took leisurely walks to admire the scenery and to give Peggy a run. In the evening I showed them the notebooks Miss Hilda insisted I keep, one for nature study and a second for Jackson's Valley Campaign.

"I haven't had a vacation," I complained, "just more school."

"You weren't bored anyway with a lot of old folks playing cards," Mrs. Houghton replied as we sat on the porch overlooking the mountains our last evening.

"I've not had time to visit the gift shop. I hoped to go to Penney's in Staunton to buy some socks. All of mine have holes in the heels from all this tramping through the forest." I said rocking my chair gently to create a little breeze.

Sadly the next morning we departed. Mr. Houghton filled his water jugs, the inn filled our thermoses: Mine with cold tea, Mrs. Houghton's with hot. We packed our suitcases and Peggy's basket and the long-handle-shovel and set out for Richmond.

Gill, Jenny and Miss Hilda waved us goodbye as we left the inn in Houghton's old Chevrolet.

"We better get a move on." Mr. Houghton said as we drove down Afton Mountain. "The backs of the leaves are showing, a sure sign of rain."

At home, in spite of Mr. Houghton's dire predictions we found everything in good order. No chickens died. Lindy Lou and Suzie Q. looked fat and sleek and contented. Lady, Jackie and Billy enjoyed the freedom of their pasture at night and their cooler stalls by day. They'd hardly noticed we'd been gone.

No one broke into the house or into Mr. Houghton's cottage.

"The electricity is still on," Mr. Houghton told us as he tried the lights.

"And the water pump still works," Mrs. Houghton reassured him in a teasing manner.

That night I sat on my hassock and wrote Father. "Taking everything into consideration we enjoyed our mountain vacation, but I never worked so hard in all my life."

A Forgotten Landscape

29

Mr. Houghton Fights a Fire

Summer 1941

One Saturday in early summer Tom Harris arrived in his old 1936 Chevrolet, his face and hands black, his Wellingtons burnt.

"Hello," Harry, "he called before the engine stopped, and Mr. Harris hopped out. "There is a big fire in the woods between Brown's Dairy and Tuckahoe Creek. It's jumped onto your side of River Road. Can you grab a shovel and come?"

Mr. Houghton met his friend as he walked out of the chicken house.

"Yes, just a minute until I get my long handle shovel."

I stood watching, pondering a moment before I scampered into the tool shed, found a hoe and joined the men.

"I am coming too."

"Sure, Kid, we need all the help we can get," Mr. Harris encouraged.

We crowded into the battered car with our tools and drove off down the gravel road.

At the fire line we found men from all over the county digging trenches and beating the flames with their shovels. But the undergrowth was dry; the pine woods made perfect tinder. Army trucks belonging to the National Guard lined River Road, and a light plane circled overhead. State Farm Prisoners, the only available man power under forty, were brought from their cells down to our woods.

"Stay close," Mr. Houghton commanded as we got out of the car and walked up the fire brake. "Here, take this hoe and clear the under brush."

The smoke blown by a strong wind, billowed up along the road in front of us. I wacked at the honeysuckle and brambles. All around me my neighbors worked digging a trench for the fire brake.

Suddenly Mr. Houghton stood up as if he saw something quite remarkable. Indeed he had. Our local hermit! A tiny, gray haired woman in jodhpurs had come out from behind her wall and iron gates. There she stood in front of us beating the ground with all the strength she could muster. The mysterious Mrs. Haunch was real. I could hardly believe my eyes.

"She's here," gasped Mr. Houghton. "She's alive with flesh and blood. I began to wonder if she really existed."

Mrs. Haunch owned forty-two dogs. James a friendly coloured man, drove a black Ford daily through her big stone gateway with mail, bread and big gunny sacks full of dog food. He went up the road about eight o'clock every morning except Sunday, and came out again about five o'clock each evening. Sometimes I sat on my pony beside the wrought iron gates and watched him come out, behind me in the woods all forty-two dogs barked at once like a chorus.

"She's too tiny to be so scary." I observed beating the ground with my hoe.

We were told not to go up the long driveway to Mrs. Haunch's house, and if we did mysterious phone calls came to my mother. These always caused trouble.

"One day," I promised myself, "I'll walk up that drive. One day while Mother is out of town, and Mrs. Haunch can't reach her." So far I'd never found the courage.

Mr. Houghton stood leaning on his shovel.

"She needs her hair done," he remarked. "It's wild and standing on her head like she has seen a ghost."

"Perhaps James does if for her. He seems to do everything else." I giggled.

Mr. Houghton still watched the frail figure welding its heavy shovel. I tore at a patch of honeysuckle, chopping it into pieces. We could hardly believe it. Mrs. Haunch was alive. A real sure person. Tiny and frail with her fly-away hair she really appeared ghost-like except she wielded her shovel with extraordinary power for a ghost. Her clothes looked dirty and her face was smudged from sweat. Thunder rattled in the sky as the tiny figure with its wild hair walked into our midst. A path immediately opened for her, but Mrs. Haunch did not pause at the store, but walked towards a black Ford and a dark figure standing by it.

"Everything's taken care of here, James," the voice commanded, "You can drive me home."

A Forgotten Landscape

30

A Strange Meeting

Summer 1941

When Mrs. Taliaferro asked an Irish friend who worked in Washington down for the weekend, I was invited to tea. She sent a note to Mrs. Houghton saying I was to appear at Alder's Point Farm by four o'clock on Saturday dressed in my church clothes. Although I loved going to Mrs. Taliaferro's elegant home, I hated to dress up.

"It sounds very mysterious," Mrs. Houghton complained, "whoever heard of sending a note?"

"Aren't you invited?" I asked her as she read the message.

"Not with an Irish person. I wouldn't go to Alder's Point if they paid me," She replied sitting down on her loveseat.

"Now, Duck, stop that talk in front of the girl. It isn't Christian. You go to St. Mary's every time the door swings open, but you refuse to drink tea with an Irishman?" Mr. Houghton looked stern as he entered the living room carrying his work boots.

"Irish woman," Mrs. Houghton corrected. " I had enough experience with the Irish in London."

She got up and slammed the door as she went into the garden to compose herself.

"Take no notice, Doc; she had an Irish boyfriend once who jilted her. She's never got over it. Get ready, and I'll drive you up. You're too dressed up to walk." He encouraged me. "Clara's not prejudiced really, just blind when it comes to the Emerald Isle. She hates anything green."

I felt uncertain if I should go. But twenty minutes later when I appeared dressed and wearing Mrs. Houghton's lipstick I'd found in the bathroom, Mr. Houghton approved.

"Don't let the Missus see that on you. It looks very grown up, I must say."

We slipped out of the house like two conspirators for the short drive to Alder's Point. Once there I stepped into a different world.

Mrs. Taliaferro and her daughters greeted me, and I was introduced to their Irish friend.

"Doc," Sally Anne said, "this is Miss Glenny."

I crossed the room to take her hand and then found an uncomfortable chair next to Jean in their beautiful living room. Sally Anne brought in a tray of tea and cookies. The silver pot gleamed and the cookies were my favourite Sand Tarts.

"I understand your mother and stepfather are now living in Washington for the duration," Miss Glenny remarked.

"Two years ago when the war broke out I was in Colraine in Northern Ireland visiting my parents. My employer sent me a telegram from America to get the first ship home." Miss Glenny took the cup of tea Sally Anne offered her and helped herself to cookies. "That's how I hurt my foot."

I noticed she wore a slipper and carried a cane. This piqued my interest.

"I got the last passenger boat from Cork, the "President McKinley." Halfway across the Atlantic we hit a tidal wave. The ship pitched and fell at such a rate I feared we'd all be killed. The crew brought the passengers into the first-class lounge where we remained for two days. As the ship spun and tossed about, the chairs and tables, which were screwed to the floor, came loose and slammed against the walls. That's how I hurt my foot. A table fell on it and broke it in two places."

"What a dreadful experience," said Mrs. Taliaferro, "you're lucky to be alive." She offered her friend some more tea.

I hadn't touched mine. It sat on a table beside me too beautiful to drink. The cup looked very delicate, and I was afraid I'd drop it. Sally Anne offered me the cookie plate, and I helped myself to three Sand Tarts. Alarmed at my boldness her eyebrows nearly touched her hair. When I put one cookie back her eyebrows returned to their usual place.

A Strange Meeting

I felt embarrassed and blushed.

Miss Glenny continued, "we stayed in semi-darkness in the lounge. The ship's doctor soon became overwhelmed by so many accidents. Luckily we found several doctors and nurses among the passengers. They were pressed into service and patched us up as best they could until we reached New York. When we sailed into New York Harbour, I felt ever so fortunate it was only my foot that was hurt. Dozens of ambulances met our ship."

"I hear you father breeds Scotties. Does he still have his dogs?" Jean asked politely. "It must be difficult now with the war on."

"Oh, yes. He's cut back considerably since dog food is hard to get. He used to breed show dogs, and one of his Scotties won best in breed at Crufts."

"What's Crufts?" I asked with my mouth full of Sand Tart.

"The big dog show in London. It's world famous." Mrs. Taliaferro explained.

During a lull in the conversation Sally Anne offered more cookies. Decorously I took only one. She nodded approval, and I felt redeemed. By now I wanted to go home and take off my good dress and stiff Sunday shoes. Miss Glenny bored me with her incessant chatter. She hadn't told us a thing about Ireland and why Mrs. Houghton felt prejudice against it. I wanted to understand why she had been upset. Mrs. Taliaferro put down her cup and went to the piano.

"Let's have a song or two," she played a few chords.

"I often hear fairy music in Ireland. My home was close to a rath or fairy fort. That's where the wee folk come to dance and play their music." Miss Glenny remarked.

I couldn't believe my ears! A grown woman who thought fairies were real. I'd never heard such a thing.

"They like to trick unsuspecting travelers and lead them astray. One night Uncle Denis spent in a field because he couldn't find his way home. He swore it was the fairies, but I suspect drink had something to do with it."

"Do you really think fairies exist?" I couldn't stop myself from asking.

"Oh, yes," she replied, "I've seen them!"

"On the evening before Samhan, November first, families place food on the doorstep for the spirits of their ancestors. These spirits come and sit around the fireside. The evening before Halloween the evil spirits are chased away so the good spirits can come unhindered. In the Irish calendar the first of November is the first day of winter," Miss Glenny explained to us.

The first day of winter is December twenty-first, Mr. Houghton's birthday. I couldn't understand why the Irish didn't know that.

"It's a very old belief," Miss Glenny continued. "It goes back into the mists of time, long before the calendar we have now was adopted."

"And the fairies?" I prompted. "When do you see them?"

"Usually they dance at night. By sun up they are gone. They go into the fairy raths where they live. No farmer will plow up a rath because it will displease the fairies, and they will seek revenge. That is why they are always called the wee people or the good people to please them."

"Do all adults in Ireland believe in the fairies?" I asked fascinated.

"Most of them. There is a house on the road between Dublin and Galway that is built on fairy grass. When the council wanted to widen the road no workman would tear the house down. Finally they built the road around the house." She explained.

"You mean grown men refused to take the house down because it was built on fairy grass?" I couldn't believe people actually thought the fairies would harm them.

"That's right. Belief in fairies is wide-spread." Miss Glenny insisted.

"What an interesting story," Mrs. Taliaferro said politely as she glared at me to stop asking questions. "The Irish are a remarkable people and have produced many clever poets and writers. I enjoy reading the poetry of Yeats and the plays of G. B. Shaw. I even read some of James Joyce's, Ulysses, a friend brought back from Paris."

"It's considered a dirty book and is not banned in Ireland," Miss Glenny said. "I've read Yeats and Shaw, but I've never read Ulysses. We do have good writers and have won Nobel Prizes with them."

"Yes, that's something to be proud of for such a small country." Mrs. Taliaferro stood up so as to end the party.

"Joyce is a strange little man," Miss Glenny would not be stopped. "He's very controversial."

I stood up and offered Miss Glenny my hand. I liked her in spite of her endless chatter. "It's very interesting to learn about Ireland and the fairies. You have some unusual customs."

Then I told Sally Anne thank you for the lovely Sand Tarts and headed for the door.

"Doc," Mrs. Taliaferro called to me, "be sure to read some of Yeats's poetry and either *St. Joan* and *Pygmalion* by G. B. Shaw. You are old enough to know these works. I'd leave Joyce alone, however, since he is accused of writing dirty books."

I felt happy as I walked home away from the talkative Miss Glenny. I found her interesting, but confusing. I couldn't fancy grown ups still believing in fairies and afraid to tear down a house built on fairy grass. I also wondered about Mrs. Taliaferro's taste in books. I thought she was a great lady with her elegant gray hair swept up from her face and her beautiful clothes. Yet she admitted quite openly that she'd read Ulysses which everyone considered a dirty book. I decided to discuss this with Mrs. Houghton when I got home. Walking through the summer evening I felt free again from social constraints. I took off my shoes and socks and strolled down the grassy verge beside the dirt road glad for a little time to myself.

At home I found Mr. Houghton raging. That summer we'd heard stories about our shipping being torpedoed by German U Boats right off the beaches. The Navy denied it and did nothing to defend the ships that sailed down our coasts. Today a ship had been torpedoed off the Virginia beaches and hundreds of people had watched it burn.

"We need a blackout along the coast, and the ships need to sail without lights. This is a disgrace. The German Wolf Packs of submarines are just waiting for any ship that clears Cape Hatteras. It's no good the Navy saying our coasts are being patrolled because they're not. It's no wonder that sea lane is called 'Torpedo Alley'", Mr. Houghton shouted as I came through the front door.

Before him on the table lay a letter from his friend, Mr. Southwell. "Sam's just returned from Savannah where he and other people stood on the dock and watched the City of Atlanta go up in flames. Tom, his son, works on her."

"Was he killed?" I asked trying to escape into my room and change clothes.

"No, just injured. What are you doing without shoes on? I told you not to go barefooted; it's dangerous on a farm."

"Yes, sir, I know, but it felt good after my church shoes. They cramp my feet."

"You do as I say or I'll send you to Washington with the rest of the shifty beggars who can't tell the truth."

I slipped into my bedroom and found some comfortable shoes. I put these on before I changed my dress. I found Mr. Houghton pacing the floor when I re-entered the living room.

"There you are with shoes too. Don't let me catch you without them again."

"No, sir. I promise to wear shoes from now on."

"You'd better or I'll send you off with Admiral King and his flunkies in our nation's capital. While those sneaky Germans are blowing up our shipping, he's wringing his hands and doing nothing."

"I didn't lie," I told him. "I told you the truth about the shoes."

"Yes, you did. Of course we're at war. America is sending munitions to Britain across the Atlantic without an escort. It's all those Germans in the Midwest who won't admit it. We reinforced the British tank force in Africa, and we're not at war? Of course we're at war. Who ever heard of being neutral and taking sides at the same time?" He strode past me and slammed the bathroom door. Then he opened it and stuck his head out. "I hope we are clear about wearing shoes. You can get lock-jaw or worms or an infection going out with bare feet."

"Who's Admiral King?" I asked.

"Some darn fool in Washington who knows nothing about running the Navy." The bathroom door slammed shut and I left the house.

I sought Mrs. Houghton in the garden to find out more about W. B. Yeats and G. B. Shaw. I also wanted to ask her how come Mrs. Taliaferro read dirty books.

31

An Interlude

September 1941

Mr. Houghton's radio blared: "From the heart of Hitler's Germany, your messenger, Paul Revere greets you again."

"Harry, do turn that off, for heaven's sakes," Mrs. Houghton resigned herself to listening to the short wave.

"Wait now, Duck, let's hear what he has to say," Mr. Houghton shushed us.

"For two years the Axis have marched from victory to victory on every front, military, diplomatic, economic. For two years, the democratic opponents of world progress, led by Churchill, the charlatan, and Roosevelt, the renegade, have sought to substitute deed, little deeds, with words. All their futility, all their shameful incompetence these men have tried to cover behind an impenetrable smokescreen of lying words......"

"Do turn it off, Harry. Who is this one?" Mrs. Houghton objected.

"He's Paul Revere. At least that's what he calls himself. Wherever do they find these fellows? I'd like to know. Anyway, they are getting the goodness out of these traitors. Nobody but a traitor would broadcast such a bucket of rot." Mr. Houghton turned the radio down and switched over to an American station. "We'll listen to something better. You like Fibber McGee and Mollie, don't you?"

September arrived, and I returned to school. Mrs. Houghton fussed over my clothes, and we'd gone downtown to buy books. Now the homework began once again, and I spent hours in the kitchen alone working on it.

"I've brought you two books from the library. One on Yeats and a second on Shaw. I know some of Yeats's poetry which I very much enjoy, and Shaw's plays are not hard to read. As for James Joyce I read some of his short stories, but I don't know Ulysses. I understand it's very difficult and not suitable for you now."

"I wouldn't think Mrs. Taliaferro would read dirty books," I replied. "She's such a great lady."

"She *is* a great lady," Mrs. Houghton agreed, "but she's got a curious mind. She reads because she's interested in knowing about things. After all, some of Shakespeare's plays are not all that clean either. I wouldn't worry about Mrs. Taliaferro. She's an educated person and understands about these things. Stick with Shaw and Yeats for now."

She started to prepare our supper, and I got up to set the table in the living room which we used as our dining room. Mrs. Houghton refused to eat in the kitchen.

"Oh, you should have seen Mrs. Owens's hair today. It's redder than ever. She's teaching history again as usual. Mrs. Stella is also back and piling on the English. Miss Hurdle is taking the math classes. Hurdle the Turtle, we call her. And Madame is back. She must be over a hundred by now. She taught French to Harriet Jones's mother and she's at least forty." I put the silver and napkins at our three places.

"I see you're taking current events. What is that about?" Mrs. Houghton inquired as she picked up my notebook.

"We talked about the Rates of Tobruk and their famous holdout of that sea port. Today we talked about the war with Russia, and we're watching Rommel in Africa. He will start his winter offensive soon. We also discussed if America will get into the war or not. That sort of thing," I told her as she served our plates and I carried them into the living room table.

"It's the Japanese we need to watch," Mr. Houghton added. "You need to watch those fellows. Germany is bad enough, but Asia is entirely different."

"We haven't said much about the Japanese in current events," I added. "We're discussing Germany and Russia right now."

"Germany and Japan have an agreement, just you wait. I don't trust those people. America's in for big trouble, believe me."

An Interlude

We ate our dinner in silence wondering what was in store for us. Finally Mr. Houghton turned on his radio. Over the airways came the oily voice of Lord Haw Haw, "Jaimany calling, Jaimany calling-."

"Turn that awful man down. He gives me the shivers," Mrs. Houghton demanded. "I am sure he's an Irishman with that fake English accent. Turn him off, Harry; I can't stand him."

Mr. Houghton winked, "And we know how she feels about Irishmen, don't we, Doc?"

A Forgotten Landscape

32

Winter Offensive

The winter offensive in Africa started on November eighteenth, and by the twentieth the Battle of Sidi Rezegh became furious. On the twenty-third the Germans had won, although both sides suffered overwhelming casualties. Now Rommel headed towards Tobruk and the Egyptian border. That evening Mr. Houghton was fairly dancing with anger when I returned from school. I met him in the front yard.

"How did it happen? How could it happen? That Desert Fox of a Rommel is too clever by far."

"What's he done now?" I asked throwing my books down.

"He's knocking on the gates of Cairo. What an everlasting mess." Mr. Houghton replied as he opened the door. "He's pushed the British back 300 miles in seventeen days!"

I ran into my room to change clothes. Miss Emma and Cary invited me to ride our horses over to Henley's store. That meant I could ride Lady. I rarely rode her alone as she was a handful sometimes, and Mr. Houghton didn't want to be responsible if I got hurt. Mrs. Houghton gave me a grocery list, and I picked up my knapsack and ran.

"Don't forget the candy. I'm packing a parcel for Mother and she loves sweets," Mrs. Houghton called after me.

"Rommel's winning in Africa," I informed Cary as we saddled our horses, "and Mr. Houghton is furious."

"It looks bad. It won't be long before we get involved. As soon as we do, I intend to join up. I plan to finish school and go straight into the Army Air Corps."

"Oh, Cary, you wouldn't do that and leave your mother." I felt tears in my eyes.

"It's time we get into it officially. We're already in it unofficially."

Cary jumped on Killybegs and I climbed on Lady. At the end of the barn lane we met his mother coming out of her stables, and together we started down the road.

"Father writes he's now a Major and is still taking courses at the War College in Washington. He says it's only a matter of time. Churchill wants us in the war, and Roosevelt agrees. It's scary." I told them.

I put the war out of my mind as we turned into the woods and trotted along a pine tag trail. The autumn afternoon was cold, the horses felt like trotting and the trees surrounded us in a blaze of colours. I felt happy in spite of Rommel winning in Africa. The horses broke into a canter, and we jumped over fallen logs. Finally at the stream we pulled down to a walk and I forgot about the world's troubles in the enjoyment of the moment.

At the store the neighbors gathered. Alvira Carthage with Sally McClain had driven down to buy some of Mr. Houghton's eggs. Catherine Hollis too was there looking very pretty in her blue suit. She had been to town and was on her way home.

"Hello, Doc," she greeted me. "What a lovely mare."

"Yes, I got her for Christmas. She's very good really."

"Then you must come up and hunt with the Colonel again. How's your mother enjoying Washington?"

"Fine," I replied. "I like your suit."

This compliment pleased her. She never had much taste in clothes, but sometimes she looked extra nice. I liked to tell her because I felt sorry for this gentle lady and was fond of her.

Alvira Carthage – I tried to avoid. She was such a gossip. I hated to say anything in case she'd repeat it. This afternoon she wasn't to be denied.

"You should help out in the Sunday school." She cornered me.

"What would I do?" I asked her.

"Why, look after the small children and teach them hymns and prayers. You're a big enough girl to help," she replied.

I went in the store to get the groceries on Mrs. Houghton's list. Mrs. Carthage followed. I tried to avoid her by picking out bread, canned goods and napkins.

"Doc," she insisted, "you need to help, you know. It's wrong not to. It's sinful to be educated in Richmond and not to share your knowledge."

I paid Mrs. Henley for the things and packed them into my knapsack.

"Did you hear, Doc, what I'm saying?"

"Yes, Mrs. Carthage, I hear. You see, I know very little about children. I find them loud and unruly. I'm not good with them," I stammered, my face turning red.

"You've done it now," whispered Cary as we left the store. "She'll have it all over the county that you hate children."

"I can't help it. I know nothing about them. It's enough to get myself to church every Sunday without minding kids."

Miss Emma laughed as she handed us the reins of our horses. Then she went into the store for her own groceries. Ten minutes later we climbed on our mounts and started down the road towards home.

"Never mind Alvira Carthage, Doc. I'll protect you from her," Miss Emma promised.

But she didn't. The next Sunday I found myself pressed into service. At Sunday school I helped Sally Anne with the beginner's class.

"You'll have stars in your crown, Doc," Mrs. Houghton comforted me. "At least you don't have to go on Thursdays to prepare the altar and take home the clothes to wash."

"She said I am sinful. I don't feel sinful at all, just stubborn," I replied.

At home we found Tom Harris waiting. Mr. Houghton parked his car and got out after driving Mrs. Houghton and me from church.

"I need your help," Mr. Harris said. "Tom, Jr. joined the Navy and left this morning for Charleston. Can you give me a hand this afternoon to cut my wood for the stove?"

"Tom's too young to enlist; did he have your permission?" Mr. Houghton asked.

"Lied about his age, and signed up about three weeks ago without our knowledge." Mr. Harris said. "His mother's devastated."

"Sure, I'll come," Mr. Houghton said and followed Mr. Harris to his car.

"We'll stay here, Doc, I'll prepare some lunch. Mr. H. won't be home for hours. How sad for Elizabeth Harris to see her son leave for an uncertain future." Mrs. Houghton entered the house and let Peggy out.

"I am not all that fired up with teaching Sunday school," I told her as we sat down to lunch. "It's hard work."

"Never mind, you'll learn as you go on, and Sally Anne is very grateful for your help. She says you are a good teacher." Mrs. Houghton passed the bread and butter. "Everyone must help out, dear, and you can try it for a month or two. If you don't like it, then you can decide to give it up or not."

"I'd have to study all those Sunday school lessons and learn *Bible* stories so that I don't disgrace myself."

"You will, dear. You are a most generous girl." Mrs. Houghton hugged me.

I felt trapped by her kindness and became a Sunday teacher.

33

"To Hell with Babe Ruth"

December 1941

It was a cold ordinary Sunday on the seventh of December. We went to church as usual and came home for lunch. At one o'clock just as we finished lunch, Mr. Houghton turned on his radio. H. V. Kaltenborne told us at a place in the Hawaiin Islands called Pearl Harbour the Japanese had bombed the American 7th Fleet early that morning in a surprise attack. Enemy pilots damaged and sank the USS Arizona and five or six other ships. They also destroyed a whole fleet of American airplanes on the ground and killed 2000 people. President Roosevelt called the attack a disaster. The country felt stunned. The next day Congress declared war on Japan and Germany, who had a treaty with her, immediately declared war on us.

I remembered what Father said, "By the time you are thirteen, we shall be at war."

My gentle life was turned upside down, and I felt very scared. The approaching Christmas Season seemed hollow now our fragile peace was shattered, and to add to our misery it became extremely cold. Father rang and told me all Reserves were now on active service. Grandmother also telephoned from Indianapolis to find out about Father. Mr. Houghton fussed over his chickens to hide his fear, and Mrs. Houghton sat in the kitchen and cried.

The following Sunday at church we were given the task of delivering coal and wood and a little Christmas candy to the Negro community which consisted of three cabins in the woods across River Road from the church.

"I'll come for you this afternoon with Paul and the wagon," Jean Taliaferro told me as we left St. Mary's. "It's just the only way to get back in the woods and deliver the stuff. You said you'd like to help."

"Yes," I agreed, "I'd like to come. At least I feel I am doing some good."

About two o'clock Jean arrived with Paul and the wagon filled with bags of coal and kindling. There were also bags of penny candy tied with red ribbons and some Christmas stockings for the children.

"I'll have her back in a couple of hours," Jean promised. "We might look for a tree. We won't chop it yet, but we'll make it ours by tying a red ribbon on it.

"Right ho," Mr. Houghton helped me up onto the high wooden seat and covered my legs with a blanket. Then Paul trotted on, his feet sounding hollow as they struck the frosty ground.

We crossed River Road and entered the woods beyond. The old saw mill trail felt marshy under the frozen crust. Out of the woods two small black boys appeared and greeted us, then led the way.

"Oh, Miss Jean," they cried in eagerness, "What you brought us?"

"Firewood and coal, and if you're very good some candy for Christmas."

"Are you Santy Claus?" asked the younger one. "You don't have a red suit, but I believe you is Santy Claus. Grandpa, Santy Claus is coming to see us."

Grievous Sin Snead stood in the snow, his galoshes opened, and split his face smiling. Jean brought Paul to a halt and the little boys climbed up into the wagon bed.

"Coal, Grandpa, bags of coal for us."

Eagerly they helped unload the 100 lb bags and handed them down to Grievous. Then they picked up the 3 piles of kindling Jean told them to take.

"Here's some Christmas cheer," I handed Grievous two brightly decorated stockings and bag of penny candy.

Mattie, Grievous's wife, joined her husband and grandsons. She peeked into the bag of candy and smiled.

"I loves sweet stuff," she told me. "This is mine, but I allows Grievous and the boys some too."

"The church will send you some food closer to Christmas," Jean told them. "It's very cold so we brought the fuel early."

Jean and I climbed back onto the wagon, and she urged Paul down the narrow snow-covered trail towards the second cabin. Our road was clear, but in these woods where the sun did not penetrate last week's snow still lingered. Three little girls ran out to meet us and taking Paul by the rein, the eldest led him into a mud-filled yard where several stunted chickens pecked hopefully at the slushy ground.

"Miss Jean, what you brought us?" cried the youngest eagerly. "Coal and wood. That's all? Ain't you got no presents from Santy Claus?"

"Yes," I replied. "Here are three stockings, one for each of you. And here's a bag of candy." I handed around the gifts.

The girls took them eagerly. "I knew he'd come 'cause I prayed ever so hard he would come. I axed and axed and Jesus heard me. Ain't that wonderful!" Cried the middle child, her face split in a big smile. "Miss Doc, you knows me from the store. I'm Emily, and that's Rosie, and that over there is Sally."

"Yes," I replied, "I remember you at the store with ice cream all over your face."

"I don't get it now," Emily said, "'cause it's winter, and we ain't got the money."

"It's too cold to eat ice cream," I told her, "but not for candy. Eat your penny candy."

"I loves candy." She looked suddenly shy as if she'd said too much.

Meanwhile, her father lifted down the heavy bags of coal and her mother took the kindling. Then the little family disappeared into their cabin.

At the third cabin Jean got down from her seat and handed me the reins.

"Hold Paul," she instructed before walking up onto the broken porch and knocking on the cabin door.

A tiny, withered old lady appeared; her head done up in a bandana, her frail body supported by a stick.

"Tis you, Miss Jean?" She inquired peering at us from behind dusty glasses. "How are you this evenin'?"

"I brought you some coal and a few little gifts," Jean explained as she lifted down a bag of coal from the wagon. "We want you to be warm in this cold weather."

A younger Negro man appeared from around the side of the house. "Wait, Miss Jean, I'll carry that. It's too heavy for a lady like you."

"That's Frank, my grandson all grown up," the old lady explained, as Jean handed her the bag of candy. "Oh, thank you, Miss Jean. I appreciates it. I surely does. Did you bring me hard candy?"

"No, chocolate," Jean replied, as she gave Frank three bundles of kindling. "We know you can't eat hard candy."

"Not with these few teeth, but I do love chocolate cherries. Did you bring me those kind?" The old lady jumped up and down like an excited bird.

"Yes," Jean said laughing, "a whole pound."

"Good gracious alive! Then I knows it will be a happy Christmas, yes ma'am. Santy Claus is good to me." Old Lucy nearly danced a jig in anticipation, as Jean handed her the candy wrapped up in red Christmas paper.

"Frank, she said, "make your grandmother a good hot fire and we'll be back before Christmas with some flour, sugar and canned goods. You let Mr. Henley at the store know if you need anything. We can't have Aunt Sally getting sick." She handed him a bag of hard candy and placed five dollars into his hand. She climbed up on the wagon beside me and took the reins.

"Wait a minute, Miss Jean. Wait one minute, please." Aunt Lucy shuffled inside and reappeared with a branch of holly in her hands. "It has lovely berries this year, big and red."

Then leaning heavily upon her stick for support, she crossed the unpainted porch and offered us the holly. Solemnly Jean got down from the wagon and accepted our gift.

"What a lovely thing to do," she said.

"That's what Christmas is all about, ain't it? I gives and receives. I likes to gives."

A chill wind blew, Aunt Lucy wrapped her tattered sweater closer around her neck and leaned on her grandson's arm beside the rickety steps of her porch.

"Ain't that the spirit of Christmas?" She asked again. "That's what I learned it was."

"You're absolutely right," I agreed, "what a lovely idea."

Jean lifted herself back onto the wagon's high seat and took the reins again from me. "Go inside, Aunt Lucy, before you freeze yourself to death. You can make a good fire and be all warm and cozy. Goodbye Frank."

"Goodbye, Miss Jean and Miss Doc. Thank you for the coal and especially for the chocolate cherries. Granny will enjoy every one." He laughed as he led her into the house.

We drove Paul back down the sawmill trail and entered River Road. Here we crossed over into our own gravel road and headed for home. I pulled the blanket closer around me and sat in deep thought. I smelled Paul's sweat and leather harness, a smell that I liked because it reflected the land and growing things.

"These people have so little," I said finally, "and yet they gave us so much happiness. I love the holly branch with its red berries; that's special. Why can't the world be like us and live at peace? Why must people kill each other? How come the Japanese said, "To Hell with Babe Ruth as they flew over Pearl Harbour? How do they know so much about our baseball?"

"They were just being hateful, that's all, putting down our heroes. It was an evil attack, but we knew it was coming eventually if not from the Japanese, then from the Germans," Jean replied.

"Father's on active duty now," I said, "and I am frightened. The world's gone mad, and I have just begun to live. The woods are beautiful and the pines smell like Christmas, yet people can't find peace. It seems strange to me that God can't stop the war. I don't want my father to go and get killed. And Cary's just as bad with his talk of flying and joining the Army Air Corps. I hate all this kind of talk; I hate it." I felt the tears prick behind my eyes.

"Let's go pick out a tree and tie this red ribbon on it so we'll find it again. Paul and I always get the tree with the wagon. He loves it. What kind of tree do you like?" Jean urged her mule into a brisk trot.

"A big one," I replied. "I want a big one that smells good."

She handed me a red ribbon which I split in two, as we reentered the woods and found an old sawmill trail to follow. Beside it were lots of trees, and soon we had selected two and tied our red ribbons on them. Then Jean turned Paul onto our gravel road once again and we trotted home.

"Enjoy Christmas, Doc," she said, "and put the war out of your mind. Grab your happiness where you can. Remember it's what you do for others that really counts."

"Yes," I replied, and breathing in the wonderful scent of pine woods I huddled under my blanket. "I believe in God, and I will pray. But the war makes everything uncertain."

34

Mrs. Haunch Appears Again

When James drove Mrs. Haunch away the afternoon of the fire we thought we perhaps would not see her again for years. But on Christmas Eve the whole neighborhood was astir. Mr. Gilley had left home at six in the morning to go fox hunting, and had not returned. Finally on Route 6, about two o'clock that afternoon, the police found Mr. Gilley's car and Mr. Gilley inside it – dead. He had suffered a heart attack.

In those days countrymen hunted from their cars or on foot to follow their hounds when in full cry after a fox. Farmers called this type of hunting, timber topping, to distinguish it from fox hunting with horses, whose riders wore pink coats.

By late afternoon everyone knew Mr. Gilley had died timber-topping during the early hours of Christmas Eve, as he rode about the countryside in his Ford car. He was much too fat to walk. He left behind a white-faced, frail-looking wife and six children.

Later that evening Mrs. Haunch, driven by James in her black car, quite unexpectedly appeared. As she came out of her road, sitting in the back seat of the Ford, huddled in a fur coat, I followed her on horseback. We headed slowly towards the Gilley's ramshackled house on River Road.

"I can't imagine what she's up to," I thought, trotting Lady through the woods, I kept an eye on the black Ford.

James pulled in at the store and asked Mrs. Henley if she had a chicken for sale. I watched curiously from the other side of the road, still seated on Lady.

"We can kill one," I heard Mrs. Henley say. "But one chicken for six children hardly seems enough."

"I hope other people in the county will not forget their Christian duty and will also bring food." Mrs. Haunch's voice sounded sharp.

I watched Mrs. Henley wring the chicken's neck and hung it up on a tree to bleed.

"Can you cook it before it goes over to the Gilley's?" The hermit asked.

"Mrs. Haunch, it's Christmas Eve, and I plan to go to Arthur's brother's house this evening," Mrs. Henley protested.

"I am sure neither James nor I are going to cook that chicken, so you must."

Mrs. Henley shrugged her shoulders.

Just then I noticed Mr. Houghton drive up and pull into the store. Mrs. Houghton, who always rode in the back seat, accompanied him. She held a hamper of food on her lap for the bereaved family.

"Merry Christmas, Mrs. Henley, I've just come for some gas."

"Merry Christmas, Harry. I'll pump it for you," Mrs. Henley offered.

"You'll pump a grown man's gas, but you won't cook my chicken," cried Mrs. Haunch hopping out of her car, fur coat open, revealing her dirty jodhpurs underneath. "Mrs. Houghton, will you cook that chicken for me so I can take it to the Gilleys?"

Mr. Houghton intervened. He met the lady hermit squarely, blocking her way.

"Clara can't bake your chicken on Christmas Eve."

"I am sure I can't. Somebody's got to cook it so I can deliver it to the poor little family who lives not a hundred yards from here."

"Bake it yourself, or get James to do it. Although it's Christmas Eve we managed to get our hamper ready," Mrs. Houghton told her.

Mrs. Henley hung up the pump handle then took the money Mr. Houghton handed her. Then she went back into the store to get change. As she went in Bertha came out. Mrs. Haunch saw her chance. Everyone knew Bertha was the best chicken fryer in the whole county. And on Christmas Eve with her large family she needed the money. In an instant Mrs. Haunch collared her. And before any of us realized it Bertha, James, Mrs. Haunch and the bloody chicken all started down River Road in the black Ford.

It was too much for me. I felt sure Mrs. Haunch had kidnapped the poor, unsuspecting coloured woman. Kicking Lady into action, I came out from my hiding place and raced towards the store.

"She's taken Bertha," I yelled at Mr. Houghton. "That old lady hermit with the astonishing hair has kidnapped Bertha."

Then I appealed to Mrs. Houghton for help. Everyone knew Bertha was mortally afraid of Mrs. Haunch, and that our laundress firmly believed the bridge over the stream near Mrs. Haunch's house was haunted. Here Bertha was sure she sensed the presence of the deceased Nellie Randolph.

"Miss Doc, I never walk over that bridge at night. And don't you neither." She often insisted.

In a dozen ways I had given her my solemn promise. Now realizing Bertha must be frightened out of her wits I turned to Mr. Houghton.

"Come on, we've got to rescue her."

"Not before I deliver these things to the Gilleys," Mrs. Houghton told me. "We won't be long. Ride on ahead, and we'll meet you at Mrs. Haunch's gate."

"Oh, do hurry, please," I begged, as panic clutched me like a vice.

Within a few minutes Mr. Houghton's car passed me on the road heading towards Mrs. Haunch's place. At the gates he waited for me to catch up.

"We'll go in together," he whispered. "So keep your horse quiet and follow me."

Slowly we wound up the long driveway through tall dark trees towards the historic house. James met us at the front door.

"I am concerned about Bertha," Mr. Houghton explained. "We have come to take her home."

"I'll do that," James insisted, walking towards us.

"No," interrupted Mrs. Houghton, rolling down her window. "We have some Christmas gifts for her and her children. We promised to pick Bertha up at the store this evening."

I could not believe my ears. Although I knew we did indeed have some gifts, the rest of Mrs. Houghton's story was a lie.

"Bertha's frying a chicken for Mrs. Haunch to carry to the Gilleys. When I bring it I'll take Bertha home," James held his ground.

"I'll wait, if you don't mind," said Mr. Houghton and got out of his car. "Tell Bertha, please, that we are waiting."

At that moment Mrs. Haunch unexpectedly appeared on her door step. She regarded me coldly, and looked at Mr. Houghton with unmasked hostility.

"What do you want?" Her voice sounded like winter.

"I have come for Bertha," replied Mr. Houghton and took a stride forward. "I've come to take her home to be with her family on Christmas Eve."

"She's cooking the chicken," Mrs. Haunch replied, as she patted Lady with her back to the Houghtons.

"Please tell Bertha I am here. She's an old woman who has suffered many hardships. You must realize she had done you a great favor," Mr. Houghton told the hermit.

Still we waited in the late afternoon cold. Mrs. Haunch continued to pay my horse attention disregarding the four people in her driveway. Finally Bertha appeared on the steps with her blue hat in her shopping bag. Suddenly into her brown hand, in front of us all, Mrs. Haunch placed a five dollar bill.

"For the chicken and for your Christmas," she mumbled looking embarrassed.

"Thank you, ma'am," Bertha replied climbing into the front seat of the Chevrolet.

"Coloured folks ride in the back," Mrs. Haunch objected.

"Since my wife always rides in the back, Bertha will sit here," Mr. Houghton's voice sounded firm and very angry.

In the half light I noticed a ghost of a smile appear on James's face. Mr. Houghton started his car and turned down the long driveway. Before he rounded the curve I saw he took one last look at Mrs. Haunch still standing on her top step dressed in her long fur coat over her riding pants. Following the Houghtons I trotted Lady slowly behind the Chevrolet to the large iron gates, where we parted.

"Goodbye Bertha, Merry Christmas," I called before galloping up the trail through the woods towards home.

I saw Mr. Houghton avoid turning down Mrs. Haunch's road over the ghost-haunted bridge, and instead he went in the other direction towards the Taliaferros and drove Bertha home the long way around.

"That's the best Christmas I've ever had," she exclaimed when later that week Bertha arrived to do the laundry. "I got a ride home on a road with no ghosties. And who in this wide world would ever believe Mrs. Haunch gave me five dollars?"

Although she needed the money badly, to prove that Mrs. Haunch was real, Bertha had her five dollar bill framed, and she hung it up in the front hall for all to see. It would be almost a year before we saw the hermit again.

A Forgotten Landscape

35

Germany Calling

"Hello, North America, Germany calling. We now present Lord Haw Haw speaking to England on 28 December 1941.

"That man again! Turn him off, Harry, for heavens sake. I can't stand him."

"Wait, let's see what he has to say," Mr. Houghton commanded.

"To say the British Empire is in danger today would be a very feeble understatement. Never before has it been in such a perilous position. Until Roosevelt and Churchill so needlessly provoke Japan into taking up arms, the greater part of the British Empire felt itself outside the war zone. Now it is all the more remarkable that the United States should be gaining such ascendancy over the British Empire; when Roosevelt's conduct of the war against Japan has been such a failure up to the present having lost his Pacific Fleet, he can hardly afford to pose as the master of the situation. And yet, Churchill will, in my opinion, bow to his wishes ever more obsequiously than in the past."

Mr. Houghton turned off the radio. We sat very solemnly in the living room wondering what would become of us and the United States. Finally Mrs. Houghton got out the cards, and we played three-handed bridge until Jack Benny came on the radio. In a week our whole world seemed to change after the air strike on Pearl Harbour, December 7th. We were now at war with Japan and Germany.

Father called to tell me things were very serious, and I must be brave. Grandmother rang to find out about father.

"I don't think Jack Benny is very funny tonight," said Mrs. Houghton. "He's out of step with the national mood, I'm afraid."

"I'll turn him off," said Mr. Houghton and got up to do so. "I'm going out to check on my chickens. It's very cold tonight."

I heard the door bang shut, and Peggy barked at something outside before I got up from my place in front of the fire.

"Doc, life will not be easy from now on. We are headed for hard times. You, my dear, must try very hard to be helpful and pleasant. People have heavy hearts and carry a lot of sadness now. The memory of the Last War is too close. We shall win and rid the world of this evil that has invaded it."

I nodded because I could not speak. I felt fear creep up my legs and around my heart. I just blew her a kiss and went to bed.

Part III
1942

Trouble on the Home Front

A Forgotten Landscape

36

"Nothing but Fear Itself"

January 1942 turned very cold. We brought extra coal and Mr. Houghton chopped up some fallen pines in the woods for the fireplace. He also caulked the windows and put new weather stripping on the doors. Still we froze. We now shared the kitchen with two baby chicks, a half-grown pheasant and a sick guinea hen. They lived in brown boxes under the stove. We kept the little creatures warm and gave them extra attention.

When the mercury dropped to 10° F. Mr. Houghton rigged a light bulb and put weather stripping around the doors and windows of the chicken house. He found extra horse rugs for Lindy Lou and Susie Q. and spent all day in the barn covering windows with old blankets and boarding up drafts.

Things became more heated at home when on January 26, America sent troops to Northern Ireland. That evening the BBC Commentator told us of a broadcast in English from Radio Hamburg: "American troops are now on Irish soil. Millions of Irish in America have sent messages to President Roosevelt affirming their loyalty to the United States. What is far more to the point the Irish shouldn't be false to their Mother Country. Ireland has remained neutral and it would be tragic if through the interference of Roosevelt or anyone else, their neutrality should be lost."

"Neutral indeed!" snapped Mrs. Houghton. "Ireland should be ashamed to be neutral and allow the Germans passage through Britain's back door."

"Now, Duck, don't get all 'het' up. The troops are there to protect Ulster, and especially Belfast from a German invasion." Mr. Houghton winked at me.

"Churchill should never have given Ireland back those ports like Spike Island on the Irish Sea. Our shipping is being torpedoed and the Irish don't care."

"It's the big shipyard at Harland and Wolfe that the Allies wish to protect," Mr. Houghton interjected as he sat down to put on his boots.

Mrs. Houghton went into the kitchen and returned with the coal scuttle.

"Get out of my way, Doc, and let me put some fuel on that fire," she snapped. "De Velara isn't going to cooperate with the Allies. If England goes under, Ireland certainly will be next. Doesn't de Velara understand that for all his German sympathy?"

"Not for heaven itself will he show loyalty to England. You can bet on that." Mr. Houghton added before he made a hasty retreat out the back door to feed his horses and chickens.

"That man will be the death of me yet. He doesn't know a thing about the Irish for all his talk."

After Mrs. Houghton got the fire banked, she prepared our supper. I spread my homework out on the hassock and started the math.

"How does that German commentator know Roosevelt got millions of messages from the Irish?" I wanted to know.

"He doesn't know; just rumours. A lot of propaganda is made up or based on half truths," she replied from the kitchen. "So don't take any notice of those people from Germany."

"Did you really have an Irish boyfriend?" I ventured to ask her in a small voice.

"I did. An attractive man, Dermot O'Kelly was his name. He could charm a snake right out of his skin. I never trusted him, being Irish. He came from Kinsale in County Cork. It didn't last," she ended reflectively.

"Were you in love with him?" I knew better than to ask such questions.

"I suppose I was really," she said softly. "Don't let Mr. H. put ideas into your head. He's as bad as any Irishman for story telling."

Just then the kettle sang and she returned to the kitchen to finish our supper. Mr. Houghton came in a few minutes later waving the newspaper Miss Emma brought from town each evening.

"Look at this," he laid the paper on the table and read out loud: "When a German Brigade surrendered in Africa, after the Allies gave the survivors a meal, and they had formed up to march off, the Free French fired on them. The French have committed one of the most shameful blunders of the African Campaign."

"Now I want to know which are worse;" Mrs. Houghton demanded, "The French or the Irish?"

"The Geneva Convention will have something to say about this. It looks as if Rommel's defeated at last," Mr. Houghton slapped the table in anger. "The garrison at Tobruk has been reinforced and the Rats saved."

"Don't be so sure about him," replied his wife. "He's a sly fox believe me."

We sat down to supper and ate in companionable silence, each in his own thoughts. Mr. Houghton got up and added another log to the fire and a shovelful of coal to the heater. He also checked the water heater in the kitchen, so we could have hot baths. It was fired by a small Franklin stove which was very efficient.

"It's very cold tonight. I hope the chickens don't freeze and die. I've fed and put blankets on Lady, Jackie and Billy which I brought over to my barn. I've hung a strip of tar paper over the double barn doors to keep out the wind. I can't remember such a wintry January. It's supposed to snow tonight," he predicted.

The next morning when I awoke at six, I discovered we were snowed in. The house felt freezing cold. I heard Mr. Houghton rattle the coal scuttle and knew he was filling the heater. I snuggled down into the covers and pretended it was Saturday. At 6:30 Cary rapped on the door to tell us his mother's car wouldn't start, and we wouldn't be going to school.

"The hill is impassable," he informed us, "and River Road hasn't been cleared. Tell Doc to enjoy her holiday."

Delighted I sprang out of bed into the chilly room. I found Mr. Houghton in his woolen cap and his thick bathrobe banking the kitchen fire.

"Sh, sh," he warned me, "the Missus is still asleep. Get dressed and we'll go look after the chickens and the horses."

Together we did the chores. Then Mr. Houghton said he would ride Lindy Lou to the store.

"Can I go with you to show you the way?" I asked, eager for adventure.

"No," he replied, "your mare is too fractious and the ponies are too small. I'll ask Cary." He went into the house to phone him.

Tears streaked down my face as I helped him saddle his mare. Mr. Houghton knew he'd hurt me, but said nothing. Not only was I too young, but he'd treated me like a girl. That was the deeper humiliation. A few minutes later when Cary arrived on Killybegs, anger replaced hurt. I was furious at them for being men and old enough to ride to the store in the snow. I hated them for belittling me. I went in the house and poured out my troubles to Mrs. Houghton.

"Harry didn't want you injured," she explained. "After all you are in our care and that makes us responsible. Later this year when you're fourteen and Lady is more easily handled, you can ride to the store in the snow."

It didn't help me. I decided being a girl wasn't fair.

37

Mr. Houghton's Wedding

The next day once again it snowed. Great white flakes came silently down and covered the landscape with a soft blanket. The pine woods and the fields, rolling gently towards the river, soon looked like an icing-covered cake. It was Mr. Houghton's wedding anniversary, and that morning Mrs. Houghton had driven into Richmond with Tom Harris to do some necessary shopping. He had a truck with chains and he also took Miss Emma to work.

Shortly after the snow started, Cary arrived at our front door. The electricity had gone out, and since nobody else was around, Mr. Houghton, Cary and I sat beside the fire. It was banked with pine logs and coal and gave off great heat. The mantle clock's musical chimes had just struck four.

"Did I ever tell you the story," Mr. Houghton asked pouring us each a cup of hot tea he'd made on the gas stove, "about how the Missus almost refused to marry me?"

"No," I answered, more comfortably settling myself in the chair to listen, while Cary stretched out on the floor in front of the fire.

Gathering his thoughts together, Mr. Houghton drank his tea, laid the saucer on the table and began his story with the cup cradled between his hands.

"When Clara came out to Canada in January 1928, we had a big snow storm. In those days, a hundred miles north of Toronto, few people owned cars. To get around in winter we used teams of horses and put our wagons on runners. That winter, in order to meet Clara, when she arrived from England, I drove a cutter, a sleigh with two horses, seventeen miles from my farm near Angus into Barrie, and caught the train for Toronto. When a big snow storm prevented my getting to Barrie until three days after Clara's boat landed, (although some friends who lived in Toronto met her) my bride was devilishly angry.

"But finally on the fourth day I hitched my two best horses, part Thoroughbred, part Perchrons, to the cutter and started out. Wind whipped the snow into drifts, it blew into our eyes and nearly blinded us. The road and fields on either side looked as if a huge white coverlet lay over them, only the tops of fence posts and trees, provided landmarks in that vast unmarked land. A man can get lost in such country and never be heard of again. Like the prairie this was wheat-growing country and almost featureless. Only a few Douglas firs broke the flat landscape and provided a little protection for the traveler. Cattle grazed in these fields in summer, but in winter no livestock was allowed out on the crusty snow. The whole landscape became a charterless sea after the storm.

"My horses, Dan and Patches, both strong and young, snorted as the wind blew snow into their noses and down their broad backs. Ice balls gathered in their feet causing the horses to stand on stilts and to slip. Slowly at a walk we crept across that frozen landscape.

"I huddled, wrapped in a parka, two hats, and three pairs of gloves, upon the wagon seat, only partly sheltered from the fierce wind. I found some old skins, once used as lap robes, and bundled them under me on the driver's box. Then I put the biggest piece of cow hide over my lap, fur side out.

"Dan and Patches tossed their great bay-coloured heads as the wind sent cold fingers down their tender ears and up their nostrils. Within minutes ice crystals formed on their black manes and tails, making the hairs stand up stiffly.

"I found it slow driving, with frequent stops to clean out, with my pocket knife, the ice balls in the horses' feet. It took us three hours to reach the farm of a preacher friend of mine. He just preached on Sundays and farmed the rest of the week – kind of free lance. The scent of wood smoke welcomed us as I turned the team into his farm lane. Just visible in front of me through an avenue of fence post tops, stood a well constructed house. Out of its chimney, smoke, blown by the wind, greeted me, an inviting sight.

"'Hello, Harry', the preacher called. 'Off to Toronto to meet your bride? Rough trip in this weather. Come, stop in awhile. Boys, take his horses'."

"Two big lads appeared, grabbed Dan and Patches by their bridles, and led them towards the barn.

"You're right, 'tis rough weather, but Clara won't like it if I wait much longer."

"Gratefully I jumped down off the cutter and followed the preacher into his house. The aroma of freshly baked bread greeted us.

"Welcome, bridegroom," the preacher's wife smiled as she met me in the hall.

"Then she poured two big mugs of hot tea and cut us each a generous piece of the freshly baked loaf she took from the oven.

"Some of this good food will warm you up. There is a terrible lot of snow out there."

"Frankly I'm more afraid of Clara than of this storm," I confessed as I munched my butter-soaked bread and washed it down with scalding tea.

"About forty-five minutes later I started out again. The ice crystals in the horses' manes and tails, now melted, had left dark furrows in their hair along their strong necks. The boys, no doubt, had rubbed Dan and Patches with gunny sacks causing the team now to smell of sweat and leather.

"Good luck, Harry. Don't forget; stop by on your way back so we can meet the bride," the preacher invited.

"After climbing up onto the driver's box, I wrapped the skins around me once more and picked up the reins. Dan and Patches leaned into their collars, and carefully we made our way up the driveway through the crusty snow. January afternoons that far north are short, and we still had about five or six miles to go. I knew around four o'clock it would be dark.

"As the afternoon wore on the snow started freezing, and its icy top soon became solid. This made the footing extremely dangerous for my horses in spite of their special shoes. Again ice balls accumulated in their feet making them stand on stilts. Dan, his heavy hooves slipping out from under him, almost fell to his knees, his soft nose cut. Intently I watched as great crimson drops of blood stained the virgin snow.

" 'Whoa', my voice sounded too loud in that empty vast country. 'Whoa.' He stood quietly, seemingly grateful for my attention. I wiped his nose with some soft snow and stopped the blood. But old Patches was of a different temperament. He hated for me to clean out his hooves. As I picked up his left hind foot, cupping it in my left hand, he jerked his leg free kicking the cutter with a smart wallop. It sounded like a pistol shot.

"This sudden motion sent me flying across the crusted snow and landing almost senseless in a huge drift. But Patches, curious about these strange goings on, merely turned his head and looked at me. Although unhurt, my anger rose as I struggled to my feet.

" 'You smart beggar, you', I yelled.

"After untangling the reins I hunted for my pocket knife which I found stuck in the snow some twenty feet away. Upon retrieving it I discovered the road ran about thirty-five yards to the west of us. We were headed in the opposite direction. Now really scared I climbed back onto the cutter, and shivering with cold and fear I turned the horses carefully towards the road. Away ahead, through the clouds, I thought I saw the lights of Barrie twinkling. The land is so flat in that region it is possible to see for a great distance.

"I felt reassured enough to let the horses trot over the icy road. But suddenly Patches slipped and went down onto his knees. The saddle pad twisted, a trace came loose, and the reins tangled in their terrets. Quickly I jumped off the cutter and slid across the ice to Patches's head. Vainly I tried to pull him onto his feet, but the big horse just sat in the snow like a dog. 'Get up, boy,' I encouraged. 'Get up.'

"In his struggle to rise Patches's feet slipped from under him, and he rolled over onto his side. Panic gripped me as I freed his collar from the pole that ran between him and Dan. Once again I pulled on the horse's head.

" 'Get up, Patches', I almost screamed. 'Please get up.'

"Gallantly Patches tried to raise himself. As he sat up, his great hooves struggling to find firm ground, the crusty snow broke under his weight, and he stood. Relieved I hugged his snow encrusted neck and unbuckled the belly band, straightened the saddle pad upon his back, and snapped the collar onto the pole once again. Inch by inch I led the frightened horses across the frozen ground until the road became less slick. Finally I climbed back onto the cutter and prayed all the way into Barrie.

"Once there, the horses' hooves, now muffled by snow, clopped through the deserted streets. Nearly dead from exhaustion I headed straight for the livery stable run by my friend, Sam. His dad boarded big teams used in the logging camps, and he usually had an extra stall or two for travelers. As I drove up to the livery stable, Sam greeted me at his door.

" 'Hello, Harry. How's the bridgegroom?'

" 'Hello,' I shouted back. 'I can tell you this darn wedding has got me more unnerved than any snow storm. Got two extra stalls for a few days?'

" 'Sure, Harry. Drive on into the barn,' Sam swung open the stable's big double doors.

"I drove the sleigh right inside onto the earthen hallway. Together we unharnessed the tired horses and bedded them down. Silently we rubbed Dan and Patches's wet backs while the stable boy rationed out oats and hay.

" 'Here, put this blanket on Dan. What time does your train leave?'

" 'Six o'clock,' I replied, handing Dan's lead to the stable boy.

" 'Good. Then there's time to drive you to the station in my best funeral rig: Black sleigh, black horses and black harness with plumes.'

" 'It's a wedding, not a burial, Sam.'

" 'About the same thing, I understand.'

Undaunted Sam hitched up his favorite team, but I insisted he leave off the plumes. Then like the wind we flew behind those horses to the station just in time for me to catch the Toronto train.

" 'Goodbye, Harry, Good luck.' Sam grabbed my bag and tossed it onto the platform.

"That night as the train sped through the darkness, the closer I came to Clara the more scared I felt. When I reached Toronto three hours later, I found my legs turned to jelly. As I strode down the platform and spied Clara dressed in a dark blue suit and a perky hat, I nearly lost my nerve. But the next instant my friend, John Curtis, appeared, took my battered case, and led me along with purposeful strides. Alice Curtis followed her husband and come up the tracks to meet me. Clara walked behind them.

" 'We became anxious since we've had no word from you in three days,' John said.

" 'So was I.' If he only realized how frightened I felt. 'But the storm knocked the telephone lines down. I finally got out this morning. I asked Sam to call you.'

"As I shyly regarded my bride, I suddenly realized I hardly knew her. I felt awkward as I leaned over and kissed her on the cheek. Clara blushed. The scarlet colour rose from her neck and finally engulfed her whole face. Suddenly I felt out of place and untutored in that big city. I had lived on my farm too long, isolated from the outside world and from women.

" 'Where have you been? I have waited for three whole days,' Clara demanded.

" 'We had a big snow, and I could not get the cutter out until this morning. It took me seven hours to drive my horses into Barrie where I caught the train. The journey here to Toronto has taken all day.' I tried to explain.

" 'If I were a proper girl, I should have gone back to England when you did not meet the ship.'

" 'But you are not a proper girl' teased John Curtis. 'Just one with an adventurous spirit which is far more suited to this rough country.'

"Clara laughed, and so did I. The tension broken, we found ourselves chatting happily together catching up on the news from England.

"About noon the following morning we got married at a small Anglican church where John knew the rector. I've forgotten its name. Alice made all the arrangements and even bought the flowers.

"First thing that day I went out and bought a new blue suit and some shoes. Clara objected to my boots. Then I got my hair cut and had a shave in a barber shop. Just before twelve thirty, we started out on foot for the church, all four of us.

"I remember Clara wore a light blue suit, a pretty pale coloured hat and white gloves. She always carried white gloves. She looked good enough to squeeze, but my knees were knocking at such a rate I was ready to hop the next train back to Barrie.

"It was snowing when we left the church. So we stood on the sidewalk and tossed snow balls at one another. Presently John insisted we go to a small hotel for lunch. Once there he ordered champagne. You know how the Missus loves a champagne cocktail.

"I remember John made an affectionate toast to Clara, praising her courage for coming so far alone to live in a strange land – a rough country about which she knew nothing. I got the feeling he thought Clara was a great lady. For many years I've known she is far too refined for me.

"So that's how we got married with Alice and John Curtis not only giving the luncheon, but also standing as witnesses. They proved to be great friends. Afterwards we remained in Toronto for a couple of days to buy household goods. Eventually on the Friday my bride and I took the afternoon train for Barrie. As the big city slipped away, Clara thought the Canadian countryside the most desolate she had ever seen. Although she did not say much, I knew she was afraid.

"I had forgotten how it was, you see, because I came out as a lad of sixteen to work in the nickel mines years before. Then I had homesteaded in Alberta for awhile, raising cattle and driving them to market at Calgary. In those days I got paid twice a year. One time on the train to Toronto I played cards for three days with cattle buyers and lost a half year's pay. But when the fellows learned I was on my way home to England to ask Clara to marry me, they let me win it all back. It was easy to spot a greenhorn in those days because he always looked so bug-eyed at this vast country. I wasn't exactly a greenhorn, just young. You see, I had forgotten how Clara would feel.

"That evening when the train pulled into Barrie I recognized Sam, his father, and Mr. and Mrs. McCarthy all standing on the platform. The McCarthy's were an older couple who owned a general store.

" 'Welcome, dear. How brave you are to come all this way in the middle of winter,' smiling Mr. McCarthy helped Clara down from the train.

" 'Thank you. How kind of you to meet us.'

" 'Not at all, my dear, we wanted to know Harry's bride. You shall spend the night with us before starting out on your long drive to Angus.'

"Delighted, Clara thanked him again.

" 'We planned a little party so we can all toast the bride,' Mr. McCarthy confided.

"Then taking Clara by the arm he guided her along the platform through the snow.

" 'Pretty little thing,' remarked Mrs. McCarthy to me as we brought up the rear.

"At this good couple's snug house next door to their dry goods store, we found the table fairly groaning under the wedding feast. Champagne corks popped, glasses were served all around, and Sam proposed a toast.

" 'To the bridegroom and his bride. May all their troubles be little ones.'

" 'To Clara,' said Mr. McCarthy as we all clinked our glasses.

" 'To Clara,' I echoed.

"Roy Williams arrived with his recent bride from Nottingham, England.

" 'I must kiss the newest English girl,' he called. 'Hello, love, welcome to Canada.' Roy planted a juicy kiss upon Clara's cheek.

"But before she could protest Clara was whisked away by Jane Williams.

" 'Don't mind him,' Jane smiled. 'He just loves English girls, that's all.'

"Then the two brides sat down together for a long chat. Every year, at Christmas, we always hear from Jane who still lives in Barrie.

"Pop went a champagne cork. Pop, pop, pop, went the bottles that Roy Williams brought. Just then Seth and Florence McAlister appeared in the doorway carrying two more bottles of champagne. Sam grabbed these also and disappeared into the kitchen.

" 'Hello, Harry,' Seth shouted to me. 'Glad to see you finally dug out of Angus.' A big man with an equally big heart, Seth slapped me across the shoulders.

"Presently the rafters rang with merriment as more glasses were filled, and other couples arrived. Soon all of Barrie seemed to be there. it was midnight before the party ended. As Mr. McCarthy let the guests out of the back door to avoid his icy front steps, the table was cleared, and we all went upstairs to bed.

"Early the next morning I awakened to the sound of sleigh bells. Opening the bedroom window I discovered Sam standing in the snow beside his fancy rig.

" 'Get up, Harry. I'll drive you to the livery stable with all of your gear.'

" 'You sure love those funeral horses,' I called back.

" 'Thoroughbreds of the best breed, right over from England, they are. Fresh from the Derby,' Sam tied up his team and entered Mrs. McCarthy's kitchen.

" 'You'll have to wait, Sam, you can't take those young folks away before they eat their breakfast,' I heard our hostess say.

"Within a few minutes we all sat down to a lovely feed of bacon, eggs and sausages. Believe me, Anne McCarthy was an exceptional cook.

"Finally after many goodbyes and an equal number of kisses, we left our kind hosts and climbed into Sam's funeral rig. With sleigh bells ringing we galloped through Barrie's snow-covered streets to the livery stable. Here I found the boy already had my team harnessed to the cutter. So after packing Clara's luggage on it and our boxes from Toronto, Sam and I stashed them all down with ropes over a big tarp. Then we rigged up a sleigh cover for Clara with just two holes in it for the reins so the wind would not freeze us to death.

" 'Now, new bride,' Sam told her, 'you should stay warm all the way to Angus. I even heated a brick for your feet.'

"(All of those years we lived in Angus and Barrie, Sam called Clara, New Bride.) Finally everything was ready, and we climbed onto the cutter.

" 'How long will it take to drive to the farm?' Clara inquired as Sam piled the lap robes over us.

" 'All day,' I replied, 'if the team is steady, and we stop at the preacher's.'

"Clara looked at me in disbelief. I realized she had no comprehension of the size of the great open prairie.

"About nine o'clock we started out. Dan and Patches, delighted to be free from their stalls, trotted eagerly through town, their big hooves throwing snow against the buck board.

" 'I reshod your horses for you, Harry,' Sam called after me. 'As a wedding present. Your team shouldn't get snow balls any more.'

"After the safe English countryside, Clara seemed amazed by the flat open Canadian landscape, now white with snow. She nestled beside me, settling the warm brick under her feet, as we fairly flew through the outskirts of Barrie. The horses, knowing they were headed home, pushed into their collars at a brisk trot and glided the cutter noiselessly over the frozen ground. I found the new shoes worked like a charm, and we did not have to stop for snow balls.

"In three hours' time I turned into the preacher's drive and met his family who walked down their lane to greet us.

" 'Welcome to Canada,' called the preacher's wife.

" 'Hello, missus, come in Harry,' the preacher laboured through the snow until he caught Dan's bridle. 'We have prepared a good meal for you.'

"Presently we sat in their warm kitchen. A grateful Clara sipped the hot cup of tea offered her. Several young children stood wide-eyed around the table and stared. None of them spoke. Shy and self conscious under their questioning eyes, Clara spilled her tea.

" 'Sit down, kids. Here, have some food,' the preacher distracted them.

" 'Take no notice, dearie,' they have never seen a real English lady before. 'Let me give you some more tea,' his wife offered.

"Clara smiled, accepted another cup of tea together with a plateful of home-grown vegetables and meat.

" 'You'll get used to it, dearie. It's a big country; the distances are long, but we are all friends here,' the wife smiled encouragingly.

"It was almost an hour later when we rose to leave. I still hoped to reach home before dark, but what with the heavy snow and gale winds, I feared it was impossible.

" 'Thank you,' Clara said politely as she put on her coat. 'You are an excellent cook.'

" 'Stop by, Harry, and visit when you're passing. You're always welcome. Goodbye, Clara, come back,' the buxom wife invited.

"Leading Dan, the preacher walked half way down his drive with us. When he let go of Dan's bridle, I picked up the reins and noticed my

Mr. Houghton's Wedding

friend stood in his drive for awhile to make sure the heavy cutter did not get stuck in the snow.

"'Goodbye, Harry,' he called finally. 'Goodbye, missus, come back.'

"I watched him turn towards his house before I guided the team onto the unmarked road to Angus. It was bitter cold. A gale force wind blew powdery snow into our faces. The unbroken prairie, with its very few trees, which grew in scattered clumps, provided us with little protection. The horses, now tired from pulling their heavy load, walked more slowly, their heads down.

"The grey afternoon wore on, and the vast landscape became less distinct as four o'clock approached. A lonely church came into view – standing forlorn beside the empty road. We passed a farm, grey smoke rising from its chimney the only sign of life. A rabbit, white and sure footed on the snow, hopped in front of the team. A flock of geese passed overhead on their journey south in their distinctive V formation. Then silence, as if the only living things in that lonely white land were the horses, Clara and I.

"My New Bride said very little. I knew she had no idea of this big country she had traveled so far to get married in. Slowly it dawned on me how frightened she must feel. Compared to England's well-ordered, lush fields with their neat hedgerows, Canada must seem to her like a waste land stretching into eternity.

"No lights blinked in the distance. No farm houses welcomed us. We saw only a vast whiteness that melted into a grey horizon. Soon the short afternoon would become dark; there was no twilight that far north. Presently I stopped the team, jumped down and lit the lanterns on either side of the cutter. Then I buckled the sleigh bells over the horses' backs so other teams could hear us coming on that dark, unlit road.

"When I climbed back onto the cutter, I realized Clara was crying. And I felt suddenly overwhelmed by confusion.

"'It's a big country,' I mumbled trying to be helpful, 'but the people are kind.'

"The wind gathered force and whipped snow into our faces, nearly blinding us. Twice the horses stopped, confused in the darkness by this whirling snow. Twice I jumped down to check the load, the lights and the harness. Everything seemed secure, but still Dan and Patches hesitated. Only the sound of the wind and a dog howling through the dark afternoon broke the stillness.

"Then away ahead, about two, maybe three miles distant, I saw a light.

"'There's the farm,' I encouraged Clara. 'We are almost home.'

"I felt triumphant. I wanted to sing, but I stole a shy kiss from my bride instead. When we at last turned into my farm lane, I realized all the lights in my house were on. Frightened lest something was wrong, I quickened the pace. Coming towards us up my road ran George Felts waving his arms.

" 'Welcome home, Harry,' he shouted against the wind.

"Out of the barn came Freddy Cofflin carrying a pitch fork, followed by James Cooper and Tom Harrison. I could not believe my eyes, apparently all of the neighbors had gathered. As I brought the team to a halt, James Cooper helped Clara down and bundled her off to the house. A great shout went up as she entered.

" 'Welcome to your new home, Clara,' a dozen voices greeted her.

"As George led the team into the barn the fellows grabbed me, pulling me from the cutter, and tossed me, more dead than alive, onto the hay loft. In a twinkling they unharnessed my tired horses and led them into their waiting stalls.

" 'Surprise,' said George, 'We fed your stock while you were gone and did your chores tonight.'

" 'How was Toronto?' Tom Harrison wanted to know. 'Did you really tie the knot, Harry?'

" 'I really did, Tom, and I wore a blue suit and new shoes.' I scrambled down from the hay loft. 'Had my hair cut too, and got a shave in a barber shop. I really was spruced up for the occasion, I can tell you.'

" 'It's grand to have you home. I am anxious to meet the new missus.' Tom slapped me upon the back.

"George led the way across the stable yard, and we entered the house. Here I found all the neighbors assembled, a fire roared up the chimney, a sumptuous meal lay ready on the table, and every one I knew for miles around was there. I could not believe it. Immediately whisked away by the women, Clara was generally admired for her clothes, for her accent and for her refined manners.

"Bottles of champagne appeared, corks popped into the air, and drinks were passed around. Tired and cold, I stood beside the fire basking in my new wife's reflected glory. Everyone thought Clara extraordinarily beautiful. It was the jolliest time I ever experienced in my entire life".

His eyes twinkled with merriment as, remembering that far-away time, Mr. Houghton ended his story. Still reminiscing, he poured us each a second cup of tea. Presently he slept – his mouth open, his honest hands relaxed at his knees. I watched him, realizing for the first time he was married in the same year I was born. Only the gentle ticking of the mantle clock broke the silence as I sat staring into the fire, savoring his story.

I did not awaken Mr. Houghton. I wanted to look at him – his blue eyes closed, his breathing rhythmic, his frame strong and angular. To me he seemed a strange figure in his old blue suit. Somehow, he did not belong in city clothes, but in a parka and boots walking over the wide-open spaces of the prairie, or driving a team of heavy horses through the snow.

A Forgotten Landscape

38

The Night The Taliaferros' Barn Burned

Our worst fear living in the country was fire. We had no fire department and once a blaze started, it usually burned itself out. Barns filled with hay and animals provided vulnerable targets for lightening. Although every one of us took great care with cigarettes, and put up several lightening rods, barn fires were the most dreaded.

The last few days of March scarcely went out like a lamb. Giant thunderstorms rattled in the skies over Goochland and brought fear to our hearts. Then one night forked lightening illuminated the sky and struck the Taliaferro's big barn.

In minutes flames leaped high into the dark sky devouring hay and corn. Animals ran in panic, screaming as they scattered across the open fields and down our road. Rain pelted upon the dry land, but it did not dampen the flames as hay and silage were instantly consumed.

"Get up, Doc," Mr. Houghton shook me; "Get up and put your clothes on. The Taliaferro's barn is on fire."

I sat up in Mrs. Houghton's dark room and switched on the light. My clock on the bedside table said three in the morning.

"Hurry up, come with me." Mr. Houghton whispered before he tiptoed out. "And don't wake the missus".

I grabbed my clothes and slipped quickly into them. Only then did I become aware of the passing cars, their motors sounding loud in the darkness. Away in the distance I heard men shouting. Through my window I saw the weird excited dance of flames as they leapt high into the sky. When I entered the kitchen, Mr. Houghton was speaking on the telephone to Tom Harris.

"We need your fire truck, Tom, at Taliaferro's barn right away," Mr. Houghton shouted into the receiver before he slammed it back onto its cradle.

"Doc, come let's go. Put on your raincoat and follow me. We need to get some leads for Jean's horses and some hose lengths from the barn."

Mr. Houghton grabbed his hat and slicker, and we let ourselves out into the wet night. Cattle crazed by the fire, stood in our front yard. Two big forms resembling Jean's horses, Tom and Huck, galloped past us on the road. In the night sky the fire shot up fifty feet into the air. I realized that the oil and grease used for farm tractors must have ignited, as sparks and cinders flew around us.

"Get out of the road, Doc, walk along the side,' cattle are everywhere. Follow behind me," Mr. Houghton strode down the lane towards his barn.

In haste we grabbed the leads and hoses before we continued up the road towards the fire. I saw in the weird light several figures of men trying to wash down William's cottage which stood only yards away from the barn. William, an older coloured man, lived on the Taliaferro's place as caretaker. The pasture gates stood open and several cars lined the road's shoulder as our neighbors from nearby farms tried desperately to contain the flames. It seemed a hopeless task.

"Tom Harris should get here in a few minutes," Mr. Houghton commented as we eased ourselves over the fence of the Taliaferros' lower pasture and started across the field.

"With his fire engine?" I asked, running to keep up and stepping into a meadow muffin.

Mr. Harris was our one-man fire department. Shortly before the war when his dairy went up in flames, he had lost six Guernsey milk cows and two heifers. Although neighbors came from far and near, fire gutted one shed in minutes and jumped to the main barn. Only the extreme effort of his neighbours and Tom Harris's quick thinking saved his dairy.

After that he bought a second-hand truck and rigged it up as a makeshift fire engine. He trained his farm workers in fire fighting, and they initiated the first fire department at our end of the county.

Tonight through the smoke and flames I saw Mr. Harris's engine arrive and recognized his familiar figure standing among the men. They poured water on the fire and turned their hoses onto William's house and the enormous silo. Other men in heavy slickers and wellingtons chased the terrified cattle down the farm lane. These animals bellowed and milled all around as we made our way into the farmyard. I saw Jean helping to man a fire hose as William tossed his few possessions out of the threatened cottage. Behind the barn the undergrowth in the woods seemed to glow with a strange light.

"Stay close, Doc, and hand me that hose," Mr. Houghton commanded as we joined the dripping, soot covered men.

Out of the confusion of men and animals I recognized Arthur Henley and Harrison Moore as they came towards us. Rain dropped from their noses and ran down their yellow slickers.

"Doc, we need you to help bring down some calves. There are two very young ones in the woods behind the barn." Harrison Moore shouted.

Running through the mud and cattle, I climbed the big double gates at the end of the pasture and followed Mr. Moore. Near William's house we found two white-faced Hereford calves. Beside them crouched Jimmy Snead, Grevious's grandson.

"You and Doc carry the smaller of the two, and I'll take this one," Mr. Moore ordered.

We picked up the calves and circled slowly around William's house towards the road. Several men with Mr. Harris's fire engine blocked our way; I almost dropped my end of the calf as Jimmy and I carefully stepped over hoses and buckets in the farm lane. My rubber boots were heavily caked with mud and my arms ached.

"Get out of the way, kids," shouted Mr. Pillar as he pumped water from the fire truck.

Rain and spray from the hoses made the lane a sea of mud, and the footing extremely slippery. Still carrying the calf, Jimmy and I made our way down the lane onto the road. Loose cattle ran everywhere bellowing and calling to each other in panic. Mr. Moore, his calf thrown over one shoulder, walked in front and cleared the way for us; then he turned into the woods. Here we found the going easier because the pine trees afforded us some shelter. On the road we heard Mr. Henley and several other men trying to round up the frightened cattle and drive them towards our pasture. Behind us on the trail I heard the sound of horses galloping, and saw two giant shadows as Tom and Huck passed us.

When we reached Mr. Houghton's farmyard, I stopped. My arms ached and I couldn't carry the calf another step. Jimmy and I laid the baby Hereford beside the watering trough. Before us a dark shadow loomed out of the night, and a soft velvet nose touched me on the hand. Instantly I reached up for the halter and held on. The big horse backed up taking me with him and then stopped. I led Huck gently forward and took him into the barn.

"The lights are out," Mr. Moore's voice said, "Let's see if I can find some matches." He put the calf down and fumbled with a box of matches.

The little flames flickered for a few seconds and allowed us to see an old lantern hanging on the wall from a stirrup leather. Although Mr. Houghton rarely used it, the lantern had some kerosene in it. Mr. Moore struck another match and lit the wick; a fragile light illuminated the barn. I could just make out the forms of Lindy Lou and Susie Q. in their stalls. Then I saw Sally Anne's horse, Tom, watching us from the doorway.

"Catch that horse, Jimmy," I commanded. But as Jimmy ran forward Tom snorted and veered back out of the stable yard. The next instant Jimmy disappeared, and I heard him gently coax the skittish horse away from the open gates. Sounds of trotting hooves and rattling chains told me that Jimmy had pushed the stable yard gates closed. Then the boy returned leading Tom by the halter. Within minutes we placed the calves and horses into loose box stalls before we stepped out into the rainy night again.

The men continued to round up the nearly hundred head of Hereford cattle still running loose. We were just in sight of the Taliaferros' barn when I heard a loud crash. Sparks and flames shot high into the sky. I watched in horror as the barn's slate roof collapsed. Smoke billowed over the woods and pastures. The giant silo exploded as fire consumed it. Mr. Harris's exhausted crew fought bravely, but the intense heat drove them back. Jean Taliaferro and William dragged the furniture away from his cottage out into the field. I saw some of the men carry it away. Mrs. Taliaferro and Sally Anne stood transfixed against the blazing sky.

"Look, Mr. Moore," I gasped holding onto his arm, "the whole world is on fire."

"Good thing it isn't winter or the stock would have gone too," he replied, grabbing Jimmy around the waist. "You stay here, boy."

"My grandfather is up there," Jimmy wiggled free and ran towards the burning barn as fast as his brown legs could carry him.

The men hosed down the barn's cinders and fought valiantly to contain the fire in the woods.

"It must be like a battlefield," I exclaimed, awed by the destruction.

"I expect so," Mr. Moore replied.

We raced across the wet pasture and joined the men. Mr. Moore picked up a fire hose. I went in search of Jimmy and found him with William and Grievous Snead. The boy stood beside the frightened black men trying to help. The intense heat forced us back to the road.

"Miss Doc," William greeted me, "There's been a great lamentation here tonight. All my clothes is still in the house. I ain't got nuffing left."

The cottage was ringed with fire. Glass popped out of the windows. Finally the house exploded, and showers of flames and glass rained down on us. Still the exhausted men poured water on the smoldering ruins of the Taliaferros' barn.

"Get back, Miss Jean, the walls are going to collapse," Tom Harris appeared masked in grime and soot. "I'm afraid the barn's gone, but I don't think you've lost any stock."

"That's a blessing," she replied, her eyes red from the intense heat. "We shall rebuild."

Two hours later as dawn broke, the fire was out. Mr. Taliaferro tramped through the fields. His face grim, his jaw set in a hard line. I had always stood in awe of him, but tonight I felt a great sorrow for this unyielding man as we surveyed the ruined barn, silo and William's house. They all lay in ashes. Only part of the barn's cinder block walls stood; the barn with its contents, the roof, its slates and walls were a twisted mass of rubble. William's house still smoldered. Grievous took him home to get some dry clothes and a bite of breakfast. The devastation before us was compounded by the smell of burning wood, silage and trees. My eyes smarted from the lingering smoke. I felt sick.

"We can gather up the hoses, men," Mr. Harris commanded. "Leave one in case the fire breaks out again."

The tired, low-spirited men began to pack up their gear. Hoses and buckets hung on the pasture fence; slickers were shed and placed over posts as Mr. Harris wound up his fire hoses and put them back on his truck. Furniture was strewed all over the pasture and the grass was blackened by fire and smoke. Harrison Moore with Jimmy walked through the undergrowth in the woods to make sure the fire was not smoldering. I went in search of Mr. Houghton. He stood with several men and Mr. Henley across the field.

In front of me out of the woods wandered several cattle, looking lost and confused. Gently I turned them towards Mr. Houghton's field and coaxed them into it. Standing beside the fire truck on the opposite side of the fence I recognized Mr. Houghton. He appeared sad and dejected.

"Come along, Doc, let's go home, away from this terrible scene. I think it's the worst day of my life." He climbed over the fence and hugged me.

The sun broke through as the last rain clouds scudded across the sky. A few minutes later the smoke cleared. Dispirited we noticed the signs of spring around us. With heavy hearts we crossed the pasture and entered the woods. Here we met Harrison Moore and several men still rounding up stray cattle.

"We got the fire out," Mr. Houghton greeted them. "But the barn's a total loss."

"Be hard to replace until after the war with building materials as scarce as they are now," Mr. Pillar remarked. "It's a darn shame."

"William's house is gone too and half the fencing with it," Mr. Houghton said.

"I believe Tom Harris's jerry-rigged fire truck saved the day," Mr. Pillar added. "It's a good thing to have since there's no other fire company between here and Richmond."

"They saved Jean's grey mules, old Paul, and her farm wagon. But she has no harness. Mr. Taliaferro appeared in shock when he saw the roof collapse. Believe me it was a terrible sight," Mr. Houghton replied.

"Everything else is gone, I suppose?" asked Mr. Moore. "Fires in the country are always devastating."

The Night the Taliaferros' Barn Burned

We parted and I followed Mr. Houghton down the path towards his house. The road was still blocked by stray cattle and cars trying to ease through them as the men started for home. The men put the cattle in our pasture at Mother's house. Several cows appeared injured and in shock. Old Dr. Sherrill arrived shortly and checked these animals over. He also looked at Tom and Huck who had taken up residence in Mr. Houghton's barn. The cattle mooed and cried all day making an awful racket. We had no electricity for hours as all the lines were burned. Mrs. Houghton greeted us at her back door and made us take off our dirty clothes in the shed before we could enter her newly scrubbed kitchen floor.

"You look like tar babies," she told us. "You are covered in mud and soot."

Then she fed us a glorious breakfast. I was never so hungry in all my life and didn't realize it until I sat down at the table to bacon, eggs, toast and homemade jam. There was no school that day. I was too tired to go.

A few days later lawyers and insurance men swarmed across the farm, poked into Mr. Houghton's stables and asked questions. These city men examined the ruined barn, the old tractor and the two scorched farm wagons. Jean's grey mules, Dilly and Dolly, unable to work without harness enjoyed a holiday. Tom and Huck who couldn't be ridden without saddles and bridles lived with Suzie Q. and Lindy Lou for a week or two. Also lost in the fire was old Paul's harness and wagon. Paul, himself, was discovered in Mrs. Taliaferro's flower garden eating the seedlings.

Within a week the barn was razed and another, a temporary one, from Sears Roebuck stood in its place. Finally the insurance men and the lawyers returned to their offices in Richmond. Meanwhile, our neighbours searched in their lofts and attics. Mr. McFarland, the County Agent, brought Jean a set of double harnesses, an unused saddle, a bridle and a girth. Mr. Harris supplied two halters. Leather goods could no longer be found in tack shops. Only rarely did they sell second-hand bridles and saddles. Those of us who owned them kept them. Mr. Kelly, up at Goochland Court House, brought down a truck load of hay, and Mrs. Clark, from the store in Manakin, sent a two-horse plow.

Shortly afterwards Tom Harris drove down to see Mr. Houghton.

"I am organizing a volunteer fire department, Harry. I want you to join."

"I don't know anything about fighting fires. You must be kidding. After the Taliaferros' I don't want anything more to do with fire."

But Tom Harris remained undaunted. He bought another second-hand truck and rigged up a water tank. Then he taught his neighbors fire fighting. Soon all the men at our end of the county had joined except Mr. Houghton.

"You are not patriotic," I teased. "Even Mr. Taliaferro joined last week."

Mr. Houghton said nothing, just continued to feed his black mares. I watched him ration out oats and hay for Tom and Huck. Then he banged the stable doors shut.

"Fire fighting takes up too much time," he complained. "I don't fancy getting myself singed to a crisp either."

But the next day he became a charter member of the Goochland Fire Brigade.

39

Store Talk

In December Churchill came to America to consult with Roosevelt and remained here a month. Shortly after his return to England, Malaya fell on February first, and two weeks later the Japanese invaded Singapore. Curtin, the Australian Prime Minister, was furious with Churchill for not sending enough arms and modern equipment so the Aussies could defend Johore on the Malay Peninsula across the Strait from Singapore. When Curtin warned Churchill to stop pushing the Australian troops around and never to send them into battle again without sufficient armament, Churchill backed down. Angry that his men had been sacrificed, Curtin recalled them home against the English Prime Minister's orders.

Mr. Houghton read this to us from the newspaper. "Churchill better be careful," he added, "he's overstepped his knowledge of war." He continued to paraphrase the paper.

When on February 15, General Wavell surrendered Singapore with 85,000 British, Indian and native troops, the home front morale hit rock bottom. Some considered this the greatest defeat in British history. The Allies hastened to protect the oil fields of the Dutch West Indies. With the combined fleets of American, British, Dutch and Australian ships under the American Admiral Chester Nimitz, they tried to prevent a complete disaster.

Mr. Houghton paced the floor and then switched on his short wave radio. Instead of the news we heard from Hamburg Radio Charlie's parody of "The Continental", a popular song:

    Japanese action, dangerous rhythm.
    It's terrific in the Pacific, the Japanese are doing very well.

> They've taken Hong Kong and Manila, their Navy and Air
> Force are swell.
> The talk of the world is the Pacific; they fight Roosevelt
> And his Jews.
> My ship whispers Franklin so helplessly, we're anything
> But strong.
> It's so terrific in the Pacific, the Japanese have taken
> Singapore.
> Terrific Pacific terrific, U.S.A., did you know that before?

"That's terrible poetry," said Mrs. Houghton. "It doesn't even rhyme much less scan. Whoever wrote that was an idiot."

Mr. Houghton turned it off.

"Get your coat, Doc, and we'll go down to the store. We need a few groceries," he told me. "I want to have a chat with the lads. This news is terrible. Radio Hamburg is having a go at the Allies. I can't stand much more."

Mrs. Houghton didn't try to stop us. In fact I thought she must be glad to get rid of us. I had pestered her with my homework, and Mr. Houghton had been pacing for over an hour. At the store we found the men gathered as usual around the pot-bellied stove. The women stood at the counter talking to Ethel and Mrs. Henley in subdued voices. The few children there played quietly in a corner beside the ice cream freezer. When he entered I sat down on a nail keg, my favourite place, near the stove while Mr. Houghton did his shopping.

"Churchill better stop meddling in this war and firing his generals," Tom Harris remarked. "Wavell isn't a bad general. He didn't have the hardware to hold Singapore. Some of the defenders were raw, untrained troops stuck out there to hold an Island. The Japs have all kinds of hardware plus air power and bombs. Once Johore, on the Malaya Peninsula, fell, it was a straight shot to Singapore."

"It was supposed to be the Gilbralter of the Pacific, a British stronghold that was impossible to capture," Colonel Hollis informed us.

"Churchill's been here begging arms from Roosevelt. What a bully that Englishman is! Roosevelt's no match for that old bulldog," said Mr. Harris.

Store Talk

A few minutes later Mr. Houghton perched on a nail keg next to mine and laid his groceries on the floor beside him. The stove was hot, but Mr. Henley added more coal before he too sat down.

"The missus puts a great deal of stock in Mr. Churchill. She reads his speeches and tells me they are written in beautiful English," Mr. Houghton joined the conversation.

"We need more than speeches to win this war," Mr. Harris replied.

"He's been a good war-time leader," said Mr. Armstrong whose daughter, Dorothy led the singing at church. I thought she sang like a hillbilly - all in her nose. His eldest daughter, Lizzie, played the organ. Mrs. Houghton told me I must not criticize because Mr. Armstrong was a "stalwart Christian." He was a lay reader and led the service when Dr. Price didn't come. "Churchill's no push over," he continued.

"I agree," concurred Arthur Henley, "but the Aussies are great fighters, and Churchill doesn't appreciate them. He's a real English snob, and he has an American mother."

"A snob like me," quipped Mr. Houghton, "only I'm a Yorkshire snob; it's not as posh as a London one." Mr. Houghton winked at Colonel Hollis, who winked back.

"Singapore has a bad time with water," commented Colonel Hollis. "I was stationed there once years ago, of course. All the Japanese had to do was to cut the water supply. On a tropical island you can't live without water. Then they walked across the causeway. They came down the Malay peninsula and Singapore sits at the bottom just waiting to be captured since the garrison lacked guns and air cover."

He sat down on the bench Mr. Henley offered and put his head in his hands. He'd fought in the First World War with the British Army, but was too old this time. Born in India of English parents, he'd lived in the Far East and knew it well. Mr. Houghton told me it nearly broke Colonel Hollis's heart when he couldn't join up again. I watched him take out his pipe, fill it and light it. Then he gave several puffs and sent sweet-smelling tobacco smoke amongst us. Mr. Armstrong lit a cigarette and offered one to Tom Harris who blew smoke rings through which I put my finger before they vanished. Nobody spoke for several minutes.

"Mr. Churchill's too old and too meddlesome to conduct a war,"

Tom Harris broke the silence. "It's his fault Singapore fell. The British fleet is in shreds. They've thousands of tons of shipping at the bottom of the sea. The Australians have headed home. The Dutch are not much better off. It's only Admiral Nimitz whose still going, but he's short on ships too. The Japs control the Pacific from the Bay of Bengal to the Bering Sea. We're nearly defeated."

"The Japanese control the Pacific," repeated Colonel Hollis. "Malaya and French Ino-China, Hong Kong and now Singapore all captured. The Philippines are hanging on by a thread. They will go too, of course. There is no way to defend them. The Japs already are on Luzon, the biggest island. We need a fighter plane like the Japanese Zero."

"It looks grave; the Philippines are doomed," said Mr. Armstrong. "We can't give up or the free world will be defeated."

"MacArthur is still there. I put great faith in him. It takes guts to retire and to re-enlist when Roosevelt needed a good general," Mr. Houghton replied.

"He lived on the Philippines as a member of the military survey when a young man. He was the department commander, out there, and finally as the Army Chief of Staff until 1935. He knows the Far East well; that's why Roosevelt picked him," Mr. Armstrong told us. I was amazed he knew so much about the army. "We just can't give up."

"I agree," said Mr. Houghton. "we're obliged for Doc's sake and others like her to defend their future. It's for the young ones that we must win."

He got up and signaled to me that we should go. We picked up our groceries and let ourselves out into the snowy night. The stars shone brightly and the moon looked full. I took a deep breath and felt better. The men's talk depressed me. I felt I was condemned to die before I'd even grown up. I choked back my tears and got into the car.

"Do you think we can win this war?" I asked as we drove home.

"Yes, you have to believe it because it's your future that's at stake. Evil wears itself out sooner or later. Hitler and the Japs are evil. They will meet their end and the war will finish. You must get the goodness out of life, as much as you possibly can."

"The Japanese frighten me even more than the Germans. The Germans are scary enough with Rommel and Lord Haw Haw's slimy voice.

I'll never forget it, if I live to be a hundred."

I tried to remain optimistic and believe with all my heart that in the end, if I rolled enough bandages at the Red Cross and sent enough parcels to England and prayed really hard, we shall win. I knew I must learn to cope with this war or it would destroy me.

February 1942

Dear Dad,

I'm in trouble again with Mrs. Owens. She claims I'll never be a lady because I bite my fingernails. I do bite them still, but I'm trying not to. I'm getting them polished and filed so they look nice. Mary Anne polishes them for me, and Mrs. Houghton says clear polish is all right. She doesn't like to see chipped nail polish. It's tacky and it's not allowed at school. I don't wish to make a career of being a lady, but it seems I must follow a great many unwritten rules of behavior. It's too confusing and boring. Mrs. Henley told me to "leave it where Jesus flung it", and not to worry. I'll grow up soon enough. Mrs. Owens thinks otherwise.

I'm lonely for you. It's been a long time since I've seen you. Mr. Houghton says war is like that. It separates people. Do write me.

Love, Doc

February 1942

Dear Doc,

The work here in Washington is very intense. I am not sure when I can get to Richmond. The weather's been terribly cold and snowy, and the traffic is snarled up with wrecks. Don't worry about the terrible Miss Owens; she's trying too hard to create a lady where a young girl still remains. Don't let her bully you into early adulthood. You need to enjoy being a child still for just a little longer. Tell the Houghtons "hello" for me. Love, Dad

A Forgotten Landscape

40

Spring Cleaning

March 1942

In March I celebrated my fourteenth birthday. We took Cary and Miss Emma out to dinner with us on Father's check he'd sent me. Then we all went to the movies. Mr. Houghton always called them "the pictures." I didn't want a party with my friends in town as transportation had become difficult and gas for domestic use was in short supply.

Mother came home for the weekend to do some spring cleaning. I didn't move back home as everything was torn up. I did go to the attic to get some lighter clothes.

"You'll have to come with me, Mrs. Houghton," I told her, "that attic is haunted."

"All right, but I'm helping your mother with the draperies and Bertha is coming to wash slip covers and summer curtains."

I promised to stay out of the way if she'd only come with me to the trunks and get my clothes.

"I'm not doing any work, and I'll be in my apple tree if you need me," I whispered. I had no intention of getting into a row with my mother, and the best policy was to stay away. Mrs. Houghton agreed.

On Sunday evening Mrs. Houghton drew a sigh of relief as she sat on her loveseat, exhausted. Mr. Houghton drove Mother to Broad Street Station to get her train, and I climbed down out of my apple tree. It took us a week to recover. Quietly I settled my spring clothes in the closet and folded up the heavier ones to return to the attic. I doubted, somehow, spring would really come before April.

Mr. Houghton put Cary and me to work the next weekend repairing his chicken house. It had taken a beating over the winter and needed a great deal of work. We ripped off old tar paper and put up new on the roof and the sides. We fixed the warped windows and added a new door to replace the one that hung crazily from a single hinge. I pounded nails until my shoulders ached, and we painted with white wash the entire chicken house inside and out. Mr. Houghton used green trim for the doors and windows, after he made sure the paint had no lead in it.

"It's the grandest chicken house in all Virginia," he declared when we'd finished. "Just think how the hens will love it and lay a lot more eggs."

"Makes them contented. Contented hens always lay more," Mr. Houghton told us. "Don't you know that?"

"Oh," said Cary, "green trim and white wash adds to their contentment, I suppose?"

"That's right. We'll have double yoke eggs every day now. I'll leave the chickens out for another two hours and allow the white wash to dry. Next week I'll plow up their yard and turn them out in the other one that has grass."

Mr. Houghton inspected our handiwork and touched up places we'd missed. "It looks grand, I tell you; we're in the chicken business now."

Cary winked at me. "Will Doc get a raise after all her work? You aren't supposed to work children without pay."

"I'll have to see about that," Mr. Houghton stammered, caught off guard.

"I expect five dollars for my contribution," Cary replied washing his hands and the brushes in a bucket. "No less than five dollars for all my hard labour."

"That's what a grown man gets. Come on Cary, it's to help the war effort." Mr. Houghton protested.

"All those contented hens will soon make up for it, Mr. H. Don't be so tight."

"Tight? You call me tight?" He looked hurt. "When you're on my doorstep for cups of tea and biscuits all the time. You must think I'm a millionaire!" He winked. "When do you ever invite me for a meal?"

"Come at Easter," Cary said impetuously. "Come and have a meal

Spring Cleaning

with us on Easter Sunday."

"That should be your mother's invitation, not yours. Suppose she's made plans?"

"I'll ask her," Cary promised, "and ring you on the phone tonight. We love you, Mr. Houghton, and I always enjoy my cups of tea at your house."

"And cookies. Don't forget the cookies. You'd eat your weight in them, Cary, if you got the chance. It all costs, you know, although the Missus bakes them."

Mr. Houghton collected his tools and put them away neatly in the feed room. The paint he carried to the shed away from his chickens because paint fumes might drop his egg production.

"We'll get the goodness out of that paint job for sure," he said as we walked home together.

The following Tuesday afternoon Mrs. Houghton took me to Miller and Rhoads after school. She had received a check from Father to buy me an Easter dress. We also got a hat and shoes. What a glorious time we had trying on and selecting my new outfit.

"Now," I told her, clutching the paper bags, "I shall look grown up."

"A lady is as a lady does," Mrs. Houghton reminded me. "A new dress won't offset bad manners."

"No," I agreed, "but this will make me feel elegant, almost as elegant as Mrs. Taliaferro."

"That will be going some because she's a real lady," replied Mrs. Houghton. "She is very cultured."

On Easter Sunday after church we all went to the Craddocks for dinner of fried chicken, okra, and tomatoes and squash casserole. Mr. Houghton really enjoyed himself. He'd dressed carefully in his grey suit and red tie for the occasion. Mrs. Houghton wore a lovely Bamburg sheer and a straw hat with field flowers. I had my new dress with daisies on it, and a straw hat with a blue ribbon around it to match. The dress was yellow with white flowers, and I thought it especially pretty. The hat had no childish streamers, but a yellow daisy tucked under the blue ribbon and sitting at a perky angle on the brim. I felt gorgeous and ever so grown up. Mr. Houghton made us each a corsage of spring flowers from the garden, and we all looked rather grand. He brought one to Miss Emma which delighted her.

"What a marvelous gift for Easter!" She told him and planted a kiss on his cheek.

"You embarrass me," he said blushing. "It's not often I get kissed anymore."

Later that evening Grandmother called from Indianapolis, and Father rang from Florida where he was now stationed.

"I'll be going overseas in a month or two," he told me. "So behave yourself, Son, 'till I get back".

"That's a long time to be good," I objected, happy to hear his voice.

"I hear Cary wants to join up when he finishes school this June. Tell him I think that's great. He always was a bright boy. Goodbye, Son, don't grow up too quickly. I hate to miss it. When I get back, you'll be a lady."

"Not quite," I replied. "It takes a long time to become a lady. One day I hope to be as cultured as Mrs. Taliaferro. When I am twenty and can speak French."

He laughed and rang off.

I felt lost. Suddenly the war, until now always so far away, took on a personal meaning. I was scared about Cary's leaving and Father's going overseas. Several men I knew at Henley's store had also joined the Armed Forces. They left shortly before my birthday. James Lucas, although barely sixteen, had lied about his age and gone too. Yet not until this evening did I realize that my personal world was changing, and I must change with it. I prayed that the people I knew would be safe and return when the war was over. But our greatest loss was yet to come.

41

Jackie Disturbs The Peace

April 1942

One Sunday in late April before it really became warm, Mrs. Houghton and I drove to church in the governess cart with Jackie. It was only a mile from our home to St. Mary's, and the donkey easily did the journey in twenty minutes. This Sunday Dr. Price, a supply minister, now retired from parish work, was to take the service. He had come several times before, and I always found him very grim.

"He likes to tell you the worst things," I complained to Mrs. Houghton as we drove along. "All about hell, and how we're headed there. I don't feel we're going to hell at all, even though the rest of the world seems to have gone crazy with this war."

"He's an old type priest. I remember several of his sort, years ago in England, who always sent everyone into brimstone and eternal fire. Dr. Price is just disappointed in life, that's all. Take no notice of him, and pray to God we'll have someone else next week."

"I wish we had a regular priest," I mused, like Dr. Clery used to be before he joined the Canadian Army."

Jackie trotted happily down our long gravel road, his head high, his pace steady. He jumped to one side as a bird flew suddenly up in front of him, and galloped a few steps until I pulled him down once again. The brisk morning made him mischievous and full of tricks. Mrs. Houghton enjoyed the bright sunshine and the song birds that chattered overhead in the pine woods. But the April wind felt cool, so we pulled on our gloves and buttoned up our coats. Presently Jackie turned out onto River

Road still trotting merrily along, sniffing at the wind. We entered the churchyard, and I found a tree away from the cars to tie him. I prayed he would behave himself and not disturb the service.

"You'd better put a blanket over him," Mrs. Houghton suggested as she got down. "This wind is cold, and heaven knows how long we will be today."

I unfolded the bright, red wool blanket and slipped it over Jackie's harness. Then I untied the check rein and filled the bucket with water from the pump. On Sundays when the service was long, as for Communion, I usually brought a pat of hay. This I offered to Jackie now. Then, hoping the donkey would remain content, I followed Mrs. Houghton into the church.

"Good morning, Doc," Alvira Carthage greeted me as I bounded up the steps. "I see you brought Jackie. Let's pray he behaves himself."

"He will," I replied.

Several parishioners gathered under the trees in the front lawn chattering together. I recognized Mrs. Sparrow, Emma Craddock, Jean and Mrs. Taliaferro. Before me in the vestibule stood Catherine Hollis offering a hymnal.

"How are you today?" she inquired as I accepted the book, straightened my hat, and took a deep breath before entering the church.

"Oh, fine," I regarded this casually dressed, rather plump woman. She always smiled and radiated a certain warmth. "It's good to see you and the Colonel here today."

"There's a vestry meeting after the service, and Carter would never miss one. We have to vote against Mr. Wickham, you know," she confided.

Haroldton Wickham's family gave the land and helped build the church, so he felt he owned it. Understanding, I nodded and went to find Mrs. Houghton in a front pew. But half way up the aisle Edna Armstrong tugged my arm.

"Can you carry in this second vase of flowers? Sally Anne arranged them, but since she has the flu, I picked them up on my way to church." Mrs. Armstrong handed me the heavy brass vase which together we placed on the altar. Then I watered the flowers carefully from a long-spouted pitcher.

"Dr. Price insists upon large vases of fresh flowers," she whispered as we took our seats next to Mrs. Houghton.

Looking out of the window I watched the tall evergreen trees blow gently in the April wind. Mrs. Houghton dropped upon her knees and closed her eyes in prayer. Mrs. Armstrong did likewise, but I spun around to see who was coming in to church.

"Pray, Doc," Mrs. Houghton whispered. "Stop looking behind you, it's impolite. You're supposed to pray."

"I've nothing to pray for," I whispered back as I watched Mrs. Taliaferro and Jean take their seats. "She's such a beautiful lady."

"Yes," agreed Mrs. Armstrong, "Laura Taliaferro certainly is."

"I hope Jackie's patience doesn't give out," Mrs. Houghton nudged me.

"God will look after Jackie."

"Don't depend upon it," she replied rising to her seat. "You'd better ask God for a special petition."

The church filled up. I recognized Cary and Mrs. Craddock who sat two pews in front. Cary's cowlick defied all combing, and this morning it stood straight up. Across the aisle sat Tom and Elizabeth Harris who drove down from Manakin. Behind them I noticed Alvira Carthage, and next to her beside the window were Colonel and Catherine Hollis. I liked the Colonel; he was great fun, but his English accent sounded quite unlike Mrs. Houghton's. How I wished he would take me hunting again with the Silver Creek Hunt Club. His wife, although sweet, was rather plump and had no taste for clothes. She wore whatever came to hand, but she loved hats. These she owned in abundance and had them especially made at Miller and Rhoads by Miss Sue. Each, I knew, cost at least twenty-five dollars, a tremendous sum. Although not cheap, Miss Sue copied the latest styles from Paris. Even in war time Catherine Hollis's hats were creations.

"Look, her hat's a basket of fruit." I nudged Mrs. Houghton. "How gorgeous."

"It always is." I was not sure Mrs. Houghton approved of such extravagance. "But this one's right from Paris." I squirmed around in my pew.

Alvira Carthage smiled at me, I smiled back. She sat straight and stiff in her black coat and her hat over faded red hair. She wore too much rouge, and I considered her lipstick far too bright for a woman of her years.

"Why doesn't Mrs. Carthage's husband ever come?" I commented.

"He goes to the Presbyterian church and rarely comes with her. He's a dour man filled with hell, fire and damnation, and considers all Episcopalians drunks. He thinks we are all going straight to you know where," Mrs. Armstrong explained. "Presbyterians believe in predestination, so he likes his own service."

"What's predestination?" I inquired.

"That it's predestined if you're saved or not, no matter what you do in good works," Mrs. Armstrong replied.

"Faith without good works is dead," Mrs. Houghton told me.

"Surely I'm not predestined for hell." This thought disturbed me. "Do you think I'm that wicked I'll go to hell?"

"Sh, sh, don't use that word in church. Really, Doc, where are your manners?"

"Sorry, Mrs. Armstrong, but I wanted to know." My cheeks felt hot from blushing.

"The service is beginning," she said.

We stood up and opened our hymnals. Lizzie, our organist, courageously pumped on her instrument, and out of it wheezed the most amazing, fretful noises that could be mistaken for music. The little church was full, and Dr. Price, grim and round, entered the sanctuary. I noticed he wore his own vestments since ours had become increasingly shabby. A wreath of gray hair encircled his pink head, bushy eyebrows framed his piercing dark eyes, and on his long nose sat a wart that bounced up and down. I watched it move. When impassioned by his sermon, Dr. Price wrinkled up his face and frowned. I was afraid of him because his eyes looked straight through me. And I knew he disliked children and found young people a nuisance. I glanced out of the window and prayed Jackie would remain content eating his hay.

But now the organ played a familiar tune:
>Stand up, stand up for Jesus
>Ye Soldiers of the cross.
>Lift high His royal banner
>It must not suffer loss.

Everyone sang, partly to help out, but mostly to cover up the sounds emitted from that old, out-of-tune organ Lizzie pumped. It was a huge task to keep those pedals moving back and forth, like the treadle of an old Singer sewing machine, in order to make the organ wheeze out its music. Not only was it old, but also no instrument should stand all week in a cold, unheated church, and then be subjected to the blazing pot-bellied stove on Sunday.

We always sang the same hymns, about twenty in number, either because Lizzie could not play any others, or we could not sing them. Perhaps Mr. Wickham, who thought he owned the church, insisted. I never found out exactly why we stuck to the more familiar tunes. This morning the organ puffed, out of breath, as Lizzie banged away on it. Then we sang a second hymn. We always did more hymn singing than other churches in town because often we had only a lay reader, and we needed the singing to fill up the service.

        Lead on, oh King Eternal
        The day of march has come.
        Hence forth in fields of conquest
        Thy tents shall be our home.

Jean and Mrs. Taliferro lent their pretty voices, and Alvira Carthage warbled, her chin shaking, her book away out in front of her. I wondered why she liked to warble like that, but thought better about asking. Then the exhausted organ gave one last, final whine and died.

Mr. Armstrong stood up to read the lessons. He was a kind, considerate man, and I liked him and his wife. Lizzie, our organist, was their daughter. Their other daughter, Dorothy, usually led the singing in her off-key voice. I thought she sang like a hillbilly, and I disliked that kind of music.

Finally the sermon began. I could tell by the thickness of the sheets of paper Dr. Price carried to the pulpit that his talk would be lengthy. After a second glance out of the window at Jackie, I intentionally dropped my quarter. It rolled under the seat in front of me, and clattered across the bare floor. I thought it made an important sounding ring as it settled in the dust at the far end of the pew. I dashed after my twenty-five cents collection money, causing not a little confusion and a great deal of noise. After crawling the length of the pew on all fours I finally retrieved the quarter. The look on Mrs. Houghton's face told me she was very annoyed. In haste I regained my seat; bang went my hymnal as it fell heavily onto the floor.

Mrs. Carthage and Catherine Hollis turned and glared at me. Mrs. Taliaferro shifted her position; even Jean regarded me with disgust. Finally Dr. Price cleared his throat. I settled myself as he began in a voice loud enough to be heard in a vast cathedral.

"Don't let us become big saints," he boomed. "Oh, Lord, just make us little saints. Being saints takes too much responsibility. It leaves us no room to tell convenient lies, to cheat our neighbors, or to drag ourselves into church late on Sunday mornings. No, Lord, just make us little saints."

The windows rattled, the congregation squirmed. I tried to remember how many lies I had told that previous week, but couldn't. As the sermon continued, Mrs. Houghton took out her handkerchief and wiped her nose in a polite way. I wondered what my neighbors thought of this rector, and prayed they realized how little he knew about people who lived in the country. Many of us did chores before we left home, and very few of us ever came to church late. I decided this old man, with his dancing wart, would never do as the permanent rector of St. Mary's. It was hard enough on us to have him come to supply, usually two Sundays a month. Still his voice droned on:

"Man has sinned against the Almighty, and look at our world today. A great war rages. Never has man experienced such destruction, or such terrible loss of young life. Now the Japanese are threatening Java, Malaya and Rangoon – places you and I never heard of until recently. And Rommel has taken the offensive in Libya. War can only be the result of sin – your sin: lies, murder and bearing false witness!"

I knew my neighbors never murdered anyone, or "beared" false witness, whatever that meant. Perhaps on occasion they lied, but only to keep from hurting someone's feelings. Once Sally Anne told Dorothy Armstrong how we missed her the Sunday she stayed home with the flu.

"The singing was just not the same," Sally graciously assured her. "You are much needed here."

I could not believe it! Sally Anne told a fib, a great big fib.

"You must be tone deaf," I remarked later. "Surely you don't think

Dorothy can sing? I thought this week's singing sounded much better without her."

"I just told her it wasn't the same," Sally Anne laughed, "And it wasn't."

Surely in this circumstance, it was better to tell Dorothy a lie. I thought it really very polite of Sally Anne to be so tactful. Then Dr. Price's voice crashed against my ears once more.

"What are you doing about it?" he demanded. "How are you making this land, this tiny spot we call Virginia, and the world we live in, a better place?"

I could hardly believe my ears! From out of the parking lot, floating over the clear Sunday air, came Dr. Price's answer:

"Hee, haa, hee, haa," brayed Jackie at the top of his voice.

The rector stopped in mid sentence. He looked around the church, puzzled. The congregation waited in expectation,. Dr. Price regarded us, unable to comprehend.

"Hee, haa, hee, haa," came the donkey tones again.

The congregation giggled; a hymnal dropped. Still the rector remained open-mouthed.

"What's that extraordinary noise?" he asked, apparently doubting his own ears.

Suppressed laughter twittered throughout the church. I put my head down pretending to pray. My face felt hot from embarrassment.

"Oh, Jackie, please stop."

Mrs. Houghton shook with laughter, but she made no sound. Only the flowers on her hat trembled, as she covered her mouth with the white handkerchief once more. Alvira Carthage had a sudden fit of coughing and sat dabbing her eyes. Catherine Hollis turned and looked at me, fur collar pressed against her mouth, tears streaming down her face. Finally the organ struck a loud, chord, decidedly off key, and we all began singing as we never sang before:

> The Church's one foundation
>> Is Jesus Christ her Lord.
>> She is His own creation
>> By water and by Word.

Our singing must have inspired Lizzie, because she jazzed up the second verse, just enough to make it sound joyful, to hide all the laughter. Then came the benediction.

"Even God's creatures opposed His word. God bless you, Father, Son, and Holy Ghost."

"Amen," we all said.

I did not wait for the last hymn when Dr. Price came down the aisle and stood at the front door to shake everyone's hand. I wriggled down my pew and slipped out of the church before anyone could stop me. I left Mrs. Houghton to do the necessary hand shaking and to exchange pleasantries. I knew I had about three minutes to untie the donkey, fold up the blanket and tuck it away with the bucket under the seat of the pony cart. But when Jackie saw me coming down the pathway, he welcomed me with a bray of great joy.

"Hee, haa, hee, haa,"

"Oh, do be quiet," I told the impatient donkey, realizing Jackie had no fear of the grim Dr. Price and just wanted to go home.

The April wind blew in gusts and leaves left from last fall struck the pony cart. Jackie jumped to one side, but I held him steady as Mrs. Houghton climbed in.

Quickly I turned the donkey out onto River Road and struck him with the ends of the reins, urging him into a fast trot. Free at last from the restraints of propriety, Mrs. Houghton laughed – loud and long. And Jackie, happy to be going home, galloped most of the way – his head high, sniffing the wind.

42

When Dr. Clery Went To War

One day in early spring the church bell rang at St. Mary's on River Road. The tolling lasted for almost an hour, and everyone wondered what had happened. Then word came, through the grapevine, that Dr. Clery was dead.

He was a young Episcopal priest when he came to our church, just out of seminary. He was dark, short and handsome. All the young girls thought so; they had a crush on him. But he stayed for only a short time before, early in 1941, he joined the Canadian Army and left for Toronto.

"We have so few priests now. Only elderly ones who supply, but no rector." Mr. Wickham told him. "We need you here."

Since Mr. Wickham's family gave the land and built the church, he thought he owned it: Cross, pews and altar cloths. But Sally Anne took care of the altar cloths. She brought them home every week and washed them. She also arranged the flowers. One Sunday when Sally Anne used only magnolia leaves, Mr. Wickham declared this lovely arrangement was inappropriate.

"It's winter, sir," she protested. "There are no more flowers in our gardens. Surely you don't wish me to buy some?"

The church was a mission and poor. It was a tradition for us to use home-grown cut flowers on the altar, a tradition which developed out of need. If there were no flowers, then greenery was used.

Mr. Wickham was the vestry. What he said was usually done, if only to avoid an argument. Dr. Clery dared to challenge this authority, and because he did, we liked our young priest more.

"It's nice to have a rector with new ideas," Mrs. Taliaferro told him one day after church. "We earnestly hope you will stay."

But Mr. Wickham, his spats and his elegant vest perfectly fitted and spotlessly clean, felt the young rector was an upstart. When he introduced some new music, Mr. Wickham became furious.

"That's not the way things were done in my mother's time. That music is far too modern. I see no need for change."

Dr. Clery was very serious, and one day last spring he joined the Canadian Army. He sincerely believed this was his duty.

"They need chaplains, and I must go," he told us.

Today the bell at St, Mary's tolled for him.

"Dr. Clery was killed," Mr. Houghton said when he returned from Henley's store. "That nice young man, who was so kind to Clara when she was ill, is dead."

Mrs. Houghton tried to write to his parents. She called the church office in Richmond for their address, but no one there could find it.

"We'll put a plaque up in the church," Mr. Armstrong suggested.

"No, we won't," Mr. Wickham told him "The only plagues in the church are for my parents. I won't allow any more."

"Then we'll give a communion cup," Mr. Taliaferro offered.

"No," said the vestry. "There is no money for such things. We need to pay old Ben for cutting the grass, and to buy wood for the stove."

So when Dr. Clery died, the sexton rang the bell for an hour on that fine spring day. Then the young man was forgotten. There was no memorial put in his church for Dr. Clery.

"He was here less than a year. It is too short a time for memorials," Mr. Wickhem insisted.

The bell tolled on. The next Sunday someone brought white flowers and put them in a silver vase on the altar. But Dr. Price did not mention their significance. He did not know Dr. Clery.

The bell finally stopped; the flowers soon died, and Dr. Clery was forgotten. Then one day I overheard Mrs. Carthage as she greeted Mrs. Taliaferro after church.

"He was a nice young man. What was his name? I am so sorry he was killed."

But I remembered. I stood with him the day we hung the bell that now tolled for him. We stood together in the sunshine on a spring morning, just a year ago, in the open porch between the church and the Sunday school. I remember his dark hair gleamed in the sun. Then shortly afterwards he went away.

Soon Father will leave for overseas. I had not seen him for almost a year. Would he be killed like Dr. Clery? Could he also just walk out of my world like this young man, and never come back? What was it like to die? What was it like to believe in a just God and to go away to a battlefield? Did the Germans pray for their boys in uniform as we prayed for ours? Did they pray for peace?

That bell on the porch of the little country church tolled several nights for me after Dr. Clery died. It tolled for my father. In my dreams I heard it. I saw a young boyish face, Dr. Clery's face, dead in Africa. I saw my father too. I saw guns and Germans and war. Then one night, several days later, it tolled no longer; it disturbed my dreams no more. And I slept once again - unafraid.

A Forgotten Landscape

43

Ilse

April 1942

After Easter a new girl came to our school. Her name was Ilse and she was Dutch. Her father was a professor and had taken a position at the University of Leyden before the war. When the Germans invaded Holland, Ilse and her family were hidden by friends, and then slipped onto a fishing boat at night and taken to England. Our Headmistress told us not to ask Ilse about her life before she came to America as she might have unhappy memories. I was dying to find out all about her, so I made friends with her.

She was shy and small for her age, but she spoke French with Madame fluently. She also knew English well, but spoke it with an accent. Sometimes when she thought we were not looking, she cried. Finally the Headmistress brought our entire class into her office.

"Girls," she said, looking very serious, "Ilse is a refugee and has some memories of war we must help her forget. You must say nothing to remind her of Holland and her experiences there. She's here at school because her father has a teaching job in Richmond. She attended another school where she felt unwelcome. You must make her feel included and part of the group. Her parents are German, but they left in 1935 when Hitler came to power and went to Holland.

"Her father is a professor of languages and her mother is also a teacher. I expect you to make her feel welcome, and don't ask her personal questions. I am counting on you. A word to the wise is sufficient."

When I tried to make friends with Ilse, she acted as if she didn't like me. Mr. Houghton came to my rescue. He brought a box of baby chicks to school to show her when he picked me up one afternoon when Miss Emma was out of town.

"How many chickens do you have?" Ilse asked him, fascinated.

"About 250 hens, and in the spring we get 100 baby chicks to raise. These came last week," Mr. Houghton told her. "We soon will have some new pullets to replace the old clucky hens who are finished laying."

"I'd like to see them. Can I come and visit you one day?" Ilse held a tiny chick in her hand and talked to it in Dutch. She told us she always spoke Dutch at home. "We rarely use English at home. May I come to see you?"

"Of course. We live a long way in the country, but you are welcome any time," he said. "Here's a young pheasant in this box. Have you ever seen one before?"

"I don't remember. I'll get my father to bring me. He'll telephone you first of course," Ilse replied in her serious voice, her face lit up with eagerness.

The next Saturday Ilse and her parents and her older brother arrived at the Houghton's cottage for a light lunch. We all met at the garden gate and brought them inside.

"I'm Manfred Becker, and this is my wife, Anne, and my son, Fredrick," Ilse's father introduced them.

I thought they were formal and dignified. Mrs. Houghton took Mrs. Becker's jacket and told me to lay it across my bed. Then we all sat down to the table which had been pulled away from the window and opened out for seven people. The dishes were Mrs. Houghton's best, taken down from the high cupboard and washed for the occasion. The lunch was simple: soup and sandwiches of beef and cheese and chicken salad. Mrs. Houghton offered us tea or coffee, and ice cream for desert.

"What a cozy home you have here," said Mrs. Becker, "I love the country. In Germany before the war we lived outside of Berlin before we went to Leyden."

"Would like to see our horses and chickens?" I offered. "We are just putting the garden in for the summer."

"Oh, yes," said Fredrick. "I like horses. I used to ride a pony in

Ilse

Germany."

"I would like to see the chickens," said Ilse. "I am afraid of horses; they are too big."

"We have a pony and a donkey. They are smaller and not scary at all." I tried to be friendly and put her at ease. Mrs. Taliaferro told me that a lady always gets the other person to talk about herself. It's impolite to tell all about oneself in formal company. These people were cultured, and I must in all ways act like a lady. I knew Mrs. Houghton would have something to say about it if I didn't, and I hated to displease her.

"How long have you been in Richmond?" Mrs. Houghton asked politely. "I am English, myself, and we've been here about six years."

"We came from England about two years ago, but moved to Richmond last September. I am a Professor at the collage. Before that we lived in Philadelphia," Mr. Becker told us.

"My father lived in Philadelphia before he joined the army and went to Florida," I tried to make conservation. "My stepmother is still there. Do you know of a place called Paoli?"

"Yes, we lived near by at Haverford. We liked it there but we like Richmond too, although they are entirely different." Mrs. Becker joined in. I found her attractive with great dark eyes and almost black hair. She spoke with a German accent. "We left to come here to an interesting job that offered more scope. Also we wished to get out of the big cities because of the war."

After lunch Mr. Houghton took the children to the barn. Ilse didn't care about the horses, and ran away from Lindy Lou and Suzie Q., but Fredrick was delighted. He patted their foreheads with great affection.

"What lovely horses you have," he said to Mr. Houghton, "What a beautifully matched pair. They remind me of the horses in London we used to see pulling the beer wagons."

Mr. Houghton took us to the chicken house. Ilse stood fascinated when he took a still warm egg from under one of his hens and handed it to her.

"May I take it home?" She asked shyly. "It's beautiful."

"I'll give you a whole dozen," he promised. "And I'll put that one in the carton just for you."

He gave her a basket and showed her how to go under the sitting hen without getting pecked to find the newly laid eggs. Then he held one of his layers for her to pat and to admire its colors and red comb. I had never seen Ilse so pleased with anything before. She no longer looked sad, but smiled at us. It was one of the few times I had ever seen her smile. I'd never heard her laugh. Fredrick, too, was delighted with the chickens, but Jackie pleased him most of all.

"He's the very devil, that one," Mr. Houghton told us. "He gets out himself and lets every other horse out. We have to keep two locks on his door. One away from his teeth at the very bottom so he can't reach it. He'll drive you crazy, that one, with his tricks."

Ilse laughed. Fredrick laughed too, but Ilse's laugh sounded like music. She was enjoying herself. Her little face lit up and her great dark eyes shone with pleasure. She even ventured to pat Jackie's nose.

"It feels like velvet," she remarked. "He's wonderful. I love him."

Later at the house Mrs. Houghton offered us a cup of tea and some homemade cookies. When our guests got ready to leave, I brought Mrs. Becker's coat and held it for her. She smiled at me, pleased at my good manners. I felt awkward, but I realized that Ilse would tell her about the eggs and the donkey, and I was glad they had come.

After they left, Mrs. Houghton turned to me.

"My dear, you've done a very good and generous thing for Ilse. Her mother told me that she never smiles anymore. You see Mrs. Becker is Jewish, and they left Germany before 1939 when a decree was passed by the government that Jews couldn't marry gentiles. Professor Becker is a gentile. Jews were also barred from careers except for the law. So they went to Holland. Then they came to England, and finally to the United States."

"Why couldn't Jews marry gentiles?" I wanted to know.

"Because Hitler wanted a pure Arian race. There is no such thing, but he wanted all blond and blue-eyed people. The Master Race, he called it." Mrs. Houghton explained.

"That's stupid. We're all mixed up. Nobody is pure anything. Except Eskimos and Gypsies, maybe." I studied the situation. "I'm many things: Scottish, English, French, and German."

"Ilse is so happy at your school, and she's beginning to come out of

Ilse

her sadness. Her mother said you have helped her by being kind. I am proud of you."

Mrs. Houghton and I cleared away the dishes and washed them. I wondered when they would come out again for another party.

After that day Ilse came to see us quite often, and each week we took a dozen eggs to school for her and her family. Soon she began to pat Jackie and finally one day she rode in the cart with me and with Jackie pulling us. Still she wasn't sure she wanted to ride him.

Mrs. Houghton knitted her a lovely white sweater for the summer so she wouldn't freeze when we took her to the movies. Ilse was delighted. One afternoon when she was visiting, Mrs. Houghton told us of the Jewish lady she'd worked for in London, during the First World War.

"I stayed with Lady Crystal the last two years of the war, after I left the factory making bullets. She was very unhappy when I left her, but she moved in with her son's family so I found another job. She had a wonderful library from which I borrowed books. I'm sorry I left her because she was elderly and alone with her only son at the Front in France. But I was young and eager to get on. I shall always remember Lady Crystal's kindness. She exposed me to culture and gave me an appreciation of art and literature."

Ilse sat on the loveseat beside Mrs. Houghton and took her hand and kissed it.

"You are very good, and I love you," Ilse said in a small voice.

Deeply touched by this sudden affection, Mrs. Houghton dabbed her eyes with her handkerchief. Then she took Ilse in her arms and hugged her.

Letters

May 1942
Richmond, Va.

Dear Dad,

A terrible thing happened. Dr. Clery was killed in Africa. He joined the Canadian Army last year as chaplain. Now he's dead, I can't believe it. We still have old Dr. Price with all his warts. He's terribly grim and full of hell. I am not sure about hell, because a loving God certainly wouldn't make such a place. I hope there is a heaven though. I'd like to meet my grandmother who died when you were seventeen. She sounds interesting. I question some of these religious ideas. Sometimes they don't make sense. Why would a loving God kill his son, or rather allow his son to die. It's too confusing, especially when we are told He loves us. If God loves us then why is there war? Surely it's a horrible thing to inflict upon many innocent people. There don't seem to be any answers.

Love, Doc

Florida 1942, May

Dear Son,

Don't try and figure out religion. It's taken great minds ages to figure it out and it's still not complete. I am sorry about Dr. Clery. I met him and liked him. What a waste of a young life! Yet he felt it was his duty and died doing what he wanted — to be with the troops. Don't grieve too much about him, Doc. There will be others you know who will die. Just pray for them, dear girl, and believe it will come out right in the end.

Love, Dad

44

Angelo

May 1942

One Saturday in early May Mr. Houghton led Jackie down our driveway with laundry hanging form his ears. The donkey had escaped form the pasture, ducked under Bertha's wash line and decorated himself with my undergarments.

"He's got a sense of humor, that donkey," laughed Mr. Houghton.

Recognizing my clothes , I blushed scarlet and tried to flee.

Convulsed with laughter, he grabbed my arm.

"Take him out in the pony cart for some exercise," he told me placing the lead in my hand, "before he gets into my garden again."

Mortified, I led the donkey towards the barn, stuffing the offending garments into my pocket. Mr. Houghton crossed the orchard still laughing. But Sally Anne Taliaferro intercepted me, at least the dog, Mike, did. A fierce Kerry Blue Terrier, he loved to run in front of the riding horses when we cantered and nip their forelegs. Often the horses would try to kick at Mike, causing him to make exciting hair's breath escapes. This morning Jackie, wary from past experience, eyed the clever dog. But Mike saw no sport in chasing a walking donkey and trotted docilely along beside us.

"Hello," called Sally Anne, "I'm headed down to the church to fix the alter for tomorrow's service. Come with me."

"I have to drive Jackie. Mr. Houghton thinks he needs exercise so he doesn't break into our gardens again," I replied.

"Where are you going?" Sally Anne stood before me carrying two shopping bags.

"Oh, no place special. I'll drive you, if you like, down to St. Mary's."

"That would be grand since I have altar cloths, vases and candles in this shopping bag and flowers in the other." She put down her bags and stretched her arms.

I harnessed up Jackie while Sally Anne tried to catch Mike. Finally he ran off to visit Emma Craddock's Kerry Blue. Jackie, now hitched to the pony cart, seeing that no dog lurked about, left the stable yard willingly. Sally Anne and I stashed her shopping bags under the seat, and hopped into the cart. I picked up the reins and clucked to the donkey. Jackie pricked his big ears forward, cantered down the hill, and finally settled into a steady trot.

"What a grand day!" I commented, pulling the donkey around a large pot-hole. "It's going to be spring."

Early this morning I went down to the low grounds for a short horse back ride on Tom. And I saw two trains carrying Italian and German prisoners of war up to Charlottesville. I hear they will help on the farms and in the apple orchards of the Shenandoah Valley," Sally Anne informed me.

"There's already some Italian prisoners here in Goochland," I told her. "They are working on dairy farms. Mr. Harris is considering getting a couple for his place."

"I wonder what these foreigners think of Virginia. It's a very different from the olive groves of Italy. We don't even grow grapes to make chianti."

"But it's safer in Goochland," I said. " I wouldn't want to be in Italy or Germany now."

"Neither would I," Sally Anne agreed. "but those prisoners must be dreadfully homesick not speaking English and being so far away from their own country."

I knew she had a tender heart. But I hoped the Italian prisoners stayed at the other end of the county. I had no intention of meeting one, even if he could speak English.

I turned Jackie onto River Road, and we drove along quite easily until we arrived at St. Mary's. Here Sally Anne jumped down and gathered up her packages while I tied the donkey to a large tree. We walked up the path, taking deep breaths of the warm spring air. When Sally Anne unlocked the church doors, a musty smell greeted us.

"It's spooky," I shivered as we entered.

"Yes, leave the doors open so the air will get in," Sally Anne instructed.

I pushed the double doors open wide and propped them ajar with two cracked bricks. Then I followed her up the aisle into the sacristy. Here she unlocked a cupboard and took down vestments, altar hangings, two brooms and a bucket. She also found some rags. We swept the church floor and dusted the windowsills. When Sally Anne reentered the sacristy, I pretended to be a bride and walked down the aisle ever so stately.

"Here comes the bride, big, fat and wide," I sang off key. "Here comes the groom as skinny as a broom."

"Perhaps we should open the window. It's stuffy in here," my friend suggested as she reappeared.

I stopped playing and pushed up the long narrow window. In that instant I noticed a movement amongst the trees near the summer house. This little structure was used during funerals when it rained, and contained a built-in bench along three sides. I used to play there, but after a prisoner from the State Farm was caught there, the Sunday School teacher told us it was off limits. The summer house stood about fifty yards from the church near some big evergreens, and was made from slats that resembled lattice work. From behind them I thought I observed a movement. I watched intently for a minute, but saw nothing.

"Can you get me a bucket of water, please?" Sally Anne's voice aroused me.

As I picked up the metal pail and started towards the door, I was sure I heard a noise as if a branch snapped – then silence. Feeling uneasy I carried my bucket outside to see if anyone was there. Gingerly I walked between the gravestones into the privy that stood at the far end of the cemetery. Nobody was around, only a squirrel which scampered across the grass and ran up the tall tree that stood beside the church.

"That's strange, I'm sure someone's here."

Then I turned towards the summer house.

"Doc, I need some water," Sally Anne called me.

Running to the outside pump, I filled the pail and re-entered the church. Here I found Sally Anne with a red scarf tied around her head, and her sleeves pushed up to her elbows, dusting the lectern and the communion rail.

"Please put some water in these two vases I brought for the flowers," she asked me.

Again I returned to the pump. This time I knew someone was in the summer house – watching me. I filled the vases and hurried back up the path splashing water over my shoes. I stopped long enough to brush a stray lock of hair from my eyes. In that instant a dark face peered at me from behind the slats of the latticework. Clutching the vases to my breast, I raced up the steps into the church.

"Sally Anne, someone's in the summer house," I whispered excitedly.

"Come on, Doc, stop playing games," she said as she rose from her knees and looked at me in disbelief.

"But someone is there, honest," I protested. "I'm going out to see."

"Go ahead," she replied playfully. "Maybe it's the Queen of Sheba."

I walked out onto the church steps, but saw nothing. Then I started down the path to the graveyard, but doubled back towards the clump of giant evergreens which stood near the summer house. When I stepped out from under the low hanging branches, a dark-haired man suddenly stood in front of me. I stopped dead in my tracks. In amazement we stood and stared at each other.

"Who are you?" I demanded. "What are you doing here?"

He spread his hands in a hopeless gesture, and I realized he was terribly frightened. His eyes looked dark and as round as pinwheels.

"Who are you?" I repeated, thinking he might be an escaped prisoner from the State Farm."

"I, Angelo," the man replied in heavily accented English. "Buon giorno."

"Angelo? What kind of name is that?" I asked.

"Italiano," the man said, his enormous eyes watching me with interest.

"Italian?" I couldn't believe it "You're an Italian?"

"Si, Italiano," he repeated.

"Oh, good Lord, you're a prisoner of war!" My first instinct was to run away, but determined not to show fear, I held my ground.

"Si, I, Angelo, a prisoner of war from Italia. Who are you?"

"I am Doc." I replied speaking slowly, and noticing his clothes, which hung from his shoulders like a sack, looked clean. His face appeared tense, but his large luminous eyes seemed kind. "How on earth did you get here?"

"Work at Brown's dairy."

I nodded, intently taking note of his straight shoulders, his military bearing and his quiet dignity. Angelo in turn watched me and took note of my wet shoes and my disheveled hair. I realized he found me not a threat because his shoulders relaxed and he smiled.

"How did you get here?" I repeated.

"Walked. I no like job."

"Why not?" I inquired, fascinated.

"Signor Brown non é sympatico."

A car drove into the churchyard and stopped.

"Doc, Doc," Sally Anne's voice called me.

"I must go, Angelo. I'll be back."

I slipped out of the summer house and bent down under the low branches of the evergreens. Then I ran through the graveyard and up the church steps.

"Was anyone there?" Sally Anne asked as I entered.

"Yes, but he's gone now." I settled for a half truth because I didn't wish to scare her.

"Who was he?" Sally Anne demanded handing me the dust pan.

"No one we know. Just a tramp." I told her as she swept a pile of dirt into the dustpan which I knelt down to hold for her so she couldn't see my face.

"A tramp?" She repeated, alarmed.

"Well, not really a tramp. A workman," I lied, flustered.

Mr. Brown stood in the doorway.

"What tramp?" He asked Sally Anne as he came down the aisle towards us.

"One Doc saw in the woods," she replied and disappeared into the sacristy.

"What did you see, kid?" Mr. Brown cornered me.

"Just an old coloured man," I tried to act disinterested and still holding the dust pan backed into the communion rail.

"Not a white man? An Italian?"

"No, sir," I lied again. That made two outright lies and one big fib.

Mr. Brown seemed satisfied. I slipped past him, picked up the bucket and dashed from the church door. He followed and stood in the doorway as I threw the dust on the ground and emptied the water from the bucket over the shrubbery.

"You haven't seen an Italian prisoner, have you kid?" the dairyman asked, "Because he works for me."

"No, sir," I placed the bucket upside down on the porch and sat on it. "Where did you get him?" I pretended to spit on my hand and hit it with my fist. Three lies.

"In Richmond, The Army supplies the P.O.W.s. The headquarters is in Richmond, why?"

"Just wondered," I replied, casting a furtive glance towards the summer house.

Mr. Brown started to leave, but turned, paused and walked down through he churchyard. He headed straight for the cemetery. I held my breath.

"What time is it, sir," I asked.

He stopped, looked at his watch thoughtfully, before replying. "Just before noon."

The dairyman turned, saw me sitting on the porch and changed direction. He walked back towards his car, and gave Jackie a resounding slap on the rear before opening the door. I breathed a sigh of relief. Still it cost me three lies and a fib, but I figured I'd got off lightly.

"If you see an Italian, call me." Mr. Brown shouted as he got into his old Dodge car, started the motor and drove away.

"Sure, Mr. Brown. Goodbye," I waved to him.

What have I done? I have harboured the enemy! Why on earth didn't I tell Mr. Brown about Angelo's being in the summer house? But I disliked Mr. Brown. Our horses sometimes got loose and went to his farm. He always called us at six o'clock in the morning and told us to come and get them at once. Yet Mr. Brown was an American, and I had

Angelo

lied to save a foreigner. I couldn't believe myself. I felt like a traitor. Still I felt deep down I'd done the right thing.

With these conflicting emotions, I picked up the bucket and went to find Sally Anne. She had locked the cupboard in the sacristy and turned out the lights. As she came down the aisle, we met halfway.

"Mr. Brown's gone," I said. I wondered how I should tell her about Angelo. She might tease me about the Queen of Sheba again.

After some thought I decided to skip it because I figured she would never see him. It's better not to alarm her, I reasoned, and I didn't wish to tell any more lies.

"Well, I'm finished here. Take the bucket in the sacristy and let's go home. Have you put away the dust pan?" Sally Anne asked gathering up her shopping bags.

"Your flowers look gorgeous on the altar," I commented as I turned from the sacristy. "You could even make a stick look artistic."

"Thank you," she replied. "I am pleased with this arrangement."

I took one of her shopping bags and turned to leave. Angelo stood in the doorway. His dark eyes regarded Sally Anne, and then he looked around the church's simple interior. It must seem very bare compared with the pictures of Italian churches Mrs. Taliaferro had shown me where every thing is decorated.

"I, Angelo," he said in his broken English. "Italiano, fiorentino."

Sally Anne suppressed a scream and covered her mouth with her hand. Frightened, she stared at our unexpected visitor. Her hand trembled, she allowed her shopping bags to clatter to the floor.

"Angelo was in the summer house," I explained. "He works at Mr. Brown's dairy."

"He's escaped, you mean. And Mr. Brown just left," Sally Anne sat down in the nearest pew. "Why didn't you tell us?"

I couldn't answer. I didn't know why. Besides I was standing in church, and I just couldn't tell another lie. I considered the porch different. It wasn't IN church, just on the church. Everything that I knew was right, I suddenly found was wrong. How could a daughter of a Major in the United States Army become such a traitor?

Father says they shoot traitors. Would they shoot me for saving Angelo? I wondered.

I couldn't believe my actions. I just felt Angelo wouldn't hurt anybody, that's all. He was certainly more of a gentleman than Mr. Brown. But how could I explain this to Sally Anne?

"It's all right," I assured her, "we're safe, but what shall we do with him?"

"I don't know," Sally Anne shook her head, her face white from fear. "What do you suggest?"

I stood in the aisle and looked at them both. Angelo remained in the doorway, watching us. Sally Anne sat, ashen-faced in the pew, her shopping bags in the aisle, their contents scattered on the floor. Suddenly I felt it necessary to introduce them.

"Angelo, this is my friend, Sally Anne." I stammered, feeling uncomfortable.

The Italian made a slight bow, and my neighbor nodded in return. This seemed to clear the air. I felt the tension relax. Still I knew I was committing a terrible crime. Angelo was my enemy. And by the same reasoning Mr. Brown should be my friend. Yet all those lies I told him wouldn't make him think much of me. I pushed that from my mind and wondered what I should do. Who should I ask for help?

"I'll go call Tom Harris," I whispered to Sally Anne.

But Angelo still stood in the doorway, blocking it. I wondered if he would let me pass. He looked unsure whether he should enter this unadorned Protestant church. I realized it must look very strange to his Roman Catholic eyes. Mrs. Taliaferro told me that Catholic churches had statues of saints and stations of the cross, some of them very ornate. Our little country church was very plain and simple.

"Come in, Angelo. Come in," I welcomed him. "My friend, Sally Anne is praying." I couldn't think of any other reason for her to remain in a front pew.

To my immense relief Angelo quietly entered the rear pew, and knelt, straight backed, in prayer. The door free at last, I dashed out, tripping over the bucket I had forgotten to put away. It rattled across the uneven boards and came to rest against the pot-bellied stove. Digging my heels into the soft ground, I flew down River Road to Red Jones's house. When Mrs. Jones opened the door, breathlessly I asked to use the telephone.

"Certainly. Come into the kitchen. It's more private," she offered;

then showed me the way and left me alone to call.

With trembling fingers I dialed Mr. Harris's number, and listened for the right combination of rings on his party line: Two short rings and a long.

"Hello," Mr. Harris's voice boomed into my ear. "What you want?"

"This is Doc, sir. I am at St. Mary's church with Sally Anne and an Italian prisoner of war. Can you please come?"

"Be there in a minute, kid," he slammed down the receiver.

"Oh, do hurry, Mr. Harris," I prayed.

"Everything all right, Doc?" Mrs. Jones entered the room.

"Yes, thank you," I looked at her, but decided she was far too old to help. "Yes, everything's fine."

She let me out waving pleasantly, and I raced back to St. Mary's. I bounded up the wooden steps, jumped over the porch and stopped. It would be unseemly to run into the church, and it might alarm Sally Anne and Angelo. Also I had committed enough sins for one day. Being disrespectful to the Lord would surely leave me without any hope of redemption. Breathless, I walked in as casually as I could manage under the circumstances. I found Angelo sitting very still in the back, and Sally Anne, equally still, at the front near the altar. They both seemed lost in prayer. I entered quietly and picked up the bucket and tiptoed into the sacristy with it. Then I picked up Sally Anne's packages that had fallen out of her shopping bags and replaced them. Finally I put the bags on the front steps, and returned to where Sally Anne sat.

"Mr. Harris is coming," I whispered as she handed me the key to the sacristy and told me to lock it.

When I'd locked the door, Angelo stirred and came towards me. I held my breath and I saw Sally Anne's fingers cover her mouth. She heard him get out of his pew. I walked straight up to her and returned the key. Angelo came down to me.

"La Signora okay?" He inquired looking at Sally Anne's face.

"Yes, she's okay," I replied, relieved Angelo meant us no harm. "We're going home."

Silently Sally Anne followed me down the aisle towards the door. She looked ill. Angelo offered her his arm. I locked the church doors and picked up the shopping bags. Then, ever so slowly we walked down the path towards the pony cart, Angelo supporting my neighbor with his arm. I wondered what Mr. Harris thought as he turned into the churchyard and got out of his car.

"You all right, Miss Sally Anne?" He inquired as he came up the path towards us.

"Yes, thank you. This is Angelo who works at Brown's dairy," she introduced them.

Mr. Harris made no significant sign, but stared at me in disbelief. I just shrugged my shoulders, and continued on down the path carrying the shopping bags.

"This is a curious kettle of fish," Mr. Harris commented as he helped Sally Anne into the pony cart.

"Yes," I agreed, "Things are not always what they seem."

I untied Jackie and slipping the reins through the turrets of the harness, hopped into the pony cart. Angelo put in the shopping bags and closed the door, then bowed as Jackie started out of the churchyard. But the donkey's near trace slipped off the singletree. Pulling Jackie to a halt, I turned to Mr. Harris for help and noticed Angelo's face blanch under his swarthy skin.

Tom Harris put his hand on Jackie's bridle, then adjusted the harness and hooked up the dangling trace. Regarding me with a twinkle in his eye, almost nonchalantly he inquired.

"Angelo work for Brown?"

"Yes, sir," I replied, "but he doesn't like it."

"So Angelo's run away," Mr. Harris sized up the situation.

"Just to St. Mary's," Sally Anne added. "Where else can he go?"

"He's not doing much work sitting around here all morning." Tom Harris observed. "You know anything about dairy cows, Angelo?"

"Dairy cows?" The dark eyes puzzled expression changed to a smile. "Il mio padre have cows a vicino Firenze."

"His father has cows near Florence," Sally Anne translated.

"Si," Angelo smiled, taking a step forward, "Si, Signora."

"You called me here for some reason, Doc, I suppose. I'm a busy man with a dairy to run with little help. So you must have had something in mind other than a tea party. Eh, kid?"

I blushed and said nothing.

Mr. Harris regarded the young Italian soldier. I knew the older man was a good judge of character, but Angelo was our enemy, a foreigner who spoke little English. Still Mr. Harris studied the strange, shabbily dressed figure. The Italian's dark eyes returned the dairyman's gaze. The ill-fitting clothes could not hide the fine features, the assured bearing, or the open countenance. Angelo was probably in his mid-twenties, for his beard was dark and his chest well developed. Still holding Jackie's bridle Tom Harris finally spoke.

"Would you like to work for me?"

Did I hear right? I wondered, caught up in conflicting emotions. Was Mr. Harris, whom we all admired and respected for his high principles, really offering this run-away prisoner a job?

I had called him to come and rescue us from any danger we might be in. Now that the danger was over, I felt embarrassed, that it hadn't been greater to bring him down from above Manakin. I hadn't expected Angelo to go and work for Mr. Harris. What would Mr. Brown say to that? Angelo had understood because he accepted.

"Si," Angelo replied, smiling in a pleased manner. "I like. But Americano Army do not know. You tell?"

This was all very strange. Not only had Angelo given Sally Anne his arm and escorted her out of the church, but he also had received a job offer from one of the most respected members of the community. I felt Angelo had bewitched us. He was a prisoner of war who had fought against the Allies in Africa and no doubt had killed some of them. Yet I knew Angelo was not going to hurt anyone. He had acted the perfect gentleman helping Sally Anne into the pony cart. I had lied to save him from Mr. Brown, and now I didn't' want him to work for Mr. Harris where he would, no doubt, be happier. I bowed my head to hide my confusion and my shame for doubting this stranger. I didn't know what to think. My thoughts were interrupted by Mr. Brown's blue Dodge as it turned into the churchyard.

"Now," I thought, "I'm in for it."

"Is this your tramp, kid?" he yelled at me. "Hello, Harris. I see you caught my Italian P.O.W."

Mr. Brown slammed his car door shut and came towards us.

"He's not much help in your dairy, Sam, seeing he's been here in

A Forgotten Landscape

the churchyard all morning," Mr. Harris greeted him.

"He's not much count. I've got two German P.O.W.'s who get along okay, even speak good English. But Angelo here just doesn't like them."

"Io sono Italiano. Io non sono Tedesco," Angelo replied in his own language.

"That's it, Brown; he's an Italian not a German. Why don't you keep your Germans and give me Angelo? We could settle it with the authorities in Richmond on Monday," Mr. Harris suggested.

"Si, si," Angelo agreed, then turned to Mr. Brown. "Okay?"

"It's not okay. How can I take it upon myself to pass this fellow around? What will the Army say about that?" Mr. Brown spat a great stream of brown tobacco.

"They have already arranged with me to send a man out when they find one with a little English and some dairy experience," Mr. Harris explained. "Since your men aren't working out, and you're not satisfied, you should have told the Army boys in Richmond to come and get Angelo. If they find out your P.O.W.'s are running around the countryside terrorizing women and children, you'll lose the Germans also. Think it over, Sam."

Tom Harris started towards his car. I tapped Jackie on the rear and turned the pony cart around. Mr. Brown caught the bridle, and stopped us.

"You and Miss Sally Anne terrorized, kid?" he snapped.

"Yes, sir," she replied, "I nearly fainted from terror."

"What about you, Doc? You nearly fainted, too, I suppose." Mr. Brown turned to me still holding Jackie.

The whole business was becoming more and more confusing.

"No," I measured my words thoughtfully and looked up at Mr. Brown all innocence, "I escaped and went to Red Jones's house for help."

Mr. Brown let go of Jackie's bridle and spat again. A smelly brown splat landed a hair's breadth from Angelo's feet, but he did not move.

"Kid," the dairyman turned again towards me. "You are disloyal to your country! You harboured the enemy, and told a lie doing it. Ain't your father in the American Army and going overseas, and you so proud of him? He isn't likely to be proud of you any more after you helped an Italian soldier to escape."

I hung my head. Everything he said was true. But there was something about Sam Brown I found offensive. Why had I helped Angelo? I couldn't understand it. I had acted against all I believed about patriotism. I had lied three times and told a fib on top of it. All of this I'd done at church. Yet, I wasn't sorry I'd helped Angelo.

"Mr. Brown," I said, determined to explain my actions. "Have you ever caught a fox in a trap? When you try to free it, the fox licks your hand. You know it kills chickens, and steals their eggs. Yet that fox trusts you because it needs help. And he believes you will help him." I stopped, not sure if I made myself clear. Anyway, I couldn't explain it in another way because I felt all churned up inside.

"What's that got to do with anything?" Mr. Brown retorted angrily.

"Well, it's the reason why I helped Angelo," I replied, trying to keep my voice steady.

I knew Sam Brown did not understand because he turned towards Mr. Harris.

"Okay, Tom, you win. Take that darn P.O.W. and use him on your farm. I prefer the Germans. You," he turned back to me, "keep your horses out of my fields or I'll sell them in Richmond, and you'll never see them again. Tell Harry Houghton to mend his fences." Mr. Brown stopped and said to Angelo, "Get your gear off my farm today."

Angelo nodded. He came over to the pony cart and bowed gracefully before Sally Anne. Then he took my hand and brought it to his lips. I saw that his dark eyes flashed with pleasure, as he said,

"Signorina Doc. Mr. Harris, this is my friend, Signorina Doc."

Tom Harris could hardly believe his ears. His mouth dropped open in amazement.

"Signorina is it now?" He asked me.

"Yes," I told him, " I am Signorina Doc. You can't call me kid any more, not in Angelo's presence."

"That's the most astonishing thing I ever heard." Tom Harris opened his car door. "A fourteen-year-old kid a Signorina, since when?"

"Since today, Mr. Harris." I replied as Angelo followed the dairyman. "I am a much admired young lady."

"Who says?" Tom Harris wanted to know as he leaned on the car door watching me with amusement.

"I do, because don't forget Angelo is Sally Anne's and my prisoner of war. After all we captured him."

45

Gossip

May 1942

At church the next Sunday everyone talked of Angelo as they stood outside on the grass waiting for the service to begin. Mrs. Houghton and I joined the rest of the congregation in front of the church steps.

"Women shouldn't come here alone during the week," said Mr. Wickham. "It's not safe."

"It's perfectly safe," said Colonel Hollis, "this is an isolated incident and nobody was hurt."

Into our midst walked Roger Schmidt looking very elegant and aristocratic. He seldom came to church, but he was highly respected because he was a financier at the Federal Reserve Bank. He was a member of the vestry and had kept our country church afloat during hard times.

"An Italian soldier in the churchyard," he told us, "is highly irregular."

"Yes," agreed Sally Anne, "but Doc and I are well able to look after ourselves. And Mr. Harris handled the situation." She turned and walked into the church.

Roger Schmidt looked at us as if we smelt bad. He detested children and animals. Sometimes he was rude to Ben, our sexton, and hurt his feelings. Some of us at church thought he was a Nazi sympathizer and felt his motives were questionable.

"He admires Lindbergh too much," Mrs. Carthage said in a whisper behind her straw fan, compliments of Bennett's Funeral Home. "And he's so pro-German that Roosevelt doesn't want him in the Air Corps in spite of his ability to fly the Atlantic."

"Lindy is pro-German?" I asked. "I didn't know that."

"He lived there and only came home when war looked inevitable. Keep an eye on Lindbergh; he's not a good American." Mrs. Carthage assured me.

I wondered how she knew so much about Charles Lindberg when she hated airplanes.

"Never get in one, Doc," she told me once. "They are very dangerous."

"How many people have keys to the church?" Mr. Schmidt wanted to know.

"Only four, I think," said Mr. Wickham. "The soldier didn't break in. He was found in the summer house. It's a one time affair. We don't' need to change the locks."

We watched Roger Schmidt enter the church and I drew a sigh of relief.

"Lindbergh's a test pilot in the Pacific," said Mrs. Houghton, "McArthur claims he's a gift from heaven."

"Still, I don't know which is worse: Lindbergh or Roger Schmidt. I don't like the idea of Nazis in America, much less in Virginia at our church." Mrs. Carthage made a face and fluttered her fan.

"I hear a lot of financiers are pro-German. They want to make money rebuilding Europe after the war," remarked Mr. Wickham as he followed behind us.

"Yes, I agree," Colonel Hollis replied. "Standard Oil of New Jersey had strong links with the international German firm, I. G. Farben. Both are interested in petroleum technology. Allen Dulles, the brother of John Foster, who is in the government, was a lawyer for I. G. Farben here in the United States. Wars make strange bed fellows."

"While young men are being slaughtered and the world's nearly conquered by the Japs and German, some business men can think of nothing else but profits."

"How disgusting," Mr. Armstrong joined in. "It's positively immoral."

"I agree," said Mr. Wickham, "but that's how things are. There is always someone after the money. It makes my blood run cold to think of it."

I listened to this conversation as Mrs. Houghton and I entered the church. I wondered how men could think of rebuilding Europe when they hadn't finished tearing it down yet. I didn't understand how anyone could do such a thing. I didn't like Mr. Schmidt and asked Mrs. Houghton to wait until he was seated so we could find a pew as far away as possible. I felt Mrs. Houghton tug my arm as we slid into a front pew. She always preferred to sit n the front so she could see and hear the sermon. She lip read well, and usually got most of it. Mrs. Carthage followed us and sat on the end.

She had on a marvelous new spring hat – all flowers on a light straw. She even out-did Catherine Hollis this morning. I wondered if "Miss Sue" had made Mrs. Carthage's hat. In fact, Miss Alvira, as she like to be called, looked elegant in her lavender dress with lace around the neck. Mrs. Hollis's dress was blue and her hat was trimmed with roses. Still Mrs. Carthage took the prize for the best-dressed in my opinion.

Mrs. Houghton looked nice, too, in a Bamburg sheer, white background with blue flowers. Her navy hat was neat, but very modest with only three daisies on it. She took off her white gloves and opened her prayer book and told me to do likewise.

I noticed Mr. Wickham entered the front pew on the other side of the isle and sat beside Roger Schmidt. I thought that strange after what Mr. Wickham had just said. Apparently, it didn't chill his blood to sit beside a pro-German. Or just maybe there was some question before the vestry that needed another vote to approve it. I wasn't sure, but it seemed that war made strange bedfellows.

Then I considered what Mrs. Carthage said about Lindy being pro-German. I hated to think he wasn't a loyal American. "But if McArthur likes him, he must be all right," I concluded.

I looked and saw Mrs. Armstrong smiling at me. She wore too much rouge. She dabbed it on in circles like a clown. Yet she was very sweet and a "devoted worker." Mrs. Houghton said if anyone would go to heaven, it was Mrs. Armstrong.

Just then, always a few minutes late, Tom and Elizabeth Harris entered the church. She looked lovely in a pink flowered dress and a pink hat. She smiled at Mrs. Houghton and me. I smiled back. Tom Harris nodded politely at Mrs. Houghton and got into the pew behind us.

We sat beside the Reilly children who always smelled of wood smoke. They lived in a shack on the other side of the creek. They were poor and couldn't afford coal, so they smelled of smoke and fatback. There were five of them. Mary was fourteen, and the youngest, Sarah, was three.

Mary was fun and good at games, but very shy. Mrs. Houghton quietly gave her some of my outgrown clothes. When Mary wore one of my dresses, Mrs. Houghton glared at me if I even hinted it was once mine. Today she had on my blue dress and my last year's Sunday hat. The dress looked very nice on her, and so did the hat.

"I must guard my tongue," I thought, "or I'll be in trouble."

Mrs. Taliaferro usually took the prize for elegance. I couldn't see what she was wearing. Sally Anne looked very feminine, and Jean liked suits and skirts. Mrs. Taliaferro preferred softer clothes with flowers on them. Their spring hats this morning looked lovely from the side. They sat near the back behind us, and I only allowed myself a furtive glance because I knew Mrs. Houghton would make me turn and face the front.

"No," I decided, "the prize today definitely belongs to Mrs. Carthage."

The first hymn, "Amazing Grace," had started when Miss Emma and Cary arrived out of breath and flustered. Their car had been giving them trouble and some days refused to start.

"That's what you call, 'fashionably late'," whispered Mrs. Houghton, "except Miss Emma is usually on time."

"Her car's acting up," I whispered back, "she needs a new one."

I noticed Cary looked very smart in a new shirt and tie. I felt a catch in my throat as I knew he would be leaving soon for the Army Air Corps. This morning he appeared manly and grown up; it made me feel sad. I wanted us to remain children forever. I knew this couldn't be, and once Cary left for the Air Corps, our lives would become different. He would become a man, and I would still be considered a child. Our paths would separate; only our memories would be the same of growing up in the country.

Roger Schmidt sang too loudly and brought me back to the present.

I looked at him and wondered if he really represented something evil. Was he making money from the war? I asked myself. People did get rich from the wars; look at the carpet baggers in the south after the War Between the States. We looked on them as evil.

Then there were people like Father whose patriotism stood for something good and upright. Since he fought in the First World War, I knew he would be one of the first to go overseas. When he went was secret, but it was to be in six or eight weeks. When would I see him again? There was no hope of saying goodbye except over the telephone. I knew he couldn't come to Richmond, and I hadn't a prayer of going to Florida.

"Kneel, Doc," Mrs. Houghton tugged my sleeve; "stop daydreaming. You are supposed to pray."

I knelt as she bid me to. But Mr. Schmidt haunted me and intrigued me. I wondered how one found out about such people. Who did you ask and what happened to you if you got too close to their secrets?

I shivered. Then I prayed that God would keep me safe and keep Mr. Schmidt honest. At least, keep him from knowing I suspected him. Finally I prayed for Cary and Father and asked God to keep them safe and send them home again. That was enough praying, and I sat up on the pew. Lizzie hit the organ once more, and we stood up to sing, "Onward Christian Soldiers."

In front of the church, after the service, stood Mr. Harris with a small bunch of wild flowers in his hand.

"Doc," he said as Mrs. Houghton and I came down the steps, "these are for you from Angelo. He asked me to give them to the 'porcina signorina'."

"Porcina Signorina?" I asked, "What does that mean?"

"Little miss," translated Mrs. Harris who stood beside us. "Angelo wishes to thank you for rescuing him."

"Oh," I said, deeply touched by this simple gesture. "Tell him, thank you."

"Come up and see him when you deliver the eggs on Saturday. He loves working in the dairy. Angelo's worth two men," Tom Harris said. We stood on the path between the church and the parking lot.

"I don't know any Italian," I confessed. "How do I write a note?"

"In English, of course," replied Tom Harris.

"No," I countered, 'in Italian. I'll ask Mrs. Taliaferro."

We walked slowly towards the parking lot as Mr. Houghton turned into it. He hated to be kept waiting.

"Signorina?" Tom Harris winked at me. "A fourteen-year-old kid, a signorina."

"Yes," I replied, stopping and drawing myself up to my five feet, two inches. "I'm growing up and am not a kid any more. Angelo appreciates me. He thinks I'm special and sends me flowers."

"Oh, Doc," said Mrs. Houghton, taking my arm. "Don't grow up too quickly. Stay just as you are awhile longer."

I said nothing, but accepted the bunch of flowers: yellow butter cups, white daisies and iris of indigo blue.

"Tell Angelo his Signorina sends her compliments," I smiled and followed Mrs. Houghton down the path to the car.

Gossip

Letters

May 1942,
Richmond, Va.

Dear Dad,

I need to ask you something serious. I've probably done something terribly wrong. I found an Italian prisoner in St. Mary's churchyard. His name is Angelo, and he's from Florence. He was fighting with Rommel in Africa, taken prisoner, and sent here to America. He worked for Mr. Brown in his dairy, and ran away because he didn't like it. That's when Sally Anne and I discovered him just after Easter. Now he works for Mr. Harris at his dairy, and has become my friend.

Is that succouring the enemy? Mr. Brown said I was a traitor, and you'd never be proud of me again. I couldn't stand that. Please tell me I've not done wrong. Angelo is a far nicer person than Mr. Brown, and he's done wonders on Tom Harris's dairy farm. He loves and understands animals. I like Angelo, but I don't know if I should.

Many years ago, (it seems like many years, but it's not) you told me there are good Germans and bad Germans. Virginia was a bad German, but my grandmother's people came from Manheim, Germany, and they are good Germans. It follows then that there are good Italians. Angelo is a good Italian even though he's a prisoner of war. I expect you might look on this differently, but that's my opinion. Love, Doc

Jacksonville, Florida
May 1942

Dear Doc,

You've asked me a very ticklish question. One I really don't wish to answer. I am not sure I would make Angelo my friend, but I am a soldier and Angelo is also a soldier on opposing sides. There is a conflict of purpose between us. As a soldier, I am trying to get rid of the Hun and Italians and the pro-Nazi French and bring peace.

You are a sensitive young girl who likes people. You didn't succour the enemy, just brought some people together who could work in harmony. It sounds as if you did both Angelo and Mr. Harris a favour and got rid of a thorn in Mr. Brown's side. I don't call that succouring the enemy. I don't consider you a traitor. You must be guided by your own conscience and not by mine. I see you've already made up your mind. Love, Dad

46

War News From The Pacific

May 1942

    Mr. Harris had a way of popping in at unexpected times for a chat. He liked to visit and got lonely with no one except the cows with whom to talk. Mrs. Houghton said he was worried sick over his two nephews who were in the Pacific, and feared for their safety. When he couldn't find peace, he began to wander seeking company. He rarely spoke of his nephews, but followed closely the war in the Far East. One Saturday in early May he landed on our door step about ten in the morning with awful news.
    "After that raid by the Americans on Tokyo in April, I thought things were getting better. But the Japanese are advancing in the Solomon Islands, and there has been a battle in the Coral Sea where our aircraft carrier, the Lexington, that grand old Lady Lex, was sunk. She suffered two torpedo hits and two bombs as well. The crew didn't even see their attackers before two internal explosions forced them to abandon ship. Luckily, the Yorktown escaped with a single bomb hit. Not only has Corregidor's fallen, but McArthur has escaped to Australia claiming, 'I shall return', and left poor Jonathan Wainwright to surrender. "The Philippines are lost, the whole world's a mess, and two of my cows are sick." Mr. Harris had to stop talking; he was out of breath.
    "Where are your nephews, Sam and Ted?" Mr. Houghton asked as he stood outside his chicken house, shovel in hand, his cheeks red from exertion and his shirt wet. We had already delivered our eggs, and now he was cleaning his chicken house.

"They are on the Yorktown. They are not on Corregidor, thank God." Mr. Harris lit a cigarette and took a puff. Then remembering Mr. Houghton disapproved of smoking around his farm buildings, Tom Harris ground out the cigarette butt and popped some gum into his mouth.

"It's a darn mess, and my tractor's out of gas. I came down to the store to find some, but Arthur Henley is rationing it out like gold."

"I'll loan you Lindy Lou and Suzie Q. Get your trailer, and I'll let you have them for a day or two, if you like." Mr. Houghton offered his prize mares.

I couldn't believe it. He never loaned out his horses, not even to the King of England, if he'd asked for them. What had prompted this generosity?

"Okay, Harry, I'll borrow them until I can get my plowing finished. I've plowed everything except that back field. It's rough and needs to be harrowed and gotten ready to seed corn. I might plant soybeans instead because the ground is poor. I'll go fetch my trailer. Tell me exactly how you feed those mares, and I'll do the same." Without another word Mr. Harris left.

"Are you really going to allow him to take your horses?" I asked as the dairyman drove off.

"He's no fool, that Tom, just frustrated. I'll take a look at his two sick cows and save him a vet bill. Might as well get the goodness out of things if you can." Mr. Houghton pushed his straw hat back to cool his head. Then he replaced it and entered the chicken house to finish his chores.

In about an hour Mr. Harris returned with his trailer. We wrapped the mares' legs in bandages and put another one on their tails so they didn't rub all the hair off during their trip. Dressed in their fancy halters, I helped Mr. Houghton lead Lindy Lou and Suzie Q. out of the barn. Their black coats glistened in the spring sunshine like a precious stone. Carefully we loaded them into the trailer. Mr. Houghton brought out their harness and gave Tom Harris a whole load of instructions for the horses' care. Mr. Houghton looked mighty sad as we watched them disappear down the road.

"I'll miss them," he told me. "I love those ladies. I just like seeing them in the pasture every day. I like to hear them nicker to me when I feed them. Horses are good for the soul."

He walked back to the barn as if he'd lost his best friends.

Mr. Harris kept the mares almost a week and got his field ready to plant soybeans. He also got in a fight with Arthur Henley at the store over gas for the tractor. Finally the mares were brought home. Mr. Houghton inspected very inch of them, but found nothing out of place; no cuts or loose shoes, so he felt satisfied.

This argument with Mr. Henley would have caused a lot of talk in the county if the Philippines hadn't fallen with the capture of Bataan and Corregidor. The Australian troops in the Solomans were thrown back to Port Moresby across the south coast of Papua, and there they held their position. The Japanese now controlled the South Pacific. The war looked very grave indeed. Mr. Harris's argument looked like small potatoes compared to these events and was soon forgotten.

A few days later Tom Harris knocked on our door at supper time. He was on one of his restless ventures or journeys through the country. The fall of the Philippines and Admiral Nimitz's losing several ships had set him off worrying about his sailor nephews.

"Don't let him in," Mr. Houghton said, annoyed at being disturbed while we ate.

Mrs. Houghton, however, got up and opened the door. The dairyman stood on the stoop with a letter in his hand.

"Look," he said excitedly, "a letter from Ted. He's fine, and so is his brother; not a bother on them. They heard rumours that the Japanese haven't treated our prisoners very well. After Roosevelt told McArthur to leave the Philippines and gave him the Congressional Medal of Honour, the troops started calling McArthur, 'Dugout Doug'." I wonder how that got through the censors. Not very flattering, to say the least. It did save face, I suppose, to give him that medal. It should have gone to General Wainwright; he's the real hero."

"Come on in, Tom," offered Mrs. Houghton, "and have a cup of tea. How's Elizabeth, these days?"

"She's fine, thank you. It's I who's been difficult. First, it was the tractor, then the cows. That stuff you gave me, Harry, worked. The cows are better. I'm fed up with shortages and with this war we keep losing. I can't live on the edge much longer. It gets to you after a while.

I've no patience with inconvenience." Mr. Harris accepted a cup of tea and some cookies Mrs. Houghton had made.

Then he turned and looked at me as if we were strangers.

"Hi, kid, where ya' been? I haven't seen you around lately?"

After that evening Mr. Harris seemed to pull himself together. He looked less worried and made up with Mr. Henley at the store. Mrs. Houghton told me long-term trouble, like war, often caused even the most stable people to crack.

"They just can't take the uncertainty. Mr. Harris's life is very certain. He milks his cows twice a day and gets it cooled for the creamery to pick it up. His life is predictable, day in and day out. War changes all that, and life is guess work," Mrs. Houghton explained. "I hope he feels better now."

Letters

May, 1942
Richmond, Va.

Dear Dad,
 I am just furious with General McArthur. He's surrendered his troops to the Japs. Only he wasn't there, but spirited away to Australia. General Jonothan Wainwright was left holding the bag, so to speak. He was left to surrender. Mr. Houghton thinks he's greater than old General McArthur. I agree. Now the Philippines are captured. It's endless defeats for us in the Pacific.
 Cary graduates this year and is talking about joining the Army Air Corps. I think he is crazy, but it's nothing but airplanes now. He makes models and has them hung by strings from the ceiling, so they look like they fly. He's terribly excited by it all; I think he's crazy.
 Love, Doc

May 1942, Florida

Dear Son,
 I am in Jacksonville where we shall be for awhile until we go overseas. Cary is very patriotic and would make a good pilot. He's smart enough to do well, and let him go if he wants to. You are too young to fight and your job is on the home front. Study hard and get good grades so you can enter a good Northern college when you graduate. You will be responsible for teaching the next generation. Learn a lot and remember what you learn, Doc, because you will nourish your mind which is important. One day the war will be over and you will grow up.
 Love, Dad

Letters

Richmond, Va.
June 1942

Dear Dad,

General MacArthur was given the Congressional Medal of Honour! I can't believe Roosevelt would do such a thing when they left poor old General Wainwright to take the surrender, and he's now a prisoner of war. I think Wainwright should have received that decoration, not MacArthur, and so does Mr. Houghton. "I shall return," is all MacArthur can say. What about General Wainwright's chances of returning? How could Mr. Roosevelt be so stupid?

I am fourteen now, and occasionally I wear silk stockings. I don't like them because they run too easily. I am getting a figure, but I'm not as curvy as Ann Sheridan, Mr. Houghton's favourite actress. We went to the movies recently, and I must admit she's very good looking. She is also a lot older than I am so she got a head start on the curves.

Rommel's up to his old tricks again. How terrible if Tobruk fell, after all our prayers last year for the brave Australians who held out for nine months. It would leave me in tears, and Mr. Houghton furious. I think God's mixing things up and answering the wrong prayers. I expect with so many people praying to him, he can't keep it all straight. I certainly couldn't keep billions of prayers sorted out. I've asked the Virgin Mary to help Him. Mrs. Houghton says only Catholics pray to her, but I find her quite comforting and less fearsome than God. She's a woman and should know how people feel when things are difficult. Do you pray to Mary in times of great stress? I'd like to find an Episcopalian who does. If they don't, I shall keep her in my prayers anyway because she's a loving and kind lady. I am sure she will help get my prayers heard by a very busy God. I am sure she will keep things straight. This war is very trying on my spiritual beliefs. I feel sorry for German mothers who have lost their sons just as I feel sorry for ours. It must be a terrible experience to lose someone close to you. Love, Doc.

Somewhere in Pennsylvania
18 June 1942

Dear Doc,

I am just as glad you don't resemble Ann Sheridan. All the boys will be massing on your doorstep, and you are far too young. It looks like I'll be going overseas soon, but I send my very best love. I should be stationed in England or Scotland or Wales, but I can't tell you the location because of security, so don't worry, I'll just write the little V-Mail letters they have now. You can reach me through the address I'll send you. We shall keep in touch that way. We can't speak on the telephone anymore, so we must become good letter writers. I'll look forward to your correspondence, my dear Son. I miss you. Love, Dad.

P.S. Don't worry about the Virgin Mary being only Catholic. I am sure she is universally loved and respected. If she brings you comfort, pray to her. God is a larger concept and difficult for one so young. I am sure your prayers will please her because they are sincere. That's what it takes: Real belief and sincerity. I am sure God is bombarded by plenty of petitions right now. Dad.

Richmond, Va.
June 22, 1942

Dear Dad,

Mr. Houghton's been in shock for three days! I can't understand why God did not hear all our prayers for the defenders of Tobruk. All last year we prayed for those Heroic Rats and they held. Then quite suddenly in June this year Rommel pounces on them and it is upsetting our flags because he's running towards Egypt. I think it's totally unfair. I wonder if God took a day off listening to us. Surely he had his back turned when Rommel was victorious.

Do you believe in a just God? I mean, you rarely go to church. Right now I am so angry at God I might never go to Church again. Why didn't he allow the British and Australians to win? Then Rommel goes and messes up everything. It will take us days to get our pins back in the right place. Love, Doc

Somewhere in England
July 4, 1942

Dear Doc,

The war news certainly looks bad with Rommel at the doors of Alexandria. Rommel, even badly beaten, is still a powerful enough force to strike fear in a fighting man's heart. I am sorry about Mr. Houghton's flags. Maybe things will settle down.

As for God. I don't have a lot of influence with the Almighty. But I do believe in Him. And He did help the Rats of Tobruk to hold out for nine months. So your prayers must have done some good. But you see, the Germans are praying too, so they must have their's answered on occasion, I suppose. I wouldn't give up church if I were you. Give the Almighty another chance and ask Him to keep Rommel out of Egypt. We must protect the Suez Canal. Tell Mr. Houghton I hope he gets his flags straight.

Love, Dad

July 1942
Richmond, Va.

Dear Dad,

I talked things over with Mr. Houghton about God. He doesn't go to church either. I thought he'd understand my wanting to stay home with him. But he doesn't. He says I'd upset the Missus terribly if I didn't go with her every Sunday. Also I am helping in the First Grade class with Sally Anne. She says she needs me. So I've decided to give God a second chance. At least until the war is over. So I'm a Christian for the Duration. I am still praying to Mary as well and ask her to keep you safe. Mrs. Houghton said that was all right since she might not be as busy as the Almighty.

Love, Doc

Somewhere in England
July 1942

Dear Doc,

We've taken over a public school for the Army's use. The main building is a three story affair with more rooms than a rabbit warren, but my quarters overlook the cricket field. It's quite comfortable. The road signs have all been taken down so in case of an invasion the Germans couldn't find their way easily. It makes for confusion.

Sometimes we hear Lord Haw Haw. He sure can get under your skin, but he's very effective spreading his propaganda. Working with the British has its problems. They are always stopping for cups of tea. Americans work right on. These tea stops can become quite disconcerting.

Love, Dad

A Forgotten Landscape

47

The Battle Of Midway

June 1942

    Mr. Harris arrived one morning in June looking white and sick. The Japanese had attacked Midway, an American island in the Pacific Ocean. On June 4th, the hero of Pearl Harbor, Admiral Naguma, sent fragmentation bombs which exploded and caused a lot of damage. It was an ambitious attack because the Japanese planned to land on Midway and capture it. The First Fleet had four carriers with 270 airplanes to throw bombs at the Americans.

    The Japanese Zeros completely annihilated a torpedo bomber squadron from the Yorktown. On June 7th the Yorktown was hit and sunk. Although Nagumo lost four of his six carriers, the American losses were devastating. Mr. Harris was beside himself with fear his two nephews had been killed. He came to us for comfort.

    "Those sneaky bastards," he shouted. "They know how to sneak in without warning. That Yamamoto and Nagumo together are poison."

    "What are they?" I asked.

    "The Japanese Admirals. Yamamoto studied English at Harvard University, and later was in Washington with the Japanese there. He and Nagumo designed and carried out the attack of Pearl Harbor – brilliant, both of them, but deadly." Mr. Harris stopped pacing long enough to tell me.

    I hated to see him so upset and went into the kitchen where Mrs. Houghton fixed him a cup of coffee. I took it in.

    "Go on outside and play with the ponies," she suggested. "Tom

Harris may be here for hours. I hope not, but he's terribly upset."

Although the Battle of Midway looked terrible for the Americans, they turned the tide and sunk four Japanese carriers. This partly avenged us for the attack on Pearl Harbor. We lost one carrier, The Yorktown; this tipped the scales in our favor. Still Mr. Harris prowled about the county trying to find sympathy, we felt sorry, but Mr. Houghton finally lost his temper.

"Tom, you're like a lion in its cage. Won't you settle on something? Go home and milk your cows. We are busy here trying to get ready to go sell our eggs. It's Saturday, and I have to take Doc and Missus to Manakin to the Red Cross and deliver eggs. Come back another time."

Mr. Harris drove away, and we didn't see him for a week. Finally he rang us to say he was sorry. He still knew nothing about the two boys. Could we come up for dinner on Sunday?

"That man is trouble. If the nephews are killed, he'll mope around here forever; if they aren't killed, he'll pester some other way." Mr. Houghton loaded up the car and we all climbed in for our trip to Manakin.

Three weeks later Cary graduated from St. Lawrence School with honors. We all went to the graduation delighted he was given such a wonderful prize. Miss Emma nearly fell off her chair when Cary's name was announced. Two days later he enlisted in the Army Air Corps, and within days, it seemed he was gone.

Miss Emma looked sad for weeks, and Mrs. Houghton cried as we told Cary goodbye. Then he drove away down our hill and into a completely different life.

"I don't know what we will do without Cary," Mr. Houghton told me one evening as we did the chores. "He's such a part of our lives. It's very difficult to see him go to war."

"He's so cocky that he'll be all right," I tried to comfort him. "He loves to fly and he loves airplanes. He'll be back."

"I must believe that," Mr. Houghton replied, as he handed me the grain for the horses. "You'll be the next to go."

"Where am I going?" I asked him. "You are stuck with me for the Duration."

"Well, I'll get the goodness out of you when you help me with the evening chores." Mr. Houghton said no more. He picked up the hay fork and climbed up to the loft. He forked down hay for the horses, and the blew his nose on his torn handkerchief.

"That's the way with loving somebody," he reappeared down the ladder. "They grow up and leave you."

"Yes," I said, "I know. Like Father. He's overseas now, you know."

"I can't make head or tail out of this war. All those Nazis here in America seem to go about scott free. Everyone knows Standard Oil is filled with German sympathizers, and Roosevelt seems powerless to get rid of them. There is a piece in the paper about it today."

A Forgotten Landscape

48

Mr. Taliaferro Dies

June 1942

One hot day in the low grounds Mr. Taliaferro had a stroke while driving his tractor. Three of the men who worked for him found Mr. Taliaferro hunched over on his tractor and although they brought him into the barn down there, he died before the ambulance arrived.

"It's the barn's burning that killed him," William told me the next evening when Mr. and Mrs. Houghton and I walked up to the Taliaferros' house with flowers from our garden.

William stood in the front yard and opened the gate for us. The overseer, Mr. Rice, was also there helping to escort the neighbors to the house. Farmers and country people filled the living room and overflowed onto the porch. Jean and Sally Anne greeted us, and someone took our flowers to put in water.

Out on the porch, dressed in all white, sat Mrs. Taliaferro. I never saw anyone look more beautiful. Every hair was in place, her lace handkerchief was the only sign of the deep emotion she felt. Her eyes, brown and always kind, had lost none of their luster.

"How beautiful you look," I gasped. "That dress is gorgeous."

Mrs. Taliaferro smiled at me, and took my hand to pull me close. "Thank you, I need your kind words," she whispered.

We left some fried chicken Mrs. Houghton had fixed with Jean and silently made our way through the crowd to the door. Then we walked home.

"You aren't supposed to tell someone in mourning she looks gorgeous," Mrs. Houghton told me when we got home. "White is for the Summer mourning. Black is for winter. The second year it's purple and lavender with white Summer dresses. But she did look lovely, I must admit."

My French classes stopped with Mrs. Taliaferro during the funeral and for about a week afterwards. Then one afternoon she rang Mrs. Houghton to send me on up to Alder's Point.

"I know exams are coming up soon and some review wouldn't hurt," Mrs. Taliaferro said. "I'll be home this afternoon between four and five, so ask Doc to come along."

When I entered the living room, it smelled of flowers. They were everywhere, in the dining room, on the porch and in the front hall. It looked as if all the florists in Richmond must have sent something. I couldn't believe there were any more left in the shops.

Mrs. Taliaferro met me at the door to the porch.

"Come out here and sit, so we can see the view of the river," she said. I sat where she told me. "I expect your exams will cover your book pretty much. Let's go over the verbs."

For the next hour we studied French. She helped me prepare the lesson and then we looked at some of her lovely books with colored pictures. Finally we gathered up our things and I prepared to leave.

"Thank you very much for your compliment the other day. I felt so distracted with all those people here that I was afraid I could not last the afternoon. You said what I needed to hear."

"I meant it. You looked beautiful; you always do. One day I hope to be a lady like you. I am afraid it's a long way off though."

49

Afton Mountain Holiday

July 1942

After all kinds of dire predictions about the farm animals, the chickens and violent storms, we finally left in early July for Afton Mountain. This year was more complicated than last because Mr. Harris's cousin had to come instead of his nephew. This took some arranging, and Mr. Houghton felt sure, right until the last minute, we couldn't leave. Finally, the cousin planned to move into his cottage and look after the farm.

We had the usual problem with packing. Water for the radiator, Peggy's basket and dog food, a long-handle shovel to ward off snakes, and a few clothes we could fit in the suitcase for a week.

"I hate to leave things unplanned. Mr. Harris will check on his cousin, so I guess it's going to be all right," Mr. Houghton said as we got into the car about six o'clock the morning of our departure.

"Oh, stop fussing, Harry; you'd think we're going to Timbuktu. It's only a hundred miles, for goodness sake." Mrs. Houghton put our picnic lunch onto the backseat before she climbed in beside it.

We started down our hill for River Road listening to a litany of things that could go wrong. Finally, we turned onto River Road and headed west towards Charlottesville. By the time we reached Route 250, Mr. Houghton had forgotten to worry about his farm.

Mrs. Houghton had bought me a book on leaves and plants in the Blue Ridge Mountains. She also decided we would picnic just outside of Charlottesville where there were tables and a shady spot.

"This old car's running well," he commented as we drove along. "It's doing all right. Those new tires we bought in the spring make a difference."

The road was all up and down hill, and soon we left Richmond behind. Our thoughts were on an eight-day holiday in the coolness of the mountains. Mrs. Houghton hoped Gill and Jenny would be back.

"Yes," I replied, "that would be nice. But Miss Hilda kept me hopping all the week last year with her nature study."

"You'll learn something useful that way, and not fritter away your time doing nothing," Mr. Houghton remarked. "You are not interested in taking drives. I am not sure we can do that now with gas at a premium."

"We'll find things to do." Mrs. Houghton said from her high back seat, "We usually do."

Finally after about two hours we stopped for a soft drink at a general store. We all trumbled out just to stretch our legs, and so we didn't have to pay a deposit on the glass drink bottles. Peggy had a little run as well. Then we returned to the hot car for the final drive to Charlottesville.

"Here's our picnic spot." Mr. Houghton pulled over and gratefully we opened fried chicken and cole slaw finished off by homemade cookies.

Mr. Houghton checked his radiator, but all was well. The old car was in good shape, but now we had hills to climb. Slowly, we didn't drive faster than 45 miles an hour, we made the final lap up the mountain stopping twice to check the radiator and allow it to cool. How happy we were when the Blue Ridge Inn came into view.

"Yes," the owner told us, "Gill and Jenny are back this summer too. Miss Hilda took them on a hiking trip in the mountains. They will be here this afternoon about four o'clock. They'll be glad to see you, Doc."

That gave us some time to explore and to sit in the rocking chairs on the back porch overlooking Rock Fish Valley. I knew once Miss Hilda got a hold of me, I'd never see a free hour.

Gill and Jenny came in later, dirty and hot from their walk. Miss Hilda came right up to me and insisted I join them the next morning.

"We're going to Luray Caverns," she told me. "You plan to come along with us."

"Miss Hilda, I don't like to be underground. It scares me. I'd rather not, thank you."

"None of that. You will learn something interesting. None of this nonsense about being afraid." She tramped off to her room to clean up.

"It's all right, Doc, please come with us. It will be fun to have you along," Jenny said. "Do say you will come."

I noticed she looked and spoke more like an American. She seemed less shy and had grown taller. Gill, her bond hair still golden, was quite a pretty girl. She also spoke with an American accent, and dressed in American clothes.

"Do come, it's great to have someone our own age along. You make things more fun." I was unable to protest because they looked so eager for me to join them. I appealed to Mrs. Houghton.

"I am scared stiff of dark and underground places," I told her. "Please make Miss Hilda leave me here with you tomorrow. I'll scream blue murder in the Luray Caverns and disgrace myself."

"No, you won't, dear. It's lighted and you see all these spiky things that form a cave. It's quite interesting."

"You mean those stalactites, calcium carbonate, which hang like icicles in caves," Mr. Houghton added.

"Yes, that's the name for them, Harry. I couldn't think for a moment." Mrs. Houghton rocked on the porch while Mr. Houghton read the newspaper.

"Whatever they are, I definitely don't wish to see them," I replied. "Suppose I yell and scream, what would Miss Hilda think of me then?"

"Well, dear, we are being called into supper. That's the gong. Mr. H. and I are going to ride over the Waynesboro tomorrow. I hardly think that would interest you." We got up to go into the dining room, and I felt defeated.

After supper we played games as we had done last year. However, Gill and Jenny knew some more grown-up games, and I eagerly joined in. Finally, we all went up to bed. Once more I asked the Houghtons to allow me to go to Waynesboro with them.

"I'll tell you what," said Mr. Houghton. "I'll give you my rabbit's foot. If you get scared just rub this foot, and it will bring you good luck."

That was all the satisfaction I received.

The following morning after breakfast we started for Luray Caverns, Gill, Jenny and Miss Hilda. Hugh and his Nannie remained at the Inn. The Houghtons waved us off, and planned a quiet day alone in the mountains. The closer we got to Luray the more I felt the hairs on my neck tingle.

"Why don't you like caves?" asked Jenny.

"I don't know why, because they are dark, I suppose. I don't like being underground." I felt silly trying to explain my fear.

"That's all right, Doc, you'll get over it today," Miss Hilda told me. "It's foolish to allow yourself such feelings. You must learn to control them."

I realized I'd get no sympathy from her.

After a pleasant drive we arrived at the caverns in about two hours. Suddenly I found myself clutching Mr. Houghton's rabbit's foot. We got out of the car and followed several other people into the entrance where we bought tickets.

"You go first, Doc," said Miss Hilda, "just behind that boy in a red shirt."

I followed instructions. Still holding tightly to my rabbit's foot, I walked, looking at my sneakers which were new. The further in we went the more panic I felt. The guide told us about the caverns and how old they were. He explained how caves are made, and I listened trying to focus my mind on what he said. We then went in deeper. We saw all the calcium carbonate stalactites, and stalacmites – one growing up, the other down. Finally, we went in very far, and panic overwhelmed me. I wanted to run back to the light; I wanted to scream for help. I clasped my hand over my mouth to prevent making a sound. I rubbed the rabbit's foot until my thumb and finger hurt. I had to get out of here.

Just then the guide doubled back and flashed his light into my face.

"What's the matter?" he asked me kindly.

"I am afraid of caves," I whispered, "please take me out of here before I scream."

He took my arm and together we walked towards a tiny speck of light.

"Hang on, now," he whispered, "you'll be all right. Please don't scream."

"Okay." I said, "only get me out into the sunshine."

He explained things as we went up towards that tiny speck. He walked briskly, and I clung to him like a drowning man. Finally, after what seemed like an age I could make out the opening and saw light. I nearly broke from his grasp and ran for the entrance.

"Why did you come?" he asked me as we walked the final yards to freedom.

"I was made to," I whispered, "in order to get over my fear. Nobody would listen to me."

Kindly, he took me out into the sunshine where I sat down on the nearest thing and put my head in my hands. I felt the tears as they streaked down my face and hastily wiped them away so Miss Hilda would not see.

"Are you all right?" she asked me when she finally came out of the caverns.

"Just a headache from the bright sun after being in the dark," I said.

"You appear quite exhausted," Miss Hilda looked around for a refreshment room. "Let's go have a soft drink."

I followed her, Gill and Jenny to a little café. I felt better once I'd eaten something. I took the rabbit's foot out of my pocket and laid it on the table. There wasn't much left of it. It looked sad and moth eaten. I'll have to get a new one.

"This is Mr. Houghton's rabbit's foot, and I've destroyed it. Is there some place near by that sells them? I can't give this one back to him."

"What's happened to it?" asked Jenny, "It was all right when we left this morning."

"It doesn't like caverns. He's lost most of his hair from fright," I explained.

Miss Hilda looked at the worn-out thing in my hand and understood.

"All right, we will find another one," she told me rather curtly.

"Yes, please. I can't take this back to him, not after he gave it to me for good luck." I began to cry, not because of the destroyed trinket, but because I could put my fear onto something else.

When we finished our snack I bought a lovely, furry rabbit's foot for Mr. Houghton. I never told him what happened to his, but just gave the new one to him that evening and thanked him for loaning it to me.

"It helped a lot," I said as we sat on the porch awaiting supper. "It kept me from screaming."

"Did you brush it? It's mighty fuzzy tonight – a lot fuzzier than it was this morning."

"Yes," I replied, "I wanted to return it in good repair. I gave it a thorough brushing to make it look neat and clean."

50

A Strange Christening

August 1942

On a communion Sunday in August Dr. Price came again to supply at St. Mary's. The day was set aside for the christening of the new Merriweather baby. His name was Horace, which I thought sounded terrible.

"Fancy naming a little baby, Horace," I remarked to Mrs. Hougton as we dressed for church.

"It's ugly, I agree," she replied.

"Horace Merriweather, how awful!"

I climbed into the front seat of Mr. Houghton's car while his wife settled herself in the back. It was too hot to drive Jackie, and since Mr. Houghton had a full tank of gas, he agreed to take us.

When he arrived outside the church, we found the young people, John and Polly, showing off their new son. The baby, was dressed in a long, white christening robe with matching bonnet made from fine batiste and trimmed with three rows of antique ace.

"What a beautiful baby, and what lovely French lace!" Cooed Mrs. Carthage.

Privately I thought three rows of French lace too fancy for a boy.

"Yes, it is beautiful," agreed Mrs. Houghton. "What a bonnie, wee lad he looks."

"But", I whispered to her, "he has an ugly name."

Mrs. Houghton led the way up the path into the church. We usually sat on the epistle side near the front, so we could hear and see what was going on.

"Good morning, Clara," greeted Catherine Hollis. "Good morning, Doc. How nice you look in that blue dress."

Since I never wore dresses except to school and on Sundays, any dress would make me appear different. But this one was new, and Mrs. Houghton had sewn my favorite lace collar on it. So I regarded this dress as rather special.

"Thank you," I replied, feeling pleased Mrs. Hollis had noticed. "Where do you suppose they got all that French lace in war time?" I whispered to Mrs. Houghton as we settled ourselves in the pew.

"People save such things, dear. A christening dress is handed down from generation to generation. The lace is probably fifty years old." Mrs. Houghton knelt down to pray.

I looked around the church and noticed Dr. Price appeared less rotund. But his wart still danced upon his nose, and his eyes glared at us with the same fierce expression. After we recited the morning prayers, he laid aside the Prayer Book and announced,

"Today we will christen the infant son of John and Polly Merriweather. Will the parents and God parents please come to the back of the church to the font."

Obediently the new parents and God parents stood up and started down the aisle towards our large christening font, a gift of the Wickham family. As Dr. Price preceded them from the altar, we all squirmed around in our seats and strained our necks to see. I watched as Polly untied the lovely bonnet and then handed her little boy to his God Mother. From the Book of Common Prayer Dr. Price intoned,

"Has this child been baptized?"

"No," replied the God parents.

"Do you renounce the devil and all his works?"

"I do," said the God parents.

After a lot of questions and replies, Dr. Price took the baby in his arms,

"Name this child."

"Horace Rodger," replied the God parents.

"Horace Rodger, I baptize you in the name of -," but Dr. Price never finished.

A Strange Christening

The baby slipped through the rector's hand and splashed head first into the font. The young mother screamed. The father looked terrified. In one breath the congregation gasped and strained forward. In an instant Dr. Price plucked the infant from the water dripping wet, but apparently unharmed. His face ashen, the screaming baby clutched at the rector's surplice with its tiny hand and hung on. After a little choking cough, the child smiled. Relieved the congregation let out its breath.

"The baby's screams will allow the devil to escape," Mrs. Houghton explained.

"I shouldn't think a little baby would have a devil," I whispered.

"An old wives' tale, don't take it seriously," she replied softly.

"I baptize you," continued the startled rector, "in the name of the Father and the Son, and the Holy Ghost, William the Conqueror. I sign you with the sign of the cross."

"He's William now," I poked Mrs. Houghton, "just plain Bill."

Polly Merriweather looked shocked. I knew she was deathly afraid of Dr. Price.

"Does that mean his name isn't Horace?" She inquired timidly.

"It most certainly does," the rector affirmed. "You can not name this infant, Horace. He's special. No other child in my forty years of experience as a priest ever swam in the baptismal font. This baby is, beyond any doubt, William the Conqueror."

"A much nicer name," said Mrs. Carthage to nobody in particular.

"Yes," Mrs. Houghton agreed, "much nicer."

Dr. Price handed the dripping infant back to his mother. I watched as Polly undressed him, handing the God mother first the christening robe with its soggy French lace, then the petticoat, and finally the little shirt. William the Conqueror, now clad only in a dripping diaper, was wrapped in a blue receiving blanket. He looked up and smiled at us, king of all he surveyed.

Lizzie got up from her organ and carried the wet dress and petticoat outside and hung them over a bush. William the Conqueror and his family returned to their pew. The little boy lay peacefully in his mother's arms. When the organ started to play, he joined in the singing. We could hear his voice above all the others.

Praise him, praise him, Jesus our blessed redeemer.

Praise him, praise him ever in joyful song.

From that day the child became known as William, and his middle name was actually changed to Conqueror.

"That's much more satisfactory," Mrs. Houghton remarked as we left the church. "William is a good old English name."

"Yes," Mrs. Carthage agreed, poking a pin into a loose strand of her red hair. "It's very Virginian. William Merriweather has a fine strong ring."

"Today I have to agree with Dr. Price," I confided to Mrs. Houghton as we got into the car. "Horace is very inappropriate for a lovely baby especially one with three rows of antique French lace."

A Strange Christening

Letters

11 August 1942
Somewhere in England

Dear Doc,

I received the socks you knitted. They are a perfect fit and well knitted. No lumps. You're improving with everything you make. The dried fruit was great. I shared it at the office with the other men. They couldn't believe the unknown angel was only fourteen years old. I am secretly delighted you are so unselfish and concerned for others.

We are still having trouble working with the British. They love to work at night, and to spend time at their clubs. As a consequence no one gets much sleep. The French, too, are difficult. They can't forget their historical dislike for the English, their ancient enemy. So we have a lot of prima donnas who get their feelings hurt for no reason. We, Americans, are the early worms and get to the office by eight o'clock and get to work. We don't stop for tea at eleven, lunch and again at four o'clock, but work right on taking an hour or a half hour usually for lunch.

This country is a mass of runours. The Irish at the back door won't help with the use of their ports. Our shipping is being sent to the bottom by the German subs which run in Wolf Packs and it's difficult to get supplies through.

Can you manage a pair of gloves? Mine are worn out. Don't forget to make them big enough for my paws. Your monthly box is very much appreciated. Rations here are very severe. Some children have never seen a banana. All that kind of food is imported. Your dried fruit is as valuable as the golden goose. I have been promoted again to Lt. Colonel. So don't forget the new title.

Love, Dad.

August 26, 1942
Richmond, VA

Dead Dad,

You must feel terribly important being promoted and all. You're almost a general. Mrs. Houghton and I packed a most glorious box for you. I hope you get it because the Germans keep sinking our ships. I've packed candies, dried fruit; apples, peaches and cherries. I am knitting your gloves. Mrs. Houghton is helping because two gloves would take an age. One I can manage. She got the biggest size, and we are almost through the ribbing. So you'll have them in a month or two. The egg business is improving and we have deliveries in town now. These are done on Friday when we go shopping for food. At least when the Houghtons go shopping, I sometimes stay with Mrs. Taliaferro that morning in order to allow the Houghtons a break since it's summer and they need to be alone sometimes. Mrs. Taliaferro has a swimming pool so that's fun. Also she is turning the collars and cuffs on her shirts. So I'm learning how to sew. I'm not much good at it. Love, Doc

51

Mr. Houghton And Jackie

August 1942

Jackie, our burro, a present from Uncle Jack, arrived from Arizona when still a baby. Rescued from a herd of wild burros after his mother died, Jackie was just three days old when Uncle Jack found him out on the hills above his ranch. After the little creature arrived, his long ears drooping, in a large crate at the railroad station in Richmond, exhausted and scared, Mrs. Houghton nursed him. Three years later when Jackie grew up and become such a nuisance, Mr. Houghton would remind his wife that it was all her fault.

"I wish you'd never saved that confounded donkey," he would tease. "You should have let him die. He lets the other horses out, makes pock marks on the grass and gets into the gardens. He's nothing but trouble."

I must admit Jackie could be aggravating, but in the summer of 1942 things reached a dangerous pitch. Jackie, snug in his stable with both locks in place, in his donkey mind planned new mischief.

One morning in August I came into the kitchen to find Mr. Houghton huddled over his radio. He looked up as I came in and pressed his finger to his mouth.

"I want to hear this," he whispered. "The Duke of Kent's been killed in an air crash."

"How?" I whispered.

"Hit a mountain in Scotland," Mr. Houghton whispered back as he turned to his crackling radio. "Don't wake the Missus. I'll tell her later."

"What's today?" I asked.

"The twenty-fifth of August, a sad day for England."

"Perhaps it's a rumor like the bombing of Canterbury Cathedral," I said.

"Not a chance; this is for real. He leaves a wife and children behind, too." Mr. Houghton pulled on his boots. "Make yourself some cereal while I go feed the horses and chickens. Let the Missus sleep."

He cut off the radio and was gone.

The last day of August we heard the account of the Duke's funeral on the radio. For once it didn't crackle. We also heard that the Duke of Windsor's offer to come home and help was refused. At this announcement Mrs. Houghton exploded.

"Surely they won't let that woman back in England, that terrible Wallis Simpson with her airs. I read she complains she can't get the clothes she wants. Fancy that, when the world is being blown to bits in Europe and Africa, she's concerned about what she wears. Her people expect her to dress well. Who does she think her people are? Surely not the British, never the British. What an almighty cheek she's got."

"Who is Mrs. Simpson?" I asked.

"A twice-divorced American woman who made the Prince of Wales give up his throne to marry her. She's a horrible woman," Mrs. Houghton nearly exploded with anger. Her face was beet red and her forehead covered with beads of perspiration.

Mr. Houghton replied by turning up the radio, as Mrs. Houghton choked with anger, disappeared into her bedroom.

"I met the present King once," Mr. Houghton said, "When he and the Queen came to Washington before the war in 1939. A big reception was given, and because I was a member of the Armed Forces during the last war, I was invited to the British Embassy to be part of the Honor Guard for a special reception there.

Seventy-six of us lined up in two long rows in front of the Embassy's main door. I was living in Maryland then just after I'd sold my farm in Canada, and was working on a cattle farm. That was before I moved to Richmond.

When the Royal visitors came down the walkway, they stopped and shook our hands. He didn't say much because of his stammer, but the Queen had a gracious smile."

"He talked about it to everyone he knew, for days after. Believe me, Doc, you'd think he was invited to tea," Mrs. Houghton, now recovered re-entered the living room.

"I was, as a matter of fact," winked her husband. "We had a lovely tea in the garden, and I even met the British Ambassador."

"You do talk so, Harry."

"It's true, every word of it is true," Mr. Houghton protested.

"Is it true?" I asked, hoping their domestic quarrel would stop. I was never sure when Mr. Houghton was teasing.

"Yes," replied Mrs. Houghton, "it is. He did go to the Embassy, and he did meet the present King and Queen. I am just upset, that's all, about the poor Duke of Kent and that awful woman, Wallis Simpson. She's no lady, even though she's a southerner from Baltimore."

That evening I did the chores. Probably with all the confusion about the Duke of Kent's death and funeral, I forgot to put the double lock on Jackie's door. Since he could open a single bolt near the top, a bottom one was added for extra security. This one I failed to shut.

While we slept, in the wee, small hours of the morning, the clever donkey worked the single bolt back with his teeth. Drunk with freedom, Billy, Jackie and Lady slipped over Mother's soft grass and trampled her flowers. Then they headed for the big vegetable garden behind the pasture. Here they helped themselves to every vegetable they could find. Then they opened the gate into Mrs. Houghton's garden and scattered carrot tops and half-eaten lettuce between rows of nearly planted vegetables and flowers. The flower garden was filled with broken heads of petunias and Zinnias. Mr. Houghton was furious.

At six o'clock the telephone rang. It was Mr. Brown who demanded Mr. Houghton bring a truck to his farm immediately and pick up our horses.

"They're over here at my dairy in one of my pastures scaring my milk cows, and cutting my milk production. I'll call Richmond's glue factory and have them come out and get these horses if you're not here in ten minutes."

Mr. Houghton woke me. "Get up, Doc, you've got to ride Lady home from Mr. Brown's farm. He's threatening to send the horses to the glue factory."

I was up and dressed in ten minutes. Mr. Houghton gave me a sticky bun and a cup of tea before we left as the dawn was breaking behind the trees. We picked up my bridle and saddle and two long leads so I could bring Jackie and Billy on long lines behind Lady. I also picked two strong halters for the pony and donkey, so they wouldn't break coming home. Then we drove in silence down our hill and out onto River Road to Brown's Dairy on Route 6.

Even this early, when we arrived we found the dairy teaming with life. Long rows of Guernsey cows stood in the milking parlor while three sleepy-looking men in wellingtons milked by hand. Mr. Brown came out of the barn as we drove up. Although he walked over to the car, I didn't think he looked especially happy to see us. Short and stocky, he was dressed in a white coat and a torn straw hat.

"Your horses are in the pasture over there," Mr. Brown waved a casual hand in the direction of his fierce bull, Diamond Head.

"Mind if I use your phone?" Mr. Houghton asked.

"I guess not, but get those animals out of here." The dairyman re-entered his barn.

Armed with two carrots, I started towards the field to catch Lady. After looking at the gate to make sure the electric fence was turned off, I let myself into the pasture. Across a second fence the Guernsey bull raised his head and regarded me with interest. I whistled, and Lady, covered with red mud, saw me and came up at a trot. As she accepted the carrot, I slipped the reins around her neck, put on the bridle and led the mare out of the field.

"Come on, Billy, here's a carrot for you, too," I called while throwing the saddle on Lady and girthing it up.

The cunning pony raised his bay head and watched me intently. But instead of coming for his carrot, he stood perfectly still. Then he lowered his head once more and continued to nibble at the grass. Jackie, meanwhile, filled with curiosity, trotted up, stuck his head over the gate and pushed his strong neck against the fence trying to get at the carrot. I broke it in two, caught his long ear and slipped the halter over his nose. Surprised, the donkey tried to back away and pulled me into the fence. Now the mare, startled by the sudden tension on her head, also backed away. I stood there holding each of them on different sides of the fence, my arms spread wide, while both horse and donkey pulled me in opposite directions.

The gate was unbolted, and I knew Jackie could easily push it open and gallop with his head in the air. Also Lady, if I let her loose, could break the reins and race around Mr. Brown's milking barn once more, scaring his cows. The next instant, I grasped the lead in my teeth and pulled it off the gate; it went flying loose and wound around the donkey's forelegs. Surprised by this sudden turn of events, Jackie stood stock still, and while I quieted the excited mare with my voice, I slipped the lead onto the donkey's halter.

"That was neatly accomplished, kid," I heard Mr. Harris say behind me.

"Good morning," I replied noticing he had brought his horse trailer.

"Here, give me that Jackie, and I'll load him."

I handed Mr. Harris the lead, but when Jackie took one look at the horse trailer, he bolted. He bucked, kicked out with one hind foot, and danced on his hind legs.

"You're a regular circus pony," Mr. Houghton observed coming up to the pasture. "I'll lead him with my car because he'll take all day to load, and Doc here has to register for school."

"Do you think that's a good idea?" I protested. "Suppose he gets hurt?"

"That tough nut? Can't hurt him. It will do him good, teach him a lesson. You ought to see my garden, and what he's done. The Missus will be furious."

Mr. Harris handed Jackie over and went into the pasture to bring out Billy. The pony loaded easily and the men closed the tall gate of the trailer before Mr. Harris drove away. I mounted Lady, and Mr. Houghton tied Jackie's long rein onto his Chevrolet's window winder. Watching from Lady's back I wondered if the donkey would tolerate this novel way of leading him. But he appeared to and trotted quite readily beside Mr. Houghton's car. Thinking all was well, I waved goodbye to Mr. Brown and trotted down the dairy's dirt road towards the sawmill trail that would take me home. I had gone barely two hundred yards when I saw the trailer bouncing wildly behind Mr. Harris's car as he came rushing back towards me.

"Come quickly," he shouted, "Jackie's kicked Harry."

I dug my heels into Lady's sides, and we galloped off down the road, jumped a small fence and pulled up beside Mr. Houghton's car. With its motor still running, the Chevrolet stood in the middle of Route 6 while Jackie pounded the driver's door with his mighty heels. The window was rolled half open and stains of red blood ran down it.

In an instance, I jumped from my horse and raced to the car. On the front seat lay Mr. Houghton, blood streaming from his forehead. I ran to the frantic donkey. His heels still banging against the car door, Jackie twisted around and caught himself in the lead. Suddenly it pulled tight around his front legs and jerked his head down nearly choking him. Slipping my hand between his chin and neck, with great difficulty I unsnapped the lead. This freed the now gasping donkey from the car, and I led him, his front legs still entwined in the rein, towards the fence. I unbuckled my belt and used it to tie Jackie to a post before I loosened the leather line from around his legs. At that moment, with Billy still in the trailer, Mr. Harris arrived.

"Harry, Harry," he called jumping out of his car. "Are you all right?"

Mr. Houghton groaned and sat up. I saw a nasty gash on his forehead, and in spite of our efforts to stop the blood, it flowed freely down his face. Frightened, I mounted Lady and galloped back towards the milking parlor.

"What do you want know, kid?" Mr. Brown snarled as I pulled the mare to a halt.

"A first aid kit," I panted. "Mr. Houghton's hurt. Cut on his head." I was too breathless to explain. "We need some bandage."

Mr. Brown handed me the first aid kit, and he jumped into his car. but I rode Lady across the fields, and reached Mr. Houghton first. Mr. Harris grabbed the first aid kit from me, found some bandage and wrapped Mr. Houghton's bleeding forehead, then pulled the gauze tight enough to stop the crimson flow.

"Doc, I'm going to take Harry to the hospital. Ride the mare on home and lead the donkey. I'll come back for the pony later," Mr. Harris instructed, and got into the front seat of the 1932 Chevrolet. Then he sped down Route 6 as if all the ghosts in Goochland were chasing him.

"You ride on, Doc," said Mr. Brown as he drove up. "I'll take this pony home, and get Mr. Harris's car off the road."

Leading Jackie by his long rein, which I unhooked from the car door handle, I turned Lady into the woods and rode at a slow trot towards home. The morning turned warm as the sun broke through the clouds. I knew I would be late to register and I had no way to get into town. Jackie trotted along beside me quietly, happy to be free of the car and beside Lady. I didn't worry about school because I knew Mrs. Houghton would call the Headmistress and explain things. I was hungry; that I felt was more important than school. I pushed Lady forward, but Jackie refused to move any faster, so we settled into a slow trot which slowly ate up the five miles we had to go. Mr. Brown passed me as I turned onto River Road and crossed it into our own woods. Jackie, sensing he was going home quickened his pace.

At the barn I found Mr. Brown unloading Billy from the trailer. I slipped from my horse and unsaddled her before I put all three of them in the pasture, double locking the gate.

"That should hold them for awhile," Mr. Brown said as he turned to leave. "He should be shot, that donkey, for causing so much trouble."

"It was my fault; I forgot to lock the bottom latch on his stall door. I am sorry about your cows and your milk production."

"I hope I don't have them visiting again. It's to the glue factory they will go." Mr. Brown got back in his car and drove off.

I raced to Mrs. Houghton's cottage to tell her what had happened. She met me at the garden gate.

"It's all right, Doc, Tom called from the hospital. It's not serious, but required a few stitches, that's all. It'll take more than a donkey's kick to crack that tough nut." She laughed. "It's my garden I'm upset about."

"I'm so very sorry about your flowers and vegetables. I forgot to lock the bottom hasp on Jackie's stall. Do I need to call school about the registration?" I hugged her because she hadn't made me feel wicked or useless.

"I called and spoke with the Headmistress. You can go in tomorrow. Classes don't start until next week, so you're okay. What am I going to do with Mr. Houghton at home all day talking and listening to his radio? He'll drive me crazy. Doc, you'll have to feed the horses and look after the chickens. It's only justice, you know, since you left the door unlocked."

"I'll do it all gladly. I am very sorry to cause so much trouble." I reached up and kissed her.

For three days Mr. Houghton sat in his easy chair and moaned. He wanted chicken for supper; then he wanted a bottle of coke to drink, with ice. He turned on his radio and let it play all day. He listed to one soap opera after the other. He gave me instructions about feeding, watering and looking after the stock. I was to be extra careful about the eggs. I had to crate them and count them and mark them for delivery with the customer's name. We nearly ran off our feet.

"I'll kill that man if he doesn't get well soon and get out of here," Mrs. Houghton confided in me. "Tomorrow he goes to the doctor again. I'll get Tom Harris to take him down to Southern States for supplies and out to lunch. Only then will we have peace."

52

When the James River Flooded

September 1942

It rained for seven days, hard driving rain – cold for September. The James River rose, left its banks and crept up over the low grounds. It covered the corn in three feet of water twenty-five miles west of us. By nightfall we knew our low grounds would also be flooded.

Mr. Harris arrived with his horse trailer shortly after eight o'clock when the rain stopped. In it he brought Nellie, his part Thoroughbred mule.

"Hello, Kid," he greeted me as he pulled up in front of the Houghtons' garden. "Where's Harry? I've come with my mule to bring in Jean Taliaferro's hay."

"He's in the barn harnessing up Lindy Lou and Suzie Q.," I replied.

"Here, help me take Nellie out, and I'll tie her to the fence. You can lead her down to the low grounds with your pony."

"Yes, sir," I said, opening the chain on the tail gate.

"Doc, this is the smartest cow-mule in the whole United States. I raised her. I know. Her mama was a Thoroughbred I owned, but Lord knows where she found the jackass."

While explaining Nellie's genealogy like any true Virginia, Mr. Harris backed his mule out of the trailer.

"Strange things can happen," I pointed out, completely disinterested, having heard the story before.

Already saddled, Nellie wore a halter over her bridle. Attached to it was a line which Mr. Harris tied to the fence.

"Remember, bring her down, in about a half hour."

Just then Mr. Houghton drove his black mares out of the stable yard at a brisk trot, their coats gleaming.

"See you later, Doc," Mr. Harris said as he swung himself up onto the wagon, and I watched it rattle down the road towards the Taliaferros.

Then I ran to our stables and saddled up Billy. I could hear Jean Taliaferro's cattle bellowing from the railroad tracks. I saw Jeb Pillar and Harrison Moore, who lived across the creek, ride up the road on their farm horses, and trot into our stable yard.

"Get on your pony, kid," Mr. Pillar greeted me. "You can open the gates for us."

"But Mr. Harris wanted me to lead down his mule."

I disliked Mr. Pillar, because he was cruel and rough with his animals. Once he shot his best hound when it chased a rabbit instead of a fox. That evening, I remember, he told the story at Henley's store as a joke. Also he smelled bad most of the time.

Harrison Moore spat a great wad of tobacco over Billy's ears just as I started to mount. It landed upon the ground in front of us.

"Hee, hee, hee. Look at dat pony jump. He'll throw you," Mr. Pillar laughed unpleasantly.

Although Mr. Moore was not really cruel, when he went about with Jeb Pillar he put on a tough act. One day when I fell from my horse and was hurt he helped me to mount and led me part of the way home. But around Mr. Pillar he acted differently.

Accompanying the farmers out of the stable yard I asked, "Don't you find floods exciting?"

They just ignored me.

"Miss Jean's cattle have been stranded on the railroad since before dawn. She was rounding up as much help as she could find when she called me," said Mr. Moore.

"She even asked me to phone Red Jones on River Road. But I couldn't reach him," Jeb Pillar replied.

I dismounted in front of Mr. Houghton's cottage to get Nellie. She never walked for very long. After a few steps she jig-trotted tossing her long ears.

"Get moving, kid," called Mr. Pillar.

Cantering to keep up with Nellie, I rode on ahead of the men. The pony and the mule matched strides, Billy's trotting to Nellie's jig. Upon reaching the low grounds' gate, I stopped and waited for the two farmers. Neither could ride his horse very well. Mr. Pillar looked like a sack of meal on his white mare. And Mr. Moore sat his black gelding in a western saddle, its stirrups far too short. Both men wore bib overalls and heavy rubber boots.

"Come on, girl, we haven't got all day," commanded Mr. Pillar as he rode through the double gates.

Recognizing the men, Jean Taliaferro came galloping up the hill to meet us. The rhythmic cadence of Huck's hooves on the gravel road frightened Nellie. She jumped to one side.

"You can't handle that fool of a mule," Mr. Pillar said, as obese and foul with sweat and tobacco, he blew his nose by holding one nostril shut.

I trotted down the hill past the men and Jean Taliaferro. The gravel road curved gently beside the disused canal which meandered out from Richmond, next to it ran the railroad. On the other side of the embankment, pastures stretched for a mile down to the James River. It was these lush, rich lands that the farmers called the low grounds. Because they lay within the flood plain of the river, they were often covered by its waters. On either side of the tracks water, about three inches deep, covered the fields. At the heavy double gates on the far side of the embankment, I met Mr. Tanner with Jean's team and loaded wagon. The men were transporting the hay stored in the low grounds' barn to put it in another barn closer to the house. This was on higher ground located on the cliffs that overlooked the river.

"Hello, Doc," Mr. Tanner greeted me.

"Hello," I replied and watched as the team of grey mules, Dilly and Dolly, crossed over the tracks with their load of loose hay.

Away in the distance I saw Mr. Houghton's team turn into the barn. His mares, docile and sure-footed, I knew placed their wagon right under the loft so the men could quickly throw down the hay and fork it into the empty wagon. Leaving Mr. Pillar and Mr. Moore on the embankment, I cantered Billy through the water towards the barn with Nellie trotting beside me. We crossed Turkahoe creek and I drew to a halt for a second double gate. These I opened still astride Billy. Then, knowing I was splashing water about and getting my legs wet, I thought I'd better trot. Besides cantering the pony in this much water with Nellie was dangerous, and both Mr. Houghton and Mr. Harris would tell me so when I reached the barn.

"You throw the hay down, and I'll stack it on the wagon," Mr. Harris shouted as I entered the barn.

Dismounting Billy I tied him and Nellie in dry stalls. They were almost dry because the barn was built on a knoll and still was not flooded. Then I climbed into the wagon to help Mr. Harris. It was sticky work, and I hated it. Hay stuck to my clothes and poked me in the neck and wrists. Quickly we filled the wagon and stacked it precariously high.

"Hurry," said Mr. Harris, "the water is rising quickly. We'd better take this load up."

"Right, Tom, I don't want my horses falling to their knees and getting hurt." Mr. Houghton slid down from the hay loft. "When did you get here, Doc?"

"Just now," I replied. "I brought Mr. Harris's mule."

"Here, give me a leg up, Tom, on Lindy Lou," Mr. Houghton seated himself in front of the saddle pad and held the short reins which usually dropped over the hames.

I brought Nellie out of her stall and held her for Mr. Harris. He unsnapped the team's driving lines and strapped them to his saddle so they could have them for the trip back. He would go first and man the gates, opening them and closing them once the team had passed through. Lightly he swung up onto his mule, and she, feeling his weight on her back, flexed her neck. Nellie, her chestnut coat gleaming, pranced through the muddy water like a war horse.

"Come on, Doc," Mr. Harris said, as I made no attempt to move so captivated by the mule, that I forgot about the flood. "Get your pony and follow us."

What a beautiful horseman he was! How skillfully he controlled that factious mule. He took a lot of ribbing, I remember, when Nellie was born. I stood there in the muddy water and thought they were the most glorious pair I'd ever seen. Mule and rider looked like they were a part of one another. I loved them.

I knew Mr. Harris could get the gates better than I could on Billy. The team's stride must not be broken because it was easier to keep moving than to stop and start. The gate man had to be clever and have the gate opened before the horses arrived. Mr. Harris and Nellie were perfect for the job. I simply trotted on behind the hay wagon.

"I'm supposed to go to the Mountains," remarked Mr. Houghton as we rode along. "I wonder if I'll make it. I hear the roads are impassable all the way to Charlottesville."

"Wait until this flood is over," suggested Mr. Harris as Nellie pranced beside the wagon.

"Got reservations at a bargain, and if we don't use them now I won't get the goodness out of the special price."

"I thought you already took your holiday in July. I am not sure my cousin can come again. Cancel your trip, Harry until this flood is over. There is flooding all the way up the James River. Go in October for the leaves, and I'll get a hold of my cousin." Mr. Harris opened the big gates that led to the railroad tracks. "Here, Doc, hold that side open, and I'll handle this one."

Leaning into their collars the big horses started up the hill. I watched the traces lose their slack and pull tight against the singletrees. The mares lowered their great heads and dug in their heels. Steadily the wagon rolled on as I swung closed the heavy gate and Mr. Harris swung his side shut and locked the gates with a chain. Then we followed the team up the embankment.

"Can't you see the cattle are loose?" Shouted Mr. Pillar.

"What's wrong with Jed?" Asked Mr. Harris. "What's old Pillar shouting about?"

"He's got a screw loose," Mr. Harris winked as he rode by.

I followed and stuck out my tongue at Mr. Pillar's retreating figure on the white mare. Pandemonium reigned on the embankment. Up and down the railroad line raced Mr. Pillar, his McClellan saddle slipped to one side. The cattle swarmed all over the tracks and ran down the path of the old canal. Waves of white faced Herefords flooded the embankment. Harrison Moore and Jean Taliaferro tried to bring the cattle up the tracks towards us. Mr. Pillar rode in the wrong place at the wrong time.

"Get out of here, you sons of bitches," he shouted.

"Shut up, Jed," I heard Mr. Houghton's voice. "There are ladies present."

"Where, Harry?" Answered Mr. Pillar, "Where? Doc there ain't nothing but a kid."

"She doesn't need to hear that kind of talk. Shut up."

Mr. Pillar galloped up the tracks towards a group of fifty young steers. Away up the line, I saw Jean turn the frightened cattle towards the gate. Every time the animals started back in the right direction Mr. Pillar's frantic galloping chased them up the tracks once again. Three steers, alarmed by his antics, jumped into the canal. Mr. Pillar's horse slipped, turning its saddle completely around. The next instance the farmer landed head first into the canal. I found myself screaming with laughter.

"I can't swim," Mr. Pillar hollered frantically. "Get me out of here."

"It ain't deep, Jed. Get out yourself," Mr. Moore yelled.

Frightened by the splashing water, Harrison Moore's black gelding bolted and dashed up the tracks.

"Whoa, whoa," yelled its rider as the gelding, out of control, sped past us.

"You sons of bitches, you confounded sons of a sea cook," shouted Mr. Pillar as he stood waist deep in the canal.

Our laughter rang across the embankment. Tom Harris sat doubled over in his saddle. Mr. Houghton nearly fell off Lindy Lou. Nellie jigged and leaped as her rider struggled for control.

"Moore," Tom Harris called, reining in his mule. "Moore, come here. Turn your horse and walk those cattle down the tracks."

Bouncing to a halt, Mr. Moore, his stirrups gone, his hat flying from his head, finally stopped his gelding. He walked the cattle down the tracks towards us. Mr. Houghton tried to position his team so the steers could not get past it onto the canal path. I placed Billy next to him.

Nellie was an incredible sight. Never taking her eyes off the cattle, she worked them like a true cow pony, her big ears pricked forward, her dainty feet light upon the ground. Far up the tracks, Jean guided the cattle down on Huck.

"Get over there, cow, that's right, steer," coaxed Mr. Harris as he cleared the tracks and brought the cattle down towards the road that led up to the high ground.

The warning signal flashed yellow. Away in the distance I heard a whistle. The morning train to Richmond came relentlessly on. Its speed terrifying, its whistle ear splitting as the engine rounded the curve about two miles up the track.

"Take these cattle to the gate," Jean Taliaferro ordered Mr. Moore as she galloped Huck up the line to stop the engineer.

Mr. Moore continued to ride down the embankment towards us. Mr. Pillar scrambled out of the canal. Wet and dripping, he fixed his saddle straight on his mare's back and remounted. Then he came up the canal path towards us.

"The train's coming. We'll all get kilt; we'll all get kilt."

"Stand over there, Jeb by the low ground gate to keep the cattle from heading down to it." Mr. Houghton pointed to where he wanted Mr. Pillar to go. Mr. Moore trotted his gelding, and the steers quickened their pace.

"Damn it, Moore, stop chasing the cattle. Walk that horse. Haven't you got any sense."? Mr. Harris lost his temper.

"We shall all be killed, if Miss Jean can't stop that train," the farmer replied.

The black gelding bolted, frightened out of his wits by a long blast on the train's whistle. He sprang straight up in the air with Mr. Moore clinging on. Then the horse galloped up the tracks, jumped the fence and flew up the road towards the high ground. Mr. Pillar followed, hanging on with all his strength, he, too, jumped the fence and lit out for home. It would have been funny if we were not in danger.

Again we heard the train's whistle. Terrified the cattle scattered along the embankment. They galloped passed us up the canal path. A steer bumped into Billy almost knocking us to the ground. Only Tom Harris remained calm. Sitting erect on Nellie, he continued to herd the cattle down the tracks. I moved stray steers at a walk down towards Mr. Houghton who sat astride Lindy Lou. The wagon was still parked across the canal path to block its entrance. In the distance I saw Jean Taliaferro wave her arms, but the train continued to race towards us.

"Hey, Doc, open the gates to the high ground," Mr. Harris shouted.

Billy and I moved forward at a walk. Carefully we treaded our way through the cattle pushing the frightened animals to one side. As we came down the path beside the canal, the road dropped steeply, its sides unguarded by fencing. Below ran the shallow water of the canal. I realized if we fell into it from this angle both Billy and I could be killed. I rode cautiously along, and gently talked to the cattle, until I reached the gate. It was about three feet. How Mr. Moore and Mr. Pillar had remained on their horses when they both rode so badly was a mystery. I felt sure neither had jumped so high before today.

"Careful, Doc," Mr. Houghton warned as he positioned his wagon once more.

I unlocked the chain, gave the gate a push and watched it swing back. The cattle surged through. They knocked Billy and me against the fence. I scraped my legs and Billy was nearly squeezed against the wire.

"Get up, Doc," Mr. Houghton called. "Quick, climb the fence."

Standing in my saddle I scrambled up the fence and sat on the gate holding Billy as tight as I could while the cattle whizzed past.

"The train isn't going to stop," shouted Mr. Harris as his strays scattered across the embankment heading towards Richmond.

By now the engine's driver was clearly visible. Still undaunted Jean rode Huck alongside the tracks, waving her arm and shouting. But the driver apparently did not see her. Mr. Houghton drove his team forward, Mr. Harris, trying to control the remaining steers, rode Nellie down the embankment towards us. From my perch on the gate I saw the frightened horses leap forward trying to escape the noise of the train.

The engineer suddenly applied his brakes. The great locomotive screeched to a halt. Lindy Lou and Suzie Q. reared up on their hind legs. Nellie flew down the tracks after the frightened cattle. Huck and Jean jumped the pasture fence into the low grounds.

"What's going on here?" Demanded the engineer sticking his head out of his cab.

"A round-up," replied Jean Taliaferro pulling Huck down to a walk, before she came back onto the embankment from the low grounds.

"A round-up? It looks more like chaos to me," observed the engineer as he climbed down from his high seat. Then he started up the tracks towards us.

"Come here, kid," he called to me. "Get down from there and help bring some cattle up."

"Miss," he addressed Jean, "you stand your horse on this side of the gates. You with the team, move over to the canal path and prevent run outs." The engineer, organized us.

Gingerly, I climbed down off the gate and remounted Billy. Then I rode slowly up the tracks towards Mr. Harris and Nellie as they brought the cattle down the embankment towards the gate to the high ground which I had chained open. With the engineer's help, we turned the skittish animals once more. They approached the train, halted, sniffed at the air and looked at the black engine with suspicion.

"Ease them around carefully with your mule. Kid, get over and guide those cattle up the road. Slowly, slowly, that's right."

When the last reluctant steer finally turned off the tracks and trotted through the gate I stood up in my stirrups and cheered.

"That's got it," said the engineer. "You'll have to take over now. Good luck."

"What are the roads like further west of here?" Mr. Houghton wanted to know.

"Very bad. This river hasn't crested yet. When it does you can expect another two to three inches of water. This will probably be the final train until the flood is over," the engineer said.

I watched him climb into his cab and pull out the throttle. He waved at us as the train quickly gathered speed and continued on its journey to Richmond. I waved back, and dismounted to pick up Mr. Moore's hat before we all passed through the gate which I swung closed and locked. Restraining his anxious horses, Mr. Houghton drove his team up the road. Tom Harris followed on Nellie, Jean walked beside him, and I brought up the rear. Billy acted exhausted, and slowly we climbed the hill to the high ground above the tracks and the canal. I knew I couldn't ride him much longer because my legs nearly touched the ground.

Mr. Moore and Mr. Pillar were nowhere in sight. Jean Taliaferro turned left towards the railroad pasture, Mr. Harris and I went with her. Mr. Houghton took his team to the barn to unload the hay. The cattle, less frightened now, stopped along the way to nibble the grass under the fence. The railroad pasture, located high on a bluff overlooking the canal was an ideal place to put the cattle.

At the top of the road by the gate sat Mr. Pillar. His horse grazed beside him, her reins broken, the saddle twisted almost under her belly. A great wad of tobacco pushed the farmer's cheek out, and I watched as he spat long stringy spits upon the grass. His big belly hung over his pants, his dirty overalls turned down exposing his skin. He looked miserable and still wet from his fall into the canal.

Mr. Moore sat on the fence, his boots off, his big toe sticking out of a hole in his sock. His black gelding grazed, free of bridle and saddle, next to the white mare. I noticed the tack hung over a fence post.

"Damn fool, cattle," Mr. Pillar commented as we approached. "I'll never cross Tuckahoe Creek again to help with cattle."

"Here's your hat, Mr. Moore," I handed him his battered head gear. "It's a bit dirty, but can be brushed up again, I suppose."

"I suppose. Thanks, Kid." Mr. Moore took his hat and placed it on the fence next to his saddle.

I followed Tom Harris and Nellie up to the railroad pasture. Jean opened the double gates as Tom Harris and Nellie drove the steers through them. I watched, marveling at the ease with which the mule handled the cattle. Finally I swung one side of the gate closed as Jean handled the other one and locked the two sides together.

Mr. Houghton returned from unloading his hay and pulled his team to a halt.

"Moore, I'll give you a ride on the wagon," he offered. "Can you tie your horse behind?"

"I don't need no help," said Mr. Pillar. "I'm going home before I get sick from the cold."

Mr. Moore put his tack in the empty wagon. He sat facing the back and dangled his feet over the side. He looked all in, and his horse's coat was streaked in sweat. Mr. Harris led the black gelding on Nellie.

We left Mr. Pillar sitting by the road side, his horse's saddle twisted, her reins broken. He was a sorry looking sight if there ever was one, I thought.

Shortly after this round-up Nellie became the talk of the county. Mr. Harris was now much sought after to move stock.

"You see, kid," he winked at me when we got back to Mr. Houghton's cottage, "She's the smartest cow-mule in the whole United States."

When the James River Flooded

Letters

September 1942
Richmond, Virginia

Dear Dad,

We had a regular round-up the other day trying to get the cattle out of the low grounds. The floods came and covered them almost up to the railroad tracks. It took a bit of doing to move the cattle, but we finally managed it with the train engineer's help.

Mr. Pillar's cattle swam to Richmond. He's been hunting all over for them. Someone found the bull in his garden. That caused a stir. Imagine a city man finding a large Hereford bull eating his plants! Mr. Pillar and Mr. Harris took their trucks into town and came back with most of the cattle. One or two steers are still missing. They may have drowned.

School started, and we have several new teachers. Some of the younger ones have joined the women's forces like the WACS and the WAVES. I guess they got fired up about this war. Now we have some retired teachers who have come back to work for the duration. Everything is for The Duration.

Miss Richards teaches math and Latin. She must be a hundred, all tiny and shriveled. But she knows about algebra and teaches it as if it's the most important subject in the world. You don't dare go in without your homework done. Mrs. Owens is still with us. She isn't as old as Miss Richards, just a few years younger. She's giving me a fit with history this year. She also asks about your part in the war. I can't tell her very much, and she doesn't like it. I told her you were in England with General Mark Clark. She thinks that's terribly exciting.

Mrs. Gilbert teaches English, and she's the best teacher left. She has a Masters Degree and knows her onions. She's got me interested in reading more of Robert Lewis Stevenson. We are doing "Treasure Island" which I like. Mrs. Owens is teaching about Ancient History. Although she's hooked on Virginia history, we are learning about the Greeks and the Romans. I can't say I like it especially. Madame retired, but has returned. She takes the French classes and I still have a terrible time pronouncing it.

Mary Ann's been very sick with Scarlet Fever. She had to be isolated so we can only speak out of her bedroom window. I went around to her house and we chatted briefly with my standing in her back garden on a bench. Mary Ann nearly fell head first out of the window until Mrs. Thornton made us quit. She looks terrible and sounded worse. I wish she'd get well and return to school because she's a whiz at math and helps me.

Mother and Rudy are still in Washington. Mother comes now about every six weeks because of the gas shortage. She came to get me settled in school so Mr. Houghton could take a long weekend in the mountains. He won a reduced rate trip, and he couldn't stand it until he made use of it. So he and Mrs. Houghton went up to some place near Afton for three days. Mother and I went shopping for clothes and books for school. The house has very little heat because coal is hard to get. We only use the furnace when the temperature goes below 65 degrees. So in September that's not at all. Mr. Harris brought the Houghtons some firewood the other day. He got it from the saw mill near his farm. We have two cords of wood for the winter. Mr. Houghton stocked up on coal last spring, so we should be all right. I don't fancy being cold, Mrs. Houghton is knitting me a pretty blue sweater, and I have some new skirts. I shouldn't freeze. That's about all my news. It's rather ordinary, I fear, but then I don't go many places. Mr. Harris's cousin came and looked after the horses and the chickens. He took the mares out in the wagon one afternoon just to show them off. I went along with him, and we ended up at the store which caused quite an sensation. We piled into the wagon some groceries and drove the mares home. Mrs. Carthage has talked of nothing else since. Wait until Mr. Houghton hears what we did. He'll skin us.

Love, Doc

53

Mr. Houghton And The Guineas

October 1942

October that year was especially colorful. The leaves blazed in crimson and in golden glory. The nights were frosty, and Mr. Houghton lost three chickens to foxes and raccoons. So one Saturday afternoon he took Mrs. Houghton and me to Goochland Court House to buy a pair of guinea hens.

"They are the best watch dogs ever," he told me as we drove through the glorious countryside in the 1932 Chevrolet.

In the back seat sat Mrs. Houghton reading the directions to Mr. Kelly's farm. She had answered an advertisement in the local newspaper, and called to arrange with Mr. Kelly when we could come up and get the pair of guineas.

"At the Court House you turn down by the high school towards Route 250. The farm's on that road about three quarters of a mile from the school." Mrs. Houghton told us.

Mr. Houghton nodded. His little dog, Peggy, sat on his lap and looked out of the window at the passing countryside. She loved to ride in the car, and whenever he could her master always took Peggy with him.

"The old car still rides well, don't you think, Doc?" he asked me. "I've had some work done on her this week. Now I know she will get us through the war."

"I am sure she will." I had heard about the inner workings of Mr. Houghton's car many times, and since I did not know one part from another I found explanations about "points" and "plugs" rather boring.

"Perhaps we should stop at the store in Goochland and buy some feed. They have those new colorful sacks there," Mrs. Houghton suggested.

After nineteen pleasant, but uneventful miles, we pulled into Sam's Place, a little general store just on the outskirts of Goochland. If Goochland, it could be said, possessed outskirts. Mr. Houghton bought us each a soft drink.

"Here's a Dr. Pepper for you. The ten, two and four quicker picker upper," he offered me a bottle as he recited the well known advertisement jingle.

After we bought feed and filled the trunk with brightly colored sacks of chicken mash, Mrs. Houghton got down from her high back seat and entered the store.

"Good morning, Clara," Alvira Carthage greeted her. "Glad to see you out and looking so well."

"Oh, dear," Mrs. Houghton whispered, "the whole county will know we were here today."

Mrs. Carthage was a gossip, harmless, but annoying. She came to church to see what news she could sniff out. Every Saturday she rode around Goochland, talked to all of the neighbors, gave them her items of gossip and picked up others. She meant no harm because she thought she was being useful, since our county was so far flung. When gas rationing curtailed her activities somewhat she drove to a general store and collared the people who came in. She was tall and striking looking with red hair, a hawk's nose and very unusual green eyes. Sometimes they looked hazel, depending upon the color she wore. Today she had on a green tweed skirt under a black coat. However, Mrs. Houghton found Alvira Cathrage offensive and often tried to avoid her.

"We would have to run into her, of all people," Clara Houghton climbed back onto her high seat.

"Don't tell her anything," I suggested as I entered the passenger side and held Peggy upon my lap until Mr. Houghton turned out onto the highway once more.

"The whole of Goochland will know I was out today. I'll have to explain why in church tomorrow," Mrs. Houghton continued.

"Just don't go to church, like me," her husband replied.

After we left the store we drove on into the little village of Goochland, turned right at the school and finally entered the dirt road

Mr. Houghton and the Guineas

that led back into Mr. Kelly's farm.

"Good morning, Harry," the farmer greeted us, as the car drew up in front of his frame house.

"Hello, John," Mr. Houghton switched off the motor and got out while I held Peggy.

"Got the whole family with you this morning, I see."

"Lovely day for an outing, a drive through the country," Mrs. Houghton opened her back window.

"Yes, Ma'am, it surely is. Well, I've got you two guineas. I put them into gunny sacks so they would go into your trunk," Mr. Kelly brought forth two wriggling brown burlap bags.

"I'm afraid my trunk is full of feed. I guess we'll have to put these bags in the back seat with the missus," Mr. Houghton teased.

"No, you don't, Harry. I'm not riding with those birds at my feet." Mr. Houghton laughed.

"Harry, you just take those sacks away from here." Mrs. Houghton looked serious. She did not like chickens although she loved our wild song birds.

"But that's why we came. Please just take one sack back there with you," Mr. Houghton begged, since it seemed the only practical thing to do.

"Just one. The other must ride in the front with Doc," Mrs. Houghton insisted.

So a wriggling sack was placed under my feet on the floorboards of the car. But when Peggy saw the burlap bag she decided it was alive and began to bark. Suddenly she tried to bite the sack but, instead, her teeth, needle sharp, sank into my ankle.

"Ouch, she bit me. That little mutt bit me," I screamed in pain.

Mr. Kelly insisted I come into the house for first aid and took me to find his wife. But Peggy continued to bark furiously, until Mr. Houghton finally snapped a leash onto her collar. In these few minutes the sack in the front seat flipped flopped out of the open car door and started off down the drive. Mr. Houghton dashed after it. But Peggy, in her excitement, wrapped the leash around his ankles and tripped him. Mr. Houghton sat hobbled upon the gravel road while the sack continued on its journey across the pasture. Mrs. Houghton and I screamed with laughter as Mr. Kelly rescued the hobbled Mr. Houghton, and together

A Forgotten Landscape

they retrieved the wriggling sack. Once more it was placed on the floor of the front seat.

"Is your leg all right?" Mrs. Houghton asked me when I returned from the house and got into the car once again.

"Sure," I replied, and pulled down my sock to show her my large bandage.

Finally we all waved goodbye to Mr. Kelly who stood in his Wellingtons at the top of his drive and watched the car rattle down the rough gravel road. Mr. Houghton held Peggy tightly by the collar as she once more sat on his lap. I clutched the sack at my feet, and Mrs. Houghton tied hers onto the rod which ran behind the front seat and was used for lap robes.

Everything seemed peaceful until we reached Goochland Court House.

As we drove through the village we found Alvira Carthage sitting in the middle of the road, her shopping bag spilled out onto the pavement, her face bleeding. Immediately Mr. Houghton stopped.

"Mrs. Carthage, are you hurt," he asked as he helped her up.

"Not really. I can move. My legs aren't broken. A black car just mowed me down and never stopped, just like I wasn't there at all." Although her hat lay on the road, and her red hair was disheveled, she stood up. "And not a soul came out of the store to help me."

"We'll take you to Dr. Lloyd's office. It's only just down the road," Mr. Houghton suggested as he half carried the frightened woman.

"Yes, yes," Mrs. Carthage sobbed as, aided by my friend, she limped towards the car.

Dressed in a long black coat, with its matching hat, Mrs. Carthage clutched at her handbag. Tall and angular, her red hair falling down onto her shoulders, she looked pitiful. I noticed her stockings were in shreds, her legs were scraped, and her white blouse had blood on its collar.

"She looks terrible," I thought as I hopped out of the front seat and took the gunny sack with me.

I held the door open for Mrs. Carthage as Mr. Houghton half lifted her into the car. Then he sent me back for her hat and groceries. These I handed to Mrs. Houghton before I squeezed my flipping flopping sack onto the floor of her back seat. Silently she handed me a piece of string to tie my sack next to hers on the bar which held the lap robes. Finally I climbed onto the high seat beside her.

Mr. Houghton and the Guineas

"What happened?" asked Mr. Houghton, not unkindly, as the car started.

"I had just come out of the store and commenced across the road when a big black automobile ran me down." Mrs. Carthage accepted the handkerchief Mrs. Houghton offered her, and wiped the blood from her face.

Mr. Houghton, with Peggy on his lap, gently drove down to Dr. Lloyd's office. It was closed.

"He's out on a call. I'm locking up for lunch. Come back at two o'clock," the nurse told us.

"I can't," Mr. Houghton protested. "Mrs. Carthage needs a doctor now."

The nurse was young, and her boyfriend, Bobby Taylor, waited for her at the store. Mr. Houghton realized this, but said nothing. He just went on.

We all wondered as we drove along how best to handle this situation. The nearest doctor was at a hospital in Richmond. That was almost thirty miles from here. Mr. Houghton looked at his gas gauge, and counted on his fingers the number of gallons it took to drive thirty miles into town and thirteen miles home again. Although his car was small and got excellent gas mileage, I knew the figuring did not come out to his advantage. For several minutes we rode along in silence.

"Mrs. Carthage," Mr. Houghton said at last, "I shall take you into Richmond to the hospital."

But our passenger had closed her eyes. Her face seemed very white. Mr. Houghton pressed down upon the gas, and I watched the speedometer creep up past the usual 45 to 50 to 55 miles per hour. We flew down Route 6, as cattle, trees and meadows raced by us. Still Mrs. Carthage did not move. The birds in the sacks stopped fluttering. I hoped they had not died, and made a secret hole in each sack, poked my finger into it and felt warm bodies. I was greatly relieved, and quickly withdrew my finger when I felt a sharp beak bite it.

At long last we arrived in Richmond. The nearest hospital was on the Boulevard, halfway downtown. Mrs. Houghton leaned over the seat and tried to open Mrs. Carthage's coat.

"Harry," my friend's voice sounded crisp with fear. "Is she dead?"

"No," Mr. Houghton replied, unconcerned. "Just fainted."

I hoped so, and prayed Mrs. Carthage would not die right here in Mr. Houghton's old car with me and two guinea hens in the back seat. I sucked on my smarting finger.

Finally we arrived at the emergency room. Nurses brought a stretcher and carried Mrs. Carthage inside.

"I'll have to go in with her," Mrs. Houghton told us. "She can't tell them who she is."

"Be quick if you can. The guineas are still in their sacks. I don't want them to suffocate after paying six dollars a pair for them." Mr. Houghton seemed to have forgotten about the forms one must sign to be admitted into a hospital. "I'm ready to get home."

We waited for an hour in the parking lot. Then we went to a nearby eating place, John's Café, and had a cup of tea and some cookies. Still Mrs. Houghton did not return. Finally, after what seemed to me an interminable time, Mr. Houghton left me with the car, the dog and the hens and went into the hospital to find out what had happened.

"Perhaps Mrs. Carthage's dead," he teased before he walked away.

I hoped not. What on earth would we do with all of her groceries and her ugly black hat? I wondered.

A few minutes later when Mr. and Mrs. Houghton both reappeared, I felt greatly relieved. Although Mrs. Houghton looked visibly shaken.

"She's just broken some ribs and the doctor wants to keep her here. I'll have to run down to Miller and Rhoads and buy her a night gown and some toilet articles."

"Then you shall have to go on the bus," Mr. Houghton told her. "Have you no pity? My gas is almost gone. And, besides, I hate to drive downtown."

"Mr. Houghton, you can't let her go downtown alone on a bus after all your wife's been through," I told him, horrified he would even entertain such a thought.

He looked at me surprised as it if were none of my business, which it wasn't.

"All right," he relented, "but first we must water those guineas."

We crossed the street and walked over to the museum where Mr. Houghton found a water fountain. Here we filled a paper cup, and we offered it to the hens still imprisoned in their sacks.

"How many miles have we come?" he asked as we watched the thirsty guineas drink before we tied the sacks up once again. "By the

Mr. Houghton and the Guineas

time we reach home tonight it will be almost forty. My gas ration for this week is gone."

"But what else could we do? We couldn't leave the poor old soul sitting in the road," Mrs. Houghton pointed out.

"No, I suppose not. But I am not very fond of Alvira. To use all that gasoline for her just makes me angry, that's all," Mr. Houghton complained as he settled Peggy and the guineas, and we all climbed into the car once more.

At Miller and Rhoads Mrs. Houghton bought the few necessities while Mr. Houghton phoned Sam's Place in Goochland, (a long distance call) to make arrangements about Mrs. Carthage's old Plymouth which still was parked in front of the store.

Then we returned to the hospital, where Mrs. Houghton once again climbed the long stairs carrying her parcels. Again we waited for her, but this time she was not long. Then we finally started home. I noticed it was alomost five o'clock by Mr. Houghton's watch when we turned into our road. Instead of taking Mrs. Houghton home first, as he usually did, we turned into the barn lane. Here Mr. Houghton stopped the car and untying the now nearly exhausted guineas he opened their sacks. Bewildered, the two birds blinked at the unaccustomed light and began to scratch at the chicken mash I offered them.

"What shall we name them?" Mr. Houghton asked me as he unloaded the feed sacks from the trunk of his car.

"Oh, do hurry, I am exhausted," Mrs. Houghton complained from the back seat.

"I shall name them," Mr. Houghton ignored her plea as he folded up the gunny sacks, "I shall name them Alvira and Mrs. Carthage."

That settled it. The two guineas were thus christened. Now they would live happily protecting Mr. Houghton's chickens from raccoons and foxes. But none of us dared tell Alvira Carthage their names.

A Forgotten Landscape

54

War News

October 1942

On October 23ʳᵈ at 9:45 in the morning the opening artillery and air bombardment on the German positions began in French West Africa. This heralded the final Battle of El Alamein. Rommel, home on sick leave was, as Father would say, 'caught with his pants down.' The German general soon came scampering back to head his Africa Corps. He pushed General Montgomery's offensive, who made stands both a Fuka and Mersa in Lybia, and Rommel did not stop until he was only a hundred miles from Alexandra in Egypt. Then suddenly the British Army was halted in torrents of rain and mud. Supplies were low, especially gas for the tanks.

On November 8ᵗʰ, with Generals Patton and Mark Clark in command of both the British and American forces, they landed and engaged the Germans in battle on the beaches of Tunisia. They met with minor French resistance, those French who had sided with the Germans. General Eisenhower was the Supreme Commander of this combined operation.

"For once the German General, Erwin Rommel, is retreating," so said Mr. Houghton's short wave radio. "We have every hope he shall be smashed at last."

"Father's with General Fredendal's staff, I think, in General Clark's Second Corps." I could never keep all the Generals straight. "Anyway, he's fighting in Africa, Frances told me."

As we watched the Allies advance from the beaches of Tunisia towards places with strange sounding names, I prayed Father was safe. The Germans held the airfields at Bizerta and Tunis from which the Allies took an awful pounding.

"Tunisia is no better than Lybia and Egypt for strange sounding names. Kaserine Pass, Bizerta, El Guettar. Even Mrs. Owens doesn't know how to pronounce them. She was in the library the other day trying to figure it out. She finally got in touch with Miss Oldfield, in the lower school who knows a lot about Egypt and could help her," I told Mrs. Houghton.

I opened my books on the table and tried to study. Finally I went back to Mr. Houghton's map of North Africa to see where my dad might be. "It's scary to think of him over there miles away in an Arab speaking country with funny sounding place names," I said.

"That Rommel is just too strong," Mr. Houghton commented as we listened to the radio. "We stopped him at Alm Halfa and at El Alamein, but Rommel at bay is still dangerous. Montgomery's afraid of him, or he would have hit the Germans again."

"Rommel can always get there with the mostest, quickly, retreat and strike again some place else," Mrs. Houghton commented. "It will take a lot of Allied power to defeat him. This General DeGaulle is making a lot of demands. He's opposed to the pro-German group under Petain in Vichy, and Admiral Darlan, who supported the French surrender in 1940. He is now the commander-in-chief of the Vichy French armed forces. He's agreed to a cease-fire on the beaches of Tunisia effective November 10th in exchange for Allied agreement that he become the high commissioner of French North Africa. Some French are fighting with us and some against us, why don't they make up their minds?"

"I received a photograph of Father in the mail yesterday. How gaunt and thin he looks," I said closing my books. "I'll set the table now for supper."

Knowing Father would never give in to illness, I felt worried and concerned for his safety."He says he's okay," but his picture told another story. "You think with all those points we have to buy meat, surely some of it must be sent to our boys overseas. At least that's what they tell us. Look at Father's photograph. He hasn't seen a square meal in weeks. I agree with him, all those politicians in Washington are nothing but squirrels going round and round in their cages."

"Don't pay any attention to what the papers say. It's mostly lies and glossed over truths. All meant to spoon feed the public," Mrs. Houghton remarked.

"You mean all those maps and troop movements we read of in the papers are lies?" I couldn't believe the editors could be so deceptive.

"No, not all. But we hardly get the whole story. Just part of it." Mrs. Houghton told me. "No, Doc, it's not all lies, but it isn't all truth either. Don't pay a lot attention to sugar and meat shortages, they are not as bad yet as the politicians tell us. Look at England; she's been fighting over two years now, and they really have shortages."

I felt better. But I hated President Roosevelt for not supplying Father with proper food. After all, I gave up meat and sugar so he could have them. Father's thin, haggard face haunted me. I'd dreamt the night before he was a ghost, and awoke screaming. I hoped I'd dream of earlier, happier days when it was always Summer or Christmas and the table groaned under food. I hated that photograph and finally threw it in the stove.

Rommel escaped! In a brilliant move he retreated along the coast towards French West Africa. The Tunisian campaign became a stalemate. I couldn't believe how stupid all those English and American generals were. Surely at West Point they'd learn the art of war.

Somewhere in England
November 4, 1942

Dear Doc,

Just a note to let you know we are moving again. I can't tell you where I am going, but just write to the address on the envelope and I'll get it.

Rest assured I love you. When you go to church on Sunday, say a little prayer for me. I assume you are churching once again. Love, Dad

November 18, 1942
Richmond, Va.

Dear Dad,

Mr. Houghton figured out where you are-North Africa with the landings of our troops there. Mr. Houghton's flags are now very crowded since we have British, French, Australian and German ones as well. So we are keeping tabs on you. I hope all goes well and you can end the war in Africa. Rommel is still running over everything. Your mittens were sent in October, I hope you got them safely and they didn't end up at the bottom of the Atlantic Ocean for a fish to wear. I don't think fish need mittens as much as you do. They were very difficult to knit – all those fingers and a thumb. It took forever. Do wear them and think of me.

Love, Doc

November 1942
Richmond, Va.

Dear Dad,

I can't make out who's fighting whom. The French seem to be fighting on both sides. What is going on? How can the French fight on both sides?

Mrs. Sparrow's nephew was wounded in Algiers. We haven't heard anything more. He was with General Patton's Task Force. We keep up with the news through Mr. Houghton's radio, but sometimes it's complicated to understand what's going on.

Must fly. Mrs. Owens is giving us a test on Monday, and I must get ready for it. I certainly find all those Greek names difficult. Why must we know what happened thousands of years ago? I'll never understand the education system. Love, Doc

North Africa
December 1942

Dear Doc,

Some of the French are pro-German, and some are not. but their resistance wasn't very important here. I am learning to say a few words in Arabic. It's a man's world here; women are thought less of than one's donkey. Donkeys are often considered more useful. Now for an Arabic lesson: Good morning is "sabhil kher"; what do you call this is "mae ism haezae." I've written these in English and not in Arabic squiggles. Of course in French West Africa I can use my French. That is far easier. We had snow, but the Hun also had snow. He's just as cold as we are. The women here are very different. Some wear the veil; some are quite westernized. The girls start wearing the headscarf at nine or ten. The Egyptians are less strict than they are here. It's a completely suppressed world. Life is very tough even without Rommel.

Love, Dad

November 22, 1942
Richmond, Va.

Dear Dad,

We had the election and Harry Byrd came back in once again. The Congress lost a lot of Democratic members, so now Roosevelt will have a hard time with so many Republicans – at least that's what people say. Stalin is angry with Roosevelt because of this invasion in Africa, Mrs. Owens told us. He wanted a second front in Europe. She claims Eisenhower never had been in battle before. According to her he's a bad choice and someone with more combat experience would have been better. Rommel's men are veterans of many campaigns, so it's going to be a hard war in Africa. I've returned to church as usual, and I've said all kinds of prayers for you. So don't worry about that.

Love, Doc

A Forgotten Landscape

November 1942
Richmond, Va.

Dear Dad,

We read about the invasion, and how the GI's landed in Algeria and Oran. I guess you were in the thick of it. The election even took second place in the newspaper. I am making you a scarf. After the mittens it's a lot easier. Grandmother called to find out if we had heard anything from you, and if we knew where you were. She's been well and sends her love. She's invited me out for Christmas if I can get a place on the train. It's very difficult for an ordinary person to travel now. It has to be an emergency or something like a death. There are troops using the train, and it's not considered safe.

We sang a new hymn in church on Sunday. Dr. Price insisted we learn some others. Things got pretty lively because Lizzie couldn't play it very well. She kept hitting wrong notes and throwing us off. Everyone ended up giggling, but the hymn is pretty and not too difficult with high notes. Do you know it?

> Sing praise to God who reigns above
> The God of all creation.
> The God of power and of love,
> The God of our salvation.

Dr. Price says there's a whole hymnal full, and we must learn some more. After Sunday's performance, I am not so sure he wants to proceed with our musical education.

I am enclosing a picture Mary Ann took of me. I've grown and am less skinny; maybe there's hope for me yet. I am tired of being an ugly duckling. Grandmother tells me, "pretty is as pretty does," and I wish she'd stop saying it. I know there is little hope of my ever looking like Ann Sheridan, but I could at least look less arms, legs and feet. Love, Doc

North Africa
December 1942

Dear Doc,

The only word you need here is "bacheesh." Something for nothing. Even the kids demand something from us poor GI's every time we meet them. I tossed a candy bar into the street and watched them scramble for it.

Any piece of equipment we leave unguarded is picked clean in minutes. Living in the desert has its problems with sand. Wind is always a threat as it blows sand over the troops and our equipment. We're constantly cleaning. Happy holidays.

Love, Dad

Christmas 1942
Indianapolis, Ind.

Dear Dad,

I came to Indianapolis after all. Someone Mother knew was going out here and brought me along with him. The train was full of troops, and it was very crowded. We had to wait forever to get into the dining room, and then they had run out of some things. Grandmother and her driver, Walter, met me at the station.

We have lots of snow, so my cousins and I are sledding and playing outside. I found it a novelty since we don't get snow very often in Richmond. We had a lovely party to go out to on Thursday afternoon. Grandmother and I got all dressed up and together we drove out to a marvelous old house not far from here. The people had children, so it was fun – not stuffy like Richmond. I enjoyed myself. We also went Christmas shopping on Wednesday. The stores here are big and very beautiful in spite of the war. Poor Walter had a lot of packages to carry. Grandmother never learned to drive a car, so we sit in the back seat and Walter sits in front. My favorite friend, Freddy, came by to see me. He's been my friend ever since I was little. You remember him, don't you? We played all kinds of games, and he taught me a new card game, Hearts. I go back home next week. Mother's friend will accompany me, so I'll be safe. I've enjoyed being here and seeing a new way of life. I haven't been out to see Grandmother for a long time. Something about my custody has caused great problems. Now I can travel out of Virginia, so I'll come again to see her in the summer. It's all arranged. I am looking forward to returning and visiting her again.

Love, Doc

PS. Grandmother still hopes I will come and live with her. Mother's opposed to it, but I'm giving it some thought. It would be a big change.

Doc

A Forgotten Landscape

55

Cary Again

Christmas 1942

In June when Cary graduated from St. Lawrence's School, the first thing he did was to volunteer for the Army Air Corps. A few days before his nineteenth birthday, he left Goochland for the duration of the war. First, he went to Greensboro, North Carolina, and then to Brownsville, Texas. He dreamed of becoming a fighter pilot and of flying the P 40 Kittyhawk. At Christmas he came home for a few days.

"No fighter pilot has got good sense," commented Mr. Harris at the store one evening shortly after Cary left. "They are all crazy, and take risks they shouldn't. I am sure Miss Emma is not pleased."

"What can she do?" Asked Alvira Carthage, pushing back her red hair under her felt hat. "Cary's old enough to make his own decisions."

Mr. Henley fired the pot-bellied stove with more coal and wood. He seemed preoccupied and silent.

"He's always wanted to fly," I added to the conversation. "He's talked of nothing else for months. He's determined to go. I shall surely miss him."

Mrs. Henley had taken down Mr. Roosevelt's picture while she put up stock. Ethel helped her replenish the shelves.

"I can't get all the things people ask for these days," she told me. "Some days I can get all the soups I want; the next time I go in, I can't find beef broth. It's difficult to run a store when you've got to restock it."

I remembered a conversation I had with Cary only a few weeks ago.

"I just want to see some action, like your dad," he insisted.

"He's too smart to stick his neck out in any old Kittyhawk," I told him. "How many pilots ever reach twenty missions?"

"Not many, I'm told, but that's where the action is up in the sky. I want to be part of it," he replied in a cocky manner.

"Besides there are other jobs in the Army Air Corps, like being a gunner or even ground crew."

"Ground crew!" Cary echoed indignantly. "That's the last thing I want. I wish to become a fly boy and really do my part in the war."

Mr. Houghton touched my elbow. I awoke from my thoughts and looked up.

"Come on, Doc," he said, "we've got to go home. The Missus will have our tea ready, and we'll be late."

Ethel came up to me and held out her hand. "These are the last of the movie star ice cream tops. They've stopped making them because of the war."

Gratefully I took them from her and smiled. She looked tired and worn. Her face was pale, and she walked as if she were in pain.

"Are you all right?" I asked her, concerned.

"I fell down the stairs to our apartment. I am badly bruised, but I didn't break anything. These tops I've kept for you. Do you still collect them?"

"Yes," I replied, "when I can find them. Thank you very much." I kissed her lightly on the cheek.

"Don't worry about Cary; he's too smart to get killed. He'll be back, just you wait. He's got too much to live for, that boy, to allow any German to kill him."

"I hate to see him go, Ethel, that's all. He's my play fellow, you know, and there are very few children my age who live near by."

"Come on, Doc," called Mr. Houghton, "the Missus will skin us."

"I've got to go, Ethel. Thanks for what you said. Pray for Cary and my dad, too. Goodbye."

I wondered if Ethel suspected I liked Cary in a special way, not in a romantic way. Mrs. Houghton would have disapproved. I liked him in a special way of friendship (I wasn't sure what a romantic way meant), not as a boyfriend, but as a friend who was a boy. His leaving had jolted me out of my feeling that the war was miles away. It was in my own back yard. It was a part of our lives. I realized that I was not just an onlooker, but I had my part to play as well. I must work at the Red Cross and knit sweaters with the rest of the women. It was my war work to deliver eggs and to go with Mr. Houghton to spot airplanes on occasion. I must pull my end. Still I was frightened about the future. Everything was uncertain now.

"You can't walk through life as if you are privileged; you have to pull your load as well. Only with everyone pulling his load will we win this war." Mrs. Houghton had told me.

Riding home from the store with Mr. Houghton that evening, I knew at fourteen I was obliged to carry my load. I hoped God would listen to me, or more likely Mary, for whom our church was named. She would listen because she was a mother and understood children. "Please keep Cary safe in his Kittyhawk, and Father too," I prayed as we turned into our road for home.

A Forgotten Landscape

56

As The Year Ends

Two days after Christmas Mother finished making my new outfit and took me into Richmond to the Rhineholds' party. I wore a blue velveteen dress with a white lace collar and silver buttons, set off by black patent leather shoes. My thick blond hair was brushed away from my face and pinned back in a clip. On my mouth I wore a faint touch of pink lipstick. Never in my whole life had I felt more miserable. Gone was any freedom of movement as I walked stiffly from fear of spoiling my dress.

"You must realize, dear, that party manners at your age are important," Mother replied turning a deaf ear to my protests.

At the Rhineholds' town house I found other young people just as uncomfortable as myself. Boys and girls of fourteen and fifteen dressed in party clothes juggled punch and sandwiches trying hard not to spill them.

"Hello, Doc, I see they scraped the stables off you for once," greeted Betty Anne James as I entered the Rhineholds' library where the young people had assembled.

"Yes," I replied, "I am practicing to become a lady. Mother tells me it's important."

"Never mind Betty, Doc. She thinks she's already a lady at fourteen. I am sure you have a great deal more fun with your horses and country friends."

Freddy Smith-Valentine, I felt sure, would some day become a diplomat because he always said just the right thing. He also taught me how to dance, something at which I was never very good.

"Yes," I replied to him now, "I do. What have you been up to?"

"Nothing much really, except school, that is. I am going away next fall, and I am busy looking at boarding schools around Virginia."

Freddy looked especially well dressed. His blond hair was combed to perfection, and his fingernails were clean. It was an unusual accomplishment, I thought, for a boy.

"Oh," I said. "Why are you going away? What's wrong with Richmond?"

"Everyone goes away, Doc, to become a man. You can't do that with your parents always hanging around." His face full of mischief, Freddy laughed.

As the library became more crowded, and the young people laughed and chattered together, the boys moved to one side of the room and the girls to the other. So after a few minutes Freddy went to join his peers and left me with the girls.

"Got any boy friends, Doc, in the country?" Betty Anne teased me.

"Sure, about six. How many do you have?" I felt uncomfortable enough stuffed into my party dress and new shoes which hurt my feet without her showing me up.

"I heard his name is Harry." Betty Anne's conversation now caught the attention of the other girls. They stopped talking and regarded me.

"Harry?" I questioned. "You must mean Harry Houghton, my neighbor. He's hardly a boy friend; he's married."

Laughter ran through the library as the girls picked up Betty Anne's cue. I felt humiliated. My private life was none of their business. Besides, I knew Betty Anne hung out at the drug store far too much after school in order to meet the boys.

"What else do you do in the country besides knowing married men?" Jean Ross asked me wickedly.

"Same as you do in the city, I suppose, except we have no drug stores in which to meet boys."

"Poor you. Then I suppose you must be terribly lonely. What do you do all day?" Sarah Taylor, never really unkind, became my friend.

"Ride horseback, help with the farm work, and meet people at Henley's store," I replied. "Of course I help spot airplanes and work at the Red Cross rolling bandages."

The girls looked amazed. I suddenly realized they never did any of these things. Nor did they correspond with someone in England as I did with Tom Phillpot. All they seemed interested in were boys, clothes and movie stars. Betty Anne wore alluring angora sweaters that cost at least twenty dollars each. But I found her empty-headed and artificial. Yet I envied her beautiful long fingernails and her poised appearance. Because of my own nervousness, I probably did not appreciate how insecure she must feel in spite of her pretty face. Somehow my country life set me apart from these girls, even with the new velvet dress I felt defenseless in front of them.

"Why do you spot airplanes?" Jean inquired.

"It's for the war effort," I replied, "in case enemy planes attack us. We report every airplane we see and tell its type and its direction. A spotter's box has a stove and a telephone in it to call Richmond."

"I've never heard of doing that before. Where do you roll bandages for the Red Cross?" Sarah asked me.

"At Manakin. You mean you don't do any of these things here in town to help the war effort?" I was amazed by their lack of community spirit.

"Oh, yes, I got out and collect pots and pans for the metal drive, but I don't go anywhere on a regular basis. I do bundle up the old newspapers, and we take them down to our church. But I never spotted airplanes. What else do you do?" Jean dropped her pose and became genuinely interested.

"Just help where ever possible. Last spring I plowed the garden for Mr. Houghton with his big horse, Lindy Lou. I also pack bundles for Britain and knit socks for the soldiers." I warmed up to my subject.

As we chatted, I finally relaxed and enjoyed myself. I forgot the velvet dress and the stiff new shoes and had fun. But later that evening I realized for the first time that my life style made me different from my friends. This worried me, I discovered, because I wanted to be like other young people. I failed to consider our interests might also be different. Yet I realized living in town would bore me.

"I enjoyed myself," I confided to Mother as we drove home. "It was fun."

"You and your friends certainly had a lot to say to each other."

"Yes, after we got over being scared to death of being all dressed up; I was quite pleased with myself for being able to carry on a conversation with the other girls." I replied.

"All you could talk about, it seems to me, was Mr. Houghton and plowing his garden. I don't consider that very ladylike conversation for a party." Mother looked at me with disapproval. "Why aren't you more like the other girls your age?"

Tears pricked my eyes. I felt I had done quite well at the party, and to have mother think I was not learning social graces crushed me. We drove the rest of the way home in silence.

"Mrs. Houghton," I asked her the next afternoon over a cup of tea, "am I different? I mean yesterday at the party I found out I am not like my friends in town. They seemed very grown up with their lipstick and their stockings. Please say I am not different."

"Little Doc, how can I tell you? Yes, my darling child, you are different in the nicest kind of way. Your being with adults so much has made you more perceptive, perhaps let's say more sensitive to the needs of others. Young girls enjoy young girls' talk, but you have not experienced much of that living out here, and your interests are different. Living in the country makes them so. Don't worry about nail polish and lipstick yet awhile, Doc. It's only surface beauty after all. It's what you are underneath that really counts. One day you will no longer be coltish and awkward as you are now. One day, my dear, you shall grow up and become a lady."

"Do you think so?" I asked, hugging her. I noticed her skin felt soft next to mine. "Oh, Mrs. Houghton, I am so afraid life will pass me by, buried out here in the country."

"Little, Doc, live life to the fullest and don't ever be afraid it will pass you by. Keep your dreams; they allow us to live with our disappointments."

Nestled in her protective arms I let my tears flow onto her new Christmas sweater.

"Yes," I echoed, "That's my secret to happiness."

Yet I craved adventure and my life seemed so ordinary. I wanted to visit Egypt and ride a camel like Mrs. Owens had done before the war. I wanted to fly a B-24 across the Atlantic and visit England before it got all smashed by German bombs. I wanted to see India like *Kim* in Rudyard Kipling's book. I wanted to do so many things I thought there would hardly be time.

Mrs. Houghton laughed, "Don't do it all at once, Doc. Spread it out over a few years. You've got enough adventure planned to last a life time."

Part IV
1943

"We Shall Fight Them on the Beaches"
Churchill

A Forgotten Landscape

Letters

January 6, 1943
Richmond, VA

Dear Dad,

Frances came through on her way to Florida. She looked like a million dollars, and she was terribly kind. She brought me some letters of yours. Your handwriting is just awful. Mrs. Gilbert would give you an F. She's always on us about writing so she can read it. And when your letters are made smaller by V-Mail sometimes I have to get a reading glass like a blind professor. Why are professors considered blind? I guess they read too much.

The new year has come, and I don't see much change with the war. I know you're doing great things in Africa, still I find it all depressing. But then war generally is, I suppose.

I went to a Christmas party. You wouldn't have recognized me all dressed up in a dress and fancy shoes. And stockings! I saw Freddie Smith-Valentine, and he's going away to school to learn to become a man. You wouldn't believe how clean he looked, even his finger nails weren't dirty. That's unusual, don't you think?

The girls like to tease me, but I tease them back. I told them about spotting airplanes and ploughing fields with Lindy Lou. They were amazed. Betty Anne was there, and she's a real pain. She calmed down after awhile, you know how prissy she is. Her clothes cost millions and here in war time, too. You can't believe her sweaters, angora and all fuzzy. She also likes the boys and meets them in the drug store – secretly. I am sure her mother disapproves.

The Hunt Club's activities are curtailed for the duration, so there is little hunting. We now have a woman MFH, and she is very good. The men are either too old or away at war. We hunt a little. I rode Killybegs and Miss Emma rode Mistress the last time we went. Cary is away learning to become a fighter pilot. I miss him ever so much. He writes us on occasion. Boot camp sounds terrible, but he's very proud to be in the Air Corps. So I have Lady who is easier to handle now, and Killybegs to ride which is wonderful. Jackie and Billy do pony cart work to church and to the store.

Mrs. Houghton has done over my room. It looks brighter now with blue bed spreads and blue and white curtains and a blue rug. It looks very pretty, and I feel more grown up. Mr. Houghton claims I am growing up too fast. He's going to put a brick on my head, if that would do any good.

I had a letter from Gil and Jenny for Christmas. Jenny is coming down for five days in March to stay with us. Mr. Houghton has arranged it with Miss Edith. I can't wait to see Jenny. She's terribly smart in school and hopes to go to Oxford or Cambridge in England, or perhaps, Harvard or Yale here. I'll be lucky to get into Slippery Rock State Teachers' College. There really is such a place in Pennsylvania. I know nothing about it, but the name sounds crazy don't you agree?

I pray to God you keep safe over there. I still believe in Him, but sometimes I find it terribly hard. He doesn't act like a God should. He often ignores my requests, but maybe He has so many He can't find time for them all. Mr. Houghton's not sure about God, but I tell him someone has to keep the earth moving and the stars in place. Mr. Houghton says it's gravity that does it. Someone had to invent the gravity, so it must be God. I love you, Doc.

57

Mr. Houghton's War Effort

January 1943

As 1942 blended into 1943 the winter brought shortages, not only gasoline, but also clothing and shoes. We had to buy meat with red points and sugar with blue ones, so people began to hoard. For us, in the country, sugar and shoes proved our worst problems, especially men's work boots. Sugar we used for canning, but for the most part we just cut it down and made do. Then even men's white shirts and tea towels became scarce in the stores, so many of my neighbours bought material and made their own. Mother turned the worn collars on my stepfather's dress shirts, and Mrs. Taliaferro even turned her frayed cuffs.

The war news began to improve. The *Richmond Times Dispatch* told us that the Allies made an air raid on Berlin, and that General Rommel was on the run in North Africa. Stalingrad, however, lay in ruins, although it still remained in Russian hands. Then, on the third of January, when Gary Craddock left for overseas, we all felt how close the war had come.

That winter, I remember, Mr. Houghton discovered horse and chicken feed, once sold in hundred pound weights in gunny sacks, now could be bought in bags of unbleached muslin. At first the muslin was just plain white, but gradually prints began to appear. So if we wanted enough material for a bathrobe or for a table cloth, we bought several bags of feed all of the same print. These feed bags also made grand tea towels, and Mrs. Houghton saved the plain muslin ones for that purpose.

One Thursday in January, Bertha stood in our kitchen cooking starch for my stepfather's white shirts. I thought it smelled good as I watched the gooey granules become smooth over the heat under her constant stirring. For years Bertha smelled of starch, even long after her retirement from doing our laundry. This morning when Mr. Houghton arrived with her dozen eggs, he also carried an armful of brightly printed feed bags.

"Good morning, Bertha," he greeted her pleasantly.

"Good morning, sir."

I've just dropped by to tell you I'll drive you home at four o'clock."

Bertha eyed the feed bags. They had pink and blue flowers on them.

"Do you need all of those sacks?" She asked.

"I am taking them home to make tea towels," he explained, handing her the box of eggs.

"They would make lovely dresses for my grands," Bertha replied.

Mr. Houghton held up the bags and regarded them in a different light. Although dirty and unattractive, each certainly would make a little girl's dress. For a moment Mr. Houghton seemed to think this over, and then retreated from Bertha's inquiring eyes.

That Thursday When Bertha arrived she seemed more quiet than usual. She washed and starched as always, but something was definitely troubling her. Mr. Houghton noticed it, too. Yet we found it hard to pry into our hard working laundress's private affairs. But that afternoon when I caught her crying over the table cloth she stood ironing, I knew something very unusual must have occurred.

"What's the matter, Bertha?" I inquired as I banged shut the laundry room door.

"Oh, Miss Doc, I've such trouble," tears cascaded down her dark cheeks. "I've been robbed."

"Robbed?" I echoed, wondering what of Bertha's few possessions was worth robbing.

"My money, my money! It was taken off of me walking home from the store last night." The tears dropped onto Mother's table cloth. "Some boys just grabbed my handbag and ran."

"What boys, Bertha?"

"There's a gang in Manakin. A gang of boys seventeen, eighteen, that's stealing from the old people. And John Payne, Thelma's husband,

Mr. Houghton's War Effort

is missing."

"How missing? What do you mean?" I knew John only slightly.

"Just gone. That's all I know, he's just gone." Bertha wiped her eyes, then replaced her handkerchief into her apron pocket.

"What do the police say about it?" I inquired laying my hand upon her arm.

"They don't care, Miss Doc, when it's coloured folks. They don't do nothing," Bertha replied folding up the table cloth.

"Maybe we can do something. I shall tell Mrs. Houghton." When I left the laundry room to tell her about Bertha's tragedy, I bumped squarely into Mr. Houghton.

"Watch out now," he caught me; then listened while I poured out Bertha's troubles to him.

Finally I explained about Thelma's husband. Mr. Houghton knew Thelma because he occasionally would drop by her eating establishment for a cold beer. Sometimes I went with him, but I never mentioned Thelma's Place to mother because I felt sure she would stop me from going there. Even though I never drank any beer, I found my expeditions there great fun.

That afternoon Mr. Houghton organized a meeting for the next evening at the Baptist church in Manakin. Really, he and Jean Taliaferro organized it. Everyone went up to Manakin, even the county police. A special officer also came out from Richmond, and everybody agreed the robberies must be stopped. But still nothing was done about Thelma's husband.

"Maybe he's run away with another woman," Mr. Harris suggested at the general store, later that week. "He always had an eye for the girls."

"That's so," Mr. Houghton agreed, "but John Payne was a good farmer, and a steady worker. I stop in Thelma's Place from time to time and have spoken to him there. He's not the sort of man to run out on his farm and home."

"It's a mystery that nobody has seen him for two whole weeks. Are you sure that he's not gone to Richmond or up to Goochland where he has a brother? Maybe he's dead," Mr. Henley suggested.

"That's hardly likely," Mr. Harris replied. "Someone would have found his body."

Meanwhile Mrs. Houghton bleached six flowered feed sacks and hung them out on the clothes line. They looked very different from those Mr. Houghton had taken home only a few days before.

The week after Bertha was robbed, Thelma's well, situated in her front yard, began to smell. Since it was the only water supply for several families, the county sent two men who arrived one afternoon to test it. After taking several samples, they found the well polluted. The following morning the county inspectors arrived and dug down into the spring hoping to find the trouble. They did, but it was hardly what we expected.

Tied up with some old ropes, at the bottom of the well they found John's decomposed body. Word of his death spread like wild fire. In a few hours all of Goochland had arrived in Manakin to see what was happening. Although the body was taken to Richmond, people looked down the well, tramped through Thelma's eating house and drank up her beer. Finally the sheriff arrived and chased everyone out. That evening Thelma lay upstairs on her bed in a state of collapse. Two days later the *Richmond Times Dispatch* told us that John had been murdered.

"Thelma's in a bad way. Her sister from Richmond came out last night," Bertha told us when she arrived the next morning.

The coloured church was packed the day of the funeral. The widow, dressed in deep black and wearing a heavy veil sat in the front pew, moaning. Those of us, who were white, stood respectfully in the back, where I stood with Mr. Houghton. The whole community had come to pay its last respects, and we all felt genuine sorrow. The casket, I remember, remained closed, an unusual feature at a Negro funeral. Usually the body lay in state in an open casket and was viewed by the mourners, as they filed by it to pay their last respects. After the long testimonials to John's character given by three of Thelma's neighbours, and the reading of the telegrams from friends not able to attend the service, Mr. Houghton took me home. I think Thelma appreciated our coming that day because she would give me free cokes afterwards whenever Mr. Houghton and I dropped by her place.

That evening after the funeral Bertha bought two locks at Henley's store. She persuaded her neighbour, Edward Green, to put these both on her front and back doors. But still she could not sleep. Finally, Mr.

Houghton went and got Bertha and drove her into town to stay with her daughter. For days all of Manakin trembled with fear.

Then in late January a second murder occurred. This time the gang attacked an old, old lady, once a slave, who lived in the woods about five miles from Manakin. Tall and thin, two or three times a week Old Mary walked to Clark's store. Sometimes we would see her trudging along the road towards Manakin carrying a sack upon her head. Although we regularly offered her a lift, Old Mary always refused. She was afraid of motor cars. On occasion I would see her get a lift in a farm wagon, but usually she walked, leaning on a cane, dressed in an old maroon hat and a long tattered coat.

When no one had seen Mary at the store for several days, a neighbour, Mr. Thomas, walked the mile and a half back into the woods to her run-down cabin. Afraid she might be ill, Martin Thomas knocked and shouted, but he got no reply and finally kicked the door open. He found Old Mary lying on her kitchen floor, half clothed. Her scant possessions lay scattered around the tiny house. Nearby lay a club with which Mr. Thomas believed Old Mary had been beaten to death. For what reason? Everyone wondered.

"Whoever killed her, thought she had money hidden somewhere," Mr. Thomas told us that evening at Henley's store.

"Yeah, I heard she buried it near her privy," added Harrison Moore. "These murders must stop. We need some more police out here to protect us. I called the authorities in Richmond and gave them hell."

"It's going to take more than that, I am afraid," remarked Mr. Henley. "There is a war on, and nobody cares if a few Negroes get murdered."

"It's very mysterious," commented the sheriff, "but we are doing all we can."

We disagreed, and appealed to our neighbour, Judge Taylor. Although the wheels of government ground slowly, finally four extra policemen were sent out from town.

"It's about time," Mr. Houghton complained, "Or we shall all be murdered in our beds."

Everyone now remained inside after dark. Henley's store sold out of locks, and several of my neighbours went into Richmond to the ASPCA to buy dogs. The bigger the dog the better, we all agreed. Still the neighbourhood trembled in fear, and Bertha remained in town.

In early February the murderers tried again. One night they tramped through the woods across River Road and beat down the door of Grievous Snead's cabin. He stood in his living room, waiting for the intruders with his gun cocked. As three black youths forced their way into his cabin. Grievous calmly took aim and fired. Screaming in pain one man fell to the floor. The others fled, with Grievous after them. They did not get far, because Grievous's sons, hearing the commotion, released their dogs, grabbed their guns and followed. The murderers were surrounded in the woods by three men with rifles and several dogs. Not far from Henley's store the gang finally surrendered. Mr. Henley told us all about it later.

Mr. Henley said he was awakened by the sound of barking dogs and came out to see what was going on. He stood in his pajamas in the back yard and listened.

"What's going on here?" he demanded aiming his rifle into the darkness.

"Call the police, Mr. Henley," Isaac shouted back, "We've caught some prowlers."

"Bring them into the store. I'll turn on the lights. You can lock those fellows up in my feed room."

"There's another man still at my house," Grievous appeared out of the darkness with his two sons holding tight to their prisoners. "Call in the dogs, Isaac, before they chew these fellows up."

After securing their captives in the feed room Isaac and his brother returned to get the third one. Wounded in the leg, this man's screams could be heard across River Road. Several neighbours, awakened by the noise, and seeing the lights on in Henley's store, appeared accompanied by dogs and carrying guns. By the time the police arrived about an hour later ten of our neighbours had gathered around the feed room door. At last the ambulance came and the wounded man was taken to the hospital in Richmond. Dawn was breaking, when the excitement finally died down and everyone returned to his bed.

The next morning when Mr. Houghton and I arrived at the store about eight o'clock, we found Grievous a hero. His two sons told their story to everyone who would listen, while Mr. Henley filled in the details.

Mr. Houghton's War Effort

Police swarmed around us; they tramped through the woods and asked us a lot of questions.

"Those fellows we captured were AWOL from the Army so they were taken off to Camp Lee. I hear Army jails are worse than regular ones," Mr. Henley told us.

"Let's hope things will calm down now. We have had enough excitement around here." Mr. Houghton and I peeked into the feed room looking for printed bags before he drove me into town to school.

About two weeks later the court sat in Goochland, and the county en masse descended upon our little court house. Mr. Houghton took Bertha and me along with him. She was to identify the man who had grabbed her handbag. Mother never knew, but I took the day off from school.

"I don't understand why Grievous must appear in court when he did not kill that man," Bertha kept repeating as we drove up through the country.

"He's got to give evidence. Don't worry, Bertha; it's just a hearing. He will get off on self defense." Mr. Houghton tried to explain.

"It seems strange to me a man who is a hero must go into court." Bertha shook her head, still puzzled by Virginia's laws. "It ain't right, Miss Doc, no one else could solve those murders, not even all those white men they sent out here from Richmond."

When we arrived at the court house, all of the county had assembled. Mr. Houghton pushed us through the crowd at the court room's door and led the way up into the balcony. Here we found a seat and Bertha, still confused by the mysteries of the law, removed her best hat.

At the table below us sat the three defendants, one with a cast on his leg. Looking around I found Grievous on the front bench seated with his sons and his wife. I noticed they had on their Sunday best, and Isaac wore a new tie.

"Hear ye, hear ye," shouted the clerk of court, and we all rose to our feet in respect for the judge's entrance.

When the three defendants stood up, I realized they were just kids. They looked scared, biting their nails and unclenching their hands.

After some "mumbo jumbo" legal talk, I watched Grievous take the stand. Bertha and I leaned forward to listen as the proceedings began.

Mr. Houghton got up from his seat and stood against the wall so he could hear better; Bertha cupped her ear.

"You swear to tell the truth, the whole truth and nothing but the truth?" The clerk of court asked Grievous, when he came forward to give the oath.

"I do," Grievous spoke quietly, with great dignity. I listened to him, his big, honest face was encircled by his closely cropped white hair, and I respected him.

"Tell the court about the men who entered your house last February sixth," Lawyer John Smith came forward from his seat and approached the witness box.

"Yes, sir, yes, sir, I understand," the colored man looked down at the cap in his hands. "These three boys here," Grievous pointed at the three youths seated at the table before him, "came through my woods about nine o'clock that night and broke down my door. Since we was all scared to death after Old Mary's murder, I took down my gun and loaded it. When these here men burst into my front room, I fired. I hit that one here in the leg."

I heard the courtroom's pot-bellied stove hiss, and the clerk's typewriter click as we all remained unnaturally still – listening. The balcony, crowded with farmers and colored people, was deathly quiet as they strained to hear.

"Please go on," instructed Mr. Smith.

"Yes, sir," the witness shifted his feet, still regarding his cap. "Well, after I shot, this here boy fell at my feet, and those two men ran out into the dark. I followed. Then I heard my sons and their dogs in the woods behind my house. We tramped around after those dogs until we almost reached Henley's store where we caught those two fellows." He pointed to the two older men. "That's about all, your honor."

"Did you think these prisoners were out to kill you?" The lawyer leaned forward.

"I thought so, sir. Because after John Payne was found in his well, and Old Mary was murdered in her cabin, we all lived in fear," Grievous explained.

"You may step down, please," the Judge instructed. " Call Arthur Henley."

I watched as Mr. Henley took the stand. He appeared nervous, because his voice quavered when he read the oath.

"What did you hear and see the night of February sixth this year?" Judge Marshall asked.

"I found Grievous and his sons in the woods behind my store on River Road. Their dogs made and awful noise and woke me up. I grabbed my gun and went out to see what was up. When I knew it was Grievous, I called to him and told him to bring those fellows into my store. Then I called the police. The third boy was still at Grievous house, screaming."

"Is that all?" The judge inquired.

"No, we locked those two fellows up in my feed room until the police came. But before they got there, several of my neighbours, upon hearing the rumpus, came to see what was going on. The next morning the police swarmed all over my store and tramped through the woods behind it."

I thought the judge looked very severe in his black robes, but he was kind. He had served on the Virginia circuit court for a long time. Now he dismissed Arthur Henley and recalled Grievous.

"For weeks we have lived in fear from these murders," Judge Marshall told him. "Our old people have been killed and robbed, and nobody seemed able to solve these crimes. You, Grievous have relieved this county of a dreadful burden, and we all wish to thank you. You are free to go. These men shall be tried for the murders of Mary Jones and John Payne, both of Manakin."

The judge had scarcely finished when the court room exploded into cheers. As the clerk escorted Grievous and Mr. Henley out, we scrambled down the narrow stairs of the balcony to speak to them. The rest of the hearing was cut and dried, and the three men went to jail. But on that day Grievous became a hero. We crowded outside under the leafless oaks to congratulate him as he stood in the winter cold, smothered by his grateful neighbours. Although the Court continued, most of us went home feeling pleased and happy that the murders were at last solved. Again, Bertha put on her favourite hat and kept Mr. Houghton waiting for ten minutes while she cried and gossiped with her neighbours about Grievous's courage.

"I am ready to go home," she finally told us stopping to speak for another few minutes with Liza Parker. "We must go now, Miss Doc, I have to finish the laundry."

Later that afternoon, about four o'clock, Mrs. Houghton came across the lawn to find Bertha. In her arms my neighbour carried three brightly coloured dresses made from feed bags. I opened the front door.

"Hello, Mrs. Houghton," I greeted her, "you missed the hearing this morning."

"I am looking for Bertha," she told me.

"I think she is still in the laundry room."

Mrs. Houghton led the way into the back of the house. I followed.

"I've brought these little things for you," she said to our laundress. "I have just finished making them."

Bertha stood up from her ironing, and Mrs. Houghton laid three pink and blue dresses in the brown arms. I watched as tears welled up in the older woman's eyes and flowed down her cheeks.

"For my grands," Bertha whispered, quite overcome by this unexpected surprise.

Then she clasped Mrs. Houghton by the hand. But, perhaps remembering the colour difference, she dropped it again. After long years of servitude in the homes of white people, Bertha knew her place.

"These bags are part of Mr. Houghton's war effort," Mrs. Houghton explained, taking the brown hand in hers. " He feels he must get the goodness out of every last ounce. But I stole three of his precious sacks and made these dresses for you."

58

When Old Sally Died

January 1943

The church was filled. The potbellied stove threw out a feeble warmth as we sat rooted to our freezing pews. The organ wheezed and puffed, while we all sang lustily, off key, the well-known hymns. Old Sally had died, and the neighbours now flocked to St. Mary's to bury her on this cold, clear January morning in 1943. She'd died two nights before, not of old age, but of the flu, for Sally was not really old, perhaps fifty.

"Rock of Ages cleft for me," we all sang. "Let me hide myself in thee."

Old Sally's favourite hymn. She always hummed it, or sang it to any kind of words. It was the only hymn she knew, for Sally could neither read nor write.

"I never knew the luxury of an education," she told me one day in the churchyard after a service. "I just didn't have time for it raising all my sisters and brothers – after Mama passed.

Old Sally never rode in a motor car until just before the war. She never had central heating in her house, and never owned a store-bought dress, except a hand-me-down, and ones she'd made herself. She raised her three brothers and saw that they had good jobs. Then she found husbands for her five sisters. Finally she too married, a man with three children who had lost his wife. And once again Sally started to raise a family that was not her own.

"It was the custom when I was young for the oldest girl to take over the household and raise the younger children. Papa depended upon me, so I gave up my schooling to look after the family. I was just fifteen. And over the years I forgot how to write and read except for the funny papers. I can still sign my name though, and write my address," Sally confided.

It was in the early fall when Sally first contracted a cough. As the winter progressed, this cough become deeper and sounded more serious. Sally's tiny frame house, old and poorly constructed, was badly heated. Also its tin roof had rusted in several places, and the chimney, cracked and without sufficient mortar, smoked. Inside Sally and her children shivered from the cold.

"John, get Sally to a doctor," Mrs. Taliaferro told the husband one afternoon just after Christmas.

"I'm a cutter with the saw mill, and since there is no work in winter I can't afford doctors."

"You can't afford to lose Sally," Mrs. Taliaferro reminded him.

Finally the doctor did come and the church paid for him in spite of Mr. Wickham's protests. But Sally was frail; she could not withstand the cold in her poor shabby clothes.

"We need to find a warm coat. We also need a dress or two in size ten," Emma Craddock called Mrs. Houghton on the telephone.

We collected the clothes and Sally wore them, but they were not enough. We bought coal and took it to her. But her cabin leaked, and we found Sally lying ill in a bed with few blankets. Although Mr. Houghton and Harrison Moore tried to repair the tin roof, and Mrs. Taliaferro took down a good wool blanket, it didn't help much. Finally two nights ago Sally died.

"We shall always remember Sally for her bright smile and for her faithful attendance here every Sunday," Dr. Price droned on. He didn't really care about country folks and never knew her. She was just a face in a pew, not a real person.

We buried Sally in a donated coffin, and laid her in a pauper's grave. She had nothing in this life and expected nothing in the next. Surely she took nothing with her.

The church managed to pay for the expenses, and donated the plot next to the back fence behind the privy. On the morning of the funeral, John and his children looked bereft and seemed broken-hearted by their

When Old Sally Died

unexpected loss. Concerned for their welfare Jean Taliaferro offered John a job on her farm working with cattle. Another neighbour offered to drive him up as far as her road so he could walk.

For several days after the funeral I hated to think of Sally lying there in the cemetery, cold and damp. She had so little in life. So one afternoon about two weeks later, I carried some flowers to her grave and placed them upon it. Old Ben, the sexton, who also worked across the road from the church, saw me and lent me a metal vase.

"What happens to you, Ben, when you die?" I wondered as we arranged the flowers.

"You rest, chile, you rest."

"Is that all?" I inquired, feeling disappointed.

"That's enough," he replied. "You just rest from your labors. And there will be no more masters and no more servants."

I thought about this for a long time, and decided that I would get mighty tired of just resting from my labors. I had come in the pony cart with Jackie; now I untied the reins and hopped up on the seat, clicked at the donkey and started home.

"Goodbye, Ben."

"Goodbye, miss," the old man tipped his battered cap.

Airplanes bombed Germany; German guns answered in Africa and England. But no word came from Father; none of those funny V-mail letters had arrived since before Christmas. Perhaps he, too, would die in some far-away land, in a strange town with a curious name.

"I wonder who will remember Sally in a year's time?" I asked Jackie. "Dr. Price said such noble things about her, but I doubt he meant them."

The donkey trotted down River Road.

"I wish there was not so much death all around me," I told the donkey as I turned into our gravel lane and headed home. "There is no end of it with people dying all over the world in this terrible war. I want to live, live, live."

So did Jackie because he galloped all the way home. But I could not shake the sadness I felt deep down inside me.

A Forgotten Landscape

59

Mrs. Houghton and I Work at the Red Cross

February 1943

In February 1943 we had two hours of daylight saving time, called War Time. We got up in the dark when the stars were still out, and dressed in the cold. Mother turned her heat back to sixty-five degrees day and night. And although the coal furnace came on at five o'clock in the morning, it took two hours for it to warm my chilled bones.

Mr. Houghton, who heated his house with a coal stove and a heater, got up in the below-freezing temperatures to start his fires. Dressed in a heavy robe and a woollen cap, he would shovel coal and kindling into his stove. Often ice formed overnight in the saucepan of water he kept on top of his heater. This ice slowly melted once the coal and wood caught which Mr. Houghton expertly lighted from a rolled up newspaper. I felt thankful we had a furnace that came on by itself. But all of us found these winter mornings terribly cold as the freezing temperatures broke all records. Mother and Rudy rarely came home now, so our furnace did me little good.

On Saturdays I did not usually get up until after the feeble sun climbed over the pine trees in the woods that surrounded our house. But this luxury ended when Mrs. Houghton and I volunteered to roll bandages at the Red Cross in Manakin. We left the house at eight-thirty with Mr. Houghton when he made his weekly trip to visit Tom Harris's dairy farm to collect milk and butter and to deliver his eggs.

Although we arrived early at the Red Cross, we found several women already gathered at the old store building near Route 6. Here we rolled bandages, knitted sweaters and packed hospital kits to be sent overseas. Some of these kits went to England to the R.A.F. These, we put into boxes marked with black letters. Although the old store was opened six days a week, Mrs. Houghton and I went only from nine to eleven on Saturday mornings, or until Mr. Houghton returned to pick us up from his deliveries and a stop at Thelma's Place for a beer. Sometimes it was almost 12:00 before he picked us up.

"I have finished my sweater," Mrs. Houghton told me one day in February as we drove down our long S curve.

"I've almost finished my socks, but I am having a terrible time with the heel." I held up a strange looking article, my teeth chattering from the cold.

"Whoever wears that sock will become crippled in the foot for life the first time he puts it on." Mr. Houghton teased. "You're not helping the war effort; you're hindering it."

"I think I can fix that mess for you," Mrs. Houghton encouraged me from the back seat, "but it does look rather strange."

As we drove through the frost-coated countryside, the car heater finally came on, and I felt warmer. But when we arrived in Manakin, and I stepped out once more into the chilly morning, again my teeth began to chatter.

"Hello," Catherine Hollis greeted us at the store as we entered the bare room furnished only with two trestle tables, six wooden chairs, a pot-bellied stove, and several brown cartons that stood against the cracked plaster walls. "Doc, please run down to Clark's store and get us matches for the stove. Also ask Mrs. Clark for some old newspaper to start the fire."

Skipping down the road which ran through the village of Manakin, I noticed my breath looked white upon the crisp morning air. Clark's store, a weathered, unpainted clapboard building, stood at the far end. Several additions hung onto its main structure in a crazy manner. Mrs. Clarke and her unmarried daughter, Mary, owned the only store in the village. Not only were they post mistresses for Manakin and the surrounding countryside, but also letter-writers and readers for several illiterate Negroes. The Clarkes acted as interpreters of government forms and as telephone operators. They generously supplied their customers with the use of one of the three telephones found in the village.

Across from the store I recognized the white folks' Baptist church, with its cemetery enclosed by a cast iron fence. Next door to this church, nestled in some high shrubbery, was the Clarkes' house, and beyond it stood the homes of several other white people. Manakin itself was a Negro hamlet. Its tiny red brick church, where Bertha attended every Sunday, provided the hub of village life. Cabins, made from wooden scraps nailed upon ancient logs, lay scattered higgledy-piggledy; like so many grains of salt, around this church. It appeared to me to be the only secure structure in the entire village. A high wind might easily have removed Manakin from the map.

"We need some paper and matches to start the stove," I told Mrs. Clarke upon entering her combination store and post office.

"You'll need more than that" she informed me. "Here's a coal-scuttle I've just filled. I can't understand why those women don't provide their own fuel."

As she handed me all the necessary things for fire making, I stuffed the matches into my coat pocket, and rolled up the newspapers so I could use them to soften the handle of the heavy coalscuttle. Thanking Mrs. Clarke, I started back towards the Red Cross building stopping every few steps to rest my load. I had gone about halfway, when sliding across a patch of ice, my feet flew out from under me, and I fell heavily, full length upon the gravel road. The coalscuttle, to which I held on for dear life, landed in front of me scattering its contents. For a moment I lay stunned upon the frozen ground, then sat up to assess the damage.

"Oh, no," I wailed cradling my legs in my arms. "Look at my knees. They're bleeding." Crying in pain I stood up. "I'm a mess. And my coat's torn."

Undaunted I collected the scattered coal as blood ran from my palms, and oozed down my legs, staining my knee socks. Anger mixed with pain enveloped me as I lifted the heavy coalscuttle by its newspaper-wrapped handle and hurried on. When I reached the Red Cross store, Catherine Hollis met me at the door.

"Good, there you are," she greeted me with her favourite expression, as she took the heavy scuttle.

Mrs. Houghton, concerned when she saw my bloody hands and

knees, came over to me and mopped up with her bandages the crimson trickles that ran down my legs and into my socks.

"Let's see if these bandages are any good. The R.A.F. might not like them," she teased.

She took me outside to the old well where we washed my legs with freezing cold water and dabbed-cleaned my bleeding, coal blackened hands. Tears ran down my face. I felt miserable. The cold water, the sticky blood, and most of all my torn coat caused me to feel deeply humiliated.

"You'll be all right now, dear," Mrs. Houghton hugged me. "Dry your eyes. Come along inside."

"None of the others even said they were sorry," I complained wiping my nose on Mrs. Houghton's lace trimmed handkerchief. "Nobody even said 'thank you'".

"They are too busy building a fire. Come on, Doc, it's all right." Mrs. Houghton led me back inside.

In a few minutes the pot-bellied stove felt hot with flames. So we all pulled our chairs closer and huddled around the fire for warmth.

"Did you know Mrs. Thomas's cow died last night?" Mrs. Carthage told us as she stacked her folded bandages. "Her nice Guernsey heifer got sick and died."

"That's too bad," replied Emma Craddock absent-mindedly.

"Yes, and Rosie finally had her baby. A boy named Winston Franklin for the English Prime Minister and for our President. Old Dr. Lloyd says it's a fine healthy boy," Mrs. Carthage continued.

"Wasn't it astonishing that Winston Churchill went to Africa and met Roosevelt at Casablanca. I think our President looks very tired. Poor man." Catherine Hollis changed the subject.

"Yes, he does," Mrs. Houghton agreed. "But fancy, Wendell Willkie going to England and accepting hospitality there, only to return home and belittle everything British."

"Some people don't like the English, my dear," Sally McClain remarked folding her pile of bandages into a small carton. "My husband claims they are natural-born snobs."

"Mr. Wilkie, I agree, showed very bad manners," Emma Craddock tried to smooth things over.

Mrs. Houghton and I Work at the Red Cross

"I, for one," Sally McClain continued, "admire Mr. Churchill. 'A marvelous brute of a man', I call him."

Mrs. Houghton gave the pile of bandages on our side of the table a savage poke with her index finger, but said nothing.

"I brought you some home-made pickles, Clara," Mrs. McClain handed her a quart jar. "Just a little thank you for taking me home last week."

"Your last gift of watermelon pickles was excellent. Harry enjoyed them ever so much," Mrs. Houghton replied placing the offered jar onto the floor beside her.

"If Mr. Willkie does not like England, that's his loss." Mrs. Hollis again changed the subject. "You certainly can't criticize the British for lacking courage. I think we need a few more lumps of coal on that fire."

"Well," replied Mrs. Carthage, "I am not for getting mixed up in Europe's war. After all they never sent the R.A.F. over here to help us fight. Why should we send our boys to get killed in Africa?"

Nobody replied to this remark. After poking at the fire and adding coal, Mrs. Hollis opened a thermos and poured herself a cup of tea. I watched her add milk and sugar before she sipped the hot liquid from the thermos lid. We continued to fold our bandages for a few minutes in silence.

"Clara," Emma Craddock finally broke the stillness, "we could use you on Thursdays to help pack the last of these R.A.F. bandages. I must send our next batch out this week.

Mrs. Craddock looked up from marking several boxes of gauze bandages for England. Fascinated, I watched as her glasses slid down her nose and perched on its tip. With her brown hair plaited in a braid around her head, and her brown eyes peering over the spectacles, she reminded me of a school marm.

Mrs. Houghton made no reply.

"You could come up with Mrs. Taliaferro on Thursdays," Emma Craddock said again.

"We can't come on Thursdays," I chimed in, hoping to settle the matter. "Mrs. Houghton goes over to the church Thursday afternoons."

But Mrs. Craddock, as chairman, needed to staff her chapter in order to assure its quota of bandages, socks and sweaters. Although she ran her little store well, I thought she often bamboozled Mrs. Houghton. Deafness made my friend shy, and her participation in groups of more than three or four people was difficult, even with a hearing aid. A fact, I thought Miss Emma appeared to overlook.

"Clara, did you hear me?" Emma Craddock continued to pack the folded bandages.

"I hear you," replied Mrs. Houghton; "Who can help but hear you?"

Although we all laughed, Emma Craddock was not to be denied.

"Then shall I put you down for Thursdays?" Miss Emma stood up and opened her record book.

"You can put me down, but I won't promise I'll come, "Mrs. Houghton said pleasantly, "Saturday mornings suit Doc and me better."

"Yes," I agreed, "Saturdays are the only day I can come at all, and Mr. Houghton can bring us."

I stood up and brought Mrs. Houghton's thermos and two china cups from where she had laid them on the windowsill. Mrs. Houghton offered me a cup filled with hot tea from her thermos and poured one for herself. No one ever brought refreshments, for all of us nor were any offered to those who had not carried a flask. For a few minutes we folded bandages in silence, Mrs. Houghton and I pausing to sip our tea.

"It's cold," observed Mrs. Carthage getting up. "I'll put some more coal on the fire."

"Yes, it's very cold indeed," Mrs. Hollis agreed opening the door of the stove while Alvira Carthage threw in several lumps of coal. "This building never seems warm."

Mrs. Houghton never went to Manakin on Thursdays. We continued to go only on Saturday mornings because Mr. Houghton could take us. Although we felt we must help the war effort, neither of us enjoyed small talk; Mrs. Houghton because of her deafness, and I because I found it boring. More that two hours a week with Mrs. Carthage's gossip and Sally McLain's stories recalled from the First World War would have driven us both mad. I thought Sally McClain very odd. She always seemed to live in the past and had never turned her clocks forward to daylight saving time, and hated Wartime. She also smelled of wood smoke and lamp oil. This morning I decided to clear up the business about time.

"How do you manage to come to places on time?" I dived in.

"We use kerosene lanterns," she explained, " and we never stay up late. Usually we get up with the sun and go to bed when it gets dark."

"But how do you know what time it is?" I found her answer unsatisfactory. "How do you get here on time?"

"Oh, that's easy. You come at nine o'clock, and I come at seven, that's all. It works out just fine. Everything is two hours earlier."

"Wouldn't it be a lot easier to change your clocks?" I persisted.

"No, I like the old time. Our animals like it too. I see no reason for us to change," she told me packing her pile of gauze bandages into their box.

I realized Sally McClain's mornings at the Red Cross were a great sacrifice. She rose at five o'clock and milked her three cows before breakfast. After finishing her chores she walked two miles across the fields to the Red Cross store. In summer she wore a big floppy hat, and in winter a bright red wool cap sat firmly over her ears. Although she rarely got a lift to the store, Mr. Houghton often took her home and so did Mrs. Carthage occasionally. This morning Mrs. McClain arrived, as she did every week, with her kind face wreathed in a red wool cap, and her cheeks bright pink.

"These boxes are ready to mail," she commented looking up at me from under her red cap.

"I think the fire's gone out," I replied. "For ten dollars I would give up these mornings."

I felt very virtuous about going to Manakin at all. Often I found these Red Cross days unpleasant, and the pot-bellied stove usually frigid. This stove never seemed to have enough wood or coal, and I found myself spending more time on the road fetching fuel that rolling bandages.

"I'll try to get this fire started again," Mrs. Hollis poured most of the remaining coal into the stove's belly. Then she added a few sticks of kindling and struck a match. A feeble fire generated itself, then died. Mrs. Hollis stuffed in most of the remaining newspaper, and we watched it blaze up.

"I know I have told you about the Battle of the Somme," Sally McClain remarked to me. "My husband fought there. He was with a Scottish regiment; they wear the kilts."

"You mean your husband wore a kilt into battle?" I replied, interested.

"He did that, and was proud of it. The highland regiments have a long history, and their soldiers are fierce fighters. The Germans called them 'the ladies from hell.'"

"I did not know your husband was Scottish."

"Oh, yes for sure. McClain is a Scottish name. I met Jim when I was nursing there during the Great War of 1918. He was wounded, you see."

I looked at her amazed. She seemed such a backward lady with her time changes and her oil lamps that I would have never guessed she was a nurse. I noticed Mrs. Houghton turned up her hearing aid.

"That's why my husband doesn't like the English. He's a Scot. You must know something about Scotland from your reading. It's a nice sort of place, but very cold. I was attached to the Navy Nursing Corps stationed near Edinburgh. That's where I met Jim when he came in after being wounded in France. I thought the kilt he wore looked marvelous. He appeared ever so handsome dressed in his regimentals."

"Fancy that, wearing a skirt into battle," sang out Mrs. Carthage. "You would never catch my Joe in any such rig up. 'Ladies from Hell' were they? Our dough boys were not cowards, I can tell you."

"In this war the Highland regiments are wearing khaki kilts," Sally McClain informed us.

"Well of all things! Men in skirts!" mocked Mrs. Carthage. "I'll stick to things like Mrs. Thomas's dead heifer and Rosies's new baby. I find them far more interesting. At least I can understand them."

Suddenly I felt angry. I felt it deep down inside me. Mrs. Houghton and I both hated gossip. We did not give a hoot about dead heifers or new babies. Besides, my knitting looked terrible, and now Emma Craddock was passing it around for all to admire. Although Mrs. Houghton usually helped me with dropped stitches and turned the heels, my socks never looked well knitted. I blushed from embarrassment. At times like this I felt Mrs. Houghton and I should give up our Red Cross mornings.

Still every Saturday we went to Manakin. I continued to sacrifice my lovely sleep, and the freedom of a non-school day. Mrs. Houghton and I had come every week for two whole years. We rolled hundreds of boxes of gauze bandages, and we knitted tons of socks and sweaters – all

Mrs. Houghton and I Work at the Red Cross

the same colour. We packed dozens of cartons, marked them and addressed them and Miss Emma mailed them. We always met our quota. I felt my sacrifice would help my father; I prayed it did. I had listened to Mrs. Carthage's gossip and Sally McClain's stories until I wanted to choke both those old ladies with my bare hands. This morning when finally Mrs. McClain told us something interesting, Mrs. Carthage had to argue. I regarded her tweed-clad figure at the other end of the table. She wore two green sweaters, one a shade lighter than the other with her gray suit. Her hair, once bright red, was now faded and mixed with gray. Her hawk-like nose and hazel eyes made her look interesting, but certainly not pretty. I did not find her attractive, and now she made me angry. My knees smarted, my palms bled, tears pricked against my eyes as I fought for self control.

"That's the last piece of coal," commented Mrs. Carthage. "Doc, will you go and fetch us some more fuel?"

"No," I shouted at her, my anger overpowering me.

The room became deathly silent, minutes crawled by. I felt suspended in time. What had caused my temper to suddenly to flare up I could not say. I knew it was justified. This morning I had fetched and carried enough coal for that particular pot-bellied stove. I resented being sent down to Mrs. Clarke's store every week for fuel. Often I went twice during the morning, and one day in January I had gone three times. But this morning when the blood ran freely down my legs I decided I'd had enough.

"No," I repeated. "My knees hurt, my hands are bleeding. You have a car, Mrs. Carthage, you can bring up the coal."

In unison the five ladies turned and stared at me. No one spoke. I stood at the table regarding them. " I might as well end this," I thought, "once and for all."

"You always talk about other people. I call that gossip," I told Mrs. Carthage.

Mrs. Houghton put her hand on my arm; I knew she was trying to restrain me. Emma Craddock peered at me over her glasses and frowned.

"Don't you like to hear what other people are doing?" Mrs. Carthage defended herself.

"Sometimes," Mrs. Houghton's hand closed firmly upon my arm. "But each week we hear the same things over and over again. I have heard about the Battle of the Somme until I am blue in the face, and about babies until you'd think everyone in the county is expecting one

"Don't you think you're being rude?" Emma Craddock asked.

"No," I replied. "I am almost fifteen, and I have given up my Saturday mornings for more than two years to come here. No one even offers us hot coffee when we arrive. I have to fetch wood and coal all the time for that stove, and listen to news I'm not interested in."

Mrs. Carthage looked amazed. Emma Craddock stood up as if to hit me, but her glasses went flying across the room, so she dashed after them instead. Catherine Hollis put the last newspaper on the fire, and I turned beet red from embarrassment.

But the next Saturday when Mrs. Houghton and I entered the Red Cross store, Emma Craddock offered us each a cup of hot coffee. And to my amazement the coal scuttle was filled, and a fire in the pot-bellied stove burned brightly.

Mrs. Houghton and I Work at the Red Cross

Letters

February 20, 1943
Richmond, Va.

Dear Dad,
We read about the Battle of the Kaserine Pass. Mr. Houghton says that the Germans licked you, and General Fredendall has been replaced. Why can't you beat Rommel once and for all? Are you all right? I heard there were a lot of losses, and we were out-gunned. Things here are as usual: little gas, less meat and freezing cold.
Love, Doc.

N. Africa
February 28, 1943

Dear Doc,
Rommel gave us a pasting. Our men fought well, but their equipment was inferior against his Panzer divisions. In spite of this we held the Kaserine Pass, but with heavy losses. In the night Rommel withdrew. "He folded his tent like an Arab and silently stole away." I can't remember who wrote it, but it's certainly true. General Patton has taken over II corps. There have been changes, but I am to remain. We can't leave any equipment unguarded these days. The Arabs pick it clean. They're the world's best scavengers. Buzzards have nothing on these birds.
Love, Dad

A Forgotten Landscape

60

Battle of El Guettar

March 26-27 1943

"The attack was launched during the night of March 26th by the 8th Armored Brigade of New Zealand and by the New Zealand Infantry. Vice Air Marshall Harry Broadhurst used Rommel's tactics of low-flying air power effectively and reached El Hamma. Here the British were checked. When morning came the enemy had disappeared to defend the American threat at his rear." Mr. Houghton's radio told us.

"At last we're getting some action," he commented as we ate our breakfast three days after the battle.

"Five thousand Italians were taken prisoner, and a thousand Germans were captured at El Hamma. Mongomery paused, but General Patton has attacked towards the coast with the U.S. 9th and 34th Infantry Divisions to open a path for his 18th Armored Division," the radio continued.

When the 34th Division fell back four miles to the west to reorganize, this withdrawal caused Rommel to remark, " The American gives up the fight as soon as he's attacked."

This made Mr. Houghton furious.

"Of all the stupid remarks, that takes the biscuit." He got up from the kitchen table and walked out slamming the back door.

"He's terribly upset," I told Jenny who was visiting us for five days from Washington while school was out. "He'll put us to work doing his horses and chickens. Quick, finish your breakfast so we can go out and ride the ponies."

I turned off the radio, and we tip-toed out and raced for our barn to get Jackie and Billy. I forgot about the Battle of El Guettar until later.

A Forgotten Landscape

March 30, 1943
Richmond, VA.

Dear Dad,

Jenny arrived by train last Saturday. Mr. Houghton and I went in to meet her, and when we returned home, lunch was ready. Mrs. Houghton out did herself. Then Jenny and I put on old clothes and went out for a ride on Killybegs and Lady. Wasn't that kind of Miss Emma to allow Jenny to ride him? She says both Hugh and Gil are fine, but Hugh is more American every day, and Nanny Grace despairs he's lost his English accent. He's now five, and still a pest, Jenny tells me.

That evening we went to the movies. Miss Emma joined us, and we all five crammed into her car because the old Chevrolet is too small. We had a big discussion about which movie to see. Miss Emma claims that Errol Flynn is a Nazi sympathizer, and she refused to go to the movie he was in. So we picked another one and had to drive all the way into Cary Street to the Byrd Theatre. Miss Emma wasn't pleased about using that much gas. After the movie we had ice cream, at White's across the street.

Cary is now overseas. He writes fairly regularly. Of course Miss Emma worries about him, but she's proud of him too. I miss him a lot because when Cary was around he made life fun. I hope he'll be all right and come home to us.

On Sunday, Jenny, Mrs. Houghton and I went to church in the pony cart to save gas. Jenny loved it, and Jackie behaved for once. In the afternoon, Tom and Elizabeth Harris dropped by for a visit because it was my birthday. He really wanted to borrow some old harness, so he can plough his garden with Nellie. He always seems to have gas, but then he has a truck and a car. Mr. Houghton says he buys it on the Black Market. The ladies, Jenny and I went for a walk down to the creek while the men talked farming. Mrs. Harris says they need another man at the dairy now that Ralph has gone to the army. Angelo can't do it all. Sometimes Grievous goes up for a day's work, but he's getting old now and isn't strong enough for the big jobs like lifting. He's always willing to go, and he's always free when Mr. Harris asks him.

After our walk Miss Emma invited us for tea. So we all trooped over there and had a birthday celebration. I love going to Miss Emma's house, it smells all leathery and painty. It's my kind of place. Quinnie, her Kerry Blue Terrier, tried to get into Jenny's lap and had to be put out. She said she didn't realize the Irish like the English so much. We all laughed. I am now fifteen, in case you've forgotten. Mr. Houghtonsays,

"Fifteen and never been kissed." He's right, I am not crazy about any boy kissing me. Maybe Cary, but then he wouldn't.

It was a really special weekend, and when Jenny left after five days with us, I cried. She's cut her braids and has curls. So although she's younger, she's growing up too. I doubt if her parents in England will recognize her. Will you recognize me? I wonder, so I'm enclosing a recent photograph of me so you won't forget. Please don't forget me. Grandmother called for my birthday and asked about news from you. She also sent me a check: a whole ten dollars.

Guess what we are collecting now? Pre-war golf balls because they have rubber in them. We are also collecting baseballs which have cork centers. Cork is scarce, so now the new baseballs have the rubber from the old golf balls inside. Can you believe it?

We also collect newspapers and cooking grease which Mrs. Houghton takes to the butcher every week. Used fat has glycerin in it and is used for dynamite and paint. She gets two extra red points for every pound of bacon drippings we take into Mr. Smith.

She also cuts the fat off the meat and takes that as well. Before Jenny came we collected two pounds of fat, so we could get extra points for cheese and butter while she was here. Usually Mrs. Tanner, the Taliaferro's overseer's wife, gives us country butter in exchange for eggs. It's unpasteurized, but Mrs. Houghton wanted store-bought butter and some cheese for Jenny. So we ate like kings and queens while she was here. I hope she comes again soon because we had fun together. It gets lonely in the country with few children my age around. Sometimes we ride into Richmond on the train. We have to flag it down at Taliaferro's Junction. Sometimes the engineer doesn't see us, or just thinks we are waving and doesn't stop. Sometimes he stops, but a mile down the line, so we have to run and be lifted up by the porter, whose name is Fred. Mary Ann comes out on the train now on a Friday evening and goes home on Sunday afternoon, so we do get together, but not as often. She's more interested in the things you can do in town. But about once a month or six weeks, she comes out on the train, and I meet her with Jackie and the pony cart. She still thinks that's fun.

I love you,
Doc

A Forgotten Landscape

61

El Guettar

March 1943

Frances telephoned from Florida to tell me that Father was wounded at El Guettar.

She didn't have many particulars, just that it was a leg wound and not life threatening. Grandmother called later to say she was sorry about this news. She knew I would be brave and not cause the Houghtons any extra worry. She also invited me out to visit her, but with school on I decided I'd miss too much and didn't go.

It was too cold for my apple tree, so I sat in Jackie's stall and talked to him that Saturday until I was too cold to stay any longer.

"It's all right, Doc," Mrs. Houghton said, "it's difficult to take this all in. You are brave and you have worked hard for the war effort. So don't feel any guilt about your father's wound."

"I don't know how I feel," I replied trying to warm myself beside her fire. "I feel numb, and angry with him and the Germans too. I'm all muddled up inside."

"Wouldn't you like to go to Indianapolis?" Mrs. Houghton asked.

"No, because school is difficult, and I must stay and get good grades. No, that would only cause me to worry more." I walked into the kitchen and put on the tea kettle. "You say a cup of tea is always a help to clear your head. I'll make us both one."

For a week I walked about the house and school in a fog. Finally the fog cleared. I decided that I must not allow myself to be sad and worried. I also told Mr. Houghton to call Mr. Harris and tell him not to call me kid anymore.

"I am sorry about his nephews on the Yorktown, but I know how he felt and why he kept coming down to see us at inconvenient times. Tell him he has a choice, I am either Catherine from now on, or Signorina. Make him understand that I've stood in his shoes.

Letters

April 1943
Richmond, VA.

Dear Dad,

I am very sorry to hear you've been wounded at El Guettar. I hope it's not too bad. Please stay away from German bullets, and don't be careless and take chances.

Frances telephoned and told me. She was very, very kind and considerate. I called Mother and told her, but she acted funny about it. Rudy didn't even care, and said he was glad to remain in Washington. I guess he's too scared to be messing around battlefields. I don't think khaki would suit his tastes. He's such a peacock.

Grandmother telephoned me and was extremely kind. She calls about once a week, just to check up on me. She and Mrs. Houghton chat about practical matters like money for clothes for me and for my keep. She always sends Mrs. Houghton a check every month. Mother's supposed to, but often forgets. So grandmother, who is more reliable, sends a check. Mr. Houghton says I cost the earth and he's about to throw me into the James River. I don't like to be a burden on them. But Mrs. Houghton says I'm not really.

I must go now. It's going to rain, the backs of the leaves are showing. Mr. Houghton claims that's a sure sign. I've left my bicycle out and must put it away.

Love, Doc

El Guettar

May 1943
N. Africa

Dear Son,

My wound is in the leg with shrapnel, and not too bad. Really in the ankle. I can't point my toe to dance anymore, but other than that I'm okay. Your grandmother would like to take you to live with her. She's written and asked my permission. What do you think about that? You'll become an Indiana hayseed in place of a Virginia one. We don't want the Houghtons to become tired of you. I am sure you are very welcome there, but the arrangement can't go on forever. Write me your thoughts about this idea, and I'll write to your grandmother.

Love, Dad

A Forgotten Landscape

62

A Letter from Tommy

June 1943

In early June a letter arrived from Tom Phillpot. After carefully examining the English stamp I ran out to the orchard and climbed up my favorite apple tree to read in peace.

> June 1, 1943
> Bedfordshire
>
> Dear Doc,
>
> I am sorry not to have written sooner to tell you how wonderful we all found your recent gift of sweets. The parcel arrived in good condition, and I passed your gift around the servant's hall for everyone to enjoy. We especially liked the chocolates with peppermint centers.
>
> In March, London took a terrific bombing, and St. Paul's Cathedral was only saved by a minor miracle. All the buildings around it were destroyed and have since been pulled down. Only the church survived.
>
> Canterbury is fine. So don't worry, you shall yet see this famous landmark. Fire bombs did fall on it, but a series of ladders on the roof allowed firemen to walk across the cathedral and to sweep these incendiaries off. We on the Home Front are trying to remain brave, but as more and more bombs fall on us, especially in London, I find it becomes extremely hard to maintain my courage.
>
> I was happy to hear that the Africa Corps had finally surrendered in Tunisia. I expect your father was glad to see this also. We have at last experienced some victories when both Tunisia and Bizerta fell to us within

a week. A recent photograph of Mussolini shows his hair is turning gray. No wonder with so many Italian soldiers taken prisoner. How terribly depressed and miserable they all looked in the pictures our newspapers printed.

I see American G.I.'s all over England. London is full of them, and I saw several in Rochester when I got off the train last week on my way to visit Mother near Cooling Castle. The sight of these young men makes me realize England is not forgotten in her hour of need. Churchill has called for volunteers for his Home Guard, and thousands have joined up. Three years ago the Home Guard had almost nothing except broomsticks to fight with, but you cannot deny the courage of these men. I found them a heart-warming sight.

Mother keeps fairly well although she is approaching eighty. I took your most recent letters and read them aloud to her. She was intrigued to hear of the murders you had in Goochland, and laughed considerably at the incident of the baby falling into the baptismal font. I agree, Horace is an ugly name, and William sounds much better. I had a friend named Horace once, long years ago. Although I like him, I found his name unpleasant. It reminds me of horses coughing. Did you know that the town of Hastings is near us in Kent where the famous Battle occurred in which Harold was defeated by William the Conqueror?

Mother thanks you very much for the stockings you sent. They are now almost impossible to buy here, and real silk ones are a rare commodity. Sheets, if we can find them, will cost nine pounds! At one time, I remember, we took all of these things for granted.

When I returned home on Sunday evening I came back through London, Victoria Station. As I walked part way to catch my train at King's Cross, I was very saddened to see the town house of the Duke and Duchess of York badly damaged in a recent air raid. Here Princess Elizabeth was born. One day in the future she shall become our Queen.

We were also considerably saddened to learn of Leslie Howard's death a few days ago. *Gone with the Wind* has always reminded me of Goochland county, since I think of you and the Duchess as my Southern Belles.

                Kind Wishes, Your Grateful
                      Tom Phillpot.

A Letter from Tommy

Slowly I folded up the letter and placed it back in its envelope. Then I surveyed the landscape stretching out below me. I wondered if Virginia looked anything like England. There, the countryside seemed very green divided into checker-board fields separated by hedgerows. Our fields had white wooden fences around them, and often looked very brown in summer. Nor did we have the centuries-old buildings dating back a thousand years. When I considered this ancient cultural heritage, it made me feel terribly small and insignificant. I wondered if our frame and brick houses would still be standing a thousand years from now. For us in America three hundred years seemed terribly old. Nothing much existed that dated from the seventeenth century except in places like St. Augustine, Florida. It seemed my country was not exceptionally venerable after all.

"I guess in the great scheme of things I am not very important," I observed out loud to a brown wren who had built a nest in a neighboring tree.

I watched her fly to and fro gathering food and fussing at me for being too close. I expected she had some babies in her nest. Not wishing to disturb this mother bird, I placed the letter in my pocket and slid down the apple tree to the ground. Receiving letters from England always made me feel important. Tommy's letter had to cross the Atlantic Ocean, now infested with German submarines, to reach me in Virginia. Sometimes overseas mail failed to arrive, so I felt fortunate. The uncertainty of a safe delivery made the contents of my pocket seem more precious. One day, I decided, I would cross the Atlantic myself and visit Tom Phillpot in England.

Letters

June 1943
North Africa

Dear Doc,

 We've mopped up things in North Africa. The surrender took place May ninth with Major General Harmon commanding the 1st Armored Division, and Major General Fritz Krause commanding the Africa Corps. Rommell escaped to Berlin, and we'll have to deal with him again. My leg wound is not healing as it should. But then I've not been off it either. I can't expect it to heal well under these conditions. I'll be glad to leave the desert and its sand behind. I'm not sure where we are going, but I'll be happy to go. Hope things are well on the home front.

 Love, Dad

June 1943
Richmond, VA

Dear Dad,

 I am glad it's all over for you in Africa. Where do you go next? Mr. Houghton says Italy. Mrs. Houghton says France. Mother and Rudy came for the weekend. They haven't been here in ages, but there was a wedding they wished to attend. I didn't bother to move back home. We are in the middle of exams, and it was too much trouble when I'm in two different places. I went into the woods to study and stayed out of their way. Mrs. Houghton didn't see them either, although Mr. Houghton did. It sees there was some trouble over the land that's leased to Harrison Moore because Mr. Houghton was upset. Rudy now wants to lease it out to Mr. Houghton to plant corn. Mr. Houghton says he doesn't wish to cultivate anymore fields. He has enough. So it was left undecided. Rudy went back to Washington in a huff because he didn't get his way. Now Mr. Moore says he will renew his lease. It's all very confusing.

A Letter from Tommy

    I need riding boots. Mine are too small, and we can't find any new ones in the stores. The riding shops are hopeless, and I have corns big time now. Mother says I was foolish to keep wearing boots that didn't fit. I find shoe rationing the most difficult. My feet are different sizes, and they keep getting longer. Pretty soon I'll have giant feet. Mr. Houghton has such a bad time finding work boots. He keeps getting the old ones resoled, but now there is nothing to resole. Mrs. Henley thinks she might have a pair she put by for a customer who never came back for them. She thinks they might fit Mr. Houghton. We also have trouble with our tires. Mr. Houghton has a spare one he kept back from the rubber drive, but the inspector people take down the serial numbers, so you have to be careful. He'll put the tire on, and take it off when we go for inspection. The shortages are difficult, but then we are not fighting like you are at the Front. We are grateful for that.

    Grandmother called yesterday to see when I can come out for a visit. Mrs. Houghton will send me out with a friend in July for two weeks. She doesn't want me to travel alone because of the vast numbers of troops on the trains now. She's afraid for my safety. She's making the arrangements so we will get the tickets now, and not find them all sold out later when I go. Grandmother's very special, and I love her.

    We all send our love, Doc.

    P.S. I am still giving my belief in God some extra thought. It's difficult to believe He cares about us struggling down here in the middle of a war. Yet without Him you'd have nothing to hang on to.. No real meaning in life, no heaven to look forward to. He could have spared the Rats of Tobruk though after all our prayers. I don't understand God sometimes, and I don't always agree with Him. Mrs. Houghton says I'm too young to tell God how to run His business. Maybe so, but I'd like to understand Him better.

A Forgotten Landscape

63

Mr. Brown's Diamond Head

Summer 1943

Angelo liked Mr. Harris's dairy and addressed it's owner in jest as "mio generale."

"Like Rommel," he explained.

Angelo had fought with this German general, and although captured after the First Battle of El Alamain, still held Rommel in high regard. The P.O.W.'s affection for Tom Harris grew into friendship. Even though we understood and accepted this new name, some of our neighbors disliked his being called after the German general, Erwin Rommel.

Several weeks later when I stopped by Henley's store, Mr. Harris came up to my pony cart.

"I am a general now, and you're a Signorina. We've both got titles, Doc," he teased.

"Yes, sir," I replied, packing the groceries under the seat before I untied the donkey.

"Well, little Doc, that makes us special with Angelo." Tom Harris winked at me.

"Yes, sir, it sure does," I agreed with a laugh.

At the dairy Angelo put in long hours. He was kind and patient with the animals and very polite to people. We heard that the authorities had come out from Richmond several times and talked to Mr. Harris. They also checked on Angelo, who seemed pleased with the new arrangement.

Everything went along fine until one morning in early summer

Angelo disappeared. Failing to locate him, Mr. Harris jumped into his old car and drove down to Henley's store to organize a search party. Here he found several farmers gathered under the trees.

"He's run away. Your wop has fled to Richmond," Mr. Brown predicted.

"You can't trust a foreigner," commented Arthur Henley. "He's just ups and gone."

But Tom Harris refused to believe them.

"Gone where?" I asked, listening to the men's comments. "Back to Italy? Where could he possibly go?"

"Probably he's hopped a train to California where wine is made," Mr. Houghton added.

"Let's get a search party together," suggested Mr. Harris to the men. "Arthur, may I use your phone to call some of the farmers at this end of the county?"

"Sure, go ahead," assented the storekeeper. "Perhaps Miss Jean and Miss Emma could bring their dogs. I know Mike and Quinnie are both good at tracking, and we might need them."

As Tom Harris disappeared inside the store the men continued to discuss Angelo's disappearance. Mr. Houghton bought gas for his car, and then telephoned Mrs. Houghton to tell her we were heading for Manakin. Within twenty minutes several men had gathered at the store, and Jean Taliaferro accompanied by Emma Craddock arrived with their Kerry Blue terriers. Even Harrison Moore came in his truck from across Tuckahoe Creek, and offered a ride to anyone who would like to go up to Manakin. After some discussion the men finally decided who was going to take his car or truck and in pairs and in threes the farmers departed. Mr. Houghton, with me in the front seat, turned his old Chevrolet out onto River Road and followed.

When we arrived at Tom Harris's dairy, it seemed that the whole county had assembled. Farmers, with dogs of every description, waited, talking in groups about Angelo's disappearance and offering their theories.

"Okay, men, let's go. The two Kerry Blues will do the tracking, so stay behind them," Mr. Harris instructed.

Just as we started out, Elizabeth Harris called her husband to the telephone.

"Mr. Brown, something about his bull," she said.

"His bull?" Mr. Harris entered the house letting the screen door bang. I watched him pick up the phone. "Hello, Sam. Tom Harris here." The dairyman's face changed expression as he listened into the receiver. "Apparently grand champion Blair's Diamond Head is also missing." Mr. Harris told us as he hung up the telephone and took down his gun.

I had heard of this vicious bull and knew it took two men to handle him. Apparently he broke loose and now roamed the countryside somewhere between Brown's dairy on Route 6 and Mr. Harris's farm near Manakin.

"That explains it," Tom Harris remarked rummaging through an oak chest in the front hall, and taking out a box of shells.

"Explains what?" Mr. Houghton wanted to know "I just hope we don't meet that bull."

"Angelo's disappearance." Mr. Harris came back out onto the porch.

"I don't see the connection," Mr. Houghton replied, looking puzzled.

"The bull broke loose about dawn and is headed this way, according to several people along Route 6 who have spotted him." The men moved off following the dogs, and I trotted behind Mr. Harris and watched him place several shells into his pocket.

"What's that got to do with Angelo?" Mr. Houghton swung along beside me walking with ground-eating strides.

But Tom Harris did not explain. Jean Taliaferro and Emma Craddock turned their dogs loose and signaled for us to follow. In groups of twos and threes we tramped after Mike and Quinnie down the driveway, crossed the dirt road and entered the woods on the far side. Here we found an old sawmill trail, and from it the men spread out in a half mile crescent. I noticed Mr. Harris had stopped and loaded his gun. Driving the shells home he snapped the barrel shut and checked the safety catch. Then he continued to follow the dogs through the pine woods. We remained on the north side of the creek since on the south side the ground was marshy and filled with briars. And there was no trail we could follow through the swamp. I entered the woods several yards behind Mr. Houghton whose long strides matched those of Tom Harris's.

"Harry, Sam Brown's promised to come up and join us with his two

P.O.W.'s at the junction of Route 6 and River Road."

"That's a pretty good way from here, about three miles," Mr. Houghton replied. "Stay close, Doc," he told me. "And watch out for snakes."

"I hate snakes," I said, running to keep up and catching my clothes upon the briars that grew in thick clumps beside the path.

We had walked perhaps a mile when Mike and Quinnie set up a terrible racket. I knew Mike's deep growling bark, and the bitch's voice, younger and more treble which now rose to a sharp howl.

Suddenly, crashing through the undergrowth in front of us I saw a gigantic bull. I gasped in fright and clutched. Mr. Houghton's hand, as we entered a clearing, really a small pasture beside the swamp. Before us stood a fawn and white bull, head down, ready to charge. Instantly Mr. Harris cocked his gun, and sighted it. At the edge of the woods twenty farmers stopped dead in their tracks. No one dared move.

Only the dogs raced through the undergrowth, then crouching nearly to their bellies, they entered the clearing. Distracted, the bull raised his head, and circled the dogs, his horns looking sharp and wicked. Suddenly the great animal lunged towards us, and charged. Mike, clever and wily, jumped aside as he did with the horses and circled the bull in the opposite direction. Momentarily confused, Diamond paused, raised his head and shook his horns.

"Stop him," I whispered to Mr. Houghton, " or Mike will be killed."

"Hush, Doc. There is no way we can stop them now." I felt his strong hand upon my arm.

Again the bull lowered his head and faced the dogs. Again Mike circled, moving ever closer to the deadly horns. The bitch took her place to one side and slightly behind. The bull charged, and she gave way. Lowering his head again Diamond sized up his opponents and then ran at the bitch. Quinnie jumped aside, but misjudged the distance, and the tip of the wicked horns grazed her flank, throwing her to the ground.

"Stop them," I stifled a scream.

But the brave Kerry Blue struggled to her feet apparently unhurt. In an instant the bull raced up the field. Mike followed, snapping at the fleeing hooves with his vicious teeth.

At the other end of the clearing smoke rose from the brick chimney of a tiny cabin. A small Negro child played in its yard. Time seemed to stop, as I watched – this scene – so silent, yet so charged with danger. In horror I stood helpless as the great fawn-coloured bull galloped towards the child. Mr. Harris's gun exploded beside me. The bullet grazed the huge horns, deflected and bounced off a tree. Diamond Head stopped, and turned. Mike stood squarely in front of him. Crouching low, the bitch took her place behind. Maddened, the bull pawed at the ground and tossed his deadly horns. He watched the dogs then the great animal lowered his head and charged.

Mr. Harris sighted his gun. At that moment a woman dashed out of the cabin, snatched up her baby and fled back into the house. I heard metal scraping metal as the door banged shut just as the bull reached the cabin's steps.

Angrily Diamond Head circled the house blowing spray from his nostrils and bellowing his frustration. Mike faced him squarely before the cabin's front steps; the bull lowered his head. I saw the deadly horns clearly visible, outlined against the pinewoods. Mike stood motionless, his brown lips opened, showing four rows of sharp white teeth. A deep growl told Diamond Head he had met his match.

The bull whirled, and charged. Nimbly the dog stepped aside. Again the bull charged, his tail switching, his great horns lowered. Again Mike skipped away; his agile footwork reminded me of a dancer's. But Mike little realized the deadly game he played.

Confused by the dog's clever movements, Diamond Head paused. Mr. Harris fired. The great bull's tan legs crumpled under him like cardboard, and he fell heavily onto his side – dead.

A fine strip of cloth dangled from the great head and blew gently in the morning breeze.

"There's something hanging from his horns," Mr. Houghton shouted as he ran up the clearing.

"A piece of Angelo's scarf," Mr. Harris jerked it from the horns. "He must be near by."

Mike sniffed the dead bull. The bitch, less adventurous, stood to one side, panting.

"Send those dogs out again," Mr. Harris shouted as he cleared his gun of empty shells.

Jean Taliaferro called Mike to her, but he bared his teeth and remained with his quarry; then realizing the sport was over, he gave one final growl and followed his mistress towards the swamp. Quinnie trotted after him. I noticed Jean carried the strip of Angelo's bloody scarf in her hand.

"Damn bull,: Mr. Harris muttered, "I'll bet he cost a bundle."

He snapped his gun shut and put on the safety lock; I saw his lips pressed tight as we re-entered the woods, and knew he was angry.

"Stay close to the dogs," Mr. Houghton commanded, as he took my arm, and pulled me along.

We tramped through the woods. A half mile west of the clearing we discovered broken branches and trampled undergrowth. Mike circled, then back tracked towards the stream that trickled through Mr. Harris's farm before it lost itself in the swamp. Near the stream bed we found the soft earth pocked with hoof prints, bovine prints with the center of the hoof split to form two. Mike picked up the scent and crawled through the briars. Not ten yards away in the swamp lay Angelo. He looked dead, covered with blood and black muck.

I hid my face in Mr. Houghton's shirt. Mr. Harris fought his way through the brambles and reached the wounded man first. I watched as the dairyman laid his gun down upon some dry pine needles and felt Angelo's pulse.

"He's still alive," Tom Harris shouted – we ploughed through the undergrowth behind him.

Mr. Houghton wet his handkerchief in the stream and bathed the death-like face. I caught hold of a sapling and prayed.

"Oh, God, please, God, don't let Angelo die."

"Doc, run get help. We need a stretcher. Hurry!" Mr. Harris commanded.

I dashed up the stream bed and ran headlong into Grevious Sin Snead.

"We found him, Grevious," I shouted at the colored man. "Get a stretcher."

He turned and flew back across the clearing towards the Negro cabin. Several yards up the stream bed I heard Jean call in Mike. Within minutes Grievous and his son, Isaac, crashed through the undergrowth carrying a wide board and a blanket. Jean Taliaferro and Emma Craddock leashed in their dogs and started up the sawmill trail towards the main road. Mr. Houghton's voice came through the trees.

"Doc, Doc," he shouted, "Go back to Tom Harris's farm and call Dr. Lloyd."

I dashed off through the woods, my legs pushing me forward, my heart pounding inside my chest. Ahead of me I saw the two women with their dogs. Fairly flying I crossed the saw mill trail, jumped over fallen trees until I came to the red clay bank which led onto the road. As I scrambled down the bank, brambles caught my shirt and cut my bare legs. Fright put wings on my heels; I jumped a ditch, landed on the gravel road, and raced through the pasture towards the dairyman's house. Mrs. Harris saw me coming, saw me fly down her farm lane, and heard me yell.

"We need a doctor. We need a doctor."

"Where, child? Where?"

"Here. Tell him to come here," I shouted back as I climbed over the pasture fence.

Breathless I arrived at her doorstep and sank down onto the porch, weak and faint. I heard Mrs. Harris enter the house and dial the telephone as I gasped for breath. When I sat up, Bobby, the big German shepherd, licked my face. Mrs. Harris reappeared and knelt down beside me.

"We found Angelo," I told her, " Down by the stream a half mile from here, gored by Mr. Brown's bull."

She dabbed my cuts with witch hazel and put a cold cloth over my forehead. I lay back down upon the cool porch and closed my eyes.

When I sat up again I saw the men. They trudged down the road carrying Angelo on the makeshift stretcher. I heard the P.O.W. groan as they lifted him over the porch and carried him into the house. Once inside they laid him, stretcher and all, on the living room floor. Angelo looked deathly pale. His large eyes remained closed; his muddy fingers lay over his chest.

Frightened, I shivered and sat down on the porch swing. Under my hundred pounds the chain made a cheerful squeak. I remained very still. Mrs. Harris drew clear water from the pump in her front yard and carried it inside. She stepped around Grievous and his son who sat on the porch steps.

Jean Taliaferro and Emma Craddock put their dogs into Jean's car and started home. The men followed. Alone and in pairs they climbed into their old Fords and pick-ups. Dust rose as they drove slowly away.

Only Grievous, his son Isaac, Mr. Houghton and I remained on the porch. Mr. Houghton sat on an old settle, his head buried in his rough, honest hands. Isaac poked the ground with a stick while Grievous lit his corn cob pipe. Only the German shepherd's tail, thumping against the floorboards of the porch, broke the silence. I remained on the swing. The mid-day sun felt oppressive; the trees blew gently in a fickle breeze.

Tom Harris stood, waiting, the gun still over his arm - forgotten. About twenty minutes later when Dr. Lloyd's car arrived, I watched it come up the driveway. Only then did Mr. Harris prop his gun against the door sill before he crossed the yard to meet the doctor. Together, without speaking, they entered the house where Mr. Harris put up his gun.

I thought the doctor looked grave when he reappeared after examining Angelo.

"Does anyone here have a station wagon or a pick-up truck?" he asked us.

Isaac Snead did. I knew that was why he had waited. Mr. Harris brought out blankets and two pillows. Tom Harris found a spare mattress, and they made a bed in the back of Isaac's truck.

"I'll ride with him," Dr. Lloyd said.

I watched Mr. Harris and Mr. Houghton carry Angelo outside and with the help of Isaac and Grievous they lifted him onto the mattress. Mrs. Harris climbed in beside Angelo on the makeshift bed, and sat on a pillow.

"I am going, too," she told them.

Dr. Lloyd heaved his bulk onto the tailgate of the truck and settled himself in a deck chair beside her. Isaac gently, quietly closed the tailgate and chained it. Then with Isaac at the wheel, they started – ever so slowly – down the driveway.

"Why didn't you go with them?" I asked Mr. Harris as he stood on the porch watching the truck drive away.

"Cause I've got to tell Sam Brown I shot his prize bull," the dairyman told me.

"Oh," I replied and sat down on the porch swing again. "That's going to be difficult."

"You said it, kid."

"Signorina," I reminded him – tears welled up in my eyes and dropped onto my scratched hands. " You can't call me kid, any more."

"Signorina," Mr. Harris repeated. He entered the house and slammed the screen door.

On the road in the distance I recognized Mr. Brown's car as it came purposefully along and turned into the driveway. Mr. Houghton stood up and leaned against a porch column. In silence we watched the car grow bigger and bigger, as Mr. Brown arrived.

"Hello, Harry," the farmer got out of his Dodge. He spit a great brown wad of tobacco into the shrubbery.

"Hello, Sam," Mr. Houghton replied.

"Harris at home?" Mr. Brown came up to the porch.

"He's inside."

Tom Harris opened the screen door and walked out onto the porch. He looked seven feet tall.

"I hear you shot my prize bull, Diamond Head." Mr. Brown spit a second splat of tobacco onto the ground.

"Yes," Mr. Harris replied. "I shot him."

"It's going to cost you, Tom."

"I expect it will," Mr. Harris seemed nonchalant as he crossed the porch and came down the front steps.

"I mean COST!" Mr. Brown shouted.

"That bull gored a man and seriously wounded him. Angelo may yet die. And that animal's been loose since dawn terrorizing the countryside." Tom Harris's voice sounded firm and angry.

"I am not sure when he got loose," Mr. Brown answered lamely.

"He was not on your land when I shot him. A dangerous bull like that can't be allowed to roam free. You're responsible," Mr. Harris took a step forward.

Sam Brown backed off.

"What about Angelo's medical expenses?"

"What about them?" Mr. Brown asked.

"You'll pay them, since your bull gored him. The Army will send a man out to investigate. We shall have to tell him what happened." Tom Harris's eyes flashed with anger. Never had I seen such fury. I sat glued in my swing.

"How much do you reckon that bull's worth?" Mr. Harris continued.

"Two thousand dollars," Mr. Brown replied, his words punctuated by a great stream of tobacco.

"That's a lot of money, Sam. You mean your bull cost you that much? Surely you got him as a two-year-old, untried in breeding?" Mr. Harris picked up a stick and struck it against his leg.

"Yes, that's right. But his calves are fetching high prices now for breeding herds. And I have lost my best bull."

"That's a lot of money for a bull," Mr. Harris protested, "Diamond's blood's not that good. No blood stock is worth $2000."

"I breed the best," Mr. Brown replied, "I buy superior cattle."

"The best bloodlines, no doubt, but hardly the best temperament." Mr. Harris tapped his leg with the stick. "Tell you what, Sam, when I get the bill for Angelo's medical expenses I'll just send it on to you."

"What about the price of the bull?" Mr. Brown protested.

"I am not responsible for your bull, even though I killed him. You can be tried for negligence, Sam, and convicted. Everyone in the county knows your bull was loose and had roamed the countryside since dawn."

"I want to be compensated for the price of my bull," shouted Mr. Brown.

"Why? Where were you this morning? Neither you nor your men tried to capture Diamond Head, a bull known for its vicious temperament." Mr. Harris pressed his point. "It charged at a young child and might have killed it if I had not shot. And Angelo's wounds may still prove fatal. The way I see it. Sam Brown, I don't owe you a penny."

Slowly, step by step, Mr. Brown retreated backwards towards his car.

"I don't see it that way," he mumbled.

"Tell your Germans to turn on your electric fences. How many more bulls do you have?"

"Just a young one," Mr. Brown replied as he tripped over the pecan tree's roots.

"Is he mean also? Tom Harris followed tapping his stick against his leg.

"No, not really." Mr. Brown reached his car.

"Sam, you need to mend your fences in this county. First, I would recommend you get rid of your Diamond Head bull. That bloodline is generally mean. Secondly, I think we should settle this among ourselves."

"I agree with that." Mr. Brown got into his car.

"Then you pay for Angelo's medical expenses if the army does not. And we shall forget the price of the bull. I figure you'll get off easy because I could take you to court and lawyer's fees don't come cheap. And Sam, with all of the men that were here today to testify against you, I doubt you'd win."

I watched as the blue Dodge turned around and saw it get smaller as it went down the driveway – taking Mr. Brown with it. Dust from the tires rose and settled upon the dry grass. Finally the car reached the road, and the air cleared.

Mr. Houghton did not move. I continued to sit on the swing. Tom Harris hit his leg three times, slowly, rhythmically, with the stick. When it broke, he spun around and regarded me.

"Well, that settles it," he said and walked back towards us.

A Forgotten Landscape

64

Angelo's Story

For several days Angelo's life hung in the balance. Mr. Harris appeared terribly worried. One day at the general store, he even snapped at Arthur Henley.

"I hear Angelo is hurt bad," the proprietor said.

"Shut up, Arthur! I don't want to hear anything about the P.O.W. I can tell you nothing more."

Without saying another word, Tom Harris walked out of the store and drove away in his car. He left us standing there shocked, and for several minutes nobody spoke. The idea of Angelo's dying had unnerved him.

"He's mighty upset over that bull," Harrison Moore finally broke the silence.

"It would be a terrible thing if Angelo should die," agreed Mrs. Henley. "Even so, Tom Harris needn't bite out heads off."

Slowly in bewildered groups we left the store. Mr. Houghton gave Ethel the money for some motor oil, and we got into his car.

"You know," he remarked as we drove along, "Angelo will speak only in Italian. It's as if he's forgotten English entirely. Tom Harris can't get the whole story how Angelo was gored, and Sam Brown is getting anxious about his insurance money. Try as they will, nobody can find out exactly what happened."

"Funny that Angelo should forget all his English," I commented, "after he seemed so proud of it."

A few days later I heard that Mr. Harris had hunted up an old, retired professor from the College in Richmond. This Professor spoke both

Spanish and French, and also knew Italian. After some reluctance, he finally agreed to accompany Mr. Harris to the hospital and speak with Angelo.

"You reckon that will work?" I asked Mr. Houghton.

"Let's hope so. Tom's becoming damned annoyed about this whole thing. He's got Sam Brown breathing down his neck about replacing his bull. He's also in bad with the Army fellows about letting Angelo get gored. Tom's sailing under a heavy cloud these days."

The next afternoon, with the Professor in tow, Mr. Harris drove into town to the Army hospital where he hoped to get the whole story of Angelo's injury.

Angelo said he was awakened that morning when the bull got loose by a great bellowing under the window of his cabin. It was barely light, but he got up and peeked out to see what was the matter.

"The cows were running back and forth along the fence line as if they were being chased by something," he explained in Italian. "I got dressed, and went out to discover a great bull roaring like an elephant."

"And then," the Professor urged, "what happened next?"

"I picked up the shovel from my porch and approached the bull. El Toro ran up the fence line and tried to break into the pasture with the cows. I followed.

"When the bull suddenly came to the end of the fence, he swerved at the corner and stopped. Huddled together in a group, the fickle cows stood watching. I walked slowly holding the shovel out in front of me and made cow noises at El Toro. I wanted to use the shovel to grab the broken chain which hung from the bull's nose, so I approached him with caution. But that mighty one just walked in the opposite direction. I tried to catch him, but couldn't reach the chain. He's a clever old fellow, that one. Keeping the shovel in front of me, I walked after the bull speaking to him in soft Italian. He turned into the woods. I walked along easily so as not to startle him and make El Toro angry. His girl friends merely raised their heads and watched him go. But I knew that clever one might turn back for another chance with those ladies."

Angelo lay back on his pillow, trying to remember what happened. In the corner of the hospital ward sat Mr. Harris, hat laid across his knees, listening. The professor translated what had been said so far. Then turning back to the patient in the bed, he spoke in Italian.

"Continue with your story, please."

"When the bull entered the woods, I'm still following him. We found the land very marshy. A streams runs through that stretch of land into a clearing. Here a young Negress and her two-year-old son lived with the grandmother who works near Manakin. El Toro jumped the stream trying to double back towards his ladies. But he sank belly deep into the marsh. After a terrible struggle this clever fellow finally freed himself and re-crossed the stream to firmer ground. Angry because he could not reach the cows he entered the clearing, but decided immediately that's not where he wished to go. The ladies were a half a mile behind us.

"Suddenly, El Toro espied the cabin. At the well drawing water stood the young mother, the bambino holding onto her skirts. The bull galloped up the field towards them.

" 'Run, run,' I yelled to the woman. Clutching her bucket she raced towards the porch. The child, unable to keep up, dropped its mother's skirts and darted under the cabin.

" My baby, my baby," screamed the young colored woman scrambling onto the porch and spilling her water.

"The baby's cries broke the stillness of early morning – the bull rushed to the cabin and tried to get his head under the porch.

" 'Help, help,' screamed the mother, 'get that bull away from here. My baby will be kilt.'

"I raced towards the cabin. I tried to divert the bull's attention away and he galloped passed me. The mother grabbed her frightened child and scrambled back onto the porch.

" 'Go inside,' I shouted at her. 'Go inside.'

"But instead, she left the baby on the steps and raced across the yard to the well to refill her bucket. The baby's cries alarmed the bull, and it turned towards the cabin again. It spotted the girl and charged at her. Using my shovel as a cape, I deflected the charge, and spun to one side as the bull passed me. The girl stood frozen as the baby's terrified cries rose from the porch. El Toro turned and charged at the moving shovel. Again I spun. The woman ran back towards the porch dragging her bucket. I drew El Toro away from the cabin towards the woods.

"The bull shifted his attention towards me. He lowered his head and charged. As El Toro flew passed, I jumped aside. We were almost to the woods now. I thought of climbing a tree to allow El Toro to forget about this bullfight. I lowered my shovel and glanced around for a stout pine tree. The bull charged, caught my shovel in his horns and sent me spinning. With a mighty toss he sent the shovel skywards and charged again. I felt his horns sink deep into my groin. He tossed me aside like a rag doll and raced back towards his ladies. I am not worthy to wear the Suit of Lights in the bull ring – enough of El Toro."

The professor slowly rose from the bed and signaling to Mr. Harris, the two men left the room.

"This is a brave man," the Professor said as they departed. "He almost forfeited his life in order to save another. That this foolish woman and her child are alive today is due to Angelo."

Then, without further comment, he translated for Mr. Harris the rest of Angelo's story. Later that evening we learned the dairyman crossed the woods to the Negro cabin and told the grandmother. For several weeks nobody spoke to the young colored girl. Mr. Houghton told me.

"She's become a persona non grata." I wasn't quite sure what that meant, but I figured it was something bad.

65

When James Broke His Arm

Summer 1943

One day in midsummer Mrs. Houghton's telephone rang. It was a Thursday, I remember, because she was washing, and her hands were covered with soapsuds. So I answered the phone and could not believe the voice on the other end.

"It's Mrs. Haunch," I said in a hoarse whisper.

Mrs. Houghton wiped her hands with a dishtowel and took the phone.

"Hello. Yes, Mrs. Haunch. I'll tell him to come right away." She replaced the receiver.

"What does she want?" I asked.

"Harry, Harry," Mrs. Houghton called. "James has fallen out of an apple tree, and Mrs. Haunch wants you to drive him into Richmond to the doctor."

Mr. Houghton poked his head out of the wood shed where he was tinkering with his lawn mower.

"Why didn't she call the Taliaferros? They live closer."

"The Taliaferros left for the mountains yesterday. Mrs. Haunch can't drive, so you'll have to go."

Mr. Houghton entered the kitchen. He moved his wife's laundry out of the sink and washed his hands in the soapy water. Then he kicked off his boots. I noticed the white socks looked clean on his long narrow feet. Thoughtfully he wiggled his toes before he slipped them into his dress shoes.

"What's the matter with James?" He asked as he tied the laces.

"Mrs. Haunch thinks his arm is broken. He's sitting in the orchard, and she can't get him to move."

I stood in the kitchen waiting. I wanted to see that old lady hermit again, but dared not ask to go. As Mr. Houghton picked up his first aid kit, his eyes met mine, and he smiled.

"Come on, Doc, let's go have another look at the mysterious Mrs. Haunch."

"Mind now, you stay in the car," Mrs. Houghton instructed me, "and don't get in the way."

We drove to Mrs. Haunch's place both of us bursting with curiosity. What would she wear in the summer, I wondered? Had she had gotten her hair done. I couldn't wait to see her.

Nor did she disappoint us. Mrs. Haunch walked down her driveway to meet us dressed in bright red shorts and a frayed white shirt. Although her hair was cut shorter, I felt sure she had not combed it since Christmas. It stood up in gray wisps all over her head. When she came over to the car I noticed her legs were skinny and her knees knocked together. I wondered how old she was.

"Sixty," I thought "or even seventy." I couldn't really tell. "She must be at least seventy."

"He's still in the orchard," Mrs. Haunch greeted us.

I could see James sitting against a tree about two hundred yards away.

Mr. Houghton left me in the car, walked down a slight hill carrying a splint and his first aid kit. I watched him wrap James's arm onto the homemade splint, then help the colored man onto his feet. They came back towards the car, where Mrs. Haunch met them. I strained my ears to listen.

"Take him to the Retreat for the Sick. I'll call Dr. Jones to meet you there. Ask him to let me know how bad the break is," Mrs. Haunch commanded.

"What about the gas?" Asked Mr. Houghton.

"What about it?" The hermit replied.

"Well, I'll need to buy some, and I'll need a ration coupon."

"I'm allowed only three gallons a week," Mrs. Haunch told him.

"So are we all. But I can't take James into Richmond without gas."

When James Broke His Arm

Mrs. Haunch thought this over. Then she entered the house, and a few minutes later reappeared carrying her ration book.

Meanwhile Mr. Houghton helped James into the back seat of the car and put one of the two pillows, Mrs. Houghton gave us, under his head. The second one I placed under the broken arm.

"Thanks, Miss Doc," James groaned as we tried to make him comfortable. Then I gently closed the back door and climbed into the front seat.

"Here's my week's ration." Mrs. Haunch tore out one of the gas coupons.

"That's illegal," Mr. Houghton told her. "But I'll explain the situation to Mrs. Henley.

"She'll take them. I've done it before. Everyone cheats a little," Mrs. Haunch told him.

"They do? Perhaps you're right." Mr. Houghton got into his Chevrolet and switched on its motor.

"Don't forget to call me," Mrs. Haunch reminded him as she leaned against the open window on her elbows.

"I won't," Mr. Houghton promised, and we started down the driveway.

Then he drove back home so he could tell Mrs. Houghton we were going to the Retreat. Standing in front of her cottage, she waited for us holding a flask and a shot glass.

"Here, take these," she put the flask into my hands. "We'll give James a shot of this whiskey now for pain. It's a long thirteen miles into the hospital."

I poured out the Scotch whiskey while Mrs. Houghton held the glass. Then I handed it to a grateful James who drank it down.

"That's my best Johnny Walker," Mr. Houghton told us.

Carefully he drove down our long hill and headed for Henley's store.

"Give me another one of them drinks," James asked from the back seat. "I hurts."

Again I poured out the golden whiskey up to the glass's rim, and handed it to him.

"Thank you, little miss," he said.

As Mrs. Henley pumped our gas, I noticed she watched James sip his whiskey.

"Harry, you'd better be careful. James doesn't drink. And Mrs. Haunch would kill you if she knew he even touched whiskey. He would certainly lose his job."

But Mr. Houghton seemed more concerned about the torn-out gas coupon. First of all it was not his, and secondly it was not attached to the book. Mrs. Henley accepted it, knowing the black Ford would be in Mrs. Haunch's garage for a long time until James could drive it again.

"It's okay, Harry," she told him. "We won't get into trouble."

We left the store with James still sitting in the back seat propped up on his pillows sipping his drink. The car started down the hill towards Tuckahoe Creek.

"How are you doing?" Mr. Houghton asked as we bumped over the bridge at Black Bottom. "You look pale; do you feel white?"

James's laughter filled the car.

"Ha, ha," he chuckled. "That's a good one. I've never heard it before. Do I feel white? How do you feel white?"

Mr. Houghton looked embarrassed. He had forgotten about James's color. But Mr. Houghton always asked that question of anyone who was sick. He pushed his gnarled fist against the seat of the car raising his body up and letting it gently down again. A motion I had often seen him do when he felt agitated. Driving with one hand he hit a pothole causing James to spill the whiskey down the front of his shirt. I leaned over the front seat of the car and took the glass.

"Here's Mr. Houghton's handkerchief," I offered.

"I smells like a brewery," James observed, mopping his shirt front. "Milwaukee's got nuthin' on me."

"A grand smell, James, don't you think?" Mr. Houghton asked him.

"Yes, Sir, it sure do smell good, but not on me." Our passenger giggled as I handed him back his refilled shot glass.

On the outskirts of Richmond, James again complained his arm hurt.

" I needs another drink, Miss Doc, if you please."

I opened the flask and filled the shot glass for a fourth time. Then leaning over the seat I handed it to the half-drunken colored man.

"It sure do help the pain," James remarked as he sipped the whiskey.

"I shall not be, I shall not be moved," he sang between sips.

"Mr. Houghton," I inquired, "What do we do now? I am afraid James is drunk."

"Good, he'll feel no more pain. Put the glass, when he finishes it, in the glove compartment, and the flask under the seat."

I did as he said. When we turned into Grove Avenue, I knew we were now only about twelve blocks away from the hospital. In the back seat James started singing again.

"Sweet low, sweet chariot, coming for to carry me home. Swing low, swing chariot, dey is coming for to carry me home."

I began to worry. Mrs. Haunch frightened me. Suppose I caused James to lose his job? I was the one who had given him the whiskey. I knew Mrs. Haunch might get me into a great deal of trouble.

"What are we going to do? I asked Mr. Houghton. "Suppose James can't get out of the car?"

"He'll be all right. You'll see."

As we pulled into the hospital at the emergency room entrance, James was singing at the top of his voice.

"What a friend we have in Jesus. All our sins and grief's to bear. What a priv-a-lidge to carry Everything to the Lord in prayer. Yes, sir, das right."

When Mr. Houghton switched off the motor, we noticed a young man in a white coat walking towards us. He stuck his head in at my window.

"I am Dr. Jones. Mrs. Haunch called me and said you were coming in with James Post." Mr. Houghton just nodded and got out of his car.

I knew Dr. Jones by reputation. He was a teetotaler, (and that in Richmond was a rarity.) He was extremely strict about his patients' drinking. His daughter, Emily, was a class above me at school. And she loved to tell us horror stories about accidents caused by people who drank too much. I agreed with her in principle, but I found Emily's constant concern with whiskey tiresome. I realized, as soon as I saw Dr. Jones, we could all be in terrible trouble. I glanced at Mr. Houghton and James.

"Oh what peace we often forfeit, oh, what needless pain we bear," song burst forth from the back seat.

Dr. Jones regarded the coloured man propped up on his pillows.

"He's drunk," the doctor realized, looking at us in wonder.

"Yes," agreed Mr. Houghton, his blue-eyes sparkling with merriment. "I am very much afraid he is."

"But James doesn't drink. Are you sure this is he?" The doctor opened the back door. "This car smells like a distillery," he cried in alarm.

"I shall not be, I shall not be, I shall not be moved," sang James, his voice cracking. "Hi, doctor. I is James Post, Mrs. Haunch's gardener."

In disbelief the doctor turned to me.

"What's happened to him? Who gave him the whiskey?"

"I did. I gave it to him for the pain."

"You gave it to him? And how old, may I ask, are you?"

"Fifteen. I was fifteen my last birthday."

"Spare me," shouted the doctor very much agitated. "Where did you get whiskey?"

"Mrs. Houghton gave it to me. I just gave him what she told me." Considering the doctor's fury, I decided to lie.

His face now crimson, Dr. Jones fiddled with the buttons on his white coat.

"And who, pray tell, is Mrs. Houghton?"

"She's Mr. Houghton's wife." I replied helpfully.

"It's a long way into town, sir," Mr. Houghton explained. "The Missus thought one shot glass full of whiskey would relax James."

"One shot glass couldn't do this," Dr. Jones pointed to the prostrate figure in the back seat.

But Mr. Houghton no longer listened and started to help James out of the car. This proved no simple undertaking, so I got out to help.

"Well?" The doctor collared me, his face scarlet with fury. "Don't ignore my question."

"What question, Sir?" I replied.

"That man has drunk more than one shot glass full of whiskey."

"Yes, sir," I confessed. "I gave him four minus the part he spilled on himself."

Dr. Jones had heard enough. Furious, he stalked back into the emergency room and slammed the door. Mr. Houghton found it impossible to get James onto his feet. An orderly arrived with a wheelchair, and all three of us helped the poor drunken gardener into it. Then Mr. Houghton insisted on pushing the chair into the hospital.

"Crown Him with many crowns, the Lord upon His throne," sang James as we wheeled him in.

I realized we would never get away with this. Everyone in Richmond would know that Mr. Houghton and I brought poor old James into the hospital drunk. Mrs. Haunch would fire him on the spot. I felt awful guilty. Mr. Houghton and I were in big trouble. I wondered if they could put me in jail since I was under age to have whiskey. Although it was not really my whiskey, I had given James four big shot glasses full of Mr. Houghton's best Johnny Walker. I though it must be very potent.

Dr. Jones drew Mr. Houghton aside.

"Don't you realize," he said," that liquor and anesthetic don't mix?"

"Yes, er, no. Not really," Mr. Houghton stammered. "I did not think about your setting the arm, just getting him here."

"I shall have to call Mrs. Haunch," the doctor looked grave.

"Oh, no. Please don't do that," I begged, "or we'll be in terrible trouble."

But Mr. Houghton had the situation under control.

"I wouldn't do that," he said. "James is cold sober most of the time. He doesn't drink. That's why Mrs. Haunch hired him. If you call her about this, James will lose his job."

Mr. Houghton followed the doctor down the hall as a nurse came and wheeled James away.

"Sir," Mr. Houghton pressed his point. "You don't know Mrs. Haunch. If it gets around I drove her man in here drunk, I could be drummed out of the county. And God only knows what will happen to Doc."

"What will happen to her?" The doctor asked.

"I'll be locked up in the barn for a week," I replied. "My mother would kill me if she knew I gave James Scotch whiskey."

I was not really afraid of the consequences, but I would rather keep the whiskey a secret.

"Okay," the doctor dismissed us. "I'll keep it quiet. I'll call Mrs. Haunch once the arm is set. But we've got to sober James up first."

Mr. Houghton and I waited. We had to explain things to James. I hoped he would be able to understand. We sat in the waiting room, then went outside and walked around the block for a half hour. When we returned to the hospital, the nurse said we could see James.

At that time the floor for the coloured people was in the basement. Eventually Mr. Houghton found James, slightly tipsy, in the far corner of a long ward. He appeared terribly frightened, because he thought he was underground. Mr. Houghton tried to reassure him everything was all right. Then we promised James we would never tell a soul about the whiskey.

"No, sir," replied the colored man, "it's better we keep that experience under our hats."

It was five o'clock before we started home. On the way Mr. Houghton practiced on me several versions of what he would tell Mrs. Haunch. He could not decide which story he liked best, but that evening she called him.

"James is fine. He's coming home tomorrow," Mr. Houghton tried to reassure her.

"I see," replied Mrs. Haunch.

I could hear her, standing ten feet away from the telephone.

"I don't understand why Dr. Jones would not let me speak to James," the hermit complained. "The doctor sounded very mysterious."

"Well," Mr. Houghton replied. I could tell he was thinking fast. "Jame's accident became a lot more complicated than we originally thought."

Then without waiting for the hermit's reply, Mr. Houghton hung up the phone.

66

Sicily

July 1943

On the evening of July tenth we learned that the British and Americans had invaded Sicily. H. V. Kaltenborne told us that evening of the two landings: one by Patton's forces and a second by Montgomery's.

"The landings are on the southeast coast and surprised the Germans who were not expecting the invasion there. Admiral Sir Andrew Cunningham is in command of the British landings and the Americans are under the command of Vice Admiral Kent Howlitt. It's the largest amphibious operation ever attempted. The Americans have encountered stiff German resistance near Gela on the south coast, but the landings were almost unopposed. The Sicilians were delighted to welcome the Americans and even helped unload their landing craft. Now the objective is Messina to prevent the Germans escaping into Italy."

"Great," said Mr. Houghton, "the armies are back in Europe, if only on a remote outpost. At least we're making progress."

Several days later we heard that after 72 hours of hard fighting the British Forces had recaptured the bridge they'd lost and had reopened the way to Catania.

"Now the Germans are concentrating on the route to Messina," the radio told us.

We watched the newspapers closely and learned General Bradley had reached Palermo first, but had to wait for Patton to catch up before they could enter the city. Meanwhile, the Germans were in full flight towards Messina, but put up stiff resistance.

"At Palermo the Sicilians greeted the Americans with great cheering and rejoicing. General Montgomery has met with fierce resistance and is delayed. General Patton is spearheaded towards Messina to cut the German retreat off so they don't cross the strait over into Italy," H. V. Kalterborne told us. "The tanks outran their supply lines and were short of gas, so hand to hand combat resulted with heavy losses on both sides."

"That General Patton," complained Mrs. Houghton as she sat on her loveseat one evening, "he's a good field commander, but he and Montgomery sure don't get along."

"They both have big egos," replied Mr. Houghton. "Patton thinks he's God. He's supposed to have said, 'if I succeed, Attila will have to take a back seat.' That's cheek for you. Monty is just as bad, but they are both good generals. Ike has his hands full with those two competing for the glory."

"Meanwhile, the Germans are escaping," I added my bit to the conversation. "Patton is at least spearheading after them so they won't flee to Italy."

In the middle of all this excitement, Frances called from Florida to tell us that Father had malaria and will be sent back to an Army Hospital in England.

"He's all right, but malaria takes time to get over," she explained.

"I am glad," I said relieved, "now I can stop worrying since he's not in the fighting."

Frances told me not to get too relieved.

"There will be more fighting, you know. Your dad will want to be in on the liberation of Europe."

"Yes, but right now with Cary gone overseas and all this fighting in Sicily I can relax about Father's well being," I explained. "It's been a great burden."

Grandmother telephoned later and I told her I was very glad not to worry every day for my father's safety.

"You deserve a rest," she said. "You've done your part in this war. So enjoy a little respite," she understood.

"Oh," Mr. Houghton exclaimed, "I wish I were young again. I'd like to be in General Montgomery's forces pushing the Germans into the sea. I had a taste of combat in the First World War, but who wants an old crock like me? I'll never see thirty-five again if I live another fifty years."

"Harry, stop moaning," said his wife, "we are too old to fight and to do factory work. We can only do what we are able. We have a job here raising food and looking after Doc. If you were thirty-five you'd be chasing the girls, never mind fighting in a war!"

I laughed. Mr. Houghton glared at me. Mrs. Houghton covered her mouth with her handkerchief. I knew she was trying not to laugh.

"I was very popular with the girls once," he told us. "I was a real lady's man, a snappy dresser too with some fancy clothes when I could afford them. The ladies found me irresistible."

"Harry, stop filling the girl's head with such tales." Mrs. Houghton snapped.

"It's true, all true. You can ask Tom Harris if you don't believe me." Mr. Houghton replied.

"No, you can't, he didn't know you at thirty-five. You were in Canada then homesteading out in Alberta before I married you. Such tales you can tell, Harry. It's a wonder you can think them all up. Doc, don't listen to half he says."

I knew she wasn't really angry, and that this banter between them was just letting off steam. He exasperated her at times, and he teased her until she couldn't take any more. I let them blow at each other and got up and left the house. I wanted to ask Miss Emma if I could borrow a book, and this was a good time to do it. When I returned all would be peaceful once again. Mrs. Houghton would have her cup of tea, and Mr. Houghton would read the newspaper in his easy chair with Peggy in his lap. The world would return to normal.

July 1943
Sicily

Dear Doc,

As you can see by the letterhead I am in Sicily. We've managed to get a toe hold here. The people are friendly, and many asked about their relations in Brooklyn, New York and Chicago thinking that's a complete address. We have several Sicilians working for us now and reward them with C-rations because they are proud and don't want money. Food is more important right now.

The country is full of ruins, one citadel that was fought over by the Saracens is of little value to us now. There is also a lot of looting, and stabbing enemy soldiers in the back is a nocturnal occupation of the Sicilians who hate the Germans.

My legs are giving me trouble. My wound is scarcely healed, and my good leg is taking the weight. So I'm an old crock, just like your teachers.

Ernie Pyle dropped in the other day. He's a shy little man with a gentle smile, but a quick wit. I consider him one of the best war correspondents we've got. He seems to understand a soldier's life and his problems. We've taken Messina and things are looking good. We didn't stop the Germans from crossing the Strait into Italy.

Patton is the over all General in the Field, and Bradley is under him. I'm still G2, but again with II Corps. Tell Mr. Houghton to get out his champagne and celebrate. We've knocked Sicily out of the war.

Love, Dad.

P.S. I don't understand God either. It's a big subject for a young girl. There are many roads to God and much philosophy concerning Him. If He gives your life meaning and promises heaven that's reason enough to keep believing in Him. I agree He could have helped the Rats of Tobruk more after their long defense. You must make your own philosophy about God and work out your own beliefs. Learn about Him before you give Him up.

Dad

67

Grandmother's Phone Call

July 1943

After the Allies landed in Sicily on July 10th we followed their progress with interest as General Patton's troops in Seventh Army steadily worked their way north towards Palermo. No word came from Father during this time, and after two weeks I wondered if he were safe. Each day I spread the newspaper out across Mrs. Houghton's living room floor and studied the maps and read the war news trying to figure out where Father might be fighting. Worried about his wounded leg and the German resistance in Sicily, one afternoon I got into a big fight with Mr. Houghton.

He had sent me down to the big garden below our house to get lettuce for dinner. I returned with two large cabbages, and Mr. Houghton exploded.

"I sent you for lettuce, and here you've brought cabbages! Can't you tell one vegetable from another? You've lived in the country most of your life, surely you know the difference."

"Make cole slaw, then," I yelled, "You said the front row was lettuce, I got these from the front row. If they are cabbages, I can't help it."

I broke into tears and ran from the room. Nor did I stop running until I reached my favorite apple tree which stood in the middle of the orchard. Once there I climbed onto the upper-most limb large enough to hold me and sat down. Hot tears streaked down my face and tasted salty on my lips. I brushed my wet face against my sleeve to wipe away the floods of tears and looked out across the valley, which stretched far below me. Cicadas accompanied by tree toads filled the hot summer afternoon with their song. A haze spread up from the river making it more humid as the temperature rose. Still I sat in my leafy perch and licked my wounded soul.

"Doc, Doc," Mrs. Houghton's voice called me. "Doc, Doc, you're wanted on the telephone. It's long distance." Her voice sounded urgent.

Reluctantly I swung down from the branch where I sat and jumped to the ground.

"Yes," I called back, "I'm coming."

I walked slowly towards the house dragging my feet in the grass.

"Quickly, it's your grandmother," Mrs. Houghton told me as she opened the door.

I entered the cottage and picked up the receiver.

"Hello, Grandmother, is that you?" I could scarce believe my ears. "It's seems such a long time since I heard your voice."

"My dear, how are you?" said the voice on the other end. "I am sure you would like to hear some news of your father. It's not very good news, but he's safe now in England."

"In England? He's in a hospital there?" I inquired on the phone.

"You know he was wounded in Africa and got malaria in Sicily, so he's been sent to hospital in England. He's better now, and sends his love to you."

"How do you know?" I asked her. "Have you heard from him?"

"I received a phone call from Frances. I wanted to tell you myself, so that's why you haven't heard from her." Her voice sounded kind and deeply concerned.

"I understand, thank you for calling me. I'm trying to be a good daughter."

"You are a good daughter, Doc, and a very sweet person. Don't let anyone tell you otherwise."

"Oh, Grandmother," I sobbed into the telephone, "do you really think so?"

"Of course, my dear," came her firm reply.

"I've been in terrible trouble this afternoon over cabbages. I got them instead of lettuce, and Mr. Houghton and I had a big fight. I can't seem to do anything right. I am just a big twit."

The telephone went dead. The gentle voice was cut off. I pressed the button up and down several times to no avail. This often happened in the country. Either they are working on the line or the old equipment had given up the ghost. I felt cheated, just when I needed her most she'd been cut off.

Again I climbed into my tree. From away up in the sky among the leaves I could see the gentle valley stretching out far below me. Beyond that to the south a tall row of pine trees marked the bed of the James River. Behind me stood Mr. Houghton's cottage, and behind it, I saw his barn with its weather vane and his chicken house. Two guinea hens ran about its roof warning the inquisitive squirrels not to come any closer. Across the road hidden in the trees I could just make out the chimney tops of Emma Craddock's house. Up here I felt free, and master of all I surveyed. I sat back against the tree's trunk and tried to remember Father.

"What does he look like?" I wondered. "He's tall, very tall and has a brown mustache. He has dark, curly hair, a long, well-formed nose, and his eyes are a hazel color, I believe, like topaz." Most of all I remembered his laugh. It was a big jolly laugh that complimented a large man. "I guess he's what people call handsome, but he's also awe inspiring."

I felt sure the soldiers in the II Corps respected him and the judgments he made in his job as G2. I knew that meant intelligence, finding out what the Germans are up to.

I pulled my legs around the branch. In so doing my blue shorts caught on a twig and ripped.

"Oh, for heaven's sake. I am a mess already, and now I've torn my clothes. I'll be in big trouble again for sure."

Try as I would I could not remember the sound of Father's voice, although I recalled the things he'd told me. I thought his laugh his most remarkable characteristic. It used to escape from his throat in a shout, and he would hold his head back to let the noise spring forth and fill the room. Other people, I remembered, caught by this infectious roar would laugh with him. My world spun with their laughter. I clung onto the tree trunk and held on tight.

"Yes, that's right; he laughs like no other person I know," I said out loud. "He also tells stories. The French have a special word for a storyteller, a raconteur. Mrs. Houghton told me that once," I remembered.

A Forgotten Landscape

I wondered what he would think of me now. I looked down at my skinned knees and at my torn shorts and realized I must look like a big over-grown kid with a terrible temper. I must learn to curb my temper. Mrs. Owens says it is very unladylike to express uncontrolled anger. I do all the time, especially when I think of Mother and Rudy. I just have to think about them to get angry. I must stop it if I wish to become a real grown-up lady.

"I don't suppose Father would consider me very worthy to be the daughter of an officer in the United States Army," I thought. "Although Angelo calls me a Signorina, so I must be pretty okay at times. I certainly don't resemble that glamourous Movie star, Ann Sheridan, Mr. Houghton likes so much. Well, there is no hope of my looking like her – ever. But, I suppose, I could look like Miss Emma. She's very neat and trim in her suits. I'd rather look like Mrs. Taliaferro. She's a real lady. I wonder if she ever gets angry. Perhaps, but it's very well controlled. Becoming a lady is very difficult. I must stop biting my nails."

I climb up higher and more comfortably settled myself in the apple tree. Below me, spread out like a carpet, lay the countryside. I found it beautiful. My feeling of mystique for the land was a part of my southern heritage. Land speaks in its own special language to southerners and has its own special feeling. My great grandfather had fought for Georgia's red earth in the War Between the States and was wounded in the cheek at Antietam. The possession of land gives a permanence to life as each succeeding generation inherits it. People come and go, are born and die, but the land remains. Without it there would be no reason for wars or for dying for one's country. I was acutely aware of this southern mystique and held the countryside I surveyed from my perch in the tree as sacred.

"When I am dead and gone, this country still shall be here, and the river will flow towards Richmond as it does today. Only people will change and grow older," I told myself. "It's the land that endures and gives us life."

"Hello, Doc," a voice called. "What are you doing up there? I'm sorry we had words, you and I."

I looked down, and found Mr. Houghton looking up at me.

"Oh, just thinking. This apple tree is a great place in which to think," I replied.

Grandmother's Phone Call

"Are you hungry?" He asked trying to hit the bottom of my feet with his shovel handle.

"Sure," I said, pulling the shovel from his hands. "What are you offering?"

"A nice cup of tea, old girl, would taste good and a home-made sugar cookie to go with it, don't you think?"

"I think it sounds great," I let go of the shovel hoping it would not hit him on the head. "Okay, I'll come down. Besides it's getting too hot up there now."

Scrambling down from my perch on the top branch, I worked my way carefully through the tree's limbs until I could jump onto the ground.

"I heard about your father," Mr. Houghton said kindly. "And I understand the telephone went dead."

"As dead as a door nail right when Grandmother was telling me about him. Country lines are so unreliable." I commented following my friend down the path towards his cottage. "You'd think to help the war effort we could get some good service out here."

"Old Mrs. Brewster's tree fell over the trunk line and knocked out the whole lower end of River Road. You know the old lady who lives across Tuckahoe Creek?" Mr. Houghton replied as we entered his garden through the wrought-iron gate he's found recently in a junk yard in Richmond.

"How long will it take to repair? We shall be cut off out here for days if I know the telephone company. Country people don't rate with these people at all." I followed Mr. Houghton into his kitchen.

"And who may I ask is this scarecrow?" laughed Mrs. Houghton when she saw me. "Go into the bathroom and wash yourself. Have you been playing in a coal bin?"

"No, just up an apple tree," I replied realizing how dirty I was.

I happened to look under Mrs. Houghton's stove which stood on old fashioned legs, and found there a tiny pink creature. At first I thought it was a dog, but upon looking more closely I discovered a baby pig.

"What is that doing under your stove?" I turned to Mr. Houghton in amazement. "Where on earth did you get a pig?"

"Oh, that's Oscar," Mrs. Houghton explained. "He's Oscar Wilde, and he's just visiting us for a few days, I hope. I could tell she was not pleased to have Oscar as a house guest.

"But where did he come from?" I asked as I knelt down beside the cardboard box and examined the sleeping piglet.

"He belongs to Tom Harris," Mrs. Houghton explained laughing. "He came by this afternoon and left Oscar here. You see the old sow tried to kill him, and broke his leg. Harry has put a splint on it."

"But a pig under your stove? Suppose he messes up the kitchen?"

"He's paper trained, Doc. Pigs are very intelligent animals, and even the Missus likes this one." Mr. Houghton picked up the tiny creature and placed him in my arms.

The piglet did not open his eyes, just snuggled against my chest and let out a great contented sigh. As I patted him behind his ears, Oscar almost purred with contentment.

"Go wash up now, Doc," Mrs. Houghton put the pig back into his box, and placed some fresh newspapers down beside it. "Let's have our tea."

My unhappiness forgotten, I went into the bathroom and applied Yardley's nice smelling soap where I needed it most – on my hands, face and knees. Then I borrowed Mr. Houghton's comb I found on the window sill and tried to take the worst of the tangles out of my hair. Feeling refreshed I reentered the living room. A lovely tea was spread before me on the dining room table.

"How wonderful it all looks," I said as I took my place in the middle facing the open window.

Suddenly from the kitchen Peggy's sharp bark broke the afternoon's stillness. She and Oscar were enjoying a furious romp under the stove. The sleepy pig grunted and jumped about on his three good legs as the dog ran in circles around the table. Oscar was not as agile as the terrier and the game ended when he was knocked over, splint in the air, he rolled against the wall. At this point Mr. Houghton got up and separated the dog and pig, who still wanted to play. He finally thought it necessary to put a leash on Peggy and tie her to the leg of his chair.

"I've never seen anything so funny," I rolled with laughter. "Who would ever think a fox terrier and a piglet would have so much fun?"

Oscar sat in his box and eyed the dog, while Peggy whined for her freedom anxious to resume their game.

"That's enough," commanded Mr. Houghton. "Oscar must grow up to become a porker, and for that he needs four good legs."

"Porker?" I inquired. "You mean Mr. Harris plans to eat him?"

"Of course, that's why Tom's gone into the pig business. It helps the war effort and supplies him with meat." Mr. Houghton laughed. "What do you expect him to do with a pig?"

"Keep him as a pet," I replied. "Surely he won't eat Oscar."

"When he grows to be five hundred pounds Oscar will no longer be a pet. Come on, Doc, don't be so sentimental. Oscar is food. We have to get the goodness out of him." Mr. Houghton eyed me from his end of the table and smiled. "But we can have fun with him now until his leg mends."

After a lovely tea with bread Mrs. Houghton had baked that morning and strawberry jam she'd canned the previous spring, I forgot about the cabbages and lettuce. Still deep down inside me I remembered Father's illness and his being in England. But I didn't wish to think about him now with Oscar in his paper carton and lovely sugar cookies to eat. Later that night when I lay in bed in the dark just before I dropped off to sleep, I'd remembered Father and heard his big merry laugh once more.

Letters

July 29, 1943
Richmond, Va.

Dear Dad,

    The summer's awfully hot, and Mr. Houghton lost six chickens from the heat. He keeps a fan going in the chicken house day and night so no more will die. So far no more have. Peggy just sits about and mopes. Even Mrs. Houghton's stopped knitting. The wool's much too itchy. Jean Taliaferro invited me up to swim in her pool. Was that ever a treat! Mrs. Houghton went too, but she didn't exactly swim, just paddled waist deep in refreshing water. All the horses are kept in during the day and turned out at night.

    Last evening we went to the movies because it was the coolest place we could find. The picture was silly, but we enjoyed it all the same. We even stayed while they played the *Star Spangled Banner*, which they do now at the end of every picture show. Everyone is supposed to stand up, but some people leave. Mr. Houghton thinks that's disrespectful, so we stand at attention until it is over. Then we leave.

    Today the thunder came bringing sheets of rain and great forks of lightning. So the heat's broken at last, and we all feel better. Mrs. Houghton says we shall go to the mountains soon, but Mr. Houghton can't seem to find the time. Mr. Harris has to get in touch with his cousin to come again and take care of the animals. I'm looking forward to going, it'll be great to be where it's cool.

    Love, Doc

68

The News

August 1943

We sat horrified by the news of General Patton's slapping two soldiers in Sicily. We couldn't believe our ears, as H. V. Kaltenborne told us the story.

"It's a very serious offense to hit an enlisted man," Mrs. Houghton replied. "It should never have happened. What was General Patton thinking when he did such a thing. No officer, not even a three star general has the right to commit such an offense. It's a wonder he wasn't relieved of his command."

"There is such a thing as battle fatigue. I've seen such cases in the First War. Men just couldn't take any more. They shake and cry and plain crack up. What's wrong with Patton? He should know that." Mr. Houghton asked again. "It is unthinkable for a man in his position to do such a thing."

Apparently General Patton had visited a hospital in Messina, and after seeing several men with very grave wounds, met this young soldier by the name of Bennett who told the General his nerves were bad. Furious at the young man, Patton had hit him with his gloves and told him he was gold-bricking, and he was a coward. Patton had to apologize to the whole Army for his actions. Then he was relieved of the Seventh Army and sent back to England.

"I'll write Father and ask him about it," I said. "Surely it's a mitake.

"It's no mistake, I'm afraid Patton has opened his big mouth once too offten," Mr. Houghton told me. "He can move troops and is a great general in the field, but he uses foul language and can't control his temper."

"Will Ike use him again, or will that be the end of Patton? I've gotten so I like him in spite of his bad language and his temper," I asked.

"It looks bad for him now. But he's too good a general to leave out when they go in to liberate Europe. They will use him again. This will blow over in a few months. People have short memories." Mr. Houghton got up to look after his chickens tossing Peggy onto the floor. She whimpered and jumped back into his chair. "You little begger," he told the dog, "taking my chair for yourself."

The newspapers made a big deal out of Patton's slapping incident, but gradually the General's troubles left the front page and he was forgotten.

69

A Mystery at Afton Mountain

Summer 1943
August

The Blue Ridge Inn looked sad. It needed paint which was now hard to come by, and it also needed repairs. Yet it was the friendly place it had always been. The Brennans greeted us as usual and showed us to our rooms.

"I am not sure Professor Morrison will be here with the children again this year. She rang us yesterday, and is booked in for tomorrow. She hopes to get here, but gas rationing is causing her a problem," Mr. Brennan told us.

After a little rest, Mr. Houghton and I took Peggy for a walk. The day was warm, but a little breeze cooled the late afternoon.

"I wonder what Miss Edith has cooked up for us to do this year," I remarked as we walked along the mountain path. "I hope not Luray Caverns again."

"She wouldn't dare take you when you acted such a fool last year. She'd be embarrassed ever to show her face there again," Mr. Houghton said.

"I'd like to see Monticello and Ashlawn near Charlottesville; that would be interesting," I commented stepping over logs and pine needles on the forest floor. "These paths are terribly overgrown since last summer."

"Got nobody to clear them with everyone of working age away at the war," explained Mr. Houghton as we made our way slowly back towards the Inn.

"The Inn, itself, was an old ramshackled building perched on the side of the mountain overlooking Rock Fish Valley. It had a long porch upstairs with rocking chairs on it and a pleasant dining room. The food was simple, but good, and the Brennans kept the place looking neat and trim. That was why I felt surprised it hadn't been painted and kept up. The same people returned year after year. Some customers were transients, but most were annual visitors. It was not expensive, and yet it was a welcoming, friendly place. Mr. Houghton didn't want to drive any long distance in his old car, so they preferred this little Inn to some untried hotel in the Blue Ridge Mountains. They returned each summer, usually in July. This summer with all the excitement at home with Angelo and James breaking his arm we just couldn't leave. Finally, Mr. Harris insisted we go, and got his cousin to come once again to look after the farm.

"Doc will be starting school before you can get you vacation," he told us. "Make you reservations and go."

And that's what we did. Mr. Houghton didn't have time enough to worry about his chickens and his horses before we were packed and on our way. He even forgot his long-handled shovel for snakes.

At dinner we met Rodger Schmidt and his wife as they came into the dining room.

"What are they doing here?" I asked Mrs. Houghton as we sat at our table.

So Mr. Houghton asked them, "What are you doing in these parts?"

"Harry, it's none of your business. Stop being nosey." Mrs. Houghton scolded him.

"We're just passing through," Mr. Schmidt replied. "This is my wife, Elaine. Mr. and Mrs. Houghton and Doc. I know them from church." He introduced us.

I'd never met Mrs. Schmidt before; in fact, I never knew there was one as she never came to church. I found her a pretty woman and less severe than her husband.

A few minutes later a distinguished-looking man joined them at their table. He wore a suit and was not at all casual looking for the mountains. I was curious.

"We've got problems," Rodger Schmidt remarked. "We've got too many pro-Germans in the financial world today. The task of financing this war is difficult, and we must keep the dollar sound and predictable."

"Yes, I agree," his companion said. "The Secretary of the Treasury, Henry Morganthau's idea of buying war bonds has helped, and now everyone is encouraged to put a little of his salary into them each month. The war bond sales have gone up."

"Morganthau is a good man. He's a Jew, who is a long-standing friend of Roosevelt's and thouroughly trusted. He was opposed to the interment of Japanese Americans on the west coast. He also helped to organize the War Refugee Board which helps Jews and other refugees who come here. He's very sympathetic and understands their plight," Mr. Schmidt replied.

"Yes, and he knows his stuff about helping agriculture too. He's been a good person in the Treasury. Roosevelt picked well." The strange man stopped talking to order his meal.

"There are too many pro-Germans in the banks. Montague Norman, the head of the Bank of England is one, and that's caused us considerable worry. Several of the petroleum companies are also pro-German, especially the boys at Standard Oil of New Jersey. Morganthau is opposed to the Swiss Banks for that reason. He doesn't trust them. He is sure they are financing Hitler and this war," Mr. Schmidt said.

Had I misjudged this man with the German name? Why was he meeting this important-looking person here at the Blue Ridge Inn? It still appeared "fishy."

Mrs. Houghton distracted me. "It's not polite to listen to other people's conversations," she said. "Doc, forget about Rodger Schmidt and eat your dinner."

"I know, but I thought he was pro-German. Apparently he's not. He seems very sympathetic to the plight of the Jews," I replied. "I misjudged him, and I'm sorry."

We continued to listen to our neighbors' conversation fascinated.

"Francis Biddle is a weak Attorney General," Mrs. Schmidt commented. "He can't seem to flush out the Nazi sympathizers."

"Harry Truman, the Senator from Missouri, is honest and has looked into things. Army waste and misspent funds are a problem, and he's put an end to that business," their friend replied. "Why can't they get Philadelphia to make ball bearings, for instance, when the Allies are short of them? It's like that America First group headed by Charles Lindbergh. It's a front for the Nazis."

"Yes, I know that," said Rodger Schmidt; "there are a lot of German sympathizers in high places. I can't believe the banking cartel; it's very anti-American. We have trouble, even in Richmond, doing business with them."

"Henry Ford and his son, Edsel, are both pro-Nazi. It's a know fact that he spreads propaganda through his company's magazine," Mrs. Schmidt explained.

"I hear Hap Arnold is having trouble getting engines and supplies for his air fleet. Our boys are getting killed over there now, and the government seems powerless to supply the necessary war goods for them," the man from Washington said between mouthfuls of his dinner. "It's a dangerous situation. We must dig out these pro-Germans in high places."

"Yes, I agree. I hear the Duke of Windsor keeps coming here on "personal business." He's another one that is pro-German. Hitler wants to make him king once he defeats England. That Wallis Simpson is dreadful with all her airs, and yet she's a hundred percent behind the Nazis too."

Mrs. Houghton heard Mrs. Simpson's name and bristled.

"That woman. That awful Simpson woman. She's caused enough trouble. The British will never accept her as queen, Hitler or no Hitler. I don't doubt she's a Nazi sympathizer if Hitler has offered her the British throne."

"Now, Duck, calm down. There's little chance of that woman ever ruling England. The Nazis just want to get the goodness out of her, that's all," Mr. Houghton said, trying to calm his wife. "They'd offer her anything, and the Duke's stupid enough to go along with their schemes."

"You two stop listening to what's being said, it's impolite as well as upsetting." Mrs. Houghton glared at us. "Finish your dessert and go take Peggy for a walk, I'm going out on the porch."

We did as we were told.

On August 17th General Patton beat General Montgomery to the Straits of Messina, but in spite of the British and American efforts the

Germans had escaped over that body of water to the boot of Italy. Although Patton had driven his troops hard and moved fast they were too inexperienced to stop the Germans. The casualties were high, and some of Pattons men had massacred unarmed prisoners of war. A few days later General Patton slapped a soldier in a hospital in Sicily suffering from battle fatigue and caused a major ruckus.

"That's certainly no way for a General in the United States Army to behave," Mr. Houghton told us at breakfast. "That's disgusting. Patton must be crazy."

"He could be sent home for that," Mrs. Houghton commented, "but Patton is too good a soldier because he gets the job done. This incident could end his career."

"General Eisenhowwer has his hands full, I agree. He won't dismiss Patton, but Ike might demote him; take away one of his four stars as a punishment." Mr. Houghton gave Mrs. Brennen our order. It was early and we were alone in the dinning room. I hoped the Schmidts hadn't left because I wanted to find out more about them.

"They allowed the Germans to escape," I added, "now what are they going to do?"

"Go into Italy, I suppose. What else can they do?" Mrs. Houghton offered me a hot biscuit.

"How many troops got away?" I asked.

"About fifty or sixty thousand," Mr. Houghton told me. "They will regroup and rearm. The they will fight again. I don't fancy being in Italy now."

"Where does the Pope live?" I asked. "Is he in Rome?"

"Yes, in a city called the Vatican within the city of Rome. Mussolini made some sort of deal with the Pope that allowed him to rule the Vatican and the Catholic Church, and Mussolini to rule the rest of Italy."

"Why doesn't the Pope speak out about the Jews?" I persisted. "If he's God's representative why doesn't he support God's Chosen People?"

We sat in silence once again eavesdropping on our neighbors at the next table who just entered the dinning room.

"It's good to see you now, Rodger," his friend said. "The mountain air has raised my spirits. It's great to get out of Washington with all its intrigues."

"We'll be here for a few more days. I can meet friends and not be bothered by the government officials I have to deal with. It's quiet, and we get a rest."

"Yes," added, Mrs. Schmidt, "it allows us a few minutes away from work. I find the pressures of Richmond very heavy. This is a nice retreat."

"She loves the mountains," Mr. Schmidt explained. "We can walk and take drives to Charlottesville, if we have the gas. It makes a nice holiday."

Shortly afterwards his friend left. I noticed the car he drove had Washington license plates, and the Congress's X ration code on its windshield allowing extra gas. Was he some biggy-wiggy who came down to consult with his friend upon the state of things? I wondered why ball bearings were so hard to come by, and what caused Hap Arnold to have so much trouble getting engines for his air fleet.

"Surely everyone is working to win this war," I said aloud.

"Apparently not everyone. The financiers are suspect, and into each other's pockets here and overseas," Mrs. Houghton replied. "I read that General Motors is also suspected of being pro-German."

"I hated to hear Mrs. Carthage when she told me Lindbergh was pro-Nazi. I just couldn't believe it. How can anyone live in America and think that way?"

"The head of the Bank of England, Mr. Schmidt said, is also suspected of being pro-German. How could he, when England has been brought so low by the German onslaught?" Mrs. Houghton asked us.

"He's a financier; you can never trust those fellows," quipped Mr. Houghton.

"You're as bad as Doc with her spies and Fifth Columnists. Where do you get such ideas? You read too many detective novels," Mrs. Houghton scolded us.

The next morning Miss Edith arrived with Gillian and Jenny. Hugh, now six years old, was still in the charge of Nanny Grace who kept him out of our hair. He was an awful pest. As usual, Miss Edith had things planned, but so did I.

"You must join us again," she collared me as she came onto the porch to greet us.

"I don't wish to return to Luray Caverns, but if you go to Monticello and Ashlawn, the homes of Jefferson and Monroe I might consider joining you," I told her straight away.

"How far is that? Gas is a problem these days," she replied. "How far is Monticello?" We could only drive thirty-five miles an hour now as the speed limits had been reduced to save gas. The trip to Monticello could take most of the day.

"I don't know," I replied, "I am sure the Brennans can tell you."

"Yes," she agreed, and left the porch to find them.

Gill and Jenny greeted me and asked me to join them.

"It's fun when you're along. Auntie Edith can get over bearing. Do come with us again," Jenny begged.

"No more caverns, please," I said, "and that's final."

Miss Edith decided we could go to Monticello and started making preparations. She asked if Mr. Brennan could pack us a picnic lunch and tell us where there was a park or picnic grounds. He must also give her detailed directions to Charlottesville.

"I've no extra gas on which to get lost. So it's straight down and straight back." She took out pen and paper and wrote down the directions and a little map marked in red where she should turn off the highway. "Now let me read this back to you," she told Mr. Brennan.

The next morning we three girls and Miss Edith all piled into her car for the trip to Charlottesville. In spite of the directions, Miss Edith got lost, and we had to double back before we discovered the road to Monticello. This did nothing to sweeten her temper, but finally we entered the mansion's gates and drove up to the parking lot behind the house. It was still early and few people were there. Miss Edith got our tickets, and we joined a tour.

"Jefferson was very clever," remarked Jenny as we learned about his life and his inventive ideas in architecture and furniture design.

"Yes," I replied, "he was extremely clever, and he had red hair."

Gill laughed, "I expect he had a fiery temper – red heads do, you know."

"He probably did. I know he wrote the Preamble to the Constitution and the Declaration of Independence."

"I love his clock in the hall that works on weights. It tells everything," Jenny said. "Time, tides and if you smell bad or not."

Miss Edith herded us back into the car, and we started down the mountain to Ashlawn, the home of James Monroe, our fifth president. Here we found a place to have our picnic. Less grand and without the marvelous view, Ashlawn is friendly like the homes of ordinary people. I preferred it to Monticello.

"I'm going into the gift shop," I announced. "Mrs. Houghton collects china teacups made in England. I shall find her a set for a little gift."

I had saved my chicken money because Grandmother had raised my allowance to a dollar a week, and I could afford to save. I was very proud of the five dollars I'd put carefully aside for the trip to Afton. Now, I wanted to spend it on Mrs. Houghton who had taken me into her home and loved me.

Miss Edith, for once, didn't seem to mind if we browsed. She took out a book and, sat under a shady tree. Jenny told me later that they resented being herded like cattle from place to place. She had informed her aunt that I refused to join them if she didn't stop treating us like small children. Apparently it worked. Gill, Jenny, and I found the gift shop interesting, and I bought an English china cup and saucer with violets on them.

"Mrs. Houghton will love these because violets are her favourite flower," I remarked. "They are very pretty. I'm lucky to find English china in war time."

The afternoon grew hot, and Miss Edith closed her book.

"It's time to go home," she said, "back to the mountain breezes."

The drive home was uneventful, but when we reached the Blue Ridge Inn, I discovered Rodger Schmidt and his mysterious friend still there. Once again I felt intrigued.

"Do you think he's here hiding from the pro-German financiers?" I asked Mrs. Houghton.

"No, he's on holiday, just as we are," she told me firmly.

I handed her my package. She sat on one of the porch swings and opened it.

"Oh, how beautiful!" she exclaimed, touched by my gift. "You know how I love violets."

She gave me a hug, then disappeared into her room to show Mr. Houghton who was lying down and reading the newspaper. I knew she would then put my present carefully away until we reached home. There she would display it in the cabinet in her living room where she kept several other cups and saucers she'd collected over the years. I felt happy I'd pleased her.

I sat down and pondered Rodger Schmidt's appearance at the Blue Ridge Inn. I felt he must be a spy or at least suspicious. A chance remark of Mrs. Brennan's explained things. Apparently Rodger Schmidt lived in a very difficult position – between the Federal Reserve Bank and Washington there had been some contention.

The Depression had caused the dollar to become unsound. In order to control the dollar, Roosevelt had closed the banks for several days. Some banks failed and others had runs on them when depositors took out their money all at one time. Rodger Schmidt had been sent to Richmond to get things back on an even keel. His wife found her husband's long hours difficult. She was Jewish, married to a Christian, which also put her into an awkward position. They had found this little Inn tucked away in the mountains and started coming. I was close enough to Washington so that people Mr. Schmidt wanted to see in the government could come down for a few days to talk over things. It was far enough away from the beaten path and inexpensive enough not to attract the people with money Mr. Schmidt knew in his business. Mrs. Schmidt found it relaxing, and she liked it. So they came every year, and every year the people from Washington came down too.

I was disappointed with this explanation. I wanted a real spy story. Mr. Houghton did also because he liked cloak-and-dagger tales too, and between the two of us, we'd hatched an exciting spy mystery.

"You see," Mrs. Houghton told us, "I knew he wasn't all that sinister. There usually is a simple explanation."

"Yes," I had to agree, "but it would have been a lot more fun if he were a spy."

A Forgotten Landscape

Letters

Somewhere in England
August 24, 1943

Dear Doc,

  I am happy you've enjoyed another trip to the mountains. I often went to the Virginia mountains as a child, but not to Afton. All I can remember are the snakes. All kinds of them lived in the woods and came out to sun themselves on the rocks. How like sticks they appeared, and once I picked one up thinking it was a stick. When Mother shrieked in horror, I threw it at her – not meaning to, of course, but it certainly went in her direction. Fascinated, I watched the snake crawl away ignoring my mother's terrified cries of alarm. When my Georgia aunts arrived they discovered nothing more dangerous than a small boy, his eyes glued to the ground, and pale and gasping mother. After that I was more careful about choosing sticks.

  My elder brother, Tad and I were never allowed to swim except on weekends when our father arrived from Washington where he was stationed with the Army. He was a career officer, you know, and a general. The place in the river deep enough for swimming was called Blue Hole. It was fed by a mountain stream and was freezing cold. Only we boys and my father ever swam since bathing costumes for ladies were made of a serge material and were unsuitable for mountain bathing. They preferred to sit on the porch of the inn and rock in white wicker chairs and talk. The same people came back year after year. We boys swam in the all-together carefully sheltered from female eyes.

  It was the most out-of-the-way place. After a train ride from Washington to Harrisonburg, Virginia, we had to take a wagon with two mules back into the mountains to Raleigh Springs. It was an inexpensive watering hole, and allowed my father to come on weekends, being close enough from Washington. It was a bad place for little boys. There was nothing for us to do.

  I never knew why Raleigh Springs was so favored by my family. It was, however, a direct line from Atlanta on the train that went to Washington. It stopped in the valley to pick up mail as well as to carry a few passengers. Then from Harrisonburg it was six or seven uncomfortable miles in a wagon to Raleigh Springs.

There was nothing there except the hotel and a few houses for visitors. It was hardly a village, more like a hamlet. The aunts, dressed in white from head to foot, sat with their lace fans on the veranda rocking like a chorus in their wicker chairs. With their fans moving in unison with their motion, they chatted and laughed about boring things until dinner. We couldn't afford Hot Springs or White Sulphur, so the aunts made the trek up to Raleigh Springs every August to get out of Atlanta's heat. Gently poor, my father paid the aunts' fares up to Raleigh Springs, and sometimes he took them on an excursion into Washington. That caused some excitement. The three old ladies fussed for days about their clothes, their hair and their anticipation. Mother, Tad, and I would watch them go on a Sunday when my father returned to the city, and see them return five days later filled with chatter about their doings in the big city. For years, I remember, my father gave these ladies a month's holiday in the mountains. All Tad and I did was to get in trouble. I have horrors of finding another place like Raleigh Springs, surely there can't be another. What memories come flooding back to me of yesterdays.

Love, Dad

A Forgotten Landscape

70

Growing Pains

September 1943

Angelo remained in the hospital for over a month. Finally he was moved into the Army Clinic for Rehabilitation. When several of the wounded servicemen there objected because he was a P.O.W., Angelo shared a room with an Italian-American named Mario. Together they spoke their own language and soon became fast friends.

During the first week in September when the Allies landed in Southern Italy, the Germans still held Rome and Florence. Then we heard a rumour that as the country became overrun with Allied soldiers, the Italians defected in great numbers. Meanwhile, fleets of planes bombed Turin and Milan, and even as far as Tuscany. This news made Angel very sad because his family lived near Florence, and he feared for their safety. For several weeks he had spoken only Italian with Mario and his English had become rusty. So Mrs. Harris borrowed an English grammar from Mrs. Tillage, the fifth grade teacher at Manakin school, and took this book into Angelo.

"You had better study," she told him, "so we can understand each other when you come home."

Several times during the summer Mr. Harris drove me into the hospital for a visit. Angelo and Mario usually chatted with me about fishing and the latest county news. Then one dull afternoon when the war news seemed especially bad, Mario taught me to play poker. We played for a penny ante, and I found this card game great fun. On my next visit, I even beat Mr. Harris from whom I'd borrow my pennies.

In September after school commenced, my time became more limited. Mary Ann invited me to go with her to St. Peter and Paul's church group and attend the dances at Camp Lee. These were chaperoned affairs to entertain our boys in uniform at the Army installation in Petersburg. To this little City, located about twenty miles south of Richmond, we drove down, usually on Friday evenings, in a chartered bus.

At first I did not really enjoy dancing with the servicemen. Then one evening I met a young sergeant from Indiana named Teddy Rohr. He was not an especially good dancer, so I did not feel intimidated. He knew all sorts of different steps and taught me several. If I tread on his toes, he only laughed and did not seem to mind. I found him a lot easier to dance with than the boys I knew at the Richmond cotillion. They always wanted their partners to dance perfectly and acted disgusted whenever I made the slightest mistake. With Teddy, I found dancing fun, and enjoyed myself.

"This is great," I told him one evening as we glided around the makeshift dance floor at Camp Lee.

"Of course," he replied, "where have you been all of my life?"

"In the country, I live eight miles outside the city limits of Richmond."

"That do make it nice; I'll come see you sometime," he suggested as we started to dance again. "This one's a rumba. That's right, just swing your hips. See how easy it is?"

"How will you get out to my house? There're no buses, so you'll have to walk from the golf course on River Road." I had a horror he might just arrive on my doorstep one day unannounced, and I would not know what to do with him.

"Suppose I come next Sunday when I get my leave?"

The music changed, and we glided across the dance floor once again to a familiar Glenn Miller tune, "Pennsylvania 6, 5000."

"It's a very long way, and you can't walk to Goochland in this heat."

Suddenly I wished Teddy would visit me in town at Mary Ann's house because she would know how to entertain him. There were many more things we could do in town, such as go to the movies or visit friends. We could even walk in Byrd Park and feed the ducks. I realized some of my city friends disliked coming to the country because they felt I had little to offer: no boys, no shops, and no drug stores.

Teddy and I sailed around the dance floor bumping into other couples and ended up laughing so hard we had to stop.

"Let's go find the refreshments," he suggested as he took my hand and led me towards a large table at the far end of the room.

"My grandmother lives in Indianapolis, do you know her?" I asked.

"I am not sure, but I went to school with your cousin, Eric," Teddy replied. "Maybe when I come on Sunday I can bring my buddy, George? I'll introduce you. So please give me your address and phone number."

I was not sure I wanted him to come, nor was I happy to give him my phone number. I was not accustomed to just pass it out and I felt somehow taken advantage of. Finally, with great reluctance, I gave it to him. Then we went in search of Teddy's friend, George, who turned out to be an unpleasant young man. I thought he had a hard northern accent and a chip on his shoulder.

"If you do come on Sunday, afternoon would be better," I suggested as the chaperones began to gather their groups together.

At exactly midnight our chaperone, Mrs. Merrick, led her group out of the dance hall into the parking lot.

"Stay together, girls," she commanded. "That's our bus over there, the yellow one, number 64."

Mrs. Merrick read our names out as we boarded the bus for the twenty mile drive over the dark turnpike back to Richmond. It was almost one o'clock when Mary Ann's mother finally picked us up at the church and drove us home.

The next morning we rose early, so we could take advantage of a big sale at the corner drug store. Everything was advertised at half price. I had 20 dollars in my purse, and I wanted to buy a new dress.

"We can buy the lipstick and powder before we catch the bus down to Miller and Rhoads. Then we will buy you a sophisticated dress in case the boys do show up on Sunday," Mary Ann bounced out of bed.

"I doubt very much if they come," I replied, hoping they wouldn't come. "Besides, I hate to get dressed up. Perhaps a new dress isn't really necessary."

Luxuriously, I stretched my legs out in the big double bed admiring the handsome canopy and the beautifully carved wood.

"I just love this four poster; it's so old fashioned and romantic with the eyelet cover and pillow shams."

"Come on, Doc, stop fooling," Mary Ann jerked off the covers and pulled me out onto the floor. "This was my great Aunt Myria's bed. Mother did it over for me about two years ago. It's pretty, don't you think?"

"It's gorgeous. What was your great Aunt Myria like? Or was she just a funny old lady who wore black dresses and cameos?" I sat down on the edge of the bed and ran my hand over the smooth rosewood.

"Oh, she was delightful, really an old Southern Belle with lots of beaux. She even had men coming to call and wanting to marry her after she became a widow. Aunt Myria loved to travel, and she met some Count in Italy on one of her trips. You can imagine how that upset the family. Her brother, my great uncle Arthur, was terribly afraid she would marry some foreigner. Eventually she came home to Virginia and lived with her sister. But Aunt Myria was an incurable romantic." I watched as my friend got into her clothes.

"Hurry up, Doc, or we shall miss the sale," Mary Ann flounced down the stairs.

I pulled myself together and got dressed. Then, looking around the big sunny room, I admired its fine old furniture. Mrs. Thornton was a very clever woman and made most of Mary Ann's clothes. She could just cut out a picture from a magazine and create a pattern in just the right size. My friend had beautiful clothes, many of them new. So Mary Ann could not understand my wearing Mother's hand-me-downs. I mostly got wool suits made over to fit me, because they always contained fine material no longer available in the stores. Mother also made some of my dresses, but I did not think they had much style. I owned few clothes because she believed I should be economical and learn the value of things.

Finally dressed, with my hair combed, I spread the bed up and carefully put on the eyelet coverlet. Its soft pink matched the curtains at the bay windows making the room appear beautiful and feminine. I envied Mary Ann's elegant bedroom. Then I hurried to follow her down the stairs.

After a hearty breakfast, we scooted down the street towards the drug store.

"Be prepared; that's my motto," Mary Ann remarked as we walked along. "A new dress will do wonders for you. Something sophisticated perhaps."

"I am not so sure about that," I told her.

"Never mind; you can always wear it on Sundays. You can't wear riding pants and shorts all of the time."

"I can't spend more than twenty dollars. That's the limit. Mary Ann, I'm worried. I am not sure what to do with city boys in the country. How do you entertain them?"

"Just ask them what they would like," she suggested as we entered the drug store. Here we discovered a whole counter full of cosmetics. Mary Ann helped me buy some lipstick before we headed down to Miller and Rhoads on the bus.

"You look just like a girl," Mr. Houghton greeted me with astonishment as he entered his kitchen later that afternoon.

"I am a girl," I reminded him.

"It's easy to forget," he teased, winking at me. "Because you're more like a boy most of the time."

"I am?" I regarded him in disbelief.

"Well, not exactly like a boy, of course," he corrected himself, flustered, "but not like a conventional young lady either."

"Angelo calls me , Signorina," I reminded him.

Suddenly I felt guilty. I had not seen Angelo since he came home. The Army had put him into Mr. Harris' custody.

"You need to visit Angelo, Doc. He asked about you again the other day when I went up to the dairy," Mr. Houghton regarded me in a serious manner. "I'll take you with us when we go up next Saturday."

On Friday afternoon we sat in Mrs. Houghton's living room and drank tea. I was still worried about Teddy and George's visit on Sunday and felt anxious to discuss it with my friend.

"Enjoy your youth while you have it, dear. It goes very quickly, but don't neglect your friends. You are growing into a young woman, and it is natural for boys to find you attractive."

Mrs. Houghton poured me a second cup of tea and offered some homemade cake. I realized I had also neglected her. I tried to tell her how sorry I felt.

"Never mind, Doc, you are still a girl. Being a woman comes slowly. It also brings responsibility for your actions. Your church group has kept you pretty busy lately. But isn't Angelo your special concern? Remember, you found him." Mrs. Houghton smiled kindly from her place on the loveseat.

I nodded. Since boys played such a small part in my life, I had found Teddy's attention a novelty. I had also discovered I enjoyed going to dances and meeting new people. It made me feel more like other girls my own age. Besides, Teddy knew my cousins in Indianapolis, and we found a lot to talk about. In recent weeks I had forgotten Angelo, but I had not meant to neglect him. In fact, I had a little gift to take him.

"Perhaps I can stay a girl for a few years longer," I told Mrs. Houghton as we sipped our tea, "but learn responsibility too. I am not ready to grow up yet. It frightens me. But I'll go to Tom Harris' dairy on Saturday." The Red Cross had made me deliver eggs less often.

This pleased her, and everything was set for us to leave about eight thirty the following morning.

But to my great surprise about eight o'clock when I walked out of the house Teddy and George met me on the driveway. They had hitched a ride from Petersburg with a farmer.

"Good morning," Teddy greeted me.

"Hello, what are you doing here? You said Sunday," I blundered, and not overjoyed to see him.

"Change of plans," he replied in a cocky manner.

I looked at the two hot young men who stood before me. Their arrival complicated things, and I was not sure how to handle these soldier boys from Camp Lee.

"You should have telephoned," I mumbled. "On Saturday mornings we usually work at the Red Cross. But today I am going to Manakin to visit a friend who was gored by a bull."

"Gored by a bull! That's a new one. Look, we left Camp at seven-thirty to get here," George unbuttoned his tunic and sat down on Mother's front steps.

"Yes," Teddy said as he took off his coat and I noticed his blond hair was plastered against his head with sweat. "I could use a drink of water."

I invited them into the kitchen and offered them each a cold drink. Then realized I should explain my plans.

"One of the P.O.W.s who works on a dairy farm here in the county was gored by a vicious bull that got loose. And Mr. Houghton has arranged to drive me up to Mr. Harris' dairy farm to visit Angelo."

I noticed the two boys exchanged glances. I started out towards Mr. Houghton's cottage leaving Teddy and George to finish their drinks.

"Wait, Doc, we'll come with you," Teddy offered as he caught up with me.

"Who is this Angelo, anyway? Maybe we can just come along."

"I am not sure," I replied, quickening my pace. "You don't know him, and Angelo might not wish to see any more American servicemen. You see, they made fun of him while he was at the Army Clinic."

Suddenly I felt awkward and unsure how to manage all of these different people who did not know one another. Just then Mr. Houghton walked across the orchard towards us.

"Hurry up, Doc, I'm ready to leave," he called.

"I've unexpected company and I am not sure what we should do," I replied.

"Hello, lads," Mr. Houghton greeted the two soldiers. "You're here early. It's too hot a day for those heavy clothes."

"Yes, sir," Teddy replied, "We could use some lighter ones."

"Doc," Mr. Houghton sized up the situation, "I'll take these lads to Mrs. Craddock's house and try to borrow some shorts. We should be ready to leave in a half hour's time. And the missus would like to see you."

I watched as they headed across the road in the direction of Emma Craddock's. Relieved to put my company in Mr. Houghton's capable hands, I returned to the house and rummaged through the shed for my fishing rod. Mr. Harris had a wonderful pond he kept stocked with bass and perch. Angelo and I often went fishing together, although we rarely caught much. Usually we just sat on the bank and watched the bobber bounce up and down as the fish nibbled our bait off the hooks. Sometimes we caught a small perch which we always threw back to grow bigger. Last evening I had dug some worms just in case Angelo and I decided to go fishing. In the search for my rod, I found two more fishing poles which I brought along with me. Carrying them over my shoulders, I entered Mr. Houghton's cottage.

"Those boys can just go fishing. That will keep them busy and out of Angelo's way," I decided.

"Harry will be here in a minute," Mrs. Houghton said as I entered her kitchen.

"Cary's clothes should just fit those boys you brought," Mrs. Houghton informed me as she bustled around getting ready. I knew she disapproved of my having boys here.

"I had nothing to do with those boys," I explained. "In fact, I think it's very inconvenient for them to turn up today. I told them Sunday, not Saturday." I rushed to explain. "I've got three rods here, and we can go fidhing in Mr. Harris's pond."

"Well, never mind. I've packed up a basket of cookies and some cheese for Angelo. Elizabeth Harris has invited us to stay for lunch," Mrs. Houghton replied as she finished getting her things ready to leave.

"I am sorry about those boys. I hope Mrs. Harris will have enough to eat. Maybe I should make some sandwiches," I felt awkward since I was not sure my guests would be welcomed.

"I have already made some for your guests. Also, I have a full carton of cokes in the pantry. We'll take them." I knew they were hard to find now.

I picked up the drinks and helped Mrs. Houghton carry her basket out to the car. Then we placed our picnic food in the trunk with the fishing poles and my can of worms. A few minutes later the boys, dressed in Cary's shorts, arrived with Mr. Houghton. I squeezed in the back with Mrs. Houghton and the two boys sat in the front. Then with Peggy on his lap, we drove down the hill and out onto River Road. I found it a very uncomfortable trip with me and Mrs. Houghton seated together and not speaking to each other. I knew she was furious.

"Who are we going to visit?" George asked as we drove past Henley's store.

"I told you, Angelo, at Mr. Harris' dairy farm, the P.O.W. who was gored by a bull," I explained.

"Oh, that one again," snickered George, opening the window.

"Do you like to fish?" I changed the subject. "I brought our rods and a can of worms, so we can go down to Mr. Harris' pond."

"Yes, I like to fish," George took a new interest. "What do you catch, minnows?"

"Perch mostly. Mr. Harris stocks his pond with several different kinds, but I've never seen any minnows," I replied seriously.

For several miles George fell into a moody silence, and I ignored him.

"I like to fish," Teddy smiled. "I used to try my luck at a pond near my home . We always threw the little ones back."

Grateful that he understood the rules, I replied, "So do we. Mr. Harris feels a fish should have a sporting chance, and he wants them to grow bigger."

"Did Angelo really get gored by a bull?" Teddy inquired.

"Yes, and very badly too. He was in the Army Clinic for several weeks. He's better now and back to work at the dairy farm. He is very good with animals. But I have not seen him for a while, since I've been spending Friday nights in town with Mary Ann. So I am not here on Saturdays when we deliver the eggs. You see, I discovered Angelo in St. Mary's churchyard."

I found this hard to explain, but Teddy nodded and seemed to understand. Then for several miles we rode along in silence. The late September morning was warm, but not hot, as we drove through the country with the windows open. Golden Rod nodded along the roadside and the dust stirred by the car's tires billowed up behind us.

Finally Mr. Houghton turned his Chevrolet down a dirt lane which ran off Manakin Road. After almost a mile, we entered Mr. Harris' farm lane. At last we came to a halt under the large pecan tree. Bobby, the German shepherd came bounding up to greet us. He and Peggy were great friends, and she barked with delight.

"Hello, there, Doc. Where have you been recently?" Mr. Harris opened the car's back door. "Oh, I see what you've been up to," he added, as he regarded the two boys.

"No, you don't," I replied. "Mary Ann's church group goes to Camp Lee for dances once a week. I have gone along only four times with her in town. That means I spend the night in Richmond," I explained.

"Boys, little Doc?" Mr. Harris winked at me.

"Yes, unexpected visitors. They said Sunday and turned up this morning. I hope it's all right."

"Angelo won't like competition," Tom Harris replied as he helped Mrs. Houghton out of the backseat.

"Good morning, Clara," greeted Elizabeth Harris as she came towards us wiping her hands up on her apron. "You have quite a crowd with you."

After Mr. Houghton unlocked the trunk, I handed each of my guests a fishing rod and the can of bait. We took out the picnic lunch and went up onto the porch. As the two women discussed the lunch, Mr. Harris put his hand on my shoulder and gently guided me into the living room.

Angelo sat on the sofa. His enormous eyes regarded me sadly. He looked very thin, and his face seemed white under his swarthy complexion.

"Have you forgotten me, little Signorina?" he asked.

"No, Angelo. I have been spending a lot of time in Richmond. I haven't forgotten you at all." I sat down in a chair next to him.

"I studied English in the hospital. You like my American accent?"

"I like it; you speak very well." I leaned forward in the chair and handed him a tiny package. "It's a little remembrance."

"Remembrance? What is that?" The word was unfamiliar.

"A little present, a gift." I slipped the poorly wrapped package into his hand. "A little gift to say I have not forgotten you."

Angelo nodded. He opened the package, and inside found a miniature picture of the Tuscan countryside.

"Bello," he whispered in Italian. "Mama mia!"

"My grandmother sent it to me. She thought you might like it," I explained.

I hardly expected the reaction to my gift that I received. Big tears ran down Angelo's cheeks. He placed his hand over his eyes. Embarrassed, I sat very still feeling sure I must have done something terribly wrong.

"Bella. Questa pittura è bella," he said softly in his own language.

"You like it?" I asked, watching the tears fall onto his lap, unchecked. "I did not mean to make you sad."

"I not sad. I happy. I thought you had forgotten me, your prisoner of war in the campo santo, your captive."

"No, I've not forgotten. My life's become so complicated recently."

We sat and talked quietly with each other for a few minutes. Then I explained about my unexpected company from Camp Lee.

"They've gone fishing down at Mr. Harris' pond."

"Then let us go too. I have a pole. Do you have any bait?" Angelo rose and went out into the hall to find his fishing rod.

Together we walked, ever so slowly, down the grassy hill to the pond. The day was fine and filled with the cicada noises of late summer. One side of the pond was shady with tall hardwood trees providing a little protection from the hot sun. Angelo and I had a favorite spot under a large oak with branches that hung over the water. Across from us, George sat with Teddy on the bank, their lines thrown lazily into the still dark pool. Although they did not see us approach, I overheard them. Their words came clearly, blown by a gentle wind.

"These people are funny people," George remarked in his loud, grating voice. "I've never heard of taking in the enemy. Most P.O.W.s go back to their base at night, and only work on the farms in the daytime. I don't understand Mr. Harris's keeping this Angelo guy here."

"They all seem to like him," Teddy replied, throwing in his line. "You'd think he was a member of the family. I don't get it."

"Perhaps we should report this to the Army when we get back to camp," George suggested. I don't appreciate this kind of Fifth Column activity when I am putting my life on the line for my country."

"No, let's not get involved. The Army guys will just make trouble. You know there's two ways of doing things: the right way and the Army way. These are innocent people and mean no harm." Teddy replaced the bait on his hook and threw it back into the pond.

"You sure meet some weirdos. The kid seems okay, but that old guy who drove us up here in his heap is a strange one and his lady is a proper old dame. Boy, what a lot of screwballs you picked."

I listened to George's conversation with mounting anger. I disliked him more with each sentence he uttered. Suddenly the thought came to me. Perhaps I am the one out of step. My friends and my world seemed so completely different from other people's. Am I really all that strange to be thought weird? I wondered.

"Lunch is ready, gang. Come and get it," Mrs. Harris called us from the garden. I pulled in my line, stuck the hook in the bobber so it would not cut my hand. Angelo also took in his line, and secured it. Then together we left the pond and slowly climbed the hill towards the house. I could see a card table and chairs placed under the trees and both Mrs. Harris and Mrs. Houghton busy carrying out dishes filled with chicken and potato salad. I thought everything looked mouth-watering and quickened my pace.

George and Teddy followed along behind us still talking about our hosts.

"Oh, damn, I bet they heard everything we just said," George's voice sounded too loud.

"I hope not," replied Teddy, "because we are their guests. And like it or not, my mother believes in good manners. As long as we are here, I wish you would shut up."

At lunch, George remained hostile. But I noticed Teddy talked quite naturally with the Harrises and the Houghtons as if he enjoyed himself. He even exchanged a few words with Angelo. Yet I wished I had never allowed those two soldier boys to invade my private world. I saw George glance at Mr. Harris as if sizing him up.

"How come you got a P.O.W. staying here?" George finally asked.

"He helps on the farm. With all the young men in the Army, I can't get help anymore. A dairy farm is considered vital for the war effort. Any place that grows food is." Tom Harris spoke evenly, ignoring the young man's open hostility.

"Why does Angelo stay here, and not go back to his base at night? Most P.O.W.s are not allowed such freedom?"

"Well, since I am so far from Richmond, a different arrangement was worked out. This is also true in the Shenandoah Valley where the P.O.W.s pick fruit crop in the apple orchards."

"Aren't you afraid Angelo might escape or even harm you and your wife?" George asked. "You're a darn fool to think it's safe to employ an Italian here."

"I don't believe that's any of your business," Mr. Harris looked at him with animosity.

"It is my business, because I am fighting for my country while you are eating a picnic with the enemy. You're probably breaking the law. I have a good mind to report you to my commanding officer. You are a fool, Mr. Harris." George sounded angry.

No one ever spoke to Tom Harris like that. I could not believe that this boy, a guest on my friend's farm would be so rude. This total disregard for good manners appalled me. I felt my face become hot as I blushed. Everyone else stopped eating, his chicken suspended in mid air. Nobody spoke and we all stared at this unexpected guest. Then Mr. Harris stood up.

"Look boy, I have Angelo here with the Army's blessing to work on my farm, so I can provide milk for the war effort. I have a dairy to run. Without me your Army could not fight, because it must eat."

"Yeah, but with a wop to do your dirty work?"

"Yes, with a wop P.O.W. I keep food on the Army's table for you and your buddies." Mr. Harris' eyes blazed with anger. "Angelo puts food on the table of his enemies."

"I am trained to fight. Don't you know how the Germans have treated the Jews? And our P.O.W.s are also being starved. The Jerries even shoot Allied prisoners. Haven't you read the newspapers recently?" George shouted.

Mr. Houghton shifted in his chair, and glanced at me. The ladies remained silent, and Angelo covered his face with his hand. I noticed his body was shaking, and he looked very pale.

"I realize that the Germans have committed some atrocities lately. I also know that you are trained to kill the enemy. That's your job as a soldier. I was a soldier once in the First World War. I went to France, and I was wounded there. At that time, I felt just like you do now. But maybe I learned a thing or two during the last twenty-five years. Angelo there was gored by a bull because someone here in Virginia failed to close a gate and allowed a vicious animal to run loose. The authorities in Richmond not only realized the seriousness of those injuries, but also my problems with help to work on this farm. A compromise was agreed, because of the difficulties in transportation and the extent of Angelo's injuries. Can't you understand that besides killing and fighting, there is also a human element in this war?"

"I can only see you are harbouring an enemy. You are as bad as any Fifth Columnist who is a traitor to his country." George's voice could have been heard at the next farm.

"Don't you come here and partake of my food and call me a traitor. You are a mere child who doesn't even shave except twice a week." Mr. Harris looked furious as he put down his chicken and walked over towards George. Nobody dared move as these two confronted each other.

"But why does this girl here come and visit the enemy? What has she to do with Angelo?" George stood and put up his fists.

"She found him. She made it possible for me to have him here. It was a brave thing she did when she saw him in the churchyard. She could have alarmed the countryside, but instead she called me. Her father is in the Army overseas, an Intelligence Officer. Don't you realize how she must have felt when she found a prisoner and did not call the authorities in Richmond. Of course I took care of such details for her. Have you forgotten Angelo is a human being? He is also a patriot. Perhaps he fought on the wrong side, but he did fight. He defended his country, and was captured in Africa, after the first Battle of El Alamain where he fought with Rommel. He's done the decent thing. He is a prisoner, but I am not a jailer. I do not chain him up each evening. I trust him. I am not a beast and shall not behave as did those people you read about in newspapers."

George retreated under Mr. Harris' fury and backed off. Then the young soldier, apparently afraid for his life, ran towards the car.

"I am an honest man. I will not stoop to such behavior. You little whippersnapper, get off my farm. Life is not black and white. It is various shades of gray. You had better learn that. It's your kind of thinking which causes trouble in this world." Mr. Harris sat down at the table.

Elizabeth Harris went after George and took him into the woods. I saw the boy's face turn ashen, and his hands shook. Teddy continued to eat his chicken, and Angelo sat in the chair with his eyes closed. Still angry, Mr. Harris crossed over to the pump and washed his greasy hands and threw water over his flushed face. I had never seen him so furious.

I now understood the difference between a boy and a man. Mr. Harris was a man; I had never doubted it. He was not harbouring the enemy, but playing fair with Angelo on a man-to-man basis. I now realized why Mr. Brown could not understand Tom Harris, and why the authorities in Richmond respected him. It was morally wrong, Mr. Harris believed, to compromise one's principles.

The picnic was over. Mrs. Houghton and I cleared the table and took the uneaten food back into the house. A few minutes later Elizabeth Harris returned and helped us.

"Teddy, George is down at the pond, if you care to join him," she whispered.

Tom Harris entered his house and slammed the screen door. Mr. Houghton kindly helped Angelo walk back into the living room. Nobody spoke as we went about our respective jobs, and I saw Teddy go down to the pond to meet his friend.

Angelo lay on the sofa and closed his eyes. A few minutes later, after helping to wash the plates, I entered the living room. The afternoon stillness seemed oppressive. The house was deathly quiet, broken only by the muffled voices of the two women chatting on the porch. Both Mr. Harris and Mr. Houghton had disappeared.

"Angelo," I said softly as I approached the figure on the sofa. "Angelo, are you awake?"

The great eyes opened, and the pale lips smiled at me.

"Am I the enemy, Signorina Doc?" he asked. "Are you afraid of me? Do you believe what George says?"

I was not sure how to answer this complex question. George's outburst this afternoon had turned things upside down for me. What had seemed extremely clear only this morning had suddenly become muddled and less defined. Suddenly I heard my voice speak.

"You are the enemy of my country, since your country and mine are at war." I chose my words carefully. "But you and I are not at war, so I am not afraid of you. Ever since I first saw you that afternoon in the churchyard, I marveled at your large eyes. They were kind even though we frightened one another. Since I am not a soldier and do not have to fight, we can be friends. Mr. Harris is right; we are first of all, human beings. That, I think, is the most important thing for us to remember."

"Si, Signorina Doc, we are people. We are, how do you say it? Sympatico."

"Si," I replied, "we are simpatico. One day, Angelo, I hope the world will become safe again, and all people everywhere can be friends. That's the way it should be."

He opened his extraordinary eyes even wider and took my hand in his. Gently and with great dignity, he brought it to his lips.

"One day, my little Signorina, you shall become a great lady."

"I hope so, Angelo. I am not sure what will become of me because I feel so unworthy."

The room was very still, and I left the exhausted Italian prisoner to rest. Slowly I helped gather up our fishing rods and the picnic hamper. Mrs. Harris called Teddy and George and told them goodbye. Then with Peggy at our heels we all started for the car. Mr. Houghton switched on the motor as everyone piled in once again. But Tom Harris did not appear.

"Goodbye, Clara. I'll meet you next week, perhaps. Goodbye, Doc, it was good to see you." Elizabeth Harris's gracious manner helped us all over this awkward moment.

"I am sorry my company caused so much trouble," I whispered before climbing into the cramped back seat. "Thank you for having us."

"You're always welcome, my dear," she smiled.

Finally we started down the driveway, and turned out onto the main road. Nobody spoke as we drove through the countryside towards home. Teddy and George stuck their heads out of the windows, and I watched the road from my high back seat. Never had my loyalties been so divided. I liked Angelo more than my own compatriots. He seemed a lot more honest and less prejudiced even though he was a foreigner. Perhaps that's what is meant about loving your enemies. Father said I must not waver hot and cold. I should make up my mind and stick to my decision. Yet, I am an American whose loyalty is to my country and to its fighting men. How could I be loyal to George? His manners were terrible, and he'd made Mr. Harris angry, especially after he arrived at their house uninvited. Being loyal to someone like that was out of the question.

"Yet, Angelo fought with the Germans and killed British soldiers. So he's really the enemy. Oh, dear, I'll never figure this out. My head's in a muddle. I only know Angelo is my friend."

When we arrived home, Mr. Houghton made the boys change back into their Army clothes, and then he drove them to the bus station. I don't know what he said to them, but he must have said something because we never heard from them again.

71

Mrs. Haunch's Last Appearance

September 1943

In September Alvira Carthage's sister died suddenly, the result of a heart attack. Mr. Houghton heard it at Henley's store, and Mrs. Houghton read it in the newspaper. I'd met this lady only once or twice at the Red Cross store when she came with Mrs. Carthage to help us meet our quota. She also had red hair and was worse than her sister for gossip.

The day the obituary came out in the paper Mrs. Haunch called us on the telephone to get information about the funeral.

"It's to be at St. Mary's for some reason because she never went there as far as I can remember," Mrs. Houghton told the hermit. "Yes, ten o'clock on Saturday."

"It's strange Dr. Price would allow Alvira's sister to be buried from a church she never attended," I remarked. "Why is Mrs. Haunch so interested?"

"She knew her. Apparently they attended school together," Mrs. Houghton replied. "I don't know all the answers, but Mrs. Haunch wants to come."

"That's strange," I said, "she never goes any place except when there is a fire or some sort of crisis."

"I expect she considers this a crisis," Mrs. Houghton went into the kitchen to prepare our supper which she always called tea.

On Saturday we drove to St. Mary's through a hot summer haze. The countryside seemed lifeless as the sultry humidity enveloped it like a cloak. White dust choked the grass along the roadside. This heavy atmosphere made me feel depressed, and Jackie jogged along slowly feeling listness. My spirits sank as we arrived at St. Mary's Church. All our neighbours were there looking hot and unhappy in the breathless morning humidity.

Catherine Hollis met us at the church steps and spoke in a whisper. Mrs. Carthage arrived carrying her fan, compliments of Bennett's Funeral Parlor. I noticed it was a new one to replace her usual Sunday one which was in tatters. Colonel Hollis escorted her in and placed her in the front pew. He still limped from his wound, but was better. In fact, he was working part-time again.

I noticed Alvira Carthage looked especially nice all in white with a big straw hat that hid her red hair. She sat alone in her pew; apparently, her husband wasn't coming.

"He didn't like the sister," Colonel whispered when he returned to the church door and led us up the aisle near the front. He knew we always sat there so Mrs. Houghton could hear.

I watched as the neighbors gathered. Mrs. Taliaferro arrived with her two daughters. She looked beautiful as always in her elegant light blue dress. She nodded to me as she took her seat behind us. Mrs. Armstrong came and sat beside me. Her cheeks had their usual round circles of rouge, but she wore a pretty yellow flowered dress. She picked up my hand and gave it a friendly squeeze. Dorothy and Lizzie took their places, one at the organ, the other next to her mother. Mrs. Armstrong took out her fan and handed it to me. Then she gave a second to Mrs. Houghton. After seeing us looked after, she opened a third fan, painted with lovely Chinese scenes, and began to move the humid air around us. Lizzie started the music and sounded as if she'd practiced some this week in preparation because she hit no wrong notes.

"Abide with me, fast fall the evening tide"

When we sang this hymn I thought the music sounded better than usual. Dorothy, I noticed, wasn't singing, so the rest of us were on key. I wondered if she had a cold. Surely Dr. Price had not told her to be quiet. He was difficult, but not to the point that he was rude.

Suddenly a great silence fell over the church. At first I thought it was out of respect for Alvira Carthage. I turned around and watched, fascinated, as Mrs. Haunch hobbled up the aisle. She was clad in a teal

Mrs. Haunch's Last Appearance

blue dress, red high heels, and a straw hat trimmed with crimson cherries. She appeared unable to walk in the high heels as she came down the aisle towards us. In her hand she carried a bright red pocket-book and grey gloves. I couldn't believe my eyes, and neither could the congregation. Every head in the church turned towards Mrs. Haunch.

"Look who's here," I nudged Mrs. Houghton.

Mrs. Houghton made no sign and appeared busy with the service. I squirmed around in my seat and stared. Mrs. Taliaferro had her handkerchief pressed against her mouth. Jean and Sally Anne had tears running down their cheeks. Mrs. Armstrong's shoulders shook, and I knew she was silently laughing. Mrs. Hollis looked amazed by this apparition as it made its way into the front pew and sat beside Alvira Carthage.

"I guess if you wear jodhpurs all the time, you don't know how to dress for the public," I whispered to Mrs. Houghton.

"Quite extraordinary," she whispered back.

I watched Mrs. Haunch open her hymnal, putting her finger to her lips before she turned the pages. Lizzie hit a strong chord and we all started the second verse, forgetting where we had left off.

"Stop wiggling," Mrs. Houghton said to me as I leaned over the pew to see this most unusual sight. "You are acting like a child, it's not polite."

I was not trying to act like anything else. I considered myself half child, half woman – some days, all woman – on others, all child. I wondered if I ever would learn to be as composed as Mrs. Taliaferro. Her dress was unwrinkled, her straw hat fit perfectly, I heard her clear voice behind me singing the hymn. I envied her, she was everything I thought a true lady should be.

I noticed that Mrs. Armstrong had dropped her fan onto the floor in front of us. Quietly I leaned over to pick it up. My eyes met Mrs. Haunch's as she reached under her pew. I nodded politely, then saw that she was sitting in the front row in her stocking feet. Her red shoes had vanished. Mrs. Houghton noticed this too and suppressed a laugh. I dared not look at her because floods of giggles would escape me. I stared at Dr. Price, hoping just looking at his ugly face would sober me.

It didn't help much. It was a great relief when the service was finally over.

I watched as Mrs. Taliaferro with her daughters walked down the aisle like a goddess, her clear brown eyes regarded me as she smiled. I nodded back. I knew her emotions were under firm control because although she saw Mrs. Haunch's stocking feet, Mrs. Taliaferro showed no sign of knowing even when Alvira Carthage slipped out a side door and left her friend still sitting in the front pew. Mrs. Taliaferro was every inch a lady and I watched as her stately figure left the church.

Furtively I stole a glance at Mrs. Haunch. She stood in the pew, clad in her strange costume and no shoes. With the utmost dignity, an older man whom I didn't know, handed back the red high heels. I watched Mrs. Haunch put them on. Very gently, Mrs. Houghton placed her hand upon my shoulder as a signal for me to move forward. With great reluctance, I walked slowly down the aisle in front of her, and we left the church.

That was the last time I ever say Mrs. Haunch, although she telephoned us from time to time. She went back into her house with her forty-two dogs and James, who came often to Henley's store to buy sacks of dog food.

Letters

September 1943
Richmond, Va.

Dear Dad,

Mrs. Haunch came out of Ballyclare and caused a sensation in church. Mrs. Carthage's sister died suddenly of a heart attack and we all went to the funeral. Mrs. Haunch came in late wearing bright red shoes and a hat with cherries. Can you believe it – cherries for a funeral? Then to top it all off she took off her shoes and lost them. It must have offended the Lord considerably since it was a very hot day. Her shoes disappeared right under her pew, and some gentleman retrieved them for her after the service. If I took off my shoes I'd surely get hell from Mrs. Houghton.

How insulting to the Almighty. He must be furious. It's the talk of the county from the Court House to Tuckahoe Creek.

I hear you are in England. Where are you? Cary is there also with the 8th Air Force. He's flying on missions. That's scary, but he loves it. How far is Cary from you? Perhaps you can visit him.

Love, Doc

P.S. About God. I've decided that I'll learn more about Him as you suggested. Anyway, I like the music and I like seeing the people I know. I could give up Dr. Price's sermons tommorow, but we are stuck with him for the duration. I like teaching Sunday school too, but I'd like God to hear me. Mary is better about that, but God often is deaf even when I shout. Mr. Houghton says that's not polite to shout at God. It makes Him angry.

Doc

A Forgotten Landscape

72

"Lilli Marlene"

October 1943

One afternoon in early October Mr. Houghton stood in the doorway of his chicken house, crying. I'd just come in from riding Lady, and as I crossed the stable yard, leading my horse, I found Mr. Houghton mopping his eyes with his big blue handkerchief.

"What's the matter?" I asked.

"Cary Craddock's missing in action," he replied stuffing the handkerchief into his trouser pocket. "His mother received a telegram this morning."

"Cary Craddock's missing?" I echoed in disbelief.

The only son of Emma Craddock, whose husband died after just seven years of marriage, was a favorite in the county. We grew up together and often shared Mrs. Houghton's bedroom whenever our mothers were out of town until Mr. Houghton thought this arrangement indecent. Over the years Cary had become more like a son to this childless couple than a neighbor.

"Shot down over France on a mission with the Eighth Air Force. That's all we know." Mr. Houghton wiped a stray tear from his cheek.

"I don't believe you," I shouted, feeling my heart plummet into my boots, "it's just not true."

"It's true all right," again he took his handkerchief and blew his nose, "When an official telegram arrives from the State Department you know it's so."

"Well, I don't believe Cary is dead. He must be safe somewhere.

You know he will come home, Mr. Houghton, I am sure of that." I brushed away the awful news with defiance. "Those Germans wouldn't dare harm Cary."

I was right, but we did not know what had happened to him until nearly two months later. Although Emma Craddock never gave up hope, I thought she looked terribly worried and seemed preoccupied most of that time.

When Cary's parachute landed him in France near the Belgium border a farmer suddenly appeared and helped to untangle the straps of his harness from around the frightened airman. Quickly Cary was bundled into a nearby barn where the burly French peasant pointed to a hay loft, a second loft high up under the roof.

"Climb up there," the farmer commanded in English," to the storage loft. Quickly before a German patrol comes."

Cary noticed the lower hay loft covered the entire length of the stone barn, and on one of its twelve supporting posts a ladder led up into a second loft. Carrying his parachute and harness he climbed with difficulty up this steep ladder to a tiny storage space under the barn's rafters. Here amid an old set of horse harness, several milk cans, long unused and old leather straps Cary hid.

"Stay there," the farmer commanded, "Be quiet. Lie down and cover yourself with the hay. Hurry."

After folding up the parachute as best he could, Cary lay beneath the hay, and watched through a crack in the rough oak floor boards as the farmer went about his chores.

The sun was just rising so Cary figured it must be about nine o'clock in the morning. Exhausted since he had flown on an air raid over France, he lay on his folded chute and watched the peasant far below.

First the old man, perhaps sixty, Cary judged, forked down some fresh smelling grass from the first loft, and then sat on a three legged stool and calmly milked his three black and white colored cows. Extremely tired, Cary had almost dozed off when suddenly a German patrol burst through the barn door.

"An American airman came this way!" Shouted the officer in charge at the gray haired peasant. Four men entered the barn bayonets fixed, their boots sounding hard against the dirt floor.

Seemingly unconcerned, the farmer continued to milk his cows. Cary heard the milk squirting against the sides of the metal pail as the white liquid frothed up. He could just see the older man's head resting against the cow's dark flank and only partly understood the French spoken to the German officer.

"I have seen no one," the farmer replied, looking surprised.

"We know an American landed not a mile from this barn. Look around men," commanded the officer in German.

Two of the soldiers climbed up onto the main loft, poked their bayonets into the recently cut grass but found nothing. Finally one of the men noticed the ladder which led into Cary's hiding place, and started to climb up, then stopped when the commanding officer spoke.

"What's in that second loft?"

"Just what you see," replied the farmer without looking up. "Broken harness, old milk cans, some hay. Storage mostly."

Only partly covered from view under the hay, Cary lay in a cold sweat, his heart thumping in his chest. Through his crack in the floor he could see the German officer brandishing a pistol and the brave, unconcerned farmer milking his cows. Cary marveled at such courage. The two Germans started up the ladder again. The first soldier's bayonet hit against the floorboards under where Cary lay, and became entangled in some long discarded leather straps which hung from a metal hook screwed into the ceiling. Unable to fee his gun the soldier gave a jerk and jumped backwards down onto the hay loft, pulling the leather reins on top of him.

The second man continued to climb the ladder climbing slowly step by step until the tip of his bayonet appeared just over the ledge of the tiny loft only a foot away from Cary's head. Inch by inch the gun's muzzle came up over the loft. Shaking with fear, Cary watched it, waiting for the man's helmet to appear. Suddenly the gun stopped. A loud crack echoed through the barn. A startled scream, then silence. Through his peephole, Cary saw the young German in mid flight as he fell backwards onto the main loft, where he landed visibly shaken, but unhurt, on top of the green hay. One of the steps of the rickety ladder had snapped in two and dangled from its rusty nails. Cary let out his breath and again looked between the floor boards. The two soldiers started up the ladder again, but this time they contented themselves by poking their bayonets at the flooring of the storage loft. Then apparently assured that nothing suspicious was there they swung themselves down onto the barn's main floor.

Meanwhile the fourth soldier opened the doors of the two box stalls and examined an old farm wagon which stood against the wall. All he discovered was an ancient white horse who stood dozing contently in his stable. The milk room beyond yielded nothing.

"No American here," said their officer sheathing his pistol. "I am warning you," he turned to the farmer speaking in French. "We shall shoot the American on sight and anyone else who helps him."

Apparently satisfied that no airmen hid in the barn, the patrol departed. Cary heard their retreating footsteps as they went down the road. Then silence. Unruffled, the farmer continued to milk his cows, moving from one to the other deliberately and speaking to each in French. Finally after what seemed to Cary an interminable amount of time, the old farmer mounted a rope ladder he kept hidden under the hay and climbed up to the tiny loft.

"Stay here. They will come back again at first light. I'll bring you some food later. Don't leave the loft." To Cary's amazement, this Frenchman spoke perfect English.

"Tomorrow," whispered Cary, "I'll try my luck with a map and work my way towards the sea. How far is it from here?"

"No," replied the farmer. "That's too dangerous. The Germans control the main roads. Be patient until nightfall. I'll see you get to the coast."

Before Cary could answer the old man climbed down the ladder and in an instant was gone.

At dawn the next morning the Germans returned. Again they searched the barn. And again they found nothing. Cary lay flat against the floor of his tiny second loft, but although the Germans poked around the floorboards with their bayonets from the lower hay loft, they seemed satisfied that no one was hidden above it and finally left. Shortly after they departed, the old man arrived to do his morning chores. Cary watched him through the crack in the floorboards as the farmer fed the horse and sat down on his stool to milk his cows.

"Good morning," Cary sat up and greeted him. "I'll be glad to help you milk. I grew up on a farm and learned how as a boy."

"Good morning, young fellow," the farmer replied. "Come down from your roost and take that bucket. A milking stool is under the bench over there."

"You were right, the Germans came back, but they did not climb up the little ladder," Cary explained.

"They rarely do," replied the farmer sitting down again on his stool. "Sometimes they climb up, and they see nothing, but they always return just before dawn."

The two sat in silence together and milked the docile French cows. The only sound was the milk hitting the metal sides of the buckets and the contented chewing of the animals. For a moment, Cary believed he was home safe in Virginia. When they finished their milking, the farmer poured the frothy warm liquid into a large metal can and rolled it into the cooling room.

"I will deliver this milk when it gets dark," he explained and closed the door.

It was about mid afternoon when Cary noticed a tall man and a tiny lady walk down the farm lane. Although they appeared to be peasants, probably neighbours, they seemed to have a certain stealth in their movements. A few minutes later the farmer reentered the barn.

"My friends are coming," he explained. "We shall talk in here. Afterwards you will come into the house for supper."

When the two peasants entered the barn, to Cary's amazement, the frail looking woman addressed him in English, spoken with an English accent.

"They're French resistance fighters," Cary thought, "or why else would they help me?"

"American airman?" she asked. "Still in your uniform. Here put these clothes on."

Cary looked down at his flight suit, and realized it was a dead giveaway. Fear pricked his neck and clutched at his heart. He accepted to dark peasant garb; she handed him a dark navy blue shirt and a baggy pair of brown trousers. He could just hear the three friends mumbling in French as he slipped into the old horse's stall to change out of his flight suit.

"We need to get rid of those Army clothes," the tall Frenchman commented. "They are dangerous indeed."

"Burn those things in the milk room. There is a large barrel for that purpose," commanded the English woman. "Then cut off any buttons and smash them with a hammer. We shall bury them. Here, take these matches, and be quick."

"I did not dare refuse," Cary told us later. "I poked those combat clothes down into the metal barrel, poured a little gasoline on them and lit a match. The whole barn damn near blew up, and in an instant the clothes were cinders."

"You speak French?" demanded the woman regarding Cary. "Not a word must you say to anyone from dark to dawn. Listen to what people tell you in French."

"I studied French in school," Cary explained, wondering how she had become a member of the French resistance.

"That's all you need. Go bury those buttons in the manure pile and come back."

The buttons charred beyond recognition, Cary smashed with an hammer and remaining close to the barn he slipped outside and buried them in the dung. Everything seemed quiet, and even peaceful.

"Now you will be given instructions. You do as you are told, and do not speak at all, even in French. Your accent is too American. You understand me?" the tall Frenchman demanded. "We'll leave now. Good luck."

Without saying another word the two peasants departed and melted into the woods nearby. Cary and the farmer finished the chores and sat down in the barn for an evening meal of thick slices of brown bread, cheese and un-pasteurized milk, still warm from the cows. Afterwards they loaded the milk cans onto the wagon and harnessed up the old horse.

Finally everything was ready, and about midnight Cary slipped into the false bottom of the wagon where he found a secret compartment between the floorboards and the axel just large enough for a man to lie down in. The farmer slid the floorboards shut and locked them by turning a piece of metal. Shortly afterwards Cary and the farmer started down the lane towards the village, about three miles distant. Only the ancient horse's clop-clop broke the stillness. In their cramped position Cary's legs soon fell asleep, and he shifted his weight.

"Silence," whispered the farmer, "Lie on your back and be still."

From his hiding place, Cary watched the village, like a strange ghost, take shape. Darkness covered the land, no light burned in the houses since blackout curtains covered their windows. Only the hollow sound of the cobblestones under the horse's hooves told Cary when they passed through the deserted streets. The wagon rolled steadily on. If left the village behind and stopped momentarily at a German sentry's command. Apparently the old man passed this way every night delivering his milk because the wagon soon rolled on again.

At the end of the cobblestones the road became gravel, and here they turned south, or so Cary thought. As they bounced over this road full of ruts and potholes, the trace chains rattled against the undercarriage of the wagon – and made an eerie sound – too loud in the dark still night, Cary thought.

The old horse turned again, and the road suddenly became smooth under the wagon's wheels. The iron tires seemed to be traveling over asphalt because Cary noticed a soft rubbing sound caused by friction, and the chains stopped clattering. Then he heard gates open, large iron ones with squeaking hinges. The wagon passed on through these and came to a halt before a large stone building. Cary could just make out the chimneys reaching up into the dark sky and could just distinguish three voices whispering to each other in French. Quickly his compartment was opened, and he was lifted up onto his feet. Before him stood three monks. Rough hands helped Cary onto the ground, then one of the monks led him silently down a dark cloister lighted only by a single candle, and through a large wooden door. The hooded figure drew the bolt and locked it before he led Cary into a small room, probably a monk's cell. In the candle light Cary saw a bed, a single chair, and a dresser. A large crucifix hung on the wall above the bed. The figure before him dressed in a long robe placed a finger on his lips.

"Here," the monk said in English, "Put these on."

Cary took the bundle of brown clothes. It contained a brown hooded robe and a long rope with three knots.

"Franciscans?" Cary inquired regarding the young face which was almost hidden by the hood.

Again the finger went to the mouth, but the brown eyes smiled. The monk nodded, as the candle light played tricks, its light sputtering and flickering almost out. Then it burned steadily once more as Cary replaced his peasant's garb with the coarse brown robe. The cowl covering his head, Cary was led into a magnificent church. A long choir full of brown clad monks flanked either side of a high altar. Windows, once stained glass, were covered with boards and supported by sand bags. Cary counted twenty or thirty brown robed figures, each with a rope around his waistband a cowl over his head. He took his place at the end of the back row. The monks sang the office, and Cary joined in the Latin service as best he could.

As the last echo of the plain song died away the church door burst open and six German soldiers entered armed with rifles. Cary's heart sank when he saw five men and an officer. The Germans counted the monks by pointing their rifles at each one and in this manner they came down the line of choir stalls. His hands trembling, Cary ducked his head as the German lieutenant struck him on the chest with a gun.

Apparently the count did not come out right because the soldiers counted again. This time they seemed satisfied. The officer turned and addressed the Abbot in French. Cary, listening intently, could just make out what they said.

"We are looking for three American airmen. We suspect you of hiding them. How many monks do you have here?"

The Abbot rose from his seat in the choir very deliberately. He was a big man, almost six feet. The brown cowl was pushed back to allow his face to show, and his very presence commanded respect.

"Our number varies," he told the officer. "We have two monks here now who have typhoid fever. They came from Lyon because there is no hospital. So that makes twenty or thirty."

"Typhoid!" The German gasped.

"Typhoid. Very serious cases. The ill men came with two, perhaps three other monks." The Abbot looked vague.

His big frame crossed the altar from the Epistle to the Gospel side. Cary watched him genuflect, then turn and face the officer.

"We also have smallpox. Just one case, I believe." The Abbot continued his vague manner.

"Smallpox!" the Germans chorused.

"Oh, yes. A very deadly illness, even in these days."

The five soldiers retreated towards the door. Their officer started backwards down the aisle and the Abbot followed slowly, deliberately walking after him. When the German reached the main door, he had enough presence of mind to stop.

"Twenty or thirty monks are here?" he inquired. "Can you be more precise?"

"No," replied the Abbot. "Some monks die in our hospital almost daily. But since we take only the most dangerous, most desperate cases, others come – quite regularly."

"Desperate cases?" the German officer repeated. "What do you mean by desperate cases?"

"Typhus, small pox, and the plague. We had a case of the plague quite recently. Quite terrible, you know." The Abbot stopped at the door of his church. "We stay quarantined most of the time. I am surprised you came here at all."

The officer fled. And Cary wondered why he had been brought to such a terrible place. Surely the underground knew what it was about. The monks left their choir stalls and silently, cowls covering their faces, in single file they retired from the church. It was two o'clock in the morning.

Ever so gently, but quite firmly, Cary was led back to his cell. Once there, two brothers, only their eyes and noses showing under their hoods, blackened his face and hands. Finally they led him down some rough stone stairs at the back of the monastery and pushed open a door half hidden in the masonry. They stepped out into the cool crisp night. A car stood waiting. Cary and two men dressed in monk's clothing climbed into the back seat, a partition was closed, and two more men got into the front. They were dressed in German uniforms! Cold fear clutched at Cary until he heard these four address each other in French.

"They are monks," Cary realized.

The car sped silently through the night, its lights out, its occupants quiet. Cary looked at the two men who sat next to him. They appeared young and scared like himself.

"Could they also be American airmen shot down in France?" He wondered.

After a half an hour's ride the car stopped. The two "German soldiers" led the way to a small cove. Cary smelled the sea. The salt water pricked at his nostrils, and through the early morning darkness he saw a small fishing boat tied to a broken pier.

The "Germans" helped the three "monks" to board and instantly disappeared up the path. A signal of some sort must have passed between them and two other men who came out of the shadows silently boarded the boat. Quickly they untied the ropes and polled their craft into deeper water.

Cary heard the motor of a patrol boat in the distance and then deathly stillness. In the darkness the two fishermen unfurled a sail, the wind caught it and pushed the boat quickly, silently seaward. The black night covered their escape.

Cary and the two monks sat in the bottom of the little boat amid the fishing nets and tackle boxes. A fresh breeze filled the sails, and the small craft skimmed through the water in the darkness. Leaning against the sail box, Cary dozed because when he awoke several hours later, the morning light was just breaking. The sound of a motor startled him as he opened his eyes and saw land. They had crossed the channel and the shores of England were just visible in the distance. Cary eyed the other "monks", but no one dared speak. They sat in the stern of the boat silently watching the land approach. In the distance Cary could make out two men standing on a pier with field glasses looking out to sea. They seemed to be waiting and watching for something.

Now the boatmen furled their sail and turned their engine on. Carefully with great assurance, they brought their boat into port at a small fishing village on the south coast. Nobody spoke as the boat was tied up and one of the waiting men swung down from the dock onto the deck of the fishing vessel and came up to Cary.

"I am Jack Andrews," he introduced himself. "Good morning. Welcome to England."

Cary pushed the cowl from his head; the two other monks did likewise. Seeing their boyish faces bright with joy, Cary knew they were also Americans.

"Jacques," said Mr. Andrews, "I see you got all three this time, and all in good shape."

"Oui, Monsieur," the fisherman replied.

As Jacques secured his small craft, Jack Andrews led the "monks" up the pier to his awaiting car. They drove in silence down the quays towards a small hotel.

"I see you've arrived safely," the frail looking English woman Cary had first seen on the farm in France greeted them.

This morning she was dressed in a blue tweed suit. Her brown hair was pinned up in a bun, swept back from her plain face. Only her eyes seemed extraordinary. Deep blue – they reminded Cary of a hawk's, so bright and alert they appeared.

"Yes," Cary replied wondering if this was really the same person he saw in France. "But how did you get here?"

"Top secret," the lady told him. "Here are your dog tags. Upstairs you will find some American uniforms. Please leave the monks' robes. Then after a good English breakfast, Mr. Andrews will drive you back to your base."

"What is your name?" The red haired flyer inquired as he and the other young man started upstairs.

"I have no name. I am called 'Lili Marlene,' or 'K K Katie,' or even Britiannia."

"But those are the names of songs," Cary protested. "'Lilli Marlene' is a song the Yanks took over from the Germans in this war. And 'K K Katie' came from the First World War."

"Yes," the English woman nodded. "I know."

"She looks so frail you could have blown away with a feather," Cary told us. "I know she went back to France or to Belgium because sometime later a man from my group disappeared and was believed to be shot down.

"When this airman returned about two months later, I asked him if he had encountered a small English woman who spoke several languages. He told me he had, and she helped him to escape. Traveling by night, she had taken him from one safe house to another until they reached the coast. Once there, he had been taken on a night with no moon, the blackest night in his memory, to a fishing boat that was tied up at a tiny cove. Then under cover of darkness in a boat with a single sail, he had been brought back to England.

"That sounded too much like Lilli Marlene, as I called her, to be a coincidence. So we went to see the Colonel in command of our squadron and asked him about it. He told us our fragile lady had once worked in Vienna in Intelligence at the British Embassy. When the war started, because her mother was ill and elderly, Lilli Marlene returned to England. Once she got her mother settled in a small village in Devon, our frail lady joined the French Resistance. Her rare courage and her knowledge of languages made her an invaluable member. Shortly after the fall of France she had been spirited out of Britain and during the last three years this shadowy figure had helped hundreds of British and American airmen to escape from German occupied France and Belgium."

Although Cary never learned this lady's name, even after the war when he tried to trace her, we always believed without the help of Lilli Marlene, our neighbour would have never seen Virginia again.

Letters

October 1943
Richmond, Va.

Dear Dad,

The saddest thing has happened. Cary Craddock's missing. Mr. Houghton cried openly for two days. I've never seen a man cry before so unashamedly. Cary's like a son, and both the Houghtons are upset by this awful news.

Miss Emma has been riding every day, and getting me to come with her on Killybegs. She's always ridden like a trooper, but I tell you recently she's been going like the wind and jumping the biggest fences around. I can hardly keep up, even on Lady. She's going to kill herself and me too. I hope we hear something soon, because I can't stand this much longer. Do you ever cry? I mean when you got hit in the ankle did you cry? Some men do, I suppose.

I appreciated your letter about Angelo. I've made my mind he's my friend. I've seen Teddy once since that awful day at the Harrises, but I refused to speak to George. Mrs. Houghton called Mrs. Overby, the leader of the church groups at Mary Ann's church, and told her I couldn't go to Camp Lee any more. Transportation was a big problem, Mrs. Houghton explained, and it was difficult to arrange for me to go. She never said she disapproved of my going at fifteen to dance with soldiers and returning home after midnight. Mary Ann found out recently that she is too young too, but she lied about her age and went anyway. I think most of the boys are scared, but put on a big act to cover up. I think that's George's problem. It's easier not going to those dances because I don't need uninvited visitors any more.

As for school. It's French and Latin as usual. I hate them both. English of course, which is fine. Math is always difficult, and history I like. Mrs. Owens is back in full swing, her hair various colours and her hairstyle's ugly. Madame still teaches French, but she looks very fragile. I'm afraid she won't last the year, and we'll get someone worse. Mrs. Gilbert is still assigning enormous amounts of homework. She always fusses about our handwriting, and mine especially is too cramped looking. Doesn't she realize our hands get to hurting when we write so long, and naturally it becomes hard to read. I suppose not, because she still fusses. She's a good teacher for English, and I've learned something this year.

Grandmother's wanting to take me has me doubtful. I like my life with the Houghtons, but I don't wish to live with Rudy and Mother. I'll give you my consent to go to Indiana, but not right away. I'm happy you are still in England. The war in Italy sounds terrible. The Battle of Salerno looks like a disaster. I am glad you were not there. I'll write to you as soon as we know anything about Cary. Pray for him please.

Love, Doc

P.S. Isn't it great the Italians have given up? They made a secret treaty with the Allies and are on our side now. Poor Angelo, he was very upset because he admired Rommel. He also felt that there must be some treachery behind the alliance with the Americans and British. I guess it's hard to switch sides once you've got used to being on one side. He's getting better now, for which we are all grateful.

Doc

A Forgotten Landscape

73

A Day to Remember

One Saturday shortly before Thanksgiving, I planned to drive into town with the Houghtons. We wanted to start our Christmas shopping, and I needed to find a birthday gift for my mother. On Mr. Houghton's radio that morning Polly Dafferine, the fashion consultant for the Richmond station, came wafting over the air waves with her high-pitched voice.

"Today's a perfect time to shop because the stores are having linen sales. Everything for your bathroom and bedroom is a fourth off. You shall find downtown Richmond very exciting. I would like to recommend Miller and Rhoads' tea room and Thalhimer's Virginia foods counter as delightful places to each lunch."

Mr. Houghton turned off the radio.

"That woman annoys me. If she isn't diving into your pocket promoting sales, she is describing those awful clothes with the padded shoulders. I think women would look like football players in some of these new styles."

"Come on, Harry, Doc and I want to go downtown early. I need to replace my towels. I have had to cut most of ours in half, because they're worn out in the middle. Now even these are wearing thin. Perhaps if we leave early, we can avoid the crowds."

"You want me to take you all the way to Miller and Rhoads?" asked Mr. Houghton, horrified by this prospect. "I hate to drive in the city."

"Yes, and we plan to shop at Thalhimer's too," I replied. "We shall need at least two hours to spend in each store."

Mr. Houghton walked out of the kitchen. Undaunted, his wife

made out a shopping list and gathered up her library books. A whole day in Richmond to browse through the shops seemed to us a royal affair. But it took endless preparation. Recently we had found the stores a disappointment because goods were scarce and the quality was often poor.

Sheets had become almost nonexistent. Ours were mostly cut down the middle, the worn sides turned out, and the centers resewn with French seams. Although these ridges could sometimes be uncomfortable to sleep on, we still managed to have plenty of muslin and percale sheets. I had heard recently on the radio, that at a sale in a Washington store several women had actually fought with each other over towels and sheets. I could not believe that adults would act in such a childish manner.

Other items we found scarce included men's white shirts, stockings, and bath towels. Silk stockings had become impossible to buy, and in winter most ladies wore cotton ones. Shoes, except those with no style, came in sizes either too big or too small. Carefully I polished my brown oxfords every night for school the next morning. My Sunday shoes I kept in their own special box, so they would not get scuffed.

Finally, by nine o'clock everyone was ready, and we started out for Richmond in Mr. Houghton's old car. I could hardly contain my excitement. In my purse I carried twenty dollars, an enormous sum. As we drove through the suburbs down Cary Street Road, I observed Mr. Houghton appeared nervous.

"I have decided," he told his wife, "to leave the car at Gregory's garage and let him repair my tail light. So you and Doc must ride the trolley car downtown."

Mrs. Houghton looked disappointed, but she said nothing. The prospect of a day in Richmond was far too exciting to spoil.

"Then leave us off on Grove Avenue. I find the trolley quite convenient, because it stops right in front of the big stores," Mrs. Houghton smiled. "And Doc loves riding it down Broad Street."

"How exciting. It'll be great fun," I agreed, scrambling out of the front seat as Mr. Houghton brought his car to a stop against the curb.

"We'll meet you at Dot's Pastry on Cary Street around four o'clock," his wife reminded him and we waved goodbye.

A Day to Remember

The trolley car ran down the center of Grove Avenue, an exceedingly practical mode of travel. For one nickel I could ride from Richmond College (located just outside of the city limits) all the way downtown to Fourteenth and Main Streets. Here the saddle shop was located. I loved swaying back and forth in the middle of the street and looking down into other people's cars. I could just peek in and see what they were up to. Although I knew this practice was sneaky, I loved doing it just the same. Riding on the trolley car added to my day's pleasure. Nor did we have to wait. In a few minutes a long yellow car came clattering down the tracks towards us.

After stepping up and allowing my nickel to slide down into the money box, I selected a seat next to the window. Mrs. Houghton joined me, settled herself and placed her shopping bag, containing the library books, on her lap. Then the trolley car glided down the rails towards town.

We decided to get out at First and Broad Streets and walk across to the main public library in order to return the books. After tip toeing around the big reading room, Mrs. Houghton selected several biographies and a new novel. Still speaking in whispers, we checked the books out and reentered the bright fall sunshine. We walked the five blocks in the crisp, bracing air down to Miller and Rhoads. Along the way, I noticed several shop windows looked bare of merchandise and instead displayed a large poster telling us "Buy War Bonds."

"When we reach Miller and Rhoads, I wish to go down to the basement first," Mrs. Houghton planned our method of attack, "because that's where the sheets and towels are on sale. Then we shall come back up to the first floor and look for a pair of gloves for your mother's birthday."

Since it was still early as we entered the store, Miller and Rhoads appeared almost empty of customers. We passed through the men's department and walked back to the elevators. When we reached the basement and the girl who ran the elevator opened the door, I clutched at Mrs. Houghton's arm. Before us stood a crowd of about fifty women who surrounded a counter heaped high with sheets and towels. Several of these shoppers pushed their way through and grabbed at the linens as if they were the last ones on earth. I saw a sales lady brace herself against the counter, her face ashen, as if she were going to faint. In vain, an elderly floor walker tried to stop the pushing, shoving women.

"Ladies, ladies," he pleaded hopelessly. But no one paid him the slightest attention.

Then three other sales people, from different departments, converged upon the towel counter. But they, too, were almost knocked down as the excited shoppers continued to snatch up everything in sight. Mrs. Houghton and I stood rooted to the floor in front of the elevator and watched this spectacle in horror. Finally a bell rang over our heads, and two policemen arrived on the scene. Still the women fought with each other, pulling the towels and jerking at the sheets. I heard ominous ripping sounds and found several torn sheets on the floor in a heap in front of me.

"Round everyone up," shouted the security officer, "and bring them down to the office."

I felt a heavy hand upon my shoulder. My heart raced with terror as Mrs. Houghton and I were escorted from the elevator, through the underwear department, and into a waiting room.

"Sit over there, miss and be quiet," the plain clothes detective commanded as Mrs. Houghton tried to explain. "Sit down please, you'll get your chance."

Rushing to and fro the security officers brought more customers into the waiting room, and confiscated their towels and sheets. Then a large, burly man slammed and locked the door. Mrs. Houghton took my hand in hers, and held it gently.

"Quiet!" shouted the security officer over the excited voices of fifty women. "Never in all my thirty years of experience have I seen anything equal to this!"

I regarded him squarely because I had done nothing. I could not imagine how we could ever explain this to Mother. Being arrested and locked up in an office with fifty screaming women was hardly the behaviour she expected of me.

"You shall be taken into the office and interviewed one by one."

I shivered at the prospect of facing the store detective. "Then you will return all of your merchandise and leave the store!" The burly officer sounded ominous. "You," he addressed me, "You're nothing but a kid, you've got no business in this kind of fracas."

I cringed against Mrs. Houghton's shoulder and tried to reply.

"Sir," I addressed the officer, "Sir."

"Never mind, Doc," Mrs. Houghton shook her head, "I'll explain."

Finally, our turn came to enter the office. The detective behind the desk regarded us with open hostility. He had spent most of the last two hours interviewing tearful women, who had given him various explanations for their conduct.

"I won't listen to any more excuses," he snorted at us.

"Please allow me to explain," Mrs. Houghton said calmly. "We have no towels or other parcels. We had just stepped off the elevator when we were confronted by chaos. We were unable to move in any direction because of the crowds of shoppers, and sheets scattered on the floor. We both felt terribly frightened and greatly relieved when you arrived. Neither this young girl nor I have anything except library books."

Mrs. Houghton offered the detective her shopping bag. Unceremoniously he dumped the books out onto his desk. When he looked up at us, I thought he seemed disappointed.

"I expect that you shall now tell me you are not from Richmond – like most of those other women, who insisted they came from Waverly or Ashland or as far away as Fredericksburg. If this ever got out to the newspapers, many reputations would be ruined."

"I am not even a Virginian," I watched Mrs. Houghton pick up the books and replace them in her shopping bag. "I come from England."

"Now I've heard everything," the detective laughed unpleasantly. Then he studied us intently before he inquired, "What language do you speak there?"

A look of disbelief crossed Mrs. Houghton's face. She opened her mouth to reply, and then closed it again. The detective wrote something down on his pad.

"Why English, of course," Mrs. Houghton finally regained her voice. "At least I don't talk like a Virginian with a plum in my mouth!"

Without saying another word she turned on her heel, and with me in tow, left the office. The next instant we marched through the waiting room, past the burly officer and out of the door. Nor did we stop until after we caught an express elevator and arrived at the fifth floor.

"We shall forget about the shopping just now," Mrs. Houghton explained, appearing quite breathless, "until after we both are revived by a cup of hot tea."

74

Fool's Faces

December 1943

The next day the paper showed a photograph of the women in Miller and Rhoad's pulling the sheets to pieces. In the corner hardly recognizable I stood in my best coat and hat. Mrs. Carthage telephoned before church to tell Mrs. Houghton my picture was on the front page of the *Richmond Times Dispatch.*

"I am sure you are mistaken, Alvira," Mrs. Houghton told her. "Doc doesn't shop for linens."

"Oh, boy," I said when Mrs. Houghton put down the phone, "I'm in for it now."

"Fools' names and fools' faces generally end up in public places," Mr. Houghton reminded me. "It will be all over Richmond that you were arrested. Just let Alvira get a hold of it."

"I simply can't go to church and face that crowd all asking me questions," I told them. "How can I ever face them again?"

"That's just what you must do; go to church and pretend it didn't happen, or else everyone will know it did. You will be accused of hiding because you are guilty," Mrs. Houghton sent me into my bedroom to dress.

Tears stained my face as I put on my best dress and shoes. I selected a jacket rather than my good coat and put on my last year's hat. I thought it looked rather nice and masked the tears.

Ten minutes later Mr. Houghton let us out of the car in front of the church.

"Now, dear," Mrs. Houghton whispered, "we shall deny you were there. The picture only shows half of you and anyway, newsprint makes your face unclear."

"But Mrs. Carthage will tell the world I was there, and Mother will know I've been arrested," I replied, speaking in an undertone.

We got away with it on Sunday, but Monday evening at the store Ethel told me she'd seen us at Miller and Rhoad's Tea Room on Saturday when she went into town with her sister.

"I saw you, Doc," she said, "all dressed up in a brown coat and hat looking ever so smart - like that girl on the fron page of the paper."

Ethel's remark made my heart leap into my throat and do flip-flops. I could not tell her a lie, she was slow-witted and very trusting. I always told her the truth.

"Yes, Mrs. Houghton and I had walked down from the library and were dying for a cup of tea," I replied. "We went into the Tea Room before we did our shopping."

"Sister was buying some china and I saw you going past us off the elevator." Ethel confirmed her belief it was us she saw.

"We were trying to shop for Christmas." I felt relieved she hadn't seen us in the basement.

"That young girl on the front page of the paper, is that you?" Ethel came from behind the counter with me newspaper in hand. "Is that your picture?"

I looked around. No one else was in the store except us. Mrs. Henley was outside pumping gas and Arthur Henley was in the feed room.

I stood between a pickle and a hard place. I didn't know what to say. I couldn't lie to her out of honor, and also because she was simple and trusting. Yet she must not tell her suspicions to anyone or I'd be in terrible trouble for years.

"Ethel," I drew her aside, "can you keep a secret?"

"I love secrets," she confided, "what is it?"

I hesitated a minute collecting my thoughts. I decided to tell her the truth straight out, no curves, no evasions.

"Well, you see that is I in the picture, but my mother would skin me if she found out. Mrs. Carthage already called us yesterday about it. If she finds out that picture was of me she'd spread it all over Goochland

and Richmond too in five seconds," I whispered. "Please, please don't breathe a word or I'll be in trouble for the rest of my life."

"For the rest of your life?" Ethel drew me closer to her.

"Yes, Ethel, for my entire life I'd hear about it."

"Were you arrested?" she asked in a whisper.

"No, just questioned. The security guard found out that Mrs. Houghton and I were not suspicious characters. He let us go," I told her.

"I won't tell a soul. It will be our secret," Ethel promised. "Now let me fix you a double decker cone."

As I handed her a dime I knew my secret was safe.

At school I was again questioned about the photograph in the newspaper. I realized our Headmistress would be very disappointed in my deportment if she knew I had been with those screaming women tearing up sheets in Miller and Rhoad's basement. I didn't want Mrs. Houghton to be questioned either about how she was bringing me up.

"Doc," said Mary Ann, "I know that picture is of you. Were you really taken into custody by the police?"

"How could you ever think such a thing?" I demanded. "I am not a criminal."

"You could have been in the wrong place at the wrong time. What really happened?" she needled me.

"Mary Ann," I told her, "I love you dearly, and I consider you my very best friend, but I can't utter a single word about this incident. Mrs.Houghton must never come under suspicion, and my Mother would kill me dead on the spot if she even heard a whisper of it."

"Since when do you buy sheets?"

"I don't. I've never bought a sheet in my entire life," I replied and walked away.

"Not so fast; wait a minute," Mary Ann caught up with me. "I promise I won't breathe a single word, but I know what happened because my mother saw you."

"Look, Virginian's push unpleasant things under the carpet. Just leave it lay where Jesus flung it," I pleaded.

Mary Ann agreed.

A Forgotten Landscape

75

Mrs. Carthage's Shopping Trip

Shortly after Thanksgiving, which at that time came on the last Thursday in November, Mrs. Carthage telephoned our house. She wanted to speak with Mrs. Houghton, but could not remember her number. I was at the house with Bertha, so I trotted across the lawn and found my neighbour in her kitchen baking.

"Mrs. Carthage is on the phone for you."

"What ever for?"

Hastily Mrs. Houghton threw a coat over her shoulders before following me back to our house. I knew she did not wish to be bothered by Mrs. Carthage, but since her accident we realized the poor, old soul was lonely. Still not able to drive the car, her weekly visits to the general stores had been curtailed.

"Hello, Alvira," I heard Mrs. Houghton pick up the telephone.

A long conversation ensued, but finally Mrs. Houghton emerged, somewhat agitated, from behind the library door.

"She wishes to go into Richmond with us on Wednesday to see the doctor and perhaps to do some Christmas shopping at Miller and Rhoads. But I am afraid of what Harry will say."

Nevertheless, early the next Wednesday morning they left for town, all three of them. Mr. Houghton dropped his wife and Alvira Carthage at the doctor's on Second Street before he drove down to the Southern States Co-operative on his own business. They all planned to meet at twelve o'clock in Miller and Rhoads tea room for lunch. This was a rather "hattie and glovie" eating establishment at one of out two big department stores.

Mrs. Houghton told me later, as she and Alvira Carthage walked down from the doctor's office, casually poking into several shops along the way, they chatted quite happily about the war, the shortages and the weather. Upon their arrival at Miller and Rhoads, Mrs. Carthage wanted to find a few little gifts for her nieces, so Mrs. Houghton went upstairs alone to the dress department. They planned to meet Mr. Houghton in the tea room just before twelve o'clock.

At noon when Mrs. Houghton walked off the elevator onto the fifth floor what should she see, but Alvira Carthage standing before her in a most extraordinary pose! Mrs. Carthage's bloomers, yes, her bloomers, had dropped around her ankles and hobbled her. Since she could not walk, Alvira Carthage just stood there rooted to the floor with her old fashioned underwear covering her shoes, and a look of horror upon her face.

"Goodness gracious! What's happened?" demanded Mrs. Houghton.

"I am afraid the elastic's broken. What do I do now?" wailed Mrs. Carthage standing immobile in her tracks.

"Alvira Carthage, don't just stay there with you britches around your ankles, get in here and take them off." Mrs. Houghton pushed the surprised woman into a phone booth.

"Suppose Harry sees me!" exclaimed Mrs. Carthage, shocked by the very thought.

Always a snob, she prided herself upon being a Virginia gentlewoman. She would never dream of appearing at Miller and Rhoads tea room without her hat and gloves.

"What size pants do you wear?" Mrs. Houghton inquired. "I'll have to buy you another pair. Just stay here in this phone booth until I return."

But Harry had seen. Punctually at twelve o'clock when he arrived for lunch, he found Alvira Carthage hobbled in her bloomers and blushed scarlet. Mr. Houghton fled down the escalator bumping into people as he ran. He did not stop until he landed in front of the tie counter on the first floor. Mr. Houghton simply laid his head down amid the piles of neck ties and Christmas shoppers and laughed. He laughed until he choked, and then he cleared his throat and laughed again.

In vain, Mrs. Houghton looked around for him before she headed

Mrs. Carthage's Shopping Trip

down to the ladies underwear department and bought poor, stranded Alvira another pair of britches. Upon Mrs. Houghton's return to the fifth floor, she found Mrs. Carthage obediently still locked in the phone booth. After some maneuvering Alvira finally disentangled herself from the encumbering underwear, and Mrs. Houghton led her friend into the ladies room.

But Harry Houghton had vanished. They entered the tea room, after the ladies waited for some time, and they ordered their meal. Still Mr. Houghton did not come. Then just as the ladies were finishing their dessert, a red-faced Harry came into the dining room.

"Where have you been?" inquired his wife.

"Down at the ties with my head on the counter," Mr. Houghton whispered. "I didn't dare appear until I could stop laughing. The sight of Alvira from the elevator was better than any picture show!"

But Alvira Carthage was not amused. She left Miller and Rhoads to sit straight and stiff in the front seat of the 1932 Chevrolet. She wished to return home immediately after she put on her new britches. Instead, Mrs. Carthage had to eat lunch in Miller and Rhoads' tea room in front of all those people, who had, no doubt, seen her standing beside the elevator in a most embarrassing position.

"Why didn't you meet us as arranged?" she asked Mr. Houghton as he drove them home. "I shall not set foot in that place again."

But Mr. Houghton, who never explained anything, made no reply.

However, about two weeks later, Alvira Carthage called our house again. Once more she needed a lift into Richmond.

"We are not going today," I told her. "But I think Mr. Houghton might."

There was a long silence at the other end of the line, but the voice finally returned.

"May I speak to Clara?"

"Can I give her a message?"

"Tell Harry I'll catch a ride with him as far a Thalhimer's," (our other big department store.)

"Not Miller and Rhoads?" I asked with all innocence.

"I wouldn't be caught dead there. I doubt I'll ever go there again."

But she did go that very afternoon.

A Forgotten Landscape

Letters

December 10, 1943
Richmond, Va.

Dear Dad,

Everyone's rejoicing, not because of Christmas, but because Cary's been found. He's back with his Group again, and everything is great. He's with the 8th Air Force in England. Miss Emma cried when she told us. I've never seen anyone cry from joy before, but she did. Everyone is light-hearted and happy once again. It's wonderful.

This Christmas was rather fun, but then again it was not. The war drags everything down. We have shortages now. Shoes are murder for me because I'm so hard on them. Mrs. Houghton says I'll have to make out until my coupon comes due next month. Sugar is the worst and gas is still a problem. I hope you are eating steak because we are not. I have never eaten so much chicken and eggs. I'm going to cackle soon. We also eat fish because Grievous catches it for us. Canned fish is rationed, so fresh ones are a treat. I've returned to peanut butter and jelly sandwiches. Mrs. Houghton puts up the jelly from the fruit trees in the orchard. It's lovely, even without much sugar in it. We have vegetables, and so we are lucky because we don't have to depend upon the stores for our food.

I hope things are better in the new year. I'm sorry to complain, but it's tiresome to give up so many things. Mrs. Houghton has been very kind and found some new fall clothes for me. She made a lovely sweater too, so I look nice. We have to be so careful with everything now. Harness, shoes, clothes, and anything made of wool is hard to get. Leather goods are impossible so it's a great sin to break anything like a bridle or a strap of leather. They can't be replaced easily. I've been good about that. Jackie's harness is in perfect condition. My saddle is too because Mr. Houghton makes me clean it and my shoes all the time. When will this war be over?

Love, Doc

P.S. Maybe God's all right after all since he brought Cary home. Mr. Houghton says it's the French Resistance, but Mrs. Houghton says it was God. Maybe it was a little of both. Doc

76

Mr. Houghton's Birthday

December 21, 1943

Mr. Houghton was born on the twenty-first of December sometime before the turn of the century. The year, however, was not important, but the day was extremely so. It became even more important from Thanksgiving onwards, and its importance increased as December arrived. Everyone in our lower end of the county, from Henley's store to Tuckahoe Creek, knew when it was Mr. Houghton's birthday.

"It's the shortest day and the longest night," he would lament as the day approached. "I've got only half a birthday. I should have been born on the twenty-first of June. That's the longest day and the shortest night."

In spite of his telling us about his birthday a month ahead of time, (to ensure we would all remember) Mr. Houghton felt cheated. Not only was it the shortest day, but his birthday fell only four days prior to Christmas.

"I don't get many presents," he complained. "Now if I were born in June, I would get them twice a year."

In fact, he did quite well where presents were concerned. As his birthday approached, we all made trips to Miller and Rhoads to shop. Usually I would go down from school on the bus to meet Miss Emma at the store's Sixth Street entrance. Finally I grew tired of hearing about Mr. Houghton's birthday.

This year, Bertha and Mr. Houghton had a run-in. Bertha celebrated her birthday in December which most of us overlooked.

One Thursday in early December, I stayed home from school because I had a cold. Bored in Mrs. Houghton's small cottage, I put my coat on and went across the orchard to my own home. I liked to chat with Bertha and hear about life in the Negro population in Manakin.

When I entered the laundry room I found Bertha seething with anger. She'd found Mr. Houghton's constant talk about his birthday too much to bear. So when he arrived at the laundry room door with a basket of freshly gathered eggs, Bertha stood waiting for him.

"Tell me why you think you own the month of December? Other folks are born then too. I's for one and Jesus. Stop worrying folks to death over your birthday. You're like a dog with a bone. I'ze fed up."

Caught off guard, Mr. Houghton made no reply. He just left the laundry room still carrying his basket of eggs and banged the door shut.

"Now, you've done it, Bertha," I told her, as I watched these proceedings with interest. "He's gone out with your eggs."

"Perhaps he'll be back, Miss Doc, I gets tired of his talk, just plain tired."

When Mr. Houghton stayed away all morning, I realized he felt deeply hurt. He put a lot of stock in his birthday for some reason. Perhaps he didn't have them as a child on a farm in Yorkshire. Bertha went cheerfully about her work, humming the hymns she sang on Sunday. Around two o'clock when I entered the laundry room again, I found her extremely worried.

"I haven't got a ride home," she confided. "And I'ze scared to walk to the store because of Nellie Randolph's ghost, to say nothin' of the headless horseman. Don't you ever walk there at night, Miss Doc, 'cause of that headless horseman."

Few colored people dared to go near that section of Tuckahoe Creek. Bertha was scared to death of this apparition even more scared than she was of Nellie Randolph's ghost.

The short afternoon wore on, but still Mr. Houghton did not appear. On occasion Bertha walked to the store and caught a ride with James. But unless she went through the woods, that meant walking over Mrs. Haunch's bridge. And the woods held other terrors – snakes and ticks in summer, and the hoot of the barn owls in winter.

Mr. Houghton's Birthday

"Miss Doc, Miss Doc," Bertha called me. "You best find Mr. Houghton and ask him to come here in an hour's time."

I wondered what Bertha was up to but did as I was bidden. Scampering across the orchard, I found Mr. Houghton in the barn sweeping and singing.

> "When I was born upon a cold and frosty morn,
> The doctor spanked me upon my little back
> And said I was a handsome little chap.
> Then after I was powder-puffed all over,
> I was dressed in the little shirt
> My mother made for me."

"Did you make that up?" I asked. I couldn't imagine Mr. Houghton being powder-puffed all over and giggled at the thought of it.

"No, I just can't remember the words," he replied as he continued to sweep down the aisle of his barn. "I learned it a long time ago."

"How are Lindy and Susie Q.?" I leaned over the loose box stall door and patted Lindy on her forehead.

"Fit as a fiddle. Fat and sassy, these two are lazy beggars with no work to do except to bring in the Christmas tree. I brought them in today early because it's calling for snow. Those horses eat, I can tell you, whether they work or not. Maybe I should sell them. They would make fine dog food, don't you think?"

I knew he was teasing, and did not reply. Then I remembered why I had come.

"Bertha sent me to ask you to please come to the house in an hour." I delivered my message, then gently stroked Susie Q.'s head. She was the more nervous of the mares and sometimes tried to nip.

My birthday falls on a Tuesday," he said, as he stopped sweeping.

"Does it?" I asked, still patting the mare. "How old will you be?"

"As old as my tongue and a little older than me teeth," Mr. Houghton replied.

He opened the tackroom door and hung up his broom on a nail. "How dare Bertha speak to me like that."

This last remark brought our conversation to a jolting halt. Not knowing what to say, I left the barn.

"Don't forget to come," I repeated and scampered away.

Upon my return to the house Bertha wouldn't let me in the kitchen. She had locked the door and pulled down the shades. This seemed very unusual because cooking starch required no special solitude. So I knocked again.

"I'm busy, Miss Doc, go away," her voice commanded from behind the locked door.

A few minutes later, Mr. Harris rolled up the driveway in his battered old car. He was dressed in a clean shirt and neatly pressed trousers at milking time. This surprised me. Bertha mysteriously allowed him in the locked kitchen for an instant. Then he was sent out.

"What's the big secret?" He asked me.

"I don't know. She's locked that door all afternoon."

"Something's up," agreed Tom Harris. "I was told to wait."

"You can sit in the library if you like. The chairs are comfortable, and you can turn on the radio."

"A fine kettle of fish; this waiting around when my cows need to be milked is tiresome."

"Can't Angelo milk the cows?" I asked him.

"Yes, I suppose he can. Let's see what's on the radio." He turned it on looking for a station.

Emma Craddock and Jean Taliaferro arrived a few minutes later and my curiosity reached its zenith.

"What are you doing here?" I demanded. "What's going on?"

"I hear there's to be a party," said Jean.

"A birthday party," Emma Craddock explained, as she arrived with two packages.

"A birthday party," I echoed. "Here, this afternoon, how do you know?"

"That was the message I received," concurred Jean.

"Come on into the library," I offered, "Mr. Harris is here too."

"This is a surprise. Hello Tom, what are you doing here?" Jean greeted him.

"How's Cary, have you heard?" Tom Harris asked Miss Emma.

"I had a telegram from the State Department that he'd been returned to his group in England." She took a seat near him. "It's been an awful worry for two months wondering where he was. He's fine and I am much relieved."

Mr. Houghton's Birthday

"He'll have some stories to tell when he gets home," Jean replied as they made themselves comfortable in the library.

I went to turn up the heat which was kept low so the pipes wouldn't freeze. Bertha was still in the kitchen behind the locked door.

"I miss Cary," continued Mr. Harris when I returned to the library. "He's a good kid to have around."

"I miss him too," I told him. "He's an awful tease, but things were fun when he was here."

"I guess he's flying missions over Europe again," Jean added to the conversation.

"Yes," said Miss Emma, "he loves flying."

I thought she looked especially nice in her blue tweed suit. Although not new, it had a longer skirt than the ones they made now. They were not long enough to be modest and Mrs. Houghton wouldn't allow me to wear them.

Finally Mrs. Houghton walked over from her cottage carrying a package wrapped in reused tissue paper and tied with a blue ribbon. She always curled the ends with her scissors, making the curls spring back when you pulled them.

"Come in," I greeted her, "everyone is here."

"Hello, neighbour," said Jean, "now turn up your hearing aid so you can join in the conversation."

I noticed for once that Mrs. Houghton was wearing it. She rarely did at home. I had got used to her deafness and had learned to talk directly to her.

I left the party and went upstairs. In a certain drawer Mother kept unwanted gifts which we used for birthday presents throughout the year. I opened this drawer and selected a gift I thought Mr. Houghton would like. Then finding some paper and ribbon, I wrapped it. Finally I discovered some stickers with Santa Claus on them and I pasted them on the paper for good measure. Then I returned to the library.

Promptly at three o'clock Mr. Houghton arrived with his boots muddy and his hands dirty. I opened the door.

"I understand Bertha wants me," he said as he entered the hall.

"Take off you boots," I said. "You look awful to come to a party."

"A party?" he asked me, removing his work boots and standing in his sock feet.

A Forgotten Landscape

"That's what I'm told," I replied as he started to leave.

"No, don't go. Just slip into the powder room and tidy yourself up." I held the door open for him and found a hand towel. "Go wash. I'm not sure there's hot water, but there might be."

I waited for him so he wouldn't escape out the front door. Meanwhile, Bertha opened the dining room doors. A great transformation had taken place. Instead of dust covers there was a table fully set with silver and plates for a party. All the curtains were drawn, the lights were off, but in the middle of the table sat a big birthday cake, a real honest-to-goodness butter, eggs and sugar birthday cake, covered in mounds of white icing, and decorated with red rosettes. Across the top in large letters, equally red, was just one word, Harry. Ten candles flickered in the darkened room.

"How marvelous," I cried, "how simply marvelous."

Mr. Houghton came out of the powder room and joined me in the hall.

"It's a wonder in War Time even to make a cake," he said amazed, "this one is a miracle."

We all trooped into the dining room and sang 'Happy Birthday' as we went. Mr. Houghton stood amazed and speechless as he inspected the cake. We watched as he blew out the candles. In a mighty effort he got them all on the first try. He stood in the dining room in his sock feet and blushed scarlet. We all laughed as we took our places around the table and Bertha opened the curtains. The late afternoon sun shone weakly as we all sat down to eat.

"Now what do you have to say for yourself?" Bertha asked as she handed him a large cake knife. "None of us forgot your birthday. How could we? It's the most important birthday of the year."

Mr. Houghton blushed again. Then he cut the first slice of yellow cake. Bertha handed him plates for the cake and gave us each a piece. Mr. Harris opened a bottle of champagne.

"This is pre-war stuff, Harry," he told us. "I've saved it for a special time, which is today."

The champagne was poured into juice glasses as we couldn't find the wine goblets, and we toasted and sipped our drink, savouring the taste and pleasure. Then Jean got up and raised her glass in a toast to Bertha.

Mr. Houghton's Birthday

"To the best cake-baker in the world!" she said.

We all clinked our glasses once again.

"To Bertha," we all cried.

"To Bertha, may all her troubles be little ones," added Mr. Houghton.

"How old am I, Miss Jean, do you reckon?" Bertha wanted to know. "My Grand Mama was born in slavery times and didn't know how to read and write. She just told me I was born the year Tuckahoe flooded out the railroad. What year was that?"

"I don't know, Bertha," Jean replied. "There have been many floods since then. I could look it up, I suppose in the newspaper. How old do you think you are?"

"I don't rightly know," Bertha said, "but I'ze 'spect about fifty. Ain't that about right?"

"That's perfect," Jean told her. "Fifty is just right."

"Yes, now I remember," Bertha continued. "Mama was born after slavery times, but before the First World War. She went to school and could read pretty well. But I ain't got no birth certificate. You didn't get them in the country when yous born in a cabin in the woods. I'll stick to fifty."

We all raised our glasses for a third time and drank to Bertha again. She saluted us with her up-raised glass and we all drank together.

Little packages for Mr. Houghton began to appear, and I ran upstairs once again and opened the present drawer. In it was a lovely green sweater, just Bertha's size. Hastily, I wrapped it, put six Santa Claus stickers on the package and returned to the dining room.

"Here, Bertha," I said upon entering, "is a birthday package for you."

"I just loves it, Miss Doc," she told us. "A Christmas sweater just the right colour, and made of wool too. Won't I be the envy of all the ladies at church on Sunday. Mr. Harris could you give me a ride home?"

Again Mr. Houghton blushed. I knew he remembered what he'd done that morning and felt ashamed after all the trouble Bertha had gone to with his cake.

"I'll take you home, Bertha," he said faintly.

"Now, Mr. Houghton, don't you trouble yourself. Mr. Harris here has offered to take me. I will take my eggs though, but I wouldn't put you out on your birthday."

A Forgotten Landscape

77

Christmas

Christmas that year was rather sad. We had a tree which we trimmed with popcorn and ornaments, but we had to use last year's tinsel. It was really the year before's that we had saved. We were invited to Miss Emma's and to Tom Harris's. We decided to go to Miss Emma's because we had little gas to go to Manakin. Tom and Elizabeth Harris joined us. We made a party of it, but Miss Emma hadn't heard from Cary and I hadn't heard from Father. So everything was uncertain.

Before Christmas we had packed three boxes for England: One for Tommy, one for Mrs. Houghton's mother and one for Father. We had a hard time finding things. Candy was impossible, pencils had no paint, the paper was cheap and unpleasant to feel. We combed the shops for small articles that would fit into our boxes. We found things in odd places, mostly in general stores in the country that had forgotten they had such things. Mrs. Houghton fussed over the boxes. She sent her mother a small Christmas pudding, the kind they make in England. She had knitted Tommy a pretty scarf, and we made some cookies, but we were hard-pressed for ideas. After a week of packing and shopping we finally got the boxes off on time.

Grandmother called us Christmas afternoon to inquire how we were getting on. Frances telephoned from Florida to say Father was in England still in the hospital. That evening Mary Ann called me from in town. She had a new beau she was dying to get my opinion about, but since I'd only met him once or twice at a party I couldn't tell her much. I think she just wanted to talk.

The war had bogged down in Italy, and the winter was again very cold. Our spirits had reached a low ebb. Even Peggy moped about trying to get warm. Mrs. Houghton finally made her a sweater and put that on when Peggy shivered.

Things at school were not much better. Classes went on as much as usual. Everyone was wearing her mother's clothes cut down to fit. At least they were made of wool which was impossible to get now. We knitted sweaters for the Red Cross and hats and gloves for ourselves. I got quite expert with socks that winter.

"Chicken feed is getting impossible," Mr. Houghton told us one day. "It's gone up too."

"Don't come here and complain, Harry, we know about the shortages. Just cut down on your chickens, that's all."

"No," he replied. "I've found a new supplier to supplement Southern States. I'll keep going with the number of layers I have now."

"Suit yourself, then, and don't ask me," she told him.

Slowly the old year ended and 1944 came in. Mr. Houghton went out into the woods to chop down some dead trees for firewood, and we kept the fires going in spite of the shortages.

"I never remember feeling so down," I told Mrs. Houghton as we drank afternoon tea together one evening. "It's difficult to think of the world not at war."

"Cheer up, Doc, you're too young to speak like that. You have you whole life ahead of you. Life is a great gift, you must use it well."

"I try to, but sometimes it's very hard to see beyond this war. I can't remember Father's voice any more and that worries me. I can remember his laugh, but his voice is gone. He's slipped away little by little, and I can't find him in my memory."

"I know, my dear, it was the same way with my father." She leaned over to where I sat on my hassock and kissed me.

Part V
1944

The End of the Beginning

A Forgotten Landscape

78

"Thy Tents Shall Be Our Home."

February 1944

At the end of the January Father was still in England on sick leave. He wrote cheerful letters from an Army Hospital somewhere in the country. At last he was able to take care of his wounded ankle and malaria

"It's great having three squares and a soft bed. The nurses make attractive scenery and most are as bright as shiny new dimes. After the fever and shakes left I am able to perambulate through the grounds. It's not half bad here, but I'll be glad to get back into action and finish off the Bosche. Do write soon. Love Dad."

"Apparently he's getting better," I assured Mrs. Houghton. "At least he's out of the fighting for a while, and I can stop worrying."

"It sounds as if he's far away from London and those terrible air raids. I expect he can't say just where the hospital is," she replied, "but I'm sure he's relatively safe."

For almost a week I forgot about Father's illness. Then on Saturday morning I wrote him a long letter.

"I am glad you're away from the fighting. Frances said you are feeling better and might even go into London. Do write me about London. What's St. Paul like, and have you seen the King and Queen? Tell Mr. Churchill, if you should meet him, Mrs. Houghton sends her best wishes. I miss you. Love, Doc."

I hoped he would receive this, because sometimes my letters did not always get through. Poking about in Mrs. Houghton's desk drawer I discovered two unused stamps, which I licked and pasted to my envelope, pounding them with my fist. Then I placed the letter on the kitchen table for Mr. Houghton to mail.

Valentine's Day, that year, dawned snowy and cold. I gathered up the cards I had written to my classmates, put them in my pocketbook, then slipped out and ran across the frosty ground to the kitchen door. I had a great, red Valentine for the Houghtons, and wished to deliver it before starting to school.

"Mrs. Houghton" I shouted, "open the door. I'm freezing. I've got a Valentine for you, special delivery."

"Hand it in here," Mr. Houghton opened the window. "Really, Doc, it's hardly eight o'clock, and you're knocking on my door. Come by after school."

"Tell Mrs. Houghton Happy Valentine's Day, when she awakes, and tell her I'll come by later to collect mine."

You might not get one. Don't be sure. Really, kids these days expect everything. Run on now so I don't freeze to death." He banged the window shut as I departed and ran back in the front door.

At school the girls exchanged cards and wrote silly verses to each other. Mary Ann decorated a big box, and we posted our cards in it for distribution that afternoon. The halls of our school were decorated in hearts made from dollies with red arrows stuck through them. Everything seemed festive, and I felt unusually happy all day. That evening I knew Mrs. Houghton would have a special surprise for me. Delivering the Valentine so early would remind her that it was the fourteenth of February.

I had not thought of Father until that afternoon when I found a letter written in his scratchy hand propped up on the table in the kitchen. I tore the envelope open and a handmade Valentine fell out and wafted towards the floor. Excitedly I caught and read the heart-shaped card, "For my special Valentine, Doc, my little daughter."

"Not so little now, Father. I've grown heaps recently. I'm almost a lady. In March I'll be sixteen." I had forgotten how he loved Valentine's Day and used to slip cards under the door and play "valentine ghost." Inside the card lay a crumpled dollar bill and a note, "Buy some candy. Little red hearts are good. Best love, Dad."

"Look, look what Father sent. A whole dollar for candy," I shouted at Mrs. Houghton as she came in from the living room.

On the kitchen table I found a cake, small and round, covered with nuts and cherries. Cherries saved for some special occasion because we could no longer buy them.

"How beautiful," I cried. "How simply beautiful. A little Valentine Cake just for me."

I threw my arms around her neck and squeezed as hard as I could.

"That's enough now, you'll choke me to death before we can enjoy the cakes. I made a second one for myself and an even bigger one for Mr. H."

We sat in her living room before the fire. Carefully she poured us each a cup of tea and put mine down on a little table beside me. I sat as usual on my hassock.

"There," she said as she settled herself on the love seat, "happy days to us, Doc."

"Happy days to you, too," I lifted my cup in salute. "What a special day this is."

"Yes," she agreed. "But it started rather too early to suit me. A little messenger arrived before eight this morning."

"Yes, I did. I hope you liked your card. I made it myself with flour paste and some old silk of Mother's. It's all pre-war stuff and terribly good."

"It is lovely. It took a great deal of thought and patience to design such a pretty card. And I appreciate you're not long on patience," she teased.

"I know, but I'm learning."

Valentine's was on Thursday and Bertha arrived as usual. But instead of her blue satin hat today she wore a new one of red felt. It had a perky feather, and a black ribbon. I noticed when she came to our house for her money.

"I like your hat, Bertha," I greeted her, "it's really stylish."

"Yes, Miss Doc, it's brand new. Store-bought with money Mrs. Taliaferro gave me. It came from Thalhimer's basement, and it's the latest, straight from Paris, France."

"Happy Valentine's. I made you a card, and I've left it on the washing machine. It's handmade by me," I told her.

"That's real sweet of you to remember old Bertha. I do likes a pretty card, and Valentine is my favourite," she sounded pleased.

"Father sent me a whole dollar all the way from his hospital in England."

"I do declare you's in luck this year, Miss Doc. All the way from England, think of that. Good Lord, and little cat fishes, who'd have thought it? All the way from England. My, my."

"I think you'd better get Mr. Houghton to take me home, Doc. He's late this evening," Bertha watched as Mrs. Houghton gave her the money.

Friday was not a very special day, I remember, just an ordinary one. It was cold and wet, and the melting snow left rivulets in our orchard. Lady and Jackie played in the pasture, and for once I did not ride them when I returned in the afternoon. The ground was soggy and the air was damp. I flopped down upon the bed and tried to study French when the phone rang. It sounded too loud as I crossed the living room to answer it.

"Hello, Doc, this is Frances. How are you?"

"Oh fine. Mrs. Houghton's not here, just me." I explained.

"No, no, I wanted to speak with you," Frances said. "I've some news about your Father.

"Is he back with his First Army? Is he out of the hospital?" I asked her eagerly.

"No, not exactly," she replied. "I've some bad news. Some very bad news."

"Surely he's all right?"

"Well, no. He's been killed in an air raid on London. I got a telegram today, and a second from the man he rescued, a Colonel with Army Intelligence like your Father. That's all I know. I've heard none of the details. Just an air raid in London on February 14th." Her voice faded away.

"Valentine's Day?"

"Yes, that's right, Valentine's Day. Sometime in the evening, I think it was."

I dropped the receiver back into its cradle. I did not want to hear any more. Perhaps if she did not tell me it wouldn't be true. It couldn't be true. I had not meant to hang up on Frances, just on her terrible news. I left the phone, feeling shattered. Killed in an air raid? Stunned and disbelieving, I ran to my room, the room Mrs. Houghton had fixed up for me. I could feel his presence all around. I stood in the middle of the blue fringed rug and looked at my familiar things. The curtains Father had selected, the white painted shelves, and the little ceramic animals his friends had sent from all over the world. Surely he was not dead, when he felt so close to me.

I didn't believe it, and couldn't cry. I sat down upon the bed and traced the pattern of the blue coverlet with my forefinger. Then I went across to the garden and found Mrs. Houghton.

"I've just had a phone call, and I need to ask you something serious," I told her.

"What do you want to ask?" She replied.

"What happens when you die?" I asked, "I mean, people just don't die and go away forever, do they?"

"What's the matter with you, Doc? What sort of question is that?"

"Well, suppose Father gets killed, will he disappear forever and ever amen?" I repeated.

"I expect he must leave something of himself behind. Like love for his children and regard for his friends." She looked at me quizzically from over her spectacles. "What do you mean? What was that telephone call about?"

"It was Frances, that's all. She had some news from Father. Nothing much. He's been in an air raid in London, that's all she knew," I lied.

"What you want to know about death for?"

"I want to know what happens to you. How do you feel when you die, and what becomes of you? Ben says you rest, but that would get boring after a while," I persisted.

"I don't know, Doc. You rest surrounded by love of God. You see your dead friends and relatives and have a grand picnic up there. She began to sing softly,

> "I'm a poor wayfaring stranger,
> I sometimes know no where to roam.
> I heard of a city called heaven, called heaven.
> I'm trying to make it my home, my home."

A Forgotten Landscape

"You think it's like that. Our home? But you don't come back, do you? You never return here again?" I wanted to make sure.

"No, you never return here once you've gone to heaven. What's all this talk about heaven?" She stopped humming.

"Nothin really. Just want to know if you thought Father would go to heaven if he died? You know, in London, in an air raid."

"I expect he would, Doc. Your father is a brave man, and he's a good man. Surely it's only a short while before he comes home again." Mrs. Houghton replied looking me straight in the face.

"I am not sure. I thought Frances said he'd been in an air raid and - -" I couldn't finish. I just stood there looking at her frozen garden and the leafless orchard beyond. She and Peggy had come out for a little walk because in February everything was dead. It was too cold for my apple tree so I returned to the cottage. That evening Mr. Houghton drove me down to the store for a loaf of bread. Everything seemed as usual; the men talked about the war, the women did their shopping. I did not speak of the awful dread I felt around my heart. The following morning I went to school as usual with Miss Emma. Nothing seemed changed, but deep down I knew all had changed. Nothing would ever be the same again.

That evening I found Rudy and Mother at home. Rudy came across the orchard to speak to the Houghtons. I watched him come and dreaded his arrival at our door. Mrs. Houghton let him in. He stood in her living room with muddy feet and one of his bird hunting hats perched on the back of his head.

"Is Doc here?" He asked.

I came from out of the bedroom and stood before him. He came straight to the point.

"Frances called to tell us about your father. He's been killed in an air raid. That's why we came home."

"I know. She called before to tell me, but I wasn't sure." My voice trailed off.

"I am sure. He's dead. There'll be a memorial service at West Point. You are to go with your grandmother." he informed us.

"West Point?" I asked. "In New York?"

"Your grandfather's buried there. Your Dad's buried in England."

"In England?" I repeated unable to believe what he said.

"They don't bring home dead soldiers in wartime." Rudy drove home his meaning.

"You are to come over to the house dressed as a lady. We are receiving guests this evening. Your mother wants you there." He turned on his heel and was gone out the door before any of us could reply.

Mrs. Houghton handed me a cup of tea and I sat down on my hassock to drink it. Mr. Houghton came in and took off his Wellingtons before he and Peggy sat in his chair. He switched on his radio and for a few minutes everything seemed the same as usual. I wanted it that way, as we had always been.

"I want to know about heaven. The kind of heaven that one has, buried in England. Is it as special as being buried in the United States? It's terribly important that I know."

I couldn't let my feelings out. I wanted to suppress them and maybe they won't be true. I knew it was true. I knew but I didn't wish to know. As long as I held my feelings in there might be hope. Somehow, in all this muddle of emotions, Mrs. Houghton understood. She gave me the much needed space I desired to come to terms with Father's death. I loved her for it, but couldn't express it, even to her.

She took my hand in hers and drew me close as I sat on the loveseat beside her.

"This is very serious," she said, "isn't it? More serious than anything else we have ever faced together?"

"Yes, it's ever so serious. I must know what heaven's like in England – for an American. For a soldier."

She held me very close to her. She smelled of lavender and roses all mixed together. Her skin was soft against my face and her arms encircled me. Never had I felt so much love except from Father. And never had I felt so safe.

"Will you come with me to West Point? I don't know when. Will you come?"

I put my head on her shoulder. Then I demanded once again to know what heaven was like in England.

"It's very green. In spring there are many flowers, and birds sing in the trees. The fields are filled with young lambs and the cuckoo whistles his tune. The rivers are swift, except the Thames, it's wide and rather slow, but is has many villages on it before it reaches London and the sea. You can go in a boat up to Hampton Court where Henry VIII lived. There is a maze there and I got lost in it once. I think you have to keep turning right to get out, sort of like the one at Tuckahoe. In Kent, where I grew up, there are oast houses where the farmers store the hops from which they make the English beer.

"My own father's there near the ruins of Cooling Castle in an old fashioned churchyard. There's a lich gate with a little roof over it. This is where they used to leave the coffins overnight in case someone was still alive. They didn't bolt down the lid until the next morning so if the corpse were alive he could get out."

I laughed and she continued.

"In spring the robins come and build their nests in the oak trees. I am sure he's content in those peaceful surroundings. One day I plan to return and see it for myself. It's also beautiful in September when they gather the hops and the harvest into oast houses. There are great Shire horses to do the heavy work. It was a grand sight to see them in the fields. It's beautiful, peaceful spot when it's not wartime."

"There are Military Cemetaries too, all over England with row upon row of white wooden crosses. There are English ones and American ones. They are beautifully kept and in the American ones the Stars and Stripes flies. It's a piece of American soil."

"American soil?" I repeated, "In England?"

"Yes, Mrs. Houghton replied, "it's a little piece of America."

We sat there together in the late afternoon twilight before her log fire. She understood from her own sorrow how I felt. I could not cry. It seemed unreal, and I did not wish to think about it. I just wanted her comforting presence. Finally the darkness enveloped us, and she took me home.

79

"Is There Room Enough for Me"
Negro Spiritual

When we reached the house it was filled with people. Several of our neighbours had arrived. Rudy met us at the front door.

"Where have you been?" he demanded.

"She's been with me," Mrs. Houghton explained.

"You shouldn't have gone out and worried your mother. She's very upset.

"So is Doc," Mrs. Houghton snapped. "You've only one father in this world however long you live."

Without saying another word she guided me upstairs.

In my bedroom with the door closed on the chatter below us Mrs. Houghton drew me to her.

"This is going to be a very tough time for you, dear. But I'll be here whenever you need me. Now change your dress and get yourself washed. You have to go down and greet your neighbours. It's expected, and you must be polite." She sat down in the blue chintz chair and waited while I washed and selected a Sunday dress. She combed my hair and pulled it back in a barrette away from my face.

"White socks and party shoes," she said as I slipped into the dress.

"Do I look all right?" I felt terrified by the prospect of talking to all those people about Father. "What do I say?"

"Just wish them good evening and that you appreciate their coming. Don't look sad, and don't cry." Mrs. Houghton hugged me affectionately.

"I can't cry, because I don't believe it. He's here all around me in this room. And until I've proof I won't believe anything Frances says."

"Now, then, we're ready for the grand entrance. Don't get into an argument with Rudy and above all be sweet to your mother. She's feeling awfully sad." Mrs. Houghton took my hand and together we walked downstairs.

The living room was filled with what seemed like dozens of neighbours, all chatting and telling Mother how sorry they felt at this terrible news.

"My dear Nancy," chirped Catherine Hollis, "do let me know if there's anything I can do. Just anything. Good evening, Doc, how are you?"

"Fine," I replied in my politest voice, "how are you?"

"There's my fine horsewoman," the Colonel gave me a hug. "When are you coming hunting again?"

"When Mrs. Craddock brings me, I guess, since Cary's gone overseas." I squirmed free from his arm. "It would be grand to go out with you again, Colonel, I'd like that."

"How are you, Doc?" Jean Taliferro tugged at my shoulder. "We've brought you a casserole. Where shall I put it?"

A casserole? What in heaven for? I wondered.

"It's customary," Jean replied. "Don't you remember bringing me one?"

"Yes," I said, but that was when your father had a stroke – before the funeral."

"That's right. It's a Southern custom."

"Oh, of course, but this isn't the same thing at all. Not really. We don't know for sure – about anything." I stared at her in disbelief.

"May I put this in the kitchen or do you wish to take it?" Jean asked.

"I'll take it. Thank you. It smells good, and I love chicken." Holding the hot casserole by its padded carrier I left the room.

The kitchen counters were covered with food. Cakes, pies, sandwiches, a roasted chicken and a small ham. I couldn't believe my eyes, and put Jean's casserole on top of the stove. A large pitcher of iced tea stood on the table, and I poured myself a glass and gulped it down.

"Whatever will we do with all this food?" I wondered, rinsed the glass and re-entered the dining room. Mrs. Sparrow stood beside the window talking with Alvira Carthage.

"Oh, Doc," Anita Sparrow caught my arm. "I am so sorry to hear this distressing news. How in the world did it happen? He was such a fine man and so terribly handsome."

We don't know the details yet. Just an air raid in London, Frances said. It may even be a mistake. You know, telegrams can get mixed up sometimes."

"Not from the War Department. When you get something for those people it's for sure." Mrs. Carthage pointed her finger at me. "Don't get your hopes up, Doc. It's not good."

"No," I agreed, "but there could be a mistake even so. I've heard of such things happening. I read about it in the paper –"

"Doc, don't believe what you read in the newspapers. They don't tell everything and not always the truth. They have to sell their rags to the public, you know, so don't take them as gospel," Mrs. Carthage said. "It's a terrible loss all the same, and I know you will miss him. He was a different sort than Rudy."

"Yes, he was – very different from Rudy." I left the room.

In the hall I found Rudy collecting more offerings of food.

"Here, take these back to the kitchen," he commanded, handing me two more dishes.

"Where's Mother?"

"In the living room, don't bother her now. She's busy with Mrs. Crosbie and Alice Dubois. Put that salad in the refrigerator and come back and get those plates I left on the hall table...." He turned his back on me, and greeted some more guests. I picked up the plates, crossed through the dining room and entered the kitchen. Alvira Carthage and Anita Sparrow were sorting out the dishes and put several in the refrigerator, and others in the cupboard. They had taken off all the cards and were entering the names in a book. I returned to the hall to collect the remaining plates. Then, confused and exhausted, I finally slumped into a kitchen chair and put my head down on the table. A few minutes later Mrs. Houghton came and took me home with her to bed.

The next morning Bertha arrived early dressed in a black uniform with a white apron and cap. She looked ever so fine, I thought. Much too dressed up to do the laundry.

"It's not Thursday, is it Bertha?" I asked her upon entering the kitchen.

"No, Miss Doc, it's Saturday. Hurry now and eat your breakfast. I 'spect there'll be a crowd of peoples here today. And I needs to get your room cleaned up and the dishes washed." She bustled about.

"What for? I don't feel like a lot of company. I just want to be alone and think." I sat down and ate my cereal. "I'm tired."

"Your mamma is receiving this morning, honey, and you's got to get ready." Bertha washed up the breakfast dishes as I used them.

"I am going out. I shall either go to the Houghtons or over to Emma Craddock's house. I can't stand this confusion. And we're not at all sure if Father's really dead. It's not right to bring food until we're sure," I protested.

"But honey, we is sure. The telegram told us so. Your Daddy is dead and will be buried in England. Ain't that what Frances said?" Bertha held the dish towel in her worn brown hand and rubbed it over the plates. "when you goin' to believe it, honey?"

"I don't believe it. And what'll happen to me? Who wants Rudy for a Father? He's stupid and mean."

Bertha did not answer. She started to hum an old song way down in her throat:

"Lord, is there room for me in dem pearly gates?
Lord, is there room for me?
My Lord says there's room enough,
Room enough in the heavens for you.
My Lord says there's room enough
Don't stay away."

"Is there room enough for me here, Bertha?" I asked her. "Is there room enough for me, now, in this house? I don't want to go to heaven. I'm not old enough to worry about that yet." I took her my cup and saucer.

"Room enough, Miss Doc, what's you saying. Sure, honey, there's room enough for you." In spite of her fancy black uniform she drew me to her and gave me an affectionate hug. "Now you goes and gets dressed."

I started upstairs to do as she requested and met Mother half way.

"Where have you been? Rudy wants you to help him get the dead flowers out of the house," she said crossly. "And you're not even dressed. Don't you realize we are expecting people?"

I stared at her. She had on a black afternoon dress, and carried a lace handkerchief. Her face was powdered too pale, and she wore only a faint pink lipstick. She looked awful, wan and fragile.

"I just had breakfast. I haven't been any place at all," I replied.

"Do hurry. Put on something nice and comb your hair, and brush your teeth," she said. "There's not time for any visits to the Houghtons this morning."

Then she swept past me down the stairs.

Once in my room I remained dressed in a wool skirt and sweater. I crossed the hall, putting on my coat, went through the back bedroom and down the back stairs, which ended in the laundry. I knew Bertha was not there.

"It's Saturday," I reasoned. "I must help deliver the eggs. I'd like to visit Mrs. Harris and see Angelo." I wanted to get away from Mother, her friends and Rudy and find some place where I felt safe.

In the laundry room I pulled on my Wellingtons, quietly slipped out of the back door and ran towards the woods, to my secret trail. I followed it around the bluff until it dropped down into the woods and rose again behind Mrs. Houghton's kitchen door. The path was muddy but I ran, slipping and sliding, in the red clay. My boots heavy, I stopped at the edge of the woods and scraped off the mud. I finished cleaning my Wellingtons on Mrs. Houghton's whitewashed fence. Globs of wet clay hung to the rails, so I knocked them off and tried to clean the fence with my mitten. Finally I entered the handsome wrought-iron gates.

Mr. Houghton was on the back porch counting his egg cartons into a large crate. He did not look up as I entered.

"Fifteen, sixteen, seventeen," he marked them on his calendar. "Seventeen dozen this week. Eight dozen for Manakin and Henley's Store and seven dozen for customers in Richmond. What do you want now?" he asked finally.

"Just to go with you and deliver the eggs. Mother's got company coming. There go the ladies now who are supposed to open the door and answer the phone." I pointed across the orchard at an old black Ford headed up our driveway.

"Just like a regular funeral," he commented under his breath. "Who'd thought there would be all this fuss?"

"I just got to get away from that house and Mother. She looks like a ghost this morning with he face all powdered white and only a little lipstick. And she's got on a black dress like she's in mourning."

"Well, Doc, I suppose she loved your Dad and naturally misses him." Mr. Houghton picked up his egg crate and entered the house. I followed.

"But it's like she's on stage or something. Like she's acting out a part. With her lace handkerchief," I protested. "I don't believe it. It's like being in a dream, and I know it's not true, and I'm going to wake up."

Mr. Houghton placed his crate on the kitchen floor and then sat down to take off his Wellingtons. He wiggled his toes and then put his gray-socked feet into his more comfortable shoes.

"People act funny sometimes, Doc. Sure, come along with us. At least you can act natural and be yourself. It's hard being on your good behavior all the time." He picked up his crate. "I'll go tell the missus. She'll call home for you. Get Peggy's leash from behind the door and let's go."

Mrs. Houghton came into the kitchen. She smiled at me and gave me a quick hug.

"Want to come?" she said.

"That's the idea, Clara, she's on the payroll again. It'll cost me a whole dollar today since she's grown so big."

Mr. Houghton and I left the house. Mrs. Houghton made the necessary phone call and locked the front door. Peggy followed at our heels. Then we all climbed into the old Chevrolet and were off to deliver our eggs. It all seemed perfectly normal, like any other Saturday, and I felt better.

We drove through the country and as the brown fields slipped by surrounded by bare dark trees I knew this land was part of me. It spoke its own special language, not always a peaceful one, since the War Between the States was fought here, but not always violent, either. Today the fields and streams lay placid along the rolling James River, and I felt the great power land can have on people. Acres of corn and oats would soon be planted and the cycle of the seasons would start again. Finally we turned into Mr. Harris's dirt road, and Mr. Houghton brought his car to a halt under the large, leafless pecan tree.

"My goodness, Harry, you have a crowd with you this morning," Elizabeth Harris greeted us. "How are you, Doc?"

"I'm back in the chicken business again. We've come out to deliver the eggs. How many do you want this morning?" I jumped out of the car and handed her two dozen I had taken from the crate at my feet.

"Clara, how good to see you. Come inside, Doc, and I'll get your money. Let me see if I can find Tom and Angelo. Run down to the barn and see if they are there," she suggested.

I dashed off over the wet ground and jumped upon the pasture fence. Across the field I recognized Angelo gently moving the milk cows towards the better grass. In a few weeks now the pastures would be green once more.

"Angelo, it's me. How are you?" I called to him.

"Get down off my fence, Miss Doc, before I paddle you. You know better than to climb on fences, it breaks them down." Mr. Harris poked his head out of the barn. "What are you doing here?"

"Delivering eggs, as usual. I want to talk with Angelo, but he didn't hear me."

"He'll be back in a minute. Now get off my fence. You're getting too heavy for climbing around on gates. How're things at your house?" He regarded me from under the brim of his battered hat.

"Busy. Really hopping last night when everyone in the county came. But I've escaped and came out to see you." I jumped down from his fence and straightened my jacket. "I've brought your eggs, and need to collect my money. Tell Angelo I'm here, will you please," I said with dignity.

"Why, you little princess, you tell him yourself. I've got work to do. This dairy doesn't run itself. Is Harry at the house?" Mr. Harris added.

"He and Mrs. Houghton both. We all came just to visit you, aren't you pleased?" I dashed off across the field towards Angelo before the dairyman could utter another word.

"Angelo, Angelo, how are you?" I caught up with him finally, out of breath.

"My goodness, what's the hurry?" Angelo asked.

He turned from the cows and came back down the field towards me "How's the egg business?"

"Booming. Mr. Houghton's hens lay like crazy, and we have Richmond customers now. They like our double yoke eggs." I walked in front of him through the pasture and entered the barn. "Angelo, I need to ask you something. What's it like being in an air raid. What happens?"

"Why you ask?"

"Father was in an air raid in London on Valentine's Day. I just wondered." I sat down on a bale of hay while Angelo took up his broom and hosed down the milking parlour.

"They can be bad, very frightening, you're Father in an air raid? I know. I remember them, and my parents are still bombed in Frienze."

Water splashed on the concrete floor as the Italian swept out the manure. Then he put down disinfectant and hosed some more. He did not say anything, just worked steadily.

"I want to know, Angelo. Tell me, please. It's very important that I know." I stood up and pushed the hay into the feed room away from the cascading water.

"Air raids are bad. Planes drop bombs and sometimes fire bombs. Everything lights up and people are killed. Buildings fall, crash down, and families in them are trapped. You must not think of such things, Doc. Let's talk of something else," he suggested.

I watched him turn off the water, and put his broom and disinfectant away then we left the barn.

"Angelo, you don't understand. Frances called me and said Father was in an air raid in London and was – hurt. I must find out what happens. You're the only person I know who has ever been in an air raid. Please, Angelo, tell me. Is it a quick way to die? I stood on the muddy path and pleaded with him. "I must know, I must know."

The tears finally came. They flowed down my face like a river. I stood on the path and silently cried, great salt tears that smarted my eyes. My face felt sticky, and the cold wind hurt.

"Doc, mamma mia, what is wrong?" Angelo sounded alarmed. Then I felt his arm around me, and we continued to walk up the path towards the house. My tears made everything blurred, but once inside Mrs. Harris led me back into her bedroom where we sat down.

"I'm not allowed to sit on the bed," I protested. "It spoils the mattress Mother says. Perhaps we could sit in a chair."

"It's all right this time, Doc. It's good to sit together on the bed because I can put my arm around you. Now, what is it you need to know?" Mrs. Harris held me close and gently patted my back."

"I want to know about an air raid. How it works. What happens. Angelo knows. He says it's full of fire. I wonder if that's the way it was in London on Valentine's night," I sobbed.

"Don't allow your imagination to run away with you. We'll hear how it happened and then you'll understand. Every air raid is different. There are no two the same. Perhaps even this coming week we shall hear. I know you want to know, and I appreciate it seems unreal to you sitting on my bed here in Manakin. It's a long way from London. But you'll be told, I'm sure."

A thought struck me I had not considered before. Perhaps I did not really want to know. Perhaps it was too awful to know. Maybe he had suffered and screamed for help and no one came. A fresh batch of tears flooded Mrs. Harris's shoulder.

"I hope it wasn't too awful for him. Perhaps it didn't really happen. Maybe there's been a mistake." I used the handkerchief she gave me and blew my nose.

"That's right, Doc, dry your eyes." She smelled of cookie dough and roses.

"Would you do me a favour?" I asked. "A great big favour. Can I have a cup of tea and a sugar cookie?"

"Of course." We stood up, smoothed down the bed and started back towards the kitchen.

"Is he really not coming home, Mrs. Harris? Will I never see him again?" I asked.

She squeezed my hand ever so tight, and her voice came in a hoarse whisper.

"I hope not, Doc, I hope not."

That evening after we had returned from the Harrises and delivered our eggs in Manakin, Mrs. Houghton asked if I wanted to spend the night with her.

"No," I replied calmly. "My room is filled with Father's presence. He's there and I want to be with him. I'll come another night if I may, please."

Mrs. Houghton understood and for several days she left me alone and I returned to school. Ten days later Frances called again. Mother and Rudy had gone out, and I was alone in the house with Bertha who was staying the night.

"I can tell you what happened, Doc. I've received a nice letter from Colonel Bennett who was with your Dad that night in London. Would you like to hear?"

"Is it awful? I don't want to know if it's terrible. I'd rather not know." I hesitated.

"No, dear, he's a hero. He saved another man's life. You should be proud," Frances replied.

"Saved another man's life? How? How do you save another man's life in an air raid when buildings are falling on top of you?"

"Colonel Bennett's letter says: "We had gone to the theater, to the Windmill, where they still have variety shows in spite of the war. John, Cliff and I met at the hospital and we all went. You see, John was returning to General Bradley at First Army, and we went to London to celebrate. We had a pleasant afternoon and arrived at the theater in great spirits. The show was good. We started walking towards Victoria Station to catch the train home. I fell on my game leg and sprained my ankle. Sirens wailed and search lights illuminated the sky, warning of an air raid. John threw me across his back, dead man style, and with Cliff on ahead we raced for the first underground station. The noise was deafening although the bombs sounded further down the river.

"Put me down, put me down," I shouted. 'Duck into the tube station. Quickly.' But John insisted upon carrying me. When we reached the tube where I jumped down, I though John was coming behind. I stopped and looked back. The next instant dust and debris flew everywhere, throwing me down the steps into the underground. Cliff was there, but John never followed. We crouched in the tube all night, and finally the All Clear sounded and people began to leave. Outside we found a sea of devastation and ambulances lined the streets. John had been picked up and placed in one of these. Cliff and I identified him. That's about it, ma'am, I am very sorry, but I thought you would want to know." Frances stopped reading.

"Are they sure it was Father?" I asked, sitting down on the floor in the upstairs hall.

"Yes, they are sure," she replied. Her voice sounded infinitely sad and thousands of miles away.

"What do we do?" I wanted to know. "Surely we must do something."

Yes, there'll be a memorial service at West Point Military Academy at the end of March, just before Easter. I hope you can arrange with your grandmother to come."

"I don't think she knows. At least I've not heard from her. I thought she would telephone. Will you call her tonight and read the letter?" I tried to sound practical.

"I will," said Frances. "Goodnight."

I put the receiver down and went into my room and packed my bag. I wrote Bertha a note and pinned it on her closet door beside the laundry. Then I slipped out the front and walked down the driveway towards the Houghtons.

"I've come to stay with you," I said when Mrs. Houghton opened the door. "Frances called and it's true. Father is dead. How can I live without him?"

"I know just how you feel. I had to leave my Dad in England, and I never saw him again." Mrs. Houghton shut the door and took me in her arms.

A Forgotten Landscape

80

Mother's Revelation

Next day Grandmother called to say how sorry she was to hear about Father.

"I'm coming down to take you to West Point. We'll make the trip together. I love you, dear, remember that." She sounded kind on the phone, and I felt grateful. "We have to change stations in New York City."

"Can we see the Empire State Building? I hear it's a wonderful sight. It's the tallest building in the world, you know, and I'm dying to visit it?"

"Yes, I'm sure we can. We'll have about two hours between trains," she said.

Excited about my forthcoming trip I thanked her, said goodbye, and I hung up the phone.

"What will the weather be like in New York?" I asked Mother. "What clothes do I take?"

"It'll be cold," she replied. "Be sure to pack warm things."

"Can you help me, please. It's terribly important I get it right."

Mother sat in the living room, her cigarette forgotten in the ash tray. A book lay open on the bench in front of her, and she leafed through it looking at photographs of gardens.

"Please," I said.

"I don't see why you can't do it yourself. Really, Catherine, you're almost sixteen and can't pack a suitcase." She continued turning the pages of her book.

"I'll ask Grandmother when she comes," I said finally.

"Don't bother her about your clothes. She'll be too tired when she arrives to worry about such things. When are you going to grow up?"

I left the room and sought Mrs. Houghton's help. She agreed gladly, and we spent the afternoon selecting skirts and sweaters, pressing and packing them. She discovered some tissue paper saved for a rainy day, and we laid it between the skirts. Then we packed Grandmother's blue dress, the one she had bought me for Mother's wedding. Mrs. Houghton thought it very suitable for a funeral. When we finished she took home my blue suit and coat to sew on a button and to repair them.

"I think we've broken the back of that job," she said as we went downstairs together. "You should be the best dressed girl there."

Mrs. Houghton gave me a hug, and I opened the front door and watched her walk home across the orchard carrying my clothes.

"You're spending too much time with the Houghtons. You practically live over there." Mother appeared in the hall behind me.

"Yes," I said, "they care about me. And we have fun together. You're always too busy to help, and we never sit down and just talk. Why can't you play games like other mothers?"

"Why should I? Children's games bore me. Really, Catherine, you expect too much." She preened herself in the hall mirror. "I don't know what's become of you. You're such a tom-boy. It's not very attractive when you grow up to behave like a boy."

"I don't care. At least I have fun. And I like the things boys like; fishing, swimming, riding horseback. I don't care for dressing up and acting like a lady. It's boring."

She stood before the mirror and regarded her image a little longer. Then she turned and without saying another word left the room abruptly.

"She just doesn't like me, that's all," I reflected. "All she thinks of are her social engagements, her clubs and Rudy."

And I couldn't stand him.

Grandmother finally arrived from Indianapolis. She made the old house seem alive once more with her giggle and her corny jokes. She was happy and brought a totally different outlook into my troubled life.

"Oh, Grandmother, how glad I am to see you." I kissed her wrinkled cheek.

"Yes, I expect this house needs a bit of livening up. Everyone looks like he hasn't smiled in a year." She walked upstairs beside me. "I

Mother's Revelation

expect I'll have the front room again that looks out over the drive. That way I can see what's going on."

"I've helped Bertha to get it ready, and put some flowers in a vase for you."

"Flowers?" Grandmother asked, surprised. "At this time of year?"

"Mrs. Houghton has flowers at any time of the year."

I watched as Grandmother took off her coat and hung it up. Then she started to unpack. Everything smelled like roses, and her underwear was in a silky-satiny bag with lace on it.

"She's a real lady," I though, "to have such nice things."

"Well, my dear, where's you Mother? Let's go down and find her. Perhaps we can have a cup of tea. It would taste good on this cold morning. It's very wintry for March."

"Yes. I guess New York will be freezing. I hope I have packed enough warm clothes." I took her hand, and we walked downstairs. Mother sat in the living room, lit a Chesterfield and blew smoke in white puffs.

"Really, my dear," Grandmother objected. "Must you smoke so much? It's very unpleasant and very bad for you. Do put it out."

"I like a cigarette every so often; it calms my nerves," Mother replied as she crushed the Chesterfield in an ash tray. "All the ladies of my age smoke. It's a different generation. Besides it's considered chic."

"It's offensive, Nancy, and I don't like it." Grandmother sat down on the sofa beside me. "Can we have a cup of tea? Shall I make it?"

"No, Catherine can get it for us. She doesn't mind," Mother said.

"We'll get it together, then. Come Doc, let's find the tea pot." Grandmother led the way into the kitchen.

It was fun fixing tea with her. We put out cookies, lemon and lovely smelling gingerbread. We prepared a tray, and I put three cups on it. The tea hot and the cookies brown and inviting, we carried the tray into the living room.

"I did not mean for you to get it," Mother said. "I just think Doc can do more around here besides spending her time at the Houghtons."

"I expect if things were more lively here she would hang around. Where there's fun, young people are bound to join in. You have to make things enjoyable, Nancy. Not just for you and Rudy, but for Doc too,"

Grandmother replied.

"John provided the fun for her. But I never could. I guess I'm not really interested in teenage pursuits. And Catherine's too young for clubs and for social gatherings. That's what I like, being the president of clubs and directing things." Mother took the cup Grandmother offered and helped herself to a cookie.

"You should try to be more concerned about your only daughter. It's really easy to like Doc because she's good company." Grandmother handed me a cup and a plate full of gingerbread.

Then she served herself, and sat back on the sofa to enjoy her tea. She had on a blue and white dress and her tiny feet looked pretty in navy shoes.

"How dainty she is," I thought as I watched her sip the hot tea. "How ladylike, and careful she is of her clothes. Yet, she seems so natural."

"Are you packed and ready to go tomorrow night? I hope you'll bring the dress I gave you," she said.

"Yes. Mrs. Houghton helped me pack with lovely tissue paper. I'll wear it with my blue Sunday coat. I can't wait to see New York City. It'll be great," I told her in eager anticipation.

"It's a funeral, not a joy ride," Mother said. "You're disrespectful to talk like that."

"Not at all," contradicted Grandmother. "She's just eager for new adventures. And you can't have a long face all day, every day. I hope we can see the Empire State Building. That would be something to tell your friends about."

"Won't Mary Ann be envious! I know she's never been to New York, although she's been all the way down to Florida." I wondered what Florida was like.

"That's right, enjoy life. Do you know what the old man said to the rooster?" she asked.

"No," I replied, although I had heard this joke many times.

"Stop crowing and get on with living," Grandmother giggled.

"Mother, why do you love those old jokes? Everyone knows them, and they are not funny."

"Nancy, corny old jokes are a lot better than your constant fussing.

Mother's Revelation

Where is the joy in your life? You are the saddest person I've ever seen. What's happened to you?"

"My happiness walked out with John. And Catherine is just like him. She reminds me of him, day and night." Mother took another cookie. "Why must you be so like him?"

"Nancy, that is enough. You must not speak in this manner. It's unChristian and extremely unkind," Grandmother's voice sounded cold and very firm. "You'll not discuss it again except in private."

I finished my tea. I know Mother did not like me. Now I realized why. I thought it was me. But suddenly I discovered it was her. She did not like me because I reminded her of Father. And I could never change that.

"She makes me feel guilty, that's all. Terribly guilty. I've neglected her, and felt jealous of her love for John. He loved Doc more than he loved me." Mother's voice sounded out of control. "He was *my* husband, not her's."

I froze in my seat. Never had I seen Mother act in this manner. I did not like her – this strange, cold, unhappy woman. That was why I had sought the Houghtons' company, they were warm and loving, and above all – they cared. Grandmother took my hand and held it tight. She said nothing. I watched in horror as Mother smashed her tea cup and walked out of the room.

Silently Grandmother picked up the broken pieces and put them in the wastebasket. I took a second cookie and bit into it. The clock in the front hall struck, sounding like a gong in the still house. After what seemed like an age Grandmother sat down and took my hand once more.

"It's true," she said softly, "it's been true for a long time. Your Mother always resented you. I only hope she can turn her feelings around before it's too late. Guilt and jealously eat into your very soul and make you bitter. Don't ever become bitter, Doc, it kills all love. Your Mother had everything she wanted and did not realize it. Now she has almost nothing because she can't love her only child and has lost the husband she adored. He was her great love, but she could not show it. Express your love, Doc. The Houghtons have given you a chance of expressing those fine feelings you inherited from your father. Always love him, and cherish his love for you. Not many girls are as lucky, to have been loved as much as you've been."

I sat on the sofa next to her and cried. I felt ever so alone. I had lost both my parents.

The next evening, dressed in my suit, a white blouse, and my blue Sunday coat I drove into the Station with Grandmother. She also wore navy and looked terribly smart, I thought. In her hands she carried white gloves, two pairs for the train.

"I wish I could go," Mother said as we rode down our lane. "I would love to see West Point again."

"Maybe later you can go up. This is just a memorial service, dear, and Frances will be there. So it's not appropriate for you to come." Grandmother settled herself in the front seat and waited for the heater to come on.

"I didn't realize when John walked out of my life it would be for good. It's terribly sad to think of him gone forever," Mother continued. "I shall miss him."

I could tell from my place in the back seat that she was crying.

"Yes, dear, we shall all miss him. He was a good man and a very loving one. Everyone liked him," Grandmother replied.

"It seems so final. So coldly final. I hate it, and I wish now I hadn't married Rudy. I don't love him, you know. It was just convenience." Mother turned the car onto River Road.

"I realized that before you married him, and I could tell you nothing."

"But an unmarried woman with a child is suspect. You're not included in things, and you're not voted president of the Women's Club. I had to get married to save face. I wish Catherine weren't so much like John. It's very difficult for me."

"You'll have to face up to that, Nancy. You can make Doc's life pleasant or unbearable. Stop and consider her feelings. Have you held her and allowed her to cry?" Grandmother asked.

"No, but then she has the Houghtons. She likes them better than she does me."

"And whose fault is that? What do you expect her to do, sit still and wait for you to love her? Children don't work that way, and you'd better learn it. Soon it will be too late, and you've lost all those wonderful childhood years," Grandmother said.

Mother's Revelation

"She's too much like her father. And I can't forget it. She reminds me of him and of my failed marriage. I don't like to be reminded." Mother drove steadily towards town.

I realized they had forgotten I was along or they would not have continued with this conversation. I stayed very quiet and small in the back seat. I had never realized Mother had any feelings about Father and me before.

"You'll have to change your attitude about things, Nancy, or you shall become a very bitter, unhappy person. You can't live with such hatred and be a loving parent. And Doc needs a loving parent, especially now."

We rode in silence for several miles. Grandmother made sure she had her tickets, and put on the pair of gloves in her handbag. Then she adjusted her blue felt hat and opened a packet of mints.

"Would you like one, Doc?, she asked.

"Oh, yes, please." I leaned forward and accepted it from her.

"The train leaves at nine-thirty and gets into new York about eight in the morning. We have a lay-over in Washington and in Baltimore. Tomorrow morning we shall see the Empire State Building. I promise." She turned and smiled at me. "What will your friend, Mary Ann say?"

"She'll die with envy. But then she's been to Florida, all the way down to the Keys. And I've never been there," I confessed. "But I think New York is far more exciting."

"At least you won't become a fried lobster from being out in the sun. Fair people like you just burn and don't tan. Too much sun is not good," Mother replied.

"Yes, and I don't like sand in my bed. It's horrid in your bathing suit too. I hate that," I said. "No, I prefer New York and getting dressed up in my best clothes."

Finally we arrived at the station and boarded the train. Mother helped Grandmother with her suitcase, and I struggled with mine. We found our seats, and I watched as Grandmother drew her daughter close and gave her a goodbye kiss.

"Goodbye, Catherine," Mother said without even shaking my hand and left the train.

I stood and watched her retreating back as we went down the

platform. She did not turn to wave, she just left. The berths were made up so Grandmother and I prepared for bed. I wondered if Mother would ever grow to like me.

In the morning we arrived in New York early. As we stepped off the train a Red Cap came and offered to carry our bags. We followed him through the crowds and out to a taxi. Then we left Pennsylvania Station and flew up Fifth Avenue towards 33rd Street. Tall buildings surrounded us and horns honked as commuters, trucks, and automobiles all dashed forward towards oblivion I felt sure. I shut my eyes, but decided I'd miss all the wonderful early morning sights. Scared to death for my life I clung to the strap beside the window and clutched Grandmother's warm hand.

"I never expected it to be like this," I gasped with fear and excitement.

"It's rather wonderful, isn't it? Very busy this time of day," the cabbie offered. "You're from the South, ain't you? A real Southern Belle, I'd say by your accent."

"From Virginia," I replied.

"Where the good horses come from. I like to bet on Virginia-bred horses. They have some good 'uns down there. Ever been to the race track?"

He parked his car, and we got out. The Empire State building before us looked like white stone. It was sleek and new. We entered and because of wartime regulations we were not allowed to go up on the observation platform but we did look around at the main floor. Then we returned to the street and craned our necks so we could see the top.

"What a great spire," I gasped. "It's wonderful. And to think I've seen it here in New York – a place I never dreamed I'd be."

Back in the cab we started up town once again towards Grand Central Station. It, too, was large and full of people scurrying to and fro. The cabbie helped us out and gave us our bags. Then Grandmother paid him, giving him a five dollar bill for taking us to the Empire State Building. Smiling, he tipped his hat and was gone.

At the ticket counter we bought roundtrip fares and hurried up the platform to a waiting train. We found seats and secured our cases under them. Out of breath we sat down and waited for the train to move.

"We shall spend the night near West Point," Grandmother explained.

Mother's Revelation

"I'm not sure we can stay at the Thayer Hotel since it's wartime. But we'll stay nearby. You'll like this trip up the Hudson River.

A Forgotten Landscape

81

West Point

The train moved through the station, entered a dark tunnel, and finally came out into brilliant sunlight. Slowly we slid past endless ranks of drab row houses, all the same. Then gathering speed we raced along the Hudson River under the Catskills, winding like a snake through brown hills of early spring, past dark, leafless trees standing black against the mountains.

"What a landscape," I thought. "How different from Virginia. This country is spooky," I said aloud.

"And filled with ghosts like the Headless Horseman of Sleepy Hollow," Grandmother added. "It's Dutch country, founded by those thrifty settlers with such names as Van Buren, Stuyvesant, and Roosevelt. Originally called New Amsterdam, it was bought by the English and renamed New York."

"Why New York?" I asked.

"After the Duke of York, I suppose," she replied. "Old York dates back to the Vikings. Have you ever heard of Yorkshire and the City of York with its famous minster?"

"Mr. Houghton comes from Yorkshire," I said. "It's in England."

My thoughts returned to Father and his final journey home. Quite suddenly my bright morning, so filled with adventure, lay in tatters. All my sadness, forgotten in the excitement of travel, came rushing back. I found this strange, shadowy country with its dark mountains and grey river, foreboding. With all my heart, I wanted to go home. Shivering, I drew my jacket closer.

"Put your coat on if you're cold," Grandmother suggested.

A Forgotten Landscape

"I don't like this place. Is West Point like this?"

"No. It has fine stone buildings, green playing fields, and a chapel that sits high on a hill above the river. It's a great fort built on a promontory guarding the Hudson."

"I wish Father would return to Virginia," I told her, close to tears.

"Your Grandpa's buried here: it's an honour to be interred at West Point," she explained. "I wonder if your Father's aunts will be there, those two remarkable old ladies who run a boarding house in Atlanta. Do you remember them?"

"Oh, yes, but they really must be ancient. Why do they always wear black?"

"It's considered very elegant, my dear, and most old ladies are widows," Grandmother replied.

"But you'd think they'd get awful tired of it. Black's a terribly dreary colour, especially for old ladies who are all white and wrinkly."

Grandmother laughed.

I wanted to escape from this gloomy, dark country with its threatening mountains and slate-coloured river. Everything about this place seemed cold and uninviting. Even in the morning sunlight the hills appeared black and their evergreens unfriendly. At home the Virginia pine woods remained green even in winter, and the sun filtered through them onto the ground making shadows. It seemed a far more hospitable place than these Catskills with their strange stories of ghosts from the Revolutionary War.

"Near here Benedict Arnold tried to give West Point to the British, and Nathan Hale gave his life for his fledgling country," Grandmother explained.

"Let's not spend the night here," I said. "Let's return to New York or even to Philadelphia."

"We'll cross the bridge at Tarrytwon near where the Tappanzee Ferry comes up from New Jersey. Then the train will head north on the east side of the Hudson towards Bear Mountain Park and Highland Springs, where we'll get off."

"Is it far?" I asked.

"It takes about an hour," she replied. Then she told me a story, I suppose to distract my attention from the landscape. "When my grandparents came over from Germany they stayed in a village near here. But after a few months they traveled west to Gettysburg, in Pennsylvania, where they settled. My grandmother had a child that died and is buried here. With her husband, a young son of five, and a new baby she rode in a wagon to Gettysburg. That young child was my papa."

"How did he get to Indiana?" I asked, not really interested.

"He grew up in Gettysburg, but before the Civil War traveled by riverboat down the Ohio to Evansville. Papa had studied law in the office of a Mr. Stevens, then went west to seek his fortune. He joined a law firm in Evansville and bought a large farm on the river. After his first wife died, he married Mamma who was ten years his junior. They had five children, and Mother raised the two young sons from the first family. With seven of us, we had merry times at our house. And Papa adored Mother whom he called his "Little Jewel.""

"Did you grow up in a cabin like Abraham Lincoln?" I asked.

"Not at all. We had a large, frame house with a garden."

"Did you have an orchard?"

"Oh yes, a lovely one, with apple trees and cherry trees. We grew wonderful cherries and made pies and cobblers, more than we could eat. I used to climb those trees, just as you do, and my brothers loved them. They would climb up and shake down the fruit for us. Both my older brothers had jobs delivering groceries after school; my sisters and I minded the house. Papa insisted we learn to make money. I became a teacher, my sister, Nannie, was a nurse, and Elsie took a typewriting course and worked as a secretary in Papa's office. The two older boys studied law like their father, and my younger brothers, Alf and John, became doctors."

"Your childhood sounds ever so nice," I replied, interested.

"It was very carefree. I had an idyllic childhood in the bosom of a large family. It was fun." She seemed to forget me and drift back into her misty past filled with children, apple trees and cherry cobbler. I envied her.

At Highland Springs we got down. It was a poky little station in an equally poky town. Not at all as I had pictured it. Undaunted, Grandmother found a taxi and instructed the driver to take us to the Military Academy. At the main gates a soldier brought us to a halt, enquired our business, then waved us through. We drove around the playing fields, past White Point with its historic cannons, and finally headed up the hill to an impressive chapel. Here all the family had gathered. I recognized Frances. Beside her stood Uncle Edward, Father's older brother, and his wife, Trudy. She was pretty and sweet, although rather flaky, I thought. She was always forgetting things. Today she came forward and gave me a big hug.

"My dear Doc, how did you get here from Virginia?"

"With Grandmother," I replied. "You remember Catherine Ferrell?" Of course, my dear. How nice of you to come such a long way."

"Doc and I had a pleasant trip," Grandmother said and shook hands.

"How are you, Southern Belle," Uncle Edward squeezed my shoulder as a sign of affection. He wasn't much on kissing, but he pinched our shoulders until we wanted to scream. The harder he pinched the more he loved us.

"Don't hurt me," I begged, spun around and hugged him close.

"My goodness, such affection. I'm overwhelmed," he cried.

How like Father he looked, even his voice sounded like him. Although older, and less slim, and not quite as tall, for a minute I was sure he was Father home safely from the war.

"Why couldn't Father have your job here at West Point instead of going overseas?" I asked. "It's not fair."

"John would hate teaching Cadets and standing on the sidelines. A man's work must be of his own choosing to be happy." Uncle Edward put his arm around me. "Don't grieve, Doc, for John got what he wanted most – adventure."

"Yes," I said, "but I'm only sixteen, and I need him."

"Life isn't always fair. It's mostly chance and hard work. But chance is everything in war. You can't control your luck."

"I wish he'd been with his troops. An air raid, a stupid air raid killed Father."

"It's just as deadly as a battlefield. Deadlier because people caught in air raids are not armed. They can't fight back; remember all those nameless civilians who have died in London?" Uncle Edward drew me closer.

"I know, that's what's so awful. He didn't have a chance. I hate it because he couldn't defend himself. It's so unfair." I hid my face in Uncle Edward's sleeve.

"Yes," he said. "That's how I feel, Doc. But we must remain brave."

"I am tired of remaining brave. I am sick to death of war, of rolling bandages and delivering eggs. Chickens are such smelly things, and oh, so stupid." My anger boiled over. "I want to drive a car and go out with boys!"

I didn't consider what I'd said funny, but Uncle Edward laughed. A great roar of a laugh, just like Father's. Again he drew me close and held me in his comforting arms.

"You're growing up, Doc. What a fine young woman you've become. I am sorry John didn't know you as an adult."

Then he led me gently towards the family grouped on the stairs and to the two awaiting aunts. How like black crows they looked. So different from Grandmother. "Here are the Merry Widows," winked Uncle Edward.

"How do you like this Rip Van Winkle country?" Aunt Agnes greeted me. "You've read Washington Irving's story set in these mountains? They're haunted, you know, and appeared ever so romantic to our early writers."

"Hello," I said extending my hand. "I like haunted places, but these mountains are terribly spooky."

"Hello, Doc," Aunt Harriet kissed the air at my cheek bone. "My, how grown up you are! I'm nearly frozen to death in this Yankee weather. Let's go inside. How are you, my dear?"

"Cold," I replied. "It's windy here on this hill."

"And I have on my unmentionables, too. New York winters are very inhospitable. Now that we're all here I think we could go inside and get out of this wind."

"And how is your dear Grandmother?" Aunt Agnes asked. "She is such a love to bring you all this way on this sad occasion. You're so like your mother, you know, with your thick blond hair and blue eyes. Really, my dear Doc, you are going to be a beauty."

I blushed scarlet.

"The boys will be knocking at your door. What a Belle you'll become." Aunt Agnes twittered in anticipation. "We always claimed that Southern women were prettier than Northern ones. It's the climate, you know, it keeps us young and soft."

"I don't really have any dates yet," I tried to explain. "I'm too much of a tomboy."

"That will pass. You will soon become a lady and put away your boyish games. It's expected, you know."

"I'm not sure I want to. You see I like my country life, riding horses and all." I regarded Aunt Agnes standing there dressed in unrelieved black, a long veil thrown back, a hat perched high on her great mass of dark hair, and wondered if she dyed it. Surely at her age it should be gray. "Just like Mrs. Owens," I thought.

Suddenly the rector appeared at the chapel door.

"Come inside," he invited, "you must be frozen. If you take your places near the front I have the heat on there. Can we begin? Has everyone arrived?"

"Yes," Uncle Edward said leading the way inside the elegant chapel with its stained-glass window – soft light and wooden pews.

Frances appeared and took me by the hand. Clad in severe black with a single strand of pearls, she looked gorgeous. Her pearls were real and all the same size. She wore a simple black hat and carried black gloves and a leather bag. It felt good to my touch; the leather was soft and supple. In her hand she held a white linen handkerchief and a small Book of Common Prayer, leather bound and trimmed in gold. She led the way to the front where we sat down. She beckoned Grandmother to sit beside us, while the family arranged behind. Frances then gave me an affectionate hug before she sat back and opened her Prayer Book. I opened mine, the one Grandmother insisted I bring.

The organ boomed forth and a small choir of men and boys appeared from a side door and entered the stalls. I did not recognize the first hymn, so didn't sing it. Although the service was short I found it extremely somber. So I let my thoughts drift back to the day we buried Old Sally at St. Mary's. I forgot about the impressive, cold chapel and remembered Father riding Cherry down to the river on summer evenings. How long ago it seemed, those halcyon days before the war!

Half-heartedly I listened as the rector intoned the service. Although the words sounded familiar, they had no meaning. I felt out of place, somehow, in this elegant chapel with strangers all around me. Even though I knew them all they didn't belong in my church. I would have felt more comfortable with Mrs. Carthage, her red hair untidy, falling out from under her black hat, and with Colonel Hollis explaining in a loud voice his latest exploits on the hunt field. I even missed our out-of-tune organ and Dorothy's hillbilly voice. Then a well-tuned organ sounded some familiar chords. I recognized a hymn I'd always associated with the War Between the States, (as Mrs. Owens insisted we call it). Now it was played for Father. With tears swimming in my eyes I stood up to sing:

> Lead on, oh, King Eternal
> The day of march has come.
> Henceforth in fields of conquest
> The tents shall be our home.

The words choked in my throat. Father's tent was no longer in Virginia, but in England. Tears streaked down my face, never in my entire life had I felt so bereft. I prayed that Father's tent, gone from me on earth, was in heaven.

"Perhaps there isn't a heaven?" I debated. "And if there is, will I end up there? Maybe I'll never see him again. Maybe he's in hell. Surely not. He must be in heaven – and I must go there and meet him."

Overcome by these thoughts, I dropped my hymnal, knelt down and sobbed.

"Dear Doc," Frances comforted me. "It's all right."

"Please, Frances," I said between sobs, "tell me, where are God's tents?"

"In heaven. It means your Father will share God's tents in heaven."

"Are you sure?"

"I'm very sure," she replied firmly. "And you, Doc, will share them one day too."

I accepted her linen handkerchief and wiped my eyes. The music swelled to a crescendo and climaxed in a long Amen. I stood up, my eyes dry, my face red from crying.

"I've ruined your handkerchief. It's all wet," I said.

"Don't worry," Frances put her arm around my waist. "Just remember that in God's tent your Father's happy and will wait for you and me. There is room for us all, my dear."

" 'His tents shall be our home.' I'll try ever so hard to become a lady so I'll enter there one day."

Outside on the steps of the chapel a bugler blew "Taps," that plantive song composed in Virginia during the Civil War and played when a soldier is laid to rest. Although sad and lonely sounding, I did not cry. Then rifle fire resounded across the valley. Finally silence. Frances stirred, placed her hand gently upon my shoulder, led me forth down the aisle and out into the cold March afternoon.

"It was very impressive," she told the rector when he came to say goodbye. "Thank you for doing the service." "We'll meet you at the Thayer Hotel for some soup and sandwiches."

Uncle Edward appeared on the top step behind us.

"Yes," Frances said, then with me in tow she walked down the long flight of steps to a waiting car. "Driver, we are going to the Thayer Hotel, but first I wish to stop briefly at the cemetery. Doc, I want you to see where he'll rest when he comes home."

"Is it far?" I asked, not sure I wanted to go.

We swung down the hill, and turned left towards the river. The cemetery was beside the Hudson amid large trees surrounded by a wall and impressive gates. The car stopped. Frances got out and led me down the frozen paths to a grassy spot under a giant oak.

"He'll lie here next to your grandfather. It's peaceful and historic here. He'd approve."

I knew she was right. Then without another word we drove to the Hotel to meet the rest of the family.

"I hope we'll always be friends," Frances remarked as we crossed the lobby. "You're the daughter I've always wanted."

"And you're great fun," I assured her.

Together we entered the dining room to find everyone already there. Soup, hot and tasty, soon warmed me up. I looked around at Father's family. Teddy, Uncle Edward's eldest son, was a favourite of mine. Even though I rarely saw him, he was good fun and always friendly. But he sat across the dining room. At my table I found Father's two aunts from Georgia with Aunt Trudy and Uncle Edward.

"I wonder if I can have a hot toddy?" Aunt Harriet remarked. "Edward, please see to it. I'm frozen stiff. Do you want one, Agnes?"

I think not, Sister. I prefer hot chocolate. It's equally warming."

"I would hardly consider it so," replied Aunt Harriet. "There's nothing like a stiff rum toddy."

"I do hope it doesn't go to your head. A lady should never display herself in such a manner."

I could tell Aunt Agnes disapproved of alcoholic drink, but was far too polite to say so. Aunt Harriet was of a more daring nature. She had traveled all over the world, ridden a camel up to the pyramids and climbed around Katmandu long before women did such things. Now a retired teacher, as was Aunt Agnes, she still craved adventure.

"Harriet should have been a man," explained her sister. "She's really lost as a woman, with all the things she likes to do."

"I am perfectly content to have been born a woman," Aunt Harriet replied, "but I find the things men do far more interesting. I adored Nepal and India, and would love to climb Mount Everest."

"I see where John got his adventurous spirit," Uncle Edward remarked, offering his aunt the hot toddy. "You've missed your calling teaching school in Atlanta."

"Not at all, I enjoyed that too. And of course I played tennis well enough to win several local tournaments. Now both Agnes and I play golf since the war has stopped us from traveling."

"Oh, Sister, you know I am just terrible at golf. I only play for the companionship. I can't really hit the ball worth a hoot." Aunt Agnes, a younger, prettier edition of Aunt Harriet, protested.

In fact, Aunt Agnes had been married once for a short time to a boy from Athens, Georgia, whose father taught at the University. Both sisters had attended the Lucy Cobb Institute where they trained as teachers. While there Agnes had fallen madly in love with Cuthbert Webb.

"He was so handsome, and ever so clever. Really terribly smart. Papa declared he would become the greatest lawyer in Georgia and even a judge. We got married on a lovely April morning when all the dogwoods and azaleas were in full bloom. Cuthbert entered the law office of Jonathan Smith. They had such high hopes for him. He joined the hunt club, and used to hunt foxes in a wonderful scarlet coat. One wet day his horse fell on him. That's how he was killed, you know, he broke his neck," Aunt Agnes remembered.

"I am so sorry, I didn't know you were married," I said awkwardly.

"Not at all, me dear, it's a long time ago. You see, Harriet and I have made a good life for ourselves. We've traveled all over the world. And I even had a ship-board romance. But since he was English and I was American, Papa didn't approve of our getting married. Rodney married Eleanor Ross, another American girl, and they came to live in New York. Isn't that ironic? He's kept in touch with me all these years. He is such a lovely man."

"Oh, Agnes, you do go on so. Really, you'd think Papa prevented it. He didn't, you know. It was your own choice," Aunt Harriet interjected.

"I would love to have lived in England. It's a very different life. I wonder sometimes if I shouldn't have married him after all."

"You would have been desperately homesick," Aunt Harriet said. "What a romantic girl you are, Agnes. It was forty years ago."

"And I remember it as if it was yesterday. Rodney has ten grandchildren now. And he still lives in New York State. Not too far from here," Aunt Agnes giggled. "Perhaps, Sister, we could see him while we're staying with Edward."

"That would be fun. We'll telephone him this evening and make arrangements."

"Oh, Sister, what a daring idea!" Aunt Agnes' eyes sparkled with delight. "And perhaps we'll go over and pay him a visit. He only lives across the river in Poughkeepsie."

"It'll be a great adventure, after forty years. Do you think he's lost his dark wavy hair and gone bald?" Aunt Harriet asked wickedly.

"Now what are you two ladies cooking up?" Uncle Edward wanted to know. "It sounds as if you're heading for trouble."

"How I love it!" Aunt Harriet crossed her arms over her ample bosom. "Edward, on the strength of Agnes' momentous decision, please bring me a second hot rum toddy."

"Oh, Sister," Aunt Agnes protested, "really, you shouldn't."

"Stuff and nonsense. I can hold my liquor. Don't be worrisome."

Uncle Edward regarded his aunt somewhat dubiously, but never questioned her demand for a second drink. When it arrived our formidable relative drank it down with considerable relish. Demurely, Aunt Agnes ordered another hot chocolate, and sipped it slowly, gracefully – every inch a Southern lady. I watched these two women, fascinated. Never before had I seen anyone like them.

"What did you teach?" I asked Aunt Agnes.

"English mostly, and some history. Sister taught chemistry and mathematics. She holds a post graduate degree, you know."

"Does she?"

"Oh, yes. She came North and studied before women in the South did such things. Papa thought it was very daring, but he let her come. He was proud of her accomplishments. Papa, you see, believed in the education of women."

"Was that unusual?" I asked.

"Very unusual at that time. That's why Harriet was such a good teacher." Aunt Agnes assured me. "She was educated like a man."

"And her husband? Did she have a husband?" I knew this was a personal question, but I was dying to know.

"Poor Sister," Aunt Agnes lowered her voice. "She married a darling man, a college professor from North Carolina who was even more brilliant than she is. He was an archaeologist, and they roamed around the world going on various digs. Sister still grieves for him."

Aunt Agnes finished her chocolate, wiped her mouth with a dainty gesture and placed the cup carefully on its saucer.

"That was good," she said, "very satisfying on such a blustery day. And now, my dear, when can you come to Atlanta and visit us?"

"I don't know," I replied. "But I'd like to come."

"Then you must, and meet all your Georgia kith and kin. I'll get Harriet to make the arrangements. And your Grandmother must come too." Aunt Agnes smiled.

Lunch over, and both her hot toddies finished, Aunt Harriet stood up. She was helped into her long black coat by Uncle Edward, and regarding us with satisfaction she remarked,

"This has been very enjoyable, seeing all the family. We shouldn't just meet at funerals; it's a rather barbaric custom, you know. We must go, Edward, please give me your arm." Then without another word she walked from the room.

Aunt Agnes, as if afraid not to comply to her Sister's wishes, picked up her coat and followed.

"Goodbye, my dear Doc," said Aunt Trudy. "Are you and

your grandmother leaving this afternoon for Virginia?"

"No, we'll go back to New York City for the night. Then we return to Richmond in the morning. I hope I'll see you again soon. Thank you for a lovely luncheon," Grandmother replied.

"We didn't have much time to talk today," my Aunt kissed me goodbye.

I went to find Teddy. I found him talking with several cousins I hardly knew.

"How did you like the old Aunts? They're out of the Dark Ages if you ask me. Here're some more Yankee cousins, Doc. You should get to know them." He put a friendly hand on my shoulder.

"Yes, I replied shyly, "I'd like to know you."

"You, a real Southern Belle?" One of my cousins inquired. What do you think of all these handsome Yankee men?"

"I don't know about that Southern Belle stuff. That's more Aunt Agnes' style," I blushed. "And I'm not sure Yankee men are more handsome that Southern ones."

"I'm sure they are," said Teddy laughing.

We crossed the hotel lobby, where I kissed my aunts goodbye. Uncle Edward gave me an affectionate squeeze on the shoulder. A few minutes later they were gone. I was delighted when Teddy drove us to the station in Highland Springs, Grandmother, Frances and me. Here we caught the train for New York, and at last left this spooky, ghost-ridden country in which Father did not belong.

West Point

Last Letter

Spring 1944
Richmond, Va.

Dear Dad,

  This is the last letter I'll ever write to you, although you won't receive it. At first I was furious at you for getting killed. It was a really stupid, jackass thing to do. Because you've left me when I needed you the very most. Bertha went around crying for days and looked terribly sad. I couldn't stand being with her. Mr. Houghton just blustered, because he was afraid to show his true feelings. But Mrs. Houghton understood how I felt. Her dad died in England years ago, and she never got back to see him. She felt guilty about that for ages. I don't feel guilty, but just angry that you could play such a dirty trick. Think of having to deal with Mother and Rudy alone, and you'll see what I mean.

  Jenny wrote me, and so did Cary. Mary Ann came out to spend the night, and we went into the woods where I cried. I feel so terribly cheated and alone. Even God had forgotten me. How could He have let you die? Now things are better, and I'm back in school trying to get ready for exams. Everyone has been extremely kind, and Mrs. Owens even gave me extra help in Ancient History to make up for the lost time. Mary Ann's helping with math and even the ancient Mrs. Smith gave me two hours tutoring in French. I couldn't believe it. I mean, she's nearly in the grave herself. I was deeply touched by her concern.

  I don't know what the future will bring, but I hope it's good. I've prayed about it enough. Oh, yes, God's back in my good graces again. If there's no God then you couldn't be in heaven. And I couldn't stand that. But I know you're not playing a harp or sitting on a cloud. Mrs. Houghton says heaven's beautiful, full of light and very, very peaceful in God's presence. If it's like that then I want you there, since you can't be here. Oh, Father, Father, why couldn't you have remained on earth just a little longer to see me become a lady?

  I'll have to become one now, you know. I'll have to grow up and stand for all those things you believed in: Honesty, loyalty, and above all, patriotism. I'll try to become what you wanted me to be and live each day fully as it comes and help build a better future. That's what you

died for. And I promise to become the great lady you'll be proud of. Goodbye, Dad.
    Love, Doc.

    P.S. Everybody at Henley's store misses you and sends their love. I never knew you had so many friends. I've decided to go live with Grandmother because I know that's what you wanted me to do. I've made my decision and will live by it. I know my new life will be different and hard to get used to, but I shall do my very best to make Grandmother happy and you too. Goodbye again,
    Forever,
    Doc

82

"The End of the Beginning"
Churchill

June 1944

In June Grandmother came to Richmond with a lawyer. He was also a family friend and a very pleasant man. Together we went downtown to a hearing when I was asked several questions.

"Answer them truthfully," Grandmother told me. "This is important, and concerns your future."

"Your grandmother wants to take you to Indiana to live with her. With wartime problems and your father's death you're allowed to choose your future." The lawyer took a paper from his briefcase for me to sign.

"What about the Houghton's?" I asked, "Can they no longer keep me?"

"You need a legal guardian, a member of your family. Your grandmother is the logical choice. The Houghtons, although kind and loving people, are not legally responsible for you. You can stay with your mother and stepfather or go to Indianapolis to live." The lawyer handed me the paper. "You sign here."

I chose Indianapolis and Grandmother. I signed the paper and that was that.

Only it wasn't. Saying goodbye to the Houghtons was the most difficult part of leaving Virginia. Mrs. Houghton and I both cried. She stood on the road waving to us holding Peggy when Mr. Houghton drove Grandmother and me to the station.

"Please stop, Mr. Houghton," I begged. "I need to hug your wife one final time."

He stopped the car, and I ran back up the road into Mrs. Houghton's waiting arms.

"How do I say goodbye?" I cried. "How do I leave you?"

"Dry your tears, Doc. Your grandmother has promised you can come for the summer and stay with us. Didn't she tell you?" Mrs. Houghton's soft English voice whispered into my ear. "That's something exciting to look forward to. You will always be our special girl, remember that."

"Yes," I said smiling at her, "you got the goodness out of me."

And we both laughed through our tears.

Selected Bibliography

Bradley, Omar, A General's Story, Simon and Schuster, New York, N.Y. 1983

Brown, Richard, Mr. Brown's War - A Dairy of the Second World War, edited by Helen D. Millgate, Sutton Publishing House, 1998. Glouchester, England

Crowley, Robert, editor, No End Save Victory, Perspectives on. World War II, G. P. Putnam's Sons, New York, N. Y. 2001.

D'Este, Carlo, Patton, Harper Collins Publishers, New York, N. Y. 1995.

Dickson, (Monk) B. A., Colonel USA Retired, G-2 Journal, Algiers to the Elbe, Copyrighted, but Unpublished, 1968.

Harman, Nicholas, Dunkirk, The Necessary Myth, Hodder and Stoughton, London. 1980.

Harrison, Frank, Tobruk, The Great Siege Reassessed, Brokhampton, London 1991

Hart, W. H. Liddell, History of the Second World War, Da Capo Press, New York, N. Y. 1971.

Higham, Charles, Trading with the Enemy, An Expose of Nazi-American Money Plot, Delacorte Press, New York, N. Y. 1983.

Jackson, W. G. P. North African Campagne

Kennedy, David M., Freedom From Fear, Oxford University Press, Oxford, England, 1999.

Maulden, Bill, Up Front, W. W. Norton, New York, N. Y. 2000.

Moorehead, Alan, The Desert War, The North African Campagne, Hamish Hamilton, London.

Nicolson, Herald, The War Years, Diaries & Letters 1939-1945, Vol II, Edited by Nigel Nicolson, Atheneum, New York, 1967

Panter-Doune, Mollie, London War Notes, edited by William Shawn, Lord Longman, 1972.

Pitt, Barrie, The Crucible of War, Western Desert 1941, Jonathan Cape, London, 1980.

Tobin, James, Ernie Pyle's War, America's Eyewitness to World War II, University Press of Kansas, 1997.

Winterbotham, F. W., The Ultra Secret, Weidenfield and Nicolson, London, 1974

Wright, Mike, What They Didn't Teach You About World War II, Presidio Press, California, 1998

Youngman, Anna, The Federal Reserve System in Wartime, Our Economy at War, Financial Research 1945

Transcripts of Radio Programs from Germany 1939-1945. Lord Haw Haw, William Joyce and Paul Revere, Douglas Chandler.

www.ingramcontent.com/pod-product-compliance
Lightning Source LLC
Chambersburg PA
CBHW032011230426
43671CB00005B/51